The General Factor of Intelligence

How General Is It?

The General Factor of Intelligence

How General Is It?

Edited by

Robert J. Sternberg
Yale University

Elena L. Grigorenko
Yale University and Moscow State University

2002

LAWRENCE ERLBAUM ASSOCIATES, PUBLISHERS
Mahwah, New Jersey   London

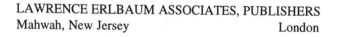

Lawrence Erlbaum Associates, Inc., Publishers
10 Industrial Avenue
Mahwah, New Jersey 07430

Cover design by Kathryn Houghtaling Lacey

Library of Congress Cataloging-in-Publication Data

The general factor of intelligence : how general is it? / edited by Robert J. Sternberg,
Elena L. Grigorenko.
   p. cm.
  Includes bibliographical references and indexes.
  ISBN 0-8058-3675-6 (alk paper)
   1. General factor (Psychology) 2. Intellect. I. Sternberg, Robert J. II. Grigorenko,
Elena.

  BF433.G45 G46 2001
  153.9—dc21

                    2001051293

Books published by Lawrence Erlbaum Associates are printed on acid-free paper,
and their bindings are chosen for strength and durability.

Printed in the United States of America
10 9 8 7 6 5 4 3 2 1

Contents

Preface   ix

PART I: PSYCHOMETRIC APPROACH

1. Tracing Psychology's Invisible g_{iant} and Its Visible Guards   3
   Andreas Demetriou

2. *g*: A Diminutive General   19
   Lazar Stankov

3. Psychometric *g*: Definition and Substantiation   39
   Arthur R. Jensen

4. Practical Implications of General Intelligence and PASS Cognitive Processes   55
   Jack A. Naglieri and J. P. Das

PART II: GENETIC–EPISTEMOLOGICAL APPROACH

5. General Intelligence: Measurement, Correlates, and Interpretations of the Cultural–Genetic Construct   87
   Lloyd G. Humphreys and Stephen Stark

6. Is There a General Factor of Cognitive Development?   117
   Jacques Lautrey

v

PART III: COGNITIVE APPROACH

7. *g* and Cognitive Elements of Information Processing: 151
   An Agnostic View
   Ian J. Deary

8. A View From Cognitive Psychology: *g*—(G)host   183
   in the Correlation Matrix?
   Jutta Kray and Peter A. Frensch

PART IV: BIOLOGICAL APPROACH

9. General Intelligence: Cognitive and Biological Explanations   223
   Douglas K. Detterman

10. The Theory of Biological Intelligence: History   245
    and a Critical Appraisal
    Douglas Wahlsten

PART V: BEHAVIOR–GENETIC APPROACH

11. The Case for General Intelligence: A Behavioral Genetic   281
    Perspective
    Stephen A. Petrill

12. Other Than *g*: The Value of Persistence   299
    Elena L. Grigorenko

PART VI: SOCIOCULTURAL APPROACH

13. *g:* Highly General and Highly Practical   331
    Linda S. Gottfredson

14. Contextual Variability in the Expression and Meaning   381
    of Intelligence
    Cynthia A. Berg and Paul A. Klaczynski

CONTENTS

PART VII: SYSTEMS APPROACH

15. *g:* Knowledge, Speed, Strategies, or Working-Memory   415
    Capacity? A Systems Perspective
      Patrick C. Kyllonen

16. Beyond *g:* The Theory of Successful Intelligence   447
      Robert J. Sternberg

Author Index   481
Subject Index   499

Preface

Is there a general factor of intelligence, and if so, how general is it? Few debates are as heated and polarized as the one centering on the answer to this question.

On the one side are the so-called "g-theorists." These theorists appear to be as convinced that there is a single general factor of intelligence as anyone could be of any scientific theory. Many g-theorists view g theory as fact, in much the way that many evolutionary theorists view natural selection as fact. Indeed, within the past several years, two books with the same title, *The g Factor,* have been published by major publishers (Brand, 1996; Jensen, 1998). The controversy surrounding the issue caused one publisher almost immediately to place the first book on the g factor out of print because of what the publisher and some others believed was an appearance of racist extensions of general-factor theory.

On the other side are theorists who believe that, to the extent that there is a general factor of intelligence, this factor represents nothing more than a factor that is general to tests of certain academic abilities, and not even the full range of these abilities. For example, both Gardner (1983, 1999) and Sternberg (1985, 1997) have suggested that the general factor applies only to the powerful range of tasks used in tests of academic abilities, and not much more.

It is difficult for any reader to evaluate the status of the debate on g theory because the available literature often seems partisan. Some researchers believe the evidence against this factor's being truly completely general is overwhelming. But the g theorists view the presentations of multiple-intelligence-type theorists as biased in much the way that the latter theorists view the presentations of g theorists as biased.

The goal of this volume is to present a *balanced* approach in presenting a variety of points of view including but not limited to the relatively extreme positions that g is either an established fact or an epiphenomenon. Thus, the book is motivated by the need to provide (a) a balanced presentation of points of view on (b) the most central theoretical issue in the field of human intelligence and one that has (c) enormous practical implications, such as whether an IQ score can be meaningful in any but a fairly trivial way.

Contributors to this book include many of the most distinguished scholars in the field of human intelligence. These scholars represent a wide variety of methodological perspectives and viewpoints regarding general ability. In particular, we have sought pairs of authors representing major points of view, with one member of the pair at least partially in favor of and the other at least partially opposed to the concept of *g* (although, of course, their positions are much more sophisticated than merely "in favor of" or "opposed to"). We also have purposively sought an *international* team of contributors to reflect the international nature of this controversy.

First representing the psychometric approach is Arthur R. Jensen, University of California, Berkeley, whose chapter entitled "Psychometric *g:* Definition and Substantiation," is largely favorable to *g.* Also representing this approach with a counter position is Jack Naglieri, Ohio State University, and J. P. Das, University of Alberta, whose chapter, "Practical Implications of General Intelligence and PASS Cognitive Processes," argues against *g.*

The genetic-epistemological approach is first represented by Lloyd G. Humphreys and Stephen Stark, University of Illinois at Urbana-Champaign, in their chapter, "General Intelligence: Measurement, Correlates, and Interpretations of the Cultural-Genetic Construct." In their chapter, they argue in favor of *g.* Questioning this conclusion is Jacques Lautrey, University of Paris V, whose chapter is entitled "Is There a General Factor of Cognitive Development?"

The cognitive approach begins with a chapter by Ian Deary, University of Edinburgh, "*g* and Cognitive Elements of Information Processing: An Agnostic View." This chapter is sympathetic to although certainly not unequivocally in favor of *g.* The chapter by Jutta Kray and Peter A. Frensch, Humboldt-University at Berlin, "A View From Cognitive Psychology: *g—(G)*host in the Correlation Matrix?" is even less favorable to the existence of *g.*

First representing the biological approach and in favor of *g* is Douglas Detterman, Case Western Reserve University, whose chapter is entitled "General Intelligence: Cognitive and Biological Explanations." Representing an opposing position is Douglas Wahlsten, University of Alberta, whose chapter is entitled "The Theory of Biological Intelligence: History and a Critical Appraisal."

The behavior-genetic approach in favor of *g* is represented by Stephen A. Petrill, Wesleyan University, whose chapter is entitled "The Case for General Intelligence: A Behavioral Genetic Perspective." Representing the opposing perspective is Elena L. Grigorenko, Yale and Moscow State Universities, whose chapter is entitled "Other Than *g:* The Value of Persistence."

The sociocultural approach is first represented by Linda S. Gottfredson University of Delaware, whose chapter is entitled "*g:* Highly General and Highly Practical." Representing an anti-*g* perspective is Cynthia A. Berg, University of Utah, whose chapter is entitled "Contextual Variability in the Expression and Meaning of Intelligence."

A systems approach is first represented by Patrick C. Kyllonen, Educational Testing Service, whose chapter in favor of *g* is entitled "*g:* Knowledge, Speed, Strategies, or Working-Memory Capacity? A Systems Perspective." This same approach is represented from a largely anti-*g* perspective by Robert J. Sternberg, Yale University, whose chapter is entitled "Beyond *g:* The Theory of Successful Intelligence."

Finally, there are two commentaries on the chapters, one from a largely pro-*g* perspective, the other from a largely anti-*g* perspective. Andreas Demetriou, University of Cyprus, whose chapter is entitled "Tracing Psychology's Invisible giant and Its Visible Guards," represents the pro-*g* stance. Lazar Stankov, University of Sydney, whose chapter is entitled, "*g:* A Diminutive General," represents the anti-*g* stance.

This book is addressed to psychologists in all areas of psychology and especially clinical, consulting, educational, cognitive, school, developmental, industrial-organizational, and other aspects of psychology who need to deal with intelligence. It will also be of interest to educators, sociologists, anthropologists, and anyone with an interest in the nature of intelligence.

The book has a number of features that we hope will make it of interest to all readers with a serious interest in intelligence. First, it concerns what is arguably the most central topic in the field of intelligence. Second it provides a uniquely balanced approach to the topic of general intelligence, pairing people who are largely for or against the notion of a general factor. Third, its authors are among the most distinguished people in the field of intelligence. Fourth, it broadly samples different approaches to the study of intelligence. Fifth, authors have been asked to write in a way that is readable to the full range of possible audiences for the book but that, at the same time, is sound and scholarly rather than aimed at selling books at the expense of scholarship.

We are grateful to Cynthia Blankenship and Sai Durvasula for assistance in the preparation of the manuscript, and to our funding agencies that allowed our spending time of this book possible. In particular, we thank U.S. National Science Foundation grant REC-9979843 and the Javits Act Program (Grant No. R206R000001) as administered by the Office of Educational Research and Improvement, U.S. Department of Education.

REFERENCES

Brand, C. (1996) *The g factor: General Intelligence and its implications.* Chichester, England, Wiley.
Gardner, H. (1983). *Frames of mind: The theory of multiple intelligences.* New York: Basic Books.
Gardner, H. (1999). *Intelligence reframed: Multiple intelligences for the 21st century.* New York: Basic Books.
Jensen, A. R. (1998). *The g factor.* Westport, CT: Greenwood/Praeger.
Sternberg, R. J. (1985). *Beyond IQ: A triarchic theory of human intelligence.* New York: Cambridge University Press.
Sternberg, R. J. (1997). *Succesful intelligence.* New York: Plume.

Part I

PSYCHOMETRIC APPROACH

Tracing Psychology's Invisible giant and Its Visible Guards

Andreas Demetriou
University of Cyprus

This book presents a fascinating array of thorough and exhaustive chapters on the nature of human intelligence. The authors of these chapters, some of the world's leading authorities in the field, were asked to evaluate the evidence available and tell us whether there is a common set of processes and abilities permeating all kinds of human understanding and problem solving or whether no such set exists. In more technical terms, the contributors to this volume were invited to elaborate on whether intelligence includes a general factor, the famous *g*, or independent domain-specific faculties of intelligence.

The volume was meant to be exhaustive. In this respect, it involves sections concerned with all of the important approaches to intelligence that have generated a satisfactory body of research and theory on the question of interest (i.e., the psychometric, the genetic–epistemological, the cognitive, the biological, the behavior–genetic, the sociocultural, and the systems approach). Moreover, the volume was meant to be fair and balanced in its treatment of the issue under discussion. In this respect, each section includes a chapter written by a scholar who is known to take a pro-*g* stance and another chapter was written by an anti-*g* (or almost) stance.

As a discussant, according to the editors' interpretation of my stance, I was invited as a member of the pro-*g* camp, most likely because in recent years I tried to identify, in my research, general abilities of the mind (Demetriou, Efklides, & Platsidou, 1993). However, a note of caution is in order here. That is, I do not ally myself with either of the two camps—either in theory or research. In fact, I have spent many years trying to specify specialized capacity spheres or abilities in the developing mind (Demetriou & Efklides, 1985, 1987). At present, my aim is to advance a theory of intellectual development that would do justice to both the general and the specific aspects of the mind, and this from the point of view of the psychometric, the cognitive, and the genetic–epistemological approaches (Demetriou & Kazi, 2001). My discussion bears this integrative approach. Thus, I try to answer the following questions:

Does a general factor really exist?
If it exists, what does the general factor include?
What is the architecture of the mind?
How is it related to development?

DOES A GENERAL FACTOR REALLY EXIST?

As an opinion poll about the existence of the g factor, this volume is certainly strongly in favor of it. In fact, only one of the 16 chapters (Berg, chap. 14, this volume) explicitly states that general intelligence does not exist. The rest of the anti-g contributors accept the presence of general abilities but believe that specialized or modular processes and abilities may be more important than the general ones to account for different aspects of intellectual functioning and understanding (see, e.g., Grigorenko, chap. 12, this volume; Kray & Frensch, chap. 8, this volume).

The pro-g contributors, as expected, stress the prominence of general abilities and processes over the specialized ones and thus argue that g is strong, ever-present, and omni-present. However, it should be noted that these contributors also made steps in the direction of the anti-g camp. That is, these contributors do not deny that other, more specialized, functions may be needed, in addition to g, to account for intellectual functioning in particular domains. Of course, the importance they ascribe to these specialized processes varies. Some believe that they add little in terms of incremental predictive validity (Humphreys & Stark, chap. 5, this volume; Jensen, chap. 3, this volume). Others believe that these specialized functions are equally important as predictors and explanations of intellectual functioning (e.g., Deary, chap. 7, this volume).

The same conclusion is suggested by the chapters concerned with the biological or genetic aspects of intelligence. That is, starting at the level of genes, it is generally accepted that a large part of variance in intelligence (50% or more) is accounted for by shared genes. At the same time, there is strong evidence that there is genetic variance in intelligence that is independent of *g* (Grigorenko, chap. 12, this volume; Petrill, chap. 11, this volume; Wahlsten, chap. 10, this volume). At the level of the brain, there are aspects of brain functioning (e.g., energy consumption as indicated by glucose metabolism) and parts of it (e.g., the frontal lobes) that seem to be directly and causally associated with all aspects of cognitive functioning. These co-exist with aspects of brain functioning (e.g., different types of neurotransmitters) and areas of the brain that are associated with different types of cognitive functioning (Naglieri & Das, chap. 4, this volume; Wahlsten, chap. 10, this volume). However, few could disagree with Wahlsten, on the basis of principle or empirical evidence, that the complexity of gene action at the molecular level does not say much about intelligence, general or domain specific, at the psychological level. This is so because, according to Wahlsten, intelligence is a property that exists at the psychological level, the level of the thinking individual who possesses a complex brain tutored in a human society. Thus, the "final theory of intelligence," if there is ever going to be one, would have to involve descriptions and premises running from the genes, to nerves, to thoughts, to society, and to history and evolutionary theory. We explore this point latter, when reference is made to the uses of intelligence to attain complex goals (Sternberg, chap. 16, this volume).

Thus, if this book represents the state of the art in the field of the psychology of intelligence, a clear conclusion is warranted: That is, a century of research on intelligence suggests that there are abilities and processes in intellectual functioning that are truly general, very strong in their effects, and always present. We can see their effects in domains as remote from each other as traffic behavior, functioning in marriage, and job performance, let alone, of course, scholastic and academic achievement. At the same time, nobody denies that there is variation across domains so that excellence and high levels of expertise in one domain may co-exist with more humble achievements in other domains. It is thus equally clear that general abilities are embedded or interleaved with domain or problem-specific abilities and processes.

This conclusion suggests that the battle between the pro-*g* camp (led by Spearman in the old days and Jensen, 1998, nowadays) and the anti-*g* camp (led by Thurstone and Guildford in the old days and Gardner, 1983, nowadays) has ended with no winner. To the satisfaction of the pro-*g* camp, *g* did stand up to the test of time. To their dismay, it cannot do the job of understanding and dealing with the world on its own. It needs completion. To the satisfaction of the anti-*g* camp, the factors needed for completion do behave systematically and consistently enough to warrant the status of independent dimensions of intelligence on a par with *g*. To their dismay, these factors may not even be able to be activated and used without the concomitant activation and use of the processes included in *g*.

Therefore, let us first specify what is included in g and the specialized factors and then specify how all of them are organized to allow intelligent functioning.

WHAT DOES THE g-FACTOR INCLUDE?

The g-factor emerges from a matrix of correlations between diverse cognitive tests as a result of the so-called "positive manifold." That is, it reflects the fact that all tests are positively correlated (see mainly Detterman, chap. 9, this volume; Humphreys & Stark, chap. 5, this volume; Jensen, chap. 3, this volume). The more variable the tests, the stronger the g-factor (Humphreys & Stark, chap. 5, this volume). This statistical construct is supposed to reflect the operation of an invisible power, which, like gravity (Detterman, chap. 9, this volume), underlies and constrains performance on all of the tests and is responsible for the positive manifold.

How is this invisible power defined? No fully agreed upon answer exists. However, there is considerable agreement on a number of functions and characteristics. First of all, there is overwhelming agreement that g can be defined in terms of a number of parameters concerned with processing efficiency and capacity. Three parameters have been systematically studied. Speed of processing is mentioned by everybody. That is, the higher the speed, the more efficient processing proves to be and this leads to better performance on cognitive tasks of all kinds. Different authors emphasize different aspects of processing speed, such as speed of searching or consulting items in short-term memory and rate of gaining information. Efficiency of inhibition is also considered to be a component of g because it is related to the thinker's ability to stay focused on goal and minimize the effects of interference. A third function, which is considered by many to be involved in g, is working memory. In fact, some authors go as far as to argue that g *is* working memory (Kyllonen, chap. 15, this volume; Detterman´s views about working memory are very close to this strong interpretation of the role of working memory). This function refers to the capacity of the system to hold information in an active state for the sake of processing. The more the capacity of working memory, the better for cognitive performance.

There is a second, more active, set of processes associated with g. These processes refer to the management of both the processing resources available and the task demands and goals. Attention is one of these processes. In fact, as discussed in the present context, attention may be conceived of as the subjectively and personally felt and controlled aspect of the inhibition processes referred to earlier. It is noted here that Stankov and Roberts (1997) have recently shown that the importance of speed of processing is not due to speed itself but to the fact that speeded tasks require selective attention. Under this perspective, directed attention is the crucial factor.

Planning is another, more complex, process. Planning refers to goal-management strategies that enable the person to analyze the task demands in a time-dependent order of goals and subgoals and match them with the resources available so that optimum performance can be achieved, given the problem, the resources available at the time, and the time constraints as such. It is interesting that these two functions, that is, attention and planning, are invoked as the building blocks of intelligence by contributors who take the anti-g stance (Naglieri & Das, chap. 4, this volume). Others (Deary, chap. 7, this volume) note that complex planning and management of complexity depends on the person's ability to generate and manage goals and subgoals in working memory. Therefore, even at this level, one finds signs of the more fundamental processes of attention, processing control, and representational capacity.

Spearman, the father of the concept of g, defined g as the ability to uncover and deal with relations at different levels of complexity and abstraction. Eduction of relations and correlates were the two basic processes he invoked to specify this ability. Nowadays very few explicitly associate g with these or other reasoning processes as such. This trend is clearly represented in this volume. Only Deary (chap. 7, this volume) has explicitly referred to analogical reasoning as a component of g and this only in order to show that this line of research did not lead to anything of substance in our attempt to crack the mysteries of the mind. It should also be noted that g is not associated with knowledge. Thus, it is natural that the model that splits the general factor into crystallized and fluid abilities is not very popular. In fact, of the 16 chapters in this volume, only one has explicitly invoked these dimensions as building constructs of g (Jensen, chap. 3, this volume).

Moreover, it is the anti-g rather than the pro-g contributors who focus on knowledge and reasoning processes as such. These contributors tend of course to think that these processes are modular and domain- or even task-specific. This is interesting because it suggests that once we come to processes that interface with real world directly, intraindividual variability and instability of performance become the rule and homogeneity and stability the exception (Berg, chap. 14, this volume; Sternberg, chap. 16, this volume). This creates the apparent paradox of having people who are high in g and have very variable performance across different domains, ranging from excellence in the domain of their expertise to moderate in many other domains. In fact, this paradox is the main reason that the struggle between the pro-g and the anti-g camps went on for about a century. I believe that we are ready to resolve the paradox and unite the two camps in one: The higher a person scores in g, the better this person could perform in his or her chosen domain. Thus, by definition, g must co-exist with a wide range of variability. We return to this point latter in the discussion.

ARCHITECTURES OF INTELLECT

Cognitive architecture may be specified in a number of ways. One way, which is common in the psychometric tradition, is to decompose the amount of variance accounted for by different kinds of factors. This is a kind of structural architecture that depicts the various components underlying performance on different kinds of tasks. A second kind of architecture is more dynamic and refers to the organization of the flow of events from the moment of encountering a task until solving it. This kind of architecture is more common in the cognitive tradition. Although different, the two kinds of architecture are complementary rather than incompatible. We first outline the two architectures and then try to show how they complement each other.

Only a few of the chapters were explicitly concerned with the structural architecture of intelligence as such. These were the two most psychometrically laden chapters (that is, Jensen, chap. 3, this volume; and Humphreys & Stark, chap. 5, this volume). However, all of the chapters were implicitly concerned with this kind of architecture as they aimed to specify how g is related to other more specialized intellectual abilities. Figure 1.1 shows, in the conventions of confirmatory factor analysis, the model that, in my view, captures the position of most of the contributors to this volume. It can be seen that this model involves three kinds of factors. First, there is a first-order factor that is common to all tests one might use to examine cognitive functioning. This factor stands for the processes and abilities that define processing efficiency and capacity, such as processing speed, inhibition or control of processing, attention, and working memory. This is the PS factor in the model. Second, there is a set of first-order factors that stand for different domain-specific abilities or modules. Spatial, verbal, numerical, and reasoning abilities, so frequently identified by tests of intelligence, may be considered examples of the abilities of this kind. These are the DS factors. Third, there is a second-order factor associated with all of the first-order factors. This refers to processes and abilities used to monitor, regulate, and coordinate the functioning of the processes and abilities represented by the other factors, both within each of and across them. Let us call this factor hypercognitive (HP) to denote its main characteristic. That is, it involves processes and abilities that stand over and above the cognitive abilities included in the others factors and are applied to them.

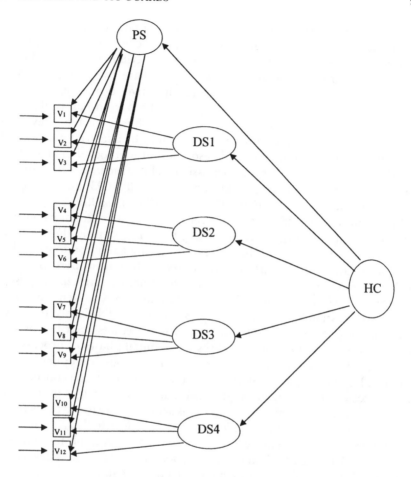

FIG. 1.1. Abstract representation of the structural architecture of the mind. Note: PS stands for a first-order factor associated with all observed variables and represents processing abilities and functions. DS stands for domain-specific factors which represent abilities and processes associated with different domains of reality or different types of relations and may be computationally and representationally specific. The HC factor stands for hypercognitive self-monitoring and self-regulation processes and functions which are applied on all other processes and functions vis-à-vis the present goals and plans. V stands for observed variables.

Of course, each of the factors in this model has its own microarchitecture, which refers to the processes and abilities involved in it. For instance, spatial reasoning may involve processes related to mental rotation and other processes related to orientation in space. Mathematical reasoning may involve processes used to perform arithmetic operations and processes used to decipher and manipulate the symbolic relations of algebraic problems. Even at the level of the fundamental processes involved in g, such as working memory, there may be several component processes, in Sternberg's (1985) classical terms. For instance, Kyllonen analyzes the architecture of working memory into a knowledge base, the strength of association between the items that are currently active in memory, and the amount of attention (or mental energy) that the person has available to give to an item at a particular point in time. Thus, each main level included in the architecture shown in Fig. 1.1 may be analyzed into several other levels and it is only aim and resolution of method of analysis that specifies what level is preferable or possible. This structure of the mind is fully consistent with modern factor analytic (Caroll, 1993) and structural equation modeling studies (Gustaffson & Undheim, 1996).

In the more dynamic, time-dependent, architectures, cognitive events are considered to be organized according to their flow from the moment of accepting to work on a problem until producing a solution to it. In this kind of architectures, events are considered to flow from perception to working memory to long-term memory to solution. For present purposes, the reader is referred to the architecture described in Kyllonen´s chapter and that is shown in Figs. 15.1 and 15.2 of his chapter. Obviously, these architectures are very similar to the structural architectures described before in that they involve the same processes at the initial phases of processing. Their only difference is that, in their case, the various component processes involved are organized in time, whereas in the structural conception, the architecture is time-neutral. Moreover, at the latter stages of processing, when working or long-term memory is activated, the two architectures may be conceived as fully complementary. That is, what is activated in working or long-term memory are, in addition to general self-monitoring and self-regulation skills, domain-specific operations, acts, and knowledge that are relevant to the particular task or goal at hand.

Moreover, the two types of architectures may interact in interesting ways. For instance, at the initial phases of processing, that is, at the perceptual phase of processing, automatic processes are more important than are controlled or domain-specific processes. When processing is passed into the working-memory phase, both domain-specific but also monitoring and regulatory processes may also be important in addition to the processing capacity dimensions. At the final stages associated with long-term memory, monitoring and regulatory processes may be more important. Note, of course, that the particular mixture of processes at the various phases of processing is affected by familiarity and experience. That is, the more familiar the task or task category, the more important the automatic processes may be. Novel tasks require slower processing at some moments and more planning, organization, and regulation.

DEVELOPMENT AND THE *g* FACTOR

Psychometrics has been distinctly nondevelopmental (see Wahlsten, chap. 10, this volume). This is due to the fact that its primary aim has always been to specify stable dimensions of individual differences and to calibrate the individuals along them rather than to understand intellectual changes within individuals. Of course, both cognitive psychology and developmental psychology have returned the favor by staying distinctly nondifferential. That is, they have focused on the kinds and structures of understanding at different phases of life and the mechanisms propelling change across phases and ignored or underestimated possible intra- and interindividual differences in the kinds and efficiency of understanding and problem solving. Some believe that these traditions cannot be integrated because the questions they ask and the methods they use to answer them are foundationally different. However, the research presented here suggests strongly that the two traditions do converge in their findings and can be integrated in their models for describing and representing reality.

The research reviewed in the chapter by Lautrey is very revealing. According to Lautrey, there seems to be a general factor in cognitive development, which reflects the synchronicity of acquisition in different domains. At the same time, there is also considerable variability in the rate of acquisition of the abilities and processes involved in different domains, so that other factors and dimensions in addition to the general factor of development must be taken into account. In fact, according to Lautrey, these other factors, which resulted from Piagetian tests, do not seem different from those found with psychometric tests. How then can we explain these findings?

Many developmental theorists define the general constraints of cognitive development in terms of working-memory capacity and processing efficiency (Case, 1992; Demetriou, 1998; Demetriou, Efklides, & Platsidou, 1993; Halford, 1993; Pascual-Leone, 1970). These theorists proposed that the development of thinking and the ensuing progression along Piagetian or other types of cognitive-developmental stages or levels is propelled by changes in one or more of the parameters mentioned before, that is, speed of processing, inhibition, and working memory. Thus, differences between individuals in any of these parameters may cause differences in cognitive development. Therefore, via this concept, three distinct traditions in the study of intelligence, that is, the psychometric, the cognitive, and the developmental, seem to converge in their interpretation of the nature and the causal functions of the *g* factor.

Moreover, recent research conducted by Case, myself, and other colleagues (Case, Demetriou, Platsidou, & Kazi, 2001), with the aim of testing what is common between the psychometric conception of the structure of the mind and the theories of cognitive development independently proposed by Case and myself, indicated that, in addition to a *g* factor, several domain-specific factors are present and common among all three theories. In particular, there were factors for spatial, quantitative, causal, logical reasoning, and social–verbal thought. These findings lend strong support and extend Lautrey's review of previous research.

The monitoring and regulatory components of cognition have been a privileged area of empirical research and theorizing in developmental psychology for many years through research on metacognition and the theory of mind (Demetriou & Kazi, 2001; Flavell, Green, & Flavell, 1995; Wellman, 1990). It is well beyond the aims and the scope of the present chapter to discuss this work. However, it must be noted that the phenomena studied by this line of research are the very same phenomena that students of intelligence in the other traditions represented in this volume call planning and control (Naglieri & Das, chap. 4, this volume), knowledge handling (Berg, chap. 14, this volume), system-handling metacomponents or self-government (Sternberg, chap. 16, this volume), or even fluid intelligence (Jensen, chap. 3, this volume). In fact, Demetriou and Raftopoulos (1999) have recently proposed that metarepresentation, that is, the dynamic aspect of the hypercognitive system, is one of the main mechanisms underlying the development of reasoning (i.e., fluid intelligence) itself. According to Demetriou and Raftopoulos (1999), metarepresentation looks for, codifies, and typifies similarities between mental experiences, thereby creating inferential schemas. Thus, the three-level architecture of the mind shown in Fig 1.1 as a representation of the mind by the psychometric tradition is also able to fully capture the representation of the mind by the developmental tradition.

Figure 1.2 presents a content-laden transcription of the model shown in Fig. 1.1. This figure illustrates how Case's (1992) and my theory (e.g., Demetriou et al., 1993) can be integrated into a unified theory. As may be seen, the theory postulates a central set of potentials, which can be seen at the center of the diagram. These potentials reflect the core capacities represented by the PS factor in Fig. 1.1. Moving out from the center of the diagram, one finds the hypercognitive processes used to monitor and regulate the processes involved in the rest of the systems. These processes reflect the second-order processes represented by the HC factor in Fig. 1.1. Finally, at the outer layer of the diagram one can see the specialized capacity systems. These correspond to the DS factors in Fig. 1.1.

Each of these systems is hypothesized to involve its own unique set of underlying operations, to be associated with a different sensory and/or neurological system, to have its own evolutionary origins, its own characteristic form of psychological operation (Demetriou, 1998; Demetriou &

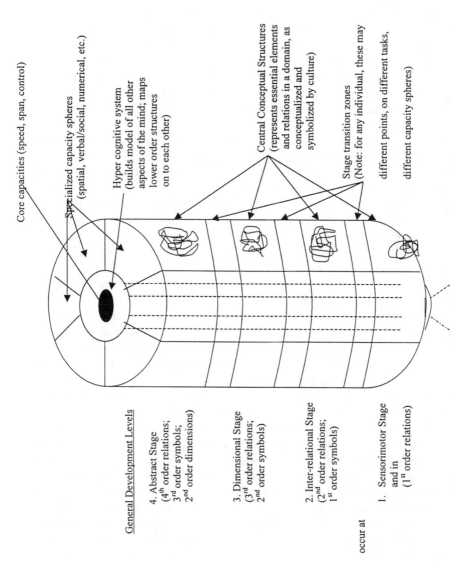

Core capacities (speed, span, control)

Specialized capacity spheres
(spatial, verbal/social, numerical, etc.)

Hyper cognitive system
(builds model of all other
aspects of the mind; maps
lower order structures
on to each other)

Central Conceptual Structures
(represents essential elements
and relations in a domain, as
conceptualized and
symbolized by culture)

Stage transition zones
(Note: for any individual, these may

different points, on different tasks,

different capacity spheres)

General Development Levels

4. Abstract Stage
(4th order relations;
3rd order symbols;
2nd order dimensions)

3. Dimensional Stage
(3rd order relations;
2nd order symbols)

2. Inter-relational Stage
(2nd order relations;
1st order symbols)

occur at

1. Sensorimotor Stage
and in
(1st order relations)

FIG. 1.2.   The proposed Demetriou and Case integrated model of the architecture of the
development mind. Based on Figure 13 in Demetriou, Efklides, and Platsidou (1993).

13

Kazi, 2001) and its own logic (Kargopoulos & Demetriou, 1998). Finally, each of these systems is hypothesized to house its own unique form of conceptual and operational structures (Case & Ogamoto, 1996).

Because of these differences between the systems, one can expect a differential rate and phenotypical form of development from one general domain of functioning to the next, notwithstanding the existence of the general capabilities illustrated in the center. The developmental hypotheses of the figure may be seen by looking down the vertical dimension of the cylinder, rather than across its top surface. That is, each of the specific capacity systems is hypothesized to develop through a series of levels, such that each successive level bears a hierarchical relationship to the previous level. In effect, then, the products at one level can be seen as second-order versions of those at the previous level, which emerge from the elaboration, differentiation, and reciprocal mapping of structures of the previous level. Although a person's rate of development is not uniform across the different capacity systems, there is a characteristic age range or "zone" in which a person makes the various transitions that are indicated, in response to their interaction with their physical and social environments, because of the reciprocal dependence of specific and general growth (Case & Okamoto, 1996; Demetriou & Raftopoulos, 1999).

Moreover, it should also be noted here that the language or models that one may use to describe the development of each of the various systems may be very different. For example, one may use graphs of processing speed as a function of age to describe changes in speed of processing and semantic analysis, as done by Case and Ogamoto (1996), to describe changes in each of the specialized domains. Admittedly, we have a long way to go before we have satisfactory information, let alone norms, about the relations between the languages or models used to describe the organization and development of the various systems.

What is the relative importance of the functions residing at each of the three levels at different phases of development? Genetic research suggests that the importance of g increases with age and novelty of problems to be dealt with (Grigorenko, chap. 12, this volume). At the same time, however, it is also clear that flexibility, probability for everyday success and wisdom in one´s domains of interest, and expertise increase with age, at least until a certain point well into the middle years, despite the fact that neurological development decelerates systematically until adolescence and it becomes negative in some parameters from young adulthood onwards. Thus, development is a process that contributes to the paradox noted above of simultaneous increases in g and domain-variability. The model proposed here and illustrated in Fig. 1.2 helps understand this paradox because it relaxes, although it does not free completely, the interdependencies between the domain-specific and the general systems.

CONCLUSIONS: FROM EXPLANATION
TO MEASUREMENT AND PRACTICE

It is clear, in my mind, that the evidence and theorizing advanced in this volume is impressively coherent and consistent. All seven approaches represented in this volume converge on the premise that general abilities do exist, they are identifiable at various levels including the genetic, the biological, the psychological, and the sociocultural, and that they enable valid and substantial predictions about the condition and prospects of valuable and valued activities in everyday performance. It may be noted here that recent studies suggest that g is projected and explicitly represented in one's self-concept (Demetriou & Kazi, 2001). This suggests that g is in fact visible by one's own mind and it thus influences behavior even from this level of the architecture of the mind.

At the same time, however, there is a consensus that these abilities co-exist and are co-activated with other more specialized abilities and processes. Some of them have already been clearly identified: spatial, mathematical, verbal, and reasoning abilities are named by almost everybody. Few would be surprised if pictographic and musical abilities would be added to the list. However, we still do not have a commonly acceptable theory about how to look, measure, demarcate, specify, and model specialized abilities or domains. We do not also have an acceptable theory for how general and specialized abilities are amalgamated into successful mixtures that lead to excellence in particular domains or in a particular course of life. There have been some attempts in both directions. For example, recent research and theorizing in the psychology of cognitive development (see the earlier example) does advance models that integrate theories about general abilities with theories about domain-specific abilities. However, we still need to answer some crucial questions. From the point of view of general processes and abilities, we need to understand how much and how each of the various processes included in g is embedded, invested, used, or employed by each of the various domain-specific systems. From the point of view of each of the domain-specific systems, we need to know what are the *truly and really* domain-specific or core abilities that belong to each one and only each one of the systems, such as particular computational or operational processes or representational and symbolic processes and functions. According to my reading of this volume, we are still far away of having satisfactory answers to these questions.

A theory of successful intelligence is highly needed. However, although Sternberg's attempts may be steps in the right direction, we still do not have this theory. The reason is that this theory cannot be attained before we have answers to the questions above. Even then, the theory would be beyond our reach because answering these questions is not enough. Intellectual success can only be evaluated vis-à-vis a person's short- and long-term goals and ambitions, this person's developmental phase and ensuing developmental tasks and obligations, this person's cultural and social environment and ensuing possibilities and constrains, and of course this person's historical time and heritage. Moreover, this theory would have to be associated with the theory of personality. In other words, we need a vast and deep theory of psychological relativity. I believe that attaining this theory will prove more difficult than it has been for physics to attain its own theory of relativity.

Lack of generally acceptable theories has been concomitant with lack of generally accepted measurement methods and practices. Understandably, therefore, many authors agree that traditional tests of intelligence measure and represent g. The pro-g authors believe that this is because g is present, strong, and integral component of every test that we can use. The anti-g authors (e.g., Naglieri & Das, Berg, Sternberg, this volume) believe that this is just because of the composition of the tests by tasks that are similar in their underlying presuppositions and even their content. These latter authors believe that, because of their construction, conventional intelligence tests cannot predict several important specialized abilities such as reading, operations on everyday rather than academically relevant tests, tests requiring creativity, and so forth. Thus, in the opinion of these authors, intelligence tests are incomplete and in need of considerable revision and revitalization.

I could not agree more. If we want to have accurate on-time measures of these abilities we do have to measure them directly. There are two reasons for this need. First, traditional tests of intelligence were not designed to provide accurate measures of these specialized abilities. Second, as argued earlier, neither theory nor practice (clinical or educational) specifies how these specialized abilities make use of g when they are acquired, developed, or put in efficient use. Thus, to the extent we are short of this knowledge we will need good specialized tests to direct our decisions, even if we do not understand how the mechanisms underlying the abilities under consideration actually work. However, we can anticipate that the more we understand the connections between g and specialized domains or abilities, the more we will be able to derive good predictions from g estimates to performances in these domains. The recent advances in our understandings of the relationships between reading and working memory can help us move from the one to the other (see Berg, chap. 14, this volume; Kyllonen, chap. 15, this volume; Grigorenko, chap. 12, this volume; Sternberg, chap. 16, this volume). Moreover, I believe that the knowledge available makes it already possible to develop tests of intellectual development and functioning that would be more successful than traditional tests to account for success or failures in different domains or activities. Constructing and using them may also produce knowledge that would be relevant to the questions raised earlier. I am sure that the present volume will prove very useful in our attempts to further our understanding, measurement, and development of the human mind.

REFERENCES

Carroll, J. B. (1993). *Human cognitive abilities: A survey of factor-analytic studies*. New York: Cambridge University Press.

Case. R. (1992). *The mind's staircase: Exploring the conceptual underpinnings of children's thought and knowledge*. Hillsdale, NJ: Lawrence Erlbaum Associates.

Case, R., Demetriou, A., Platsidou, M., & Kazi, S. (2001). Integrating concepts and tests of intelligence from the differential and developmental traditions. *Intelligence, 29*, 307–336.

Case, R., & Okamoto, Y. (Eds.). The role of central conceptual structures in the development of children's thought. *Monographs of the Society for Research in Child Development, 61*(1–2, Serial No. 246, pp. 103–130).

Demetriou, A. (1998). Nooplasis: 10 + 1 Postulates about the formation of mind. *Learning and Instruction: The Journal of the European Association for Research on Learning and Instruction, 8*, 271–287.

Demetriou, A., & Efklides, A. (1985). Structure and sequence of formal and postformal thought: General patterns and individual differences. *Child Development, 56*, 1062–1091.

Demetriou, A., & Efklides, A. (1987). Towards a determination of the dimensions and domains of individual differences in cognitive development. In E. De Corte, H. Lodewijks, R. Parmentier, & P. Span (Eds.), *Learning and Instruction: European research in an international context* (Vol. 1, pp. 41–52). Oxford, England: Leuven University Press and Pergamon Press.

Demetriou, A., Efklides, A., & Platsidou, M. (1993). The architecture and dynamics of developing mind: Experiential structuralism as a frame for unifying cognitive developmental theories. *Monographs of the Society for Research in Child Development, 58*(5–6, Serial No. 234).

Demetriou, A., & Kazi, S. (2001). *Unity and modularity in the mind and the self: Studies on the relationships between between self-awareness, personality, and intellectual development from childhood to adolescence*. London: Routledge.

Demetriou, A., & Raftopoulos, A. (1999). Modeling the developing mind: From structure to change. *Developmental Review, 19*, 319–368.

Flavell, J. H., Green, F. L., & Flavell, E. R. (1995). Young children's knowledge about thinking. *Monographs of the Society for Research in Child Development, 60*(1, Serial No. 243).

Gardner, H. (1983). *Frames of mind. The theory of multiple intelligences*. New York: Basic Books.

Gustafsson, J. E., & Undheim, J. O. (1996). Individual differences in cognitive functions. In D. C. Berliner & R. C. Calfee (Eds.), *Handbook of educational psychology* (pp. 186–242). New York: Macmillan.

Halford, G. (1993). *Children's understanding: The development of mental models*. Hillsdale, NJ: Lawrence Erlbaum Associates.

Jensen, A. R. (1998). *The g factor: The science of mental ability*. New York: Praeger.

Kargopoulos, P., & Demetriou, A. (1998). Logical and psychological partitioning of mind. Depicting the same map? *New Ideas in Psychology, 16*, 61–87.

Pascual-Leone, J. (1970). A mathematical model for the transition rule in Piaget's development stages. *Acta Psychologica, 32*, 301–345.

Stankov, L., & Roberts, R. (1997). Mental speed is not the 'basic' process of intelligence. *Personality and Individual Differences, 22,* 69–84.

Sternberg, R. (1985). *Beyond IQ: A triarchic theory of intelligence.* Cambridge, England: Cambridge University Press.

Wellman, H. M. (1990). *The child's theory of mind.* Cambridge, MA: MIT Press.

g: A Diminutive General

Lazar Stankov
The University of Sydney

Galileo wrote his *Dialogue Concerning the Two Chief World Systems* in 1632 as a discussion between three friends Sagredo, Saliati, and Simplicio that took place over 4 days in Venice. At a time when no canons for scientific writing (e.g., APA Publication Manual) were available, this work was not only scientific, but also a literary accomplishment. The two chief world systems were, of course, the Ptolomaic and Copernican. For a psychologist interested in individual differences it may be tempting to compare these world systems to one-factor (i.e., general plus specifics, aka Spearman) and multifactor (i.e., Thurstonian) theories of the structure of cognitive abilities and intelligence. As witnessed by the contributions to this volume, these issues remain debated with considerable fervor today and there are even religious overtones present—opponents of the *g* factor have been called creationists! The analogy, of course, does not quite hold inasmuch as views about the structure of intelligence are not as existentially important as those of the "chief world systems" and it would be pointless to push comparisons too far, even as a purely literary exercise. Besides, although the heliocentric world system did prevail over the geocentric view, neither an extreme one-factor nor multifactor position are likely to succeed.

From the scientific point of view (i.e., meaning I intend neither to be diplomatic or a fence-sitter), my reading of the evidence suggests that an in-between position, rejecting strong versions of either one-factor or multifactor theories, is most tenable. "Strong versions" are: one-factor theories that deny (or significantly minimize) the role of group factors and multifactor theories that do not acknowledge the plausibility of g. In this chapter, I focus on factor analytic evidence and aspects of its interpretation. In my opinion, this is the critical evidence, and issues related to any other aspects of this book (cognitive, biological, etc., underpinnings of intelligence), take on a completely different complexion if this factor-analytic basis is accepted.

It is necessary to stress that Spearman did accept the existence of broad (or group) factors in addition to g and Thurstone acknowledged the existence of g, in effect, by accepting oblique factors. Subsequent accounts of their respective contributions have often neglected such "subtleties." In view of the issues raised in the contemporary debate over the importance of g, it is worth noting that Thurstone was able to show that positive manifold may arise from a suitably chosen set of independent components (see Horn, 1998). Thus, in theory at least, positive manifold by itself is not sufficient to prove the existence of g. Nevertheless, some prominent researchers investigating cognitive abilities and intelligence have remained unimpressed by Thurstone's argument and have maintained a conviction that positive manifold attests convincingly to the importance of g (Guttman, 1992).

The reason for my own *neutral* position is due to theoretical developments and empirical evidence that has accumulated over the past 30 years or so. This leads me to conclude that g is not as conceptually important as some writers want us to believe (see pro-g chapters in this volume). At the same time, I am unable to dismiss it completely, as some anti-g advocates argue. Crucial to each one of these views are design issues related to the definition of the domain of cognition and, in particular, the effects of sampling from this domain. In the first part of this chapter, I outline the reasons for my position. If the role of g in cognition is smaller than its advocates surmise, it is not surprising that no agreed *basic* process, either psychological or physiological, has been identified to date. In the second half of this chapter I argue that searching for such a single process underlying g may be a futile exercise. Finally, as pointed out many times by the proponents of the theory of fluid and crystallized intelligence, focusing on the second-stratum factors and leaving g aside, can lead to theoretically deeper understanding of individual differences in cognitive abilities.

g IS WEAK WITHIN THE UNIVERSE OF ALL COGNITIVE TESTS

There are two major influences on the size of correlation coefficients in psychological research: Sampling of participants, and sampling of cognitive tasks. Biased selection of either can affect the size of coefficients and can therefore affect the amount of variance accounted for by the g factor. Both effects have operated in past psychometric studies and have influenced theorizing about the structure of cognitive abilities. It would thus seem worthwhile considering lessons learned from these experiences.

Selection of Participants

The use of samples selected for high levels of ability (college samples, airforce pilots) may lead to a restriction in range that could cause lower correlations overall and therefore mitigate against the g factor. One of the most extreme proponents of the multifactor position was Guilford who, in the 1950s and 1960s, presented a large amount of data based on his work for the US Air Force, including the selection of pilots, in support of his Structure of Intellect model (see Guilford, 1967). According to the 1980s version of this model, there exist (or there should be), some 150 cognitive ability factors and no general factor. However, critics have pointed out that samples of participants in Guilford's work consisted of people of high ability (see Carroll, 1972; Horn & Knapp, 1973). This type of selection, coupled with the practice of overextraction of factors and the use of orthogonal rotations, might have affected a number of Guilford's findings. Some recent work, however, indicates that selection of participants may not be very important, to which issue I now turn.

A renewed debate about the role of selection of participants took place in the 1990s, following the work of Detterman and Daniel (1989), whose evidence points to the fact that low IQ-groups (i.e., 1.5 SD below the mean) give higher correlations among different tests than more representative samples. The subsequent work of Deary, Egan, Gibson, Brand, and Kellaghan (1996) agreed with this general finding, but the overall effect was very small indeed—the difference between the amount of variance accounted for by the first principal component in low- versus high-ability groups was only 2%! Furthermore, Fogarty and Stankov (1995) showed that within a high-ability group, low correlations might be due in part to poor power of discrimination among the available tests, and not to genuine individual differences. In other words, IQ tests are not well suited to discriminate between those scoring 130, as opposed to those scoring 140 points. For example, Fogarty and Stankov (1995) demonstrated that, with difficult competing tasks (two complex tasks performed simultaneously), high-ability groups might show higher correlations than low-ability groups. Similarly, tasks that are equally difficult for all individuals—for example, perceptual speed tasks—show a uniform size of correlation over IQs that vary from low to very high.

In conclusion, this body of research indicates that correlations among ability tests may be somewhat higher in low-ability samples as compared to the rest of the population. However, there is no reliable evidence of systematic differences in the size of correlations in samples of average to high-ability groups. For example, we obtained a similar factorial structure from inmates of Colorado State Penitentiary, whose IQ scores tend to be around 90 on the average (Stankov & Horn, 1980), adult and elderly samples of typical individuals with average IQ scores (Stankov, 1988), and from samples consisting mostly of university students, whose Full Scale WAIS IQ scores had a mean of 115 (Roberts & Stankov, 1999). Despite considerable differences in the overall levels of IQ, these studies produced essentially the same factorial structure. I hasten to add that they all provided support for the theory of fluid and crystallized intelligence, rather than the theory of g.

Consequently, a restricted selection of participants may not be a sufficient cause to dismiss Guilford's (1967) Structure of Intellect model. It is frequently overlooked, however, that Guilford's work has also been characterized by a broader selection of tasks than in many contemporary studies of intelligence. This feature may have been more important for the outcomes of his work than the selection of participants. Indeed, the design of his studies called for the presence of marker tests for several, often many, different primary mental abilities, in addition to those new ones he was trying to identify in any given study. Essentially the same strategic approach has been employed in empirical research within the theory of fluid and crystallized intelligence and this, in turn, provides a challenge to the current notion of g. The use of a single test, or a few tests from a limited area of cognition, is often present in research supportive of g.

Selection From the Universe of Tests Is Important

The strength of g can be significantly affected by the composition of an intelligence test battery. Two related issues are of particular interest: The possibility of representative sampling and the delineation of the domain of cognition.

Representative Sampling From the Domain of Cognition and Its Implications for the Existence of g

Typical quantitative training in psychology tends to emphasize statistics and the machinery associated with the representative sampling of participants (or experimental units) from the population. Valid conclusions, as we are taught in our undergraduate classes, can be reached only if such representative sampling can be accomplished. Advanced quantitative training in psychology may bring out the fact that an analogue of the representative sampling of participants exists with respect to psychometric notions of reliability and validity. The relevant population may be the domain of cognition and representative sampling of measures from the "universe of tests" is certainly a reasonable proposition, at least in theory, albeit probably impossible to achieve in reality. Representative sampling implies the enumeration of all members of the population and the use of a well-defined random process in order to choose the sample for study. Because enumeration of all cognitive processes may be an impossible task, due to lack of agreement on the definition of what constitute cognition, it follows that true representative sampling may also be impossible. Faceted theories of intelligence like Guilford's (1967) and Guttman's (1992) were attempts to circumscribe cognition but provided different, and essentially arbitrary, definitions of the domain.

To some, this state of affairs provides a powerful argument that places a huge question mark over the existence of *g*. Any arbitrary collection of tests is not representative (but rather a biased sample), from the domain of cognitive processes, and the *g* obtained with one sample of tests is clearly different from the *g* obtained from another sample. A battery that contains mostly fluid reasoning tasks will provide a *g* that is akin to Gf and an analogous situation will arise with any arbitrary collection of tests producing a *g* that is akin to Gc, Gv, and the like. Without representative sampling, every empirically defined *g* will be different from any other *g*. The position can be described from the perspective of a "purist agnostic"—*g* may exist but we shall never be able to establish it empirically without reasonable doubt (see Horn, 1998). In other words, a definitive study containing a representative sample of the many, many tests possible within the cognitive domain, with an even larger number of participants, would be impossible to carry out. Only this kind of study would provide a definite proof for the existence of *g*.

Curiously, Humphreys (1962; see Humphreys and Stark, chap. 5, this volume), who has also been concerned with the issues related to the selection of tests, has embraced the construct of *g* enthusiastically. His *g*, however, is based on the idea that tests subjected to factor analysis should be as heterogeneous as possible. This approach is not only "philosophically" different from Jensen's (chap. 3, this volume) position, but also implies a different empirical approach to the study of intelligence. A logical extension of the notion of heterogeneity would suggest the broadening of the definition of the universe of tests advocated later, but this is not the direction Humphreys has taken. Viewed in this light, the opening paragraphs of Humphreys and Stark's chapter seem to overemphasize their similarities with Jensen's position.

At this juncture, I wish to alert the reader to the fact that some recent developments in the methodology of missing data analysis have opened the possibility of designing strategic studies that would contain larger-than-usual batteries of tests. These batteries can be given to sufficiently large samples of participants and valid conclusions regarding the structure of human abilities can be derived. Although this represents a welcome practical development that will bring us close to the ideal, empirical studies based on that approach have not been carried out as yet. It is therefore difficult to assess the potential theoretical impact of this new procedure.

Lower Order Cognitive Processes and the Strength of *g*

Studies of individual differences aim to uncover the structure of psychological traits within the domains of intelligence and personality. Such studies are usually based on the a priori assumption that there are a large number of cognitive tasks, and that there is a need to classify them using the generally accepted methodology. Taxonomy is one of the primary goals of multivariate research. Again, the first step in this process has to be the demarcation of the domain of cognition but, because faceted theories of intelligence have failed, it may be thought that a reasonable approximation is provided by the general approach embodied in the work of Carroll (1993). After defining cognitive tasks according to convention (i.e., as "any task in which correct or appropriate processing of mental information is critical to successful performance" [Carroll, 1993, p. 10]), he proceeded with his re-analyses of the data sets that employed such tasks. The logic behind this approach was that a large number of studies, and variables employed within these studies, were likely to have covered a good chunk of the area of cognition. This may be fine, except for the fact that, in my opinion, a restricted and biased selection of tasks in intelligence research was employed throughout most of the last century. This biased selection of tasks has led to an overemphasis on *g* in contemporary research in human abilities.

A Quick Look at History

Two positions that are relevant for the present discussion have been discernible since the second half of the 19th century. Thus, Francis Galton was quite happy to study the relationship between the "keenness of senses" and genius, while Alfred Binet laid the foundation for the successful testing of intelligence by focusing on thinking processes. Much of the work in the area of intelligence throughout the 20th century was largely restricted to the latter and the term *higher mental processes* was used in order to point out that lower order sensory and motor processes are excluded from consideration. Guilford (1967) himself separated psychomotor processes from the rest of cognition. Jensen (1998) also excluded both sensory and psychomotor processes from his considerations of the structural aspects of *g*. Finally, Carroll (1993) characterized psychomotor (but not sensory) processes as belonging outside the ability domain. Obviously, although there is some disagreement about the inclusion of sensory processes, there appears a consensus that psychomotor processes should be excluded from discussions about intelligence.

Burt's (1949) theory was at odds with much of the literature on cognitive abilities in that he did not commit himself to higher mental processes only, but included sensory and, indeed, motor processes as well. His hierarchical model is depicted as an inverted tree diagram with four main nodes, or levels, where different branches of the tree meet. At the lowest mental level, there are two main groups of processes: Elementary *sensory* processes and elementary *motor* reactions. The next level includes more complex processes of *perception* and equally complex *reactions* on the motor side. The third is the level of mechanical associations—*memory* and *habit*. Finally, the fourth level involves thought processes: the apprehension and application of relations. It is quite important to note that here intelligence is the "integrative function of the mind" that encompasses processes at *all* levels.

Our own empirical studies did include both sensory and psychomotor processes. We found it difficult to exclude psychomotor processes from consideration mainly because it is hard to distinguish between these and tactile/kinaesthetic processes, especially since "active touch" is an important aspect of the latter (Roberts, Stankov, Pallier, & Dolph, 1997; Stankov, Seizova-Caijic & Roberts, 2000). Also, studies of stimulus–response compatibility effects (see what follows) implicate the pairing of stimulus and response as an important aspect of cognitive task's difficulty. Gardner (1983) also kept bodily kinaesthetic intelligence in his list of multiple intelligence because of its links to high level accomplishments in dance and sports.

Renewed Interest in Lower Order Processes

Today's literature on intelligence contains frequent references to Elementary Cognitive Tasks (ECTs; Carroll, 1980). These are contemporary labels for the "lower order processes." Carroll (1980) assumed that there is a very large number of such tasks, all of which are characterized by "a relatively small number of mental processes." A major feature of ECTs that distinguishes them from traditional views about lower order processes is that they are measured in terms of time (speed) rather than accuracy. Obviously, the appearance of ECTs in the literature is directly linked to the seminal componential analysis of Bob Sternberg (1977) and the cognitive correlates approach advocated by Earl Hunt (1980), which provided the impetus for enumerating the ingredient processes of ECTs.

ECTs are nowadays often studied in relationship to intelligence because a researcher may hold a Spearmanian view of g and thus needs a link to physical properties in order to argue for its importance (see Deary, chap. 7, this volume). Alternatively, for researchers following Thomson's (1939) idea of g, there is an expectation that ECTs will bring us closer to an understanding of the notion of "bonds." Thus far, only a relatively small number of such tasks, certainly a far cry from what I believe Carroll (1980) envisioned, have been correlated with tests of intelligence (see Roberts & Pallier, 2001). Nevertheless, it is clear that Galton's hope that lower order mental processes will provide an explanation of individual differences in intellectual tasks is very much alive at the beginning of this new millennium, with the idea of reductionism looming large. The prevalence of the ECTs in the literature today suggests that the traditional distinction between lower and higher order processes in intelligence needs to be re-examined.

NEGLECTED ROLE OF LOWER-ORDER PROCESSES

Issues related to the delineation of cognitive processes that enter into the definition of intelligence (higher order or both higher and lower order) are inevitably a source of tension. The main problems arise from:

1. *Arbitrariness of classification.* In our studies of intelligence we can focus arbitrarily on higher order processes, but it is hard to dismiss lower order processes into a shaded area between psychology and physiology. What are the criteria for deciding that something is a lower order process? To the best of my knowledge, this has never been specified. At least since the time of the Gestaltists, it has been known that principles identified in the study of perceptual processes can be translated into the domain of thinking and problem solving. Is anyone going to propose that we should throw away some items from the matrices tests because they can be solved using lower order perceptual process? If a putative lower order process shows a moderate, or even high, correlation with measures of intelligence, should it be re-classified into a higher order category? Arbitrary exclusion of some sensory domains from the study of intelligence, for example, has for a long time kept aside higher order processes that are unique to particular modalities. For example, sequential aspects that are characteristic of auditory stimuli have been neglected because of the focus on visual modality and the role of auditory, tactile/kinesthetic, and olfactory imagery in in-

telligence has attracted no attention whatsoever. These, and other similar processes, have thus been denied their rightful place within the repertoire of human cognitive abilities.

2. *Assumption that lower order processes are more tractable than higher order processes.* Researchers who have followed the work Inspection Time (IT) know that tractability is a myth. We still do not know for sure what is the role of practice, strategy, or attention in IT (Bors, Stokes, Forrin, & Hodder, 1999), or the extent to which it measures *g* as opposed to visualization or mental speed (Crawford, Deary, Allan, & Gustafsson, 1998; Nettelbeck & Burns, 2000). One has to wonder about the reasons for investing so much effort into something that has been unable to provide theoretical enlightenment for such a long period of time. Just like IT, most other ECTs are typically more complex than we tend to assume (see Carroll, 1980), and parameters derived from such tasks sometimes behave in a way that is not predicted by the theory underlying their construction (see Roberts & Pallier, 2001).

If it is psycho-logically impossible to separate lower and higher cognitive processes in a meaningful way, we have no choice but to accept lower order processes within our studies of intelligence. I do not think that they will necessarily provide a better explanation of individual differences in cognitive abilities, as hoped for by some advocates of reductionism. Their inclusion is necessary for taxonomic reasons. We are still far from mapping out the whole domain of cognition using individual differences methodology and there remains a huge amount of uncharted territory.

My argument, also, is not against reductionistic approach per se. The true meaning of reductionism is in terms of explaining a scientific construct in one science by constructs from another science. Thus, biological explanations may be useful for psychology, even though much more careful thinking and research needs to be invested in this link (see Mackintosh, 1998). I have difficulties in accepting what may be called "psychological reductionism"—using one psychological process to explain another psychological process. Explaining biological events in terms of chemistry or physics is reductionism, but replacing one biological process by another, perhaps simpler and more parsimonious, is not. Can anybody claim that the Copernican system is not only more parsimonious, but also reductionstic in relationship to the Ptolomaic system? The same phenomena are explained in a more coherent way, but not in terms of lower order physical processes. In the same way, lower order cognitive processes, working memory, attentional resources, and mental speed, for example, are all useful for an improved understanding of the nature of individual differences in cognitive processes. However, these are not reductionistic constructs in the sense that biological accounts based on the neural efficiency hypothesis, plasticity, or the like may be. The individual differences approach is on an equal footing with the experimental approach in psychology, the latter does not "explain" the former. In fact, Carroll (1993) treated many of the processes that had been proposed as an explanation of individual differences in the same way as the processes they were supposed to explain.

CONSEQUENCES: REDUCED POSITIVE MANIFOLD AND g AS THE CHAIRPERSON OF AN OLIGARCHY

If it is hard to distinguish in a meaningful way between lower order and higher order processes, and if *microlevel reductionism* (Brody, 1999; Ceci, 1990; Deary, chap. 7, this volume) is taken seriously, a re-evaluation of the g construct is necessary. Since the time of the abovementioned shift from Galton's to Binet's approach, it has been known that lower order processes correlate lowly [*sic*] among themselves and they do not account for much of the variance in either school marks, job performance, or intelligence. Although it is almost axiomatic that this broadening of the definition of the domain will lead to a reduction in the role of g, it is necessary to get a "feel" for the amount of that reduction.

There are only a few studies in the literature that report on the average correlation between tests of cognitive abilities—the basis for positive manifold. Guilford (1964) reported such correlations in a paper with a somewhat misleading title "Zero correlations among tests of intellectual abilities." He noted that out of some 7,000 correlation coefficients derived from his own studies, virtually all values were positive, but also rather small. Thus, some 25% of correlation coefficients were not statistically significant and 18% were less than .10 in size. The average correlation coefficient was .22. This was one of the reasons why he dismissed g.

In Carroll (1993), the average correlation from 322 data sets was reported to be around .29 (Table 4.14, p. 132). He found that only 6.8% of all coefficients are smaller than .11. Apparently, both the average and the percentage of close-to-zero correlations are different in Guilford's and Carroll's reports, with the latter relying on a much more extensive database. As mentioned earlier, Guilford's studies deliberately included a great variety of marker tests, but not lower order processes, for different factors. This could account for the lower average correlation.

Stankov and Roberts (1999) argued that a representative sample of, say, 11 tests from the population that has an average correlation coefficient of .29, reported by Carroll (1993), would produce a first principal component whose latent root will be slightly less than four, taking over 35% of the total variance. Similar values for the latent root are frequently reported in the literature, supporting a "lion's share" of variance for the general factor. Under the same assumptions, Guilford's average correlation of .22 would lead to the first latent root accounting for about 29% of the variance. Although lower than 35%, this is still respectable and certainly not dismissive of the general factor.

Table 2.1 presents the percentages of variance accounted for by the general factor (either the first principal component or the second-order factor) in seven studies that contained measures of both higher order processes *and* a sizable proportion of ECTs or lower order sensory tasks. The percentage of variance accounted for by the general factor ranges from 20.5% to 26%, and the average from these seven studies is 24%. Working backwards under the same assumptions as before, this implies that the average correlation within the seven studies is smaller than .20.

It is well known that Spearman's one-factor theory was flawed because his statistical tests, based on the distribution of tetrad differences, did not support it. The situation has not changed: Only 6 studies out of 461 in Carroll's (1993) survey indicated a single factor. The application of confirmatory factor analytic procedures is in full support of these findings (see McArdle, Hamagami, Meredith, & Bradway, 2000). The only reason I can see for disregarding such strong statistical evidence is the claim that *g* is mighty *by comparison* to the other factors. But its strength depends on definitional aspects regarding the universe of tests. Because we cannot exclude lower order processes from the universe of cognitive tests, it follows that factors additional to *g* cannot be disregarded either. For example, 18% of the variance that is accounted for by the second factor may appear small when compared to the 36% accounted for by *g*. The same value cannot be disregarded in comparison to a *g* that takes only 24% of the total

TABLE 2.1
Percentage of Total Variance Accounted for
by the First Principal Component (Studies 1–5)
or the Second-Order Factor (Studies 6 & 7)

Study	% Accounted for by *g*
1. Auditory sensory/perceptual processes (Stankov & Horn, 1980)	25.9
2. Tactile/kinesthetic sensory/perceptual processes (Pallier et al., 2000)	25.8
3. Tactile/kinesthetic sensory/perceptual processes (Stankov et al., 2001)	22.8
4. Olfactory sensory/perceptual processes (Danthiir et al., 2001)	20.5
5. ECTs (Roberts & Stankov, 1999)	24.0
6. ECTs (Nettelbeck & Burns, 2000)	23.0
7. ECTs (Luo & Petrill, 1999)	26.0
Average	24.0

variance. Continuing investigations, using the full range of cognitive abilities, may reduce this percentage even further.

Although the data presented in Table 2.1 do not impinge on the position of a strict "purist agnostic" (virtually no amount of empirical data can be completely satisfactory) I feel that there is enough accumulated evidence to accept the existence of g within the cognitive domain. In reality, however, the role of g is much weaker than its advocates claim.

THE PSYCHOLOGICAL NATURE OF COGNITIVE FACTORS

However strong or weak g is, it is difficult to defend the proposition that there exists a single process that is responsible for its emergence. In a sense, g is devoid of any meaningful psychological conceptualisation.

Much confusion has been caused by failing to appreciate the complexities that are implied by the hierarchical structure of cognitive abilities. For example, by identifying fluid intelligence with g, and by claiming that reasoning ability is a little more than working memory (see Kyllonen, chap. 15, this volume), we are piling one simplification upon another. Research on Inspection Time, again, is a good example of a somewhat wasted effort because of the failure to consider the full hierarchical structure. Even a casual examination of the IT tasks would indicate that measures of perceptual processes of Gv (and Ga), in addition to measures of mental speed (Gs), may be implicated in performance on such tasks. If perceptual measures had been properly incorporated into the studies of the relationship visual and auditory IT and intelligence (for the most part, Gf), a much clearer picture would have emerged two decades ago. In other words, Gv and Ga processes in addition to, or instead of, g, are likely to play a role in IT.

Careful reading of the chapters in this volume clearly shows that there is no agreement on the underlying, basic psychological or biological process of g. At best, the proposed accounts in terms of working memory, mental speed, and the like, are relevant for fluid reasoning ability (Gf), not g. Because neither working memory nor mental speed plays a significant role in Gc, or in other broad organizations of the Gf/Gc theory, how can they be the "ingredient parts" of g?

COMPLEXITY MANIPULATIONS

In order to understand the nature of a factor, any factor, one needs to examine the pattern of factor loadings. Although, in the interpretation of the factor, we are trained to follow the practice of hypothesis testing and separate loadings into salient and nonsalient, much can be learned from the examination of the trends on factor loadings within the same factor. After all, Spearman claimed to have done precisely that when he formulated his noegenetic laws. Some variables may tend to have a consistently low loading on a given factor, others may tend to have high loadings on it. In principle, not only *g*, but also any other factor can be examined for such trends on loadings.

Furthermore, it may be possible to devise experimental procedures within a particular task (or several tasks) to systematically influence changes in factor loadings. These may be referred to as complexity manipulations. Such procedures might provide an improved understanding of the nature of the processes captured by the factor of interest.

Effective complexity manipulations currently exist for the processes captured by the broad fluid reasoning ability, Gf. They include competing tasks (Stankov, 1983), changes in the number of working memory place-keepers in series completion problems (Myors, Stankov, & Oliphant, (1989), card sorting with manipulations designed to capture parameters of Hick's law (Roberts & Stankov, 1999), stimulus–response compatibility effects, and tasks that require an increasing number of steps (e.g., pairwise mental permutations) to reach a solution (Schweizer, 1996). (Some of these processes also show their effects on the broad factors of short-term acquisition and retrieval [SAR] and aspects of broad speediness (Gs), but the effects on these latter functions are either inconsistent or weak.) On closer scrutiny, all these manipulations implicate different kinds of ingredient processes, and it is hard to single out any particular one as being the "basic" process of Gf. In a way, they are similar to ECTs in that they are conglomerates of relatively simple processes. There is, nevertheless, an impression that these different processes relate to what we have come to call Gf. If pushed, I would probably agree that the term *attention*, in all its diverse meanings, captures what we mean by Gf. Working memory is certainly a very important aspect of it, but it could not be the whole story. It is quite to be expected that these different aspects of Gf will have a biological basis that can be studied experimentally.

In order to gain a better understanding of the processes involved, similar systematic experimental manipulations should be employed with other broad factors of the theory of fluid and crystallized intelligence. It is to be expected that each broad factor will be influenced by several different kinds of manipulations, each consisting of different sets of ingredient processes.

In our laboratory, we have never attempted to carry out complexity manipulations that would affect the acculturated knowledge factor of crystallized intelligence (Gc). Interestingly, Gottfredson (chap. 13, this volume) seems to have provided an example which, although based on "classification" rather than experimental manipulation, suggests a way forward. Meta-analytic studies of personnel selection indicate that g is a good predictor of job performance, especially for jobs of high cognitive demand, because it captures the cognitive complexity required for such jobs. Thus, if we classify jobs from those imposing low cognitive demand to those requiring high demand, the predictive validity of g systematically increases. This is analogous to the manipulations we have employed with Gf tasks.

The problem in this case derives from the fact that she, and other people working in this area, never raise serious questions about the nature of g. They seem to think that this issue has been resolved, because the importance of one alternative, practical intelligence, pales in comparison to the role of g. And she is not alone in this refusal to look beyond g. One may wonder about the reasons for the practice of disregarding the distinction between Gf and Gc in meta-analytic studies of personnel selection. Likewise, one may wonder about the message from *The Bell Curve*. I raise these questions here because both Gottfredson's chapter and *The Bell Curve* were based on data obtained from the ASVAB (or its predecessor). This test battery, my colleagues and myself believe, measures Gc more than anything else (see Roberts, Goff, Anjoul, Kyllonen, Pallier, & Stankov, 2000). If the ASVAB measures mostly Gc, it is possible that a significant proportion of the literature on personnel selection that lumps all cognitive tests under the umbrella of g has a Gc quality.

Thus, for cognitively demanding jobs, acculturated knowledge (Gc) predicts successful performance better than it does for jobs that place low cognitive demand. If it is indeed largely Gc that is being measured by tests used for such prediction, one may be somewhat less impressed by the finding of high predictive validity. This is because jobs that impose high cognitive demands (i.e., criteria to be predicted), also imply a heavy reliance on formal education, precisely as would be predicted from the definition of Gc.

g glosses over important distinctions between abilities. Too much parsimony can only result in conceptual oversimplification. Its strong supporters seem to neglect the diversity of human cognitive processes.

AN UNAMBIGUOUS, SINGLE-PROCESS, ACCOUNT OF g IS UNACHIEVABLE

Being a factor, g can be examined using complexity manipulations. What changes in the features of cognitive tasks make them more g-loaded? Spearman's noegenetic laws are an aspect of Gf, and therefore they do not encompass everything we mean by g. In some of our own work, competing, or dual, tasks (two ability tests presented simultaneously), showed higher average correlations among themselves than their single counterparts. They also had higher correlations with outside measures of intelligence, such as WAIS–R scores. Because of their theoretical link to divided attention, and therefore to the capacity theory of attentional resources, these trends on correlations were thought to provide evidence that attention may be the basis of *g*. Put simply, the *g* loading depends on a tasks' processing demands. This has a strong "mental energy" flavor, and therefore it should be appealing to many people. It also has a connotation for ECTs and Thomson's theory of bonds.

Interpreting *g* in terms of attentional resources, or in terms of complexity (Jensen, chap. 3, this volume), is still a possibility, but more work needs to be done. In particular, only a limited number of competing tasks have been investigated. Such tasks are not easy to devise and administer. Also, competing tasks can lead to higher loadings not only on *g*, but on the Gf factor as well. Theoretically, too, their effects are akin to processes captured by Gf. It may, therefore, be practically impossible to reach unambiguous conclusions as to whether *g* or Gf is affected by competing task manipulations. Indeed, some other factors, such as short-term acquisition and retrieval (SAR), may be affected as well.

This methodological difficulty needs to be taken into account in the interpretation of *g*. It appears that virtually all factors at the second stratum can be interpreted in a meaningful way, but an unambiguous interpretation of *g* in terms of a limited number of manipulations and ingredient processes may be very difficult, if not impossible, to achieve.

It may be the case that the generality of *g* limits its chances of being linked to any particular cognitive or biological process. Furthermore, as mentioned previously, as it is likely that more then one ingredient process is always involved in the operation of a factor, the general factor is likely to involve a larger number of these processes than lower order broad and primary factors. After all, the increased diversity of cognitive processes captured by *g* would have to be the consequence of the inclusion of lower order processes in research on intelligence. Given these circumstances, it is probably futile to search for a single process underlying *g*.

As argued by Stankov and Roberts (1997), mental speed is not a good choice for such a "basic" process. In some of our recent work, for example, mental speed (Gs) and fluid intelligence (Gf) were assessed using several different tasks, and complexity manipulations were employed using an independent task. We have frequently observed an increased correlation of more complex versions of our manipulated task with independent Gf scores, but no systematic change in correlation with external Gs scores. This has happened even when the dependent measure for the manipulated task is mental speed (e.g., a stimulus–response compatibility task).

To illustrate this point, a compatible pairing of stimulus and response (choose "down" arrow when you hear word "down") might produce a correlation of .20 with both Gf and Gs measures. An incompatible pairing (choose "down" arrow when you hear word "up") might produce a .30 correlation with Gf but .20 correlation with Gs.

An interpretation of this finding may be that something else, not speed of mental processing by itself, is the cause of individual differences in Gf-type processes. For stimulus–response compatibility findings, this may be an interference effect due to unnatural pairings of stimuli and responses. If speed is not the basic process of Gf, how can it be the basic process of *g*?

g AS AN OUTGROWTH OF HISTORY IN THE SENSE USED BY CATTELL AND HORN

In a way, a hierarchically defined *g* that is located on the third stratum, is something that is three-times removed from the raw test scores. Some, perhaps many, tests will have most of their reliable variance taken by the primary factors and broad factors at the second order. In other words, *g* gains its strength from the fact that it captures a little bit of variance from many tests. What remains within each test to be picked up by *g* is a distillate that may be psychologically uninterpretable, and any effort to seek an understanding of its deeper nature may be doomed to failure.

According to Jensen (chap. 3, this volume), Gf, Gc, and *g* are not clear-cut constructs. It is worth noting that all constructs within Gf/Gc theory are better defined than *g* itself. Cattell's investment theory provides a clue as to the possible nature of *g*: It may be conceived of in terms of broad sets of influences that go beyond the cognitive domain. An early proposal of Cattell (1971), was that Gf and "provincial powers" (largely sensory processes captured by broad visualization, Gv, broad auditory function, Ga, and similar processes from other modalities) interact with the environment from early stages of human development. Interests play a very important part in the choice of these interactions, by reinforcing some types of activities, and eliminating others. The outcome of these interactions is the development of crystallized intelligence (Gc) and all primary factors. The full structure of human abilities is, therefore, the result of history. In his many writings on the development of cognitive abilities, Horn (1985) extended the list of influences beyond interests to include a host of proximal and distal causes. His subsequent renaming of crystallized intelligence (Gc) as acculturated knowledge is an explicit acknowledgment of its historical nature. Ackerman (1996) proposed a model of intelligence that is more involved, but conceptually similar to the ideas of Cattell and Horn.

In historical terms *g* is the outcome of ontogenesis consisting of many loosely related elements that have been selected by processes that have relatively little to do with cognitive abilities. Whatever is being captured by the *g* factor, thus, has to be different from "pure" Gf processes and provincial powers. Likewise, Gc is different from *g*, and the same conclusion can be reached with respect to all other broad factors of Gf/Gc theory. At any point in development *g* captures a mishmash of different things that are continuously changing. Searching for a single process underlying *g*, psychological or biological in nature, is a chimera. Perhaps *g* should be left uninterpreted forever.

If we accept a true hierarchical model of cognitive abilities, and define the universe of tests to cover all cognitive processes, many properties attributed to *g* will turn out to be properties of the existing second- or first-stratum factors. One has to ask if it is worthwhile glorifying a factor that emerges from frequently small correlations among broad factors. (Correlations between Gf and Gc range from .10 to more than .50, typically falling between .20 and .40. They both show different patterns of correlations with other broad factors, many of these correlations being lower in size.) In a substantive sense, *g* can be seen as a residual—whatever process remains after one takes account of cognitive processes captured by factors we understand well. By focusing on *g* rather than broad organizations of abilities located on the second-stratum, we gloss over many important aspects of human cognition.

CONCLUSIONS

g is not strong, but it does exist. It will become considerably weaker when the universe of tests is defined in terms of the totality of cognitive processes. This re-definition of the domain is called for by concerted efforts to explain performance on cognitive tests in terms of the ECTs. Since it is totally arbitrary to divide processes into higher order and lower order, and ECTs are deemed to be useful, the overall impact will be a reduced role for *g*.

As acknowledged by virtually every contributor to this volume, the cognitive basis of *g* is poorly understood. There is no single cognitive process that can explain the presence of *g*. Even a small number of core processes is unlikely to suffice for this purpose. It is a mixture of many different processes (including noncognitive influences) that are known to change in the course of development. The search for a single biological basis of *g* might be a futile exercise. Second-stratum factors, like Gf and Gc, are much better understood than *g*, and biological and sociological processes and influences can easily be related to these.

ACKNOWLEDGMENTS

I am grateful to G. Pallier and Dr. R. Roberts for their comments on an earlier draft of this chapter.

REFERENCES

Ackerman, P. L. (1996). A theory of adult intellectual development: Process, personality, interests, and knowledge. *Intelligence, 22*, 227–257.

Bors, D. A., Stokes, T. L., Forrin, B., & Hodder, S. L. (1999). Inspection time and intelligence: Practice, strategies, and attention. *Intelligence, 27*, 111–129.

Brody, N. (1999). What is intelligence? *International Review of Psychiatry, 11*, 19–25.

Burt, C. (1949). The structure of the mind: A review of the results of factor analysis. *British Journal of Educational Psychology, 19*, 100–111, 176–199.

Carroll, J. B. (1972). Stalking the wayward factors: Review of J. P. Guilford & Hoephner's *The analysis of intelligence* (New York: McGraw-Hill, 1971). *Contemporary Psychology, 17*, 321–324.

Carroll, J. B. (1980). *Individual difference relations in psychometric and experimental cognitive tasks*. Chapel Hill, NC: The L. L. Thurstone Psychometric Laboratory, University of North Carolina, Report No. 163. [ERIC Doc. 191 891]

Carroll, J. B. (1993). *Human cognitive abilities: A survey of factor-analytic studies*. New York: Cambridge University Press.

Cattell, R. B. (1971). *Abilities: Their structure, growth and measurement*. Boston: Houghton-Mifflin.

Ceci, S. J. (1990). On the relation between microlevel processing efficiency and macrolevel measures of intelligence: Some arguments against current reductionism. *Intelligence, 14*, 141–150.

Crawford, J. R., Deary, I. J., Allan, K. M., & Gustafsson, J. -E. (1998). Evaluating competing models of the relationship between inspection time and psychometric intelligence. *Intelligence, 27*, 27–42.

Danthiir, V., Roberts, R. D., Pallier, G., & Stankov, L. (2001). What the nose knows: Olfaction and cognitive abilities. *Intelligence, 29*, 337–361.

Detterman, D. K., & Daniel, M. H. (1989). Correlations of mental tests with each other and with cognitive variables are highest for low-IQ groups. *Intelligence, 13*, 349–359.

Deary, I. J., Egan, V., Gibson, G. J., Brand, C. R., & Kellaghan, T. (1996). Intelligence and the Differentiation Hypothesis. *Intelligence, 23*, 105–132.

Fogarty, G. J., & Stankov, L. (1995). Challenging the "law of diminishing returns." *Intelligence, 21*, 157–174.

Galilei, Galileo. (1953). Dialogue concerning the two chief world systems, Ptolemaic & Copernican [Dialogo . . . dove . . . si discorre sopra i due massimi sistemi del mondo]. Translated by Stillman Drake, with a foreword by Albert Einstein. Berkeley: University of California Press.

Gardner, H. (1983). *Frames of mind: The theory of multiple intelligences*. New York: Basic Books.

Guilford, J. P. (1964). Zero correlations among tests of intellectual abilities. *Psychological Bulletin, 61*, 401–404.

Guilford, J. P. (1967). *The nature of human intelligence*. New York: McGraw-Hill.

Guttman, L. (1992). The irrelevance of factor analysis for the study of group differences. *Multivariate Behavioral Research, 27*, 175–204.

Horn, J. L. (1985). Remodeling old models of intelligence: Gf-Gc theory. In B. B. Wolman (Ed.), *Handbook of intelligence* (pp. 267–300). New York: Wiley.

Horn, J. (1998). A basis for research on age differences in cognitive capabilities. In J. J. McArdle, & R. W. Woodcock (Eds.), *Human cognitive abilities in theory and practice* (pp. 57–91). Mahwah, NJ: Lawrence Erlbaum Associates.

Horn, J. L., & Knapp, J. R. (1973). On the subjective character of the empirical base of Guilford's Structure-of-Intellect model. *Psychological Bulletin, 80*, 33–43.

Humphreys, L. G. (1962). The organization of human abilities. *American Psychologist, 17*, 475–483.

Hunt, E. B. (1980). Intelligence as an information-processing concept. *British Journal of Psychology, 71*, 449–474.

Jensen, A. R. (1998). *The g factor: The science of mental ability*. Westport, CT: Praeger.

Luo, D., & Petrill, S. A. (1999). Elementary cognitive tasks and their role in *g* estimates. *Intelligence, 27*, 157–174.

Mackintosh, N. J. (1998). *IQ and human intelligence*. Oxford, England: Oxford University Press.

McArdle, J. J., Hamagami, F., Meredith, W., & Bradway, P. (2001). Modeling the dynamic hypotheses of Gf-Gc theory using longitudinal life-span data. *Learning and Individual Differences, 34*.

Myors, B., Stankov, L., & Oliphant, G. W. (1989). Competing tasks, working memory and intelligence *Australian Journal of Psychology, 41*(1), 1–16.

Nettelbeck, T., & Burns, N. (2000, April). *Reductionism and "intelligence": The case of inspection time*. Paper presented at the Australian Experimental Psychology Conference in Noosa, Queensland.

Pallier, G., Roberts, R., & Stankov, L. (2000). Biological versus psychometric intelligence: Halstead's (1947) distinction re-visited. *Archives of Clinical Neuropsychology, 15*, 205–226.

Roberts, R. D., Goff, G. N., Anjoul, F., Kyllonen, P. C., Pallier, G., & Stankov, L. (2000). The Armed Services Vocational Aptitude Battery (ASVAB): Not much more than acculturated learning (Gc)!? *Learning and Individual Differences, 34*.

Roberts, R. D., & Pallier, G. (2001). Individual differences in performance on Elementary Cognitive Tasks (ECTs): Lawful vs. problematic parameters. *Journal of General Psychology*.

Roberts, R. D., & Stankov, L. (1999). Individual differences in speed of mental processing and human cognitive abilities: Toward a taxonomic model. *Learning and Individual Differences, 11*, 1–120.

Roberts, R. D., Stankov, L., Pallier, G., & Dolph, B. (1997). Charting the cognitive sphere: Tactile/kinesthetic performance within the structure of intelligence. *Intelligence, 25*, 111–148.

Schweizer, K. (1996). The speed-accuracy transition due to task complexity. *Intelligence, 22*, 115–128.

Stankov, L. (1983). The role of competition in human abilities revealed through auditory tests. *Multivariate Behavioral Research Monographs*, No. 83-1, pp. 63 & VII.

Stankov, L. (1988). Single tests, competing tasks and their relationship to the broad factors of intelligence. *Personality and Individual Differences, 9*, 25–33.

Stankov, L., & Horn, J. L. (1980). Human abilities revealed through auditory tests. *Journal of Educational Psychology, 72*, 21–44.

Stankov, L., & Roberts, R. (1997). Mental speed is not the 'basic' process of intelligence. *Personality and Individual Differences, 22*, 69–84.

Stankov, L., & Roberts, R. D. (1999). *Hierarchical models of human abilities and basic and elementary cognitive processes*. Paper presented at the conference of the European Society for Psychological Assessment. Patras, Greece.

Stankov, L., Seizova-Cajic, T., & Roberts, R. D. (2000). Tactile and kinesthetic perceptual processes within the taxonomy of human abilities. *Intelligence, 29*, 1–29.

Sternberg, R. J. (1977). *Intelligence, information processing, and analogical reasoning: The componential analysis of human abilities*. Hillsdale, NJ: Lawrence Erlbaum Associates.

Thomson, G. A. (1939). *The factorial analysis of human ability*. Boston: Houghton-Mifflin.

Chapter 3

Psychometric *g*:
Definition and Substantiation

Arthur R. Jensen
University of California, Berkeley

The construct known as psychometric *g* is arguably the most important construct in all of psychology largely because of its ubiquitous presence in all tests of mental ability and its wide-ranging predictive validity for a great many socially significant variables, including scholastic performance and intellectual attainments, occupational status, job performance, income, law abidingness, and welfare dependency. Even such nonintellectual variables as myopia, general health, and longevity, as well as many other physical traits, are positively related to *g*. Of course, the causal connections in the whole nexus of the many diverse phenomena involving the *g* factor is highly complex. Indeed, *g* and its ramifications cut across the behavioral sciences—brain physiology, psychology, sociology—perhaps more than any other scientific construct.

THE DOMAIN OF *g* THEORY

It is important to keep in mind the distinction between *intelligence* and *g*, as these terms are used here. The psychology of intelligence could, at least in theory, be based on the study of one person, just as Ebbinghaus discovered some of the laws of learning and memory in experiments with $N = 1$, using himself as his experimental subject. *Intelligence* is an open-ended category for all those mental processes we view as *cognitive*, such as stimulus apprehension, perception, attention, discrimination, generalization, learning and learning-set acquisition, short-term and long-term memory, inference, thinking, relation eduction, inductive and deductive reasoning, insight, problem solving, and language.

The g factor is something else. It could never have been discovered with $N = 1$, because it reflects *individual differences* in performance on tests or tasks that involve any one or more of the kinds of processes just referred to as *intelligence*. The g factor emerges from the fact that measurements of all such processes in a representative sample of the general population are positively correlated with each other, although to varying degrees.

A *factor* is a hypothetical source of individual differences measured as a component of variance. The g factor is the one source of variance common to performance on all cognitive tests, however diverse. Factors that are common to only certain groups of tests that call for similar mental processes, or a particular class of acquired knowledge or skills, are termed *group factors*.

The g factor should be thought of not as a *summation* or *average* of an individual's scores on a number of diverse tests, but rather as a *distillate* from such scores. Ideally, it reflects only the variance that all the different tests measure in common. The procedure of "distillation" that identifies the common factor, *g*, is *factor analysis*, a class of mathematical algorithms developed following the invention of principal components analysis in 1901 by the statistician Karl Pearson (1857–1936) and of common factor analysis in 1904 by Charles Spearman (Jensen, 2000). These methods are now used in a great many sciences besides psychology, including quantum mechanics, geology, paleontology, taxonomy, sociology, and political science. Readers who want a brief introduction to the workings of factor analysis are referred to the tutorial articles by John B. Carroll (1979, 1983, 1997).

FACTOR MODELS

Factor analysis can represent the correlational structure of a set of variables in different ways, called factor *models*. Depending on the nature of the variables, certain models can represent the data better than some other models. Factor models fall into two main categories: *hierarchical* and *nonhierarchical*.

The simplest model represents Spearman's *two-factor theory* of abilities, in which each test variable reflects only two sources of true-score variance—a *general* factor (*g*) common to all of the variables in the analysis and a *specific* factor (*s*) peculiar to each test. A variable's *uniqueness* (*u*) (shown for each of the nine variables in Fig. 3.1) consists of the variable's specificity (*s*) and random measurement error (*e*). In this simplest model,

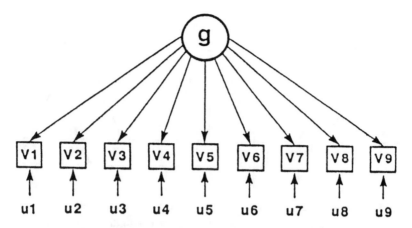

FIG. 3.1. The *two-factor model* of Spearman, in which every test measures only two factors: a general factor *g* that all tests of mental ability have in common and a factor *u* that is unique (or specific) to each test. From Jensen and Weng (1994). Used with permission of Ablex.

only one factor, *g*, accounts for all of the correlations among the variables. The correlation between any two variables is the product of their *g* factor loadings. Although it was seminal in the history of factor analysis, Spearman's model has usually proved inadequate to explain the correlation matrix of a large number of diverse tests. When *g* is statistically partialled out of the correlation matrix and many significant correlations remain, then clearly other factors in addition to *g* are required to explain the remaining correlations.

Burt (1941) and Thurstone (1947), therefore, invented multiple factor analysis. Illustrated in Fig. 3.2, it is not a hierarchical model. The three group factors (*F*1, *F*2, *F*3) derived from the nine variables are also called *primary* or *first-order* factors. In this illustration there is no general factor, only three independent (uncorrelated) factors, each comprising three intercorrelated variables. This model, originally hypothesized by Thurstone, didn't work out as he had hoped. Thurstone had believed that there is some limited number of independent primary mental abilities, so he *rotated* the factor axes in such a way as to make them uncorrelated with each other and to equalize as much as possible the variance accounted for by each of the factors, a set of conditions he referred to as *simple structure*. But this model never allowed a clear fit of the data, because every test battery he could devise, however homogeneous the item content of each of the diverse cognitive tests, always contained a large general factor. Though he tried assiduously to construct sets of uncorrelated tests, he found it absolutely impossible to construct mental tests that were not positively correlated with each other to some degree. In order to achieve a clean fit of the

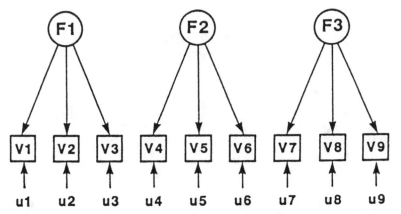

FIG. 3.2. The *multiple factor model* originally put forth by Thurstone (1887–1955), in which different sets of related variables (*V*) form a number of uncorrelated factors (*F*1, *F*2, *F*3, etc.). This model, therefore, has no general factor. From Jensen and Weng (1994). Used with permission of Ablex.

first-order factors to the separate clusters of tests, instead of orthogonal rotation of the axes he resorted to *oblique rotation* of the factor axes (i.e., the angle subtending any pair of axes is less than 90°), thereby allowing the first-order factors (e.g., *F*1, *F*2, *F*3) to be intercorrelated. The one factor common to these first-order factors, then, is a *second-order factor*, which is *g*. The first-order factors thus are *residualized*, that is, their common variance is moved up to the second-order factor, which is *g*. This is a hierarchical analysis, with two levels.

A nonhierarchical approach to multiple factor analysis that reveals the group factors as well as *g* was proposed by Karl Holzinger, one of Spearman's PhD students and later a professor at the University of Chicago. His bifactor model is now only one in a class of similar solutions called nested factor models. As shown in Fig. 3.3, a nested model first extracts the *g* factor (i.e., the first principal factor, which accounts for more of the total variance than any other single factor) from every variable, and then analyzes the residual common factor variance into a number of uncorrelated group factors. Note that there is no hierarchical dependency between *g* and the group factors in the nested model. Discussion of the nested model's theoretical and technical advantages and disadvantages as compared with the hierarchical model is beyond the scope of this chapter, but this has been nicely explicated elsewhere (Mulaik & Quartetti, 1997).

In the abilities domain, the *orthogonalized hierarchical model* has gained favor, especially with respect to identifying the same group factors across numerous different studies often based on different tests of the same basic abilities (Carroll, 1993). When a small matrix (fewer than 15 tests) is ana-

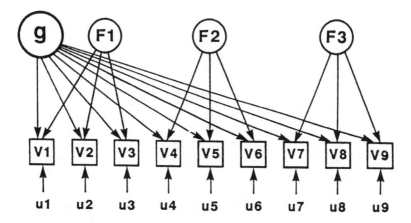

FIG. 3.3. A *nested multiple factor model*, which has a general factor *g* in addition to multiple factors *F*1, *F*2, etc. Holzinger's bifactor model was the first of this type of model. From Jensen and Weng (1994). Used with permission of Ablex.

lyzed the factor hierarchy usually has only two strata—the first-order factors and *g* appearing at the second order. When there is a large number of diverse tests there are many more first-order factors. When these are factor analyzed, they may yield as many as six to eight second-order factors, which then yield *g* at the third order.

Applying the hierarchical model to several hundred correlation matrices from the psychometric literature, Carroll (1993) found that *g* always emerges as either a second-order or a third-order factor. Inasmuch as *g* is ubiquitous in all factor analyses of cognitive ability tests, Carroll was more concerned with the identification of the other reliable and replicable factors revealed in the whole psychometric literature to date. He found about 40 first-order factors and 8 second-order factors, and, of course, the ubiquitous *g*. None of the hundreds of data sets analyzed by Carroll yielded any factor above a third-stratum *g*. He refers to the model that embraces these empirical findings as the "three-stratum theory" of human cognitive abilities.

A simple two-strata hierarchical analysis is illustrated in Fig. 3.4. The three first-order factors (*F*1, *F*2, *F*3) might be identified by the tests loaded on them, for instance, as verbal, numerical, and spatial ability factors. The numbers on the arrows are the *path coefficients* (correlations) between factors and variables at different levels of the hierarchy. A variable's *g* loading is the product of the path coefficients leading from the second-order factor (*g*) to the first-order factor (*F*), then to the variable (*V*). The *g* loading of V1, for example, is $.9 \times .8 = .72$. The correlation between any two variables is the product of the shortest pathway connecting them. For exam-

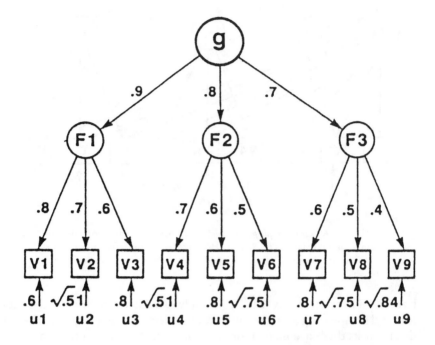

FIG. 3.4.   A hierarchical factor model in which the group factors (*F*) are correlated, giving rise to the higher order factor *g*. Variables (*V*) are correlated with *g* only via their correlations with the group factors. The correlation coefficients are shown alongside the arrows. The *u* is a variable's "uniqueness" (i.e., its correlation with whatever it does not have in common with any of the other eight variables in the analysis). Reproduced from Jensen and Weng (1994) with permission.

ple, the correlation between *V*1 and *V*9 is $.8 \times .9 \times .7 \times .4 = .2016$. The factor structure is completely *orthogonalized*, apportioning the variance accounted for in each variable by *g* and by *F* independently by means of an algorithm known as the *Schmid-Leiman orthogonalization transformation*, which leaves all the factors that emerge from the analysis perfectly uncorrelated with one another (Schmid & Leiman, 1957). The final result is shown as a *factor matrix* in Table 3.1. The percent of the total variance accounted for by each factor is in the last row and the communality (h^2) of each variable is shown in the last column; it is the proportion of a single variable's total variance that is accounted for by all of the common factors in the set of variables subjected to the factor analysis. In this example, only 37.33% of the total variance in all of the variables is accounted for by the common factors, of which 68.1% is accounted for by *g*. The correlation between any two variables is the product of their *g* loadings plus the product of their loadings on the first-order factors.

TABLE 3.1
An Orthogonalized Hierarchical Factor Matrix

| Variable | Factor Loadings | | | | Communality |
| | 2nd Order | First Order | | | |
	g	F_1	F_2	F_3	h^2
V_1	.72	.35			.64
V_2	.63	.31			.49
V_3	.54	.26			.36
V_4	.56		.42		.49
V_5	.48		.36		.36
V_6	.40		.30		.25
V_7	.42			.43	.36
V_8	.35			.36	.25
V_9	.28			.29	.16
% Var.*	25.4	3.1	4.4	4.4	37.33

*Percent of total variance accounted for by each factor = the sum of the squared factor loadings. Besides *g*, which is common to all of the variables, there are three uncorrelated group factors (F_1, F_2, F_3).

HOW INVARIANT IS *g*?

An important question regarding *g* as a scientific construct is its degree of invariance. If *g* varied across different methods of factor analysis, or different batteries of diverse mental tests, or different populations, it would be of relatively little scientific interest. Although this question has not been studied as thoroughly as the importance of the subject warrants, the answers based on the most relevant data available at present indicate that *g* is indeed a remarkably stable construct across *methods*, *tests*, and *populations*.

Across Methods

Applying the 10 most frequently used methods of factor analysis (and principal components analysis) to the same correlation matrices, both for artificial data in which the true factor structure was perfectly known and for real data, it was found that every method yielded highly similar *g* factors, although some methods were in slightly closer agreement with the known true factor loadings than were others (Jensen & Weng, 1994). The mean correlation between *g* factor loadings was more than +.90, and the different *g* factor scores of the same individuals were correlated across the different methods, on average, +.99. It makes little practical or theoretical difference which method is used to estimate *g* for a given battery of tests. The group factors, however, are generally less stable than *g*.

Across Tests

Thorndike (1987) examined the stability of *g* across different test batteries by extracting a *g* factor by a uniform method from a number of nonoverlapping test batteries, each composed of six tests selected at random from a pool of 65 exceedingly diverse ability tests used in the U.S. Air Force. Included in each battery was one of the same set of 17 "probe" tests, each of them appearing once in each of the test batteries. The idea was to see how similar the *g* loadings of the probe tests were across the different batteries. The average correlation between the probe tests' *g* loadings across all the different test batteries was +.85. From psychometric principles it can be deduced that this correlation would increase asymptotically to unity as the number of tests included in each battery increased. This implies that there is a true *g* for this population of cognitive tests, of which the obtained *g* is a statistical estimate, just as an obtained score is an estimate of the true score in classical measurement theory.

Across Populations

Provided that all the subtests in a test battery are psychometrically suitable for the subjects selected from two or more different populations, however defined, the obtained *g* factor of the battery is highly similar across the different populations. By *psychometrically suitable* is meant that the tests have approximately the same psychometric properties such as similar reliability coefficients, absence of floor and ceiling effects, and quite similar correlations between each item and the total score (i.e., the *item-total correlation*). When such criteria of adequate measurement are met, the average congruence coefficient between the *g* loadings obtained from representative samples of the American Black and White populations in a wide variety of test batteries is +.99, or virtual identity (Jensen, 1998, pp. 99–100; 374–375). The same congruence coefficient is found between the *g* loadings of the Japanese on the Japanese version of the Wechsler Intelligence Scale subtests (in Japan) and the *g* loadings in the American standardization sample. Similar congruence is found in European samples (Jensen, 1998, pp. 85–86).

FLUID AND CRYSTALLIZED INTELLIGENCE (Gf AND Gc)

These terms and their symbols were coined by Spearman's most famous student, Raymond B. Cattell (1971). They emerge as group factors at the stratum just below *g*, as second-order factors. *Gf* is most highly loaded on nonverbal tests that call for novel problem solving (e.g., Wechsler Block

Designs, Raven's matrices, figural analogies), inductive reasoning, and short-term memory for newly learned material (e.g., the backward digit span test). *Gf* is aptly defined as what you use when you don't know what to do. It enters into new learning and solving novel problems for which the individual has not already acquired some specific algorithm, strategy, or skill for tackling the problem. Also, response times (RT) to elementary cognitive tasks (ECTs) that involve a simple decision (e.g., press the left-hand button when the red light goes on; press the right-hand button when the green light goes on) are typically more loaded on *Gf* than on *Gc*.

Gc is loaded in tests of acculturation and past acquired verbal and scholastic knowledge, general information, and problems for which individuals have prior learned relevant concepts and specific solution strategies (e.g., general information, vocabulary, arithmetic problems). *Gc* is especially characterized by the individual's having to draw on long-term memory for past-acquired information and skills.

In a homogeneous population with respect to education and cultural background, measures of *Gf* and *Gc* are always highly correlated. Along with other second-order factors, therefore, they give rise to the higher order factor *g*. In Cattell's *investment theory*, the correlation between *Gf* and *Gc* comes about because persons *invest Gf* in the acquisition of the variety of information and cognitive skills that constitute *Gc*, and therefore over the course of interacting with the total environment, those who are more highly endowed with *Gf* attain a higher level of *Gc*.

In a number of very large hierarchical factor analyses of a wide variety of tests where *g* is the highest-order factor and the group factors at lower levels in the hierarchy have been residualized (i.e., their *g* variance has been removed to the next higher stratum), the *Gf* factor disappears altogether. That is, its correlation with *g* is unity, which means that *g* and *Gf* are really one and the same factor (Gustafsson, 1988). The residualized *Gc* remains as a first-order or second-order factor, loading mainly on tests of scholastic knowledge and skill. Nevertheless, *Gc* is of great practical importance for a person's success in education, in employment, and in the specialized expertise required for success in every skilled occupation.

When a large collection of highly varied tests of crystalized abilities is factor analyzed, a general factor emerges that is much more like *g* than it is like *Gc*. It is obvious that *Gf*, *Gc*, and *g* are not clear-cut constructs and that Cattell's claim that he had split Spearman's *g* into two distinct factors is misleading. The generality of *g* is remarkably broad, with significant loadings in tests and tasks as disparate as vocabulary, general information, reaction time, and inspection time (Kranzler & Jensen, 1989; Vernon, 1989).

Because the ability to *acquire* new knowledge and skills (hence *Gf*) typically declines at a faster rate in later maturity than the *memory* of past acquired and well practiced knowledge and skills (hence Gc), the Gf–Gc distinction has proved most useful in studies of the maturation and aging of cognitive abilities. This increasingly important topic is beyond the scope of this chapter; references to the relevant literature are given elsewhere (Horn & Hofer, 1992).

THE EXTERNAL VALIDITY OF g

If the g factor were related only to purely psychometric variables, or were only a result of the way cognitive tests are constructed, or were solely an artifact of the mathematical procedures of factor analysis, it would be of little scientific or practical interest. But this, in fact, is not the case.

First of all, it should be known that a general factor is not a necessary characteristic of a correlation matrix, nor is it the inevitable result of any method of factor analysis. The empirical finding of positive correlations among all cognitive tests is not a methodological artifact, but an empirical fact. It has proved impossible to construct cognitive tests that reliably show zero or negative correlations with one another. In the personality domain, on the other hand, although there are a great many measures of personality and these have been extensively factor analyzed by every known method, no one has yet found a general factor in the personality domain.

Moreover, g is not a characteristic of only certain cognitive tests but not of others. If one examines the g loadings of all of a great many different mental ability tests in current use, it is evident that g factor loadings are a continuous variable, ranging mostly between $+.10$ and $+.90$, and the frequency distribution of all the loadings forms a fairly normal, bell-shaped curve with a mean of about $+.60$ and a standard deviation of about $.15$ (Jensen, 1998, pp. 380–383). Yet factor analysis has been used in the construction of very few of the most widely used IQ tests, such as the Stanford–Binet and the Wechsler scales. It so happens that IQ and other cognitive ability tests that are constructed to meet the standard psychometric criteria of satisfactory reliability and practical predictive validity are typically quite highly g loaded. And they are valid for a wide range of predictive criteria precisely because they are highly g loaded.

Spearman (1927) said that although we do not know the nature of g, we can describe the characteristics of the tests in which it is the most or the least loaded and try to discern their different characteristics. But that cannot tell us what g actually is beyond the properties of the tests and the operations of computing correlations and performing a factor analysis. Comparing the g loadings of more than 100 mental tests, Spearman characterized those with the largest g loadings as involving the "eduction of relations and correlates," or inductive and inductive reasoning, and as having the quality of "abstractness."

But it is not the tests themselves, but g as a major source or cause of individual differences in mental tests that is still not adequately understood, although we do know now that it involves more than just the properties of the tests themselves, because it is correlated with individual differences in a number of wholly nonpsychometric variables (Jensen, 1987, 1993b).

As for the tests themselves, and for many of the real-life tasks and demands on which performance is to some degree predictable from the most g-loaded tests, it appears generally that g is associated with the relative degree of *complexity* of the tests' or tasks' cognitive demands. It is well known that test batteries that measure IQ are good predictors of educational achievement and occupational level (Jensen, 1993a). Perhaps less well-known is the fact that g is the chief "active ingredient" in this predictive validity more than any of the specific knowledge and skills content of the tests. If g were statistically removed from IQ and scholastic aptitude tests, they would have no practically useful predictive validity. This is not to say that certain group factors (e.g., verbal, numerical, spatial, and memory) in these tests do not enhance the predictive validity, but their effect is relatively small compared to g.

The Method of Correlated Vectors

This is a method I have used to determine the relative degrees to which g is involved in the correlation of various mental tests with nonpsychometric criteria—variables that have no necessary relationship to mental tests or factor analysis. IQ tests and the like were never constructed to measure or predict these extrinsic variables, and the fact that IQ is found to be correlated with them is an informative phenomenon in its own right, suggesting that the tests' construct validity extends beyond the realm of psychological variables per se (Jensen, 1987; Jensen & Sinha, 1993). The key question posed by this finding is which aspects of the psychometric tests in terms of various factors or specific skills or informational content is responsible for these "unintended" correlations?

Two methods can be used to answer this question. The first is to include the nonpsychometric variable of interest in the factor analysis of the test battery and observe the factor or factors, if any, on which it is loaded and the relative sizes of its loadings on the different factors. This method requires that we have all of the measurements (including the extraneous variable) and all of their intercorrelations based on the same group of subjects.

The second method, *correlated vectors*, consists of obtaining the column vector of, say, the g factor loadings on each of the tests in a battery (e.g., the first column [g] in Table 3.1) and correlating the factor loadings with a parallel column vector consisting of each test's correlation with the external variable. The size of the correlation is an index of the relative degree (as compared with other tests in the battery) to which g (or any given factor) enters into the test's correlation with the external variable. The advantage of the correlated vectors method is that the factor loadings and the tests' correlations with the external variable need not be based on one and the same subject sample. It is often preferable to use factor loadings based on the test battery's standardization sample, which is usually larger and more representative of the general population than is the data set of any single study. Hence data reported in the literature that show various tests' correlations with some external variable but were never intended to relate the external variable to g or other common factors in the test battery can be used for the correlated vectors analysis even if a factor analysis of the tests (not including the external variable) has to be based on a different subject sample, for example, the standardization sample of the Wechsler Adult Intelligence Scale.

An example of correlated vectors is shown in Fig. 3.5, based on a study of the habituation of the brain's evoked electrical potentials (Schafer, 1985). Subjects sit in a reclining chair in a semidarkened room and hear a series of 50 "clicks" at 2-second intervals, while the amplitude of the brain's change in electrical potential evoked by the click is measured from an electrode attached to the vertex of the subject's scalp and is recorded on an electroencephalograph. In normal subjects, the amplitude of the evoked brain wave gradually decreases over the course of the 50 clicks. The rate of this decrease in amplitude is an index of the *habituation* of the brain's response to the auditory stimulus. In a group of 50 young adults with IQs ranging from 98 to 142, the habituation index correlated +.59 with the WAIS Full Scale IQ. But what is the locus of this correlation in the factor structure of the 11 WAIS subtests? We see in Fig. 3.5 that the various subtests' g loadings predict the subtest's correlations with the evoked potential habituation index with a Pearson $r = 0.80$ and a Spearman's rank-order correlation $\rho = 0.77$. Because the differing reliabilities of the various subtests affect both their g loadings and their correlations with the habituation index, it is necessary statistically to remove the effect of correlated errors in the variables' g loadings and in their correlations with the habituation index. (The procedure of correlated vectors and its statistical variations are explicated in detail in Jensen, 1998, Appendix B.) After the g factor was statistically partialled out of the 11 subtests, none of them showed a significantly non-zero correlation with the habituation index; g was the sole factor responsible for the correlation between the WAIS IQ and the habituation of the evoked potential.

The same kind of correlated vectors analysis as illustrated earlier has been used to determine whether a number of different genetic, chronometric, anatomic, and physiological variables are related to the g load-

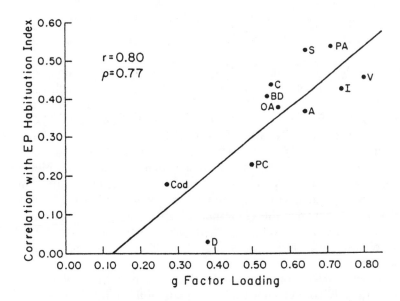

FIG. 3.5. Scatter diagram showing the Pearson correlation (*r*) and the Spearman rank-order correlation (ρ) between the correlations of each of the 11 subtests of the Wechsler Adult Intelligence Scale with the evoked potential (EP) Habituation Index (on the vertical axis) and the subtests' loadings on the *g* factor. The subtests are V–Vocabulary, PA–Picture Arrangement, S–Similarities, I–Information, C–Comprehension, BD–Block Designs, OA–Object Assembly, PC–Picture Completion, Cod–Coding, D–Digit Span. From Jensen (1998) with permission of Praeger.

ings in different batteries of mental tests, including the Wechsler scales. These are listed below, with the typical vector correlations shown in parentheses. Details of these studies are provided elsewhere (Jensen, 1998, chaps. 6–8).

- *Assortative mating* correlation between spouses' test scores (.95).
- The genetic *heritability* of test scores (.70).
- *Inbreeding depression* of test scores in offspring of cousin matings (.80).
- *Heterosis*-outbreeding elevation of test scores in offspring of interracial mating (.50).
- *Reaction time* (RT) on various elementary cognitive tasks (ECTs) (.80).
- *Intraindividual variability* in *RT* on ECTs (.75).
- *Head size* as a correlated proxy for brain size (.65).
- *Brain evoked potentials*: habituation of their amplitude (.80).
- *Brain evoked potentials*: complexity of their waveform (.95).

- *Brain intracellular pH* level; lower acidity → higher *g* (.63).
- *Cortical glucose metabolic rate* during mental activity (−.79).

It is a fairly certain inference that *g* is also mainly responsible for the simple correlation between scores on highly *g* loaded tests, such as standard IQ tests, and a number of other brain variables: brain volume measured *in vivo* by magnetic resonance imaging (MRI); brain wave (EEG) coherence; event related desynchronization of brain waves, and nerve conduction velocity in a brain tract from the retina to the visual cortex (Jensen, 1993b, 1997, 1998). There are also many physical variables that have less clearly brain-related correlations with IQ, such as stature, myopia, body and facial symmetry, blood chemistry, and other odd physical traits that somehow became enmeshed with the more direct neural and biochemical causes of individual differences in mental abilities in the course of human evolution or in ontogenetic development (Jensen & Sinha, 1993).

The functional basis of how and why all these physical variables are correlated with *g* is not yet known. The explanation for it in causal rather than merely correlational terms is now the major research task for the further development of *g* theory. Some of the as yet inadequately investigated and unproved hypotheses that have been put forth to explain the relationship of *g* to brain variables involve the total number of neurons, the number of connections between neurons (dendritic arborization), nerve conduction velocity, the degree of myelination of axons, the number of glial cells, and brain chemistry (neurotransmitters, ionic balance, hormonal effects, and so on).

The *g* factor at the level of psychometrics is now well established. Discovering its causal explanation, however, obviously requires that investigation move from psychology and psychometrics to anatomy, physiology, and biochemistry (Deary, 2000). This is now made possible by the modern technology of the brain sciences and will inevitably lead to the kind of reductionist neurophysiological explanation of *g* envisaged by its discoverer, Spearman (1927) who urged that the final understanding of *g* ". . . must come from the most profound and detailed direct study of the human brain in its purely physical and chemical aspects" (p. 403).

REFERENCES

Burt, C. (1941). *The factors of the mind.* New York: Macmillan.
Carroll, J. B. (1979). How shall we study individual differences in cognitive abilities? Methodological and theoretical perspectives. In R. J. Sternberg & D. K. Detterman (Eds.), *Human intelligence: Perspectives on its theory and measurement.* Norwood, NJ: Ablex.

Carroll, J. B. (1983). Studying individual differences in cognitive abilities: Through and beyond factor analysis. In R. F. Dillon & R. R. Schmeck (Eds.), *Individual differences in cognition* (Vol. 1, pp. 1–33). New York: Academic Press.

Carroll, J. B. (1993). *Human cognitive abilities: A survey of factor analytic studies.* New York: Cambridge University Press.

Carroll, J. B. (1997). Theoretical and technical issues in identifying a factor of general intelligence. In B. Devlin, S. E. Fierberg, D. P. Resnick, & K. Roeder (Eds.), *Intelligence, genes, & success: Scientists respond to 'The Bell Curve.'* New York: Springer-Verlag.

Cattell, R. B. (1971). *Abilities: Their structure, growth, and action.* Boston: Houghton Mifflin.

Deary, I. J. (2000). *Looking down on human intelligence: From psychometrics to the brain.* Oxford: Oxford University Press.

Gustafsson, J. -E. (1988). Hierarchical models of individual differences in cognitive abilities. In R. J. Sternberg (Ed.), *Advances in the psychology of human intelligence* (Vol. 4, pp. 35–71). Hillsdale, NJ: Lawrence Erlbaum Associates.

Horn, J. L., & Hofer, S. M. (1992). Major abilities and development in the adult period. In R. J. Sternberg & C. A. Berg (Eds.), *Intellectual development* (pp. 44–99). New York: Cambridge University Press.

Jensen, A. R. (1987). The *g* beyond factor analysis. In R. R. Ronning, J. A. Glover, J. C. Connoley, & J. C. Witt (Eds.), *The influence of cognitive psychology on testing* (pp. 87–142). Hillsdale, NJ: Lawrence Erlbaum Associates.

Jensen, A. R. (1993a). Psychometric *g* and achievement. In B. R. Gifford (Ed.), *Policy perspectives on educational testing* (pp. 117–227). Boston: Kluwer.

Jensen, A. R. (1993b). Spearman's *g*: Links between psychometrics and biology. *Annals of the New York Academy of Sciences, 702,* 103–129.

Jensen, A. R. (1997). The neurophysiology of *g*. In C. Cooper & V. Varma (Eds.), *Perspectives in individual differences* (pp. 108–125). London: Routledge.

Jensen, A. R. (1998). *The g Factor: The science of mental ability.* Westport, CT: Praeger.

Jensen, A. R. (2000). Charles E. Spearman: Discoverer of *g*. In G. A. Kimble & M. Wertheimer (Eds.), *Portraits of pioneers in psychology* (Vol. IV, pp. 92–111). Washington, DC: American Psychological Association and Mahwah, NJ: Lawrence Erlbaum Associates.

Jensen, A. R., & Sinha, S. N. (1993). Physical correlates of human intelligence. In P. A. Vernon (Ed.), *Biological approaches to the study of human intelligence* (pp. 139–242). Norwood, NJ: Ablex.

Jensen, A. R., & Weng, L. -J. (1994). What is a good *g*? *Intelligence, 8,* 231–258.

Kranzler, J. H., & Jensen, A. R. (1989). Inspection time and intelligence: A meta analysis. *Intelligence, 13,* 329–347.

Mulaik, S. A., & Quartetti, D. A. (1997). First order or higher order general factor? *Structural Equation Modeling, 4,* 191–211.

Schafer, E. W. P. (1985). Neural adaptability: A biological determinant of behavioral intelligence. *Behavioral and Brain Sciences, 8,* 240–241.

Schmid, J., & Leiman, J. M. (1957). The development of hierarchical factor solutions. *Psychometrika, 22,* 53–61.

Spearman, C. E. (1904). 'General intelligence' objectively determined and measured. *American Journal of Psychology, 15,* 201–293.

Spearman, C. E. (1927). *The abilities of man.* London: MacMillan.

Thorndike, R. L. (1987). Stability of factor loadings. *Personality and Individual Differences, 8,* 585–586.

Thurstone, L. L. (1947). *Multiple factor analysis.* Chicago: University of Chicago Press.

Vernon, P. A. (1989). The generality of *g*. *Personality and Differences, 10,* 803–804.

Chapter 4

Practical Implications of General Intelligence and PASS Cognitive Processes

Jack A. Naglieri
George Mason University

J. P. Das
University of Alberta

This chapter discusses how the extent to which the concept of general intelligence or *g* is adequate for both a theoretical understanding of human cognitive function and for practice. We specifically focus on the value of *g* in comparison to an alternative and contemporary conceptualization that includes assessment, delineation of individual differences in cognitive processing, and serves as a guide for instruction and remediation when a deficit is diagnosed. We review the background literature on the alternative conceptualization that divides mental processes into Planning, Attention, Simultaneous and Successive processing (PASS; Naglieri & Das, 1997b), and discuss its advantages over a single-score measure of general intelligence.

Theoretical Understanding of Intelligence

There was never any doubt that intelligence was a function of the brain, but what has been disputed is exactly what intelligence may be. Initial conceptualizations have only gradually yielded to an increasing willingness to accept contemporary advances in unraveling the workings of the brain. Whereas old conceptualizations focus on general intelligence, newer attempts to better understand intelligence have begun to focus on cognitive functions or processes. These functions have sometimes been conceptualized as independent constructs that work interdependently. We begin with a discussion that sets the stage for considering cognitive functioning in segments rather than as an undifferentiated mass. We propose that contemporary thinking about the brain, and therefore intelligence, has focused more on functional segmentation. Frackowiak, Friston, Dolan, and Mazziotta (1997) argued this when they stated: "The brain consists of a great many modules that process information more or less independently of each other" (p. 5).

Functional Organization

Does the brain function as a whole or are different processes of the brain associated with specific regions dedicated to them? This question received early attention from both Lashley and Pavlov in the early part of the 20th century. In an article "Reply of a Physiologist to Psychologists," published in *Psychological Review* in 1932, Pavlov responded to several issues in psychology, one of which was Karl Lashley's theory of mass action. Lashley concluded from his experiments with white rats that the brain works as a whole, and the results of damage to different parts of the rat's brain were dependent not on the region of the brain that was damaged but on the amount of brain tissue that was destroyed. Pavlov and later Luria took strong exception to the theory of mass action. Although Luria had much greater clinical evidence on human brain function than Pavlov, both questioned Lashley's conclusion that specific regions of the brain do not relate to specific mental functions, even in the rat.

Lashley's conclusion was that "specific cortical areas and association of projection tracks seem unessential to the performance of such functions which rather depend on the total mass of normal tissue" (Pavlov 1941, p. 133). In contrast, Pavlov's view was as follows:

> . . . it is not permissible to carry out at once any far-reaching correlation between dynamic phenomena and details of structure; but this correlation is by all means admissible, for the structure of the cortex is so variegated throughout its whole extent, and there is the fact, which we already know certainly, that only certain phases of synthesis and analysis of stimuli are admitted to one portion of the cortex and to none other. (p. 132)

Luria (1966), following Pavlov, showed through clinical studies on neurological impairment that it is quite conceivable to divide the brain into different areas and furthermore, to broadly locate certain functions within those areas. Luria's (1966) view on separate functional organizations described as the three blocks of the brain has considerable implications for the consideration of intelligence as a general construct or from a multiability perspective.

Although the brain works as a whole, it cannot be conceived to have one general function that is identified with intelligence. Neuropsychologists and their predecessors, the neurophysiologists, such as Sechenov and Pavlov, like current neuropsychologists, were convinced by repeated findings that some specific cognitive functions can be impaired while others remain largely intact. Arguments against a general factor of intelligence arise from clinical observations and logical considerations. For example, it is well documented in the literature that individuals with frontal lobe damage can earn average scores on a traditional IQ test (Lezak, 1995). Similarly many dyslexic children earn average or higher IQ scores but experience significant difficulty in reading (Siegel, 1988). These examples clearly illustrate that whereas these persons may have specific cognitive problems that relate to performance deficiencies, little value is obtained from a measure of general intelligence. This is also shown in the following case illustration.

Case Illustration

Larry is an 8-year-old boy in third grade who has had considerable difficulty reading during his elementary school years. His third-grade teacher initiated an evaluation by the school psychologist in order to attempt to assist him with his reading problem. The school psychologist evaluated Larry with the Wechsler Intelligence Scale for Children–3rd ed. (WISC–III; Wechsler, 1992) and other measures. This test is based on the concept of general intelligence and provides a single score (a Full Scale) that is often used as a good measure of *g* or general ability. Larry obtained a Full Scale score of 106 (Verbal IQ = 97, Performance IQ = 115) on this test and scores of 81 and 79 in reading decoding and reading comprehension, respectively. The discrepancy between Larry's Full Scale IQ and achievement could be used to qualify him for special education services as a learning disabled child in many locations around the United States. But the Full Scale score provides little information about the nature of the child's disability because no cognitive problem was detected to explain the academic failure—only a discrepancy was found. Thus, the Wechsler failed as a predictor of achievement for this young man. Without evidence of an intellectual problem it can only be assumed that the child can learn if provided instruction and that there is no apparent reason for the failure. In this case, as shown at the end of this chapter, there is a serious cognitive problem that was not detected by the general intelligence approach because this approach was developed during a period when little was known about specific human cognitive abilities.

HISTORICAL BACKGROUND

During this century, intelligence has been defined by the tests that have been used to measure it, especially tests like the Stanford–Binet IV (Thorndike, Hagen, & Sattler, 1986) and WISC-III (Wechsler, 1991). These tests provided structured and useful methods to evaluate children and adults since the early part of the 20th century. Research has shown that the IQ scores these tests yield are significantly correlated with achievement, related to acquisition of knowledge in employment settings, and related to acquisition of knowledge in nonacademic settings (Brody, 1992). Because of these results and the practical utility of IQ tests, general measures of intelligence have enjoyed widespread use for nearly 100 years.

Currency of Traditional IQ Tests

The Wechsler and Binet tests represent a traditional IQ testing technology that rests on the concept of general ability and has not changed since Binet and Simon introduced their first scale in 1905 and Wechsler published his first test in 1939. Despite cosmetic modifications and improved standardization samples the Fourth Edition of the Stanford–Binet and the latest revisions of the Wechsler Scales (e.g., Wechsler Adult Intelligence Scale–3rd ed., Wechsler, 1997) are essentially the same as their respective early versions. Moreover, the content of the Wechsler scales was largely based on the seminal work of Alfred Binet whom Yoakum and Yerkes (1920) recognized as the person responsible for the "origin of general intelligence tests" (p. 1). Binet, Wechsler, and others in the field at that time, deserve recognition, as visionaries who laid the groundwork for those who would follow.

Even though "early attempts at mental measurement were concerned with the measurement of separate faculties, processes or abilities" (Pintner, 1925, p. 52), the early researchers gravitated to the concept of general intelligence without a clear definition of what it was. As Pintner (1925) wrote, psychologists "borrowed from every-day life a vague term implying all-round ability and knowledge" (p. 53). Interestingly, Pintner also stated that "in the process of trying to measure this trait he has been and still is attempting to define it more sharply and endow it with a stricter scientific connotation" (p. 53). Thus, the psychologists who are mainly responsible for the content and form of tests still used some 80 years later had vague conceptualizations of what intelligence might be, but their methods gained and retained popularity to this day.

Ironically, the argument about intelligence as a general ability or separate abilities (e.g., Spearman's work) was a point of disagreement even at this early stage of the development of the field of intelligence testing. Researchers suspected that there could be separate abilities but they settled on general ability (Pintner, 1923). Unfortunately, some researchers noted that the arguments about general intelligence obscure the real issue, which is that intelligence tests built during the early part of the 20th century are incomplete and are in need of considerable revitalization (Naglieri, 1999; Sternberg, 1999).

There has been stagnation in the evolution of IQ tests and our understanding of intelligence has suffered because the tests which defined the construct have not changed during this century. A considerable amount of research has been conducted on human abilities during this century, but especially during the past 50 years. The study of specific abilities that extend beyond the poorly defined concept of general intelligence have been especially important. In the 1960s, in particular, a growing number of cognitive theorists studied neuropsychology, neuroscience, and higher mental processes. These efforts, described as the cognitive revolution (Miller, Galanter, & Pribram, 1960), had a substantial influence in theoretical psychology and some influence in applied psychology as well. The impact of the cognitive revolution was first felt with the publication of the Kaufman Assessment Battery for Children (K–ABC; Kaufman & Kaufman, 1983) and most recently with the publication of the Cognitive Assessment System (CAS; Naglieri & Das, 1997a). These authors have provided alternatives to traditional IQ tests that have dominated the field during most of this century. In the remainder of this chapter, we focus on the PASS theory and CAS.

PASS: AN ALTERNATIVE TO GENERAL INTELLIGENCE

Luria's Foundation

Luria's work (1966, 1970, 1973, 1980) was used as a blueprint for defining the important components of human intellectual competence corresponding to the functional aspects of brain structures included in the PASS theory. Luria described human cognitive processes within a framework of three functional units. The function of the first unit is the regulation of cortical arousal and attention; the second unit codes information using simultaneous and successive processes; and the third unit provides for planning, self-monitoring, and structuring of cognitive activities. These units provide separate abilities that are associated with different regions of the brain.

The first functional unit of the brain, the Attention–Arousal system, is located mainly in the brain stem, the diencephalon, and the medial regions of the cortex (Luria, 1973). This unit provides the brain with the appropriate level of arousal or cortical tone, and "directive and selective attention" (Luria, 1973, p. 273). That is, when a multidimensional stimulus array is presented to a subject and she or he is required to pay attention to only one dimension, the inhibition of responding to other (often more salient) stimuli and the allocation of attention to the central dimension depends on the resources of the first functional unit. Luria (1973) stated that optimal conditions of arousal are needed before the more complex forms of attention involving "selective recognition of a particular stimulus and inhibition of responses to irrelevant stimuli" can occur (p. 271). Moreover, only when an individual is sufficiently aroused and when attention is adequately focused can he or she utilize processes in the second and third functional units.

The first functional unit is not an autonomous system but works in cooperation with, and is regulated by, higher systems of the cerebral cortex, which receive and process information from the external world and determine an individual's dynamic activity (Luria, 1973). In other words, this unit has a reciprocal relationship with the cortex. It influences the tone of the cortex and is itself influenced by the regulatory effects of the cortex. This is possible through the ascending and descending systems of the reticular formation, which transmit impulses from lower parts of the brain to the cortex and vice versa (Luria, 1973). For the PASS theory this means that Attention and Planning are necessarily strongly correlated because attention is often under the conscious control of Planning. That is, our plan of behavior dictates the allocation of our limited attentional resources.

Luria's description of the second functional unit of the brain follows the work of Sechenov (1952). This unit is responsible for the reception, coding, and storage of information arriving from the external (and partially from the internal) environment through sensory receptors. It is located in the lateral regions of the neocortex, on the convex surface of the hemispheres, of which it occupies the posterior regions, including the visual (occipital), auditory (temporal), and general sensory (parietal) regions (Luria, 1973). Luria (1966) described "two basic forms of integrative activity of the cerebral cortex" (p. 74) that take place in this unit: simultaneous and successive processing. Simultaneous processing is associated with the occipital–parietal areas of the brain (Luria, 1966) and its essential feature is surveyability, that is, each element is related to every other element at any given time (Naglieri, 1989). For example, in order to produce a diagram correctly when given the instruction, "draw a triangle above a square that is to the left of a circle under a cross," the relationships among the different shapes must be correctly comprehended. Successive processing is associated with the frontotemporal areas of the brain (Luria, 1973) and involves the integration of stimuli into a specific serial order (Luria, 1966) where each component is related to the next component. That is, in successive synthesis, "each link integrated into a series can evoke only a particular chain of successive links following each other in serial order" (Luria, 1966, p. 77). For example, successive processes are involved in the decoding and production of syntagmatic aspects of language and speech articulation.

The third functional unit of the brain is located in the prefrontal areas of the frontal lobes of the brain (Luria, 1980). Luria stated that "the frontal lobes synthesize the information about the outside worlds . . . and are the means whereby the behavior of the organism is regulated in conformity with the effect produced by its actions" (Luria, 1980, p. 263). Planning processes that take place in this unit provide for the programming, regulation, and verification of behavior, and are responsible for behaviors such as asking questions, solving problems, and self-monitoring (Luria, 1973). Other responsibilities of the third functional unit include the regulation of voluntary activity, conscious impulse control, and various linguistic skills such as spontaneous conversation. The third functional unit provides for the most complex aspects of human behavior, including personality and consciousness (Das, 1980).

PASS Theory

Naglieri and Das (1997b) and Naglieri (1999) state that Planning, Attention, Simultaneous, and Successive cognitive processes are the basic building blocks of intelligence. These four processes form an interrelated system of functions that interact with an individual's base of knowledge and skills and are defined as follows:

- *Planning* is a mental activity that provides cognitive control, use of processes, knowledge and skills, intentionality, and self-regulation;
- *Attention* is a mental activity that provides focused, selective cognitive activity over time and resistance to distraction;
- *Simultaneous* is a mental activity by which the child integrates stimuli into inter-related groups; and
- *Successive* is a mental activity by which the person integrates stimuli in a specific serial order to form a chain-like progression.

Planning. Planning is a mental process that provides the means to solve problems of varying complexity and may involve attention, simultaneous, and successive processes as well as knowledge and skills. Planning is central to activities where the person has to determine how to solve a problem. This includes self-monitoring, impulse control, and generation of solutions as needed. Success on planning tests in the CAS requires the child to develop a plan of action, evaluate the value of the method, monitor its effectiveness, revise or reject the plan to meet the demands of the task, and control the impulse to act impulsively. All of the CAS planning subtests require the use of strategies for good performance and the use of strategies to solve CAS planning tests is amply documented by Naglieri and Das (1997b).

Attention. Attention is a mental process by which the person selectively focuses on specific stimuli while inhibiting responses to competing stimuli presented over time. All CAS tests on the Attention scale demand focused, selective, sustained, and effortful activity. Focused attention involves directed concentration toward a particular activity and selective attention is important for the inhibition of responses to distracting stimuli. Sustained attention refers to the variation of performance over time, which can be influenced by the different amount of effort required to solve the test. All CAS attention subtests present children with competing demands on their attention and require sustained focus.

Simultaneous Processing. Simultaneous processing allows the person to integrate separate stimuli into a whole or see parts as an interrelated group. An essential dimension of simultaneous processing is that all of the separate elements are interrelated into a whole. For this reason, simultaneous processing tests have strong spatial and logical aspects. The spatial aspect of simultaneous processing includes perception of stimuli as a whole as in a recognizable geometric design. Simultaneous processing is similarly involved in grammatical statements that demand the integration of words into a whole idea. This integration involves comprehension of word relationships, prepositions, and inflections so the person can obtain meaning based on the whole idea. Simultaneous processing tests in the CAS require integration of parts into a single whole and understanding of logical and grammatical relationships. These processes are used in tests that involve nonverbal and verbal content, and recall of the stimuli, but the essential ingredient is simultaneous processing.

Successive Processing. The essence of successive processing is that stimuli must be organized into a specific serial order that forms a chainlike progression. Successive processing is required when a person must arrange things in a defined order where each element is only related to those that precede it and these stimuli are not interrelated. Successive processing involves both the perception of stimuli in sequence and the formation of sounds and movements in order. For this reason, successive processing is important to any activity with sequential components such as memory of digits as well as the comprehension and use of the syntax of language. All CAS successive tests demand use, repetition, or comprehension based on order.

Cognitive Assessment System

The PASS theory was used as the theoretical basis for the CAS (Naglieri & Das, 1997b). This places the CAS in contrast to traditional tests based on the general ability concept. The PASS theory was used during the development of the items and subtests and as a guide to the conceptualization and construction of the CAS scales. The arrangement of subtests to their respective scales is supported by confirmatory factor analytic research (Naglieri & Das, 1997b) but it is important to recognize that the test was conceptualized according to the theory then examined using statistical analyses. The main purpose of the CAS was to integrate a theoretical view of human abilities based on neuropsychology and cognitive psychology with a test built within the psychometric tradition.

The CAS (Naglieri & Das, 1997a) is a recently published individually administered test standardized on a nationally representative sample of 2,200 children aged 5 to 17 years. The test is organized into four scales (Planning, Attention, Simultaneous, and Successive) according to the PASS theory. Each scale is made up of three subtests designed to assess the corresponding process. The Planning subtests require the child to devise a plan of action, apply the plan, verify that an action taken conforms to the original goal, and modify the plan as needed. There is considerable data to show that children use strategies to solve these tests. In fact, Naglieri and Das (1997b) reported that about 75% to 80% of 5- to 7-year-olds and more than 90% of children aged 8 to 17 years used strategies to complete the CAS Planning subtests. The Attention subtests require the focus of cognitive activity, detection of a particular stimulus, and inhibition of responses to competing stimuli. Subtests included in the Simultaneous processing scale all require the synthesis of separate elements into an interrelated group. The subtests vary on the basis of content (verbal and nonverbal) and some involve memory. The Successive processing subtests demand the repetition or comprehension of the serial organization of events. All the Successive subtests require the individual to deal with information that is presented in a specific order and for which the order drives the meaning. These subtests have been subjected to extensive validation examination (for summaries see Das, Naglieri, & Kirby, 1994; Naglieri, 1999; Naglieri & Das, 1997b).

Evidence for the PASS Theory Relevant to *g*

There are three aspects of the PASS theory that have special relevance to the current discussion regarding limitations of the concept of general ability, or *g*. The first is the issue of sensitivity to the problems of exceptional children, second is the question of prediction to achievement, and third is the relevance g has to intervention. In this section we argue that measurement of g is insufficient for examination of special children's cognitive problems and that although g has been shown to be a good predictor of achievement for groups of children, a more complete conceptualization of intelligence can predict achievement more effectively. Finally, we return to the case illustration provided in the first part of this chapter and show the child's PASS scores and how these can be used to generate interventions.

Sensitivity to Children's Cognitive Variation

Traditional measures of general intelligence like the WISC–III have been shown to be insensitive to the problems exceptional children experience (Siegel, 1988). The failure of the Wechsler Scales to accurately identify, for example, learning disabled (LD) children is well documented despite the widespread use of scale and attempts to identify specific types of children using scale or subtest profiles (Kavale & Forness, 1984; McDermott, Fantuzzo, & Glutting, 1990). Naglieri (in press) argued that the Wechsler Scales do not show sensitivity to the problems that many exceptional children have because the concept of general intelligence that is used is both ill defined and incomplete. This is why repeated attempts to validate the Wechsler profile analysis have met with failure. Moreover, evidence is needed to show that a recent reanalysis of the Wechsler subtests, for example, using the cross battery approach advocated by McGrew and Flanagan (1998) offers any advantage. In fact, the Gf–Gc approach utilized by Woodcock was also diagnostically ineffective. This is consistent with limited presentations of the discriminant validity evidence on Gf–Gc provided by McGrew, Flanagan, Keith, and Vanderwood (1997) and Horn and Noll (1997). These data are more fully described later.

Naglieri (1999) provided a review of cognitive profiles for children with Attention Deficit and Learning Disabilities for the WISC–III (Wechsler (1991), WJ–R Cognitive (Woodcock & Johnson, 1989a), and CAS (Naglieri & Das, 1997b) based on information taken from the test Manuals and a recent publication by Woodcock (1998). Wechsler (1991) reported studies involving children with Learning Disabilities ($n = 65$) and Attention-Deficit Hyperactivity Disorder (ADHD; $n = 68$), which showed that the profiles of WISC–III Index scores for the LD and ADHD children were essentially the same. Similarly, Woodcock (1998) reported profiles for the seven Gf–Gc clusters for children with learning disabilities ($n = 62$) and attention deficit disorders ($n = 67$). His results also showed similar profiles for the groups. These data illustrate that the seven factor Gf–Gc, like the WISC–III four Index level scores, do not yield distinctive profiles of scores for the LD and ADHD samples used. In contrast are the results for the CAS. In the studies reported by Naglieri and Das (1997b) children with

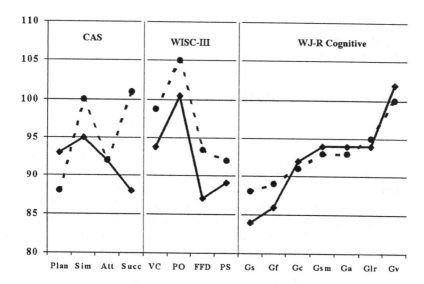

FIG. 4.1. Profiles of Standard Scores earned by children with Learning Disabilities and Attention Deficit Hyperactivity Disorder for the WISC–III, WJ–R Cognitive, and CAS.

Reading Disorders ($n = 24$) and Attention Deficit ($n = 66$) earned PASS scores that show a different pattern (see Fig. 4.1). The performance of ADHD children was more fully examined by Paolitto (1999).

Paolitto (1999) studied matched samples of ADHD ($n = 63$) and LD ($n = 63$) children and found that the CAS "is a useful tool in the assessment and identification of children with ADHD. The CAS was able to successfully identify about three of every four children having AHDD" (p. 4). He also reported that the CAS showed a total classification accuracy of about 70%. These findings also support the view of Barkley (1997, 1998) that ADHD involves problems with behavioral inhibition and self-control, which is associated with poor executive control (from PASS, Planning processing).

The data presented here illustrates that the traditional general intelligence model represented by the Wechsler Scales and the hierarchical g model represented by the WJ–R Cognitive do not appear to be sensitive to the cognitive problems these exceptional children exhibited. The Wechsler and WJ–R Cognitive were not effective for identification of the children with ADHD because these tests do not measure Planning. These results are consistent with suggestions by Barkley (1998) that the Wechsler is ineffective for identification of ADHD children. The results also illustrate that measurement of Successive processing is important for evaluation of children who have reading failure (this is discussed more fully later in the chapter). In total, the comparative results suggest that sensitivity to the cognitive problems these children have support suggestions by Naglieri (1999) and Sternberg (1999) that the general intelligence model is insufficient and incomplete.

Relationships to Achievement

One of the arguments in favor of traditional tests of intelligence based on general intelligence is that they predict outcomes in school and in the workplace (Jensen, 1998). Some researchers suggested that an important dimension of validity for a test of cognitive ability is its relationship to achievement (Brody, 1992). Naglieri (1999) studied this question for a variety of IQ tests and found that the correlation between the Full Scale scores obtained from various tests of ability with tests of achievement does vary. Naglieri (1999) summarized large-scale studies of the relationship between intelligence test composite scores and any and all achievement tests reported by the test authors. He found that the median correlation between the WISC–III (Wechsler, 1991) FSIQ and Wechsler Individual Achievement Test scores (WIAT; Wechsler, 1992) was .59 for a national sample of 1,284 children aged 5 to 19. A similar median correlation of .60 was found between the Differential Ability Scales (Elliott, 1990), General Conceptual Ability, and achievement for a sample of 2,400 children included in the standardization sample. The median correlation between the Woodcock–Johnson Revised Broad Cognitive Ability Extended Battery (Woodcock & Johnson, 1989) score with the Woodcock–Johnson Revised Achievement Test Batteries (data reported by McGrew, Werder, & Woodcock, 1991) as .63 ($N = 888$ children aged 6, 9, and 13 years). This value was very similar to the median correlation between the K–ABC (Kaufman & Kaufman, 1983) Mental Processing composite and achievement of .63 for 2,636 for children aged 2½ through 12½ years. Importantly, the K–ABC only has two scales and content that does not include verbal/achievement content like that found in the first three tests. The median correlation between the CAS Full Scale and the WJ–R Test of Achievement (Naglieri & Das, 1997b) was .70 (for a representative sample of 1,600 children aged 5 to 17 years who closely match the U.S. population). These results, shown in Fig. 4.2, suggest several important conclusions. First, that the general intelligence model illustrated by the Wechsler scales predicted achievement adequately, accounting for about 35% of the variance, but not as much as the CAS, which accounted for nearly 50% of the variance in achievement. This is a 40% increase in the amount of variance accounted for. Second, that when intelligence is viewed as a multidimensional construct it may (in the case of the CAS) or it may not (in the case of the WJ–R Cognitive) improve the prediction of achievement. Interestingly, the WJ–R has the largest number of scales and corresponding

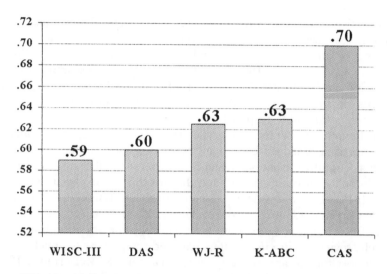

FIG. 4.2.   Median Correlations Between the WISC–III, DAS, WJ–R Cognitive, K–ABC, and CAS with Achievement.

factors, yet it did not predict achievement better because of that. In fact, the two factor K–ABC did about as well as the seven factor Gf–Gc model of Woodcock. Third, the two cognitively based tests of intelligence that are not rooted in general intelligence (K–ABC and CAS) and which were not designed to measure *g* showed the best prediction to achievement. This is even more important when it is recalled that both the CAS and K–ABC do not include subtests that can easily be considered measures of achievement (e.g., Information, Arithmetic, Vocabulary) and which overlap in content with the achievement test scores being predicted. That is, the WISC–III, DAS, and WJ–R Cognitive all contain subtests that have clear achievement items very similar to those found in the achievement tests that they were correlated with.

Relevance of g and PASS to Intervention

One of the most important practical uses of an IQ test is making the connection between assessment results and intervention. The relationship between IQ and instruction is often conceptualized within the context of an aptitude–treatment interaction (ATI). ATI assumes that the variation in a person's cognitive ability can have relevance to the type of instruction provided (Cronbach & Snow, 1977). The concept of using intelligence test scores for the purpose of instructional decision making has had considerable intuitive appeal for some time. Unfortunately, researchers have found that tests of general intelligence have not been useful for "providing effective aptitude–treatment interactions (ATIs) for evaluating how children best learn, or for determining how a particular child's style of learning is different from the styles manifested by other children" (Glutting & McDermott, 1990, p. 296). Although this research is difficult to conduct and replicate (Peterson, 1988), Snow (1976) concluded that students low in ability generally respond poorly to instruction and those high in general ability respond well.

The limited support for ATI led Peterson (1988) to suggest that an aptitude approach based on cognitive processes, which defines the persons ability as cognitive processes instead of general intelligence, could hold more hope for success. One method that fits the process treatment interaction (PTI) is the dynamic assessment approach designed to measure a child's learning potential (see Feuerstein, Rand, & Hoffman, 1979 or Lidz, 1991). Dynamic assessment has received some attention but, unfortunately, reviews of its effectiveness have led researchers to conclude that the support for the approach is limited (Glutting & McDermott, 1990). Another application of the PTI concept involves the PASS theory, which is covered in the remainder of this section.

Naglieri and Das (1997b) and Naglieri and Ashman (1999) described a number of methods that link information about a child's PASS characteristics with interventions in order to improve educational outcomes. Naglieri and Ashman (1999) summarized several approaches including the PASS Remedial Program (PREP; Das, 1999), Process Based Instruction (Ashman & Conway, 1997), and Planning Facilitation (Naglieri & Gottling, 1995, 1997) methods. They also describe how the PASS theory is related to and can be used with cognitively based instructional methods described by Kirby and Williams (1991), Pressley and Woloshyn (1995), Mastropieri and Scruggs (1991), and Scheid (1993). In this chapter we focus on the Planning Facilitation Method described by Naglieri (1999) and the PREP (Das, 1999) methods because they have the closest connection to the PASS theory.

Planning Facilitation

The PTI concept is well illustrated by research that has examined the relationship between strategy instruction and CAS Planning scores. Four studies have focused on planning and math calculation (Hald, 1999; Naglieri & Gottling, 1995, 1997; Naglieri & Johnson, 2000). The methods used by these researchers are based on similar research by Cormier, Carlson, and Das (1990) and Kar, Dash, Das, and Carlson (1992). These researchers utilized methods designed to stimulate children's use of planning, which in turn had positive effects on problem solving on non-academic as well as academic tasks. The method was based on the assumption that planning processes should be facilitated rather than directly taught so that children discover the value of strategy use without being specifically told to do so.

The results of the Cormier et al. (1990) and Kar et al. (1992) investigations demonstrated that students differentially benefited from a technique that facilitated planning. They found that participants who initially performed poorly on measures of planning earned significantly higher scores on progressive matrices than those with good scores in planning. The verbalization method encouraged a planful and organized examination of the demands of the task and this helped those children that needed to do this the most (those with low planning scores). This is in direct contrast to ATI research suggesting that children with low ability improve minimally but those with high ability improve the most (Snow, 1976).

The Cormier et al. (1990) and Kar et al. (1992) studies formed the basis for three experiments by Naglieri and Gottling (1995, 1997) and Naglieri and Johnson (2000) that focused on improving poor math calculation performance by teaching children to be more planful. The instruction focused on how children did the work rather than on mathematics instruction. The first two research studies by Naglieri and Gottling (1995, 1997) demonstrated that an intervention that facilitated planning led to improved performance on multiplication problems for those with low scores in planning, but minimal improvement was found for those with high-planning scores on the CAS. These learning disabled students benefited differentially from the instruction based on their CAS Planning scores, which suggested that matching the instruction to the cognitive weakness of the child was important.

Description of the Planning Facilitation Intervention. The planning facilitation method has been applied with individuals (Naglieri & Gottling, 1995) and groups of children (Naglieri & Gottling, 1997; Naglieri & Johnson, 2000). Tutors or classroom teachers provided instruction to the students about 2 to 3 times per week and consulted with the school psychologists on a weekly basis to assist in the application of the intervention, monitor the progress of the students, and consider ways of facilitating classroom discussions. Students completed mathematics worksheets that were developed according to the math curriculum in a series of baseline and intervention sessions over a 2-month period. During Baseline and Intervention phases, three-part sessions consisted of 10 minutes of math followed by 10 minutes of discussion, followed by 10 minutes of math. During the Baseline phase discussion was irrelevant to the mathematics problems but in the intervention phase, a group discussion designed to encourage self-reflection was facilitated so that the children would understand the need to plan and use efficient strategies when completing the mathematics problems. The teachers provided questions or observations that facilitated discussion and encouraged the children to consider various ways to be more successful.

Teachers made statements such as: "How did you do the math," "What could you do to get more correct," or "What will you do next time"? The teachers made no direct statements like, "That is correct," or "Remember to use that same strategy." Teachers did not provide feedback about the accuracy of previous math work completed and they did not give mathematics instruction. The role of the teacher was to facilitate self-reflection and encourage the children to complete the worksheets in a planful manner. In response to teacher probes, students made statements such as: "I have to keep the columns straight or I get the wrong answer," "I have to go back and study my math facts," "I have to remember to borrow," and "Be sure to get them right not just get it done." Naglieri (1999) provided additional details about the planning facilitation intervention method.

The application of the Planning Facilitation method is well illustrated in a recent investigation by Naglieri and Johnson (2000). These authors followed similar procedures as those used by Naglieri and Gottling (1995, 1997) but with a larger sample. The purpose of their study was to determine if children with specific PASS profiles would show different rates of improvement. For this reason subjects were organized into groups based on their PASS scores. Naglieri and Johnson (2000) formed groups of children with a cognitive weakness (an individual PASS score significantly lower than the child's mean and below a standard score of 85) in Planning, Attention, Simultaneous, or Successive Scales. The experimental group (those with a cognitive weakness in Planning) was contrasted to groups of children with cognitive weakness in Simultaneous, Attention, or Successive processing as well as a no cognitive weakness group. The results showed that the five groups of children responded very differently to the intervention. Those with a cognitive weakness in Planning improved 143% in number of math problems correct per 10-minute interval over baseline rates, whereas those with no cognitive weakness improved only marginally (16%). Similarly, lower rates of improvement were found for children with cognitive weaknesses in Simultaneous (−10%), Successive (39%), and Attention (46%).

Finally, a study by Hald (1999) was conducted using the Planning Facilitation method for children with high (>92) and low (<83) scores on the CAS Planning Scale. Mathematics worksheets were developed in accordance with the children's curriculum and five baseline and 11 intervention sessions conducted using the method. The results showed that children with the lowest Planning scores improved considerably more in math calculation than those with high planning scores (see Table 4.2 on p. 71).

TABLE 4.1

Percentage of Change From Baseline to Intervention for Children
with Good or Poor Planning Scores in Five Research Studies

Study	High Planning	Low Planning
Cormier, Carlson, & Das (1990)	5%	29%
Kar, Dash, Das, & Carlson (1992)	15%	84%
Naglieri & Gottling (1995)	26%	178%
Naglieri & Gottling (1997)	42%	80%
Naglieri & Johnson (2000)	11%	143%
Hald (1999)	−4%	29%
Average percent change baseline to intervention	16%	91%

A summary of the findings for the Cormier et al. (1990), Kar et al. (1992), Naglieri and Gottling (1995, 1997), Naglieri and Johnson (2000), and Hald (1999) studies is provided in Table 4.1. The results illustrate that Planning scores are relevant to intervention and predictive of which children would improve the most. The results of these studies, particularly the Naglieri and Gottling (1995, 1997), Naglieri and Johnson (2000) and Hald (1999) are in contrast to ATI research in important ways. First, in this research the children with the lowest planning scores improved the most, whereas in past ATI research the children with the highest scores improved the most. Second, the results showed that there was evidence for a process treatment interaction based on the PASS characteristics of the child.

As a group, these studies suggest that a cognitive strategy instruction that teaches children to better use planning processes is especially useful for those that need it the most. The effectiveness of this approach, however, was sometimes demonstrated for children who did not have planning problems. This has been found for other cognitive strategy training math studies (e.g., Van Luit & Naglieri, 1999), but the results of the studies summarized here showed that the greatest effect was found for those with poor Planning Scale scores on the CAS. This suggests that information about the child's specific, as opposed to general, ability, when defined by PASS, had relevance to the intervention provided.

These intervention findings support Naglieri and Gottling's (1997) suggestion that the PASS theory addresses calls for a theoretical model of cognitive processing that influences learning (Geary, 1989). These results also support the view that PASS may meet the need for a "theory of the initial properties of the learner which interact with learning . . . [and] accounts for an individual's end state after a particular educational treatment" (Snow, 1989, p. 51). By changing the way aptitude was conceptualized (e.g., from general intelligence construct used in past research to PASS) evidence for an ATI, or more precisely a PTI was suggested.

Although the Planning Facilitation method is one of several intervention options, another is the PASS Reading Enhancement Program (PREP) by Das (1999). This program is based on the PASS theory and is specifically recommended for those with reading failure and poor scores on the CAS Simultaneous and/or Successive processing scales. The PREP program was designed to improve simultaneous and successive processing that underlie reading, while at the same time avoiding the direct teaching of word reading skills. PREP is also founded on the belief that the transfer of principles can be made easier if the child experiences the tasks through guided discovery rather than by direct teaching and learning rules. Accordingly, the program is structured so that strategies are learned tacitly and not through direct teaching.

The PREP program consists of 10 tasks that vary in content and processing emphasis. Each task involves both a global training component and a curriculum-related bridging component. The global component includes structured, nonreading tasks that require the application of simultaneous or successive strategies. These tasks (see Fig. 4.3) also provide children with the opportunity to internalize strategies in their own way, thus facilitating transfer (Das, Mishra, & Pool, 1995). The bridging tasks involve the same simultaneous or successive cognitive demands as their global counterparts, which have been closely linked, to reading and spelling (Das et al., 1994). Children are encouraged to develop their own strategies and focus on the most relevant dimensions of the tasks. The global tasks begin with content that is familiar and nonthreatening so that strat-

PREP - Joining Shapes (Successive)

Global Task	Bridging Task
	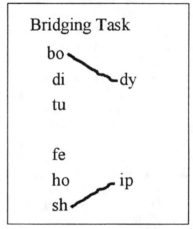

FIG. 4.3.   Illustration of PREP Global and Bridging Tasks.

egy acquisition occurs in small stages (Das et al., 1994). The global and bridging components of PREP also encourage children to apply their verbal mediation strategies to academic tasks such as word decoding.

The PREP program includes a system of prompts that are integrated into each global and bridging component. The series of prompts creates a scaffolding network that supports and guides the child to ensure that tasks are completed with a minimal amount of assistance and a maximal amount of success. A record of these prompts provides a monitoring system for teachers to determine when material is too difficult for a child or when a child is able to successfully progress to a more difficult level. A criterion of 80% correct responses is required before a child can proceed to the next level of difficulty. If this criterion is not met, an alternate set of tasks, at the same difficulty level, is used to provide the additional training required.

Efficacy of PREP

The efficacy of the PREP program was examined in recent research studies with good results. Carlson and Das (1997) and Das et al. (1995) conducted studies of the effectiveness of PREP for children with reading decoding problems in the United States. The Carlson and Das (1997) study involved Chapter 1 children who received PREP ($n = 22$) or a regular reading program (control $n = 15$). The children were tested before and after intervention with measures of Word Attack and Word Identification. The intervention was conducted in two 50-minute sessions each week for 12 weeks. The results showed that the students who received PREP remediation gained significantly more than control children in word identification and word attack. This study provides strong support for the utility of PREP in improving word reading by teaching students to use appropriate processes.

The Das et al. (1995) study involved 51 Reading Disabled children who were divided into PREP ($n = 31$) and control ($n = 20$) groups. There were 15 PREP sessions given to groups of four children. The experimental group was administered PREP approximately twice a week for a total of 15 sessions. Word Attack and Word Identification tests were administered pre and posttreatment. The PREP group improved significantly more in word identification and word attack than did the control group, even though both groups experienced the same amount of additional instructional time.

Boden and Kirby (1995) reported a study of a version of PREP modified for older children. A group of fifth- and sixth-grade students were randomly assigned to either a control or an experimental group. The control group received regular classroom instruction and the experimental group received PREP. Poor readers were identified from the overall sample based on their average grade equivalent scores on the Gates–Mac-Ginitie Comprehension and Vocabulary tests. Half of the students received PREP from one instructor and half from the other. Each group, which consisted of four students, received remediation for approximately 3 hours a week over a 7-week period. This provided each student with an average of 14 hours of remediation. Again, the results showed differences between the control and PREP groups on the Word Identification and Word Attack subtests of the Woodcock Reading Tests. In relation to the previous year's reading scores, the PREP group performed significantly better than the control group.

Finally, the most recent study by Papadopulous, Das, and Parrila (1997) involved a sample of 58 Grade 1 children who were among those who had been considered at-risk for reading disability and scored below the 26th percentile in either word identification or word attack. This sample was divided into two remediation groups—one group was trained in PREP, the other group was given a meaning-based intervention (shown pictures in the stories and discussed the stories without any reading of the words). The PREP group again outperformed the control group.

The investigations by Carlson and Das (1997), Das et al. (1995), Boden and Kirby (1996), Papadopulous et al. (1999) suggested that word decoding improved after completion of the PREP program. These results suggest that PREP appears to be effective with elementary school-aged students who have reading decoding problems that are especially related to successive or simultaneous processing difficulties. These findings also "suggest that process training can assist in specific aspects of beginning reading" (Ashman & Conway, 1997, p. 171).

CASE ILLUSTRATION OF A PASS PROCESSING APPROACH

We now return to the case illustration that was presented at the start of this chapter. The child's scores, provided in Table 4.2, show important variation and document the processing and academic problems this child has. It is clear that the WISC–III Full Scale score of 106 (66th percentile rank) suggests good performance as do the verbal and nonverbal measures of general ability. No general intelligence failure was found, so following from an ATI perspective, it would be predicted that this child should benefit from instruction at least at an average level. This is, of course, not the case, as evidenced by his very poor scores in Reading Decoding (81, 10th percentile rank) and Reading Comprehension (79, 8th percentile rank) on the Kaufman Test of Educational Achievement (K–TEA, Kaufman &

TABLE 4.2
Case Illustration—Larry, Age 8 years 3 months

Scale	Standard Score	Percentile Rank
WISC-III		
Full Scale IQ	106	66
Verbal IQ	97	42
Performance IQ	115	84
CAS Planning	108	70
Simultaneous (Relative Strength)	120	91
Attention (Cognitive Weakness)	80	9
Successive (Cognitive Weakness)	88	24
Full Scale	99	47
DSMD		
Conduct	54	66
Attention (Significant Problem)	68	96
Anxiety	43	24
Depression	43	24
Autism	44	27
Acute Problems	51	54
Externalizing	59	82
Internalizing	43	24
Critical Pathology	47	38
K-TEA		
Math Applications	104	61
Reading Decoding (Significant Weakness)	81	10
Spelling	87	19
Reading comprehension (Significant Weakness)	79	8
Mathematics Computation	101	53

Note. Child's mean PASS score was 99.5. Child's mean DSMD Scale T-Score is 50.5. Differences that are significant from the child's mean are noted.

Kaufman, 1998). A more complete picture of this child emerges when a nongeneral intelligence approach is used.

The case of Larry is typical of many, which illustrates that the general intelligence approach is incomplete in its coverage of the important variables that are related to academic failure. This boy has a cognitive weakness on the CAS Attention scale and consistently poor performance on the Attention scale of the Devereux Scales of Mental Disorders (DSMD; Naglieri, LeBuffe, & Pfeiffer, 1994). These two different sources of information indicate attentional problems in behaviors observed by parents and teachers (the DSMD is a behavior rating scale) and impaired performance of the child on the CAS Attention Scale. Importantly, the child's low scores in Attention (CAS and DSMD) are consistent with the child's poor reading performance. Problems in the Attention area of PASS are related to the child's reading failure because the deficit interferes with his ability to focus on the details of the stimuli (leading to misreading of words). In such cases the child gets distracted by the global meaning of sentences and fails to read the words precisely. Failure to control attention to the subject matter results in disorganized search strategies necessary for good reading comprehension, and in general, selective attention and resistance to distraction are impaired (Kirby & Williams, 1991). In this illustration, Larry's low scores on the K–TEA demonstrate the depth of the academic problems he has in reading and these are consistent with poor scores on the CAS Attention and DSMD Attention Scales.

The use of a general intelligence approach or *g* score for the case of Larry provided a view of the child that suggested good overall ability. Similarly, the CAS Full Scale score of 99 does not provide enough information about this person. In contrast, the PASS profile and achievement test data indicated problems in reading and the DSMD results suggested that those who have observed Larry noted a significant attention problem. In this scenario the child might be considered learning disabled (due to the ability–achievement discrepancy) or attention deficit (due to the poor achievement scores and problematic attention ratings). Teachers and parents would work under the assumption that the child has at least average ability with poor academics. The ability–achievement discrepancy results provided no explanation of the nature of the child's deficit and the DSMD data might be interpreted (with other findings) to suggest an attention deficit disorder. Guidelines for the construction of interventions for reading would likely focus on behavioral methods to control the child's classroom behavior.

Results from the PASS scales of the CAS suggest a different picture. The child does not have the type of attention deficit hyperactivity disorder (ADHD) found for children with a deficit in Planning on CAS (Paolitto, 1999). That type of problem is consistent with Barkley's (1997, 1998) theoretical model of ADHD, which describes the population as having a loss of behavioral inhibition and self-control, which is related to planning in PASS. Larry has a problem of inattention which, according to the DSM–IV (APA, 1994), includes problems with focus of attention, resistance to distraction, and poor attention and concentration. This is in contrast to the pattern of disinhibition, loss of control, and generally disruptive behaviors found with the hyperactive–impulsive type of ADHD. Poor attention in this case has blocked adequate examination of reading stimuli, interfered with the child's ability to selectively attend while reading, and disrupted the extent to which the child can examine a group of letters, organize it into sounds or patterns to adequately decode the word (Kirby & Williams, 1991).

In addition to poor attention, Larry also has a cognitive weakness on the CAS Successive processing scale. This score (88, 24th percentile) indicates that he has difficulty working with information that is presented in or requires working with things in order. For example, the sequences of sounds used to make words and the sequences of letters corresponding to the sequences of sounds for decoding as well as spelling. In order to help Larry better use successive processing when reading the PREP program is recommended (Das, 1999). This will teach him to recognize the sequences of letters and sounds in reading decoding and to better focus on the important serial nature of reading.

Additional interventions should focus on improving reading performance and skill acquisition by addressing other important findings—his cognitive weaknesses on the CAS Attention and Successive scales and relative strength on the Simultaneous scale. The child's difficulty with the CAS Attention Scale and DSMD Attention rating, along with the poor academic performance indicates that his problems with Attention (and Successive processing) are related to the specific areas of academic difficulty. One way to help him improve his attentional processing is to utilize a cognitive training program designed to help children better understand their attention difficulty and overcome it through a variety of compensatory skills. The Douglas Cognitive Control Program (Douglas, 1980) could be implemented to help teach Larry strategies for paying attention to his work through providing successful experiences and teaching him general rules about how to approach tasks. The program, described in Kirby and Williams (1991), involves a series of levels summarized in Table 4.3.

One advantage of using a cognitive processing perspective to examine basic psychological processing disorders that are related to academic failure is the explanatory power the view gives. In the current illustration, Larry's low score in Attention and Successive processing along with reading failure gives an explanation about why the child has had such difficulty. Attention is critical to maintenance of focused cognitive activity and resistance to distraction while reading (Kirby & Williams, 1991) but also in spelling. The child must maintain attention to the details of words and spelling, divide attention between the meaning and specific task of decoding, and not become distracted by extraneous material. In addition to the intervention for inattention, a second ("Word Sorting" from Zutell, 1988) for spelling and reading decoding problems should be implemented, and a third for reading comprehension ("Story Mapping" from Pressley & Woloshyn, 1995) is discussed. Both of these interventions take advantage of Larry's relative strength in the CAS Simultaneous processing scale.

Larry's strength in Simultaneous processing can be used to help him better attend to what he reads, more closely examine how words are spelled, and focus on the sounds that are associated with different letter combinations. In order to help Larry learn the sequence of spelling and sound–symbol associations needed for spelling (and reading decoding) a

TABLE 4.3
Illustration of the Methods That Could Be
Used to Improve Larry's Attention

Level I: Help children understand the nature of their deficits including:
  1. attention, resistance to distraction, and control of attention;
  2. recognition of how these deficits affect daily functioning;
  3. that the deficit can be overcome
  4. basic elements of the control program
Level II: Improve Motivation and Persistence
  1. Promote success via small steps;
  2. Ensure success at school and at home
  3. Teach rules for approaching tasks
    • Define tasks accurately
    • Check work carefully
    • Develop your own test strategy (see Pressley & Woloshyn, 1995)
  4. Discourage passivity and encourage independence
  5. Encourage self-reliance (Scheid, 1993)
  6. Help children avoid
    • Excessive talking, working fast with little accuracy, and sloppy disjointed papers
  7. Level III: Teaching Specific Problem-Solving Strategies
  8. Model and teach strategies that improve attention and concentration
  9. Child must recognize if he is under or over attentive
 10. Teach the use of verbal self-commands (e.g., "OK, calm down and think about what the question is.")
 11. Teach focusing strategies such as checking for critical features and careful listening for basic information
 12. Teach strategies that increase inhibition and organization
 13. encourage the use of date books and special notebooks for keeping papers organized
 14. teach the child to stop and think before responding
 15. Teach strategies to increase alertness
 16. teach the child to be aware of levels of alertness
 17. teach the child to use calming self statements
 18. Teach other relevant strategies
 19. teach rehearsal and mnemonic devices (Mastropieri & Scruggs, 1991)
 20. teach reading or math strategies (Pressley & Woloshyn, 1995)

Note. The information in this table is summarized from Kirby and Williams (1991).

technique called Word Sorting is recommended because it relies heavily on Simultaneous processing (seeing patterns in things). Word sorting is an intervention in which "students organize words printed on cards into columns on the basis of particular shared conceptual, phonological, orthographic, and meaning-related features" (Zutell, 1998, p. 226). This teaches students to generate concepts and generalizations about the features of how words are spelled, and it helps them connect new words to ones they already know (Pinnell & Fountas, 1998). The Word Sorting technique draws on the similarities among word spellings and encourages children to see words in groups based on the sounds the letters make. Because Larry is good at Simultaneous processing, the method draws on his strength and encourages him to see these patterns of sound–symbol associations. For example, the teacher may provide a list of words (e.g., grape, he, tree, knee, save, and tube) and request that Larry sort them according to how the e at the end of the word sounds (e.g., grape, save, and tube all have silent e whereas he, be, and knee all end in long e sound). This approach fits Larry because it has an emphasis on simultaneous processing, which is his strength. This intervention, in addition to application of the PREP Program should help him with the successive dimensions of reading and allow him to learn to better use these important processes during reading.

Larry's strength in simultaneous processing can also be used to help him with reading comprehension. Understanding of the meaning of a paragraph requires that the information in the sentences be seen as an interrelated whole, which demands simultaneous processing. Larry has difficulty with decoding and his attention to the details of the information provided in the paragraph is poor, which is why he is not able to get the facts needed to comprehend the paragraph. To help him attend to the relationships in the paragraph a technique called "Story Mapping" should be used (Pressley & Woloshyn, 1995). This technique requires that the child complete a diagram that organizes the paragraph (or story) into parts and draws attention to how these parts are interrelated.

Finally, Larry's instructional environment should be carefully monitored. Special efforts should be made to provide a supportive environment that is not overly punitive for inattentive moments, which will occur. Teachers should be knowledgeable about inattention and willing to accommodate the child (Goldstein & Mather, 1998). Classrooms should be well-organized and structured with separate working areas and clearly articulated rules. Academic materials should vary but should be of maximum interest to Larry. Attention should also be paid to what times of the day he can work most efficiently (Goldstein & Mather, 1998). Larry should also be taught plans for attending better to the work he is assigned which would include the following questions: What am I supposed to be doing? Did I complete the task? Did I miss anything? Are there any errors? Is the work neat and organized? Can I hand in my work now? (Naglieri & Ashman, 1999).

This illustration demonstrates that the outcome of the use of the CAS and PASS theory are very different from that which would result from a general intelligence approach. The results from the CAS showed cognitive processing deficits in Attention (also shown with the DSMD rating scale) and Successive processes that were related to academic failure. Interventions that addressed low Attention and poor Successive processing were proposed and one that utilized the strength in Simultaneous processing were provided. The examination of the child's PASS profile was considerably more informative than any single score that would be obtained from the merging of these components.

CONCLUSIONS

The time has come to move beyond the general intelligence model that has dominated the profession for nearly 100 years. Although these instruments have served an important purpose of establishing testing as one of the most important contributions psychology has made to society (Anastasi & Urbina, 1997), the way intelligence is conceptualized and measured needs substantial reinvention. Evidence provided in this chapter suggests that conventional g-based theories are incomplete and limited in their utility. Improved prediction of achievement, identification of the cognitive problems associated with academic failure, and connections between assessment and intervention were achieved when the PASS theory was applied using the CAS. Other advantages, such as increased fairness to minority populations also when this theory and test are used result (Naglieri & Rojahn, 2001; Wasserman & Becker, 1999).

It is important to carefully examine the advantages of newer approaches to intelligence. Researchers and practitioners should examine the evidence for validity of these alternatives in order to arrive at the most advantageous alternatives. Dillon (1986) suggested that a model should be evaluated on such dimensions as standardizability, reliability, validity, and diagnostic utility. In addition, a model's application to intervention should be added to better address current demands in school psychology and psychology for more defensible connections between assessment and educational programming. The alternative to general intelligence proposed here and elsewhere (Naglieri, 1989, 1999; Naglieri & Das, 1990, 1997b) is based on a modern conceptualization of ability (cognitive processes) rooted in cognitive and neuropsychological findings since the 1950s. The PASS theory fares well along a variety of tests of validity (Gutentag, Naglieri, & Yeates, 1998; Naglieri, 1999; Naglieri & Das, 1997b; Paolitto, 1999; Wasserman & Becker, 1999) and intervention applications (Hald, 1999; Naglieri & Gottling, 1995, 1997; Naglieri & Johnson, 2000). These studies suggest, at least, that the PASS theory as operationalized in the CAS warrants consideration. Ultimately, the success of the PASS theory rests in the advantages it provides to practitioners who use the CAS for important diagnostic and intervention decisions. These users will be able to judge if the expanded conceptualization of ability yields the kinds of information that extends beyond conventional notions of intelligence that have dominated the field to date. These users will also determine the value added by this attempt to revolutionize how intelligence is defined and measured.

REFERENCES

American Psychiatric Association. (1994). *Diagnostic and statistical manual of mental disorders* (4th ed.). Washington, DC: Author.

Anastasi, A., & Urbina, S. (1997). *Psychological testing.* Upper Saddle River, NJ: Prentice-Hall.

Ashman, A. F., & Conway, R. N. F. (1997). *An introduction to cognitive education: Theory and applications.* London: Routledge.

Barkley, R. A. (1997). ADHD and the nature of self-control. New York: Guilford Press.

Barkley, R. A. (1998). *Attention-Deficit hyperactivity disorder: A handbook for diagnosis and treatment* (2nd ed.). New York: Guilford Press.

Boden, C., & Kirby, J. R. (1995). Successive processing, phonological coding, and the remediation of reading. *Journal of Cognitive Education, 4,* 19–31.

Brody, N. (1992). *Intelligence.* San Diego: Academic Press.

Carlson, J., & Das, J. P. (1997). A process approach to remediating word-decoding deficiencies in Chapter 1 children. *Learning Disability Quarterly, 20,* 93–102.

Cormier, P., Carlson, J. S., & Das, J. P. (1990). Planning ability and cognitive performance: The compensatory effects of a dynamic assessment approach. *Learning and Individual Differences, 2,* 437–449.

Cronbach, L. J., & Snow, R. E. (1977). *Aptitudes and instructional methods.* New York: Irvington.

Das, J. P. (1980). Planning: Theoretical considerations and empirical evidence. *Psychological Research (W. Germany), 41,* 141–151.

Das, J. P. (1999). *PASS Reading Enhancement Program.* Deal, NJ: Sarka Educational Resources.

Das, J. P., Mishra, R. K., & Pool, J. E. (1995). An experiment on cognitive remediation or word-reading difficulty. *Journal of Learning Disabilities, 28,* 66–79.

Das, J. P., Naglieri, J. A., & Kirby, J. R. (1994). *Assessment of cognitive processes: The PASS theory of intelligence.* Needham Heights, MA: Allyn & Bacon.

Dillon, R. F. (1986). Information processing and testing. *Educational Psychologist, 21,* 161–174.

Douglas, V. I. (1980). Treatment and training approaches to hyperactivity: Establishing internal or external control. In C. K. Whalen & B. Hencker (Eds.), *Hyperactive children: The social ecology of identification and treatment.* New York: Academic Press.

Elliott, C. D. (1990). *Differential ability scales: Introductory and technical handbook.* San Antonio: The Psychological Corporation.

Feuerstein, R., Rand, Y., & Hoffman, M. B. (1979). *The dynamic assessment or retarded performers: The Learning Potential Assessment Device, theory, instruments, and techniques.* Baltimore: University Park Press.

Frackowiak, R. S. J., Friston, K. J., Dolan, R. J., & Mazziotta, J. C. (Eds.). (1997). *Human brain function.* San Diego: Academic Press.

Geary, D. C. (1989). A model for representing gender differences in the pattern of cognitive abilities. *American Psychologist, 44,* 1155–1156.

Glutting, J. J., & McDermott, P. A. (1990). Principles and problems in learning potential. In C. R. Reynolds & R. W. Kamphaus (Eds.), *Handbook of psychological and educational assessment of children: Intelligence & Achievement* (pp. 296–347). New York: Guilford Press.

Goldstein, S., & Mather, N. (1998). *Overcoming underachieving: An action guide to helping your child succeed in school.* New York: Wiley.

Gutentag, S., Naglieri, J. A., & Yeates, K. O. (1998). Performance of children with traumatic brain injury on the cognitive assessment system. *Assessment, 5*, 263–272.

Hald, M. E. (1999). *A PASS Cognitive Processes Intervention Study in Mathematics.* Unpublished doctoral dissertation, University of Northern Colorado.

Horn, J. L., & Noll, J. (1997). Human cognitive capabilities: Gf-Gc theory. In D. P. Flanagan, J. L. Genshaft, & P. L. Harrison (Eds.), *Contemporary intellectual assessment: Theories, tests and issues* (pp. 53–92). New York: Guilford Press.

Jensen, A. R. (1998). *The g factor: The science of mental ability.* Westport, CT: Praeger.

Kar, B. C., Dash, U. N., Das, J. P., & Carlson, J. S. (1992). Two experiments on the dynamic assessment of planning. *Learning and Individual Differences, 5*, 13–29.

Kaufman, A. S., & Kaufman, N. L. (1983). *Kaufman assessment battery for children.* Circle Pines, MN: American Guidance.

Kaufman, A. S., & Kaufman, N. L. (1998). *Kaufman test of educational achievement.* Circle Pines, MN: American Guidance.

Kavale, K. A., & Forness, S. R. (1984). A meta-analysis of the validity of the Wechsler Scale profiles and recategorizations: Patterns or parodies? *Leaning Disability Quarterly, 7*, 136–151.

Kirby, J. R., & Williams, N. H. (1991). *Learning problems: A cognitive approach.* Toronto: Kagan and Woo.

Lashley, K. S. (1930). Basic neural mechanisms in behaviour. *Psychological Review, 37* (Cited in Pavlov, 1932).

Lezak, M. D. (1995). *Neuropsychological assessment* (3rd ed.). New York: Oxford University Press.

Lidz, C. S. (1991). *Practitioner's guide to dynamic assessment.* New York: Guilford Press.

Luria, A. R. (1966). *Human brain and psychological processes.* New York: Harper & Row.

Luria, A. R. (1970). Functional organization of the brain. *Scientific American, 222*, 66–78.

Luria, A. R. (1973). *The working brain: An introduction to neuropsychology.* New York: Basic Books.

Luria, A. R. (1980). *Higher cortical functions in man* (2nd ed., revised and expanded). New York: Basic Books.

Mastropieri, M. A., & Scruggs, T. E. (1991). *Teaching students ways to remember.* Cambridge, MA: Brookline Books.

McDermott, P. A., Fantuzzo, J. W., & Glutting, J. J. (1990). Just say no to subtest analysis: A critique on Wechsler theory and practice. *Journal of Psychoeducational Assessment, 8*, 290–302.

McGrew, K. S., & Flanagan, D. P. (1998). *The intelligence test desk reference: Gf-Gc cross-battery assessment.* Boston: Allyn & Bacon.

McGrew, K. S., Keith, T. Z., Flanagan, D. P., & Vanderwood, M. (1997). Beyond g: The impact of Gf-Gc specific cognitive abilities research on the future use and interpretation of intelligence tests in the schools. *School Psychology Review, 26*, 189–210.

McGrew, K. S., Werder, J. K., & Woodcock, R. W. (1991). *WJ-R technical manual.* Itasca, IL: Riverside.

Miller, G., Galanter, E., & Pribram, K. (1960). *Plans and the structure of behavior.* New York: Henry Holt.

Naglieri, J. A. (1985). *Matrix Analogies Test—Expanded Form.* San Antonio: The Psychological Corporation.

Naglieri, J. A. (1989). A cognitive processing theory for the measurement of intelligence. *Educational Psychologist, 24*, 185–206.

Naglieri, J. A. (1997). *Naglieri Nonverbal Ability Test.* San Antonio: The Psychological Corporation.

Naglieri, J. A. (1999). *Essentials of CASAssessment.* New York: Wiley.

Naglieri, J. A. (2000). Can profile analysis of ability test scores work? An illustration using the PASS theory and CAS with an unselected cohort. *School Psychology Quarterly, 15,* 419–433.

Naglieri, J. A., & Ashman, A. A. (1999). Making the connection between PASS and intervention. In J. A. Naglieri, *Essentials of CASAssessment.* New York: Wiley.

Naglieri, J. A., & Das, J. P. (1990). Planning, attention, simultaneous, and successive cognitive processes as a model for intelligence. *Journal of Psychoeducational Assessment, 8,* 303–337.

Naglieri, J. A., & Das, J. P. (1997a). *Cognitive assessment system.* Itasca, IL: Riverside.

Naglieri, J. A., & Das, J. P. (1997b). *Cognitive assessment system interpretive handbook.* Itasca, IL: Riverside.

Naglieri, J. A., & Gottling, S. H. (1995). A cognitive education approach to math instruction for the learning disabled: An individual study. *Psychological Reports, 76,* 1343–1354.

Naglieri, J. A., & Gottling, S. H. (1997). Mathematics instruction and PASS cognitive processes: An intervention study. *Journal of Learning Disabilities, 30,* 513–520.

Naglieri, J. A., & Johnson, D. (2000). Effectiveness of a cognitive strategy intervention to improve math calculation based on the PASS theory. *Journal of Learning Disabilities, 33,* 591–597.

Naglieri, J. A., LeBuffe, P. A., & Pfeiffer, S. I. (1994). *Devereux Scales of Mental Disorders.* San Antonio: The Psychological Corporation.

Naglieri, J. A., & Rojahn, J. (2001). Evaluation of African-American and white children in special education programs for children with mental retardation using the WISC-III and cognitive assessment system. *American Journal on Mental Retardation, 106,* 359–367.

Papadopoulos, T. C., Das, J. P., & Parrila, R. K. (1997, August). *Long-term benefits of a reading remediation program with an at-risk population.* Paper presented to 7th European Conference for Research on Learning and Instruction, Athens, Greece.

Paolitto, A. W. (1999). Clinical validation of the cognitive assessment system with children with ADHD. *ADHD Report, 7,* 1–5.

Pavlov, I. P. (1932). Reply of a physiologist to psychologists. *Psychological Review, 39.* In I. P. Pavlov (1941). *Lectures on conditioned reflexes, Vol. 2: Conditioned reflexes and psychiatry.* W. Horsely Gantt (Trans.). New York: International Publishers.

Peterson, P. L. (1988). Selecting students and services for compensatory education: Lessons from Aptitude-treatment interaction research. *Educational Psychologist, 23,* 313–352.

Pintner, R. (1925). *Intelligence testing.* New York: Henry Holt.

Pinnell, G., & Fountas, I. (1998). *Word matters: Teaching phonics and spelling in the reading/writing classroom.* Portsmouth, NH: Heinemann.

Pressley, M. P., & Woloshyn, V. (1995). *Cognitive strategy instruction that really improves children's academic performance* (2nd ed.). Cambridge, MA: Brookline Books.

Raven, J. C. (1947). *Standard progressive matrices.* London: H. K. Lewis.

Scheid, K. (1993). *Helping students become strategic learners.* Cambridge, MA: Brookline Books.

Sechenov, I. (1952). *Selected physiological and psychological works.* S. Belsky (Trans.) and G. Gibbons (Ed.). Moscow: Foreign Languages Publishing House.

Siegel, L. S. (1988). IQ is irrelevant to the definition of learning disabilities. *Journal of Learning Disabilities, 22,* 469–479.

Snow, R. E. (1976). Research on aptitude for learning: A progress report. In L. S. Shulman (Ed.), *Review of research in education* (pp. 50–105). Itasca, IL: Peacock.

Snow, R. E. (1989). Aptitude-treatment interaction as a framework for research on individual differences in learning. In P. L. Ackerman, R. J. Sternberg, & R. Glasser (Eds.), *Learning and individual differences: Advances in theory and research* (pp. 13–60). New York: Freeman.

Sternberg, R. J. (1999). The theory of successful intelligence. *Review of General Psychology, 3,* 292–316.

Thorndike, R. I., Hagen, E. P., & Sattler, J. M. (1986). *Stanford-Binet Intelligence scale: Fourth edition.* Itasca, IL: Riverside.

Van Luit, J. E. H., & Naglieri, J. A. (1999). Effectiveness of the MASTER Strategy Training Program for Teaching Special Children Multiplication and Division. *Journal of Learning Disabilities, 32,* 98–107.

Wasserman, J. D., & Becker, K. A. (1999). *Recent advances in intellectual assessment of children and adolescents: New research on the cognitive assessment system (CAS): Research Report #1.* Itasca, IL: Riverside.

Wechsler, D. (1991). *Wechsler Intelligence Scale for Children Third edition* manual. San Antonio, TX: The Psychological Corporation.

Wechsler, D. (1992). *Wechsler Individual Achievement Scale.* San Antonio, TX: The Psychological Corporation.

Wechsler, D. (1997). *Wechsler Adult Intelligence Scale.* San Antonio, TX: The Psychological Corporation.

Woodcock, R. W. (1998). *The WJ-R and Bacteria-R in neuropsychological Assessment: Research Report Number 1.* Itasca, IL: Riverside.

Woodcock, R. W., & Johnson, M. B. (1989a). *Woodcock–Johnson Revised tests of cognitive ability: Standard and supplemental batteries.* Itasca, IL: Riverside.

Woodcock, R. W., & Johnson, M. B. (1989b). *Woodcock-Johnson revised tests of achievement: Standard and supplemental batteries.* Itasca, IL: Riverside.

Yoakum, C. S., & Yerkes, R. M. (1920). *Army mental tests.* New York: Henry Holt.

Zutell, J. (1998). Word sorting: A developmental spelling approach to word study for delayed readers. *Reading & Writing Quarterly: Overcoming Learning Difficulties, 14,* 219–238.

Part II

GENETIC–EPISTEMOLOGICAL APPROACH

General Intelligence: Measurement, Correlates, and Interpretations of the Cultural–Genetic Construct

Lloyd G. Humphreys
Stephen Stark
University of Illinois at Urbana–Champaign

Our contribution to general intelligence in this chapter is highly similar to the development of the topic by Jensen (1998). One of us (LGH) has written in support of the hierarchical model for many years. An early systematic account is presented in Humphreys (1962). It is rewarding to see the acclaim that Jensen's very able account of the model and the supporting data received. We do differ occasionally from Jensen in what we say about the model and the accompanying data, but differences are relatively minor. They reflect primarily a difference in philosophical orientation toward data and theory. There is no conflict with respect to the importance of the individual differences measured by the test of general intelligence.

Readers may find the first portion of our chapter to be repetitious of Jensen's discussion of the same topics. After a brief historical account of the factor analytic origin of the hierarchical model of intelligence, we start our definition with the same behavioral observations, the positive correlations among cognitive tasks, as Jensen. The complete definition represents an objective set of operations. We list its properties and briefly describe its correlates.

A major portion of our chapter, however, is reserved for a discussion of the major kinds of errors made by critics of the construct, its measurement, and its correlates. The construct of general intelligence cannot be discussed in full without discussing the errors made by many psychologists. They are picked up and quoted by opinion shapers, and their repetition falls on receptive eyes and ears of many Americans.

FUNDAMENTALS OF THE CONSTRUCT

A Glimpse at History

For a number of years in the 20th century, factor methods were used almost exclusively by British and American psychologists, but there was a difference in their approaches. British psychologists followed Spearman and emphasized a general factor that they extracted before defining narrow group factors. Most American psychologists were influenced by the multiple factor analysis of Thurstone and extracted no general factor. However, Thurstone shortly abandoned orthogonal rotation of multiple group factors to improve the fit of his factors to the data. This better fit, however, was obtained at a cost. Large positive correlations among the obliquely rotated factors were the norm, but were disregarded when interpreting the first-order factors. Thurstone and Spearman were converging because these correlations clearly showed a great deal of generality among so-called primary abilities, which is the empirical basis for the general factor of intelligence. Schmid and Leiman (1957) completed the rapprochement by using correlations among factors to define objectively a hierarchical model with a general factor at its apex. In sets of dependable data, the factor at the apex can be replicated among samples of persons from a defined population and from different sets of tests that sample the population of cognitive tasks.

We view our task in this chapter as one of fleshing out the approach to the measurement of general intelligence proposed by Schmid and Leiman. A unique definition emerges when their approach is followed. The definition is operational in the best sense of that measurement concept. It also has the important property that it does not force either a research person or a user into a premature unrealistic choice between general ability and narrow abilities.

Defining General Intelligence

Operational definitions of general intelligence were dropped many years ago from serious discussions of research involving human attributes, but this was due to the original simplistic use. The statement, "Intelligence is what intelligence tests measure," was sufficient to dismiss operational definitions. Our definition, adopted from Schmid and Leiman, is more complex. It starts with empirical, easily replicable observations of positive correlations among cognitive tasks. The replicable quantitative operations provide a unique definition without preconceptions about "real" intelligence.

The Observations Required. The necessary and sufficient condition to define a general factor in a set of cognitive measures (tests, tasks, problems) is that the intercorrelations are all positive; that is, they form a positive manifold. This phenomenon is most dramatic when the measures, by inspection, are widely different from each other. Higher levels of positive correlations occur among variates when, again by inspection, the variates are cognitively complex. The positive manifold does not disappear when chronological age is held constant, or when the sample is drawn from a population representing less than the full range of intellectual talent. Even if a cognitive task poses relatively simple problems for which there are demonstrably correct answers, the number correct score will be correlated with scores on more complex tasks. On the other hand, speed scores of various kinds may have a few small negative correlations with cognitive problem-solving tasks, and it seems reasonable to exclude these variates from the cognitive problem-solving domain.

For a common factor to become *the* general factor requires a domain of cognitive tests or tasks highly heterogeneous in content, operation, and product from which to select a representative set of variates for analysis (Humphreys chap. 5, 1985). Guilford's structure of intellect model provides an excellent guide to the variety needed (Guilford chap. 6, 1985). Two or more broadly based selections of variates from this domain can define, given standard psychometric methods, a common factor sufficiently close to identical in two or more analyses to be called the general factor. There are a series of examples of this near identity, extending over more than 50 years, in the reanalyses of Carroll (1993) of the basic R-matrices of many early investigators.

Standard Psychometric Methods. The discussion of standard psychometric methods starts with components of variance of test theory. Total raw score variance can be broken down into component variances in different ways. If the attribute being measured is X, its distribution can be described by $\bar{X}$ and $S_X = 1.00$. The classical analysis of the variance of X is $1 = t^2 + e^2$, in which t is true score and e is random error. In a factor analysis involving $X_1, X_2, \ldots, X_n$, $1 = h^2 + s^2 + e^2$ for each X_i. The total variance is now composed of the communality, the amount that a given X has in common with the other Xs, a broadly defined methods factor specific to the measuring instrument, and random error. Thus $t^2 = h^2 + s^2$. The communality, h^2, may contain the variances of n common factors.

Factor Methods. Two quite disparate methods of analysis of the evidence provided by the observed data are used. Statisticians seem to prefer the analysis of a matrix of variances and covariances. Psychologists prefer, or should prefer, a matrix of estimated communalities and correlations.

This preference is free of the units of measurement, which are typically highly arbitrary. The latter method is called principal factors; the former is principal components. Principal components describe raw score variances, whereas principal factors suggest possible behavioral constructs to those interested in individual differences.

In a common factor analysis, the initial diagonal entry must be estimated. Squared multiple correlations of each measure with all of the rest represents an estimate that is frequently and deservedly used. The decision concerning the number of factors to retain and rotate can be made by the parallel analysis criterion of Montanelli and Humphreys (1976) and the differences in size among the ordered successive roots of the R-matrix, the so-called scree criterion. The easy, highly quantitative "roots greater than one" criterion of Kaiser (1960) for examining the principal factors/components of the R-matrix can be very misleading (Carroll, 1993).

The factors retained are rotated obliquely by computer program to the simple structure criterion of Thurstone. Then the intercorrelations of these first-order factors are analyzed by the same procedures used with the original correlations. The analysis of the second-order factors usually finds a single third-order factor.

An exception to finding a single factor in the third order can occur if the sampling of the cognitive domain is seriously biased toward one type of content or operation. In the early years of research on Thurstone's primary mental abilities, several doctoral dissertations showed that a concentration of numerous different tests of one primary mental ability could break down the ability into several common factors. An R-matrix containing a concentration of tests needed to define the constituent factors can move a previous factor's location in the first order to the second order. This can appreciably reduce the fit of the single factor needed in the third order (Humphreys, 1962). Carroll did find three stages consistently in his many reanalyses of earlier first-order only analyses.

The Hierarchical Transformation.   The final step in the Schmid and Leiman (1957) procedure transforms, by two matrix multiplications, the factors in three orders into a hierarchy in which all of the factors are uncorrelated. The single third-order factor becomes the general factor (e.g., see Humphreys, 1962). Each measure in the analysis has a positive nonzero loading on this factor. The factors that appeared in the second order now have loadings on major subsets of the measures in the original R-matrix. These are major group factors. The first-order factors have loadings much smaller in the hierarchy in the first order. They are minor group factors.

Following the transformation, the loading in the hierarchical model for one of the major group factors can become essentially null. This occurs if that factor has a loading approaching unity on the third-order factor. This possible outcome can be readily misinterpreted as that particular second-order factor being identical with the general factor. That interpretation is erroneous because factor loadings in three orders enter the transformation to the hierarchy. The measures in the first order have the same communalities as in the more numerous hierarchical factors. The validity of a given measure for use in a test of the general factor is described by one number, the size of the correlation with the general factor. Every first-order test contains a substantial component of nonerror variance that is independent of its general factor variance.

Properties of the General Factor

The general factor obtained by the Schmid and Leiman orthogonalization procedure describes less variance than either the first principal factor or the first principal component of the R-matrix. No residual correlation between any two cognitive tests is reduced to a nontrivial negative value when the general factor has been removed. The general factor is also independent of varying numbers of tests defining first-order factors. For example, if verbal tests outnumber quantitative ones, the first principal component is affected. The general factor represents what highly varied tests, in terms of content and cognitive operations required, have in common with each other. Variance due to the several kinds of content and operation has been diminished. However, the general factor cannot be interpreted as representing pure biological capacity. It is still a phenotypic construct.

Measurement of the General Factor. The general factor can only be estimated, and there is only one way to diminish the error of estimation. Every potential item must contain general factor variance, whereas the unwanted variance that items inevitably bring to the total score is made as *heterogeneous* as possible. Heterogeneity produces small covariances so that the covariances due to the general factor accumulate more rapidly. A highly valid test of general intelligence can be described as measuring one dominant dimension with the inevitable nonerror unwanted variance kept small by diversifying it. Such a test is not attained by striving for the highest possible correlations among the items. Because the correlation between parallel forms of a test is also affected by the size of item intercorrelations, the highest possible reliability at a particular point in time is not a desirable goal.

We can now add a relationship of the first principal component to estimating the general factor. In the first place, the general factor is defined by the intercorrelations of behavioral measures, and the score that estimates individual differences in the underlying construct is the raw score on a behavioral measure. There is no way in which the general factor can be directly measured. Second, when the items in the estimate are selected in terms of size of loading on the general factor *and* by minimum overlap of nonerror variance independent of the general factor, the raw score on such a test becomes the first principal component of this special matrix. Only under these circumstances does the first principal component estimate the general factor without bias. The first component inevitably extracts nonerror unique and random error variances that appear in the raw score of the test. The amount of each source of unwanted variance, as well as the size of the total, decreases as the number of comparable, equally heterogeneous items is increased.

The Rest of the Hierarchy.   Each factor below the general factor in the hierarchy is a residual. Major factors have had the variance of general intelligence removed. Narrow, minor factors have had the variances of factors above them in the hierarchy removed. A composite of verbal tests may be called a measure of verbal comprehension or crystallized intelligence, but a substantial proportion of its nonerror variance is general factor variance. A composite of figural reasoning (fluid intelligence) also measures the general factor plus substantial nonerror unique variance. Both become residuals in hierarchical theory. Such residual scores may well add information of predictive significance to that furnished by a valid estimate of the general factor, but this requires quantitative research, not armchair speculation.

The total common variance of the factors in the hierarchical model is identical with communalities of the variables in the matrix of correlations that defined the first-order principal factors. The n factors in the first order are increased in number in the full hierarchy, but the communalities remain invariant. A large factor drastically reduces the amount of communality available to define subordinate factors.

A Statistical Criticism.   Statistically sophisticated critics tend to reject the hierarchical model of intelligence on grounds that factors higher in the hierarchy than those defined in the first order do not add information beyond what is already available in the first-order factors. The statement as such is true, but the conclusion that there is no need for the higher order factor tests is fallacious. The same reasoning would lead to ignoring factoring because all the information in the first-order factors is in the R-matrix. There is merit in reducing the number of variates needed in research if it can be done with little or no loss of usable information. The general factor at the top of the hierarchy not only describes a large portion of the total variance in R-matrices, but an even larger portion of the variance with personally and socially important criterion measures. The major group factors do add dependably to both total and psychologically important variances, but minor group factors add such a trivial amount to variance that they can be ignored in most applications. The result of this way of evaluating the hierarchical model does provide a substantial reduction, with little loss of useful information, in the number of variates needed in research.

The Criterion for Item Selection. The definition of general intelligence and the resulting tests that define the factor with the least nonerror unwanted variance does not include any preconceptions about the content of the items or the operations required. If a given type of item has a large loading on the general factor and meets the requirement of heterogeneity, it is acceptable. It does not matter that a critic might label some items as measuring achievement. Reading comprehension and arithmetic reasoning items are examples. They do measure achievement when the persons in the population are in the process of initial acquisition of the necessary skills. First and second grade reading are not as highly correlated with the general factor as later reading beyond the skill acquisition phase. See Cleary, Humphreys, Kendrick, and Wesman (1975) for a more extended discussion of the aptitude–achievement distinction.

The principle clearly rules out a criterion of equal opportunity to learn, or fairness, in selecting items for an intelligence test. Exposure to the materials in the items in a broad cultural area such as the United States is necessary. Raven's Progressive Matrices or other nonverbal tests are not, ipso facto, more effective measures of the general factor than a verbal or quantitative test. Such tests do contain substantial general factor variance, but each also measures a nonerror component that can be broadly described as a methods factor. Each item in the test of general intelligence also contains nonerror variance independent of the general factor. The sum of the contribution to variance of unwanted nonerror is smaller than any of its components when its origins are sufficiently heterogeneous.

IMPORTANCE OF THE CONSTRUCT

Applied Correlates of Proficient Cognitive Performance

The construct called general intelligence might be expected to have a wide range of correlates beyond those with cognitive problems solving tests. This is indeed the case. We start with educational and occupational correlates and add correlates with performance in military assignments. This material is followed by a discussion of the small correlations found with a wide variety of measures of human characteristics.

Educational Correlates.   Scores on a test of general intelligence are positively and substantially correlated with academic grades at every level of education. The many predictive correlations are worth more theoretically than the concurrent ones. There are additional correlations of a different research design predicting the amount of education that is reached years later, whether an undergraduate degree or a graduate or professional degree. The prediction of amount is made more accurately than the favorite alternative predictor of critics, the socioeconomic status of the parents (SES). Even decisions to enter higher education are predicted more accurately by the test than by SES (Humphreys, Jones, Davenport, & Lubinski, 1991).

Proficiency in Civilian Occupations.   There is little that can be added here to the findings and conclusions of Schmidt and Hunter (e.g., Schmidt & Hunter, 1998). They have published a great deal of data, much from the Department of Labor's General Aptitude Test Battery (GATB). They showed for a variety of occupations that an estimate of proficiency on the job is consistently correlated to a useful degree with scores on any test that estimates the general factor reasonably well. The criterion is frequently a supervisor's rating. If a second supervisor is available, the second rating is used to estimate a parallel forms reliability. A correction for attenuation raises the validity of the test from about .40 to the upper fifties for an infinite number of supervisors. This gain cannot be realized, but it can be approached by adding the two ratings. Working on the *validity* of the rating estimate can result in a larger gain that becomes an empirical reality. The validity of a rating is far from perfect. Ratings are influenced in a nonerror manner by factors that are not related to job proficiency. Adding more supervisors, even if possible, produces less gain than can be obtained by adding a valid measure of proficiency containing different method variance. Additional valid criterion information can come from peer ratings, performance tests, and printed proficiency tests. In other words, measuring job proficiency can be treated like the measurement of general intelligence. If each possible component measures something in common with the rest, total nonerror methods variance is reduced by the linear combination of components, while the common variance is increased. Thus, the correlations with general intelligence tests increase markedly.

Proficiency in Military Assignments.   The Schmidt and Hunter findings about civilian occupations are modified only a little in the military. The test of general intelligence predicts everything, and it is very difficult to find a cognitive measure that increases the validity of the intelligence test for either civilian or military assignments. The analyses reported in Campbell (1990) found that one well-known factor, spatial visualization, added consistently to the validities of the then current Armed Services Vocational Aptitude Battery for mechanical and technical military assignments. The findings were highly ironic, however, because the AFQT and its 1942 predecessor, the Army General Classification Test (AGCT) had contained a spatial component until the Carter administration. During that period, removal was initiated by women, at the level of the Department of Defense, on the grounds that the test discriminated against women. There is a sex difference in means, but there is also a good deal of overlap in the scores of men and women. The spatial attribute is critical for careers in physical science and engineering (Humphreys, Lubinski, & Yao, 1993; Humphreys & Yao, 1993).

Spatial visualization is a component of Vernon's (1960) major group factor that he called mechanical–spatial–practical. It is distinguished from another major factor called verbal–numerical–educational. The addition of mechanical to spatial does nothing to reduce the size of the sex difference, but ninth-grade girls who are high on the factor are the ones who enter the hard sciences years later. An additional benefit of being guided by data rather than ideology is the factor scores have substantially smaller correlations with social class than the scores on the other major group factor. The dropping of spatial visualization was self-defeating. If more women were wanted in the technical–mechanical job families, dropping qualifying scores a little, if necessary, would have been more effective than trying to sell young women, high in verbal ability, on that option.

Miscellaneous Correlates of General Intelligence

A dramatic attribute of the construct of general intelligence is the wide gamut of moderate positive correlations with the test of the general factor. Jensen considers one class of these correlates of high importance for the construct of the general factor on logical and empirical grounds. This class, however, does not stand out from the rest with respect to the size of its correlations.

Correlations With Neural Events. Estimates of the general factor are positively correlated with reaction time, discrimination reaction time (larger), variability of reaction time, speed of nervous conduction, movement time, evoked response potentials in the cortex, and so forth. These correlations are reported more fully in Jensen (1998). A gap of the research in this domain is there are few if any intercorrelations of two or more of these neural measures and general intelligence. Such correlations, depending on the size of one of the three, can lead to quite disparate interpretations of the data. The relative sizes of these correlations are important to their evaluation, so sample size is critical in answering research questions. Con-

TABLE 5.1
Models of Three-Variable R-Matrices and Their Factor Loadings

Model A				Model B			
1	2	3	Factor Loadings	1	2	3	Factor Loadings
	0.40	0.40	1.00		0.40	0.40	0.63
0.40		0.16	0.40	0.40		0.40	0.63
0.40	0.16		0.40	0.40	0.40		0.63

Intercorrelations and Factor Loadings of Three Variates for 10th Grade Boys and Girls

	Boys				Girls			
	1	2	3	Factor Loadings	1	2	3	Factor Loadings
General Intelligence		0.37	0.42	0.87		0.41	0.41	0.82
Health Key	0.37		0.20	0.42	0.41		0.26	0.50
SES	0.42	0.20		0.48	0.41	0.26		0.50

sider the following hypothetical R-matrices and their factoring in Table 5.1. The A matrix shows that the common variance of the three variates is defined by one of the three and shared by small parts of the variances of the remaining two. The B matrix shows that the three variates are each equally valid measures of what they measure in common. Individually, they do measure something at a modest level. The three could be equally weighted in a composite to measure that something more effectively. If one of the three variates is a measure of general intelligence, the something does not have the unique characteristics of general intelligence.

A Test of the Two Models.　　This method of evaluating correlations can be illustrated in data published several years ago (Humphreys, Davey, & Kashima, 1986). These data also present a second miscellaneous correlate and amply confirm an almost 80-year-old finding (Terman, 1925). Empirically keyed tests composed of items from the Project Talent background questionnaire concerned with physical health and well-being were used. The keys were formed on 10,000 cases and cross-validated on a separate 10,000. The item correlations with the Talent measure of general intelligence were keyed independently for boys and girls in their own samples. The intercorrelations of the two health scores, the Talent intelligence composite, and the score on the Talent composite measuring the socioeconomic status of the parents were computed and evaluated in the fashion just described. The data appear in Table 5.2 with the results for high school boys on the left and high school girls on the right.

TABLE 5.2
Effect Sizes and Their Corresponding Point Biserial Coefficients
of Correlation When Two Treatment Groups Have Equal Ns

Effect Size	Description	Correlation
.20	Small	.100
.50	Medium	.243
.80	Large	.371
1.00		.447
1.50		.600
2.00		.707
2.50		.781
3.00		.832
3.46		.866

Note. Based in part on (1988, p. 22)
From "Intelligence: A Neglected Aspect," by D. Lubinski and L. G. Humphreys (1997), *Intelligence, 24*, p. 175. Reprinted with permission from Ablex Publishing Corporation.

The fitting of one factor to each table of correlations by a little trial and error, not computer iteration, is very accurate. The results for boys and girls are quite similar. For each sex the communality among the three variates as being due in its entirety to general intelligence cannot be rejected. The health keys and the measure of SES seemingly have nothing in common when their shared general intelligence variance is accounted for.

Brand's Review of Correlates. Brand (1987) listed a full page of correlates, along with a source for each entry (p. 254). Entries are arranged alphabetically and range from achievement motivation to values. Artistic preferences and abilities, emotional sensitivity, field-independence, health and longevity, interests of several varieties, leadership, marriage partner's intelligence, migration, moral reasoning, motor skills, perceptual abilities, social skills, and socioeconomic status achieved fill in some of the rest of the list.

Social Ills. General intelligence has small, but still important, nonzero correlations with a variety of social phenomena. When the focus is on social ill rather than social health, the correlations are negative. Herrnstein and Murray (1994) presented these data on Whites so that they are not confounded with the Black–White difference in tested intelligence. They made social comparisons at different levels of adult intelligence and socioeconomic status of the parents of the research participants, the latter variable being a widely accepted causal source of social problems. In one comparison after another, these authors showed that general intelligence test scores were more predictive than SES.

Height and Intelligence. Standing height has been studied extensively. See Tanner (1966) for an excellent review. By the time young adulthood is reached, a correlation of standing height with general intelligence in the low twenties is common. Husen (1959) found a correlation of .22 in a large sample of military conscripts in the racially homogeneous population of Sweden. It should be noted that other measures of physique also have positive correlations with intelligence.

Humphreys, Davey, and Park (1985) studied relations between height and intelligence on measures obtained every year between 8 and 17. They used data from the Harvard Growth Study (Dearborn, Rothney, & Shuttleworth, 1938). More than 700 girls and 500 boys from the Boston area participated in that study. The sample was longitudinal and the investigators attempted to measure each child every year.

Humphreys et al. (1985) reported a relatively wide range of correlations in the two longitudinal samples as a function of the 10 ages during which both variates were measured and the 100 correlations relating height to intelligence. Some of the variability results from chance, some from the different tests of intelligence used, and some from the sex differences. We have now computed mean correlations of intelligence with height at each age from 8 to 17 to control for the differences in the tests. For girls there was gradual drop in the mean correlations from .33 at age 8 to .20 at age 17. For boys the largest differences in mean correlations as a function of age was .02, and .23 was the mean on 8 of the 10 occasions. The correlations with SES were etas computed from only three categories. Those for intelligence and SES in both sexes had means of .24, but those for height and SES were .12 for girls, .23 for boys. Samples are not large enough, however, to support a difference in fit of the two models from Table 5.1. On the other hand, correlations of intelligence with anatomical features of the central nervous system may be little if any higher than those with standing height.

Differences With Jensen

Use of g. We do not use *g* in place of the general factor among cognitive tasks. It is interpreted much too freely as an entity, such as a fixed capacity, by psychologists and people in general. Spearman started the reification of the general factor in describing his own research. He defined intelligence as "mental energy." It seems to us that Jensen also reifies *g*. Reified concepts frequently lead to erroneous interpretations.

Neural Correlates. We do not agree with Jensen's concentration on neural correlates, including brain size revealed by head size. He seems to have been motivated by a presumed need for a biological basis for general intelligence. If that were his motivation, there was no need. All behavior has both genetic and environmental substrates, or making a slightly different cut, biological and cultural substrates.

The general factor is a highly replicable mathematical dimension possessing a large number of correlates. Many of the correlates are personally and socially important. This is sufficient for the construct to be welcome in science. Despite this difference we view neural research as important, but not essential. Reductionism has been a source of argument in psychology since at least the time of Watson in the 1920s and is not likely to go away.

Information Processing.   Jensen leans toward defining intelligence as the speed and accuracy of information processing. His choice of reaction time (RT) for each item in a test, in much of his research, seems to follow from his definition. But consider the following. If the number right score measures individual differences from low to high well, speed of response to items reduces correlations with recognized measures of the general factor. Furthermore, when an external criterion of performance is available, the correlations of number right with the criterion are generally higher than those with the mean RT. Information processing is an appropriate term to subsume the acquisition, storage, and retrieval of information. No matter how large a genetic component to individual differences of test scores may be, the behavior sampled by a psychological test was acquired by the processing of information.

Content Criteria.   In addition to the size of the correlation of a variate with the general factor, Jensen adds a content criterion for the items in an intelligence test. This is illustrated by his preference for Raven's Progressive Matrices over verbal content in tests for measuring the general factor. The Raven test is supposedly less culturally influenced. In factor analyses involving figural reasoning, such as the Raven, such tests are shown to contain substantial methods variance.

A fair test is one that allows substantially accurate inferences, on average, about performance in individual and social roles without regard to race, ethnicity, social status, religion, or sex. The persons tested must of course belong to the population for which the test was intended.

Spearman's Hypothesis About Race Differences.   Jensen has tested many times the hypothesis he attributes to Spearman by comparing the size of race differences on a small number of tests with the size of the correlations with the general factor of the same tests. High correlations are typically found. The conclusion is that the phenotypic difference between the races is primarily genetic. We criticize the results because his test is not very powerful, not necessarily because of the conclusions drawn. There is a more powerful test on record that is based on similar reasoning. The test does not involve the factor analytic method, but it does require inferences from the factor model.

In a previous study involving a nonorthogonal ANOVA, Humphreys, Lin, and Fleishman (1976) formed 24 groups of high school students in a $3 \times 2 \times 2 \times 2$ design of demographic variables using data from Project Talent. In that project, there had been a stratified random sample of the nation's high schools. Students in the four high school classes were tested on 75 cognitive measures and composites of those measures. The year was 1960. Samples of about 15,000 Black students, 15,000 low-SES Whites, and 70,000 high-SES Whites were selected for a test of interactions involving race and SES. The race–SES samples were further divided into low (9 and 10) grades and high (11 and 12) grades in school, residing in the south or nonsouth, and sex of the students.

For the test of Spearman's hypothesis, the intercorrelations of the means of the 24 groups were computed. The correlations among the three groups were extracted from the 24×24 matrix by a process that held grade in school, area of the country, and sex approximately constant. The three correlations were –.90 for the SES comparison, –.61 for Black and high-SES White, and –.19 for Black and low-SES White (Humphreys, Fleishman, & Lin, 1977).

The correlation close to unity for the SES comparison indicates that the mixture of biological and cultural influences on test scores is much the same for low and high SES Whites. The two groups are separated almost entirely on the general factor. It is inconceivable that a combination of two or more independent factors could produce a correlation of the magnitude observed between means of such a heterogeneous set of cognitive measures. In contrast, although there is evidence that Blacks and high-SES Whites do differ on the same general factor, even the correlation with the high-SES White group is small enough (–.61) to provide for distinctive cultural differences between the races. This conclusion is reinforced by the small (–.19) correlation between Blacks and low-SES Whites. It is also clear that the cultural component is not represented by poverty per se.

Behavioral Definition of General Intelligence. A behavioral definition of what an intelligence test measures was proposed by Humphreys (1971). He stated that intelligence was the behavioral repertoire of cognitive skills and knowledge at a particular time in development. The intelligence test samples the repertoire. This has satisfied few psychologists. Jensen (1994) declared this definition involved merely the epiphenomena of intelligence in his commentary on a more recent article by Humphreys (1994).

We prefer to call the Humphreys approach a behavioral definition. It is clearly not false, but it is not as deep within the organism as many prefer.

A test of general intelligence does sample the cognitive behavioral repertoire. It is congruent with the data on the degree of stability of individual differences during development. It is congruent with the increasing stability of individual differences with age. It is congruent with recent behavioral genetic findings of increasing heritability of intelligence from early childhood to adulthood.

It is also congruent with Thomson's (1919) approach to the interpretation of the general factor and other subordinate factors. The debate between Spearman and Thomson started in the early part of this century. Gould (1981, 1986) used the argument flippantly to discount the importance of tested general intelligence, but the nature of the construct does not affect the important personal and social correlates of the test. Gould is, to borrow a Freudian mechanism, in denial of their importance.

ERRORS THAT DIMINISH SPURIOUSLY THE IMPORTANCE OF GENERAL INTELLIGENCE

We now discuss two major, independent statistical–psychometric errors and one basic conceptual error, that of reification. This error places a unitary thing (entity) within the organism to "explain" individual differences in measurement data. We discuss three situations in which reifying commonly occurs: naming tests scores, estimating proficiency of persons in social roles, and identifying variates in causal models. The all too free use of "construct" today in discussing research findings does not avoid the error of reification. A scientific construct is built, piece by piece, from many research findings over a period of time, just as a house is constructed of components over a period of time. Constructs can be held with greater confidence the longer the time and the greater the number of components that fit. Nevertheless, an established construct can be abandoned by well-designed research findings. Scientific constructs are not modified or abandoned, however, because critics make errors.

Errors in Interpreting Correlations

One of the most egregious errors in interpreting data arising from intelligence tests, as well as from tests in general, is in the interpretation of r itself. Our focus on the product–moment correlation, however, does not deny that some of the relations among psychological attributes may not be linear. It is empirically true that most correlations among measures of psychological attributes are approximately linear as long as both measures that are correlated have low enough floors and high enough ceilings to measure the full distribution of talent in the population being sampled.

Our discussion is also applicable to nonlinear relations that can also be expressed by a number varying from 0 to 1.00.

What r^2 Provides. The measure, r^2, is the residual obtained when the variance of the linear estimates of Y are subtracted from the total variance of Y. As in the analysis of variance, this quantity is called the variance of error. In each design it is necessary to remember, however, that there are two kinds of error affecting X and Y. One is random measurement error; the other is systematic variance that is independent of both random error and the common variance of X and Y. Depending on one's goal, it might also be called unwanted true score variance.

The interpretation of r^2 does not stop with an overall variance. A user commonly assumes that $1 - r^2$ can be used to estimate the variance of the Y scores at each level of X. That is, the arrays of Y scores at each level of X are assumed homoscedastic. The standard deviation, $(1 - r^2)^{1/2}$, becomes the standard error of estimate in each array of X. Typical use of this statistic requires an estimate of a mean of the Y's about which the errors of estimate are distributed.

What r Provides. The correlation unsquared defines the regression line that is actually a series of estimates of Y means. These estimates are obtained with the linear regression equation that involves r_{xy}, s_x, and s_y. It is at least as important to estimate a mean of Y as it is to estimate the variance about that mean. Of course, the sole interpretation of r as its square is only an error of omission, but it omits by at least one-half the information provided by the statistic. When the task is to estimate the Y score of a person knowing that person's score on X, a mean and a standard deviation are both needed. Use of these statistics for prediction for a single person, knowing that person's score on X, is a highly probabilistic undertaking. On average, if the r is .4, the standard deviation of the Y's in any array of X is .92, $(1 - .16)^{1/2}$, of the total standard deviation of all Y scores. However, prediction is not quite as chancy as the .92 suggests because it is about an estimated mean of Y that is .4 of the difference, in standard score units, from the mean of X toward the X score. If X is 2.00, the Y scores are distributed around a mean of .80. The proportion of the observed Y scores below the Y mean is expected to be .19. An equal proportion is expected above $Y = 1.72$.

A Different Use of r. Most correlations involving psychological attributes are based on scores made by individuals. These correlations can be called individual difference correlations, but the data do not have to be used solely for the prediction of performance of individuals on Y from their scores on X. The alternative is to predict the mean performance on Y

from the common score of the group on X. Personnel psychologists have been doing this from the beginning of their subdiscipline, but they still report individual differences correlations. They argue correctly that their small correlations become quite useful when there are more applicants than positions to be filled. They have avoided the perception of absence of lawfulness when Y is a dichotomy, such as pass–fail, by portraying the biserial correlation with a continuous predictor in a graph in which the percentage passing (or failing), which is a mean, is plotted at each level of a convenient number of arrays of X. Furthermore, if the sample size is sufficient to produce dependable data, a so-called small correlation is seen as lawful. This correlation can have important consequences.

Lubinski and Humphreys (1996) recognized this fact and, going a step further, advocated the use of correlations between means of continuous variates when the *primary* interest is the prediction of *mean* performance. This is, by the way, the standard method of epidemiology. An example of the lawfulness of correlations between means is provided in their Figure 2, which is reproduced here as our Fig. 5.1. Linear prediction of mean performance is almost perfect in two of the three examples, but requires a more complex equation for the third. A dependable slope requires an acceptable fit of the linear regression line and a large sample. The r between means is independent of the size of the r for individuals, but the slope of the Y means on the levels of X is identical to the regression in individual differences data. There are no false positives or negatives, and the only question is the utility of the relation in predicting the performance of the groups. The essential relation between X and Y is not obscured by a seemingly random clutter about the regression in individual differences data. The correlation between means provides at a glance the amount of gain or loss on Y of a unit of change on X when both X and Y are measured in meaningful units.

Mean levels of intelligence have been shown repeatedly to be well-nigh perfect predictors of means of job performance, scholastic achievement, and other socially desirable outcomes. Yet, in the report of the Task Force of the APA (American Psychological Association, 1995), correlations that range in absolute value from about .20 to .55 are implied to be only marginally important. The reports states as follows:

> The correlations [of IQ with] most "negative outcome" variables are typically smaller than .20, which means that test scores are associated with less than 4% of their total variance. . . . [Intelligence test scores] do in fact predict school performance fairly well: the correlation between IQ scores and grades is about 0.50. . . . Note, however, that correlations of this magnitude account for only about 25% of the overall variance. . . . [The corrected correlation of IQ with job performance is] 0.54. . . . This implies that across a wide range of occupations, intelligence test performance accounts for some 29% of the variance in job performance. (p. 11)

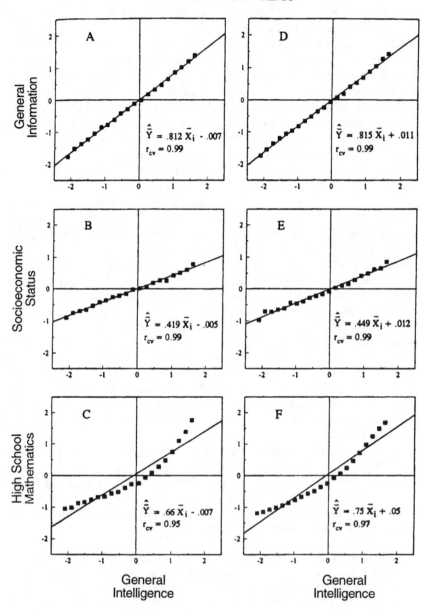

FIG. 5.1. Reproduction of Figure 2 from Lubinski and Humphreys (1996).

A public health research person would be delighted if the slope of the means on a measure of a public health problem were as large as .50. The individual false positives and false negatives are not seen as problems when the concern is reducing the size of a public health problem.

Correlations and Effect Sizes. As the minimizing of correlations with intelligence tests has proceeded unchecked, the reporting of effect sizes in experimental research has become more popular. Effect size, *d*, is the difference between the means of the treatment groups divided by the pooled standard deviation within treatments. It is an important way of demonstrating the social or psychological significance of research outcomes independently of sample size. This property, independence of sample size, is also a property of correlations. The two measures can be used to achieve the same goal, and effect size can also be transformed directly into an unsquared point biserial correlation having a range from 0 to 1.0 (see Cohen, 1988). They differ with respect to their range of values because effect sizes can range from zero to infinity, but there is a one-to-one numerical correspondence. The need to understand the essential identity is well illustrated by the following quotation from the APA Task Force on intelligence:

> *Large* differences favoring males appear on visual–spatial tasks like mental and spatio-temporal tasks like tracking a moving object through space (Law, Pellegrino, & Hunt, 1993; Linn & Petersen, 1985). The sex difference on mental rotation tasks is *substantial*; a recent meta-analysis (Masters & Sanders, 1993) puts the effect size at $d = 0.9$. (p. 27; italics added)

An effect size of .80, widely described as large, corresponds to an *r* of .37 when Ns for the treatment groups are equal. Interpolating in Table 5.2, the *r* for an effect size of .9 is about .42. In variance accounted for this is .18. This is similar in size to the correlation between intelligence and the fallible rating of job performance made by a single supervisor. Experimenters ignore the equivalent in their studies of $1 - r^2$, which is $1 - SS_B / SS_T$. The *r* unsquared measures effect size; *r* squared does not.

Error Arising From Restriction of Range of Talent

Most psychologists are aware of the attenuation of correlations as a function of range of talent in the personnel selection paradigm. (Talent is used generically to include attributes besides the cognitive ones.) There are many errors, however, in recognizing its presence elsewhere and in appraising the size of this effect. Restriction of range is ubiquitous in psychological research, and investigators need to draw their conclusions accordingly.

The breadth of the problem can be ignored in much of selection research, but it is of high importance for theory. A measure of intelligence has many correlates with the personal and social variables that produce restriction. If one problem-solving task is restricted, all are restricted. Another problem for theorists is that there are three kinds of restriction, each of which occurs commonly. They can be substantial and can occur at any time during development.

Kinds of Restriction.   In our discussion, we use X to represent the score on a test being investigated as a possible predictor (independent) variable and Y for the scores of the measure being predicted (criterion, or dependent) variable. Direct restriction occurs when a measure of either is categorized into acceptable or not acceptable segments of the scores. When this happens on X, it represents the personnel selection paradigm. When it occurs on Y, it represents students' grade point averages (GPAs) of those who passed a previous educational hurdle.

Indirect restriction occurs on X when there is direct restriction on Y; indirect restriction on Y occurs when there is direct restriction on X. Related indirect restriction, and the most common type, occurs on all Zs correlated with X when X is directly restricted or Y when Y is directly restricted. Given sufficient data, and linearity of regressions, sample correlations can be corrected accurately to the range of talent in the population from which the sample was drawn. To do this, three quite different equations are required. Two are needed for direct and indirect restriction on either X or Y; the third equation is required for the indirect restriction on a third variable, Z, correlated with X or Y. A discussion of restriction of range of talent, as well as the presentation of the three equations, is available in Thorndike (1949).

Although most psychological data are influenced by range of talent, little can be corrected because needed quantitative information is not available. An investigator does need to be aware of the problem. For example, to conclude that intelligence is not related to success in graduate school because correlations are small and are not statistically significant is absurd. The problem of expected small correlations is compounded by statistical naiveté in interpreting sample correlations as zero merely because the null hypothesis cannot be rejected. It is pertinent that correcting either X or Y for either direct or indirect restriction cannot change the sign of the correlation. In contrast, the sign of a corrected correlation can differ from that of the restricted correlation for a Z highly correlated with X. This is essentially the suppressor effect in multiple regression.

A measuring instrument that has too low a ceiling or too high a floor in an "unrestricted" range of talent produces a skewed distribution that obviously restricts the spread of scores at one end of the distribution or the other. However, this does *not* represent restriction of range of talent. Talent is in the examinees, not the measurement metric. The metric chosen must reveal the full range of talent in the population sampled.

Restriction in Longitudinal Perspective.   There is a published source of relevant data (DuBois, 1947) on successive restrictions of range of talent. The data extend from a starting value somewhat restricted on general intelligence through final proficiency in pilot training. Entrance to pilot training in WW II, as well as training for other aircrew positions, started with entry to military service and measurement on the Army General Classification Test (AGCT). The next step required volunteering for training and passing the Aircrew Qualifying Examination (AQE). Qualifiers were sent to a classification center where the decision was made, based on scores on the Aircrew Classification Battery (ACB), to accept the candidate for pilot or other forms of training. After 2 months of training in preflight, future pilots spent 2 months each in primary, basic, and advanced flight training. Upon graduation, candidates were awarded pilot wings and commissions as second Lieutenants.

Cogent data for evaluating the effects of restriction of range of talent came from 1,311 volunteers for training who were randomly selected. Of this total 1,152 entered training without regard to scores on the AQE and the ACB. The candidates in this group were not identified in training and were widely scattered among the regular candidates across many different training bases. Their distribution statistics on the AGCT, from which they were not exempt, were $\overline{X} = 113$, $S_x = 14$, as compared to the standardization statistics, $\overline{X} = 100$, $S_x = 20$. This indirect restriction arose from the process involved in volunteering. Direct restriction on the AQE and ACB would have failed about 40% on the first followed by 50% of those remaining on the second.

The candidates in the experimental group placed pilot training as their overwhelming first choice, as did trainees in general. Thus, the sample available for pilot training was reduced trivially in size in biserial correlations with the three test scores and the dichotomy of graduation and cumulative failures from the three stages of flight training. Correlations of this criterion with AGCT total score, AQE total score, and ACB score on the pilot composite were, respectively, .31, .50, and .66.

Correlations were also regularly computed between tests and the pass–fail criterion at a given stage of flight training for which failures are restricted to that stage. Sample sizes for the experimental group became too small to obtain dependable results after the primary stage and a correlation of .64. Only 20% of the entering class of 1,152 graduated from pilot training. It is more revealing to report the observed correlations of this sort for a representative class, the 8,137 trainees of the last class to graduate in 1944.

The observed validity of the pilot composite of the ACB was .37 at the end of primary training. It corrected to .51 for direct restriction on the pilot score in classification. Observed validities of .27 and .21 in basic and advanced, respectively, corrected for indirect selection on the pilot score to .33 and .27. In each case, the direct restriction was on performance in flying in the immediately preceding stages as measured by the number of eliminations from training at that stage. If restriction of range of talent is ignored except at an advanced stage, the importance of individual differences on a test can be drastically undervalued. In these data, a correlation of .21 that corrected to .27 is essentially the equivalent of a correlation in the middle sixties in a much wider, but still not full, range of talent. The essential identity between these pilot training data and progression in our educational system seems obvious.

What to Do About Restriction.   Small correlations between intelligence tests and criteria of proficiency of graduate or professional school students are not evidence of the unimportance of intelligence. Such groups were directly restricted on tests when entering college and entering postgraduate education. They were also restricted on academic performance by dropouts in high school, by dropouts from undergraduate college, from transfers out of their undergraduate major, and by the same criterion restrictions at the postgraduate phase. There is a close parallel between the multiple stages in education and those in WW II pilot training. Suitable statistical corrections cannot be made because the data to do so are not available, but recognition of the problem is a minimum requirement for a sophisticated presentation of one's data.

It would be helpful in recognizing the problem if scores on college entrance tests and graduate and professional entrance tests could be related to the adult Wechsler norms. Many years ago, as a first step, one of us (LGH) compared the Officer Quality scale of the Air Force to the Armed Forces Qualifying Test (AFQT) by the equipercentile method. The highest score in the lower 4% of the officer test was at the upper seventies of the centile ranks of the AFQT. The highest score in the next 7% (from a stanine distribution) was in the upper eighties. This left the remaining 89% of the officer scores crowded into the highest 10% of the AFQT. Another indication of the selection that is present in higher education is from Thomas Sowell's (1992) report about Black students at MIT (see also Lubinski & Humphreys, 1997). Selection of Blacks in engineering places them in the top 10% of scores in the total White distribution, but they have academic difficulties and drop out at a disappointing rate. The reason is not the popular one of hostile atmosphere. Instead, their White counterparts, with many fewer academic problems, have entrance scores at a substantially higher level within the upper 10%. The White and Black *mean difference* in academic achievement is predictable with complete confidence from the *difference in mean* entrance examination scores.

Reification Errors

Reification is defined as treatment of an abstraction as substantially existing, as a concrete material object or entity. There are numerous examples. Reification of measures of named factors is so widespread that it is difficult to find an exception. In factor analysis, factors quickly become entities. A personality test is constructed in accordance with some vague theoretical rationale and given the appropriate name. A new attribute of human personality is the immediate result. The following historical example of gross reification is only a little extreme. A popular personality test provided four scores from the same set of differentially keyed items. A young doctoral student obtained the intercorrelations of these scores on a suitable sample and extracted two principal components that described most of the variance of each of the four scores. The two essentially orthogonal components were given names that did not repeat any of the four existing names. In a subsequent edition of the test manual, the publisher included six keys producing scores having six different names and descriptions of what each meant psychologically. Many psychologists were pleased to have measures of six attributes to discuss with students and other clients.

Reification and Intelligence Tests

Reification of scores on tests of intelligence takes more than one form. For most users different tests of intelligence are interchangeable. The raw score of each measures the same entity. For many the entity is a basic biological capacity measured by IQ. There is widespread neglect that IQ measures *relative* intelligence and is not synonymous with the attribute of intelligence that grows and changes with age. The problem is compounded by the conversion to IQ. Any numerical IQ can remain constant as children grow. As a consequence, it is easy to confuse the constancy of the scale with an entity in the child.

An Example of Reification. The report of the Task Force contains the following statement that illustrates how persons ranging from *g* theorists to critics treat intelligence as an entity:

One way to represent this structure is in terms of a hierarchical arrangement with a general intelligence factor at the apex and various more specialized abilities arrayed below it. Such a summary merely acknowledges that performance levels on different tests are correlated; it is consistent with, but does not prove, the hypothesis that a common factor such as g underlies those correlations. Different specialized abilities might also be correlated for other reasons, such as the effects of education. (p. 8)

The general factor cannot be so readily dismissed. It exists as a replicable factor based on psychometric theory and on the empirical reality of positive correlations among cognitive problem solving tests. It is defined by objective computational routines applied to objective behavioral measures. Of course, there is more to this factor than a replicable mathematical dimension. As discussed earlier, it meets minimum requirements for use in both application and theory. The construct of the general factor has both a genetic and an environmental substrate. It is a linear composite of its components that also have both genetic and environmental substrates. An entity, such as Spearman's "mental energy," is not required to explain the large number of external correlates of the general factor or to explain the positive correlations that define it.

Flynn's Research on Mean Gains. Flynn (1987) reported that Jensen advised him to use Raven's Progressive Matrices in a proposed study of change in means from generation to generation in intelligence. This recommendation was the outcome of the cultural fairness doctrine. Flynn did find large gains on the Raven. Other tests of intelligence showed smaller gains. Flynn concluded that the gains, especially on the Raven, were too large for a test of "real intelligence." Note that it is possible for a critic to reify a construct as real intelligence even though no measuring instrument exists.

For those who avoid the errors that reification can produce, it is not surprising that mean scores on estimates of the general factor show gains over a period of several generations. The estimate of the general factor is as much a phenotypic attribute as any of its components. It should also not be surprising that mean gains on different estimators would differ. There is a psychometric basis for an expectation that mean gains on the Raven would be larger than on more effective estimators. The loading on the general factor for a test like the Raven is much less than unity. It is much higher for a test like the Wechsler. Reliability is high for both, so the residual part of the total variance is legitimately called nonerror. The latter is a combination of group and specific factors. In the hierarchical model, both are independent of the general factor. Both have their independent correlates. Thus, Flynn's gains are an unknown mixture of two major sources of variation, and the source of the gains is not known. More than generalized experience with tests and testing contribute to the nonerror uniqueness of a test.

Reification and Performance in Social Roles

Reification of Academic Performance. Grade point average is rarely questioned as a measure of academic success, and the correlations of intelligence with GPA are considered the largest correlates of the test. These correlations are also considered by critics as quite modest in size in comparison to all of the important attributes of success that are not being measured. All criterion measures are fallible, however, and GPA is especially so. On one large university campus, the correlation, across the population of independent colleges, between the mean entrance examination scores of their students and the mean grades awarded by their faculties was almost −.80.

There are similar differences among curricula within a college. The liberal arts and sciences college on the same campus has more variability of this sort than the college of engineering. Within curricula, faculty members assign grades that differ in some degree in the location of the zero and the size of the units of measurement. Although the differences exist, there is still enough commonality in course grades that correlations with intelligence are certainly not abolished, but they are substantially attenuated. It is not surprising that grades in single courses awarded by conscientious instructors can be predicted more accurately than the mean grades (GPA) in all courses. In such a course, grades are awarded on a scale that has the same zero and same units of measurement from one student to another.

Reification of Job Performance. Proficiency on a job is typically measured by ratings, frequently from a single supervisor. A committee of the National Research Council used an estimate from published data of the average correlation between the tests of the Department of Labor's General Aptitude Test Battery and occupational success as no larger than .40 (Hartigan & Wigdor, 1989). This provided a convenient basis for their proposal for a modified affirmative action hiring procedure: the lower the validity of the test, the lesser the decrease in productivity (not proficiency rating) from lowering the hiring standards for minorities.

If the problem of measuring proficiency is approached by considering a given measure as an estimate of the construct, the problem is to increase the accuracy of a given estimate. There is support for the following statements extending from the early years of applied psychology: An independent rating provided by a second supervisor who is in an equally good position to evaluate has the same validity as that of the first. The correlation between the two ratings is sufficiently low (the reliability referred to), though larger than either rating's validity, that the mean rating is substantially more highly correlated with the selection test. At times, also, it is possible to obtain peer ratings of proficiency of each person rated. Ratings by peers are imperfectly correlated within the members of the group and with those of the supervisors. Again, the correlation with the selection tests is frequently increased when ratings of peers are added to those of supervisors. Both printed and hands-on proficiency tests are imperfectly correlated with each other and with the several sources of ratings. Different types of tests and different sources of ratings are all prime candidates for a composite measure of job performance. Correcting one component, a supervisor's rating, for unreliability is useful, but does not tell the full story. There is every reason to approach the estimation of the construct of job proficiency in the same fashion as the measurement of general intelligence.

Causal Modeling Errors

Probably most psychologists know that a nonzero correlation between X and Y might represent X causing Y, Y causing X, or Z, or a series of Z's from 1 to n, causing the correlation. However, this knowledge is ignored in many uses of causal modeling when an "acceptable fit" to the observed correlations is obtained (see Loehlin, 1998).

The elaborate computer programs for causal models constitute a complex way of computing partial, semi-partial, and multiple correlations. For example, a stepwise multiple regression is a possible causal model. Let X_1 be family background, X_2 amount of education, X_3 general intelligence, and Y a dependent measure or criterion. The stepwise procedure evaluates each predictor in turn by the amount the squared multiple correlation is increased when the next predictor is added. The square root of the added variance is a semi-partial correlation. If X_1 is entered first, the square of r_{YX1} is the squared correlation with the criterion. If X_2 is second, the square root of the added variance is $r_{Y(X2.X1)}$, or the correlation of education with the criterion after the variance of family background has been removed from education. Similarly, the semipartial correlation with family background and education removed from general intelligence is $r_{Y(X3.X1.X2)}$.

The six possible orders of three predictors provide for a variety of causal interpretations. The problem is how to choose. Causation cannot be supported by reifying each of the three variables as independent agents: SES as family environmental privilege, education as privileged access to formal education, general intelligence as a residual biological component, and then computing the stepwise semipartial correlations in that order. The three cannot be reified validly as named because they share cultural–genetic components of variance. The order selected must be justified by independent, dependable, well-designed research. The accuracy of fit of a given model is entirely secondary.

Quasi-Experimental Data. One source of less ambiguous information than concurrent correlations is a social experiment. Charles Murray (1998) published convincing results from a quasi-experiment in which siblings of the target group served as controls. The analyses support a conclusion that the primary direction of causation is from a child's intelligence to years of education rather than the reverse. We call it a quasi-experiment because there was no random assignment of persons to treatment groups. The genetic mechanism, however, is a random mechanism that operates within a family.

The Primary Basis for the Errors

The primary basis for the prevalence of the misinterpretations of information from intelligence tests appeared to Coleman (1991) to be native (traditional) American egalitarianism. Secondarily, specific errors are associated with the emphasis on the analysis of variance and hypothesis testing in statistics courses, the absence of training in psychometrics and individual differences for most psychologists, and the quite different goals of cognitive and psychometric psychologists.

When Coleman called attention to the prevailing egalitarianism, he added the phrase "conspicuous benevolence" as a correlate of the prevailing attitudes toward the downtrodden. Conspicuous was borrowed from Thorsten Veblen, an economist of the turn of the century, who had teamed it with consumption to describe the patterns of America's nouveau riche. Coleman associated conspicuous benevolence with political correctness on college and university campuses and with the failure of those who practice this form of censorship to see any conflict with a university's mission of research and scholarship in a democratic society.

REFERENCES

American Psychological Association (1995). *Intelligence: Knowns and unknowns: Report of a Task Force established by the Board of Scientific Affairs of the American Psychological Association.* Science Directorate, Washington: District of Columbia.

Brand, C. (1987). The importance of general intelligence. In S. Modgil & C. Modgil (Eds.), *Arthur Jensen: Consensus and controversy.* New York: Falmer.

Campbell, J. P. (1990). An overview of the Army selection and classification project. *Personnel Psychology, 43,* 231–240.

Carroll, J. B. (1993). *Human cognitive abilities: A survey of factor analytic studies*. New York: Cambridge University Press.

Cleary, T. A., Humphreys, L. G., Kendrick, S. A., & Wesman, A. (1975). Education uses of tests with disadvantaged students. *American Psychologist, 30*, 15–41.

Cohen, J. (1988). *Statistical power analysis for the behavioral sciences*. Hillsdale, NJ: Lawrence Erlbaum Associates.

Coleman, J. (1990–1991). The Sidney Hook Memorial Award Address: On the self-suppression of academic freedom, *Academic Questions*, Winter, 17–22.

Dearborn, W. F., Rothney, J. W. M., & Shuttleworth, F. K. (1938). Data on the growth of public school children. *Monographs of the Society for Research on Child Development, 3*(1, Serial No. 14).

DuBois, P. (1947). *The Classification Program: Report No. 2*, Army Air Forces Aviation Psychology Program, Washington DC, U.S. Government Printing Office.

Flynn, J. R. (1987). Massive IQ gains in 14 nations: What IQ tests really measure. *Psychological Bulletin, 101*, 171–191.

Gould, S. J. (1981). *The mismeasure of man*. New York: Norton.

Gould, S. J. (1996). *The mismeasure of man* (2nd ed.). New York: Norton.

Guilford, J. P. (1985). The structure-of-intellect model. In B. Wolman (Ed.), *Handbook of intelligence: Theories, measurements, and applications*. New York: Wiley.

Hartigan, J. A., & Wigdor, A. K. (Eds.). (1989). *Fairness in employment testing: Validity generalization, minority issues, and the General Aptitude Test Battery*. Washington, DC: National Academy Press.

Herrnstein, R. J., & Murray, C. (1994). *The bell curve: Intelligence and class structure in American life*. New York: The Free Press.

Humphreys, L. G. (1962). The organization of human abilities. *American Psychologist, 17*, 475–483.

Humphreys, L. G. (1971). Theory of intelligence. In R. Cancro (Ed.), *Intelligence: Genetic and environmental influence*. New York: Plenum.

Humphreys, L. G. (1985). General Intelligence: An integration of factor, test, and simplex theory. In B. Wolman (Ed.), *Handbook of intelligence: Theories, measurements, and applications*. New York: Wiley.

Humphreys, L. G. (1994). Intelligence from the standpoint of a (pragmatic) behaviorist. *Psychological Inquiry, 5*, 179–192.

Humphreys, L. G., Davey, T. C., & Kashima, E. (1986). Experimental measures of cognitive privilege/deprivation and some of their correlates. *Intelligence, 10*, 355–376.

Humphreys, L. G., Davey, T. C., & Park, R. K. (1985). Longitudinal correlation analysis of standing height and intelligence. *Child Development, 56*, 1465–1478.

Humphreys, L. G., Fleishman, A. I., & Lin, P. (1977). Causes of racial and socioeconomic differences in cognitive tests. *Journal of Research in Personality, 11*, 191–208.

Humphreys, L. G., Jones, L. V., Davenport, E. C., & Lubinski, D. (1991). *The influence of college enrollment patterns on the U.S. science and engineering talent pool in three decades (Res. Rep. 91-1)*. L. L. Thurstone Psychometric Laboratory. Chapel Hill: University of North Carolina.

Humphreys, L. G., Lin, P., & Fleishman, A. I. (1976). The sex by race interaction in cognitive measures. *Journal of Research in Personality, 10*, 42–58.

Humphreys, L. G., Lubinski, D., & Yao, G. (1993). Utility of predicting group membership and the role of spatial visualization in becoming an engineer, physical scientist, or artist. *Journal of Applied Psychology, 78*, 250–261.

Humphreys, L. G., & Yao, G. (1999). Manuscript submitted for review.

Husen, T. (1959). *Psychological twin research*. New York: The Free Press.

Jensen, A. R. (1994). Humphreys's "behavioral repertoire" an epiphenomenon of g. *Psychological Inquiry, 5*, 208–210.

Jensen, A. R. (1998). *The g factor: The science of mental ability.* Westport, CT: Praeger Publishers/Greenwood Publishing Group.

Kaiser, H. F. (1960). The application of electronic computers to factor analysis. *Educational and Psychological Measurement, 20,* 141–151.

Law, D. J., Pellegrino, J. W., & Hunt, E. B. (1993). Comparing the tortoise and the hare: Gender differences and experience in dynamic spatial reasoning tasks. *Psychological Science, 4,* 35–40.

Linn, M. C., & Petersen, A. C. (1985). Emergence and characterization of sex differences in spatial ability: A meta analysis. *Child Development, 56,* 1479–1498.

Loehlin, J. C. (1998). *Latent variable models: An introduction to factor, path, and structural analysis* (3rd ed.). Mahwah, NJ: Lawrence Erlbaum Associates.

Lubinski, D., & Humphreys, L. G. (1996). Seeing the forest from the trees: When predicting the behavior or status of groups, correlate means. *Psychology, Public Policy, and Law, 2,* 363–376.

Lubinski, D., & Humphreys, L. G. (1997). Intelligence: A neglected aspect. *Intelligence, 24,* 159–201.

Masters, M. S., & Sanders, B. (1993). Is the gender difference in mental rotation disappearing? *Behavior Genetics, 23,* 337–341.

Montanelli, R. G., Jr., & Humphreys, L. G. (1976). Latent roots of random data correlation matrices with squared multiple correlations on the diagonal: A Monte Carlo study. *Psychometrika, 15,* 341–348.

Murray, C. (1998). *Income inequality and IQ.* Washington DC: The AEI Press.

Schmid, J., & Leiman, J. (1957). The development of hierarchical factor solutions. *Psychometrika, 22,* 53–61.

Schmidt, F. L., & Hunter, J. E. (1998). Validity and utility of selection methods in personnel psychology: Practical and theoretical implications of 85 years of research findings. *Psychological Bulletin, 124,* 262–274.

Sowell, T. (1992). *Inside American education: The decline, the deception, the dogmas.* New York: The Free Press.

Tanner, J. M. (1966). Galtonian eugenics and the study of growth: The relation of body size, intelligence test score, and social circumstances in children and adults. *Eugenics Review, 58,* 122–135.

Terman, L. M. (1925). *Genetic studies of genius: Vol. I. The mental and physical traits of a thousand gifted children.* Stanford, CA: Stanford University Press.

Thomson, G. H. (1919). On the cause of hierarchical order among correlation coefficients. *Proceedings of the Royal Society (A), 95.*

Thorndike, R. L. (1949). *Personnel selection: Test and measurement techniques.* New York: Wiley.

Vernon, P. E. (1960). *The structure of human abilities.* London: Methuen.

Chapter 6

Is There a General Factor of Cognitive Development?

Jacques Lautrey
University of Paris 5

The first tests of intellectual development, those imagined by Binet or Wechsler, were not based on very elaborated theories of intelligence. The approach of these pioneers of psychometry was, of course, inspired by some general ideas on intelligence, but the way in which they searched for tasks likely to measure it was very empirical. Binet, for example, tried various items and retained those that discriminated well between mentally retarded and nonretarded children, between older from younger children, and good from not so good students. The construction of tests was guided by their empirical validity, in particular relating to criteria like academic performance, more than by their theoretical validity. "Psychometric" tests (i.e., intelligence scales or factorial batteries), are the product of this very empirical approach to the measurement of intelligence.

The approach that led to the construction of the so-called "Piagetian" tests has been rather different. Piaget's goal was not to measure individual differences in intelligence, nor to predict academic success, but to verify hypotheses about cognitive development. The experimental situations that he imagined for this purpose were intended to track the stages of construction of operational structures in various fields of knowledge: logic, physics, space, time, causality, etc. The tasks of conservation, of class inclusion, or of coordination of perspectives, to cite only some of them, were directly inspired by his theory of cognitive development and had no equivalent in psychometric intelligence scales. Initially, the idea to use these experimental situations to assess the general level of development of chil-

117

dren germinated in the Genevan school itself. The first research on mental retardation using Piagetian tasks was done in Geneva by Inhelder (1943). An attempt at standardizing the Piagetian tasks was led by Vinh-Bang (1966), but never published. A quantitative analysis of the results of a large set of Piagetian tasks was also conducted in a thesis defended in Geneva (Nassefat, 1963). Nevertheless, the first attempts that really succeeded in developing Piagetian tests were made outside of Geneva at the end of the 1960s (e.g., Kaufman, 1971; Laurendeau & Pinard, 1968; Longeot, 1969; Tuddenham, 1971), one of the reasons being probably the disinterest of Piaget for all that could resemble a psychometric, quantitative approach to the development of intelligence.

Piagetian tests had their partisans. One of the arguments most often advanced in favor of these tests was their theoretical basis. This theoretical basis was seen as making possible a kind of exchange, between the data collected with the tests and the theory from which they were drawn; psychometric tests had no equivalent. Another argument was that Piagetian tests did not characterize subjects by their rank in the population but by their stage of development. This latter form of characterization appeared preferable because of its transitory nature and because it seemed more adapted to evaluations made with an educational purpose.

The question that arose immediately was whether Piagetian tests measured the same intelligence as psychometric tests. Was the factorial structure of these tests the same? If so, were the contents of the various factors in which they loaded the same? If there was a factor common to all Piagetian tasks, was it g?

Only a few empirical studies were undertaken to answer these questions. The first reason is that Piagetian tests generally suppose an individual application. Questions are asked about transformations carried out on objects (pouring of liquids, classification of objects, changing the point of view in a landscape, etc.) and the questioning is often a true discussion, in which the arguments of the child are followed by counterarguments of the experimenter. This makes it difficult to examine a sufficient number of subjects to be able to carry out a factor analysis. The second reason is that the period during which these studies were conducted was somewhat limited. Research was conducted during the 1970s and early 1980s, when Piaget's theory was still dominant in the field of developmental psychology, but ceased when this theory gave way to information-processing models of cognition. The same questions, however, arose within neo-Piagetian research, which retained certain aspects of the Piagetian framework, in particular the concept of stages, but reinterpreted them within the conceptual framework of information processing. In this trend, developmental stages were no longer explained by the operational structures advocated by Piaget, but by the limits imposed by the processing capacity of the child in a given period of development. The question that arose was that of the relationship between this general processing capacity and the general factor of intelligence.

Examination of the various experiments in which the relations between the factorial structure of the psychometric and of the Piagetian tasks were studied, reveals three sets of studies, which tackled this question in a rather different way. The first set includes the studies carried out in the United States to determine if psychometric and Piagetian tests did measure the same intelligence. The second set, which was in fact the first chronologically, includes studies undertaken in France and in French-speaking countries. This set of studies was initiated by the hypotheses advanced by Reuchlin (1964) in a paper trying to articulate the Piagetian and the factorial approach to intelligence. The third, more recent, set of studies raises the same question within the framework of the neo-Piagetian approach. First, the results gathered within these three research trends are reviewed and then their implications concerning the general factor of intelligence is discussed.

THE AMERICAN APPROACH: DO PSYCHOMETRIC AND PIAGETIAN TESTS MEASURE THE SAME INTELLIGENCE?

The first studies, which included Piagetian, and psychometric tasks in the same factor analysis, concluded that these two kinds of tasks did not measure the same form of intelligence.

The First Studies

Stephens, Mc Laughlin, Miller, and Glass (1972) administered Piagetian, psychometric, and achievement tasks to a sample of 150 subjects. This sample was composed of three age groups with 50 subjects in each group: 6- to 10-year-olds, 10- to 14-year-olds, 14- to 18-year-olds. Each of these groups was further divided into 25 mentally retarded subjects (IQ between 50 and 75) and 25 nonretarded (IQ between 90 and 110). All subjects completed a battery of 27 Piagetian tasks, a Wechsler scale of intelligence (WISC or WAIS according to the age), and a general achievement test, the Wide Range Achievement Test (WRAT), including subtests of spelling, arithmetic, and reading.

Among the 27 Piagetian tasks, there were 11 conservation tasks (substance, weight, length, volume, etc.), 7 tasks of logical classification (intersection, inclusion, etc.), 8 tasks of spatial operations (rotations of beads, rotation of squares, coordination of perspectives, etc.), and a task of assessment of formal operations (combination of liquids). The explanation advanced by the subject for each task was scored on a 6-point scale. Whereas the Piagetian tasks were noted in raw scores, the subtests of the Wechsler and the WRAT were noted in standard scores (this point was later criticized).

A factor analysis was carried out on all these variables (principal factor and oblique rotation). Five factors were extracted: The subtests of the Wechsler and the WRAT loaded on the first factor, the conservation tasks on the second factor, the class inclusion tasks on the third, and the spatial operations on the fourth factor; loadings on Factor 5 were unclear. The correlations between these four factors ranged from .22 to .39, the correlation between the first and the second being .37.

From these results, Stephens et al (1972) drew the following conclusion: "Review of the matrix indicates that Piagetian operativity as determined by measures of reasoning does indeed measure performance distinct from that measured by the Wechsler scales and the Wide Range Achievement Test" (p. 347).

A rather comparable study was undertaken by DeVries (1974). The whole sample of 143 subjects included mentally retarded and nonretarded subjects, but we focus here on the results obtained with a subsample of 50 nonretarded subjects, 5 to 7 years old, having completed two tests of intelligence (the Stanford–Binet and the California Test of Mental Maturity (CTMM)), a general achievement test (the Metropolitan Achievement Test (MAT)) and a battery of 15 Piagetian tasks. The factor analysis (orthogonal rotation Varimax) retained three factors. The psychometric tests of intelligence (Stanford–Binet, CTMM), and a few Piagetian tasks (class inclusion, left–right perspective) loaded on the first factor (35% of the communality). The conservation tasks loaded on the second factor (12%), and the achievement test (MAT) loaded on the third factor (7%). An oblique rotation indicated that the first factor, interpreted as corresponding to psychometric intelligence correlated .33 with the second factor (interpreted as Piagetian intelligence), and .34 with the third factor (interpreted as an achievement factor). Factors 2 and 3 did not correlate. DeVries (1974) concluded: "To a very large extent, Piagetian tasks do appear to measure a different intelligence and a different achievement than do psychometric tests" (p. 753).

Criticisms and Reanalyses of These First Studies

The results and the conclusions of these two studies were criticized on two main points. Humphreys and Parsons (1979) stressed that in the study of Stephens et al. (1972), the scores analyzed for the WISC were standard scores (thus independent of age), whereas the scores in the Piagetian tasks were raw scores (thus related to chronological age). This error could explain why these two categories of tests, psychometric and Piagetian, loaded on two different factors. The second criticism made by Humphreys and Parsons was to have stopped the analysis after the extraction of the first-order factors, without seeking to see whether an analysis of second order made it possible to extract a general factor, common to Piagetian and psychometric tests.

Humphreys and Parsons (1979) presented a reanalysis of the data of Stephens et al. (1972). The bias coming from the use of raw and standard scores in the same analysis was removed by partialling out chronological age from the correlations. A hierarchical factor analysis was then conducted. After orthogonalization of second and first-order factors, a general factor was isolated, in which all the tests had substantial loadings. There were also four first-order factors on which loaded respectively the achievement subtests (WRAT) and the WISC subtests (Factor 1), the conservation tasks (Factor 2), the class inclusion tasks (Factor 3) and, less clearly, the spatial tasks of the Piagetian battery and the Wechsler tests. In addition, the correlation between the sum of the scores of the 11 subtests of the WISC and the sum of the scores of the 27 Piagetian tasks was .88. Humphreys and Parsons concluded: "The showing of a substantial communality in function measured by intelligence tests and Piagetian tasks, however, opens the way for their interchangeable use or, better, for their joint use in developmental and educational psychology" (p. 380).

Going in the same direction, Humphreys, Rich, and Davey (1985), in a later reanalysis of the same data, calculated the correlations between the four following global scores: Wechsler verbal IQ, Wechsler performance IQ, Piagetian tasks, and tests of academic achievement. A hierarchical factor analysis of this table of intercorrelations again showed a general factor accounting for 94% of the variance and two small group factors, one with loadings for verbal IQ and achievement tests, and the other with loadings for performance IQ and scores on the Piagetian battery.

This divergence in the interpretation of the data caused a polemic between the authors (see Glass & Stephens, 1980; Humphreys, 1980; Kohlberg & DeVries, 1980) and a symposium was organized, at the 1981 SRCD Congress, to clarify this confused question. For this occasion, Carroll, Kohlberg, and DeVries (1984) reanalyzed the data of DeVries (1974) and of DeVries and Kohlberg (1977) in applying the recommendations of Humphreys and Parsons (1979): partialling out chronological age from the correlations and carrying out a hierarchical factor analysis. This analysis yielded three first-order factors and one second-order general factor. The three first-order factors concerned respectively the psychometric tests (Stanford–Binet, CTMM, and two Piagetian tasks—class inclusion and magic thought), the conservation tasks, and the achievement tasks. This factor structure is similar to that found by Humphreys and Parsons (1979), but the part of variance accounted by the group factor of Piagetian tasks (mainly conservation tasks) was much more important in their results (the loadings of these tasks were stronger for their group factor than for the g factor, whereas the reverse was found in the reanalysis of Humphreys and Parsons). Carroll et al. (1984) concluded: "The net result of the two reanalyses may be said to be, therefore, that Piagetian intelligence, especially as measured by Piagetian tests, is somewhat distinct from psychometric intelligence. Piagetian conservation ability can be likened to a primary factor of intelligence alongside verbal, spatial, and numerical ability. It is entirely possible that Piagetian conservation ability is closely allied with some primary factor of reasoning ability" (p. 89).

Other Studies

Two other studies deserve to be mentioned in this trend of research. First, is Kaufman (1971), who administered to 103 kindergartners (5 and 7 years old) a Piagetian Battery (PB) of 13 tasks, the Gesell School Readiness Test (GSRT) and the group-administered Lorge–Thorndike (L–T). The score on the PB correlated .64 with the score on the GSRT and .62 with the score on the L–T.

The factor analysis of the PB (principal components and orthogonal rotation) yielded three group factors corresponding respectively to the tasks of conservation, classification, and seriation. The factor analysis (principal factors), including psychometric, achievement, and Piagetian tests, yielded a general factor accounting for 70% of the communality, and three bipolar factors. After orthogonal rotation of these four factors, the three subtests of the L–T loaded on Factor 1, conservation tasks on Factor 2, GSRT subtests on Factor 3, and seriation tasks on Factor 4.

Inman and Secrest (1981) developed a few years later a revised and extended version of Kaufman's Piagetian Battery. This new battery, the Cognitive Development Inventory (CDI), is comprised of 35 items corresponding to six operations: conservation, seriation, numeration, temporal reasoning, spatial reasoning, and classification. The CDI was administered with an achievement test, the General Concept Test (GCT), to a sample of 660 children attending the last year of kindergarten. The hierarchical factor analysis of the 35 items of the CDI yielded, in a first step, five oblique factors, each of them showing loadings for the items corresponding to one of the abovementioned operations (except that the items of classification and numeration loaded on the same factor). The correlations between these five factors ranged from .21 to .49. The second-order analysis specified two factors, that were interpreted as corresponding respectively to logico-mathematic and infralogic operations.[1] The first one showed loadings for the primary factors of classification–numeration and seriation, the second involved spatial and temporal reasoning. Number conservation had average and approximately equivalent loadings on these two factors. These two second-order factors correlate .66, so the third level analysis yields a general factor. After orthogonalization, this general factor accounted for 34% of the communality, the second-order factors, logico-mathematic and infralogic, accounted respectively for 10% and 4%, and each of the five first-order factors accounted for approximately 10%.

Inman and Secrest also regressed the total GCT score on these factors in a stepwise analysis. The multiple correlation was R(3) = .665 when entering only the general factor, R (3 + 2) = .666 when the second-order factors were added, and R (3 + 2 + 1) = 681 when the first-order factors were added. Part of the sample (441 of the 660 subjects) completed other achievement tests 15 months later, at the end of Grade 1—the Primary Reading Inventory (PRI) and the Diagnostic Mathematics Inventory (DMI). Regression of the total score on the achievement tests (PRI + DMI) on the different factor scores described earlier yielded the following multiple correlations: R(3) = .629, R (3 + 2) = .639, R (3 + 2 + 1) = .652. These results led the authors to conclude that only the general factor of their Piagetian battery was related to the total score on achievement tests.

Discussion

The first studies concluding that Piagetian and psychometric tasks measured different forms of intelligence had errors and weaknesses that were clearly addressed by Humphreys and Parsons (1979) and Humphreys (1980). When age was controlled in the same way for the two types of tests and when the method of factor analysis allowed a general factor to be extracted, such a factor was found, and the two types of tests had substantial loadings (Carroll et al., 1984; Humphreys & Parsons, 1979; Kaufman, 1971).

When the variance of this general factor was removed, the Piagetian and psychometric tests loaded loaded generally on different group factors. It should be noted that Piagetian tasks are themselves not homogeneous. When the sample of Piagetian tasks was sufficiently varied, they

---

[1]Piaget used the term *logico-mathematic* to refer to operations bearing on the relationships between discrete objects (the logical domain is hence that of discontinuous entities) and the term *infralogical* to refer to operations bearing on relationships between parts of a continuous object (e.g., space or time, in which subjects must isolate parts from the continuum before operating on them). Nevertheless, Piaget considered that logical and infralogical operations were isomorphic and arose from the same overall structure.

loaded on at least two distinct group factors, one corresponding to tasks involving the logic of classes and relations, the other corresponding to conservation tasks (Humphreys & Parsons, 1979; Kaufman, 1971; Stephens et al., 1972). When there were also tasks of spatial and temporal reasoning in sufficient number, they loaded on a different factor (the second-order factor interpreted as infralogic in Inman & Secrest, 1981).

There were nevertheless important variations between the studies concerning the relative importance of the general and Piagetian factors. The two studies involving a hierarchical factor analysis that included both Piagetian and psychometric tasks can be compared from this point of view. In Humphreys and Parsons' (1979) study, the contribution of the group factors seems very reduced and the authors considered that the variance specific to Piagetian tests was not important. They did not give the relative parts of variance in the hierarchical factor analysis but one can see that, in the principal components analysis, the eigenvalue of the first factor was 19.86 whereas those of the three following factors ranged between 1 and 2. The part of variance specific to the Piagetian factor—in fact, a conservation factor—was more important in Carroll et al.'s (1984) analysis because the loadings of Piagetian tasks were stronger on their own group factor than on the general factor. These variations cannot be explained, in principle, by the difference in the range of ages in the two studies (6–18 years in the first and 5–7 years in the second) because age is controlled by partialling it out from correlations. Nevertheless, one can wonder—as do Carroll et al.—if Piagetian variables were appropriately scaled to measure growth from ages 6 to 18 years. These differences can likely also be explained by differences in the composition of the samples. Half of Stephens et al.'s subjects (reanalyzed by Humphreys and Parsons) were mentally retarded children. This can reinforce the correlations—and thus the part of the general factor—due to increased dispersion of the variables, or due to the fact that intellectual task performance is known to be more homogeneous in mentally retarded subjects than in nonretarded ones.

These studies provide some indications on the relations between IQ or the general factor drawn from psychometric tests and the general factor drawn from the analysis of Piagetian tests. To tell the truth, the correlations were more often calculated between the total scores of the batteries concerned than between factors, but the total score can be considered as an approximation of the score in the general factor. Humphreys and Parsons (1979) found a correlation of .88 between the total score of the Piagetian battery and the total score of Wechsler's tests. In Kaufman (1971), the correlations between the total score of the Piagetian Battery and the total scores of the Gesell and Lorge–Thorndike were respectively .64 and .62. In Inman and Secrest (1981), the correlation between the general factor of the CDI (the Piagetian battery) and the GCT (a general test of achievement) was .66. Here again, the exceptionally strong correlation of .88 in Humphreys and Parsons' study was probably due to the particular composition of their sample. However, the correlations between .60 and .70 found in the other studies are about the same order of magnitude as those usually found between various psychometric scales of intelligence.

It is less easy to establish possible correspondences between the group factors drawn from the factor analysis of Piagetian tests and the group factors generally found with psychometric tests. The psychometric tasks used in these studies are not factorial tests, but intelligence scales, whose factorial structure is less clear. We return later to this point. The same can be said about the relations between Piagetian group factors and achievement tests. The results of Inman and Secrest showed that adding these group factors to the general Piagetian factor in the regression analysis did not improve the correlation with a total achievement test score, but the correlations between these specific group factors and achievement in specific fields of knowledge were never calculated.

THE FRENCH APPROACH: ARTICULATING
PIAGETIAN AND PSYCHOMETRIC CONCEPTS

The French or French-language studies that, in the same period as the American studies, compared the factorial structure of Piagetian and psychometric tests were guided by theoretical considerations on the relations between these two conceptual frameworks.

The Hypotheses of Reuchlin

The so-called "French-connection" (Larivée, Normandeau, & Parent, 2000) takes as its source the hypotheses formulated by Reuchlin (1964) on the correspondences between the psychometric and the Piagetian conceptual frameworks. The first of these hypotheses was that the Piagetian concept of "overall structure" could provide a theoretical explanation of the psychometric concept of a general factor:

> In the course of development, reaching a new stage, controlling a new operational structure, constitutes an acquisition of a very general nature. Becoming able to handle formal thought is, for a given child, to ensure a considerable advantage over less advanced children. It ensures especially a general advantage, which certainly appears whatever the nature of the task. For all the period in which chronological decalages exist between children as for these acquisitions, one thus conceives that the most important differentia-

tion between these children is of a general nature, the general superiority of some over others translating simply the fact that some already have powerful and universal intellectual tools which are still lacking for others. To express this fact in factorial language, is to say that, for all the period in which these individual decalages in the chronology of stages exist, the general factor of differentiation will have a great importance compared to other factors. (p. 121)

The second hypothesis formulated by Reuchlin concerned the relations between the psychometric concept of a group factor and the Piagetian concept of horizontal decalage:

> if the factorial approach has much to learn from the genetic epistemological framework with regard to these general processes, and consequently with regard to the general factor which translates them, it does not find the same support with regard to the group factors. There are, admittedly, the horizontal decalages, about which we already spoke. Following a reasoning that we will examine in a moment, they can account for the appearance of group factors during the period of development. But it remains to be understood why these group factors are still here after the period of development. It remains also, especially for the Piagetian approach, to enrich its observations concerning the decalages and to explain them. The basic problem that one can see in this direction is the following: Does there really exist a single pathway to carry out this walk towards equilibrium of the cognitive structures? Or should it be admitted that this walk towards equilibrium constitutes only the most formalized schematization of processes which can, from one individual to another, be carried out preferably in a domain or an other. . . . (p. 119)

Empirical Studies Testing Reuchlin's Hypotheses

Longeot (1969, 1978) devoted two sets of studies to test these hypotheses on the relations between the concepts of stage and the general factor on the one hand and the concepts of decalage and group factors on the other hand. To achieve this goal, Longeot constructed several Piagetian tests centered on the period of transition from concrete to formal operations: an individually administered scale, the Logical Thought Development Scale (LTDS; EDPL in French; Longeot, 1974), and group administered tests, the Formal Operations Tests (FOT; TOF in French), adapted to the examination of the large samples of subjects that are needed to carry out factor analyses. Six FOT were devised, two for each of the three main types of formal operations identified by Piaget: Combinatorial operations, operations of proportionality (supposed to rely on the formal operational structure that Piaget called the INRC group, which is a specific case of the Klein group), and propositional operations (supposed to rely on combinatorial as well as INRC operations). Each one of these tests is composed of a dozen problems whose resolution implies, in principle, the use of the corresponding formal operations.

In a first study, Longeot (1969, chap. V) focused on the relations between group factors and decalages, the six FOT were given to a sample of 200 children in sixth grade. This same sample, in addition, completed factorial tests (numerical ability, spatial ability, verbal ability) and two achievement tests (French and mathematics). The factor analysis of the Piagetian tests (principal factors and oblique rotation) yielded two interpretable factors, one on which the two combinatorial tests loaded and one on which the tests of proportionality and propositional operations loaded. Longeot interpreted the first factor as combinatorial and the second as INRC. These two group factors were regarded as confirming the hypothesis of decalages corresponding to differences of pathways in the access to formal operations; some subjects appeared to master first combinatorial operations whereas others appeared to master first the operations corresponding to the INRC group. Factor analysis of the psychometric tests passed by these same subjects (principal factors and then oblique rotation) also yielded two factors, one on which numerical aptitude and spatial aptitude tests loaded, which Longeot interpreted as a reasoning factor, the other on which the verbal aptitude test and the two achievement tests loaded, interpreted as an academic factor. The Piagetian tests were then projected in the space of the psychometric factors. In this space, the six Piagetian tests had substantial and equivalent loadings on the reasoning factor but not on the achievement factor.

In a second study (Longeot, 1969, chap. VI) focusing on the relations between the general factor of the psychometric tests and stages in Piagetian tests, Longeot used three Piagetian tests of formal operations (combinatorial operations, proportionality, propositional operations) and six tests of a psychometric battery (two verbal, two numerical, and two spatial) with a sample of 250 subjects. In order to maximize the general factor in this study, the dispersion of ages was increased by including subjects from Grades 5, 6, and 7 in the sample.

The factor analysis (principal factors, oblique rotation, and hierarchical analysis), yielded a second-order general factor accounting for 77% of the commonality and three first-order factors, one on which the two verbal tests loaded (10%), one on which the two spatial tests loaded (9%), and one on which the two numerical tests and the three Piagetian tests loaded (4%). Longeot interpreted this third factor as "operational-numerical." The fact that very little variance was left by the general factor for this operational–numerical factor, indicated that in this study, Piagetian tests loaded practically only on the general factor. Returning to the first hypothesis of Reuchlin, Longeot (1969) thus concluded:

When the general factor is that of a battery in which prevail psychometric tests, this factor is defined by the operational level of the children, i.e., by the general stage of the development that they reached. Subjects being at the formal stage succeed better than the others in all kinds of tests of efficiency of all kinds, whatever the support. Then, on equal operational level, some obtain better results in the verbal tests, some others in the spatial tests or in the numerical tests. (p. 149)

The second research project, carried out some years later by Longeot (1978), aimed at clarifying the relations between group factors and what Piaget called "horizontal decalages." To articulate these two concepts Longeot proposed a model of development in which several routes are possible. In the preparation phase of a stage, several paths can be followed according to whether a child constructs the new cognitive structure in one domain or another. At the completion phase of the stage, these various routes would converge. This model thus comprised, at the final phase of each stage, nodal points of passage corresponding to the fact that all ac-quisitions of one stage must be completed before those of another stage can begin. But between these nodal points, in the preparation phases of the stages, this model admits that the order in which a structure general-izes to various domains is not universal. The corresponding decalages are "individual," meaning that they are not in the same direction for all sub-jects. They are distinguished from the "collective" decalages (horizontal or vertical), which are in the same direction for all subjects.

Figure 6.1 schematizes this model with a simple example in which the pathways followed by four subjects (S1 to S4) are represented in the course of mastering the various items of two domains: four items of the logico-mathematic domain (LM1 to LM4) and four items of the infralogic do-main (IL1 to IL 4). For each of the two stages represented, Stage II and Stage III, the figure distinguishes a preparation phase and a completion phase. Two different routes are represented, one (top) in which LM items of a stage are mastered before IL items, the other (bottom), in which the order of mastering for LM and IL items is reversed. Subjects S1 and S2, who are in the preparation phase of Stage II, succeed on items of varied difficulty, but inside only one field (LM for S1, IL for S2). These decalages are "individual" because they are in different directions for the subjects S1 and S2 and, from the factorial point of view, they are at the origin of two group factors in which are respectively loaded tests of the LM and IL domains. The subjects S3 and S4, in contrast, are in the completion phase of Stage II, and even if they had previously followed different routes, they master all of the items of Stage II and are thus at the origin of a general factor of performance. The hypothesis of Longeot was that the joint presence of a general factor and of group factors in Piagetian tests resulted from the mixture, in the same sample, of subjects

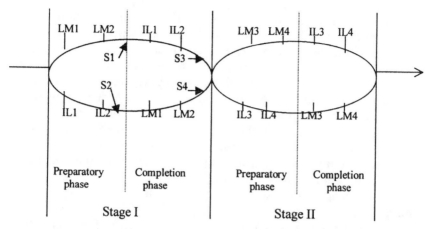

FIG. 6.1. Schematic representation of Longeot's model of cognitive development.

being in the preparatory phase and of subjects being in the completion phase of the various stages.

To test this model, Longeot did not rely on factor analytic methods, but on hierarchical analyses. His goal was to show that the expected hierarchical relation between items belonging to different stages is preserved when one admits in the preparation phase of each stage permutations between items belonging to different domains. His data showed, however, that despite this less-constrained version of the Piagetian concept of stage, it was not possible to order items of different domains in the same hierarchical scale.

Group Factors and Individual Differences in Developmental Pathways

The distinction between the preparatory and the completion phases of a stage was thus an attempt to make the hypothesis of overall cognitive structure compatible with the existence of individual decalages between domains, provided that these decalages did not exceed one stage (e.g., it was not possible that subject S1 of Fig. 6.1 responded correctly to item LM3 before having mastered items IL1 and IL2). This model predicted also an increase in intraindividual variability of the developmental stage across domains for the preparation phase of a stage, but a decrease of this variability for the completion phase. These two predictions were tested by Lautrey (1980) by reanalyzing the data collected by Longeot when elaborating his Logical Thought Developmental Scale (EDPL in French).

To develop this Piagetian scale, Longeot (1967) examined individually 210 subjects from 9 to 16 years old, with five subscales whose items made it possible to locate the children at five different stages: preoperational, concrete, preformal, formal A, and formal B. The five subscales were: (a) Conservation (weight, volume, dissociation heaviness-volume), (b) mechanical curves (tasks requiring the coordination of two distinct systems of reference in the representation of space), (c) quantification of probabilities (problems of proportionality, the more complex ones were supposed to require the INRC group), (d) permutations (combinatorial operations), and (e) pendulum (a task requiring in principle propositional operations to find which of four factors modifies the frequency of pendulum oscillations: weight, length of the string, height of the launching point, force of pushing).

Correspondence analysis (Benzecri, 1973; Greenacre, 1984), a multidimensional method of analysis for nominal data, was applied to the table having as columns the 20 items of this scale and as lines the 210 subjects aged 9 to 15 (30 by age group). Three factors were found. The first was a general factor of cognitive development, accounting for 21% of the variance and opposing the concrete stage items and the formal stage items. The second factor accounted for 12% of the variance and opposed the items of permutation (combinatorial operations) to those of quantification of probabilities (INRC group). The third factor accounted for 9% of the variance and was interpreted as opposing logical operations (items of permutation and of quantification of probabilities) with infralogical operations (items of conservation and of mechanical curves). The oppositions found on the second and the third factor are the expression of individual decalages, which can be noteworthy for some developmental patterns. Only 16% of the subjects were in fact at the same developmental stage for the five subscales. Among the rest of the sample, the maximal amplitude of the observed individual decalages was one stage for 44%, two stages for 33%, three stages for 4%, and four stages for 1% (Lautrey, 1980).

The hypothesis of a reduction of intraindividual variability in the completion phase of a stage, followed by an increase in the preparation phase was also tested. The sample was divided into three age groups: 9 to 10 years ($N = 60$), 11 to 13 ($N = 90$), and 14 to 16 ($N = 60$). These three age groups were selected to correspond respectively to the completion phase of concrete operations, the preparatory phase of formal operations, and the completion phase of this stage. The results did not confirm the alternation predicted by Longeot's model in terms of phases of decreases and of increases in intra-individual variability with developmental level, but rather showed a regular tendency toward an increase in the frequency and extent of the intraindividual decalages during this period of development.

The study of the relations between the factorial structure of Piagetian tests and the individual differences in developmental pathways continued in a longitudinal research project carried out by Anik de Ribaupierre and Laurence Rieben, of the University of Geneva, and Jacques Lautrey, of the University of Paris V.

The developmental period studied was that of concrete operations. A sample of 154 children representative of the Genevan population was examined twice with a 3-year interval. These children were between the ages 6 to 12 on the first evaluation (22 subjects per age group) and thus between 9 to 15 on the second evaluation. Because the tasks described later only discriminate ages 6 to 12, only subjects who were between 9 and 12 at the time of the second evaluation were re-examined with these tasks. Of the 88 subjects aged 6 to 9 at the first evaluation, 76 were relocated 3 years later.

Subjects were individually administered eight operational tasks adapted from Piaget and Inhelder. Testing adhered as closely as possible to the "critical questioning" technique developed by Piaget. These eight tasks were selected in order to sample four domains: The logico-mathematical domain (class intersection, quantification of probabilities), the physics domain (conservations and Islands), the spatial domain (sectioning of volumes, intersection of volumes), and mental imagery (folding of lines, folds, and holes). Each of the eight tasks measured a given operation and was comprised of several items corresponding to different levels of mastery of that operation. For example, the conservation task included four items known to be of increasing difficulty: conservation of substance, conservation of weight, conservation of volumes, and dissociation between heaviness and volume. In total, subjects were tested on 38 items on two occasions. A complete description of the material, instructions, and scoring criteria can be found in Rieben, de Ribaupierre, and Lautrey (1983) and a more succinct version in Lautrey, de Ribaupierre, and Rieben (1986) or de Ribaupierre, Rieben, and Lautrey (1985).

Correspondence analysis was applied again. The 154 individuals tested on the first occasion appear in the rows and the 38 items they were administered appear in the columns. For each item, subjects were scored 1 if they succeeded and 0 if they failed (in fact, there are 76 columns, because success and failure are represented as two disjunctive modalities for each item). The correspondence analysis of the first occasion yielded three factors accounting respectively for 30%, 14%, and 9% of the variance. The first one can be interpreted as a general factor of complexity (as regards items) and as a general factor of development (as regards subjects). The next factor contrasts logical and infralogical items. The items loading on the logical pole of this factor were those of class intersection and of quantification of probabilities and the items loading the infralogical pole were those of unfolding of volumes, sectioning of volumes, and line foldings.

The infralogical items that contributed most to the definition of the second factor were those for which the parts of objects on which the subjects had to perform mental actions were visible. On the contrary, the items contributing most to the third factor were infralogical tasks for which the parts of objects to be manipulated mentally could not be seen. Within this set of infralogical items, axis 3 contrasts items from the physical domain (e.g., conservation of volumes) with some items of mental imagery (e.g., folds and holes).

One of the advantages of correspondence analysis is that it is possible to represent simultaneously items and subjects on the same axes. This technique was used to locate, on each pole of each axis, the items and the individuals that contributed most to the part of the chi-square value that this axis contributed. For example, Table 6.1 gives this simultaneous representation for Axis 2 (logical/infralogical factor). Reading horizontally this table shows the developmental profiles of the five individuals contributing the most to each pole of this factor; reading it vertically shows profiles of the items contributing the most to each pole of this factor for these individuals.

The items are presented in the columns. Those contributing the most to the definition of the "logical" pole of Axis 2 appear on the left-hand side of the table and are denoted L. These items are tasks of varying difficulty and are about class intersection and quantification of probabilities. The items that contribute the most to the definition of the infralogical pole of Axis 2 appear on the right hand side of the table and have been labeled IL. They cover tasks on the sectioning of volumes and mental

TABLE 6.1
Success Patterns of the Five Subjects Contributing
the Most to Each Pole of Factor 2

Subjects			Logical items							Infralogical items					
			L1	L2	L3	L4	L5	L6	L7	IL1	IL2	IL3	IL4	IL5	IL6
Sex	Age	N	100	76	68	44	40	18	18	64	45	39	32	24	19
M	7		1	1	1	1	1	0	0	0	0	0	0	0	0
M	9		1	1	1	1	1	1	1	0	0	1	0	0	0
M	9		1	1	0	1	1	0	1	1	0	0	0	0	0
F	12		1	1	1	1	1	1	0	0	0	0	0	0	0
M	10		1	1	1	1	1	1	0	0	0	0	0	0	0
F	11		0	0	0	0	0	0	0	1	1	1	1	0	0
M	12		1	0	0	0	0	0	0	1	1	0	0	0	1
F	10		0	0	0	0	0	0	0	1	1	1	1	1	1
G	12		1	1	0	0	1	0	0	1	0	0	1	0	0
F	6		0	0	0	0	0	0	0	1	0	0	1	0	0

imagery. The columns were reclassified within each of the two groups of items, according to their order on the first factor. The indices of the items (e.g., L1, L2, . . . LN) correspond to the order of their coordinates on this factor. The number of subjects N (out of 154) who succeeded on them follows.

The subjects, identified by sex (M or F) and age (6 to 12), are presented in the rows. The five subjects contributing the most to the logical pole of Axis 2 appear at the top and the five subjects who contributed the most to the infralogical pole appear at the bottom. Within each of these groups, the rows were reclassified as a function of the order of their coordinates on Axis 2.

For example, reading the developmental profile of subject M7 (a 7 year-old boy) in line 1 shows that he succeeded coherently at nearly all logical items, including L6, which is an item of quantification of probabilities belonging in principle to the formal stage and passed by only 18 out of the 154 subjects, but that subject M7 failed coherently all the items contributing to the infralogical pole of this factor, including IL1, which is a rather easy item of sectioning of volume, belonging in principle to the concrete stage and passed by 64 subjects. The profile of subject F11 (a 11 year-old girl) is exactly the reverse: She fails at all the items contributing to the logical pole, including L1 which is an easy item of class intersection of the concrete stage, but succeeds coherently at infralogical items. The shape of such developmental patterns is entirely characteristic of what were earlier termed *individual decalages*. These patterns are of course extreme. The majority of subjects present decalages that are smaller, but the fact that some subjects, who do not suffer of any pathology (all of them attended regular classes), can present such asymmetric patterns of development as well in one sense that in the other, argues for the relative specificity of the developmental mechanisms in these two domains. Such patterns can be seen as different pathways of development in the multidimensional space defined by the three factors revealed by the correspondence analysis.

The profile of each child on the 38 items for the first occasion gives only one point of his or her developmental pathway in this multidimensional space. The follow-up, 3 years later, of this sample provided another point in the developmental trajectory of each individual, allowing us to see if there was some stability in the form of this trajectory. As explained earlier, only children who were 6- to 9-year-olds at the first occasion were reexamined with the same tasks when they were 9- to 12-year olds. The method of correspondence analysis gives the possibility of plotting "supplementary individuals" into a previously conducted analysis. This possibility was exploited in projecting the 76 subjects examined at the second occasion as supplementary individuals in the analysis of the first occasion. The sample examined at the first occasion is an appropriate base of reference because it included subjects of 9 to 12, who can be used for purposes of comparison. This procedure has the additional advantage of situating each subject in terms of his or her own coordinate position 3 years later on an identical system of axes. The stability and change in subjects' relative position has been assessed by computing correlations, for each axis, between coordinates for individuals on the first evaluation (where they appear as main elements) and on the second evaluation (where they appear as supplementary elements).

For the first three factors, these correlations were respectively .76, .35, and .34 (Lautrey & Cibois, 1991). It appears thus that during this 3-year time period, the order of subjects' coordinates on the first factor, interpreted as a general developmental factor, remained fairly stable. The value of .76 is comparable to that obtained with IQ for the same time period in childhood. The stability on the two other factors, which are group factors, and correspond to differences in developmental pathways, is weaker and suggests that there is an important fluidity in the form of the decalages in the course of development. It is nevertheless possible that this kind of study underestimates stability in the form of the developmental trajectory. Because subjects who have very asymmetric patterns of development succeed at almost all the items of the domain in which they are in advance, three years later, there is a ceiling effect for them in this domain and, as they generally have progressed in the other domain, their pattern can only become less asymmetric than at the first occasion (this is, for example, what happened for subject M7 of Table 6.1). This problem could be avoided by using other tasks, more discriminant ones, at the second occasion, but this solution can create another problem because it may be more difficult to retrieve exactly the same factorial structure when using different tasks at different occasions.

In a more recent longitudinal study of the factorial structure of Piagetian tasks, Bradmetz (1996) did not replicate the results concerning the differences in pathways of development. In this study, 104 children were tested five times, once a year, from 4 to 9 years of age, with 25 Piagetian tasks. The factorial structure of these 25 tasks on the five occasions was analyzed through structural modeling using LISREL. Bradmetz found for each year a general factor accounting for approximately 30% of the variance and group factors each accounting for approximately 7% of the variance. The correlations between the overall scores (obtained by summing up the scores of the 25 tasks) at two successive occasions were high, approximately .85. The pattern of correlations between the five occasions suggested a simplex model; the amplitude of the correlation decreased as the interval between occasions increased. With an interval of 3 years, between 5;6 and 8;6, the correlation was .72, a value very close of that found with the same interval for the general factor in the foregoing study (.76). Additionally, as in the previous study, Bradmetz found an important intraindividual variability, reaching two stages for certain subjects, some of these decalages being individual decalages (i.e., decalages whose direction is different for different subjects).

But what differs from the foregoing study is that Bradmetz failed to find stable group factors corresponding to a stable distinction between domains, as, for example, the distinction between logic and infralogic factors in Inman and Secrest (1981) or Lautrey et al. (1986). The content of group factors varied from one occasion to another and, as a consequence, there were no stable individual differences in the form of cognitive development. This instability in the content of group factors, from one year to the next, accompanies the fact that the content of the general facor also varied from year to year. For example, at 4;6, the highest loadings on Factor g were those of numerical tasks; at 5;6, the seriation task had also a high loading; at 6;6, conservation tasks had the highest loadings.

Bradmetz's failure to find stable group factors, and thus to find stable individual differences in the form of cognitive development, seems thus due to the fact that most of the tasks he used were discriminant for only a short age period. This led to variations on both the content of the general factor and the content of the group factors over occasions. This problem was not present in Lautrey et al.'s study because each task included items of various level of difficulties. The conservation task, for example, included items of conservation of substance, of weight, of volume, of dissociation between heaviness and volume, so that between ages 6 and 12 there was always one of the conservation items that was discriminant, and the same was true for the other tasks. This is probably the reason why stable group factors and stable developmental pathways could be found in one study and not in the other.

Discussion

The studies undertaken in what has been called the "French connection" (see Larivée, Normandeau, & Parent, 2000, for review) have their origin in the hypotheses formulated by Reuchlin (1964) on the correspondences between the Piagetian and psychometric conceptual frameworks. The first hypothesis was that the Piagetian concepts of overall structure and stage could explain the general factor of cognitive development observed with psychometric tests. By showing that the psychometric and the Piagetian tests loaded on the same general factor, Longeot thought to have empirically confirmed this assumption.

However, the studies that followed led us to question the concept of general stage itself. The extent of intraindividual variability of developmental level across domains was such that it was difficult to explain the general factor by an overall structure common to different domains of knowledge.

The analysis of the form of this intraindividual variability, and, in particular, of the decalages that we called *individual*, has shown that, as suggested by the second hypothesis of Reuchlin, the group factors correspond to individual differences in the pathway of development. The extent of these individual decalages in the developmental pattern of some individuals suggests a relative autonomy in the development of the various cognitive domains. All these domains are certainly under the influence of a set of common maturational and environmental factors that give rise to a general factor of development, but they do not seem interrelated by a general cognitive structure that would lead to a common and single form to cognitive development. These reflections were extended in a pluralistic model of development, in which the plurality of the processes likely to fulfill the same cognitive function account for variations in the trajectories of development (Lautrey, 1990, in press; Lautrey & Caroff, 1996).

GENERAL DEVELOPMENTAL FACTOR
AND PROCESSING CAPACITY:
THE NEO-PIAGETIAN APPROACH

The difficulties encountered with the Piagetian concept of overall structure led some of the disciples of Piaget to search in information processing models for another explanation of the sequential order of acquisitions in the course of cognitive development. There are different neo-Piagetian theories in this trend (see, e.g., Case, 1987; Fischer & Farrar, 1987; Pascual-Leone, 1987) but all of them share some fundamental postulates (Case, 1992). All of them keep the stage model of cognitive development advocated by Piaget. Nevertheless, the developmental stages are no longer explained by the construction of an operational structure that is common to different domains of knowledge. These theories rather explain the relative synchronism of development by the existence of an upper limit in the processing capacity of children, and they explain the sequence of developmental stages by the increase of this processing capacity with age. This increase is conceived as a necessary condition to reach the following stage of development but is not considered as sufficient. Optimal environmental conditions of familiarity, training, and exercise are necessary to reach the optimal level of performance allowed by the upper limit of the processing capacity (Fischer & Farrar, 1987). This model of a general ceiling in performance has the advantage of being compatible with both the relative synchronicity and the important situational and individual variability reported earlier.

The models of processing capacity differ among neo-Piagetian theories, but all of them can be related to one or the other of two conceptions. The first one, mainly advocated by Pascual-Leone, is a model of attentional capacity. The metaphor used is that of "Mental Power." The capacity of this Mental Power, named M capacity, is defined as the number of schemes that can be simultaneously activated in a single operation. The range varies from one scheme at age 3 to seven schemes at age 15, in principle, at the rate of one more scheme every 2 years. According to Pascual-Leone, this increase relies essentially on brain maturation. In the second conception, mainly advocated by Case (1985), the processing capacity is defined by storage space in working memory. The metaphor used here is that of mental space. Working memory is conceived as a limited space, in which there is a tradeoff between the space used for processing (Operating Space, OS) and the space used for momentary storage of the products of processing (Short Term Storage Space, STSS). The complexity of the problems that can be solved depends thus of the number of goals and subgoals that can be kept simultaneously activated (i.e., momentary stored in STSS) while processing a mental operation (in OS). According to Case (1985), the increase of STSS with age is probably not due to the growth of the whole working memory space, but to the increase of processing speed. Due to exercise, automatization, reorganization, as well as maturational factors, this acceleration of processing decreases the size of operating space and so doing, increases STSS.

As noted by de Ribaupierre (1995), the first kind of model is close to those general models of cognition viewing working memory as a strongly activated subset of long-term memory (e.g., Cantor & Engle, 1993; Cowan, 1993), whereas the second kind of model is close to those models viewing working memory as a system with its own specific processes (e.g., Baddeley, 1986). But despite their differences in the interpretation of working memory development, all the researchers of the neo-Piagetian trend define developmental stages by the upper limit in the number of schemes that can be simultaneously activated and use the same set of tasks in order to measure this upper limit. In the following, this upper limit is named "processing capacity," whatever the theoretical background of the studies considered (working memory span or attentional capacity or M capacity)

Tasks Measuring Processing Capacity

Some examples of tasks that have been developed in the neo-Piagetian framework are briefly presented below.

Compound Stimuli Visual Information Task (CSVI). This task was developed by Pascual-Leone (e.g., 1970). In a learning phase, the subject learns to associate some attributes of a set of simple stimuli (such as square, red, circle, etc.) to a specific button of a keyboard (e.g., associate the square with the round, white button). In the test phase, once these associations are overlearned, the simple stimuli are nested in a composite stimulus and the task of the subject is to respond to all the elements that can be remembered (e.g., press the four appropriate keys when the compound stimulus is a red big square with a cross in the middle). Item complexity is defined by the number of simple elements embedded in the complex stimulus.

Figural Intersection Task (FIT). This task was also developed by Pascual-Leone (see Pascual-Leone & Baillargeon, 1994). Each item consists of two to eight simple figures on the right-hand side of the page and one compound figure on the left-hand side of the page. The participant's task for each item consists of two subtasks. First, he or she is required to place a dot inside each simple figure. Second, he or she is asked to search successively for each simple figure in the compound figure and to place a dot at the point where the simple figures intersect. The factors intervening in the M demand of an item are the number of task-relevant simple figures and the presence of task-irrelevant simple figures in the compound figure.

Mr. Peanut Task. This task was developed by Case (1985) and adapted again by de Ribaupierre and Bayeux (1994). Children are presented with a clown figure with colored dots painted on different body parts. The picture is then removed and replaced by a blank figure on which children had to place colored chips on the parts that were painted in the previous picture. Item complexity is defined by the number of colored dot.

Counting Span. This task was developed by Case (1985). Children are presented with a series of cards, each containing green and yellow dots. They are instructed to count the green dots and retain that total while counting the number of green dots on subsequent cards, the preceding ones being removed. At the end of each series, subjects had to report the total. Item complexity is defined by the number of sets to count or totals to report.

Reading Span. This task was developed by Daneman and Carpenter (1980). Subjects are presented with a series of sentences. They are instructed to read each sentence, decide whether it is semantically correct, and to retain the last word while reading the subsequent sentence. At the end of the series, they had to report all the final words.

The *listening span task* has been adapted from this task for children who do not master reading. The principle is the same except that they have to listen to the series of sentences rather than to read them.

If these different tasks all measure the same general processing capacity they should load on a common factor. If, in addition, the upper limit of processing capacity underlies the general factor observed in developmental studies, this common factor of processing capacity should be the same as the general developmental factor. As for Piagetian tasks, there are few studies having performed factor analyses on neo-Piagetian tasks. Some of them conclude that these tasks measure effectively the same capacity and others that they do not.

Studies Pointing to the Unity of Processing Capacity

The first published factor analytic study of processing capacity tasks was conducted by Case and Globerson (1974). In this study, 43 children aged 7½ to 8½ years were administered seven tasks. Four of them were considered as measuring Field Independence–Dependence (FID)—Rod and Frame Test, Children Embedded Test, Block design subtest of the WISC, Colored version of Raven's Progressive Matrices—and the three others were considered as measuring Processing Capacity (PC)—CSVI, Digit placement, and Backward Digit span. Different methods of factor analysis were used on the intercorrelation matrix of these seven tasks, all of them resulting in two factors, one loading the four FID tasks and the other loading the three PC tasks. With a principal factor analysis followed by an orthoblique rotation, for example, the FID factor accounted for 34% of the variance and the PC factor for 17%; these two factors correlated .61. This result was interpreted as demonstrating that the three PC tasks loaded on a common factor corresponding to M capacity.

In an unpublished study cited by Case (1985), Collis and Romberg observed a similar result. In their study 139 children aged 5 to 8 years were administered four PC tasks (Mr. Peanut, Digit Placement, Counting Span, Backward Digit Span). According to Case, the factor analysis yielded only one factor in which the four PC tasks had substantial loadings.

Morra (1994) examined 191 children aged 6- to 10-year-olds with 17 tasks including M capacity tests as well as psychometric tests. There were 5 PC tasks(FIT, Mr. Peanut, Counting span, Backward Digit Span, Backward Word Span) and 10 psychometric tasks some of them considered as spatial tests (e.g., Block design, Googenough Draw-A-Man, Corsi's tests, Raven's Matrices, etc.) and the others as verbal tests (Vocabulary, Word Span, verbal fluency, etc.). A factor analysis of these 17 tasks (principal components with orthogonal rotation) yielded three factors that accounted for 44% of the total variance, respectively 20%, 14%, and 10%. Spatial tasks loaded on the first factor, verbal tasks on the the second, and PC tasks on the third (except the FIT test, which had stronger loadings on the spatial factor). The correlations among the five measures of PC when age was partialled out were significant, but rather weak (ranging from .21

to .33). Morra's conclusion was that despite their specificities, these five tasks measure the same processing capacity.

The foregoing studies have been criticized by Pulos (1997). The point is that these studies suggest that there is convergent validity of the PC measures but do not establish the divergent validity of these measures. In other words, it is not clear how measures of PC are related to other cognitive constructs and one can not to dismiss the hypothesis that the common factor of PC measures corresponds in fact to one of these other cognitive constructs. This hypothesis could be dismissed if it could be shown that there is no relation between the PC factor and the others, but othogonal rotations are not appropriate to give an answer to this question.

Reanalyzing the data with a promax rotation, Pulos found that the PC factor and the other factor (that he interprets as a Gv/Gf factor) correlated at .46 in Case and Globerson's study, and at .42 in Morra's study. According to Pulos, this result suggests a hierarchical factorial structure with a second-order factor relating PC and Gv/Gf. This point is reminiscent of that made by Humphreys concerning factor analysis including psychometric and Piagetian tasks (but see Morra & Scopesi, 1997 and Pascual-Leone, 1997 for replies).

Finally, a single factor loading all the PC tasks was also found in a longitudinal study conducted by de Ribaupierre and Bayeux (1995). Four age groups composed of 30 subjects each, aged 5, 6, 8, and 10 years old at the onset of the study, were examined once a year over 5 years with four PC tasks. Three of the tasks were administered each year (CSVI, Mr. Peanut-P, Mr. Peanut-C), the fourth task being different each year (FIT, Counting Span, Listening Span, Reading span). In the confirmatory factor analysis (LISREL) performed on these data, a single factor model proved satisfactory each year, except for age 5. In addition, a simplex model was able to account for the correlation between the five occasions on this factor.

However, as de Ribaupierre and Bailleux themselves acknowledge, the size of the sample constrained them to put the four age groups together in their analyses of each occasion. Given the extent of these ages (from 5–10 years), it is possible that this single factor reflects mainly the influence of age (the correlations between age and this single factor ranges from .76 to .91).

Studies Supporting a Plurality of Processing Capacities

Some studies on working memory (WM) in adult samples have yielded results that have also been interpreted as consistent with the unitary resource position (Engle, Cantor, & Carullo, 1992; Kyllonen & Christal, 1990). According to Shah and Miyake, this interpretation is debatable because the working memory tasks used in these studies have contents that, although different (words or numbers), are verbally coded.

The aim of the study carried out by Shah and Miyake (1996) was to show that working memory ressources for verbal and nonverbal processing is separable. Thus, they developed a spatial analog of the Reading Span task inspired by the experimental paradigm of mental rotation. Series of capital letters and of mirror-images of these letters were presented on a computer, one at a time, rotated in various orientations. For each letter, the participants had to say if it was *normal* or *mirror-imaged* (component of treatment), while keeping track of the orientation of the previously presented letters (component of storage). At the end of each set, they were asked to recall the letter's orientations in the correct serial order. The participants (54 undergraduate students) were administered this task and Reading Span as a verbal WM task. In addition they were administered three visuospatial tests, for which was computed a composite score of spatial ability, and verbal SAT. The results show that the Spatial Span task correlated significantly with the Spatial Composite score (.66), but not with Verbal SAT (.07). Reciprocally, the Reading Span task correlated significantly with Verbal SAT (.45), but not with the Spatial Composite score (.12). In addition, the correlation between the Spatial Span task and the Reading Span task was weak (.23). According to Shah and Miyake, these results suggest the separability of the cognitive resources for verbal and spatial processing at the central executive level.

The same criticism can be made with the PC tasks used in the developmental studies reviewed earlier. In general, these tasks privilege a verbal content (numbers or words), and even when their material is spatial they lend themselves to verbal coding strategies. In addition, some of them are short-term memory tasks rather than working-memory tasks, because they do not require simultaneously storage and processing. In the Mr. Peanut task, for example, the material is spatial but nothing prevents the child from making a verbal coding of the positions of the dots; secondly, this task requires mainly the storage of the dots' positions on the clown's body, but no real concurrent processing.

On the basis of these considerations, Bardon (1999) adapted two PC tasks so that they required simultaneously storage and processing. In the Mr. Peanut task, the requirement for processing was increased by presenting sequentially, one at a time, the figures of the clown, each having one painted dot placed on one part of the figure. On each drawing, there were in fact two pink dots playing the role of distracters and one non-pink dot (the color of which varied on each drawing). The children's task was to point their finger, for each drawing, to the non-pink point (processing component) while retaining the position and the color of the dots in the preceding figures (storage component). At the end of each set of drawings (whose size varied from 2 to 5), children were asked to recall the position and the color of dots by putting chips of the appropriate color at the appropriate positions on a blank figure of the clown.

The second task of spatial working memory, the Spatial Span task, was adapted from Oakhill, Yuill, and Parkin (1986) and from Seigneuric (1998). Children were presented series of cards, each having a grid of 3 × 3 cells. Each grid contained two dots of the same color and the task of the children is to point with their finger to the box in which it would be necessary to add a third point so that these three points form a straight line (as in the game of tic tac toe). Children must store the orientation of this line and its color while processing the following card. At the end of each set of cards they are asked to position these lines on a blank grid (they had colored strips of cardboard at their disposal).

To prevent strategies of verbal coding and subvocal rehearsal, these two WM tasks were administered under the condition of articulatory suppression. The children had to count aloud from 1 to 5, in a repetitive way, as quickly as possible, while carrying out the task.

In the framework of a study on the relations between reading and working memory, 48 fourth-grade children were administered these two tasks with two verbal WM tasks, the Reading Span task, and the Counting Span task. The intercorrelations of these four WM measures are presented in Table 6.2. In a confirmatory factor analysis (LISREL), a good fit was obtained with a hierarchical model comprising two first-order factors, one loading the two verbal WM tasks and the other the two spatial WM tasks, and a second-order general factor loading the four WM tasks. This result goes in the same direction as that obtained by Shah and Miyake (1996) with adult subjects, with the difference that the mean correlation between verbal and spatial WM tasks were higher here (around .40).

Discussion

The assumption that the various PC tasks measure the same general cognitive resource has probably to be reconsidered. It seems that when the PC tasks imply both storage and processing, and when the nature of both processing and storage required is systematically varied, the structure of

TABLE 6.2
Intercorrelations Between the Four Working
Memory Tasks in Bardon and Lautrey's Study

	RS	CS	SS	MP
RS		.67	.41	.35
CS			.43	.46
SS				.65
MP				

RS = Reading Span, CS = Counting Span, SS = Spatial Span, MP = Mr. Peanut.

their intercorrelations is compatible with a hierarchical model. In such a model, the first-order factors should correspond to domain-specific cognitive resources, and the second-order factor, to general purpose resources that can be assimilated to the central executive capacity.

This hierarchical structure appears so close to the factorial structure of intelligence that—as for the Piagetian tests—one can wonder whether the factors found with the two sets of tasks do not correspond to the same constructs. This similarity raises, in particular, the question of the identity between the general factor of PC tasks and the general factor that has been observed with psychometric tests. There are not yet sufficient empirical data to give a firm answer to this question but the reanalyses of Pulos (1997), showing that psychometric tasks and PC tasks loaded on the same second-order factor, are compatible with this hypothesis. The results of Pennings and Hessels (1996), who found that the processing capacity (here, M capacity) evaluated with the FIT correlated at .72 with the M capacity evaluated in Raven's Progressive Matrices, also goes in this direction.

CONCLUSION

Is there a general factor of cognitive development? In a certain sense, yes, and in an other sense, no.

In developmental studies, the general factor expresses the relative synchronicity of the acquisitions observed in various aspects of cognition. The greater the dispersion of ages in the sample considered, the more commonplace is this factor (nobody doubts that adolescents have, in all aspects of cognition, better performance than preschoolers). A common factor of development is, however, found also when the dispersion of ages is narrower and even when the effect of age is removed, either by studying children having the same age (e.g., Inman & Secrest, 1981), or by partialling out the correlation with age (e.g., Humphreys & Parsons, 1979). This common factor then reveals a less commonplace synchronicity in cognitive development.

Such a common factor of development was found both within batteries of Piagetian tasks and within batteries of psychometric tasks. As mentioned at the beginning of this chapter, these two kinds of tests were developed in very different theoretical frameworks. The existence of strong correlations between the common factors of these two kinds of tests (or between the total scores of these two kinds of batteries) thus suggests that they measure the same latent variable and widens its "general" nature. The common factor observed in these two kinds of developmental tests can be considered relatively general in this precise sense.

Furthermore, the group factors that are observed with Piagetian tests do not seem different from those found with psychometric ones (cf.

Carroll, 1993). The Infralogic factor, frequently found when Piagetian batteries include tasks requiring spatial and temporal operations, seems to correspond to the Gv factor (visuospatial representation) and the Logico-mathematic factor seems to correspond to the Reasoning factor and thus to the Gf (fluid intelligence) factor (cf. Gustaffson, 1984). The batteries of Piagetian tests thus assess a more restricted subset of factors than the psychometric batteries or scales; they do not include, in particular, verbal or achievement tests corresponding to the Gc factor (crystallized intelligence). Their specificity is to assess the development of logical reasoning in a much more detailed way.

The relative importance of these group factors, compared to the general factor, depends of course on the sampling of the subjects (in particular from the point of view of the dispersion of chronological or mental ages) and of the sampling of the tasks. When these two aspects of sampling are satisfactory, the group factors account for substantial parts of variance. In developmental studies, these group factors express differences in developmental pathways, which correspond to asynchronisms of development. The extent of these asynchonisms, in the developmental pattern of some subjects, suggests that cognitive development is in part domain specific. The results of a recent study integrating neo-Piagetian and psychometric tasks in the same factorial analysis allows us to generalize this conclusion to the neo-Piagetian tasks (Case, Demetriou, Platsidou, & Kazi, in press).

How then can the relative synchronicity that underlies the general factor of development be explained? Given the asynchronisms observed, this general factor cannot be explained by the construction, at certain stages of development, of a general purpose structure, which would be common to the various fields of knowledge. The notion of an upper limit in the processing capacity fits better with the observations. It should not, however, be inferred that this processing capacity corresponds to a unitary cognitive mechanism. Many assumptions, which are not exclusive, have been advanced to explain the development of working memory capacity with age (see Cowan, 1997; Dempster, 1981). There are of course explanations that depend on the maturation of the central nervous system, for example, the myelinization (Case, 1985) or the periodical waves of dendritic connections, in particular, those relating the frontal lobes to the other areas of the brain (Fischer & Rose, 1994; Thatcher, 1992). Other explanations have emphasized the effects of environmental factors like the automatization of information processing with exercise, the discovery of metacognitive strategies, and the influence of instruction which increases knowledge simultaneously in various fields.

All these factors, maturational and environmental, covary with age and there are interactions between some of them, for example, via pruning, between the waves of dendritic connections and exercise. It is thus illusory to search for a single, general purpose, elementary process, that would account for the upper limit of processing capacity and thus for the existence of a general factor of development. The increase in processing speed, sometimes advanced as an elementary mechanism susceptible to play this role (cf. Kail & Salthouse, 1994) results from changes in the complete set of these factors and is thus only one global indicator of development, as global as mental age. Explaining the general factor of development by an increase in processing speed adds little more than explaining it by an increase in mental age.

Whether psychometric, Piagetian, or neo-Piagetian, all the tasks included in the factor analyses reviewed here concern the understanding of the relations between objects or between more or less abstract symbols. These factor analyses did not include tasks assessing, for example, the development of the competence to communicate with other people, or the practical intelligence developed in everyday life (Sternberg, Wagner, Williams, & Horvath, 1995). We do not have results of factor analyses including all these various aspects of cognitive development. If such a study could be conducted, would there be a general factor of development? When asked in this sense, the only answer that can be given to the question raised in the title of this chapter is that we don't know.

REFERENCES

Baddeley, A. (1986). *Working memory*. Oxford, England: Oxford University Press.

Bardon, G. (1999). Relations entre modes de traitement préférentiels en mémoire de travail et dans l'apprentissage de la lecture [Relationships between preferential processing modes in working memory and in learning to read]. Unpublished doctoral dissertation. Université René Descartes. Series V.

Benzecri, J. P. (1973). *L'analyse des données* [Data analysis] (Vol. 2). Paris: Dunod.

Bradmetz, J. (1996). The form of intellectual development in children age 4 through 9. *Intelligence, 22*, 191–226.

Cantor, J., & Engle, R. W. (1993). Working memory as long term memory activation: An individual differences approach. *Journal of Experimental Psychology: Learning, Memory, and Cognition, 19*, 1101–1114.

Carroll, J. B. (1993). *Human cognitive abilities*. Cambridge, England: Cambridge University Press.

Carroll, J. B., Kohlberg, L., & De Vries, R. (1984). Psychometric and Piagetian intelligences: Toward resolution of controversy. *Intelligence, 8*, 67–91.

Case, R. (1985). *Intellectual development. Birth to adulthood*. New York: Academic Press.

Case, R. (1987). The structure and process of intellectual development. *International Journal of Psychology, 22*, 571–607.

Case, R. (1992). Neo-Piagetian theories of intellectual development. In H. Beilin & P. B. Pufall (Eds.), *Piaget's theory: Prospects and possibilities*. Hillsdale, NJ: Lawrence Erlbaum Associates.

Case, R., Demetriou, A., Platsidou, M., & Kazi, S. (in press). Integrating concepts and tests of intelligence from the differential and developmental traditions. *Intelligence*.

Case, R., & Globerson, T. (1974). Field dependency and central computing space. *Child Development, 45*, 772–778.

Cowan, N. (1993). Activation, attention, and short-term memory. *Memory and Cognition, 21*, 162–167.

Cowan, N. (1997). The development of working memory. In N. Cowan (Ed.), *The development of memory in childhood*. Hove, UK: Psychology Press/Lawrence Erlbaum Associates.

Daneman, M., & Carpenter, P. (1980). Individual differences in working memory and reading. *Journal of Verbal Learning and Verbal Behavior, 19*, 450–466.

Dempster, F. (1981). Memory span: Sources of individual and developmental differences. *Psychological Bulletin, 89*, 63–100.

DeVries, R. (1974). Relationships among Piagetian, IQ, and achievement assessments of intelligence. *Child Development, 45*, 746–756.

DeVries, R., & Kohlberg, L. (1977). Relations between Piagetian and psychometric assessments of intelligence. In L. Katz (Ed.), *Current topics in early childhood education* (Vol. 1). Norwood, NJ: Ablex.

Engle, R. W., Cantor, J., & Carullo, J. J. (1992). Individual differences in working memory and comprehension: A test of four hypotheses. *Journal of Experimental Psychology: Learning, Memory, and Cognition, 18*, 972–992.

Fischer, K. W., & Farrar, M. J. (1987). Generalizations about generalization: How a theory of skill development explains both generality and specificity. *International Journal of Psychology, 22*, 643–677.

Fischer, K. W., & Rose, S. P. (1994). Dynamic development of coordination of components in brain and behavior: A framework for theory. In G. Dawson & K. Fischer (Eds.), *Human Behavior and the Developing Brain*. New York: Guilford Press.

Glass, G. V., & Stephens, B. (1980). Reply to Humphreys' and Parsons' "Piagetian tasks measure intelligence and intelligence tests assess cognitive development." *Intelligence, 4*, 171–174.

Greenacre, M. J. (1984). *Theory and applications of correspondence analysis*. New York: Academic Press.

Gustaffson, J. E. (1984). A unifying model for the structure of intellectual abilities. *Intelligence, 8*, 179–203.

Humphreys, L. G. (1980). Methinks they protest too much. *Intelligence, 4*, 179–183.

Humphreys, L. G., & Parsons, C. K. (1979). Piagetian tasks measure intelligence and intelligence tests assess cognitive development: A reanalysis. *Intelligence, 3*, 369–382.

Humphreys, L. G., Rich, S. A., & Davey, T. C. (1985). A Piagetian test of general intelligence. *Developmental Psychology, 21*, 872–877.

Inhelder, B. (1943). *Le diagnostic du raisonnement chez les débiles mentaux* [The diagnostic of reasoning abilities in mentally handicapped persons]. Neuchâtel: Delachaux & Niestlé.

Inman, W. C., & Secrest, T. (1981). Piaget's data and Spearman's theory—An empirical reconciliation and its implications for academic achievement. *Intelligence, 5*, 329–344.

Kail, R., & Salthouse, T. (1994). Processing speed as a mental capacity. *Acta psychologica, 86*, 199–225.

Kaufman, A. S. (1971). Piaget and Gesell: A psychometric analysis of tests built from their tasks. *Child Development, 42*, 1341–1360.

Kohlberg, L., & De Vries, R. (1980). Don't throw out the Piagetian baby with the psychometric bath: A reply to Humphreys and Parsons, *Intelligence, 4*, 175–178.

Kyllonen, P., & Christal, R. E. (1990). Reasoning ability is (little more than) working memory capacity? *Intelligence, 14*, 389–433.

Larivée, S., Normandeau, S., & Parent, S. (2000). The French connection: Some contributions of French-language research in the post-Piagetian era. *Child Development, 71*, 823–839.

Laurendeau, M., & Pinard, A. (1968). *Les premières notions spatiales de l'enfant* [The first spatial notions of children]. Neuchâtel: Delachaux & Niestlé.

Lautrey, J. (1980). La variabilité intra-individuelle du niveau de développement opératoire [Intra-individual variability of the operational development level]. *Bulletin de Psychologie, 33*, 685–697.

Lautrey, J. (1990). Esquisse d'un modèle pluraliste du développement cognitif [Outline of a pluralistic model of cognitive development]. In M. Reuchlin, J. Lautrey, C. Marendaz, & T. Ohlmann (Eds.), *Cognition: l'universel et l'individuel*. Paris: P.U.F.

Lautrey, J. (in press). Variability: A key to models of cognitive development and differentiation. In R. J. Sternberg, J. Lautrey, & T. Lubart (Eds.), *Models of intelligence for the next millenium*. Washington, DC: American Psychological Association.

Lautrey, J., & Caroff, X. (1996). Variability and cognitive development. *Polish Quarterly of Developmental Psychology, 2*(2), 71–89.

Lautrey, J., & Cibois, P. (1991). Application of correspondence analysis to a longitudinal study of cognitive development. In D. Magnusson, L. R. Bergman, G. Rudinger, & B. Törestad (Eds.), *Problems and methods in longitudinal research—Stability and change*. Cambridge, England: Cambridge University Press.

Lautrey, J., de Ribaupierre, A., & Rieben, L. (1986). Les différences dans la forme du développement cognitif évalué avec des épreuves piagétiennes: Une application de l'analyse des correspondances [Individual differences in the form of cognitive development assessed with Piagetian tasks: An application of correspondence analysis]. *Cahiers de Psychologie Cognitive, 6*, 575–613.

Longeot, F. (1967). Aspects différentiels de la psychologie génétique [Differential aspects of genetic psychology]. *Bulletin de l'Institut National d'Orientation Professionnelle*. N° spécial.

Longeot, F. (1969). *Psychologie différentielle et théorie opératoire de l'intelligence* [Differential psychology and operational theory of intelligence]. Paris: Dunod.

Longeot, F. (1974/1979). *L'échelle de développement de la pensée logique* [The logical thought development scale]. Paris: Éditions des Établissements d' Applications Psychotechniques.

Longeot, F. (1978). *Les stades opératoires de Piaget et les facteurs de l'intelligence* [Piaget's operational stages and factors of intelligence]. Grenoble: Presses Universitaires de Grenoble

Morra, S. (1994). Issues in working memory measurement. *International Journal of Behavioral Development, 17*, 143–159.

Morra, S., & Scopesi, A. (1997). Issues in testing for processing capacity with oblique rotations in the background. *International Journal of Behavioral Development, 20*(4), 739–742.

Nassefat, M. (1963). *Etude quantitative sur l'évolution des opérations intellectuelles* [A quantitative study of the evolution of intellectual operations]. Neuchâtel: Delachaux & Niestlé.

Oakhill, J., Yuill, N., & Parkin, A. (1986). On the nature of the difference between skilled and less skilled comprehenders. *Journal of Research in Reading, 9*, 80–91.

Pascual-Leone, J. (1970). A mathematical model for the transition rule in Piaget's developmental stages. *Acta Psychologica, 32*, 301–345.

Pascual-Leone, J. (1987). Organismic processes for neo-piagetian theories: A dialectical causal account of cognitive development. *International Journal of Psychology, 22*, 531–570.

Pascual-Leone, J. (1997). Divergent validity and the measurement of processing capacity. *International Journal of Behavioral Development, 20*(4), 735–738.

Pascual-Leone, J., & Baillargeon, R. (1994). Developmental measurement of mental attention. *International Journal of Behavioral Development, 17*, 161–200.

Pennings, A. H., & Hessels, M. G. (1996). The measurement of mental attentional capacity: A neo-Piagetian developmental study. *Intelligence, 23*, 59–78.

Pulos, S. (1997). Divergent validity and the measurement of processing capacity. *International Journal of Behavioral Development, 20*(4), 731–734.

de Ribaupierre, A. (1995). Working memory and individual differences: A review. *Swiss Journal of Psychology, 54*(2), 152–168.

De Ribaupierre, A., & Bayeux, C. (1994). Developmental change in a spatial task of attentional capacity: An essay toward an integration of two working memory models. *International Journal of Behavioral Development, 17*(1), 5–35.

De Ribaupierre, A., & Bayeux, C. (1995). Development of attentional capacity in childhood: A longitudinal study. In F. E. Weinert & W. Schneider (Eds.), *Memory performance and competencies: Issues in growth and development.* Hillsdale, NJ: Lawrence Erlbaum Associates.

de Ribaupierre, A., Rieben, L., & Lautrey, J. (1985). Horizontal decalages and individual differences in the development of concrete operations. In V. L. Schulman, L. C. Restaino-Bauman, & L. Butler (Eds.), *The future of Piagetian theory: The neo-Piagetians.* New York: Plenum Press.

Rieben, L., de Ribaupierre, A., & Lautrey, J. (1983). *Le développement opératoire de l'enfant entre 6 et 12 ans.* Paris: Editions du CNRS.

Reuchlin, M. (1964). L'intelligence: Conception génétique opératoire et conception factorielle [Intelligence: Operational genetic and factorial conceptions]. *Revue Suisse de Psychologie, 23,* 113–134.

Seigneuric, A. (1998). *Mémoire de travail et compréhension de l'écrit chez l'enfant* [Working memory and reading comprehension in children]. Unpublished doctoral dissertation. Université Paris V – René Descartes.

Shah, P., & Miyake, A. (1996). The separability of working memory resources for spatial thinking and language processing: An individual differences approach. *Journal of Experimental Psychology: General, 125,* 4–27.

Stephens, B., McLaughlin, J. A., Miller, C. K., & Glass, G. V. (1972). Factorial structure of selected psycho-educational measures and Piagetian reasoning assessments. *Developmental Psychology, 6,* 343–348.

Sternberg, R. J., Wagner, R. K., Williams, W. M., & Horvath, J. A. (1995). Testing common sense. *American Psychologist, 50*(11), 912–927.

Thatcher, R. W. (1992). Cyclic cortical reorganization during early childhood. *Brain and Cognition, 20,* 24–50.

Tuddenham, R. D. (1971). Theoretical regularities and individual idiosyncrasies. In D. Green, M. P. Ford, & G. B. Flamer (Eds.), *Measurement and Piaget.* New York: McGraw Hill.

Vinh Bang (1966). La méthode clinique et la recherche en psychologie de l'enfant [Clinical method and research in child psychology]. In *Psychologie et épistémologie génétiques. Thèmes piagétiens* (pp. 67–81). Paris: Dunod.

Part III

COGNITIVE APPROACH

g and Cognitive Elements of Information Processing: An Agnostic View

Ian J. Deary
University of Edinburgh

PROLOGUE

Searching for cognitive elements of human mental ability differences, and focusing that search on *g*, has a venerable record in our field of inquiry. The search, which Hunt (1980) compared with the search for the Holy Grail, is an interesting one to document, partly because researchers' opinions on the same data can be diametrically opposed. In 1904 Spearman found small to medium-sized correlations between mental ability estimates and measures of sensory discrimination. He speculated that, after correcting for unreliability in the measures, the correlation between discrimination and mental ability was near to 1.0, and that discrimination was the psychological basis of human mental ability differences. (Although he withdrew the comment a few years later [Burt, 1909–1910], he repeated it in his magnum opus [Spearman, 1927]). In 1909 Thorndike, Lay, and Dean found very similar correlations to those of Spearman when they examined sensory discrimination and higher level mental abilities, and they remarked that it was tenable to conclude that discrimination and mental ability differences were unrelated (a correlation = 0.0). Such is the violence that prior theory may wreak on congruent data.

Introduction

This author sits enthusiastically as a spectre at this feast of an edited volume. The structure first proposed for the book, that we authors be broadly pro- or anti-*g*, had the same principal attraction as a jousting contest between knights in "olde" England: namely, that the mob loves a good scrap, and the more blood spilt the better. However, academic debates also share the same demerits as the chivalric contests: They tend to emphasize disagreement over agreement; and they obscure the good qualities of the two sides, with only one seen as a winner. Going back to the prologue, it would have been much more memorable to watch Spearman and Thorndike aim big lances at each other than to hear a timid exposition on how one might further investigate the small-to-medium effect size of the association between sensation and intellect. But the present chapter exhorts the reader to eschew entertainment value and to prize those replicated, if at times small, effect sizes and to question psychologists' theories about how correlations have come about. In a research topic where "theory" at times comes close to meaning "poorly substantiated prejudice" it is helpful to keep a close eye on the empirical data and to appreciate its strengths and weaknesses. Therefore, in what follows, I have consciously avoided partial subscription to g or non-g theories of mental ability differences. I have essayed a disinterested weighing-up of the importance and relevance of the finding of general psychometric ability variance in the search for cognitive contributions to mental ability differences.

First, the broad "lie of the land" (see Neisser et al., 1996). There are three main types of mental ability research: psychometric studies, predictive validity research, and reductionistic validity research. This chapter concentrates on the last of these. In service to the particular theme of this book one may address g within each type of research, but also emphasize that there is more to all three types of mental ability research than g.

With regard to psychometric studies of human mental abilities there is much that is known. When a large sample of the population, at any age from childhood to old age, is administered a diverse battery of mental tests the covariance structure forms a hierarchy. At the peak of the hierarchy there is a general factor, typically accounting for about 40% to 50% of the test score variance. Below this, there are correlated group factors of ability. These do not attract full agreement between studies, reflecting the different salads of tests' contents in different batteries. At a still lower level in the hierarchy there are specific abilities, which form correlated but separable aspects of the group factors. This hierarchical structure is found in single large experiments (Gustafsson, 1984) and in surveys of large numbers of psychometric studies, including many classic databases, some of which originally were thought not to contain g (Carroll, 1993). With regard to predictive validity studies, mental ability differences are significant predictors of educational, occupational, and social outcomes, with effects sizes that are typically moderate to large (Gottfredson, 1997).

For researchers interested in reductionistic validity studies the latter findings suggest that the mental tests whose information-processing origins are being sought have at least some practical importance. The psychometric studies suggest that there might be different targets for cognitive or broader information processing studies: general variance, and group and specific factor variance (see Roberts & Stankov, 1999, for strong advocacy of this approach). On the other hand, people conducting reductionistic validity studies need to be aware of the limitations of psychometric studies. Any human mental abilities not included in typical psychometric tests might need additional information-processing accounts (Gardner, 1983; Sternberg, 1999). And it must be recalled that the hierarchical structure of the covariance of ability test scores exists as a finding that is not necessarily isomorphic with anything in people's heads; the three-level hierarchy is a taxonomy of tests, not of human's mental structures (not necessarily, anyway). These, therefore, are the first three limitations facing information-processing research into human mental ability differences: that one must be aware of what ability level is being "explained," that the psychometric enterprise might leave some abilities untouched, and that psychometric structures are not necessarily reflected in the brains of humans. In each of these limitations is an explicit agreement that there is more to mental life, and its cognitive underpinnings, than g.

Information-processing constructs, be they more cognitive or biological in their level of description, are meant to index important aspects of brain processing; there is no guarantee that psychometric structures do any such thing. But, the fourth warning for the would-be reductionist is even more gloomy; that there might be no current cognitive or biological model of mind from which to cherry-pick information processing parameters, the interindividual variance which might account for variance in mental test scores. That is, despite Spearman's (1923) search for a "mental cytology" that would provide a parameterization of mind, despite the cognitive revolution promising a catalogue of "mental components" (Sternberg, 1978), "microscopes of mind" (Massaro, 1993), and ways to "parse cognition" (Holzman, 1994), despite psychophysics promising some "benchmark tests" (Vickers & Smith, 1986) of human mental operations, and despite elaborate artificial intelligence models of 'general intelligence' (Laird, Newell, & Rosenbloom, 1987) we are still a long way off Galton's (1890) aim of being able to drive a few shafts at critical points in the mind to gauge its working efficiency.

To recap on the remit for this chapter, in which the author was asked to reflect on the importance that g has in cognitive accounts of mind, there are three things that need addressing after agreeing that g does at least emerge from analyses of psychometric test score batteries. The other matters to be considered are: What cognitive theories and variables have been used to try to account for psychometric mental ability differences?; what is the place of g versus more specific abilities in this search?; and what validity do the cognitive variables and theories have, given that they do provide variables that correlate with psychometric g?

In terms of cognitive candidates to account for human ability differences, it is worth discerning three broad approaches. Cognitive variables have emerged at three different levels of reduction, which shall be called psychometric, cognitive–experimental, and psychophysical.

PSYCHOMETRIC-LEVEL COGNITIVE CONSTRUCTS AND g

Sometimes psychometricians appear to get ideas beyond their stations. They act as if their tweakings of mental tests' contents are facets of human cognitive assemblies and functions. It's not impossible that the lineaments of mind might be read in a pattern of test performances, just unlikely. However, in the meantime, such psychometricians have come up with some ingenious ways to calibrate the grades of difficulty within mental tests. A good early example is provided by Furneaux (1952) who manipulated the content of mental tests and divined people's reactions to them and saw among people differences in mental speed, persistence, and error checking. Here, too, was the possibility of a disunitarian g, because these three mental characteristics combined to give people's ability test scores. Furneaux's ideas, although championed by Eysenck (1967), never were rendered in full detail and failed widely to influence psychologists. But the idea that the nature of ability test performance, not least g, might be revealed through dissecting mental tests themselves did catch on. Since then, although the idea that g might comprise unrelated or at least separable cognitive components has been acceptable even to its strongest protagonists (Jensen, 1998a), others have asserted that a single process might underlie g (Brand, 1996).

One research program that promised to change the face of intelligence research to a more cognitive complexion was Sternberg's (1977a, 1997b). His vision was of factors of mental ability (including g) being replaced by mental components (Sternberg, 1979). Mental components were the consecutively turning cogs, or serial mincing machines, that took in mental test items at one end and produced answers at the other. The first assault of "componentman" on "factorman" (Sternberg, 1979) was on analogical reasoning, although he subsequently took on classification and series continuation reasoning (Sternberg & Gardner, 1983). For someone who was avowedly cognitive, Sternberg was historically very well aware of the history of the psychometric disputes surrounding g and he chose to examine analogical reasoning precisely because it was viewed by landmark psychometricians as close to the heart of what *g*, cognitively, was. And Sternberg's scheme of mental components and their activities stayed close to the ideas of *g*'s inventor–discoverer (Spearman, 1904, 1923). According to Sternberg, analogical reasoning items were solved by a series of operations—mental components—called encoding, inferring, mapping, application (and responding, justification, etc., which appeared later, on occasion). Take the analogical reasoning item,

fish is to swim as bird is to [robin, fins, fly, wing, feather]

Progressing beyond the perhaps-true-in-some-sense-but-ultimately-unhelpful statement that people who did well on such tests had a lot of *g*, which leaves the problem of unpacking *g* untouched, Sternberg (1977a, 1997b) described the cognitive components involved in such reasoning. The analogy's items were "encoded." A relation was "inferred" between the first and second items. Mapping was performed between the first and third items. The relation between items 1 and 2 was then "applied" to item 3 and the correct answer (fly) was chosen from the answer options. These cognitive elements or components were akin to Spearman's (1923) rationalist–philosophical cognitive account of mental activity. Indeed, Spearman's lesser known book which produced this cognitive architecture has been dubbed the first book on cognitive psychology (Gustafsson, 1992). Spearman's economical cognitive architecture, designed to account for much of human thinking, contained only three components: the apprehension of experience, the eduction of relations, and the eduction of correlates. Apply these to Sternberg's analogy items. The apprehension of experience might equate to encoding items. The eduction of relations means finding general rules or relations from more than one instance: thus, the higher order, relational concept of "mode of movement" emerges from fish and swims. Taking up the third term in the analogy—bird—we can then apply Spearman's third principle. This is the eduction of correlates, the mental activity that takes an example and a relational rule and generates an outcome. Applying mode of movement to bird gives fly.

Sternberg (1977a, 1977b) did more than merely revive and expand Spearman's principles of cognition. He invented a method for discovering the amount of time it took for each component to operate within an individual. Thus, if analogical reasoning was close to what psychometricians thought of as a *g*-loaded test, here was a multicomponent account and, to boot, a way of measuring people's differences in each component. If the scheme works, *g* is relegated to a kind of arithmetical summary of components' efficiencies. The method was called "partial cueing" and its essence was in allowing subjects to study one, two, or three analogy terms prior to viewing the whole item and responding as fast as possible. From a series of simultaneous equations and a regression method, subjects' efficiencies for each of the components could be ascertained.

But *g* didn't fracture along the lines drawn by the Sternbergian components. The enterprise lost steam along the way and there is little current interest in the components. The proper attempts were made to show that the same components could be extracted from different tasks and that different components were distinct from each other. However, parameters of the *same* components from different tasks tended to correlate at about 0.3 and different components' parameters tended to correlate at about 0.2 (Sternberg & Gardner, 1983). Given that the samples were typically small and often involved students, these were not significantly different, leaving the possibility of a general factor permeating the components' efficiencies. The same components did not always emerge from the tasks, additional components were introduced seemingly on an ad hoc basis, and at times conglomerate components—like a *reasoning* component—were introduced that seemed almost to admit reductionistic failure (Sternberg & Gardner, 1983). It became clear that the monophrenic strictures of the componential model did not fit the pluralistic mental wanderings of different people as they thought their various ways through reasoning problems (Alderton, Goldman, & Pellegrino, 1985). For example, high-ability people seemed to have different task structures than lower ability people, and they were differently advantaged and disadvantaged by viewing answer alternatives. Although there were criticisms that the components were self-evident and did not need empirical studies to validate them, the truth was precisely the opposite (Kline, 1991). There was insufficient evidence that the components were anything other than arbitrary choppings-up of the time taken to perform highly *g*-loaded tasks. To establish the validity of mental components required a research program that demonstrated the existence of the components as brain processes independent of the psychometric tasks from which they were extracted. That didn't happen and the components have remained as clever slices of test scores rather than validated mechanisms of mind.

Three widely cited research programs that followed Sternberg's path-breaking work also peered within psychometric test items for the nature of individual differences in mental functions, with potentially strong implications for *g*.

Raven's Progressive Matrices (RPM; Raven, 1938) is a psychometric test constructed according to Spearman's (1923) cognitive principles of the eductions of relations and correlates, principles that Spearman deduced from armchair musing rather than empirical investigation. Scores on the RPM tend to load very highly on *g* (Marshalek, Lohman, & Snow, 1983) and understanding the constituents of differences in RPM performance might unpack some of the general factor's variance. Using subjects' verbalizations and their eye movements while solving RPM items, an explicit series of rule-finding and other imputed mental functions was written into two computer programs, which were thereafter average and good, respectively, at solving RPM items (Carpenter, Just, & Shell, 1990). In general terms the better computer program, reflecting the higher scoring subjects' performances on the RPM, found more correct rules in the items and could concurrently handle more transformations demanded by the rules at any one time. This research seemed to indicate that RPM performance, and *g* to the extent that it is captured in the RPM test, was something to do with working memory and goal management strategies. According to Carpenter et al.,

> One of the main distinctions between higher scoring subjects and lower scoring subjects was the ability of the better subjects to successfully generate and manage their problem-solving goals in working memory. (p. 428)

> Thus, what one intelligence test measures, according to the current theory, is the common ability to decompose problems into manageable segments and iterate through them, the differential ability to manage the hierarchy of goals and subgoals generated by this problem decomposition, and the differential ability to form higher level abstractions. (p. 429)

It is shown later that working memory and *g* must conceptually be brought closer together; they are closely linked concepts yet their researchers work in almost nonoverlapping agendas. In addition, the management of mental goals is also some researchers' favored cognitive account of *g*. For example, it was suggested that the location of *g* differences lies in the frontal lobes and that the chief psychological function of this area is goal management (Duncan, Emslie, & Williams, 1996). The suggestion comes from research based on a cognitive test involving a "second side instruction." In this test the subject reads a column of numbers, ignoring letters interspersed with the numbers within the column, and also ignores an adjacent column of letters and numbers. Every so often in this busy mental stream of thinking and responding there comes a second side instruction: a plus or minus sign tells the subject to stick with one side or switch to the other. The finding was that people with lower ability and people with frontal lobe damage were less able to implement the second side instruction, even when they saw and understood it. The authors urged that *g* be viewed as a cognitive property of frontal lobe functioning.

Back to the computer implementation of RPM (and *g*) performance (Carpenter et al., 1990). What did such an elaborate exercise achieve? At best it might have revealed aspects of mental performance that have validity in a mental architecture, reducing or dissolving *g* into more brain-anchored cognitive mechanisms. That doesn't seem likely, for in the published account of the research there is a clear trail from the RPM items to the computer programs that does not seem to fractionate the mind. The principles used to construct the successful programs appear rather too similar to the original principles that Raven used (which he got from Spearman) when he constructed the test. And it is likely that subjects' verbal reports and eye movements had some isomorphism with the tests' principles of construction. Although the investigators came up with some imputed mental functions that were more or less efficient in solving RPM items in differently abled subjects, they did this largely by commenting on what, subjectively, is required to think about in order to solve RPM items. The real opportunity for reduction was not this type of rationalism, which might in fact represent more armchair musing along the lines of Spearman's original principles of cognition, but lay, instead, in the details of the computer programs. The selected alterations in the program between the high and the low-ability subjects, had the computer program details been tied to a theory of cognitive architecture, might have provided hypotheses about the brain differences between higher and average ability subjects. But no such parallels seem to have been drawn or intended, and the qualitative differences between the computer programs, which involved one program being unable to induce a given rule and one program having elements that the other lacked, seem unlikely to reflect the quantitative brain differences among human subjects.

A successor to the Sternberg (1977a, 1977b) approach of mental components has been to construct mental tests with a manipulable aspect of content (perhaps thereby indexing a cognitive component) whose difficulty levels are explicitly graded to put a putative mental function under increasing pressure. Thus working memory has been manipulated in psychometric mental tasks to allow the extraction of a latent component that indexes the strength of different subjects' working memory efficiency (Embretson, 1995). In this task a second latent trait was extracted—it provided a sump for the other sources of individual difference—and was called *general control processes*. Perhaps not *g*, then, as a focus for research into mental ability differences, but these two more cognitive-psychology friendly components? They certainly performed well in accounting for the covariance among a battery of different mental tests (Fig. 7.1). But the author recognized explicitly that the success of these components relies not just on their psychometric performance but on their being part of a strong prior theory of cognitive architecture and function; just what is presently lacking.

Working memory differences take center stage as an alternative, more cognitively oriented, construct to *g* in another cognitive model of mental performance (Kyllonen, 1996a, 1996b; Kyllonen & Christal, 1990). This model is founded on a simple mental architecture and, although it con-

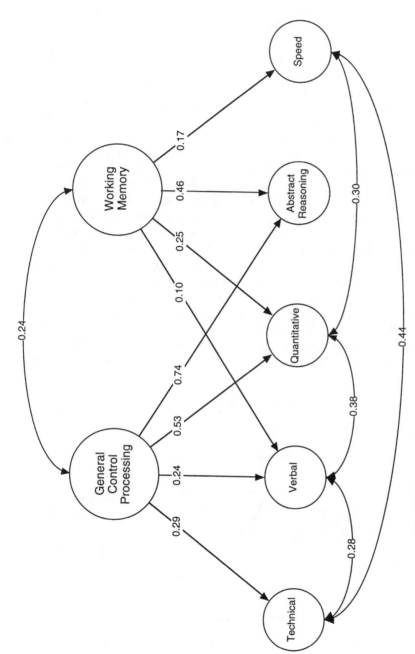

FIG. 7.1. Structural model showing that latent components of 'working memory' and 'general control processing' mediate the associations between factors from the ASVAB battery and scores on Embretson's abstract reasoning task. This figure was redrawn from Embretson (1995).

tains boxes and processes that most psychologists would recognize, it does not describe a modern, accepted mental architecture (Fig. 7.2). The model has been used to formulate a cognitive assessment battery which, rather than possessing a *g* factor, delivers scores on four factors: working memory, general knowledge, processing speed, and reasoning. Various large samples of armed forces applicants and recruits have been tested on the battery and other tests and the general result is that reasoning by analogy and other means (mental effort assessed by tests that are reckoned to be close to *g*) has a very high (> 0.8) correlation with a latent trait from the working memory subtests in the battery derived from the four sources model (Fig. 7.3). This has the effect of emphasizing the importance of *g* and at the same time diverting attention away from it, for it says that working memory might be the more useful, tractable cognitive construct to explore in asking about the meaning of the general variance in mental tests. Scrutiny then attaches to the tasks used to assess working memory: They turn out to be very psychometric-looking tests. Indeed some of the working memory tests are called *reasoning* tests. The model does show two separable constructs from two sets of psychometric tests (the set that is supposed to be a standard psychometric reasoning battery and the set that is supposed to assess working memory), but the nature of the tests does not make one more cognitively tractable looking than the other. Naming one factor *working memory* and the other *reasoning* does not confer causal precedence, nor does it securely attach the label to validated brain processing mechanisms, and the two are almost too closely correlated (the *r* value of-

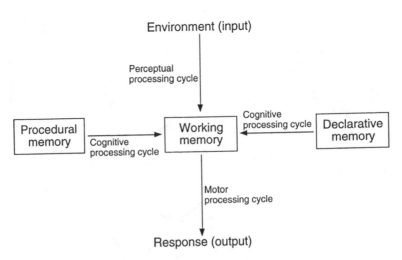

FIG. 7.2. The cognitive architecture used by Kyllonen and Christal to examine associations between working memory and psychometric intelligence. This figure was redrawn from Kyllonen and Christal (1990).

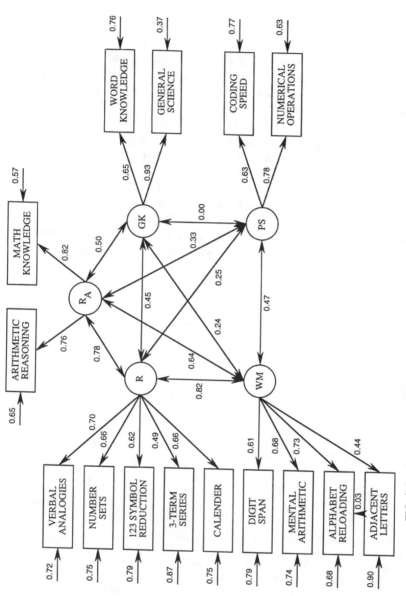

FIG. 7.3. Structural model showing the associations among latent variables of reasoning (R), working memory (WM), processing speed (PS), general knowledge (GK) and ASVAB reasoning R_A. Rectangles represent manifest variables (test scores). This figure was redrawn from Kyllonen and Christal (1990).

ten approaches unity). These concerns raise the question of whether this is just another discovery of g or whether it truly begins to reveal g's essence(s). Indeed, an investigation of the general factor extracted from this four-sources cognitive battery and a general factor from a standard psychometric test battery resulted in a correlation of 0.994 (Stauffer, Ree, & Carretta, 1996; Fig. 7.4), suggesting pleonasm rather than explanation. The four-sources cognitive battery, then, clearly emphasises the importance of g, but its contents are not sufficiently theoretically tractable to inspire confidence that any distance down the road toward understanding g has been traveled. Perhaps the most positive aspect of this cognitive-level research has been to signal the fact that research on working memory, with its wealth of data from neuropsychology, cognitive psychology, and functional brain scanning, may be brought to bear on our thinking about the nature of g: no matter what we call them, two constructs as closely empirically related as working memory and g have a promising future as a couple (Baddeley, 1992a, 1992b; Baddeley & Gathercole, 1999). Engle, Tuholski, Laughlin, and Conway (1999) claimed "very strong evidence" (p. 328) for the association between working memory and fluid general intelligence.

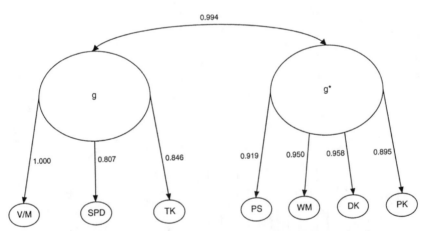

FIG. 7.4. Structural model with maximum likelihood estimates showing the association between general factors obtained from a set of paper-and-pencil tests, the ASVAB and computerised cognitive components measures, the CAM. The first order factors of the ASVAB are verbal/mathematical (V/M), clerical speed (SPD), and technical knowledge (TK). The first order factors for the CAM are processing speed (PS), working memory (WM), declarative knowledge (DK), and procedural knowledge (PK). Note the almost perfect correlation between the two general factors and the very high loadings of the first order factors on the respective general factors. This figure was redrawn from Stauffer, Ree, and Carretta (1996).

COGNITIVE–EXPERIMENTAL-LEVEL COGNITIVE CONSTRUCTS AND *g*

Sternberg's building a componential model of mental performance may be seen on the backdrop of a wider change in psychology in the 1970s (Deary [1997] reviewed this movement). With the rise of cognitive psychology came renewed impetus toward understanding the processes that linked to give the melodies of human thought. Really, the search was on for cognitive-level constructs that would provide what some called "microscopes of mind" or a "parsing" of human thought. With differential psychologists' realizing that factor models of ability might always be limited to describing and construing aspects of the tests that gave rise to them, many visited cognitive models to select those constructs that might account for some of the variance in mental test score differences.

In advance of the empirical evidence there is no reason to emphasize *g* over other factors in this approach. Isolable cognitive elements might relate solely or more strongly to *g* or to other ability factors. Early on in the cognitive–differential communion aimed at intelligence differences Hunt and MacLeod (1978) saw that, if there were many independent cognitive operations that linked to different psychometric abiltities, then *g* could lose much of its interest and importance. Although the constructs of working memory and goal management are current cognitive favorites to account for mental ability differences, there are three cognitive constructs that attracted attention during the years since the cognitive revolution. First, there was the slope parameter from the Hick (1952) reaction time task, which was hypothesised to index a person's "rate of gain of information." Second, there was the slope parameter from the Sternberg (1966) memory scanning task which was reckoned to measure the speed of scanning of items in short-term memory. Third, there was the difference between name-identity and physical-identity reaction times in the Posner reaction time task (Posner & Mitchell, 1967), which some researchers thought might measure the time to consult an item in long-term memory. Therefore, individual differences researchers had the opportunity to measure differences in people's ability to absorb environmental information of different levels of complexity and differences in the efficiency with which they could consult their long and short-term memory stores. Might these apparently elementary parameters of the mind relate to higher level cognitive performance differences, and perhaps to *g*?

An important distinction is between the aforementioned constructs and the tasks from which they arise. In each case, as the cognitive procedures became adopted by individual differences researchers, one can discern a progressive pattern of cognitive obfuscation. First, interest from differential psychologists focused on a single parameter that could be shelled out from the subject's performance on the cognitive task. Thus the first attachment is to some theoretically powerful element within the overall task. This is often a slope parameter; that is, the cognitive variable of interest is the subject's performance on one aspect of the task relative to another. One can easily see how such an enterprise threatened to water down g's standing in mental ability research. If particular mental processes/parameters/components/mechanisms could be measured, there might turn out to be many of them, all related to different psychometric abilities. A modular story might thereby fit the cognitive and the psychometric data. An early success in this mode occurred with verbal ability and its relation to performance in reaction time tasks related to verbal materials (Hunt, Lunneborg, & Lewis, 1975). But this processes of filleting out key cognitive processes, usually slope parameters derived from reaction times, from the fat and gristle of overall reaction times and indigestible intercepts ran into problems and has failed to deliver an account of g or any other cognitive factor. Early on it was emphasized that those wishing to weld cognitive and differential approaches to ability differences should consider the implications of drifting from the purity of the derived cognitive parameters to the adoption of overall reaction times in cognitive tasks (Hunt & MacLeod, 1978). The latter outcomes owed little to cognitive models of task performance and, if they did prove to have significant correlations with ability test scores, they would not be understood in cognitive terms, unlike the slope parameters. What happened, though, was that so-far cognitively intractable variables such as overall reaction times and intraindividual variability in reaction times proved to be better correlates of mental ability test scores than did the theoretically more interesting slope parameters. This may be seen in the review of the Hick reaction time procedure and mental test scores that was carried out by Jensen (1987, see also 1998a) and in the review of the Hick, Sternberg, and Posner reaction time tasks and cognitive ability test scores carried out by Neubauer (1997). The slope of the Hick reaction time procedure has no special correlation with psychometric ability test scores and is usually outperformed by more mundane measures such as overall reaction time and the intraindividual variability of reaction time. Correlations between individual reaction time parameters and psychometric ability test scores tend to have small to medium effect sizes. Now, the correlation between these aspects of reaction times and mental test scores is surprising and not without considerable interest, but it betokens a redirection of interest, because the reason that differential psychologists adopted the task in the first place was that the slope parameter might be a human information-processing limitation. Although there has been less published research, a similar story emerges for the Sternberg memory scanning task and the Posner letter matching task. In both cases there are significant and modest correlations with mental ability test scores but they tend not to be with the theoretically attractive cognitive components assessed in the reaction time slopes; rather it is the intercept or overall reaction times and/or their intraindividual variabilities that correlate with psychometric test scores (Neubauer, 1997). Again, this is of interest in itself. Reaction times are a different type of task to psychometric tests and it is reasonable to suggest that reaction times might prove more amenable to understanding than mental test scores. Therefore, for the smallish part of mental test variance that they represent, reaction times might offer some information about what distinguished the less from the more able performers on mental ability tests.

But will reaction times tell us about *g* or more specific factors of mental ability? Although some suggest that reaction time tasks form their own specific factors in the hierarchical structure of mental abilities (Carroll, 1993; Roberts & Stankov, 1999; Stankov & Roberts, 1997) there is evidence suggesting that they have a place within an account of *g*. A large general factor, often between 50% to 60% of the variance, may be extracted from a battery of reaction time tasks' variables, such as those from the Hick, Sternberg, and Posner procedures (Neubauer, Spinath, Riemann, Borkenau, & Angleitner, 2000; Vernon, 1983). Some find that much of the association between a battery of mental tests and reaction time tests can be attributed to general factors in both (Jensen, 1998a, p. 235; Vernon, 1983; see also Neubauer & Knorr, 1998). However, in a large sample of adults that may be noted for its unusual representativeness (many other studies have used university students), reaction time variables had a stronger association with a fluid as opposed to a crystallized *g* factor (Neubauer et al., 2000; although one must recall that Gustafsson [1984] found that the second stratum Gf loaded perfectly on the third stratum *g*]). The associations between psychometric *g* and reaction time *g* (e.g., from the batteries of reaction time tests used by Vernon [1983, 1989]) can reach effects sizes that are large, with *r*'s above 0.5. Vernon (1985; Vernon & Kantor, 1986) tested and refuted hypotheses that factors such as shared content-type, the need for speeded responding, and general complexity level of task were the key factors that produced correlations between psychometric test scores and reaction time variables,

> Rather, it is the *g* factor common to all psychometric variables that accounts for the bulk of the relationship between IQ and reaction time. Further, given the degree of this relationship, it appears that a moderately large part of the variance in *g* is attributable to variance in speed and efficiency of execution of a small number of basic cognitive processes. (p. 69)

However, such extracting of a general factor from a set of reaction time tests would seem to obscure the theoretical interest that the individual parameters were supposed to contain. Often, when reaction time parameters are used as independent variables to predict psychometric test scores in multiple regression equations, there is little additional independent variance added after the first variable has been entered. This result goes against a model that states that each reaction time task is indexing a separate function or set of functions. Partial dissenters from the view that g is the locus of most variance accounted for by speed of information processing tests or elementary cognitive tasks are Roberts and Stankov (1999). They found that the chief correlate of speed of processing is the second stratum factor of fluid g and that speed of processing itself has a taxonomic structure within the hierarchy of mental abilities (Carroll, 1993). However, they also leaned toward emphasizing the special association between a third stratum g and chronometric variables,

> The third-stratum factor extracted from the factor analysis of broad abilities in this study was interpreted as an "inflated" Gf, and subsequently designated GF . . . Table 25 includes the correlations between MTx, DTx, and RTx [movement, decision and reaction times, respectively, of the given chronometric task] with GF for each of the 10 chronometric tasks. Consistent with the assertion that the relationship between processing speed and cognitive abilities occurs at a higher stratum of the taxonomy circumscribing intelligence, these coefficients are among the highest obtained for any psychometric factor extracted in the investigation. (p. 71)

The correlation between psychometric test scores and reaction time parameters from Hick, Posner, and Sternberg tasks, although it is modest, seems largely to be mediated by genetic factors (Rijsdijk, Vernon, & Boomsma, 1998). In one large study of German twins the genetic contribution to the association between the general factor extracted from variables produced by the Sternberg and Posner reaction time tasks was 0.97 for a fluid intelligence factor and 0.81 for a crystallized intelligence factor (Neubauer et al., 2000). This is strong evidence for some causal link between the general variance in psychometric g and the cognitive processes measured in the aforementioned tasks. More evidence for the relevance of g to currently employed cognitive tasks comes from the finding that adding so called elementary cognitive tasks to batteries of psychometric tests does not alter the predictive validity of g (Luo & Petrill, 1999):

> The predictive power of g will not be compromised when g is defined using experimentally more tractable ECTs. (p. 157)

It is precisely this theoretical tractability that must now be addressed. From the foregoing selection of evidence, reaction time-type tests have relevance to our understanding of g, and g is relevant to cognitive models of ability that look to reaction time-type measures. The use of theoretically unspecified variables within reaction time measures (in most cases the slope-type variables that attracted initial interest in the reaction time measures do not perform well as predictors of psychometric test variance) and the increasingly common tendency to use conglomerate measures that bundle together several reaction time variables would seem to be moves away from tractability. It is not that the correlation between the *g* factor from psychometric and reaction time tests is uninteresting, it is just that theoretically understanding a factor common to many reaction time variables seems less likely than understanding a single slope measure. If these issues are combined with the fact that reaction time variables often involve response times of several hundred milliseconds it becomes difficult to defend the epithet "Elementary Cognitive Task" that is often used alongside Hick, Sternberg, and Posner procedures (Jensen, 1998a; Luo & Petrill, 1999). Whereas some have suggested that slope measures can be revived with procedures to increase their reliability (Jensen, 1998b), others have tried to explain that slope measures could never contain much variance that would attach itself to psychometric test score differences (Loman, 1994, 1999). Efforts to explore the psychophysiological associations of reaction time-type tasks that relate to psychometric tests scores, including *g*, are laudable but rare (McGarry-Roberts, Stelmack, & Campbell, 1992).

PSYCHOPHYSICAL-LEVEL COGNITIVE CONSTRUCTS AND *g*

If there is to be a valid estimate of some elementary aspect of cognitive functioning we might expect that the psychophysical level would be a good place to look. Spearman (1904) reckoned that sensory discrimination was a fundamental mental activity and Vickers (Vickers and Smith, 1986) thought that the psychophysical measure of inspection time might provide a 'benchmark' test of mental functioning. Measures of sensory discrimination feature in two current fields of research that are relevant to the theme of this chapter: work on inspection times and mental ability test scores, and measures of sensory discrimination in studies of cognitive ageing.

Inspection Times and Cognitive Ability Test Scores

If a subject is asked to make a simple, forced choice discrimination between two equally likely alternative stimuli, in which the feature to be discriminated is well above the threshold for visual acuity, the relationship between the duration of the stimulus and the probability of a correct response is well described by a cumulative normal ogive (Deary, Caryl, &

Gibson, 1993; Vickers, Nettelbeck, & Willson, 1972). The duration of the stimulus, as available to the subject for the processing of information, is assured by its being backward masked after offset. Individual differences in the efficiency with which visual discriminations of this type take place are measured by a procedure called inspection time. In this task the stimulus is two parallel, vertical lines of markedly different lengths. The longer line may appear on the left or right of the stimulus with equal probability. It is well established that there are individual differences in the stimulus duration that subjects require in order to make a discrimination to any given level of correctness (between 50% [chance] and 100% [perfect]). These individual differences correlate with psychometric intelligence test scores with a medium effect size (about 0.4 with some types of ability test; Deary & Stough, 1996; Kranzler & Jensen, 1989; Nettelbeck, 1987). We thus again pass the starting point for a consideration of these findings within the present remit. With such an association between a putatively elementary cognitive ability and psychometric intelligence what emphasis need there be on the construct of g?

A semiquantitative review and a meta-analysis of inspection time research suggested that there were stronger correlations between inspection time and nonverbal as opposed to verbal abilities (Kranzler & Jensen, 1989; Nettelbeck, 1987). Whereas the former associations were around or above .4, the latter tended to be around or below .2. This was replicated in a single study involving otherwise healthy people with diabetes who were tested on 9 of the 11 subtests of the WAIS–R (Deary, 1993). In this study a two-factor model of Performance and Verbal ability, in which the two factors correlated strongly and in which inspection time loaded only on the Performance ability, fitted better than a single g factor model onto which all nine subtests plus inspection time loaded. A subsequent study examined inspection time and all eleven WAIS–R subtests in a sample of more than 100 people whose age, sex, and social class characteristics were well matched to the Scottish adult population (Crawford, Deary, Allan, & Gustafsson, 1998). This was the first report in which a moderately large general population sample of normal adults had been tested on a recognized battery of tests alongside a valid inspection time measure (based on a light emitting diode device rather than a computer screen). Several competing models of the association between inspection time and factors from the WAIS–R were tested. The best fitting model is shown in Fig. 7.5. This is a nested factors model fitted by structural equation modeling using EQS. The chi square for the model was 61.7 with 43 d.f. The average off-diagonal standardized residual was 0.037 and the comparative fit index was 0.971. By all of these criteria the model fits well. Thus, inspection time has a loading of almost 0.4 on the perceptual–organizational factor of the WAIS–R and a loading of almost 0.2 on g. This model performed better

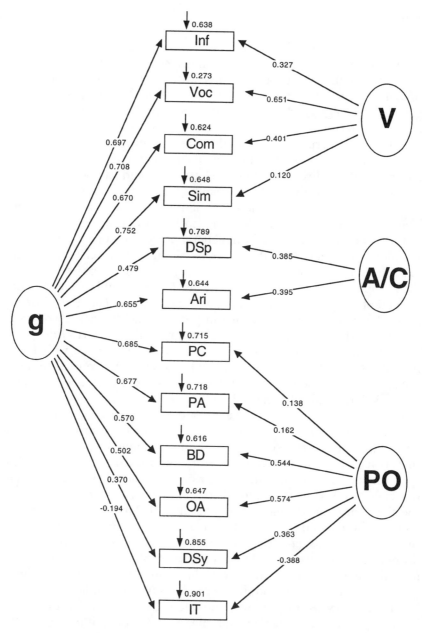

FIG. 7.5. Nested factors structural model of the associations among subtest scores of the Wechlser Adult Intelligence Scale-Revised and inspection times. Note that the general factor (g) of the WAIS-R is orthogonal to the verbal (V), attention/concentration (A/C) and perceptual-organisational factors. Inspection time loads −0.388 on the PO factor and −0.194 on the general factor. This figure was redrawn from Crawford, Deary, Allan, & Gustafsson (1998).

than models that posited the following: (a) a g only model; (b) a similar model to that in the figure but in which inspection time loaded on no factors; (c) as (b) but inspection time was constrained to load only on g; (d) as (b) but inspection time was constrained to load on only the perceptual/organisational factor; and (e) as (b) but inspection time was allowed to load on all four factors.

Some have interpreted these findings as indicating that inspection time has a special association with fluid intelligence in the Horn–Cattell model. However, data collected by Burns, Nettelbeck, and Cooper (1999) suggested another possibility. They examined inspection time's associations with tests indexing five second-order abilities outlined in Gf–Gc theory. The tests were drawn from the Woodcock–Johnson battery. Inspection time's highest association was with general processing speed (above .4 in a sample of 64 adults) and there was no significant correlation with the marker test for Gf. Note, however, that only one subtest was used to index each supposed factor. The data in the last few paragraphs were obtained on modest sample sizes undertaking only modest-sized batteries of mental tests. They agree to the extent that inspection time's highest correlations might be with some second-order factors rather than a third-order g factor. But they impel researchers to conduct more research with larger psychometric batteries, in which several markers tests are used to index each ability factor, so that a better location for inspection time's explanatory possibilities may be charted.

In the model in Fig. 7.5 the factors are orthogonal, which means that inspection time has a significant association with g but a stronger association with a factor orthogonal to g. The tests among competing models show that g cannot be left out of the story with regard to the impact of inspection time, and also that the closer association lies elsewhere. As an endorsement of this, another study (Deary & Crawford, 1998) examined inspection time's performance within Jensen's (1998a) method of correlated vectors. This method examines the correlation between two vectors of correlation coefficients: (a) the strengths of association (loadings) between individual psychometric mental tests and g, and (b) the correlation of those mental tests with another indicator of ability (in this case inspection time). The usual result is a high positive correlation (i.e., the indicator typically has the strongest associations with those tests that have the largest g loadings). This works for reaction time measures (Jensen, 1998a, pp. 236–238). Inspection time bucks the trend. Three moderately sized studies—involving inspection time or tachistoscopic word recognition, the WAIS–R battery and a near-normal samples of adults—were re-examined (Deary & Crawford, 1998). In all three cases the psychophysical measure failed to show the expected correlated vectors association, with the sign typically being negative: Tests with higher g loadings had lower correlations with inspection time. However, others have used Wechsler-type batteries and found that inspection time-type tasks load principally on *g* and/or find a positive correlated vector association (Jensen, 1998a, p. 223; see also Kranzler & Jensen, 1991; Luo & Petrill, 1999).

These results take the inquiry on to some tricky ground. First, it is recollected that psychometric ability test score models do not represent, necessarily, the brain's processing structures. Next, it is asked whether inspection time has validity as a measure of brain processing, and whether, therefore it can inform about the nature of the psychometric factors it associates with. To answer, using the foregoing data, the question of whether a major element of *g* is some form of processing speed begs the questions of, (a) whether the WAIS–R provides an adequate *g* factor and (b) whether inspection time may be said solely or largely to index speed of information processing.

Even if inspection time and other psychophysical processing tasks showed individual differences that were substantially related to psychometric *g*, that association might be more or less interesting. It might be less interesting, especially to those for whom cognitive task–psychometric correlations were a step toward reducing psychometric intelligence differences to something nearer to the brain, if all that was being shown was that some type of general, higher level psychological factor was responsible for the correlations. Candidate higher level factors might be attention, motivation, persistence, test anxiety, other personality traits, cognitive strategy usage, and so forth. These top-down explanations for cognitive/psychophysical–psychometric ability test correlations have competed with so-called bottom-up accounts which assert that the correlations are caused by some shared information processing elements in cognitive/psychophysical tasks and psychometric tests. Discussions of the empirical studies that addressed this issue (Deary, 1996; Jensen, 1998a; Neubauer, 1997) find little evidence that personality, motivation, strategies, or other higher level factors account for the relationships. Progress, though, would be easier if, instead of attempting to refute all such high-level explainings-away of cognitive/psychophysical task-psychometric task correlations, researchers could come up with a validated model of a cognitive task and point to the source of variance that affords the correlation with psychometric test scores. Even for the seemingly simple inspection time the original model of task performance has been seriously questioned and all but abandoned by its originator (Levy, 1992; Vickers, Pietsch, & Hemmingway, 1995). Proper attention is being given to integrating inspection time with other backward masking tasks and theories (Deary, McCrimmon, & Bradshaw, 1997; White, 1996) and the psychophysiological underpinnings of inspection time performance and its association with psychometric ability tests scores have been explored (Caryl, 1994).

Sensory Discrimination, g and Cognitive Aging

A fillip to the idea that mental ability differences may largely be captured in a general factor and positive evidence that the general factor to some substantial degree might underpinned by differences in a speed of cognitive processing come from research into cognitive aging. In a number of influential empirical, review, and theoretical papers Salthouse (1996a, 1996b) and colleagues (Kail & Salthouse, 1994) have adduced evidence that supposedly different mental abilities, those often assumed to be subserved by different modules, do not age independently. In fact, cognitive aging tends largely to occur in the factor that is general to a number of different factors of mental ability (see the abovementioned papers and Lindenberger and Baltes, 1997; Fig. 7.6). Next, these authors have shown that age-related changes in cognitive ability test scores may in large part be accounted for by changes in processing speed. That is, the variance shared between mental ability test scores and chronological age is mostly mediated by quite simple tests of speed of processing, such as the WAIS–R digit symbol and similar tests, and various tests of reaction time. Salthouse's review and theoretical articles are particularly impressive for their integration of huge numbers of data sets and their fixedness on the processing speed theory of cognitive aging.

With regard to a cognitive account of g, these results from the aging literature are of potentially great importance, even though the cognitively oriented research on cognitive aging tends to take place apart from other information-processing research into psychometric ability test differences in young adults. If cognitive aging occurs largely in g (whatever it represents about the brain) rather than specific cognitive modules, and if most of the age-related variance in cognitive aging is mediated via simple measures of speed of information processing, then there is a clear case for stating that g is of central importance in this aspect of cognitive life and that a cognitive account (an information-processing account) must address g as the main target for explanation. Without detracting from the care and industry that has been involved in amassing the huge data sets that formed these powerful and convincing regularities (Salthouse, 1996b), two factors relating to the mechanisms and implications of these startling regularities should be raised.

First, the account stating that aging of cognitive functions (largely g) is mediated mostly via speed of processing is only as convincing as the measures used to index speed of processing. These measures tend to be either digit symbol-type tests (i.e., tests akin to the Digit Symbol subtest of the Wechsler Intelligence battery) or various reaction time tests. The former is a psychometric test and the latter is more clearly taken from the experimental psychology tradition. By absorbing much of the age-related variance in diverse mental abilities these so-called speed of processing tasks

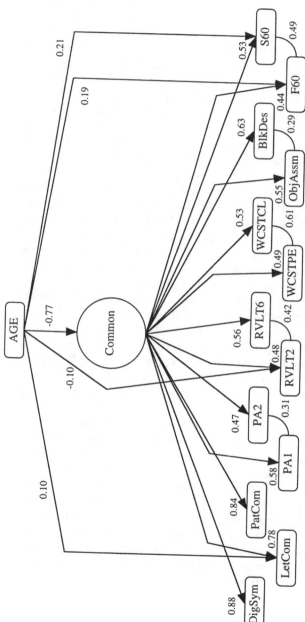

FIG. 7.6. Structural model demonstrating the effects of age on a battery of cognitive abilities. Note that the influence of age is largely on the general (common) factor extracted from the battery of tests. Significant effects of age on specific tests, beyond those effects which are mediated by the general factor, are limited to four relatively small contributions. The tests are: digit symbol from the Wechsler Adult Intelligence Scale-Revised (DigSym), letter comparison (LetCom), pattern comparison (PatCom), Trials 1 & 2 in paired associates memory (PA1 & PA2), Trials 2 and 6 in the Rey Auditory Verbal Learning Test (RVLT2 & RVLT6), percent perseverative errors and conceptual level responses in the Wisconsin Card Sorting Test (WCSTPE & WCSTCL), WAIS-R object assembly and block design score (ObjAssm & BlkDes), and numbers of words produced beginning with F and S in 60 seconds (F60 & S60). This figure was redrawn from Salthouse (1996a).

help us to focus on what might be central to cognitive aging. They cut down much of the complexity surrounding cognitive aging from the cognitive test battery level to the individual task level but they themselves are not understood in mechanistic terms. We are not in a position to offer an elementary account of how humans perform digit symbol or reaction times. The research to date goes as far as our understanding of the brain processes that supports differences in the performance of these tasks.

Second, as long as one inquires after only speed of processing as the mediating variable that accounts for cognitive aging (especially g) then one will assume that that is the cause, or that the cause lies in the processes underpinning the tasks that were used to index speed of cognitive processing. But it is possible that processing speed measures appear to mediate age-related changes in cognition because they both correlate highly with something more general about brain changes with age. Relevant to this possibility are the results from the Berlin studies on aging which find that even simpler measures of sensory acuity—vision, hearing, and balance—can largely or entirely mediate the age-related variance in diverse mental abilities (Baltes & Lindenberger, 1997; Lindenberger & Baltes, 1994; see Fig. 7.7). Again, the aging of diverse mental abilities is mediated through g. More general still is the finding that the aging of specific abilities, almost entirely mediated through g, may be further mediated through biological age acting as a surrogate for chronological age (Anstey & Smith, 1999). This biological age is a latent trait with the following marker variables: physical activity, vision, hearing, grip strength, vibration sense, forced expiratory volume (a respiratory system measure). The authors viewed the marker variables as, "general indicators of the integrity of the central nervous system as well as being sensitive to the aging process" (p. 615).

The foregoing studies on cognitive aging find that the aging of g is the bulk of age-related variance, but the field has now come to an interesting point in looking at the mechanisms underlying this aging. Much data suggest that speed of processing might be the key element in age-related change. But growing data sets show that the general decrements in the senses, in psychomotor performance, and even in respiratory function can account for much of cognitive aging. With one stream of research aiming at a specific mechanism underpinning age-related change in the g factor, and another insisting that the age changes in g are a reflection of general brain (or even wider bodily) integrity, an integration and reconciliation of the two projects is a research priority.

CONCLUSIONS

The question addressed by this chapter is ultimately a rather arbitrary one. Finding associations between psychometric ability factors and validated cognitive elements is an interesting and practically important enter-

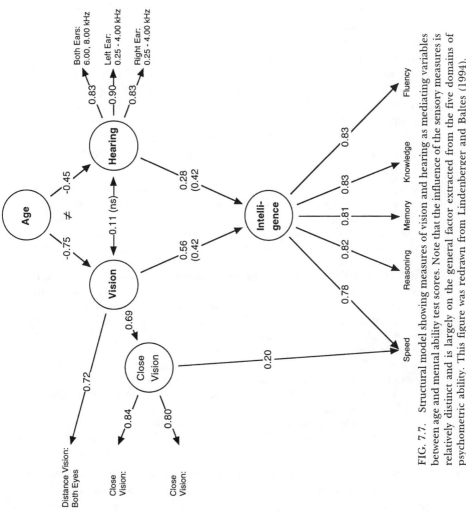

FIG. 7.7. Structural model showing measures of vision and hearing as mediating variables between age and mental ability test scores. Note that the influence of the sensory measures is relatively distinct and is largely on the general factor extracted from the five domains of psychometric ability. This figure was redrawn from Lindenberger and Baltes (1994).

prise. It tries to tie aspects of molar human mental performance to parameters of a cognitive architecture. But the psychometric and the cognitive sides of the equation provide their own brakes to the progression of the field.

Psychometric factors might or might not have isomorphism with the brain's processing mechanisms. Therefore, when cognitive elements correlate with these factors it must be remembered that all that is thereby shown is that the cognitive parameters have a correlation with a test score/factor that has some predictive validity.

Cognitive tasks achieve their importance from two things. First, when they correlate significantly with molar cognitive performance as captured in psychometric tests they obtain a *prima facie* interest. However, to convert this interest into a substantive finding requires that the cognitive task has validity as a parameter within a believable cognitive architecture. How far has cognitive neuroscience progressed in offering such an architecture?

> Exciting new findings have emerged in recent decades concerning the neural underpinnings of cognitive functions such as perception, learning, memory, attention, decision-making, language and motor planning, as well as the influence of emotion and motivation on cognition. With very few exceptions, however, our understanding of these phenomena remains rudimentary. We can identify particular locations within the brain where neuronal activity is modulated in concert with particular external or internal stimuli. In some cases we can even artificially manipulate neural activity in a specific brain structure (using electrical or pharmacological techniques) and cause predictable changes in behavior. But we encounter substantial difficulties in understanding how modulations in neural activity at one point in the nervous system are actually produced by synaptic interactions between neural systems. Thus our current state of knowledge is somewhat akin to looking out of the window of an airplane at night. We can see patches of light from cities and town scattered across the landscape, we know that roads, railways and telephone wires connect those cities, but we gain little sense of the social, political and economic interactions within and between cities that define a functioning society. (Nichols & Newsome, 1999, p. C35)

g stands unassailed as a big concretion of mental test variance. It is a psychometric triumph and a cognitive enigma. When a validated biocognitive model of human mental function finally does arrive, with measurable performance parameters, then we shall begin to understand whether *g* represents some general aspects of brain function or some conglomerate of specific processing functions. Those who want to assert *g*'s pre-eminence possess more empirical support than those who want to wash their hands of it, but that's only because the psychometrics have bedded down far in advance of any cognitive understanding of *g*. In summary, given the current state of knowledge, it is difficult either to disagree with or to state much more than Jensen (1998a), who commented on "The question of the unity or disunity of *g*," as follows,

> The question of whether *g* is the result of individual differences in some single process or in a number of different processes is probably answerable only if one takes into consideration different levels of analysis. At the level of conventional or complex psychometric tests, *g* appears to be unitary. But at some level of analysis of the processes correlated with *g* it will certainly be found that more than a single process is responsible for *g*, whether these processes are at the level of the processes measured by elementary cognitive tasks, or at the level of neurophysiological processes, or even at the molecular level of neural activity. If successful performance on every complex mental test involves, let us say, two distinct, uncorrelated processes, A and B (which are distinguishable and measurable at some less complex level than that of the said tests) in addition to any other processes that are specific to each test or common to certain groups of tests, then in a factor analysis all tests containing A and B will be loaded on a general factor. At this level of analysis, this general factor will forever appear unitary, although it is actually the result of two separate processes, A and B. (pp. 260–261)

REFERENCES

Alderton, D. L., Goldman, S. R., & Pellegrino, J. W. (1985). Individual differences in process outcomes for analogy and classification solution. *Intelligence, 9,* 69–85.

Anstey, K. J., & Smith, G. A. (1999). Interrelationships among biological markers of aging, health, activity, acculturation, and cognitive performance in late adulthood. *Psychology and Aging, 14,* 605–618.

Baddeley, A. (1992a). Working memory. *Science, 255,* 556–559.

Baddeley, A. (1992b). Working memory: The interface between memory and cognition. *Journal of Cognitive Neuroscience, 4,* 281–288.

Baddeley, A., & Gathercole, S. (1999). Individual differences in learning and memory: Psychometrics and the single case. In P. L. Ackerman, P. C. Kyllonen, & R. D. Roberts (Eds.), *Learning and individual differences: Process, trait, and content determinants* (pp. 33–54). Washington, DC: American Psychological Association.

Baltes, P. B., & Lindenberger, U. (1997). Evidence of a powerful connection between sensory and cognitive functions across the adult life span: A new window to the study of cognitive aging. *Psychology and Aging, 12,* 12–31.

Brand, C. R. (1996). *The g Factor.* Chichester, UK: Wiley.

Burns, N. R., Nettelbeck, T., & Cooper, C. J. (1999). Inspection time correlates with general speed of processing but not with fluid ability. *Intelligence, 27,* 37–44.

Burt, C. (1909–1910). Experimental tests of general intelligence. *British Journal of Psychology, 3,* 94–177.

Carpenter, P. A., Just, M. A., & Shell, P. (1990). What one intelligence test measures: A theoretical account of processing in the Raven's Progressive Matrices Test. *Psychological Review, 97*, 404–431.

Carroll, J. B. (1993). *Human cognitive abilities: A survey of factor analytic studies.* Cambridge, England: Cambridge University Press.

Caryl, P. G. (1994). Event-related potentials correlate with inspection time and intelligence. *Intelligence, 18*, 15–46.

Crawford, J. R., Deary, I. J., Allan, K. M., & Gustafsson, J. -E. (1998). Evaluating competing models of the relationship between inspection time and psychometric intelligence. *Intelligence, 26*, 27–42.

Deary, I. J. (1993). Inspection time and WAIS–R IQ subtypes: A confirmatory factor analysis study. *Intelligence, 17*, 223–236.

Deary, I. J. (1996). Reductionism and intelligence: The case of inspection time. *Journal of Biosocial Science, 28*, 405–423.

Deary, I. J. (1997). Intelligence and information processing. In H. Nyborg (Ed.), *The scientific study of human nature: Tribute to Hans J. Eysenck at eighty* (pp. 282–310). New York: Pergamon Press.

Deary, I. J., Caryl, P. G., & Gibson, G. J. (1993). Nonstationarity and the measurement of psychophysical response in a visual inspection-time task. *Perception, 22*, 1245–1256.

Deary, I. J., & Crawford, J. R. (1998). A triarchic theory of Jensensim: Persistent, conservative reductionism. *Intelligence, 26*, 273–282.

Deary, I. J., McCrimmon, R. J., & Bradshaw, J. (1997). Visual information processing and intelligence. *Intelligence, 24*, 461–479.

Deary, I. J., & Stough, C. (1996). Intelligence and inspection time: Achievements, prospects and problems. *American Psychologist, 51*, 599–608.

Duncan, J., Emslie, H., & Williams, P. (1996). Intelligence and the frontal lobe: The organisation of goal-directed behavior. *Cognitive Psychology, 30*, 257–303.

Embretson, S. E. (1995). The role of working memory capacity and general control processes in intelligence. *Intelligence, 20*, 169–189.

Engle, R. W., Tuholski, S. W., Laughlin, J. E., & Conway, A. R. A. (1999). Working memory, short-term memory, and general fluid intelligence: A latent variable approach. *Journal of Experimental Psychology: General, 128*, 309–331.

Eysenck, H. J. (1967). Intelligence assessment: A theoretical and experimental approach. *British Journal of Educational Psychology, 37*, 81–97.

Furneaux, W. D. (1952). Some speed, error and difficulty relationships within a problem solving situation. *Nature, 170*, 37–38.

Galton, F. (1890). Remarks on 'Mental tests and measurements' by J. McK. Cattell. *Mind, 15*, 380–381.

Gardner, H. (1983). *Frames of mind: The theory of multiple intelligences.* New York: Basic Books.

Gottfredson, L. S. (1997). Why *g* matters: the complexity of everyday life. *Intelligence, 24*, 79–132.

Gustafsson, J. -E. (1984). A unifying model for the structure of mental abilities. *Intelligence, 8*, 179–203.

Gustafsson, J. -E. (1992). The relevance of factor analysis for the study of group differences. *Multivariate Behavioral Research, 27*, 239–247.

Hick, W. E. (1952). On the rate of gain of information. *Quarterly Journal of Experimental Psychology, 4*, 11–26.

Holzman, P. S. (1994). Parsing cognition: The power of psychology paradigms. *Archives of General Psychiatry, 51*, 952–954.

Hunt, E. (1980). Intelligence as an information processing concept. *British Journal of Psychology, 71*, 449–474.

Hunt, E., Lunneborg, C., & Lewis, J. (1975). What does it mean to be high verbal? *Cognitive Psychology, 7,* 194–227.

Hunt, E., & MacLeod, C. M. (1978). The sentence-verification paradigm: A case study of two conflicting approaches to individual differences. *Intelligence, 2,* 129–144.

Jensen, A. R. (1987). Individual differences in the Hick paradigm. In P. A. Vernon (Ed.), *Speed of information processing and intelligence* (pp. 101–175). Norwood, NJ: Ablex.

Jensen, A. R. (1998a). *The g factor: The science of mental ability.* New York: Praeger.

Jensen, A. R. (1998b). The suppressed relationship between IQ and the reaction time slope parameter of the Hick function. *Intelligence, 26,* 43–52.

Kail, R., & Salthouse, T. A. (1994). Processing speed as a mental capacity. *Acta Psychologica, 86,* 199–225.

Kline, P. (1991). Sternberg's components: Non-contingent concepts. *Personality and Individual Differences, 12,* 873–876.

Kranzler, J. H., & Jensen, A. R. (1989). Inspection time and intelligence: A meta-analysis. *Intelligence, 13,* 329–347.

Kranzler, J. H., & Jensen, A. R. (1991). The nature of psychometric *g*: Unitary process or a number of independent processes? *Intelligence, 15,* 397–422.

Kyllonen, P. C. (1996a). Is working memory capacity Spearman's g? In I. Dennis & P. Tapsfield (Eds.), *Human abilities: Their nature and measurement* (pp. 77–96). Mahwah, NJ: Lawrence Erlbaum Associates.

Kyllonen, P. C. (1996b). Aptitude testing inspired by information processing: A test of the four sources model. *The Journal of General Psychology, 120,* 375–405.

Kyllonen, P. C., & Christal, R. E. (1990). Reasoning ability is (little more than) working memory capacity? *Intelligence, 14,* 389–433.

Laird, J. E., Newell, A., & Rosenbloom, P. S. (1987). SOAR: An architecture for general intelligence. *Artificial Intelligence, 33,* 1–64.

Levy, P. (1992). Inspection time and its relation to intelligence: Issues of measurement and meaning. *Personality and Individual Differences, 13,* 987–1002.

Lindenberger, U., & Baltes, P. B. (1994). Sensory functioning and intelligence in old age: A strong connection. *Psychology and Aging, 9,* 339–355.

Lindenberger, U., & Baltes, P. B. (1997). Intellectual functioning in old and very old age: Cross sectional results from the Berlin Aging Study. *Psychology and Aging, 12,* 410–432.

Lohman, D. F. (1994). Component scores as residual variation (or why the intercept correlates best). *Intelligence, 19,* 1–11.

Lohman, D. F. (1999). Minding our p's and q's: On finding relationships between learning and intelligence. In P. L. Ackerman, P. C. Kyllonen, & R. D. Roberts (Eds.), *Learning and individual differences: Process, trait, and content determinants* (pp. 55–76). Washington, DC: American Psychological Association.

Luo, D., & Petrill, S. A. (1999). Elementary cognitive tasks and their roles in *g* estimates. *Intelligence, 27,* 157–174.

Marshalek, B., Lohman, D. F., & Snow, R. E. (1983). The complexity continuum in the radex and hierarchical models of intelligence. *Intelligence, 7,* 107–127.

Massaro, D. W. (1993). Information processing models: Microscopes of the mind. *Annual Review of Psychology, 44,* 383–425.

McGarry-Roberts, P. A., Stelmack, R. M., & Campbell, K. B. (1992). Intelligence, reaction time, and event-related potentials. *Intelligence, 16,* 289–313.

Neisser, U., Boodoo, G., Bouchard, T. J., Boykin, A. W., Brody, N., Ceci, S. J., Halpern, D. F., Loehlin, J. C., Perloff, R., Sternberg, R. J., & Urbina, S. (1996). Intelligence: Knowns and unknowns. *American Psychologist, 51,* 77–101.

Nettelbeck, T. (1987). Inspection time and intelligence. In P. A. Vernon (Ed.), *Speed of information processing and intelligence* (pp. 295–346). Norwood, NJ: Ablex.

Neubauer, A. C. (1997). The mental speed approach to the assessment of intelligence. In J. Kingma & W. Tomic (Eds.), *Advances in cognition and education: Reflections on the concept of intelligence.* Greenwich, Connecticut: JAI press.

Neubauer, A. C., & Knorr, E. (1998). Three paper and pencil tests for speed of information processing: Psychometric properties and correlations with intelligence. *Intelligence, 26,* 123–151.

Neubauer, A. C., Spinath, F. M., Riemann, R., Borkenau, P., & Angleitner, A. (2000). Genetic and environmental influences on two measures of speed of information processing and their relation to psychometric intelligence: evidence from the German Observational Study of Adult Twins. *Intelligence, 28,* 267–289.

Nichols, M. J., & Newsome, W. T. (1999). The neurobiology of cognition. *Nature, 402,* C35–C38.

Posner, M. I., & Mitchell, R. F. (1967). Chronometric analysis of classification. *Psychological Review, 74,* 392–409.

Raven, J. C. (1938). *Progressive matrices.* London: Lewis.

Rijsdijk, F. V., Vernon, P. A., & Boomsma, D. I. (1998). The genetic basis of the relation between speed-of-information-processing and IQ. *Behavioural Brain Research, 95,* 77–84.

Roberts, R. D., & Stankov, L. (1999). Individual differences in speed of mental processing and human cognitive abilities: Toward a taxonomic model. *Learning and Individual Differences, 11,* 1–120.

Salthouse, T. A. (1996a). Constraints on theories of cognitive aging. *Psychonomic Bulletin and Review, 3,* 287–299.

Salthouse, T. A. (1996b). The processing-speed theory of adult age differences in cognition. *Psychological Review, 103,* 403–428.

Spearman, C. (1904). "General Intelligence" objectively determined and measured. *American Journal of Psychology, 15,* 201–293.

Spearman, C. (1923). *The nature of intelligence and the principles of cognition.* London: MacMillan.

Spearman, C. (1927). *The abilities of man.* London: MacMillan.

Stankov, L., & Roberts, R. D. (1997). Mental speed is not the 'basic' process of intelligence. *Personality and Individual Differences, 22,* 69–84.

Stauffer, J. M., Ree, M. J., & Carretta, T. R. (1996). Cognitive-components tests are not much more than *g*: An extension of Kyllonen's analyses. *The Journal of General Psychology, 123,* 193–205.

Sternberg, R. J. (1977a). Component processing in analogical reasoning. *Psychological Review, 84,* 353–378.

Sternberg, R. J. (1977b). *Intelligence, information processing, and analogical reasoning: The componential analysis of human abilities.* Hillsdale, NJ: Lawrence Erlbaum Associates.

Sternberg, R. J. (1978). Intelligence research at the interface between differential and cognitive psychology: Prospects and proposals. *Intelligence, 2,* 195–222.

Sternberg, R. J. (1979). Six authors in search of a character: A play about intelligence tests in the year 2000. *Intelligence, 3,* 283–293.

Sternberg, R. J. (1999). Successful intelligence: Finding a balance. *Trends in Cognitive Sciences, 3,* 436–442.

Sternberg, R. J., & Gardner, M. K. (1983). Unities in inductive reasoning. *Journal of Experimental Psychology: General, 112,* 80.

Sternberg, S. (1966). High speed scanning in human memory. *Science, 153,* 652–654.

Thorndike, E. L., Lay, W., & Dean, P. R. (1909). The relation of accuracy in sensory discrimination to intelligence. *American Journal of Psychology, 20,* 364–369.

Vernon, P. A. (1983). Speed of information processing and general intelligence. *Intelligence, 7,* 53–70.

Vernon, P. A. (1985). Reaction times and speed of processing: Their relationship to timed and untimed measures of intelligence. *Intelligence, 9,* 357–374.

Vernon, P. A. (1989). The heritability of measures of speed of information processing. *Personality and Individual Differences, 10,* 573–576.

Vernon, P. A., & Kantor, L. (1986). Reaction time correlations with intelligence test scores obtained under either timed or untimed conditions. *Intelligence, 10,* 315–330.

Vickers, D., Nettelbeck, T., & Willson, R. J. (1972). Perceptual indices of performance: The measurement of "inspection time" and "noise" in the visual system. *Perception, 1,* 263–295.

Vickers, D., Pietsch, A., & Hemmingway, T. (1995). Intelligence and visual and auditory discrimination: Evidence that the relationship is not due to the rate at which sensory information is sampled. *Intelligence, 21,* 197–224.

Vickers, D., & Smith, P. L. (1986). The rationale for the inspection time index. *Personality and Individual Differences, 7,* 609–624.

White, M. (1996). Interpreting inspection time as a measure of the speed of sensory processing. *Personality and Individual Differences, 20,* 351–363.

Chapter 8

A View From Cognitive Psychology: *g*—(G)host in the Correlation Matrix?

Jutta Kray
Peter A. Frensch
Humboldt University at Berlin

> *How can human intelligence be understood? The question is an old one, but age does not necessarily lead to wisdom, at least not in the sense that long-standing interest has led to a large body of accumulated knowledge and understanding.*
> —Norman (1991, p. 327)

Toward the end of the 19th century, Francis Galton (1888; see Diamond, 1997) introduced the concept of a "correlation coefficient," a concept that immediately generated new avenues for studying a variety of, among many other things, complex psychological phenomena (Diamond, 1997). The new concept led to Charles Spearman's fundamental observation that the intertest correlations among psychological tests, all believed to measure some aspect of intelligence, "although widely varying in magnitude, were at least regularly positive in sign" (Spearman & Jones, 1950, p. 7). The observation made by Spearman implies that a person who shows good performance on one task, will also show good performance on many other tasks. Conversely, a person who demonstrates poor performance on one task is also likely to demonstrate poor performance on many other tasks. This "positive manifold," as it has come to be known, seemingly indicates the presence of some general ability that underlies performance on many, if not all, tasks requiring intelligence, a suggestion that has aroused a debate about the nature of intelligence in all major research traditions within psychology. As is amply shown by the present volume, this debate is still going strong at the beginning of the 21st century.

In this chapter we discuss theoretical approaches in the area of Cognitive Psychology that have some bearing on the question of whether or not a general ability, henceforth also called g, underlies all intelligent human behavior. The chapter is divided into three main sections. In the first section, we briefly define what exactly we mean when we state, from the theoretical view of Cognitive Psychology, that a "general ability g might underlie intelligent behavior." In the second section, we review some of the most important paths cognitive psychologists have traveled to pin down—theoretically and empirically—the nature of g. In our view, none of the paths has turned out to be successful. In the final section, we discuss some of the most prominent modern theoretical conceptions, or models, of cognition to find out to what extent a general ability g has been realized in (i.e., is part of), the proposed functioning of the human cognitive system. Our main argument throughout is one that is consistent with the Norman (1991) citation that opened the chapter: We argue that there exists no convincing empirical evidence that would support the existence of a general ability, or g, at least when viewed from the perspective of Cognitive Psychology. Furthermore, we argue that the equivalent of g cannot be found in most of the modern theoretical (cognitive) conceptions of human mind.

DEFINITIONS AND CLARIFICATIONS

It is helpful to distinguish at least two different interpretations of the statement that "there exists a general ability of intelligence," a strict and a loose interpretation. According to a strict interpretation of the statement, there exists one and only one source of all intelligent behavior. (Notice that we use the term *behavior* in a very general sense that includes cognitive activity as well.) The strict interpretation of the general statement thus implies that the quality of all intelligent behavior is *determined* by a single source or ability. Individuals who possess more of this source or ability, act more intelligently than persons possessing less of the source or ability.

According to a looser interpretation of the statement, there exists one source that *affects* all intelligent behavior. In the latter case, it is quite possible that intelligent behavior is influenced by other sources as well. Figure 8.1 depicts just two realizations the loose interpretation of the statement can take. In the upper part of Fig. 8.1, the impact of a general ability on intelligent behavior is indirect because the general ability directly affects a number of other abilities which, in turn, determine intelligence. In the middle part of the figure, the impact of the general ability is direct and either adds to, or interacts with, the influence of other abilities. Of course, other realizations of the loose interpretation of the statement are possible. The lower part of Fig. 8.1 depicts one constellation, again of many possi-

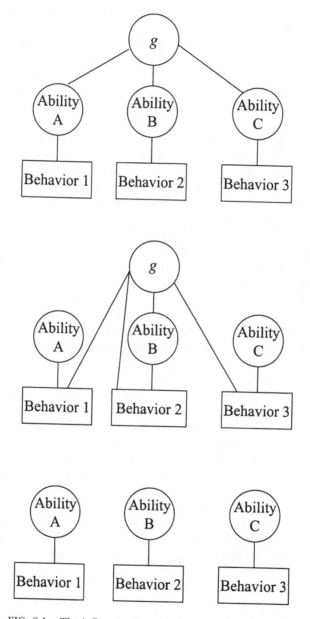

FIG. 8.1. The influence of *g* on behavior: three possibilities.

ble constellations, in which a general ability g of intelligence does not exist. Instead, intelligence is determined by many different abilities that do not share commonalities.

The reader might notice that, if one accepts a loose interpretation of g, then the size of the relative influence of the general ability (relative to the influence of the other abilities) on intelligent behavior may vary from very little to very much. To us, the assumption of a general ability g makes sense only as long as the impact of this g on all forms of intelligent behavior is large relative to the impact of other abilities. In our discussion of the existence of a general ability of intelligence in this chapter, we do therefore not differentiate between the two possible, strict and loose, interpretations of the concept. Instead, we interpret the concept of a "general ability g of intelligence" as meaning that *there exists a source or ability such that the influence of this source or ability on all forms of intelligent behavior is large relative to the impact of other sources or abilities*.

Which kind of empirical finding might constitute support for our interpretation of g? At least three different possibilities come to mind immediately. First, as mentioned earlier, one would expect to empirically observe positive correlations among different measures of intelligent behavior. The "positive manifold" should hold both within as well as between persons. Thus, for example, a person's standing (relative to other persons' standings) with regard to his or her performance on intelligence-demanding tasks should remain relatively constant across all tasks.

One main problem with accepting an empirically observed positive manifold as evidence for g is that positive manifolds do not automatically reveal their meanings. For example, it is quite possible to obtain a positive manifold due to an overlap of task demands, rather than due to the influence of a general ability (e.g., Ceci, 1990). Thus, tasks that all require substantial visual processing, to take an example, will generate a positive manifold that points to the existence of a specific "visual processing" ability that has little to do with the existence of g. Although the empirical persuasion of a positive manifold increases with the number of different tasks across which the manifold holds, it should be clear that the unambiguous interpretation of positive manifolds is difficult, to say the least.

A more convincing empirical result supporting the assumption of a general ability of intelligence would be the finding that persons possessing more of this ability would do better in tasks requiring intelligence than persons possessing less of the ability, but would not necessarily do better in tasks requiring little or no intelligence. Aside from the fact that the separation of tasks requiring more or less intelligence is difficult, the envisioned empirical finding also requires a theoretical clarification of what the general ability underlying intelligent behavior might be. Therefore, the third and key empirical evidence supporting the assumption of a general ability of intelligence, in our view, is the clarification of the exact nature of this general ability.

In the next section we consider and discuss attempts aimed at unraveling the nature of the general ability, *g*. The reader should notice that we limit our discussion to attempts that originated from within the perspective of Cognitive Psychology. Thus, we do not consider possible biological, physiological, or neurological interpretations of a general ability. We do also not consider sociological, behavior–genetic, or cultural attempts to qualify the nature of a general ability; many of these attempts are discussed in other chapters of the present volume.

What does it mean to take the perspective of Cognitive Psychology when addressing the question of a general ability of intelligence? Cognitive Psychology may be defined as "a general approach to psychology emphasizing the internal, mental processes. To the cognitive psychologist behavior is not specifiable simply in terms of its overt properties but requires explanations at the level of mental events, mental representations, beliefs, intentions, etc." (Reber, 1995, p. 135). Thus, by asking what the nature of *g* might be, we are searching for a cognitive manifestation of a general ability. More specifically, we are asking which mental processes and representations or which properties of mental processes and representations might be primarily responsible for intelligent behavior. To provide an example that is discussed in more depth later, some cognitive psychologists have argued that the speed with which mental processes can be carried out is relatively constant within persons but differs between persons. Because many, though not all, of the existing intelligence tests (e.g., Wechsler Adult Intelligence Scale, WAIS; Wechsler, 1982) use response times on different tasks as indicators of intelligence, it is at least conceivable that more intelligent persons might differ from less intelligent persons primarily in terms of their mental speed. In other words, mental speed is one, of many, possible manifestations of a general ability of intelligence at the cognitive level.

Next we discuss some of the more prominent attempts to characterize a general ability of intelligence in terms of the language and concepts of Cognitive Psychology. Our focus and leading question will be on the extent to which the particular attempts have been successful in unraveling the nature of *g*.

g IN COGNITIVE TERMS

Ever since the days of Spearman and Thurstone, researchers in the psychometric tradition have been arguing about the organization of the mental abilities that underlie intelligent behavior (for three different possibilities, see Fig. 8.1). However, psychometric approaches to describing the *structure* of intelligence have not fostered our understanding of the *nature* of intelligence. New hope for a better understanding of the latter arose with the introduction of information-processing theory (e.g., Miller, Galanter, & Pribram, 1960). According to information-processing theory, human behavior is the result of a chain of elementary information processes. The hope arising with the ascent of the new theory with respect to understanding the nature of intelligence was both theoretical and practical. Theoretically, it was hoped that cognitive theories based on information-processing assumptions might provide the theoretical basis for an explanation of intelligence. Empirically, it was hoped that the nature of *g* could be determined on the basis of correlations between scores measuring specific information-processing parameters (e.g., speed of mental processing) and scores assumed to measure intelligence (e.g., Raven's Progressive Matrices; Raven, Court, & Raven, 1987; see also Sternberg & Frensch, 1990).

Within the perspective of the information-processing framework, the nature of *g* has been tied, theoretically, to at least four different general properties of the information-processing system, (a) structural properties (e.g., attentional resources), (b) general processing properties (e.g., mental processing speed), (c) procedural or strategy properties (e.g., metacognition), and (d) specific processing properties that sometimes are assumed to be located in specific brain regions (e.g., the inhibition function). Next, we review theoretical and empirical treatments of *g* for these four properties of the cognitive system. Notice that our empirical focus is on new findings, that is, findings that have been reported roughly within the last 10 years (for a review of previous findings, see Sternberg & Frensch, 1990).

To evaluate the various proposed theoretical accounts, we use five evaluation criteria. We argue that each of the five criteria must be met before any cognitive construct can truly be considered a cognitive manifestation of *g* (for a similar set of criteria, see Deary & Stough, 1996; but see Sternberg, 1997).

Criterion 1: The Account Must Be Theoretical Rather Than Empirical (Need for Multiple Measures of the Account).

Criterion 1 implies that any proposed account must have a theoretical basis. Following an example that was introduced earlier, if the assumption that speed of mental processing is a potential cognitive manifestation of *g* is to be acceptable, it needs to be spelled out how exactly speed of processing is realized in the cognitive system. Criterion 1 also implies that the proposed account should, in principle, be measurable via different psychometric tests or experimental tasks. Thus, the theoretical status of a proposed account can be partly evaluated on the basis of the validity of its measures.

Criterion 2:   In Empirical Research Relating g to the Proposed Account, g Must Be Measured in Multiple Ways (Need for Multiple Measures of g).

Most intelligence researchers today accept traditional psychometric IQ tests, often the Raven's or the WAIS, as indicators of *g*. The Raven's, for instance, is one of the best known markers of fluid intelligence (Marshalek, Lohman, & Snow, 1983), but, like most IQ tests, captures only a part of intelligent behavior. Criterion 2 demands that researchers use multiple measures of *g* (e.g., IQ tests, experimental tasks) to enhance the validity of measurement. The latter demand is consistent with many modern intelligence theories that allow for multiple types of intelligence (e.g., Eysenck, 1992, 1998; Gardner, 1983; Sternberg, 1985a).

Criterion 3:   Any Empirically Observed Relation Between the Proposed Account and g Must Not Be Due to the Influence of Third Variables (Control of Third Variables).

It is well known, for example, that individual differences in dual-task performance (as one potential marker in so-called attentional-resource-accounts of *g*) are likely to be confounded by individual differences in strategy use. Thus, substantial relations between individual differences in *g* and individual differences in dual-task performance (i.e., attentional resources) can also be due to individual differences in strategy use. Several methods have been proposed to overcome the third-variable problem, for instance experimental manipulation of potential third variables, and training or testing-to-the-limits studies (e.g., Ackerman, 1986; Lindenberger & Baltes, 1995). Hence, one important evaluation criterion will be whether potential third variables that might modulate an empirically observed relation between an account and *g* have been controlled for.

Criterion 4:   The Direction of Causality Must Be Demonstrated Empirically.

All of the proposed theoretical accounts establish a causal direction between the construct of interest and *g*. At the same time, empirical studies are usually based on cross-sectional data and unlikely to prove the assumed direction of causality. Hence, longitudinal research designs are required to clarify whether the proposed account is a cause rather than a consequence of intelligent behavior.

Criterion 5: The Proposed Theoretical Relation Between the Account and g Must Be Plausible.

The plausibility of a theoretical relation is an admittedly loosely defined criterion for the evaluation of theoretical accounts. It refers to the rationale for why a relation between the construct of interest and *g* should actually hold.

Of course, other criteria than those described earlier are both thinkable and plausible, such as, for example, the magnitude of an obtained empirical relation (typically a correlation coefficient) between a theoretical construct and *g* (see Deary & Stough, 1996). We have chosen not to use the latter criterion because a comparison of correlation coefficients between studies that differ in ability ranges and sampling strategies does not make sense to us (see Sternberg, 1997). Table 8.1 provides a summary of the extent to which we believe the five criteria are to be met by the various theoretical accounts discussed next.

Attentional Resources

Description of the Account. According to attentional-resources-accounts of *g*, the amount of attentional resources that are available to individuals is a major determinant of intelligence (Fogarty & Stankov, 1982; Hunt, 1980; Hunt & Lansman, 1982; Stankov, 1983). Note that the term *attentional resources* is very loosely defined and refers to structural properties within the information-processing system, such as a hypothetical workspace, energy pool, mental energy, or workload, that are all assumed to be limited in an individual (e.g., Kahneman, 1973).

Proponents of an attentional-resources-account often use a dual-task methodology to examine whether individual differences in attentional resources predict individual differences in intelligence (e.g., Hunt, 1980; Hunt, Pellegrino, & Yee, 1989; Stankov, 1989). Attentional resources are measured in terms of the costs of performing two tasks together as compared to performing each of the tasks alone. The general idea underlying this approach is that persons who perform well on intelligence-requiring tasks suffer less from performing a secondary task in addition to the primary task because they have more attentional resources for cognitive activities available than do persons performing less well on intelligence-requiring tasks.

For example, Hunt (1980) cited a study in which the primary task, Task A, consisted of performing a subset of 18 Raven problems (Marshalek et

TABLE 8.1
Some Cognitive Manifestations of g

Construct	Criterion 1 Theoretical Rationale	Criterion 2 Dependent Variables	Criterion 3 Third Variables	Criterion 4 Causality	Criterion 5 Rationale of Relation
Attentional resources	medium	single	Yes, strategies	—	low
Speed of information processing	medium	two/three	No	—	low
Speed of visual processing	low	two/three	No	Yes	low
Cognitive components	medium	multiple		—	medium
Metacognition	medium	multiple	Yes, contents	—	medium
Goal selection	low	two/three		—	medium
Inhibitory processing	medium	multiple	—	—	medium

191

al., 1983). The secondary task, Task B, was a simple psychomotor task that was assumed to require little intelligence. The presentation of Raven items was in ascending order of difficulty. Participants practiced Tasks A and B alone before they performed both tasks concurrently. The results showed that the quality of performance on the psychomotor task declined when the Raven items became more difficult, suggesting that performance on the intelligence-requiring Task A relied on attentional resources.

Over the years, several problems have led to researchers' disengagement from resource-accounts of g. First, as already stated, the concept itself is very loosely defined (for a review, see Navon, 1984). Therefore, different researchers rarely agree with each other on what is the "appropriate" measure of attentional resources. Second, a variety of empirical findings has led researchers to believe that attentional resources may not constitute a single unitary concept but may come from different sources (Wickens, 1978).

Evaluation of the Account.   Evaluation Criterion 1 (need for multiple measures) is not met by attentional-resources-accounts of g. For example, on the one hand, researchers have been able to demonstrate dual-task costs in many different tasks, such as memory or reasoning tasks (Hunt, 1980). On the other hand, however, dual-task costs seem to be absent in certain situations. For instance, Allport, Antonis, and Reynolds (1972) found no interference between two tasks that were presented in different modalities indicating that the processes involved rely on separate pools of resources. Thus, the assumption of a general attentional resource that underlies all kinds of intelligent behavior seems at least highly questionable.

Regarding Criterion 2 (need for multiples measures of g), proponents of an attentional-resource account have typically used a single traditional IQ test as a marker of intelligence in their research. Furthermore, third-variable explanations of the empirically obtained relations between dual-task costs and g (Criterion 3) are often possible, if not likely. That is, the interpretation of empirical findings is difficult in this area because participants may differ in assigning priorities to the two tasks in a dual-task situation (Hunt, 1980; Stankov, 1989). It may be that some persons try to divide their attention equally across the primary and secondary tasks, whereas others focus more on the primary than on the secondary task or vice versa. Thus, an attentional resource cannot be viewed as cognitive manifestation of g—at least not as long as individual differences in strategy use are equally plausible alternative factors that produce high correlations with g (Stankov, 1989). Moreover, to our knowledge there exists no single longitudinal study investigating the causal relation between attentional resources and g; thus, the direction of causality (Criterion 4) remains unclear. In sum, most of the five evaluation criteria are not met by the attentional-resources-account of *g*. Therefore, an attentional resource cannot be considered a likely manifestation of *g* at the present time.

Speed of Processing

Description of the Account. In terms of speed of processing, we distinguish two properties of the cognitive system that have been proposed to underlie *g*—speed of information processing and speed of visual processing.

Typical proponents of a speed-of-processing explanation of *g* are Jensen (1984, 1987) and Vernon (1987, 1989). Jensen (1987), for example, has reported that simple and choice reaction time measures (using Hick's paradigm) are substantially correlated with intelligence as measured by the Raven's. Moreover, higher correlations are observed when task complexity is increased via an increase of the number of response alternatives in Hick's paradigm (see also Larson & Saccuzzo, 1989; Neubauer, 1991; Vernon, 1987). In addition, Jensen (1984) reported that interindividual differences in reaction times are correlated with intelligence measures at about −.35.

Evaluation of the Account. The theoretical concept underlying a speed-of-processing account (Criterion 1) is rather straightforward. Based on his empirical findings, Jensen (1984), argued for a low-level processing explanation of *g*. In his theory, the cognitive manifestation of *g* is a global property of the brain. More specifically, Jensen suggested that *g* is associated with the neural efficiency of the cerebral cortex. The neural efficiency of the cerebral cortex is dependent on two factors, (a) the number of neurons activated by the environment, and (b) the rate of oscillation between refractory and excitatory phases of neural processes. Individual differences in reaction time are viewed as reflecting a "hardware" component of the cognitive system that is independent of knowledge, skills, or cultural background. Other researchers using choice reaction time paradigms share this general view on individual differences in intelligence (see Eysenck, 1998; Vernon, 1987).

Furthermore, speed of processing has been measured in a wide variety of studies using different tasks and tests (Jensen & Weng, 1994). Nevertheless, there is also empirical evidence, for instance in the domain of insight problems (see Sternberg & Davidson, 1983), indicating that taking *more* time sometimes leads to a greater likelihood of solving a problem.

Criterion 2 is generally met by proponents of a speed-of-processing account because researchers typically use more than one IQ test as indicator of *g* (see Kranzler & Jensen, 1991; Vernon, 1989). In addition, alternative accounts, based on the possible influence of third variables (Criterion 3), for the relation between speed of processing and *g* are rare. For instance,

Ceci (1990) proposed that substantial speed–g correlations are due to their sharing variance of a common knowledge base, but empirical research (e.g., Neubauer & Bucik, 1996) has not confirmed this hypothesis. Furthermore, researchers sometimes argue that reaction time measures should be more highly correlated with timed than with untimed IQ tests. However, research has not confirmed this argument either; RT–IQ relations do not seem to vary for speed and power versions of IQ tests (e.g., Vernon & Kantor, 1986).

Criterion 4 asking for empirical evidence confirming the assumed direction of causality, is not generally met by speed-of-processing accounts. Equally critical seems to be the lack of a plausible theoretical reason for the relation between mental speed and g (Criterion 5). Thus, although many cognitive psychologists would probably agree that mental speed may be a major determinant of individual differences in intelligence test performance, the more radical view that mental speed is the single source of individual differences in g, as proposed by Jensen and others, seems to be implausible (e.g., Nettelbeck, 1998; Sternberg, 1984).

Interestingly, Jensen himself seems to have moved from a strict to a looser interpretation of the mental-speed account of g. Kranzler and Jensen (1991), for instance, investigated a variety of elementary cognitive tasks (ECT), and used a stepwise hierarchical regression analysis to predict psychometric intelligence. The authors report that four independent components lead to a significant increment in multiple R^2. Thus, mental speed seems not to be the only source of variance accounting for individual differences in intelligence test performance. Unfortunately, the interpretation of the four isolated components remains unclear (for methodological criticisms of the study, see Carroll, 1991). In sum, at best, three of the five evaluation criteria are met by speed-of-processing accounts of human intelligence.

Speed of Visual Processing (Inspection Time)

Description of the Account.   The speed with which visual information is taken in by the human cognitive system (i.e., inspection time) has been proposed as another processing property of the cognitive system that might underlie g and explain interindividual differences in g (Bates & Eysenck, 1993; Brand & Deary, 1982; Deary & Stough, 1996; Nettelbeck, 1987). To measure inspection time, two-choice discrimination tasks are used in which participants are asked to decide, for example, which one of two vertical lines is longer. The exposure time for discriminations is varied randomly. Inspection time is determined as the stimulus duration that is needed by the participant to reach a given accuracy level. Meta-analytic studies indicate a strong relationship between inspection time and intelligence measures of about .50 (e.g., Nettelbeck, 1987). Hence, inspection time has been found to account for approximately 25% of intelligence-test variance, but despite that fact, the concept has not (yet) caught on in the intelligence research community (Deary & Stough, 1996).

Evaluation of the Account. A theoretical analysis of the concept of inspection time has been provided by Vickers and others (Criterion 1; Vickers, 1979; Vickers & Smith, 1986). Like the construct of mental speed, inspection time is viewed as a low-level hardware component, namely, the amount or quanta of perceptual information perceived by the cognitive system in a certain time. However, inspection time has been measured via a single category of tasks only (see also Sternberg, 1997). Hence, the validity of the construct may be questionable. Probably aware of this limitation, Deary (1995, 1999) introduced an auditory version to measure inspection time, and has shown that this measure is highly correlated with *g*.

The inspection-time-account of *g* generally meets Criterion 2. That is, researchers in this area often use multiple IQ tests as markers of *g* (e.g., Deary, 1999). Furthermore, the potential influence of third variables (Criterion 3) has been examined empirically. For instance, some researchers (e.g., Howe, 1988) argue that the relation between inspection time and *g* may be confounded by individual differences in strategy choice. However, recent studies have demonstrated that inspection time–*g* relations do not seem to be influenced by strategy choice (Egan, 1994; Evans & Nettelbeck, 1993; Simpson & Deary, 1997).

To determine the direction of causality linking inspection time and *g* (Criterion 4), Deary and colleagues conducted longitudinal studies providing first evidence that inspection time measured at a young age predicts intelligence at an older age, at least better than the reverse (Deary, 1995; but see Nettelbeck & Young, 1990).

Criterion 5, calling for a theoretical rationale supporting the obtained correlation between inspection time and general intelligence, appears to be the most problematic criterion for this concept. It is important to see that, in this regard, Deary and Stough (1996) concluded that "to explain effectively why inspection time correlates with IQ and, thereby, truly to understand more about the causation of individual differences in intelligence, inspection-time performance must be understood in terms of validated psychological or biological constructs" (p. 605). In our view, the lack of a theoretical rationale for the empirically observed relation between inspection time and intelligence measures is more serious than seems at first glance—because it essentially leaves us where we started. The positive manifold between performances on many tasks observed by Spearman, such was our argument, can only be attributed to a general ability *g* if the nature of this ability can be clarified. Similarly, the empirically observed correlation between inspection time and intelligence measures is only useful to the extent that the involvement of inspection time in tasks demonstrating intelligent behavior can be clarified. Moreover, in comparison to speed of processing, the speed of visual processing seems to be a much too specific property of the cognitive system to be taken as a convincing possible manifestation of g at the cognitive level.

Cognitive Components

Description of the Account. In the late 1970s, Sternberg (1977) introduced a new research strategy, componential analysis, that can be used to study the nature of intelligence (for details, see Sternberg, 1985b). The general idea underlying componential analysis is to decompose a task that is known to rely on intelligence and to identify those components (e.g., inference, encoding, justification) of the cognitive system that are significant predictors of individual differences in intelligence. Sternberg has stressed the point that intelligence tests, such as the Raven's, measure only a part of intelligent behavior. Therefore, componential analysis can be, and has been, extended to other facets of intelligent behavior as well such as induction problems (e.g., Pellegrino & Glaser, 1980; Sternberg & Gardner, 1983), deductive reasoning problems (e.g., Guyote & Sternberg, 1981), and vocabulary learning (Sternberg & Powell, 1983).

Sternberg and Gardner (1983), for example, used three inductive reasoning problems—analogies, series completion, and classifications—to identify which cognitive components are possible sources of g. The authors reported that seven components—encoding, mapping, justification, inference, comparison, application, and response—accounted for individual differences in g. In general, persons with more efficient information processing components also showed better performance on inductive reasoning problems.

Evaluation of the Account. Evaluation Criterion 1 is met by the componential approach. Indeed, Sternberg (1977) suggests a hierarchical theory of intelligence in which multiple components underlie g. The components are quite similar to those originally proposed by Spearman (1927). However, there exists a lack of taxonomy of how many and which information-processing components account for individual differences in g, that is, researchers using componential analysis have failed to identify a set of fundamental components that explain individual differences across multiple subsets of intelligent behavior. A further problem of this theoretical account is that many information-processing components required for performing cognitive tasks may not be independent of each other (e.g., Keating & Bobbitt, 1978).

Researchers using a componential approach typically use multiple indicators of *g*; thus, Criterion 2 is also met by this approach. On the other hand, individual differences in strategies seem to influence assessment of *g* (Criterion 3). This aspect is discussed in more detail in the next section. To our knowledge, Criterion 4 is not met, that is, there exists no longitudinal study examining the direction of causality.

Criterion 5, the theoretical relation between cognitive components and *g* appears to be a problematic criterion as well. On the one hand, it is, of course, plausible to assume that various components are related to individual differences in intelligence; on the other hand, the questions arise (a) whether different components explain individual differences in *g* to the same or differing extents, and (b) whether a predictive pattern differs across intelligence-requiring tasks (e.g., inductive reasoning tasks or classifications). This point is even more important when metacomponents are assumed to underlie *g* as well (see next section).

Metacognition

Description of the Account. If indeed, as was suggested by Sternberg and Gardner (1983), multiple information-processing components are associated with *g*, then it is not unreasonable to assume that higher level processes required for deciding which and how elementary processes are combined, may be related to *g* as well. Hence, some cognitive researchers have claimed that a major source of individual differences in *g* is due to individual differences in metacognition.

The term *metacognition* has quite different meanings in psychology[1] (for a review, see Brown, Bransford, Ferrera, & Campione, 1983). Sternberg (1980), for instance, has defined "metacomponents" as "higher order processes used for planning how a problem should be solved, for making decisions regarding alternatives courses of action during problem solving, and for monitoring solution processes" (p. 573). Proponents of the metacognitive account of *g* argue that persons who use metacomponents more efficiently are more intelligent and, thus, show higher performance on psychometric intelligence tests than persons who use metacomponents less efficiently. Indeed, Haygood and Johnson (1983) reported that persons who switch earlier to a more efficient strategy in novel task situations reach higher scores on the Raven's than do persons who switch later to a more efficient strategy.

Evaluation of the Account. Regarding Criterion 1, a theory of metacognition has been outlined in the componential approach to intelligence

---

[1]Brown (1987) distinguishes three meanings of metacognition, (1) the strategy use itself, (2) monitoring and planning activities, and (3) the application of knowledge in which situation a certain strategy is adequate.

(Sternberg, 1977). What remains unclear in this approach is how exactly cognitive components and metacomponents can be separated. Criterion 2 is met; researchers in this research area often use multiple markers of *g*. Furthermore, the potential influence of third variables has been examined (Criterion 3). A cognitive training approach (see Campione & Brown, 1978; Campione, Brown, & Ferrara, 1982), has been applied to investigate whether correlations of higher level or lower level processing components with *g* are enhanced or reduced after extensive training (Ackerman, 1986, 1988; Necka, 1999). Ackerman (1988), for example, postulated that cognitive ability–general intelligence correlations decline with practice because content-specific variance is reduced during skill acquisition. In several experiments, he demonstrated that ability–intelligence correlations indeed decline with increasing task training. Other researchers have tried to enhance intelligence by teaching the use of metacognitions, instructions, and strategies. The results of this literature seem to indicate, in general, that interventions lead to an increase in cognitive skills but do not necessarily improve intelligence test performance (Perkins & Grotzer, 1997; Sternberg & Williams, 1998).

Evaluation Criterion 4 is not met by the metacognition account of *g*, that is, longitudinal research designs determining whether individual differences in metacognition are a cause of individual differences in *g* are still lacking. Finally, the concepts of intelligence and of metacognition seem to refer to a similar range of behavior; thus, a relation between individual differences in the efficiency of metacomponents and individual differences in intelligence-requiring tasks seems to be rather plausible (Criterion 5).

Specific Processing Properties That Are Located (Presumably) in Subsystems of the Human Brain

In recent years, attempts have been made to integrate many findings described in the literature by assuming that the efficiency of processing within a certain brain region, predominantly the frontal lobe system, is related to individual differences in general intelligence. Typical proponents of this new approach are Duncan (1995), who focused on the process of goal or action selection, and Dempster (1991, 1992), who stressed the role of inhibitory processing.

Description of the Goal-Selection Account.   Duncan and his colleagues (Duncan, 1995; Duncan, Emslie, & Williams, Johnson, & Freer, 1996; Duncan, Johnson, Swales, & Freer, 1997) have argued for a close relation between three empirical phenomena, behavioral deficits after frontal lobe lesions, individual differences in fluid intelligence, and performance costs in divided-attention tasks. Cognitive researchers often explain these observations by referring to a general distinction between automatic and controlled processing (e.g., Atkinson & Shiffrin, 1968; see also next section). Duncan (1995) suggested that a "process of goal or abstract action selection under conditions of novelty or weak environmental prompts to behavior" is related to all three phenomena (p. 721).

In his research, Duncan investigated goal-selection processes with a specific paradigm in which pairs of letters and digits are presented side by side on the computer screen. Participants are asked to read aloud, for instance, the digits either on the left or the right side. A cue in the middle of the screen indicates which side, left or right, should be read aloud. Duncan and colleagues use the term *goal neglect* to describe the disregard of certain task requirements (i.e., cues) that are observed in frontal lobe patients, and individuals with lower fluid intelligence, such as older adults compared to young adults (Duncan et al., 1996). Goal-neglect behavior is interpreted as a simple goal or task activation function that seems to have a central function in intellectual behavior. Similar theoretical considerations and empirical findings were recently provided by Engle, Tuholski, Laughlin, and Conway (1999). Engle et al. argued that individual differences in *g* are closely related to individual differences in keeping mental task representations active, especially in situations of interference, and that this type of processing is performed in the prefrontal subsystem.

Evaluation of the Goal-Selection Account. The theoretical view of Duncan and his colleagues is based on many empirical findings from different research areas, and relies on a consistent theoretical framework (Criterion 1). However, to investigate action–selection processing, Duncan and colleagues use only a single task, the goal-neglect paradigm. Clearly, the development of parallel versions or additional experimental tasks is necessary if the validity of the proposed construct is to be ensured.

Evaluation Criterion 2 concerns the use of multiple markers of *g*. For the present concept, the selection of IQ tests is problematic and has been shown to lead to inconsistent empirical findings. For example, on the one hand, empirical findings have indicated that executive or control functions are involved in measures of *g* and in so-called frontal lobe tests (Reitan & Wolfson, 1994; Tranel, Anderson, & Benton, 1994). On the other hand, there is also evidence that patients with frontal lobe damage show normal performance on psychometric intelligence tests (e.g., Shallice & Burgess, 1993). This apparent paradox was resolved by Duncan (1995; see also Duncan, Williams, Nimmo-Smith, & Brown, 1993) who demonstrated that patients with lesions in the frontal lobe often show low Raven scores but normal WAIS IQ scores. The WAIS measures aspects of both fluid and crystallized intelligence (Cattell, 1971; Horn, 1982). In contrast, the Raven's is a prototypical test of fluid intelligence (Marshalek et al., 1983). The obtained paradoxical finding points, of course, to a more general problem in the search for cognitive manifestations of g, namely the question of how g should be measured.

Little is known about the potential effect of third variables, such as individual differences in strategy use or practice and training, on the relation between goal selection and g (Criterion 3). In addition, longitudinal research designs that might clarify the assumed direction of causality have not been conducted yet (Criterion 4). Problematic is also the assumed association of goal selection with the frontal lobe system because there exists no accepted taxonomy of frontal lobe functioning. Recent neuropsychological studies seem to suggest that inhibition, switching, and goal maintenance are "located" in separate frontal subsystems (e.g., Fodor, 1983; Gazzaniga, 1989). At present, however, we still know little about the mapping of action selection or other executive functions to underlying brain subsystems (Baddeley, 1996; Duncan et al., 1996). Consequently, it is simply not possible (yet) to determine with certainty whether g is associated with a specific frontal subsystem or arises from the cooperative activity of distinct frontal subsystems (Duncan et al., 1996).

Description of the Inhibitory-Processing Account. Based on developmental changes in cognitive performance and neuropsychological observations of patients with lesions in the frontal cortex, some researchers consider the efficiency of inhibitory processing as a major determinant of g (Dempster, 1991, 1992; Hasher, Stoltzfus, Rypma, & Zacks, 1991; Zacks & Hasher, 1994). Inhibition is defined as the ability to activate task-relevant and to inhibit task-irrelevant information (Bjorklund & Harnishfeger, 1995). Evidence from neuroscience research has shown that brain functioning may indeed be based on two categories of mechanisms, inhibitory and excitatory.

A variety of tests, such as the Stroop Test (Stroop, 1935), seem to involve the ability to inhibit task-irrelevant information. However, correlations between these tests and typical IQ tests are rather low (Dempster, 1991). On the other hand, the ability to inhibit task-irrelevant information may be a critical component of traditional reasoning tasks. For instance, Marr and Sternberg (1986) found that intellectually nongifted students spend more time attending to irrelevant information than did intellectually gifted students.

Evaluation of the Inhibitory-Processing Account. Although individual differences in the efficiency of inhibitory processing may account for individual differences in intelligence, the construct has been relatively ignored by the intelligence research community. One reason for this lack of attention seems to be that there exists no generally accepted definition of *inhibition* in the current literature, and that it is probably not a unitary construct

(Criterion 1; Kane, Hasher, Stoltzfus, Zacks, & Conelly, 1994). In addition, the relation between activation processes (measured by reaction time) and inhibition processes (measured by reaction time differences) remains unclear. As already mentioned, the relation between *g* and reaction time becomes closer with increasing task complexity (Jensen, 1984; Larson & Saccuzzo, 1989, Vernon, 1987). Dempster (1992) suggested, in this context, that task complexity is often induced by dual-task conditions which imply an increase of interfering stimuli. Thus, dual-task measures may reflect the efficiency of inhibitory processing as well as speed of processing. Hence, proponents of the inhibition account to general intelligence provide no tasks that clearly represent the inhibition construct.

Researchers in this area typically use more than one IQ test to measure *g* (Criterion 2). However, only a few empirical studies relate "inhibition tasks" to standard measures of intelligence and the obtained empirical correlations are rather low. Not surprisingly, therefore, Criteria 3 and 4 are not met. Proponents of this approach often provide rational arguments for a relation between the efficiency of inhibitory processing and human intelligence that are based on advances in neuroscience and evolutionary considerations about the development of the brain, especially the frontal lobe. Nevertheless, it remains rather unclear which psychological tasks or tests should be taken to be predictors and which ones criteria.

Developmental Considerations

Why would it be useful to consider developmental changes in intellectual abilities if one is interested in understanding the nature of *g*? Developmental researchers have shown that changes in two components of intellectual abilities are not uniform, but multidirectional, across the life span (e.g., Baltes, Staudinger, Lindenberger, 1999). More specifically, many cross-sectional and longitudinal studies have demonstrated a decline of fluid intelligence (*g*) but stability or moderate increase of crystallized intelligence with increasing age (e.g., Schaie, 1996). To explain age-related decline in fluid intelligence (measured with traditional tests, such as the Raven's), most of the sources or abilities discussed earlier have been put forward (for a review, see Lindenberger & Baltes, 1994), such as age-related declines in (a) attentional resources (Craik, 1983; Craik & Byrd, 1982), (b) speed of information processing (Cerella, 1991, Lindenberger, Mayr, & Kliegl, 1993; Salthouse, 1991), (c) executive or control components (Frensch, Lindenberger, & Kray, 1999; Mayr & Kliegl, 1993; Kray & Lindenberger, 2000), and (d) efficiency of inhibitory processing (e.g., Dempster, 1992; Hasher et al., 1991; Zacks & Hasher, 1994). The critical question in most of these studies is which of the possible determinants is the best predictor, that is, explains most of the age-related variance in fluid intelligence.

A variety of empirical findings has indicated that speed of processing may be the single most important predictor of age-related decline in g (Cerella, 1991; Hartley, 1992; Salthouse, 1991). However, recent studies have shown that the magnitude of age-related decline in mental speed may not be constant across task and content conditions (Ferraro & Moody, 1996; Mayr & Kliegl, 1993; Lima, Hale, & Myerson, 1991). The question of whether mental speed is the sole source of, or whether other sources also have an impact on, age differences in g has fueled a general debate on many theoretical and methodological issues in cognitive aging research (e.g., Cerella, 1994; Fisk & Fisher, 1994; Kliegl, Mayr, & Krampe, 1994; Lindenberger & Pötter, 1998; Molenaar & van der Molen, 1994; Myerson, Wagstaff, & Hale, 1994; Perfect, 1994). The most recent consensus in the cognitive-aging community seems to be that (a) speed is an important source of age-associated decline in g but not the only one, and (b) a better research strategy is needed to determine the relative importance of possible sources underlying age differences in fluid intelligence (e.g., Lindenberger & Pötter, 1998).

The Differentiation Hypothesis.   As stated in the Introduction, one pattern of empirical findings that suggests, though does not prove, the existence of g, is a positive manifold. The developmental differentiation hypothesis, in contrast, assumes that individual differences in g vary as a function of ability level or age (e.g., Burt, 1954; Deary et al., 1996; Spearman, 1927). The terms *differentiation* and *dedifferentiation* mean that intellectual abilities are more differentiated in early and middle adulthood than in childhood or old age. Specifically, differentiation refers to the extent to which a general ability g explains variance among intellectual abilities (Lienert & Faber, 1963). Lienert and Faber (1963) observed a divergence of mental abilities, that is, higher correlations between mental abilities at lower IQ levels and higher ages (e.g., Lindenberger & Baltes, 1994; but see Kray & Lindenberger, 2000). Most empirical findings confirm the differentiation hypothesis that individual differences in g account for a greater amount of variance in psychometric test batteries at lower ability levels and at lower and higher age ranges (Carroll, 1993; Deary et al., 1996; Detterman & Daniel, 1989; Lynn, 1992). However, important for an interpretation of these findings is that the structure of intelligence and the reliability of measurement are comparable across ability levels and age. Empirical findings have demonstrated that the structure of intelligence does indeed not change with age (e.g., Bickley, Keith, & Wolfe, 1995), but most of the developmental studies are based on cross-sectional data. Thus, cross-validation analyses, and especially longitudinal research designs, are desperately needed to come to a conclusion on this particular issue.

Based on the empirical findings in the developmental literature, should we reject the assumption of *g*? It seems that we cannot. Theoretical accounts of the differentiation of intellectual abilities have been provided that are consistent with the assumption of a general ability *g*. For instance, higher correlations among mental abilities are explained by the low efficiency of general cognitive processes. In contrast, lower correlations among mental abilities are explained by a higher efficiency of general cognitive processes, and therefore performance in particular tasks is more influenced by the efficiency of specific processes. For instance, Anderson (1992) proposed a model of two mechanisms, a Basis Processing Mechanism (BPM) and Specific Processors (SP). The BPM as a general mechanism constraints the operations of all specific processors when the speed of the BPM is slowed (see also Spearman, 1927).

Summary

In this section we discussed some of the most important theoretical approaches that have been taken to capture the nature of *g*. The various approaches differ with regard to the properties of the information-processing system they consider essential for capturing *g* (i.e., structural, general processing, strategy, or functional subsystem). None of the concepts that have been proposed meets all five criteria we applied (cf. Table 8.1).

Theoretical Status of the Proposed Accounts. Most of the theoretical accounts have a more or less convincing theoretical rationale. Where limitations of the offered rationale exist, they often are related to (a) the lack of a clear definition of the account (e.g., attentional resource or inhibition), and (b) low validity (e.g., inspection time, goal selection; Deary & Stough, 1996). Psychometric and experimental tasks are often used as indicators of individual differences in hypothetical constructs that generally involve a relatively complex sequence of processes. For instance, traditional perceptual speed tests measure not only speed of processing; they also measure the ability to coordinate visual and working memory processes (Laux & Lane, 1985; Lindenberger et al., 1993). As a result, "the search for a 'true' single information-processing function underlying intelligence is as likely to be successful as the search for the Holy Grail" (Hunt, 1980, p. 457).

*Psychometric **g** as Dependent Variable.* Neisser (1979) already pointed to the need to overcome Boring's definition of intelligence, namely, that intelligence is what the tests measure. Correlational approaches to understanding the nature of *g* are used almost exclusively in the research discussed earlier. These approaches search for high correlations between scores on a hypothetical construct and scores on general intelligence tests. The correlations obtained, however, cannot be interpreted unless one accepts that the intelligence tests indeed measure intelligence (see Neisser, 1979).

Most of the empirical studies reviewed here try to measure intelligence via multiple indicators, that is, they typically use the Raven's, WAIS, and other tests. The selection of traditional IQ tests can be a fundamental problem in this research, as has been amply demonstrated by the paradoxical finding of Duncan. The paradoxical finding can be resolved when one considers that different IQ tests measure different aspects of intelligence.

The Influence of Third Variables.   Only for some of the discussed theoretical accounts are possible alternative sources of individual differences that might affect the amount of variance in g explained by the proposed construct empirically examined. When this is done, researchers typically examine the influence of individual differences in strategy choice, training, or pre-experimental knowledge.

The Direction of Causality.   Although in all theoretical accounts it is assumed that the proposed construct is the source rather than the consequence of human intelligence, most of the reported empirical findings are based on cross-sectional studies. There exist only a few longitudinal studies (e.g., Deary, 1995). Longitudinal research is, however, needed to (a) clarify the direction of causality, and (b) determine the relative impact of the proposed construct to individual differences in g (see also Lindenberger & Pötter, 1998).

Plausibility of the Theoretical Relation Between the Proposed Construct and g.   One of the main difficulties in finding determinants of human intelligence consists of coming up with theoretical accounts that capture the full range of intelligent behavior. Thus, the proposed construct should be not too specific (e.g., visual inspection time) but also not too broad (attentional resources) to be considered a serious candidate for capturing the essence of g. Many of the accounts discussed earlier fall way short on this criterion.

In the next and final section of this chapter, we discuss some of the prominent modern theoretical conceptions, or models, of the human (cognitive) mind. Our goal is to examine to what extent a general ability g has been realized in the proposed functioning of the human cognitive system.

MODERN THEORIES OF COGNITION

Which mechanisms or mental processes underlie human intelligence? Modern theories of the human mind focus their theoretical considerations and empirical research on the question of whether intelligent behavior is the result of processing in more or less independent subsystems or whether it is the result of processing within an integrated whole. It seems that modern approaches have undergone a similar development as have traditional approaches to the understanding of human intelligence. At the beginning of differential research on intelligence, the focus was on providing a taxonomy of mental abilities that best describe the construct of intelligence. The seemingly endless debate about what the best methods and models to describe intelligence are has led to a decline of interest among many researchers in the area. Interests shifted toward the search for mental processes that might underlie intelligent behavior. Similarly, research in the field of Cognitive Psychology has shifted from a focus on the architecture of the information-processing system toward a focus on the questions of (a) how cognitive processes are controlled or organized, and (b) what exactly it is that turns a cognitive architecture into an intelligent system.

The debate about whether a single component or multiple components underlie intelligent behavior is cast in modern cognitive models as a debate about the modularity or unitary of the human mind. Following, we discuss two modern approaches that provide explanations for intelligent behavior—attentional control models and computer simulation models. The two approaches differ in their conceptualization of intelligent behavior. In theories of attentional control, higher level processing allows for the flexible and adaptive response to continuous and multiple changes in the environment, the maintaining of goal-relevant activities, and the inhibition of irrelevant activities. Such cognitive activity is usually subsumed under the headings of (intentional) control processes or central executive processes. To control its own processing, a cognitive system must be able to (a) represent alternative activities and their consequences; (b) plan, select, and organize cognitive operations; and (c) monitor the execution of those activities (for reviews, see Goschke, 1996; Kluwe, 1997). The benefit of intention control is that the regulation of behavior can occur independently of changes in the environment or motivational states in the organism. One of the mysteries of intelligence is that intelligent systems find a balance between attending to external cues from the environment and integrating external information with current internal goals or intentions. That is, the system "knows" which is the most appropriate task or action (operation) to perform at the present time.

Cognitive researchers who strongly rely on the computer metaphor, such as Newell, Rosenbloom, and Laird (1989), defined intelligence in terms of characteristics that an intelligent system (i.e., a computer simulation) should be capable of showing. The system should be able to (a) be flexible as a result of rapid changes in the environment, (b) be adaptive in the sense of demonstrating goal-directed behavior, (c) operate in complex and detailed environments, that is, perceive an immense amount of changing details, (d) use a mass of knowledge, (e) control the motor systems to various degrees of freedom, (f) form symbols and abstractions, (g) use language, (h) learn from the environment and experience, (i) acquire abilities through development, and so on.

Our main goal in this section is to review and discuss the extent to which a general ability g has been conceptualized in modern models of attentional control and in computer simulation models of the cognitive system.

Models of Attentional Control

Theoretical Considerations. Many cognitive researchers assume that control processes are required in intelligence-demanding situations, such as learning responses that require novel sequences of actions, overcoming strong habitual responses or prepotent response tendencies, planning, error correction, generating action choices, and decision making in difficult situations (Allport, 1993; Jonides & Smith, 1997; Shallice & Burgess, 1993). Note that this list comes quite close to Duncan's view that cognitive control processes are concerned with problems of goal or action selection under conditions of novelty or weak environmental cuing of appropriate behavior (Duncan, 1995; see previous section).

Several models of cognitive control have been proposed in recent years, such as the Two-Process Model of Atkinson and Shiffrin (1968), the Working-Memory Model of Baddeley (1986), the Supervisory System of Norman and Shallice (1986), and the Executive-Process/Interactive-Control (EPIC) architecture recently promoted by Meyer et al. (1995). What these models have in common is that they propose a functional distinction between two different classes of cognitive processes: control or executive processes, on the one hand, and automatic, stimulus-triggered processes, on the other hand. Control processes are generally characterized as active, slow, capacity-limited, and effortful. Additionally, they are often associated with voluntary, intentional, or conscious aspects of human behavior. In contrast, automatic processes are characterized as fast, parallel, and effortless (Atkinson & Shiffrin, 1968; Baddeley, 1994, 1995; Norman & Shallice, 1986; Schneider & Shiffrin, 1977).

Thus, in most modern theories, intelligent behavior is conceptualized as resulting from efficient control processing in a capacity-limited central system, such as Baddeley's (1986) "central executive" or Shallice's (Norman & Shallice, 1986) Supervisory Attentional System. For instance, within the framework offered by Norman and Shallice, behavior is based on the selection and activation of action schemata. Schemata are usually triggered automatically by external cues, and compete with one another, with the most dominant schema determining the actual behavior (i.e., contention scheduling). The supervisory attentional system modulates contention scheduling through top-down activation. The biasing of contention scheduling is necessary in situations of novel environmental cues or inappropriately activated schemata (Shallice, 1992, 1994).

The most convincing empirical evidence for the assumption of a unitary, capacity-limited executive system sensu Norman and Shallice comes from neuropsychological observations of patients with lesions in the frontal cortex (Reitan & Wolfson, 1994; Shallice, 1994; Shallice & Burgess, 1993; Tranel et al., 1994). A typical example of failures in control functions is the "utilization behavior" demonstrated by frontal lobe patients (Lhermitte, 1983). These patients are often unable to inhibit entire action patterns (schemata) associated with everyday objects.

Contrary to the theoretical view of a unitary, capacity-limited system, proponents of the "late-selection-theory" assume that the capacity of the cognitive system is limited by problems in the "selection-for-actions" (Allport, 1987; Neumann, 1987, 1992). According to these authors, the cognitive system is limited by the interplay between sensory information and action planning. Two selection mechanisms are relevant in this context: First, the system must decide from one moment to the next which action needs to be performed. Second, the system needs to decide where the action is to be directed. Allport (1987) argued that the limitation on the simultaneous control of independent actions by different sensory inputs is dependent on the difficulty of preventing crosstalk between streams of information. Allport, Styles, and Hsieh (1994) further elaborated the hypothesis of decentralized and distributed control. Specifically, these authors suggested "that voluntary or intentional control of task set is realized through interactions among a variety of functionally specialized components, each responsible for specific features of executive control" (Allport et al., 1994, p. 432). Hence, *g* is realized in this model in terms of an interaction between independent functionally specialized subsystems.

Empirical evidence supporting these theoretical assumptions comes from neuropsychological research (see next subsection) and experimental studies (Allport et al., 1972; Meyer et al., 1995). For instance, using the psychological refractory-period procedure (PRP), Meyer et al. (1995) obtained evidence that two tasks can be executed without between-task interference for many experimental manipulations, which is inconsistent with the notion of a bottleneck at the central level of the human cognitive system. Based on these empirical findings, Meyer et al. (1995) proposed a new theoretical framework based on two basic assumptions, (1) cognitive capacity is not limited when multiple concurrent tasks are performed, and (2) decrements in multiple-task performance are attributable to interference in peripheral sensory and motor mechanisms.

Neuropsychological Research. Researchers like Duncan (1995) or Dempster (1992) have suggested a close relation between general intelligence *g* and executive control functions associated with the frontal lobe area in the human brain. To clarify whether cognitive control processing is attributed to the frontal lobe area, a variety of neuropsychological studies have been conducted in recent years, either using data from PET or rCFB studies or collecting behavioral data from patients showing lesions in a certain area of the frontal lobe.

Neuropsychological studies strongly suggest that the prefrontal, dorsolateral cortex is involved in the selection and generation of human behavior. PET studies show an increase of activation in prefrontal lobe areas, for instance, in fluency tasks (Frith, Friston, Liddle, & Frackowiak, 1991) that are assumed to involve the internal control of cognitive processing. Moreover, neuropsychological observations of patients with lesions in the frontal cortex indicate (a) typical control failures, such as the "utilization behavior" (see earlier; Lhermitte, 1983; Shallice, 1988) or perseveration errors (Anderson, Damasio, Jones, & Tranel, 1991; Milner, 1965), (b) impairments in planning (Stuss & Benson, 1986) or prospective memory tasks (Shallice & Burgess, 1993), and (c) performance deficits in various so-called *frontal lobe tests* (Reitan & Wolfson, 1994; Shallice, 1994; Tranel et al., 1994).

Evidence from these studies strongly supports the notion that a possible source of intelligent behavior is the efficiency to execute or control cognitive processing, which is primarily associated with the prefrontal lobe subsystem. Nevertheless, there are major methodological and theoretical problems with this approach. First, most neuropsychological tests (i.e., frontal lobe tests) developed to measure executive/control function deficits in the frontal lobe have only face validity, and only few attempts have been made to support other aspects of validity (e.g., construct validity). Second, not all patients with frontal lobe lesions show impairments on tasks and tests supposed to be indicative of frontal-lobe functioning; that is, current neuropsychological tests and cognitive tasks have failed to demonstrate high sensitivity in the assessment of frontal lobe dysfunction (Reitan & Wolfson, 1994). Third, executive functions and frontal lobe functions are often only loosely defined, and the two terms are used interchangeably without further clarification (e.g., Tranel et al., 1994). In light of the problems identifying neuroanatomical correlates of cognitive control functions, Baddeley (1996) explicitly proposed not to use "anatomical localizations as a defining criterion for the central executive" (p. 7). Finally, some researchers in this field suggest that the frontal lobe system may involve separate functions for the regulation of human intelligent behavior, such as selection for action, planning, monitoring, stopping, activation, and inhibition of schemata (Jonides & Smith, 1997; Shallice & Burgess, 1993).

Hence, cognitive neuroscientists argue that it is very implausible that only one unitary subsystem in the cerebral cortex is responsible for the organization of higher level processing (Allport et al., 1994; Fodor, 1983; Gazzaniga, 1989). They propose an alternative view, that of multiple, specialized subsystems within the frontal lobe system that are required to interact to produce human intelligent behavior. Recent neuropsychological evidence has supported the existence of multiple, specialized, and parallel subsystems in the frontal cortex. Dissociations between conscious and unconscious information processing, such as are observed with blind sight patients (Weiskrantz, 1986), are consistent with a theoretical view of specialized subsystems.

Still, serious problems associated with the interpretation of neuropsychological research methods remain. For instance, the interpretation of activation patterns of PET scans is sometimes difficult because most studies use tasks that compare externally triggered behavior with internally triggered behavior. The tasks compared often differ in many aspects, such as in working memory demands or the retrieval of semantic information, which could affect the observed activation patterns (Buckner & Tulving, 1995). Furthermore, cognitive tasks typically do not only activate regions of the frontal lobe but activate also different regions within the cortex, or different cognitive tasks lead to activation of the same area in the frontal lobe. The only common single attribute of those tasks seems to be that they are new, unusual human activities (see Frith & Grasby, 1995).

Computer Simulation Models

Some cognitive scientists have argued that computer simulations can be useful for constructing theories of human intelligence. Just like in the attentional theories discussed earlier, the regulation of intelligent behavior in the computer simulation model of Newell and Simon (1972), to take an early example, is limited by a central component, a program called *central executive*, that organizes the interplay of different heuristics within the information-processing system. The introduction of an additional organization, called control structure, in the system was useful to compare behavior on diverse tasks (Newell, 1973). By comparison, Anderson's model of the cognitive architecture, Adaptive Control of Thought (ACT), does not include such a control structure. Nevertheless, Anderson (1983) argued that the control of higher level processing and the principles underlying control are some of the most important issues to be dealt with in Cognitive Psychology. In his production-system framework (Anderson, 1983), the control of actions occurs as a choice of which production (condition-action pairs) to execute next. Productions are triggered either by external stimuli or by internal goals. Conflicts between two simultaneously activated production rules are resolved by five conflict resolution strategies (degree of match, production strength, data refractoriness, specificity, goal dominance) which modulate the activation levels and selection probabilities of these productions. The notion of many powerful special-purpose "peripheral" systems for processing perceptual information and coordination motor performance is inconsistent with the theoretical assumption of a central system underlying human intelligence. Similar cognitive architectures have been proposed, such as the general problem-solving systems (e.g., Newell & Simon, 1972), general interference systems (e.g., McDermott & Doyle, 1980), and general schema systems (e.g., Schank & Abelson, 1977). All in all, the cognitive architecture proposed by Anderson (1983) seems to be very powerful for explaining human intelligent behavior because a single set of principles simulates cognitive performance across many computational tasks.

SOAR is a cognitive architecture that was specifically developed with the purpose to model human intelligence. Laird, Newell, and Rosenbloom (1991) state that "the goal is to provide the underlying structure that would enable the system to perform the full range of cognitive tasks, employ the full range of problem solving methods and representations appropriate for the tasks, and learn about all aspects of the tasks and its performance on them" (p. 463). Like Anderson (1983), Laird et al. (1991) conceptualized the brain (system) as a functional whole. Central assumptions of SOAR are that (1) intelligent behavior is based on a physical symbol system, (2) there is a single, universal architecture, a long-term memory, and a learning mechanism; and (3) the architecture consists of a set of orthogonal mechanisms.

Some central assumptions of SOAR as a cognitive architecture modeling intelligent behavior have been criticized (cf. Norman, 1991). First, it seems implausible that a single computational architecture underlies all subsystems in the human brain, such as the cortex, the cerebellum, or the thalamus. Second, there exists empirical evidence against the assumption of a single memory system, such as a functional distinction between episodic and semantic memory (Tulving, 1983) or a distinction between declarative and nondeclarative memory systems (Squire & Zola-Morgan, 1988; but see Greene, 1992). Third, the fathers of SOAR postulated only one common learning mechanism—chunking—that is quite powerful in learning. Nevertheless, other computational systems that use more than one learning mechanism are much more powerful in the ability to learn across a wide variety of tasks.

In sum, computer simulation models provide a theoretical structure of how human intelligence might operate. In contrast to Anderson's cognitive architecture, SOAR is based on one single computational structure that is assumed to efficiently run a system that involves abilities such as perception, motor control, and problem solving. We believe that the notion of a single computational structure is rather implausible partly because it makes a cognitive system very slow and inefficient. This inefficiency is quite inconsistent with the definition of human intelligent behavior as flexible and adaptive to rapid changes in the environment.

SUMMARY AND CONCLUSIONS

On the basis of our discussion of the various theoretical attempts to capture the essence of *g* (see pp. 190ff), can we say that Cognitive Psychology has produced compelling theoretical and empirical evidence supporting the assumption of a general intelligence *g*? Although many, if not most, of the proposed explanatory concepts discussed here show moderate to substantial correlations with intelligence-test performance, we are in agreement with Hunt (1980) that "the argument between the generalist and the specialist view does, at times, take some of the aspects of an argument over whether a glass is half full or half empty" (p. 466). Researchers preferring a strict interpretation of *g* (see p. 184) often interpret correlations between their proposed construct and psychometric test performance that are above .4 as supporting their view (Hunt, 1980). On the other hand, researchers opposing a strict interpretation of *g* often interpret correlations of less than .2 in favor of their own view. Needless to say that, in light of these controversial discussions, the magnitude of obtained empirical correlations cannot be taken as a reasonable basis for evaluating the appropriateness of the many differing accounts of what the cognitive manifestation of *g* might be. For this reason, we chose five different evaluation criteria. None of the information-processing concepts that we considered meets all five criteria. Therefore, none of the accounts discussed can be considered a cognitive manifestation of *g*.

In the final section, we reviewed the extent to which two complete modern theories of cognition conceptualize a general ability *g*. We argued that the long historic controversy regarding the nature of *g* manifests itself in these theories as a debate about the modularity or unitary of the human mind. Those participating in this controversy are in agreement that limitations in information processing exist, but strongly disagree about their location and character. In some models of cognitive control, for instance, it is assumed that the capacity of the cognitive system is limited at a central level (e.g., Baddeley, 1986; Norman & Shallice, 1986). In contrast, in other models, it is hypothesized that the capacity of the cognitive system is limited at a peripheral level (e.g., at the motor level; Meyer et al., 1995). In recent years, more and more cognitive researchers turn to neuro-physiological and neuropsychological research methods to clarify the question of the modularity unity of the human mind. Although there exists neuropsychological evidence for both views on the human mind, the notion of multiple, specialized subsystems in cognitive functioning seems to be the more plausible one. The use of neuropsychological research methods is still plagued, however, by serious problems in the interpretation of data. Any conclusion regarding the modularity of the mind should therefore be taken with extreme caution.

Computer simulation models can be useful tools for constructing theories about general intelligence. We have argued that in computer-simulation frameworks, the debate about how human behavior is controlled mirrors the debate discussed for attentional control models. Laird et al. (1991), for instance, suggest a single, unitary architecture for human intelligence, whereas Anderson (1983) proposes multiple, specialized subsystems. To us, the latter approach seems to be more plausible. Nevertheless, we are also in agreement with Neisser (1979) who prophesied that,

> different intelligent behaviors may be based on the same underlying processes. Cognitive researchers may indeed be successful in identifying those processes, and thus account for some of the observable correlations among the attributes of intelligence. Such research is certainly worth pursuing. We must be wary, however, of believing that it will enable us to define intelligence itself. Otherwise, we may find ourselves acting on a new scenario in the year 2000, when someone defines intelligence as what the model models. (Neisser, 1979, p. 226)

RECOMMENDATIONS FOR FUTURE WORK

First, we believe it to be useful to combine an individual-differences approach with the mainstream cognitive approach, an idea originally proposed by Cronbach (1957), but still rarely realized. Indeed, any good theory about human intelligence needs to explain both, the results of experimental manipulations and individual differences (see Cohen, 1994; Eysenck, 1995). This is especially important if there exists a single underlying mechanism, a general factor g. Most empirical approaches discussed in this chapter use either experimental methods or test for individual differences, but rarely are the two methods used in conjunction.

Second, we also believe it to be helpful to apply neuroscientific research methods if a better understanding of intelligent behavior is to be gained and the unitary or modularity of mind to be clarified. In this context, Dempster doubts that the currently favored computer metaphor of the human mind will lead to an understanding of human intelligence. Dempster (1991) argued that "the critical complement to behavioral evidence in the study of human intelligence are constructs consistent with what is known about cerebral structure and function" (p. 168). Indeed, in recent years, more and more cognitive researchers stress the necessity for modern theories to formulate ideas about human behavior that are neurologically plausible (Allport, 1987; Jensen, 1984; Meyer et al., 1995). Regardless of which route is taken, understanding human intelligence demands an understanding of the mechanisms underlying intelligent behavior. As long as we do not understand this point, we shall always end where we started.

REFERENCES

Ackerman, P. L. (1986). Individual differences in information processing: An investigation of intellectual abilities and task performance during practice. *Intelligence, 10*, 101–139.

Ackerman, P. L. (1988). Determinants of individual differences during skill acquisition: Cognitive abilities and information processing. *Journal of Experimental Psychology: General, 117*, 288–318.

Allport, A. (1987). Selection-for-action: Some behavioral and neurophysiological considerations of attention and action. In H. Heuer & A. F. Sanders (Eds.), *Perspectives on perception and action* (pp. 395–419). Hillsdale, NJ: Lawrence Erlbaum Associates.

Allport, A. (1993). Attention and control: Have we been asking the wrong questions? A critical review of twenty-five years. In D. E. Meyer & S. Kornblum (Eds.), *Attention and performance XIV* (pp. 183–218). Cambridge, MA: Bradford.

Allport, A., Styles, E. A., & Hsieh, S. (1994). Shifting intentional set: Exploring the dynamic control of tasks. In C. Umiltà & M. Moscovitch (Eds.), *Attention and Performance XV*. Cambridge: Bradford.

Allport, D. A., Antonis, B., & Reynolds, P. (1972). On the division of attention: A disproof of the single channel hypothesis. *Quarterly Journal of Experimental Psychology, 24*, 225–235.

Anderson, J. R. (1983). *The architecture of cognition*. Cambridge, MA: Harvard University Press.

Anderson, M. (1992). *Intelligence and development: A cognitive theory*. Oxford, England: Blackwell.

Anderson, S. W., Damasio, H., Jones, R. D., & Tranel, D. (1991). Wisconsin Card Sorting Test performance as a measure of frontal lobe damage. *Journal of Clinical Experimental Neuropsychology, 13*, 487–495.

Atkinson, R. C., & Shiffrin, R. M. (1968). Human memory: A proposed system and its control processes. In K. W. Spence & T. J. Spence (Eds.), *The psychology of learning and motivation: Advances in research and theory* (Vol. 2, pp. 89–105). New York: Academic Press.

Baddeley, A. (1986). *Working memory*. Oxford, England: Clarendon Press.

Baddeley, A. (1994). Working memory: The interface between memory and cognition. In D. L. Schacter & E. Tulving (Eds.), *Memory systems 1994*. Cambridge, MA: Bradford.

Baddeley, A. (1995). Working memory. In M. S. Gazzaniga (Ed.), *The cognitive neurosciences*. Cambridge, MA: Bradford.

Baddeley, A. (1996). Exploring the central executive. *The Quarterly Journal of Experimental Psychology, 49*, 5–28.

Baltes, P. B., Staudinger, U. M., & Lindenberger, U. (1999). Lifespan psychology: Theory and application to intellectual functioning. *Annual Review of Psychology, 50*, 471–507.

Bates, T. C., & Eysenck, H. J. (1993). Intelligence, inspection time, and decision time. *Intelligence, 17*, 523–531.

Bickley, P. G., Keith, T. Z., & Wolfle, L. M. (1995). The three-stratum theory of cognitive abilities: Test of the structure of intelligence across the life span. *Intelligence, 20*, 309–328.

Bjorklund, D. F., & Harnishfeger, K. K. (1995). The evolution of inhibition mechanisms and their role in human cognition and behavior. In F. N. Dempster & C. J. Brainerd (Eds.), *New perspectives on interference and inhibition in cognition* (pp. 141–173). New York: Academic Press.

Brand, C., & Deary, I. J. (1982). Intelligence and "inspection time." In H. J. Eysenck (Ed.), *A model for intelligence* (pp. 133–148). Berlin, Germany: Springer-Verlag.

Brown, A. (1987). Metacognition, executive control, self-regulation, and other more mysterious mechanisms. In F. E. Weinert & R. H. Kluwe (Eds.), *Metacognition, motivation, and understanding* (pp. 65–116). Hillsdale, NJ: Lawrence Erlbaum Associates.

Brown, A. L., Bransford, J. D., Ferrera, R. A., & Campione, J. C. (1983). Learning, remembering, and understanding. In J. H. Flavell & E. M. Markham (Eds.), *Handbook of child psychology* (pp. 77–166). New York: Wiley.

Buckner, R. L., & Tulving, E. (1995). Neuroimaging studies of memory: Theory and recent neuropsychology. In F. Boller & J. Grafman (Eds.), *Handbook of neuropsychology* (Vol. 10, pp. 439–466). Amsterdam: Elsevier.

Burt, C. (1954). The differentiation of intellectual ability. *British Journal of Educational Psychology, 24*, 76–90.

Campione, J. C., & Brown, A. L. (1978). Toward a theory of intelligence: Contributions from research with retarded children. *Intelligence, 2*, 279–304.

Campione, J. C., Brown, A. L., & Ferrara, R. (1982). Mental retardation and intelligence. In R. J. Sternberg (Ed.), *Handbook of human intelligence* (pp. 392–490). Cambridge, England: Cambridge University Press.

Carroll, J. B. (1991). No demonstration that *g* is not unitary, but there's more to the story: Comment on Kranzler and Jensen. *Intelligence, 15*, 423–436.

Carroll, J. B. (1993). *Human cognitive abilities: A survey of factor-analytic studies* Cambridge, England: Cambridge University Press.

Cattell, R. B. (1971). *Abilities: Their structure, growth, and action*. Boston: Houghton Mifflin.

Ceci, S. J. (1990). On the relation between microlevel processing efficiency and macrolevel measures of intelligence—Some arguments against current reductionism. *Intelligence, 14*, 141–150.

Cerella, J. (1991). Age effects may be global, not local: Comments on Fisk and Rogers (1991). *Journal of Experimental Psychology: General, 120*, 215–223.

Cerella, J. (1994). Generalized slowing in Brinley plots. *Journal of Gerontology: Psychological Sciences, 49*, 65–71.

Cohen, R. L. (1994). Some thoughts on individual differences and theory construction. *Intelligence, 18*, 3–13.

Craik, F. I. M. (1983). On the transfer of information from temporary to permanent memory. *Philosophical Transactions of the Royal Society of London, 302*, 341–359.

Craik, F. I. M., & Byrd, M. (1982). Aging and cognitive deficits: The role of attentional resources. In F. I. M. Craik & S. Trehub (Eds.), *Aging and cognitive processes* (pp. 191–211). New York: Plenum.

Cronbach, L. J. (1957). The two disciplines of scientific psychology. *The American Psychologist,* *12*, 671–684.

Deary, I. J. (1995). Auditory inspection time and intelligence: What is the direction of causation. *Developmental Psychology, 31,* 237–250.

Deary, I. J. (1999). Intelligence and visual and auditory information processing. In P. L. Ackerman, P. C. Kyllonen, & R. T. Roberts (Eds.), *Learning and individual differences: Process, trait, and content determinants* (pp. 111–130). Washington, DC: American Psychological Association.

Deary, I. J., Egan, V., Gibson, G. J., Austin, E. J., Brand, C. R., & Kellaghan, T. (1996). Intelligence and the differentiation hypothesis. *Intelligence, 23,* 105–132.

Deary, I. J., & Stough, C. (1996). Intelligence and inspection time: Achievements, prospects, and problems. *American Psychologist, 51,* 599–608.

Dempster, F. N. (1991). Inhibitory processes: A neglected dimension of intelligence. *Intelligence, 15,* 157–173.

Dempster, F. N. (1992). The rise and fall of the inhibitory mechanism: Toward a unified theory of cognitive development and aging. *Developmental Review, 12,* 45–75.

Detterman, D. K., & Daniel, M. H. (1989). Correlations of mental tests with each other and with cognitive variables are highest for low-IQ groups. *Intelligence, 13,* 349–359.

Diamond, S. (1997). Frances Galton and American psychology. In L. T. Benjamin Jr. (Ed.), *A history of psychology: Original sources and contemporary research* (2nd ed., pp. 231–239). Boston: McGraw-Hill.

Duncan, J. (1995). Attention, intelligence, and the frontal lobes. In M. S. Gazzaniga (Ed.), *The cognitive neurosciences* (pp. 721–733). Cambridge, MA: MIT Press.

Duncan, J., Emslie, H., Williams, P., Johnson, R., & Freer, P. (1996). Intelligence and the frontal lobe: The organization of goal-directed behavior. *Cognitive Psychology, 30,* 257–303.

Duncan, J., Johnson, R., Swales, M., & Freer, C. (1997). Frontal lobe deficits after head injury: Unity and diversity of function. *Cognitive Neuropsychology, 14,* 713–741.

Duncan, J., Williams, P., Nimmo-Smith, I., & Brown, I. (1993). The control of skilled behavior: Learning, intelligence, and distraction. In D. E. Meyer & S. Kornblum (Eds.), *Attention and performance XIV* (pp. 323–341). Cambridge, MA: The MIT Press.

Egan, V. (1994). Intelligence, inspection time, and cognitive strategies. *British Journal of Psychology, 85,* 305–316.

Engle, R. W., Tuholski, S. W., Laughlin, J. E., & Conway, A. R. (1999). Working memory, short-term memory, and general fluid intelligence: A latent-variable approach. *Journal of Experimental Psychology: General, 128,* 309–331.

Evans, G., & Nettelbeck, T. (1993). Inspection time: A flash mask to reduce apparent movement effects. *Personality and Individual Differences, 15,* 91–94.

Eysenck, H. J. (1992). Intelligence: The one and the many. In D. K. Detterman (Ed.), *Current topics in human intelligence: Is mind modular or unitary?* (pp. 82–116). Norwood, NJ: Ablex.

Eysenck, H. J. (1995). Can we study intelligence using the experimental method? *Intelligence, 20,* 217–228.

Eysenck, H. J. (1998). *Intelligence. A new look.* New Brunswick, NJ: Transaction.

Ferraro, F. R., & Moody, J. (1996). Consistent and inconsistent performance in young and elderly adults. *Developmental Neuropsychology, 12,* 429–441.

Fisk, A. D., & Fisher, D. L. (1994). Brinley plots and theories of aging: The explicit, muddled, and implicit debates. *Journals of Gerontology, 49,* 81–89.

Fodor, J. A. (1983). *The modularity of mind.* Cambridge, MA: MIT Press.

Fogarthy, G., & Stankov, L. (1982). Competing tasks as an index of intelligence. *Personality and Individual Differences, 3,* 407–422.

Frensch, P. A., Lindenberger, U., & Kray, J. (1999). Imposing structure on an unstructured environment: Ontogenetic changes in the ability to form rules of behavior under conditions of low environmental predictability. In A. Friederici & R. Menzel (Eds.), *Learning: Rule extraction and representation* (pp. 139–162). Berlin, Germany: De Gruyter.

Frith, C. D., Friston, K. J., Liddle, P. F., & Frackowiak, R. S. J. (1991). A PET study of word finding. *Neuropsychologia, 29,* 1137–1148.

Frith, C. D., & Grasby, P. M. (1995). rCBF studies of prefrontal function and their relevance to psychosis. In F. Boller & J. Grafman (Eds.), *Handbook of neuropsychology* (Vol. 10, pp. 383–403). Amsterdam: Elsevier.

Gardner, H. (1983). *Frames of mind: The theory of multiple intelligences.* New York: Basic Books.

Gazzaniga, M. S. (1989). Organization of the human brain. *Science, 245,* 947–952.

Goschke, T. (1996). Wille und Kognition: Zur funktionalen Architektur der intentionalen Handlungssteuerung [Will and cognition: On the functional architecture of intentional action control]. In J. Kuhl & H. Heckhausen (Eds.), *Motivation, Volition und Handlung [Motivation, volition, and behavior]* (pp. 583–663). Göttingen: Hogrefe.

Greene, R. L. (1992). Unitary and modular approaches to human memory. In D. K. Detterman (Ed.), *Current topics in human intelligence: Is mind modular or unitary?* (pp. 231–250). Norwood, NJ: Ablex.

Guyote, M. J., & Sternberg, R. J. (1981). A transitive-chain theory of syllogistic reasoning. *Cognitive Psychology, 13,* 461–525.

Hartley, A. A. (1992). Attention. In F. I. M. Craik & T. A. Salthouse (Eds.), *The handbook of aging and cognition.* Hillsdale, NJ: Lawrence Erlbaum Associates.

Hasher, L., Stoltzfus, E., Rypma, B., & Zacks, R. (1991). Age and inhibition. *Journal of Experimental Psychology, 17,* 163–169.

Haygood, R. C., & Johnson, D. F. (1983). Focus shift and individual differences in the Sternberg memory-search task. *Acta Psychologica, 53,* 129–139.

Horn, J. L. (1982). The theory of fluid and crystallized intelligence in relation to concepts of cognitive psychology and aging in adulthood. In F. I. M. Craik & S. Trehub (Eds.), *Aging and cognitive processes* (pp. 237–278). New York: Plenum Press.

Howe, M. J. A. (1988). Intelligence as an explanation. *British Journal of Psychology, 79,* 349–360.

Hunt, E. (1980). Intelligence as an information-processing concept. *British Journal of Psychology, 71,* 449–474.

Hunt, E., Pellegrino, J. W., & Yee, P. L. (1989). Individual differences in attention. In G. Bower (Ed.), *The Psychology of learning and motivation: Advances in research and theory* (pp. 285–310). Orlando, FL: Academic Press.

Hunt, E. B., & Lansman, M. (1982). Individual differences in attention. In R. J. Sternberg (Ed.), *Advances in psychology of human intelligence* (Vol. 1, pp. 207–254). Hillsdale, NJ: Lawrence Erlbaum Associates.

Jensen, A. R. (1984). Test validity: g versus the specificity doctrine. *Journal of Social Biological Structures, 7,* 93–118.

Jensen, A. R. (1987). Psychometric g as a focus of concerted research effort. *Intelligence, 11,* 193–198.

Jensen, A. R., & Weng, L. -J. (1994). What is a good g? *Intelligence, 18,* 231–258.

Jonides, J., & Smith, E. F. (1997). The architecture of working memory. In E. D. Rugg (Ed.), *Cognitive neuroscience. Studies in cognition* (pp. 243–276). Cambridge, MA: MIT Press.

Kahneman, D. (1973). *Attention and effort.* Englewood Cliffs, NJ: Prentice-Hall.

Kane, M., Hasher, L., Stoltzfus, E., Zacks, R., & Conelly, S. (1994). Inhibitory attentional mechanisms and aging. *Psychology and Aging, 9,* 103–112.

Keating, D. P., & Bobbitt, B. L. (1978). Individual and developmental differences in cognitive-processing components of mental ability. *Child Development, 49,* 155–167.

Kliegl, R., Mayr, U., & Krampe, R. T. (1994). Time-accuracy functions for determining process and person differences: An application to cognitive aging. *Cognitive Psychology, 26,* 134–164.

Kluwe, R. H. (1997). Intentionale Steuerung kognitiver Prozesse [Intentional control of cognitive processing]. *Kognitionswissenschaft, 6,* 53–69.

Kranzler, J. H., & Jensen, A. R. (1991). The nature of psychometric *g*: Unitary process or a number of independent processes? *Intelligence, 15,* 397–422.

Kray, J., & Lindenberger, U. (2000). Adult age differences in task switching. *Psychology and Aging, 15,* 126–147.

Laird, J. E., Newell, A., & Rosenbloom, P. S. (1991). Soar: An architecture for general intelligence. In P. S. Rosenbloom, J. E. Laird, & A. Newell (Eds.), *The Soar papers: Research on integrated intelligence* (Vol. 1&2, pp. 463–526). Cambridge, MA: The MIT Press.

Larson, G. E., & Saccuzzo, D. P. (1989). Cognitive correlates of general intelligence: Toward a process theory of g. *Intelligence, 13,* 5–31.

Laux, L. F., & Lane, D. M. (1985). Information processing components of substitution test performance. *Intelligence, 9,* 111–136.

Lima, S. D., Hale, S., & Myerson, J. (1991). How general is general slowing? Evidence from the lexical domain? *Psychology and Aging, 6,* 416–425.

Lhermitte, F. (1983). "Utilization behavior" and its relation to lesions of the frontal lobes. *Brain, 106,* 237–255.

Lienert, G. A., & Faber, C. (1963). Über die Faktorenstruktur der HAWIK auf verschiedenen Alters- und Intelligenzniveaus [On the factor structure of the HAWIK at different levels of age and intelligence]. *Diagnostica, 9,* 3–11.

Lindenberger, U., & Baltes, P. B. (1994). Aging and intelligence. In R. J. Sternberg (Ed.), *The encyclopedia of human intelligence* (pp. 52–66). New York: Macmillan.

Lindenberger, U., & Baltes, P. B. (1995). Testing-the-Limits and experimental simulation: Two methods to explicit the role of learning in development. *Human Development, 38,* 349–360.

Lindenberger, U., Mayr, U., & Kliegl, R. (1993). Speed and intelligence in old age. *Psychology and Aging, 8,* 207–220.

Lindenberger, U., & Pötter, U. (1998). The complex nature of unique and shared effects in hierarchical linear regression: Implications for developmental psychology. *Psychological Methods, 3,* 218–230.

Lynn, R. (1992). Does Spearman 'g' decline at high IQ levels? Some evidence from Scotland. *Journal of Genetic Psychology, 153,* 229–230.

Marr, D. B., & Sternberg, R. J. (1986). Analogical reasoning with novel concepts: Differential attention of intellectually gifted and nongifted children to relevant and irrelevant novel stimuli. *Cognitive Development, 1,* 53–72.

Marshalek, B., Lohman, D. F., & Snow, R. E. (1983). The complexity continuum in the radex and hierarchical models of intelligence. *Intelligence, 7,* 107–127.

Mayr, U., & Kliegl, R. (1993). Sequential and coordinative complexity: Age-based processing limitations in figural transformations. *Journal of Experimental Psychology: Learning, Memory, and Cognition, 19,* 1297–1320.

McDermott, D., & Doyle, J. (1980). Non-monotonic logic I. *Artificial Intelligence, 13,* 41–72.

Meyer, D. E., Kieras, D. E., Lauber, E., Schumacher, E. H., Glass, J., Zurbriggen, E., Gmeindl, L., & Apfelblat, D. (1995). Adaptive executive control: Flexible multiple-task performance without pervasive immutable response-selection bottlenecks. *Acta Psychologica, 90,* 163–190.

Miller, G., Galanter, E., & Pribram, H. (1960). *Plans and the structure of behavior.* New York: Holt, Rinehart & Winston.

Milner, B. (1965). Visually-guided maze learning in man: Effects of bilateral hippocampal, bilateral frontal, and unilateral cerebral lesions. *Neuropsychologia, 3,* 317–338.

Molenaar, P. C. M., & van der Molen, M. W. (1994). On the discrimination between global and local trend hypotheses of life-span changes in processing speed. Special Issue: Life span changes in human performance. *Acta Psychologica, 86,* 273–293.

Myerson, J., Wagstaff, D., & Hale, S. (1994). Brinley plots, explained variance, and the analysis of age differences in response latencies. *Journal of Gerontology: Psychological Sciences, 49,* 72–80.

Navon, D. (1984). Resources—A theoretical stone soup? *Psychological Review, 91,* 871–882.

Necka, E. (1999). Learning, automaticity, and attention: An individual-differences approach. In P. L. Ackerman, P. C. Kyllonen, & R. T. Roberts (Eds.), *Learning and individual differences: Process, trait, and content determinants* (pp. 161–181). Washington, DC: American Psychological Association.

Neisser, U. (1979). The concept of intelligence. *Intelligence, 3,* 217–227.

Nettelbeck, T. (1987). Inspection time and intelligence. In P. A. Vernon (Ed.), *Speed of information processing and intelligence* (pp. 295–346). Norwood, NJ: Ablex.

Nettelbeck, T. (1998). Jensen's chronometric research: Neither simple nor sufficient but a good place to start. *Intelligence, 26,* 233–241.

Nettelbeck, T., & Young, R. (1990). Inspection time and intelligence in 7-yr-old children: A follow up. *Personality of Individual Differences, 11,* 1283–1290.

Neubauer, A. C. (1991). Intelligence and RT: A modified Hick paradigm and a new RT paradigm. *Intelligence, 15,* 175–193.

Neubauer, A. C., & Bucik, V. (1996). The mental speed-IQ relationship: Unitary or modular? *Intelligence, 22,* 23–48.

Neumann, O. (1987). Beyond capacity: A functional view of attention. In H. Heuer & A. F. Sanders (Eds.), *Perspectives on perception and action* (pp. 361–394). Hillsdale, NJ: Lawrence Erlbaum Associates.

Neumann, O. (1992). Theorien der Aufmerksamkeit: von Metaphern zu Mechanismen [Theories of attention: from metaphors to mechanisms]. *Psychologische Rundschau, 43,* 83–101.

Newell, A. (1973). Production systems: Models of control structures. In W. G. Chase (Ed.), *Visual information processing* (pp. 463–526). New York: Academic Press.

Newell, A., Rosenbloom, P. S., & Laird, P. S. (1989). Symbolic architectures of cognition. In M. I. Posner (Ed.), *Foundation of cognitive science* (pp. 93–131). Cambridge, MA: MIT Press.

Newell, A., & Simon, H. A. (1972). *Human problem solving.* Englewood Cliffs, NJ: Prentice-Hall.

Norman, D. A. (1991). Approaches to the study of intelligence. *Artificial Intelligence, 47,* 327–346.

Norman, D. A., & Shallice, T. (1986). Attention in action: Willed and automatic control of behavior. In R. J. Davidson, G. E. Schwartz, & D. Shapiro (Eds.), *Consciousness and self-regulation* (Vol. 4, pp. 1–18). New York: Plenum Press.

Pellegrino, J. W., & Glaser, R. (1980). Cognitive correlates and components in the analysis of individual differences. In R. J. Sternberg & D. K. Detterman (Eds.), *Human Intelligence: Perspectives on its theory and measurement* (pp. 61–88). Norwood, NJ: Ablex.

Perfect, T. J. (1994). What can Brinley plots tell us about cognitive aging? *Journal of Gerontology: Psychological Sciences, 49,* 60–64.

Perkins, D. N., & Grotzer, T. A. (1997). Teaching intelligence. *American Psychologist, 52,* 1125–1133.

Raven, J. C., Court, J. H., & Raven, J. (1987). *A manual for Raven's Progressive Matrices and Vocabulary Tests.* London, England: H. K. Lewis.

Reber, A. S. (1995). *Dictionary of Psychology.* London, England: Penguin.

Reitan, R., & Wolfson, D. (1994). A selective and critical review of neuropsychological deficits and the frontal lobes. *Neuropsychology Review, 4,* 161–197.

Salthouse, T. A. (1991). *Theoretical perspectives on cognitive aging.* Hillsdale, NJ: Lawrence Erlbaum Associates.

Schaie, K. W. (1996). *Intellectual development in adulthood: The Seattle Longitudinal Study*. New York: Cambridge University Press.

Schank, R. C., & Abelson, R. P. (1977). *Scripts, plans, goals, and understanding: An inquiry into human knowledge structures*. Hillsdale, NJ: Lawrence Erlbaum Associates.

Schneider, W., & Shiffrin, R. M. (1977). Controlled and automatic human information processing: 1. Detection, search, and attention. *Psychological Review, 84*, 1–66.

Shallice, T. (1988). *From neuropsychology to mental structure*. Cambridge, England: Cambridge University Press.

Shallice, T. (1992). Information processing models of consciousness in contemporary science. In A. J. Marcel & A. J. Bisiach (Eds.), *Consciousness in contemporary science* (pp. 305–333). Oxford, England: Clarendon Press.

Shallice, T. (1994). Multiple levels of control processes. In C. Umiltà & M. Moscovitch (Eds.), *Attention and Performance* (pp. 395–417). Cambridge, MA: MIT Press.

Shallice, T., & Burgess, P. (1993). Supervisory control of action and thought selection. In A. Baddeley & L. Weiskrantz (Eds.), *Attention: Selection, awareness, and control* (pp. 171–187). Oxford, England: Clarendon Press.

Simpson, C. R., & Deary, I. J. (1997). Strategy use and feedback in inspection time. *Personality and Individual Differences, 23*, 787–797.

Spearman, C. (1927). *The abilities of man*. London, England: MacMillan.

Spearman, C., & Jones, L. W. (1950). *Human ability. A continuation of 'The abilities of man.'* London, England: MacMillan.

Squire, L. R., & Zola-Morgan, R. (1988). Memory: Brain systems and behavior. *Trends in Neurosciences, 11*, 170–175.

Stankov, L. (1983). Attention and intelligence. *Journal of Educational Psychology, 75*, 471–490.

Stankov, L. (1989). Attentional resources and intelligence: A disappearing link. *Personality and Individual Differences, 10*, 957–968.

Sternberg, R. J. (1977). *Intelligence, information processing, and analogical reasoning: The componential analysis of human abilities*. Hillsdale, NJ: Lawrence Erlbaum Associates.

Sternberg, R. J. (1980). Sketch of a componential subtheory of human intelligence. *The Behavioral and Brain Sciences, 3*, 573–614.

Sternberg, R. J. (1984). Does "simplicity breed content"? A reply to Jensen. *Journal of Social and Biological Structures, 7*, 119–123.

Sternberg, R. J. (1985a). *Beyond IQ: A triarchic theory of human intelligence*. New York: Cambridge University Press.

Sternberg, R. J. (1985b). Componential analysis: A recipe. In D. K. Detterman (Ed.), *Current topics of human intelligence. Research methodology* (pp. 179–201). Norwood, NJ: Ablex.

Sternberg, R. J. (1997). Inspection time for inspection time: Reply to Deary and Stough. *American Psychologist, 52*, 1144–1147.

Sternberg, R. J., & Davidson, J. E. (1983). Insight in the gifted. *Educational Psychology*, 51–57.

Sternberg, R. J., & Frensch, P. A. (1990). Intelligence and cognition. In M. W. Eysenck (Ed.), *Cognitive psychology. An international review* (pp. 57–103). Chichester, England: Wiley.

Sternberg, R. J., & Gardner, M. K. (1983). Unities of inductive reasoning. *Journal of Experimental Psychology: General, 112*, 80–116.

Sternberg, R. J., & Powell, J. S. (1983). Comprehending verbal comprehension. *American Psychologist, 38*, 878–893.

Sternberg, R. J., & Williams, W. M. (Eds.). (1998). *Intelligence, instruction, and assessment*. Mahwah, NJ: Lawrence Erlbaum Associates.

Stroop, J. R. (1935). Studies of interference in serial and verbal reactions. *Journal of Experimental Psychology, 18*, 643–662.

Stuss, D. T., & Benson, D. F. (1986). Neuropsychological studies of the frontal lobes. *Psychological Bulletin, 95*, 3–28.

Tranel, D., Anderson, S. W., & Benton, A. (1994). Development of the concept of "executive function" and its relationship to the frontal lobes. In F. Boller, H. Spinnler, & J. A. Hendler (Eds.), *Handbook of neuropsychology* (Vol. 9, pp. 125–148). Amsterdam: Elsevier.

Tulving, E. (1983). *Elements of episodic memory*. New York: Oxford University Press.

Vernon, P. A. (1987). *Speed of information processing and intelligence*. Norwood, NJ: Ablex.

Vernon, P. A. (1989). The generality of g*. *Personality of Individual Differences, 10*, 803–804.

Vernon, P. A., & Kantor, L. (1986). Reaction time correlations with intelligence test scores obtained under either timed or untimed conditions. *Intelligence, 10*, 315–330.

Vickers, D. (1979). *Decision time in visual perception*. London, England: Academic Press.

Vickers, D., & Smith, P. (1986). The rationale for the inspection time index. *Personality and Individual Differences, 7*, 609–624.

Wechsler, W. (1982). *Handanweisung zum Hamburg-Wechsler-Intelligenztest für Erwachsene (HAWIE) [Manual for the Hamburg-Wechsler Intelligence Test for Adults]*. Bern, Switzerland: Huber.

Weiskrantz, L. (1986). *Blindsight: A case study and implications*. Oxford, England: Oxford University Press.

Wickens, C. D. (1978). The structure of attentional resources. In R. Nickerson (Ed.), *Attention and performance VIII* (pp. 239–257). Hillsdale, NJ: Lawrence Erlbaum Associates.

Zacks, R., & Hasher, L. (1994). Directed ignoring: Inhibitory regulation of working memory. In D. Daggebach & T. H. Carr (Eds.), *Inhibitory process in attention, memory, and language* (pp. 241–264). New York: Academic Press.

Part IV

BIOLOGICAL APPROACH

Chapter 9

General Intelligence: Cognitive and Biological Explanations

Douglas K. Detterman
Case Western Reserve University

In this chapter, I consider the status of the concept of general intelligence and its explanations with special emphasis on biological explanations. First, I discuss *g* as a scientific construct and itemize the objections that have been raised against *g*. Second, I consider cognitive explanations of general intelligence and whether or not such explanations are capable of explaining *g*. Third, I survey attempts to relate *g* to brain functioning and consider the acceptability of various explanations that have been proposed. The emphasis in this chapter is on the potential of explaining *g*.

Many researchers make an assumption about *g*. They assume that it follows a logical, hierarchical chain of explanation: *g* can be explained by cognitive processes that, in turn, can be partly explained by biological variables. On the surface, such an explanatory chain seems reasonable. But is it? This issue deserves more consideration than it has received.

THE CURRENT STATUS OF *g*

When most people discuss intelligence, what they really mean is *g*, or general intelligence. Among researchers, *g* has become synonymous with intelligence. No concept in the social sciences is better established or more substantially validated than *g*. Jensen's (1998) recent book, *The g Factor*, provides overwhelmingly extensive support for the concept and its importance. Despite the support for this construct, a number of objections are frequently raised against it. Before considering how g can be explained, it would probably be wise to consider if it is worth explaining. Do any of the objections raised about g negate its use as a valid scientific construct?

g AS A SCIENTIFIC CONSTRUCT

One way of asking if g is a valid scientific construct is to compare it to other scientific constructs that are generally agreed to have validity. The construct that suggests itself as obvious for comparison is the other g, gravity. I think few would argue with gravity as a valid scientific construct. If the g of general intelligence has the same scientific characteristics as the g of gravity, by analogy, we can conclude that both have equal scientific status. In the following sections, I compare general intelligence to gravity with respect to many of the objections raised against general intelligence. To avoid confusion and subscripts, I use g to refer to general intelligence and spell out gravity.

Nobody Knows What g Is

One of the common arguments against g is that nobody really knows what it is or how to explain it. This comment is true at a theoretical level. Empirically, g is well defined but, theoretically, we have only vague ideas about how to explain it. At the empirical level, g is the first general factor of a battery of mental tests. Theoretically, there are numerous speculations about what g could be but none are presently considered completely adequate.

How does this compare to gravity as a scientific construct. It may come as a surprise to many that gravity has a scientific status almost identical to g. Empirically, gravity is well defined but theoretically, there is no scientific agreement about how to explain it. Gravity has been mathematically defined at least since Newton and its effects were well understood even before that. It is well known that bodies attract each other in direct proportion to their mass and in indirect proportion to the distance between them. However, why this occurs is one of the great puzzles of modern physics. After Einstein presented his general theory of relativity, he spent the rest of his life attempting to develop a unified field theory. The goal of this theory was to unify physical forces into a single explanatory theory. Neither Einstein nor anyone else has accomplished this goal. So gravity is as much of a mystery as g. Being unable to explain a scientific construct is hardly grounds for objecting to it.

There are numerous other examples of scientific constructs that were widely accepted before they were understood. Genes were so completely accepted as a scientific construct that their effects were described in detail before anyone had seen a gene or even knew their composition. When atomic microscopy was finally used to photograph a single gene, the event went largely unheralded.

In summary, a scientific construct is still valid even if it cannot be completely explained. Indeed, if a complete explanation were required to accept a construct as valid, there would be few or no valid constructs.

g Is Based on Factor Analysis

Another argument against *g* is that factor analysis is used to demonstrate it. This argument generally takes the following form: Factor analysis has a number of technical ambiguities and there is no exactly agreed upon method of measurement. Often investigators will find somewhat different results with the same data set because they use different methods. Because no one is able to measure *g* precisely and exactly, it is not useful as a scientific construct.

This argument amounts to suggesting that bad math invalidates the construct of general intelligence. What the argument fails to do is separate the construct from the measurement method. Even if everything critics say about factor analysis is true, there is no denying that mental tests are positively correlated among themselves. This is the fundamental insight provided by the concept of *g*.

The scientific concept of gravity had its mathematical problems in its development. From Keppler to Galileo to Newton to Einstein, many of the debates about gravity were really arguments about mathematical representation. How should orbits of planets be characterized? How should falling bodies be described mathematically? Indeed, the history of physics is intimately intertwined with the history of mathematics. Despite imprecision in the mathematical representation of gravity, it is hard to argue that imprecision invalidated the construct. The fundamental insight advanced in the concept of gravity is that bodies exert an attractive force on each other. Scientific advancement is certainly related to the precise description of any scientific construct. But inadequacies in the construct's measurement hardly invalidate the construct.

There have been similar advances in the measurement of *g*. Spearman's (1904) first efforts to describe *g* were very crude. Factor analysis has developed into a much more mathematically sophisticated method than those first early efforts. Some would even argue that most of the mathematical arguments about how to define *g* have been settled (Carroll, 1993, Jensen & Weng, 1994). However, the concept of *g* has not changed significantly since those first efforts. *g* simply summarizes the positive relationship between mental tests just as gravity summarizes attractive forces between objects. Again, we find substantial similarity between g and gravity.

Mathematics is the language of science. Many mathematicians would say that the history of science is the history of mathematics. This seems to be an oversimplification. Concepts exist independently of the mathematics that define them. Mathematics helps us to define the concept and communicate it. However, the idea of gravity being an attractive force between masses was well established from the time the effort to describe it began. Certainly there were those who resisted the concept. The clergy resisted the idea even after it had become a scientifically and mathematically established fact. It wasn't gravity that they objected to but the change from a geocentric to a heliocentric solar system. Man was no longer at the center of the universe. This change in perspective challenged basic assumptions of organized religion.

Similarly, the idea of g has been resisted. Although no one I know of has spent time under house arrest as Galileo did, there has certainly been strong, emotionally laden resistance (Gould, 1981). I think the real reason for this resistance is that g appears to limit individual choice. g implies that if you are good at one thing, you will be good at everything. It implies that some people will be better than others. This suggestion is anathema to those who believe in a literal interpretation of a fundamental principle that "all men are created equal." They regard a literal equality of ability as fundamental to political equality and, ultimately, democracy or socialism, depending on the writer. In my opinion, this objection is a misinterpretation of what the goals of equality, democracy, and socialism should be. Individual differences exist and the current challenge to social philosophies is how those differences will be accommodated. Social philosophies must adjust to empirical realities.

g Is a Statistical Artifact

Another argument against g is that it is a statistical artifact. According to this argument, g can be demonstrated statistically but has no existential reality. That is, although one can make a good case for g with statistical evidence, there is no such thing as g. No one will ever find a place in the brain where g is located or even specific cognitive processes that reflect g.

The identical thing can be said of gravity. It is unlikely that anyone will ever show you a jar of gravity. Although there have been some suggestions that gravity is a substance, most current theories make no such claims. Obviously, it is important whether a thing exists or not. However, with respect to the scientific status of a construct, existential reality is only important to the purest of scientific realists and there are very few of those.

There are many useful scientific constructs that do not exist as a thing. Examples are hunger, extroversion, and heat to name a few. Even if g can only be demonstrated statistically, it is still a legitimate scientific construct. Scientific legitimacy is determined by the extent to which a construct provides explanations for observed phenomena. A massive amount of data show that g is a powerfully explanatory construct.

g Depends on the Test Battery

One objection often raised against g is that it is dependent on how it is measured. To determine how g-loaded a particular test is (call it Test X), one must factor analyze Test X within a battery of other mental tests. The factor loading of the first principal component for Test X indicates its g-loading. This g-loading will be somewhat dependent on what other tests are included in the battery. Change the other tests in the battery but still include Test X and the g-loading of Test X will change slightly.

One reply to this argument is that the change in g-loading is only experimental imprecision. If the battery of tests is made very large, the addition or deletion of a few tests will have little or no effect on other tests. If the battery could be made infinitely large, every test would have a fixed g-loading.

Comparisons of g with gravity show remarkable similarities. Gravity has been notoriously difficult to measure exactly. Gravity varies from place to place. The value of gravity is different on the moon than on the surface of the earth. In fact, gravity differs over the surface of the earth. There is a long history in experimental physics of attempts to obtain accurate measures of gravity. Initially, measurements were taken using pendulums. The history of these experiments is an interesting one progressing toward increasingly accurate measurement. Gravity is still very difficult to measure though more sophisticated instruments have been developed. None of the problems with measuring gravity had any substantial impact on the status of gravity as a scientific construct. Even though nobody knows exactly what gravity is and even though it is not possible to accurately measure gravity, the force of gravity on the moon was predicted and well known before any human set foot there.

There Is No Such Thing as g

This issue was touched on earlier. When this criticism is made, it could mean two possible things. The first and most severe criticism is that the operations used to specify g fail to show it. This would essentially be an argument that factor analysis shows no g and by extension that mental tests are not correlated with each other. To my knowledge, this is one criticism that has never been seriously made. As mentioned earlier, the evidence for g is overwhelming and very easy to find.

The second form of this argument is the more common one that was discussed briefly before. In this form of the argument, it is said that g has no existential reality. As indicated earlier, g need not exist to be a valid scientific construct just as gravity need not exist to be useful as a construct. A variant on this argument accuses those who study intelligence of reifying g. Reification is the process of treating a construct that may not exist as if it does exist. The major problem with reification is that it can cause scientists to look for things that don't really exist. For example, the reification of gravity would cause scientists to look for some substance called gravity. If no such substance existed, much time could be needlessly wasted. There are many examples in science of searches for things that had no existential reality. Although such searches may complicate the course of science, they do not invalidate a construct.

Variance Beyond g

Some researchers have argued that additional or new constructs are necessary to explain intelligent human behavior. In recent years, such conceptions have rapidly multiplied. They include constructs like practical intelligences, emotional intelligence, social intelligence, and multiple intelligences. There are two ways to look at these constructs. First, they can be viewed as replacing standard conceptions of g. To support this stand, any alternative conception of intelligence would be subject to the standard scientific tests that any scientific concept must pass. The proposed construct would have to be more explanatory than any other established construct, including g. No construct that I am aware of has come close to meeting this test. In fact, the inventors of these constructs, to my knowledge, have never intended that these constructs replace g.

The second approach is to regard new constructs as supplemental to g. In this approach, the construct is viewed as an addition to the prediction made by g. There is no doubt that such constructs are needed. At its best, g can predict only about 50% of the variance in any particular outcome. More usually, g predicts about 25% of the variance. This leaves between 50% and 75% of the variance to be explained and something must explain it. The test of whether such constructs are scientifically useful is if they can add predictive validity to what g already predicts. This is sometimes called incremental validity. Some of the concepts that have been proposed as supplements to g do add incremental validity. Unfortunately, so far this incremental validity seems to be small, usually under 10%. However, even small amounts of incremental validity can be useful in the appropriate prediction situation.

Is there any parallel to this situation with respect to gravity? Yes. As mentioned earlier, Einstein attempted to develop a theory of forces that would include not only gravity but all forces of nature. He was never able to do it but others are still trying. Besides attempts to find concepts that would replace or subsume gravity, there have been other forces identified in the physical world that add "incremental validity" to gravity. These forces are familiar to anyone who has taken a basic physics course (e.g., magnetism).

In the previous sections, I examined the status of g as a scientific construct by comparing it to gravity. As a scientific construct, g seems nearly identical to gravity in its scientific status. Although arguing by analogy can be dangerous, there seems to be no valid reason to believe that g should be rejected as a scientific construct. The next thing to be considered is if basic cognitive processes can be used to explain general intelligence. Like gravity, general intelligence presents an empirical riddle, a scientific juggernaut. We know that mental tests are correlated with each other, but why are they?

COGNITIVE EXPLANATIONS OF g

Since the 1980s, perhaps more attention has been given to studying the relationship between cognitive processes and general intelligence than any other area of research on intelligence. Those who have examined cognitive processes as an explanation for g have taken several different approaches based on different assumptions. These assumptions and the appropriateness of the approaches they generate are seldom examined.

Can g Be Explained in Terms of Cognitive Processes?

The first question to be addressed is if general intelligence can ever be explained by cognitive processes. Although it is a prevalent assumption that cognitive processes can explain g, there are those who argue that it may not be possible. In fact, there is no strong evidence for a necessary connection between cognitive processes and g. For the most part, correlations between basic cognitive processes and g are low, often under .30. It is possible that cognitive skills like memory, attention, and basic learning processes have nothing to do with intelligence. It could be that intelligence tests test something different than basic cognitive processes. Intelligence tests do appear to depend heavily on learned information like vocabulary and other kinds of acquired information. The assumption has generally been that even if intelligence tests do rely on learned information, that learned information depends ultimately on a person's basic cognitive skills because they must use those skills to acquire information. However, some have argued that the acquisition of information does not depend on basic skills so much as opportunity and the development of appropriate strategies for information acquisition (e.g., Ceci & Liker, 1986).

There are several arguments strongly suggesting that cognitive skills must underlie and be responsible for the information we learn. First, and most important, it is possible, using twin samples, to determine if general intelligence and cognitive abilities are based on common genes. When this is done, it is found that tests of basic cognitive ability have a common genetic basis with more complex tests of intelligence (e.g., Petrill, Luo, Thompson, & Detterman, 1996). Further, general intelligence and academic achievement share a common genetic base (Thompson, Detterman, & Plomin, 1991). These findings argue for a common biological basis for a path from basic cognitive tasks to general intelligence to academic achievement.

Second, there are literally thousands of studies from infancy to adulthood that show basic cognitive skills like attention, memory, and perceptual skills determine rate of learning for individuals in experimental situations. To assume that such skills have no impact on the learning of information like that found on intelligence tests defies credibility. Such an assumption would suggest that basic attentional, memorial, and learning skills are entirely learned and that ability is a transitory concept. However, we know that large individual differences can be demonstrated shortly after birth and are reasonably stable throughout the lifespan (e.g., Fagan & Detterman, 1992; Fagen & Haiken-Vasen, 1997).

For these reasons, it seems very likely that cognitive abilities will be involved in the prediction of general intelligence. How, exactly, might g and cognitive abilities be related? Several possibilities have been suggested or implied. First, g might be predicted by a single cognitive ability. A second possibility is that g might be predicted by a set of cognitive abilities. A third possibility is that g might be predicted by the relationship among cognitive abilities, that is, by the characteristics that derive from the configuration of cognitive abilities within a complex system. I consider each of these possibilities in order.

Explanations in Terms of a Single Cognitive Process

What would be necessary to show that a single cognitive process was the cause of g? As a preliminary, it would be necessary to show that the candidate cognitive process had a high correlation with general intelligence, preferably above .80 before correction for unreliability. Such a correlation would indicate that the process in question accounted for most of the reliable variance of g. In fact, there are statistical tests to determine if two variables are actually perfectly correlated with each other once reliability of each test has been taken into account. Application of such a test would be a much stronger criterion than just a high correlation. To the best of my knowledge, no one has ever applied such a high criterion.

A second criterion for accepting any cognitive task as explaining *g* is that the task is a basic cognitive task. What the task measures must be clear and it must be simpler than the complex tests that usually constitute measures of *g*. It would not be explanatory to include tasks as complex as those found on most intelligence tests and then consider this a basic cognitive task. It would simply be a case of one intelligence test correlating highly with another and that is not surprising news.

Several candidates have been suggested as possibilities for a single cognitive process that could explain *g*. Most common of these is speed of processing as indexed by measures of reaction time and other speeded tests. Most measures of speed of processing have not correlated with *g* more highly than about .60 even when unreliability has been taken into account (Kail, 2000; see Vernon, 1987 for reviews). These correlations are not high enough to regard speed of information processing as a possibility for accounting for *g* on its own. In most studies, correlations between *g* and measures of speed of information processing are more often around .30, which is about average for most cognitive tasks.

Another concept closely related to speed of information processing is efficiency of processing (Bates & Stough, 1998). Efficiency not only includes speed but also usually some measure of accuracy. Efficiency of information processing has fared no better than speed of information processing in explaining *g*. Even when modifications in the reaction time procedure are made to improve measurement characteristics, the maximum absolute correlation between the measure of efficiency and *g* is not over .60.

Still another class of cognitive tasks that have been suggested as explaining *g* are those that measure cognitive capacity. In particular, working memory has been identified as one possibility (Embretson, 1995; Kyllonen, 1996). Measures of working memory often do provide the requisite high correlations for explaining *g*. However, when the tasks used to operationalize working memory are examined, they are found to be quite complex. The tasks that have been used to define working memory are often as complex as IQ tests, themselves. For example, Embretson (1995) used indices of progressive matrices-like items to define working memory load.

When the tasks are not as complex, the correlations are substantially lower. Although working memory capacity offers an interesting possibility of a variable that can explain *g*, to be convincing the fundamental processes that compose these tasks will have to be identified. Until that is done, saying working memory explains *g* is nearly the equivalent of saying that *g* explains *g*.

Another idea that has been advanced to explain *g* is complexity. It has been noted that as cognitive tasks become more complex, the correlation between the cognitive tasks and *g* rises. Obviously, task complexity itself is not a cognitive variable. It is simply a description of stimulus characteristics. There must be some single underlying cognitive process that might explain why complexity increases a task's correlation with *g*. One possibility, suggested by Spearman, was the deduction of relationships. As tasks become more complex, it may be more difficult to deduce the relationships involved in the task. However, when the tasks become complex enough to correlate highly with *g*, they are as complex as items that compose *g*. Like working memory, unless a model that specifies the exact cognitive processes involved in complexity is developed, complexity is not a good explanatory construct.

In summary, none of the single variable constructs that have been proposed to explain *g* do so convincingly. Of those that have been considered, working memory and complexity offer the most potential for further exploration. They provide the requisite high correlations but when they do, the tasks used to define these concepts are often as complex as items on intelligence tests that define *g*. Therefore, they are not very explanatory of *g*. To be useful, these constructs will have to be supplemented by a model of exactly what it is that causes them to correlate with *g*.

Explanations in Terms of Multiple Cognitive Processes

Another possible way of explaining *g* is in terms of multiple cognitive processes. That is, multiple basic cognitive processes might contribute separately to explain *g*. If this is so, then it should be possible to combine the contributing cognitive processes in a multiple regression equation and predict *g* at high levels, above .80. It should also be possible to devise a model in which each contributing cognitive process is uncorrelated with others, that is independent. Such a model would describe the sources of individual differences that produce *g*. It would specify the various processes that contribute to attention, learning, and memory.

Detterman et al. (1992) and Detterman (1992) developed a set of cognitive tasks that were computer administered. The development of these tasks was based on a model of information processing developed after a review of the literature. The tasks included measures of reaction time, learning, memory, and other basic cognitive tasks known to be related to intelligence. Each task provided several measures of performance including both speed and accuracy measures. The battery of 10 tasks was given to persons with mental retardation and college students along with a standard intelligence test. The measures from the battery of basic cognitive tasks were then combined in a multiple regression equation to predict general intelligence. It was found that the measures combined to predict general intelligence. The basic cognitive measures predicted intelligence as well as intelligence tests predict each other. In nearly all cases, the multiple correlations were above .80. This finding has been confirmed in larger samples (Detterman, 2000).

Unfortunately, when an attempt was made to fit the data to the original model used to select the variables, the fit was not good. The data also failed to fit several modifications of the original model. The reason the data failed to fit any of the models considered may have to do with measurement of the processes in question. Although the different measures from the 10 tasks had low correlations with each other, they were still correlated. That means they were not pure measures of a single psychological process. If they had been, they would have been uncorrelated with each other.

Logical consideration of any single measure suggests that it will be very difficult, if not impossible, to get a "pure" measure of a cognitive process. The reason is that in any behavioral measure there must always be some kind of sensory stimulus input (encoding) and some kind of motor output (response). Both encoding and response factors must be included with whatever process is being measured. Even if two processes being measured are completely independent of each other, they can still be correlated because of common encoding and response factors. Until adequate methods are found to factor out encoding and response factors, the best measures of independent cognitive processes will remain correlated because of this contamination.

Another problem in identifying basic cognitive processes is that much of what we know about cognition was learned in an effort to develop general laws of cognition. This is what has been called nomothetic research. Most individual differences researchers draw from the knowledge base developed by nomothetic researchers, at least in the early stages of their work. Most of the concepts of attention, learning, memory, and perception used in individual differences research have been directly obtained from nomothetic research.

Although it would seem logical to adopt models from nomothetic research to study individual differences, there can be serious problems. Nomothetic researchers consider individual differences only as "error variance" and regard differences between subjects' performance as nuisance. Because they have no interest in individual differences, they pay little attention to task reliability. Even worse, from a nomothetic perspective the best tasks are those that show little or no individual differences. So tasks developed by nomothetic researchers may be unreliable.

Because of these problems, models developed to describe nomothetic research outcomes may be completely useless when it comes to explaining individual differences. That means that if multiple cognitive processes are required to explain *g*, the most familiar models of cognition may not be very useful. New models may have to be devised with special reference to individual differences.

Kranzler and Jensen (1991) attempted to determine if *g* is actually composed of independent basic cognitive processes. They administered a set of basic cognitive tasks and a measure of psychometric *g* to a group of subjects. They reasoned that if *g* was a single thing, the battery of cognitive tasks would yield a single factor, a general factor. Further, this single factor from the basic cognitive tasks should correlate highly with psychometric *g* obtained from more complex intelligence tasks. On the other hand, if there were multiple independent cognitive processes underlying psychometric *g*, then the battery of basic cognitive tasks should yield multiple factors and each of these factors should be correlated significantly with psychometric *g*. This second result is one they obtained. Even though the battery of basic cognitive tasks was somewhat restricted in the processes measured, they obtained four factors each of which correlated significantly with psychometric *g*. They concluded that psychometric *g* is composed of a number of independent cognitive processes.

Carroll (1991) argued that the Kranzler and Jensen demonstration was not sufficient to show that psychometric *g* was composed of independent processes. Basically, Carroll asserted that the factors Kranzler and Jensen had obtained from the battery of basic cognitive tasks were cross-contaminated causing them all to correlate with psychometric *g*. Because of this contamination, Carroll considered it more parsimonious to regard psychometric *g* as represented by a unitary underlying process. Despite several exchanges between Kranzler and Jensen and Carroll, Carroll remained unconvinced by the Kranzler and Jensen argument even though the Kranzler and Jensen argument became increasingly more refined as the debate progressed.

Despite Carroll's arguments, Kranzler and Jensen support the possibility that a set of independent cognitive processes may be required to account for psychometric *g*. At the very least, the methodology they employed should be a useful one for resolving the issue in the future. It would be interesting to see what would happen if a larger, more diverse set of cognitive tasks than used by Kranzler and Jensen were employed.

In summary, there are some good reasons to believe there are at least several underlying cognitive processes that contribute to *g*. There are several reasons for this conclusion. First, it is possible to use a battery of basic cognitive tasks to predict *g*. Even though the measures obtained from the basic cognitive tasks have moderate to low correlations with *g*, these tasks combine to predict *g*. Second, when a battery of basic cognitive tasks are factor analyzed, factors beyond the first are significantly correlated with psychometric *g*.

There are also some problems in concluding that g consists of a set of independent processes. First, it has been very difficult to identify exactly what the independent processes underlying g actually are. Second, none of the models of cognitive processing have had much success in fitting the data. Third, the findings that support independent basic cognitive processes, some have argued, can also be explained by a unitary construct and measurement errors.

Explanations in Terms Derivative of Cognitive Systems

Even if g is composed of a set of independent cognitive processes, g may not be derived from those processes. It could be that g results not because of any particular set of basic cognitive processes but because of the relationship among those processes. Detterman (1987, 1994a) proposed a system theory of general intelligence that suggests that g really results from the relationship among components of the cognitive system. According to this theory, cognitive components are independent but are integrated together into an interactive system with a high degree of wholeness. In system terminology, wholeness means that the parts of the system are highly interdependent on each other. Some of the components are more central to the operation of the system. If a process is a central one, it is used by a high proportion of the system's other parts. Thus, many system paths lead through a central process. Therefore, if a central process is congenitally weak or has been damaged, it will have a widespread effect on the system because so many other parts of the system rely on the central process. Detterman proposed that g resulted from a defect in one or more central processes. The damaged central process has the effect of lowering the efficiency of the entire system. In a sense, the damaged central process sets a limit on performance for the whole system.

If this speculation is correct, then a particular pattern of results should obtain. Subjects who have damaged or inefficient central processes should perform more similarly on all tasks because the damaged central process causes the whole system to perform inefficiently. On the other hand, those who show highly efficient central processes will be more variable on all tasks because any limitation on those tasks will be dictated by more peripheral processes, not central processes that affect the entire system. If such effects actually occur, then mental tasks including basic cognitive tasks will be more highly correlated among low IQ subjects than among high IQ subjects.

To investigate this possibility, Detterman and Daniel (1989) divided up the distribution into five equal parts. Within each division of the distribution, they correlated subtests of IQ tests with each other. They did the same for basic cognitive tasks from a battery of basic cognitive tasks. They found that correlations were as much as twice as large for low IQ subjects as for high IQ subjects. This finding provides tentative support for the idea that the origin of g is not in defective processes, themselves, but in the relationship of the defective processes to other parts of the system.

SUMMARY OF COGNITIVE EXPLANATIONS OF g

In the previous sections, I considered three possible cognitive explanations for g. The first is that g results from a single cognitive process that varies among individuals. Cognitive processes that have been suggested as a single process that could explain g are working memory, cognitive complexity, and speed or efficiency of processing. The second possibility is that g can be explained by a set of independent cognitive processes. Although no one has yet identified the specific cognitive processes that might be implicated in this explanation, there is evidence that multiple cognitive processes might explain g. A third possibility is that g is not explained by cognitive processes themselves, but rather by the relationships between processes within the cognitive system. There is also evidence that supports this position.

In general, it can be concluded that there is no single agreed upon cognitive explanation for g. Each of the potential explanations has some support and some negative evidence. This is a serious problem for finding a biological explanation of g. If we do not know how to explain g at the behavioral level, it will be much harder to discover the biological basis of g.

EXPLANATIONS OF g IN TERMS OF BRAIN FUNCTIONING

Now to the main topic of interest: How can g be explained in terms of biological processes? There must be some relationship between general intelligence and properties of the brain, but what could it be? We have already seen that there is no agreed upon explanation of g in terms of cognitive processes. It might be possible to find a biological explanation of g without ever developing a cognitive explanation of g. However, understanding the cognitive basis of g could tell us where to look in the brain or, at least, what classes of explanation might be most appropriate. Lacking an agreed upon cognitive basis of g means that the search for a biological basis of g must go forward without guidance from cognitive processes.

Given the uncertainty about the cognitive explanations of g, it is not surprising that biological explanations of g have taken a parallel route of development. In fact, as we shall see, each class of cognitive explanation has an identical class of biological explanation. Biological explanations fall into almost exactly the same categories as cognitive explanations. They include g explained by a single thing, g explained by multiple processes, and g explained by system characteristics.

Andrist et al. (1993) and Detterman (1994b) have reviewed the many studies that have attempted to relate brain processes to g. The following discussion does not repeat this information. Instead, the purpose of this discussion is to critically consider the potential for explaining g from each perspective.

Explanations of g in Terms of Single Brain Processes

There have been a number of attempts to explain g in terms of single brain processes. Perhaps best known of those is the work of the Hendrickson's (A. Hendrickson, 1982; D. Hendrickson, 1982; Hendrickson & Hendrickson, 1980). They developed what came to be known as the "string" measure of the complexity of evoked potentials. To obtain this measure, a string was placed to be congruent with the tracing of an evoked potential for a subject. The more elaborated the evoked potential, the longer the string would be. This unique method of measurement was combined with an interesting theory that described how errors in transmission could occur to reduce complexity of transmission (A. Hendrickson, 1982). This theory was one of neural efficiency.

In the original studies, the string measure correlated around .80 with measures of intelligence. Unfortunately, the original study had a number of methodological problems (Detterman, 1984) and subsequent efforts failed to replicate the high correlations found by the Hendricksons (Haier, Robinson, Braden, & Williams, 1984). It is interesting to note that the studies of neural efficiency explaining g have had a very similar course in both the biological and cognitive domains.

Another proposed explanation for general intelligence has been dendritic sprouting and neural pruning. Infants are born with a large excess of dendrites that are "pruned" during the first years of life (Huttenlocher, deCourten, Garey, & Van der Loos, 1982). This mechanism has been suggested as the possible origin of differences in g. Unfortunately, when persons with mental retardation are compared to those of normal intelligence, pruning does not appear to be very different (Huttenlocher, 1984) thus eliminating it as a possible explanation for g.

A number of other processes have been suggested as the single variable that could explain g. These include neural transmitters, brain size, speed of transmission, and others. Like most cognitive variables, no single biological variable has been able to reliably establish correlations with g that are consistently above .80 or even close to it.

Explanations of *g* in Terms of Multiple Brain Processes

Unfortunately, there is no single agreed upon model of exactly how the brain works or even what its functional parts are. However, there have been a number of techniques that have been developed that hold great potential for understanding how *g* is related to brain processes. Each of these methods has its strengths and weaknesses.

Averaged evoked potentials are recordings of current changes taken from the skull. These recordings are thought to indicate changes in brain activity. The major advantage of averaged evoked potentials is that they can record instantaneous changes in brain activity. The major disadvantage is that it is difficult or impossible to localize the exact source of the electrical activity in the brain.

Positron emission tomography (PET) can provide pictures of the functional activity in the brain. An uptake substance, such as glucose or oxygen, that has been radioactively tagged is administered to the subject. The subject then does a task of some sort during the time the uptake substance is being used by the brain. After the uptake period, the decaying radioactive material can be recorded. Those areas of the brain that were most active during the uptake period have the highest level or decaying material. It is the decaying material that is detected by the scanner after the uptake period is finished. This technique provides what amounts to a time-lapse photograph of activity in the brain during the uptake period. The advantage of this technique is that it provides very accurate estimates of activity levels of each part of the brain, because the mechanism of uptake of the tagged substances used is well known and mathematically described. The disadvantage of the method is that temporal resolution is dependent on the half-life of the uptake material used and can vary from a few minutes to more than 30 minutes. It would be impossible to identify very brief brain activity or the sequence of brain activity using PET.

Functional magnetic resonance imaging (fMRI) can also provide functional pictures of activity in the brain. This technique actually measures changes in blood flow that occur in the brain. Because blood flow takes time, the temporal resolution of fMRI is in the range of seconds and this is a major disadvantage inasmuch as many psychological processes occur in the range of milliseconds. The major advantage of this method is exceptional spatial localization of brain activity.

Both PET and fMRI have poor temporal resolution but excellent spatial resolution. On the other hand, averaged evoked potentials have poor spatial resolution but excellent temporal resolution. One suggestion that has been made is to combine these two techniques. For example, one could combine the information available from fMRI and average evoked potentials and obtain both good spatial and temporal resolution.

Both PET and fMRI have an additional difficulty. Changes in functional activity during experimental tasks must be compared to some control condition where the brain is "at rest." The active brain is then compared to the brain at rest in order to determine which areas of the brain show the greatest change in activity level. What constitutes the appropriate control condition to measure a brain at rest is not entirely clear. In some pilot work we have done, we have had subjects report thinking about all kinds of things from problems with boy friends to baseball. We have even had subjects who were falling asleep during the control condition. The control condition is an important determinant of the outcome of experiments in functional brain imaging as all such methods use subtraction to determine activity. That is, activity levels in the experimental condition are subtracted from those in the experimental condition to determine what areas of the brain were most active in the experimental condition.

Although techniques for observing thinking brains in action are most impressive and will certainly provide important information about the relationship between g and brain processes, the most impressive work identifying multiple parts of the brain as causing g comes from an older technique: brain lesions. In this technique, damage is experimentally produced in the brain by lesioning it. The results of the experimental lesion on behavioral tasks are then studied. Thomson, Crinella, and Yu (1990) systematically lesioned a large number of rats and then put them through an experimental battery of tests that was the rat equivalent of an intelligence test. They were able to identify brain areas that were most important to the psychometric g they identified. These areas came from different functional systems of the brain suggesting that no single functional system of the brain was responsible for g. These data provide strong support that multiple areas of the brain contribute to general intelligence. To what extent these findings will generalize to humans is not known.

In summary, there are numerous techniques that promise an interesting future for identifying multiple brain sources for g. These techniques are in the earliest stages of application and it is still not clear how useful they will be. However, there are already animal data from lesion experiments that suggest what portions of the brain may be most important to understanding g.

Explanations of g in Terms of Derivatives of Brain Processes

Interestingly, there have been few speculations that I am aware of in the neurological literature about how system characteristics of the brain might affect behavior. There is one interesting set of experiments suggesting that system characteristics of the brain may be important for understanding *g*. Haier et al. (1988) used PET to observe which portions of the brain were most active as subjects took the Raven's Progressive Matrices test. Although no particular area of the brain was implicated in solving the problems on the test when total activity level was analyzed, a counterintuitive result emerged. Subjects who had the highest IQ levels showed the lowest level of brain activity. That is, high-IQ subjects actually used less brain power than lower IQ subjects. This finding was confirmed in another study by Haier, Siegel, Tang, Abel, & Buchsbaum (1992). In this study, subjects were given a PET scan playing Tetrus, a video game. After extensive practice playing Tetrus, they were given another PET scan. As predicted from the first experiment, subjects' brains were less active during the second scan than during the first. This study suggests that the prepared, knowledgeable brain is more efficient than the less prepared, less knowledgeable brain. Evidently, there are some system organizing principles at work that make a brain more efficient.

SUMMARY OF ATTEMPTS TO EXPLAIN *g* ON THE BASIS OF BIOLOGICAL VARIABLES

In general, there have been fewer systematic efforts to account for *g* on the basis of biological variables than to account for *g* using cognitive variables. Those attempts that have been made fall into the same categories as attempts to explain *g* using cognitive variables. Like cognitive explanations, none of the biological explanations is entirely convincing as an explanation of *g*. And like cognitive explanations of *g*, they each present interesting possibilities for future research.

In some ways, attempts to explain *g* using biological variables are less impressive than explanations based on cognitive behaviors. That is probably because biological explanations require a longer inferential chain because they are more molecular than cognitive behaviors. Each biological explanation, either explicitly or implicitly, suggests a cognitive behavior that is related to *g*. Cognitive explanations of *g*, on the other hand, seldom suggest a biological mechanism. In that sense, biological explanations of *g* are often more complete than cognitive explanations.

CONCLUSIONS

There are several conclusions that can be made.

1. *g* is a scientific concept with a status much like gravity. Despite its critics, it seems a concept worthy of explanation.

2. Biological and cognitive explanations fall into three separate categories: g as a single thing, g as several things, and g as a derivative construct resulting from the interaction of system parts. Biological and cognitive explanations that fall into any one of these three categories have much in common.

3. None of the explanations considered here provides an entirely satisfactory explanation of g. None even is so plausible as to rule out other potential explanations.

4. The research done so far offers interesting possibilities for further research.

What is the best way to go about understanding g? In my opinion, the cognitive explanations of g are currently the best developed and most thoroughly researched. However, even these are none too sophisticated. Ultimately, any satisfactory theory of g will have to include both cognitive and biological levels of explanation. Those theories that have well-developed cognitive models associated with underlying biological mechanisms will ultimately be the most powerful. This is easy to say but hard to do. We have no adequate cognitive model of how the mind works. We have no adequate biological model of how the brain works. Our knowledge about how behavior interfaces with biology is rudimentary. Explaining g either in cognitive terms or in biological terms will be difficult so coming up with both cognitive and biological explanations at once will be even harder. What must be kept in mind is that g is, empirically, the most well-established phenomenon in the social sciences. If any social science construct is capable of explanation in either cognitive or biological terms, it should be g. Efforts to explain g are to be encouraged.

REFERENCES

Andrist, C. G., Kahana, M. J., Spry, K. M., Knevel, C. R., Persanyi, M. W, Evans, S. W., Luo, D., & Detterman, D. K. (1993). Individual differences in the biological correlates of intelligence: A selected overview. In D. K. Detterman (Ed.), *Current topics in human intelligence: Vol. 2. Is mind modular or unitary?* (pp. 1–59). Norwood, NJ: Ablex.

Bates, T., & Stough, C. (1998). Improved reaction time method, information processing speed and intelligence. *Intelligence, 26,* 53–62.

Carroll, J. B. (1991). No demonstration that g is not unitary, but there's more to the story: Comment on Kranzler and Jensen. *Intelligence, 15,* 423–436.

Carroll, J. B. (1993). *Human cognitive abilities: A survey of factor analytic studies.* Cambridge, England: Cambridge University Press.

Ceci, S. J., & Liker, J. (1986). A day at the races: A study of IQ expertise, and cognitive complexity. *Journal of Experimental Psychology: General, 115,* 255–266.

Detterman, D. K. (1984). 'g-Whiz' [Review of *A model for intelligence*]. *Contemporary Psychology, 29,* 375–376.

Detterman, D. K. (1987). Theoretical notions of intelligence and mental retardation. *American Journal of Mental Deficiency, 92,* 2–11.

Detterman, D. K. (1992). Mopping up: The relation between cognitive abilities and intelligence. *American Journal of Mental Retardation, 97,* 295–301.

Detterman, D. K. (1994a). A system theory of intelligence. In D. K. Detterman (Ed.), *Current topics in human intelligence: Vol. 4. Theories of Intelligence* (pp. 85–115). Norwood, NJ: Ablex.

Detterman, D. K. (1994b). Intelligence and the brain. In P. A. Vernon (Ed.), *Handbook of the neuropsychology of individual differences.* San Diego, CA: Academic Press.

Detterman, D. K. (2000). General intelligence and the definition of phenotypes. In G. R. Bock, J. A. Goode, & K. Webb (Eds.), *The nature of intelligence, Novartis Foundation Symposium 233* (pp. 136–148). Chichester, UK: Wiley.

Detterman, D. K., & Daniel, M. H. (1989). Correlations of mental tests with each other and with cognitive variables are highest for low IQ groups, *Intelligence, 13,* 349–359.

Detterman, D. K., Mayer, J. D., Caruso, D. R., Legree, P. J., Conners, F., & Taylor, R. (1992). Assessment of basic cognitive abilities in relation to cognitive deficits. *American Journal of Mental Retardation, 97,* 251–286.

Embretson, S. E. (1995). The role of working memory and general control processes in intelligence. *Intelligence, 20,* 169–189.

Fagan, J. F., III, & Detterman, D. K. (1992). The Fagan Test of Infant Intelligence: A technical summary. *Journal of Applied Developmental Psychology, 13,* 173–193.

Fagan, J. F., III, & Haiken-Vasen, J. (1997). Selective attention to novelty as measure of information processing across the lifespan. In J. A. Burack & J. T. Enns (Eds.), *Attention, development, and psychopathology* (pp. 55–73). New York: Guilford Press.

Gould, S. J. (1981). *The mismeasurement of man.* New York: W. W. Norton.

Haier, R. J., Robinson, D. L., Braden, W., & Williams, D. (1984). Evoked potential augmenting-reducing and personality differences. *Personality and Individual Differences, 5,* 293–301.

Haier, R. J., Siegel, B. V., Nuechterlein, K. H., Hazlett, E., Wu, J. C., Paek, J., Browning, H. L., & Buchsbaum, M. S. (1988). Cortical glucose metabolic rate correlates of abstract reasoning and attention studied with positron emission tomography. *Intelligence, 12,* 199–217.

Haier, R. J., Siegel, B., Tang, C., Abel, L., & Buchsbaum. M. S. (1992). Intelligence and changes in regional cerebral glucose metabolic rates following learning. *Intelligence, 16,* 415–426.

Hendrickson, A. E. (1982). The biological basis of intelligence. Part I: Theory. In H. J. Eysenck (Ed.), *A model of intelligence* (pp. 151–196). New York: Springer-Verlag.

Hendrickson, D. E. (1982). The biological basis of intelligence. Part II: Measurement. In H. J. Eysenck (Ed.), *A model for intelligence* (pp. 197–228). New York: Springer-Verlag.

Hendrickson, D. E., & Hendrickson, A. E. (1980). The biological basis of individual differences in intelligence. *Personality and Individual Differences, 1,* 3–33.

Huttenlocher, P. R. (1984). Synapse elimination and plasticity in developing human cerebral cortex. *American Journal of Mental Deficiency, 88,* 488–496.

Huttenlocher, P. R., deCourten, C., Garey, L., & Van der Loos, H. (1982). Synaptogenesis in human visual cortex: Evidence for synapse elimination during normal development. *Neuroscience Letters, 33,* 247–252.

Jensen, A. R. (1998). *The g factor: the science of mental ability.* Westport, CT: Praeger.

Jensen, A. R., & Weng, L. -J. (1994). What is a good g? *Intelligence, 18,* 231–258.

Kail, R. (2000). Speed of information processing: Developmental changes and links to intelligence. *Journal of School Psychology, 58,* 51–61.

Kyllonen, P. C. (1996). Is working memory capacity Spearman's g? In I. Dennis & P. Tapsfield (Eds.), *Human abilities: Their nature and measurement* (pp. 49–57). Mahwah, NJ: Lawrence Erlbaum Associates.

Kranzler, J. H., & Jensen, A. R. (1991). The nature of psychometric g: Unitary processes or a number of independent processes? *Intelligence, 15,* 397–422.

Petrill, S. A., Luo, D., Thompson, L. A., & Detterman, D. K. (1996). The independent prediction of general cognitive tasks: Genetic and environmental influences. *Behavior Genetics, 26,* 135–147.

Spearman, C. (1904). General intelligence, objectively determined and measured. *American Journal of Psychology, 15,* 201–293.

Thompson, L. A., Detterman, D. K., & Plomin, R. (1991). Associations between cognitive abilities and scholastic achievement: Genetic overlap but environmental differences. *Psychological Science, 2,* 158–165.

Thompson, R., Crinella, F. M., & Yu, J. (1990). *Brain mechanisms in problem solving and intelligence: A lesion survey of the rat brain.* New York: Plenum Press.

Vernon, P. A. (Ed.). (1987). *Speed of information processing and intelligence.* Norwood, NJ: Ablex.

Chapter 10

The Theory of Biological Intelligence: History and a Critical Appraisal

Douglas Wahlsten
University of Alberta

Human intelligence has an intimate relationship with the anatomical structures and physiological functions of the nervous system, and psychologists often refer to the brain as the basis for or substrate of intelligence. At the same time, intelligence is a very complex psychological phenomenon that is not easily understood in terms of the properties of nerve cells and brain circuitry. Several significant neural correlates of IQ test scores have been documented, but it is not at all clear that variation in IQ is actually caused by variation in these aspects of the nervous system. Genetic variation is undoubtedly important for individual differences in both brain structure and intelligence, yet mounting evidence also demonstrates that differences in environment have major influences on both brain structure and intelligence. A limited set of genes or a distinct array of features of the nervous system cannot encapsulate the concept of intelligence or provide a better way to measure intelligence. Whether population variance in intelligence arises largely from a single, general factor (*g*) or from many specific factors therefore is not a question that can be answered decisively by examining the brain or the genes. The present chapter does not purport to refute or affirm the reality of *g* as a psychological concept. Rather, it argues against the theory of biological intelligence—the assertion that intelligence is essentially a genetically determined biological entity.

INTELLIGENCE AS AN EMERGENT PROPERTY

A one-cell embryo contains a complete set of the organism's genes but does not possess a nervous system or intelligence. The vertebrate embryo differentiates into three kinds of tissue, one of which (ectoderm) eventually forms the neural tube that gives rise to neurons in the central nervous system. The neurons are generated at the surface of fluid-filled ventricles inside the nascent brain, and they migrate to regions where they begin to form dendrites that will receive synaptic connections from other neurons (Purves & Lichtman, 1985). During migration, they send out axons that will later make connections with distant neurons. After inputs from sensory receptors are received, synapses are made with skeletal muscles, and circuits of neurons begin to form, the fetus gains the capacity for simple movements but it does not yet have intelligence.

Intelligence is generally believed to involve cognitive processes, and cognition is usually seen as a function of the cerebral cortex (Kuljis, 1994). The cortex begins to form organized assemblies of neurons that can sustain electrical activity (the electroencephalogram or EEG) prior to birth (see Table 10.1). In debates about the ethical and legal status of abortion and infanticide, the presence of cortical EEG is viewed by some scholars as a sign of brain-life comparable to the brain-death criterion used to make decisions about turning off life support or donating organs (Sass, 1994), although others question its validity for this purpose (Jones, 1989; Kuljis, 1994). Intelligence, however, involves more than an EEG, and it is doubtful that genuine intelligence appears until the infant or the species has acquired the rudiments of language (Calvin, 1999). Binet and Simon (1905b), for example, held that "one can not make tests of judgment on children of less than two years when one begins to watch their first gleams of intelligence" (p. 43).

Thus, intelligence is an emergent property of a nervous system that has become sufficiently complex and has been exposed to an adequate amount of speech. The age at which intelligence emerges is difficult to de-

TABLE 10.1
Major Events in the Prenatal Development
of the Human Cerebral Cortex

Event	Weeks After Conception	Reference
Closure of the neural tube	3–4	Kuljis, 1994; O'Rahilly & Müller, 1987
Cerebral hemispheres appear	5–6	Kuljis, 1994; O'Rahilly & Müller, 1987
Birth and migration of neurons	7–12	Bayer, Altman, Russo, & Zhang, 1995
Formation of cortical plate	8	Kuljis, 1994
Formation of fissures and gyri	18–28	Encha-Razavi, 1995
First synapses in cortical plate	22	Kuljis, 1994; Huttenlocher et al., 1982
Formation of distinct layers, columns	24–40	Encha-Razavi, 1995
Beginning of myelination of axons	30	Encha-Razavi, 1995
Sustained electrical activity (EEG)	32–36	Jones, 1989; Laget, 1979

termine, at least partly because psychologists have no consensus definition of intelligence (Neisser et al., 1996) but also because the emergence is probably gradual. The period when intelligence emerges is a period of rapid changes in the brain. Most of the neurons are already present in the cerebral cortex at the time of birth, but during the first 2 years after birth vast numbers of synaptic connections form and many are then pruned away (Huttenlocher, de Courten, Garey, & Van der Loos, 1982), the my-elin sheaths around the axons between cells grow rapidly (Yakovlev & Lecours, 1967), and the forms of cortical evoked potentials to sensory stimuli change markedly (Laget, 1979).

Although there are psychological tests of mental and motor develop-ment for infants from shortly after birth to 2 or 3 years of age (e.g., Bayley, 1993; Hart, 1992), these are not always regarded as tests of intelligence, and they show very low correlations with later scores on bona fide intelli-gence tests for school-age children (Brody, 1992; Cohen & Swerdlik, 1999; Vandenberg, 1977). Fagan (1985) argued that the low correlations occurred because the items administered to young infants were mainly tests of sensorimotor function and that continuity of intelligence from in-fancy to childhood will be observed if more appropriate tests are used. Several investigators have devised tests that rely on stimulus habituation to assess infant cognition, and correlations of these tests with later childhood IQ scores are generally positive. A meta-analysis by McCall and Carriger (1993) found that the weighted average correlations of infant habituation and recognition memory measures versus later IQ for nonrisk samples of children were about .4, but there was a strong tendency to find smaller correlations of .3 or less with larger samples. These correlations are well above zero but also far below IQ test–retest reliabilities of .8 or more seen after age five. The infant habituation tests may reflect processes that are important for later intelligence, but they are not indicators of intelligence per se. Rather, they are early signs of incipient intelligence.

Children commonly speak their first word at 8 to 9 months of age and utter complete sentences around the age of 3 years (Gesell & Amatruda, 1947). The Stanford–Binet intelligence test may be used with children 2 years of age or older, the Goodenough–Harris Drawing Test is recom-mended for children at least 3 years old (Harris, 1963), and the Wechsler Preschool and Primary Scale of Intelligence (WPPSI–R) is suitable for chil-dren from 3 to 6 years old. As the child's vocabulary and linguistic abilities expand, the correlation of the IQ score with IQ assessed in the teen years increases. Thus, it appears that intelligence arises gradually in infancy and early childhood (see Fig. 10.1).

Intelligence as an emergent property of the nervous system is also ap-parent during the evolution of species (Calvin, 1999). There must have been a remote human ancestor that did not evidence intelligence even in

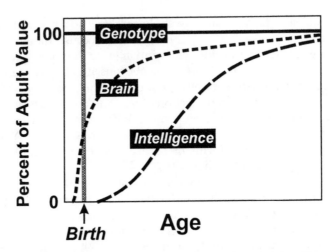

FIG. 10.1.   Profiles of changes in different human characteristics with age.
Genotype is established when sperm and egg unite at conception and is effectively constant throughout life. Gross brain structure begins to form in
the late embryo and early fetus (see Table 10.1), progresses very rapidly in
the third trimester and infancy, then gradually decelerates, never becoming
fixed. Intelligence emerges in late infancy or early childhood when the first
signs of competence in language appear and then grows steadily for many
years. Changes in the finer details of the nervous system that occur well into
middle-age are not indicated in this diagram.

the adult. As the nervous system became larger and more complex over
millions of years, it eventually reached a state where cognitive functioning
warranted a designation as intelligent. There is continuing controversy
about the existence of intelligence in birds and nonhuman mammals
(Gould & Gould, 1999). If language is accepted as essential for intelligence, then only humans may be properly regarded as possessing language (MacWhinney, 1998) and therefore intelligence. Many species have
high levels of learning ability in situations adapted to their capabilities
and needs, but there is more to intelligence than simply learning associations, spatial relations, or rudimentary concepts.

From both the developmental and evolutionary perspectives, there
must be something special about a nervous system that can form the basis
for intelligent behavior. Furthermore, as a tenet of materialist philosophy,
there must also be something different about the nervous systems of people who differ greatly in intelligence. In this chapter I question whether
the study of the biological or neural bases for intelligence can help us to
understand intelligence better. Two issues are addressed. First, the theory
of the biological basis of human intelligence is examined. Second, the theory of a general factor (g) of intelligence accounting for most of the variance is compared with multiple factor theories from a genetic perspective.

THE THEORY OF BIOLOGICAL INTELLIGENCE

The theory of biological intelligence entails four propositions.

1. Heredity (genes) specifies the structure and physiology of the nervous system.
2. The structure and physiology of the nervous system determine cognitive and learning abilities that constitute genuine intelligence.
3. Because a person's heredity is a constant throughout life (Fig. 10.1), his or her intelligence relative to same-age peers is essentially fixed, and psychological changes related to environment cannot reflect changes in intelligence per se.
4. Psychometric tests measure genuine, biological intelligence indirectly and imperfectly, and experimental control plus statistical adjustments to test scores are needed to yield a better estimate of the person's true intelligence.

Although the proposal that human mental ability is rigidly determined by heredity can be traced in psychology to Galton (1892), who claimed somewhat crudely that "men who achieve eminence, and those who are naturally capable, are, to a large extent, identical" (p. 78), a more completely elaborated theory that today has many adherents was formulated by Spearman (1904, 1923; see Fancher, 1985). He focused on "*natural innate faculties*. By this definition, we explicitly declare that all such individual circumstances as after birth materially modify the investigated function are irrelevant and must be adequately eliminated" (Spearman, 1904, p. 227; emphasis in original). For this purpose, he invented a method to adjust for test unreliability. "The result actually obtained in any laboratory test must necessarily have in every case been perturbed by various contingencies which have nothing to do with the subject's real general capacity" (p. 223) and "the total effect of all such errors can be measured *en masse* and mathematically eliminated" (p. 226). In his more lengthy treatise on intelligence, Spearman (1923) asserted that the "ultimate basis" for mental abilities was "the influences of heredity and of health" (p. 347). One of his three "noegenetic" principles involved "apprehension of experience" that could change behavior, whereas "eduction of relations" and "eduction of correlates" were held to be independent of experience. "Hence, judged from the standpoint of modifying behaviour, just these two *non*-experiential principles most conspicuously deserve the name of intelligence" (Spearman, 1923, p. 352; emphasis in the original). Tentatively, he proposed that the physiological basis for intelligence was a "general energy" that was constant in a person, wherein the brain is "able to switch the bulk of its energy from any one to any other group of neurons" (p. 346).

Spearman's ideas were strongly endorsed and applied by Cyril Burt (1909), whose expressed interest was in "general, innate endowment, as distinguished from special knowledge and special dexterities, that is to say, from post-natal acquisition" (p. 97). For Burt, the challenge was to un-cover the innate: "Thus the prime difficulty in psychological research is the elimination of the factors that are irrelevant. In investigating General Intelligence by means of experimental tests the essential relations between the functions to be observed are liable to be distorted or obscured by such accidental conditions as the personality of the conductor of the experi-ments, the age, sex, social status, education, zeal, and practice of the sub-jects of the experiments" (p. 99). From the outset, he believed: "that we may eventually seek the psycho-physical basis, underlying this capacity, in a particular characteristic of general neural constitution; the accentuation of such a neural characteristic would then produce the type of mind known as intelligent, while its biological inheritance would form the con-dition of the transmissibility of the mental trait" (p. 169). Burt adhered to these beliefs throughout his career: "By intelligence, the psychologist un-derstands inborn, all-round, intellectual ability. It is inherited or at least innate, not due to teaching or training" (Burt, 1934, p. 28). In his final statement on the matter, he claimed that "individual differences in mental ability depend largely on differences in physical structure of the brain" (Burt, 1972, p. 422).

Thorndike (1924) concurred with Spearman and Burt: "Psychologists would of course assume that differences in intelligence are due to differ-ences histological or physiological, or both, and would expect these physi-cal bases of intelligence to be measurable" (p. 229). He proposed that the number of connections in the brain was the basis for intelligence: "The gist of our doctrine is that, by original nature, the intellect capable of the highest reasoning and adaptability differs from the intellect of an imbecile only in the capacity for having more connections" (Thorndike, Bregman, Cobb, & Woodyard, 1926, pp. 421–422). He thought that heredity would effectively dictate the structure of the brain, but this might not be fully ap-parent in a test score: "The contribution of original nature is all there in the individual at three years, or at three days. How much of it is revealed in external behavior, and how much is hidden in the constitution of the neurones, is a question for investigation" (p. 461).

His unshakeable belief in biological intelligence helps to understand the scientific misconduct of Cyril Burt. When Kamin (1974) scrutinized the entire corpus of Burt's scholarly writings, he was shocked to read in one footnote by Burt and Howard (1957) that adjustments to the test score were used "to reduce the disturbing effects of environment to relatively slight proportions" (p. 39). For Kamin (1974), this data fudging and other irregularities rendered Burt's data useless for scientific purposes. Burt (1972) defended the practice against earlier criticisms: "Fuller and Thompson (1960, pp. 2, 323), in discussing these results, evidently suppose that the purpose of our analysis was to discover how much 'the variability of intelligence is attributable to heredity,' and describe our figures as 'estimates of the hetability [sic] of intelligence.' This is a frequent misinterpretation. The word 'intelligence' was merely used as a convenient shorthand label for 'the innate, general, cognitive factor'. In this sense the whole of it would by definition be inheritable" (p. 436). So Burt (1972, p. 346) advocated various devices to eliminate the influences of "the varying health and emotional attitude by many of the pupils," "the cultural background of the home," and other aspects of the environment, which Burt (1972) lightly dismissed as "irrelevancies." "Hence the final assessment cannot be called 'test score;' it is rather an estimate of a certain 'factor measurement' " (Burt, 1972, p. 437). Only after Kamin's (1974) thorough critique of Burt's work was it realized that Burt had not adjusted actual IQ test scores but instead had fabricated the published IQ distributions and correlations altogether (Dorfman, 1978; Fancher, 1985; Hearnshaw, 1981; Samelson, 1992).

Many psychologists then and now adjust correlations among raw scores for "attenuation" by test unreliability or average results from more than one IQ test in order to analyze "true" or biological intelligence. The testing situation may be arranged and other statistical corrections employed to eliminate other "irrelevancies" of the kind mentioned by Burt. The consequence of these practices in quantitative genetic studies is to increase the apparent influence of heredity by dispensing with sources of environmental variation. This was done in a prominent report on the Minnesota Twin Study in *Science* (Bouchard, Lykken, McGue, Segal, & Tellegen, 1990). Viewed from one perspective, that study was a model of well-controlled research. Monozygotic (MZ) twins raised apart were brought to the same laboratory and tested simultaneously by personnel trained to use the same criteria. They were given several IQ tests and average scores were used. The twins had been reunited as adults and had contact with each other from time to time during a period on average of almost 10 years prior to testing, but the researchers dismissed this environmental source of covariance as inconsequential because their adult subjects supposedly had passed through the "formative years" for environmental effects on intelligence before being reunited. The raw IQ scores were adjusted for changes with age (the cohort effect; see Neisser, 1997) and gender. Every one of these procedures and statistical devices had the effect of ejecting a source of environmental variance from the final equation or, in the case of environmental covariance, merging it with the term for genetic covariance, thereby increasing the estimation of "heritability." Viewed from outside the IQ testing fraternity, this might be seen as injecting a serious bias into the research, nudging the coefficient of heritability upwards. To many psychologists, however, the goal is to study a hypothetical and unseen biological intelligence that is not directly measured by IQ test scores.

GENETICS AND PHYSICAL STRUCTURE

The principles of Mendelian genetic inheritance were re-discovered, elaborated, and popularized in the first two decades of the 20th century (Sturtevant, 1965), a period when intelligence tests were also being invented and popularized. It was widely believed at the time that heredity somehow specifies the physical structure of the organism, including the nervous system. Mendel (1970) himself believed that "constant differentiating characters," not genes, were transmitted from parent to offspring. Bateson (1913) used the term *character-unit* or *factor* to represent that which was transmitted by heredity. For him, the characteristic was itself embodied in a microscopic and durable entity, termed the *gene*. From the perspective of Mendelian genetics, development was rigidly specified by heredity and thus was of little interest; attention instead focused on laws of transmission and resemblance among relatives. This doctrine resurrected a kind of preformationism previously buried by embryologists (Gottlieb, 1992; Jacob, 1973).

Early geneticists usually concentrated their efforts on situations where animals showed distinct and stable variants of traits such as color, size, or shape, and they frequently observed that those variants obeyed Mendel's laws quite faithfully. Instances were known where differences in animal behavior also followed Mendelian patterns (e.g., Yerkes, 1907), but behavior typically showed considerable variation among animals of the same strain and almost always occurred on a continuum where individuals differed only by degree. Close observation also revealed substantial variation in morphological traits even in pure lines of plants.

Bateson (1913) acknowledged that among pure lines there sometimes "are intermediates due to the *disturbing effects* of many small causes not of genetic but presumably of environmental origin" (p. 239), and these variations "are due to *interference which is external,* or environmental in the wide sense" (p. 240; emphasis added). Concerning the character-units, he wrote: "They are the *fundamental* elements, and consequences of *environmental interferences are subordinate* to them" (p. 203, emphasis added). That is, hereditary units were held to specify the outcome of development, and environmental influences were seen merely as subordinate disturbances that interfered with preordained form.

The Mendelian view of physical characters determined by hereditary units apparently influenced the thinking of pioneers of intelligence testing in psychology. Belief in genetically specified brain structure has persisted for decades in psychological and behavioral science. For example, Lorenz (1965) proposed that the genes contain a "genetic blueprint" for the structure of the brain. Wilson (1983) argued that "the brain is the ultimate structure underwriting human behavioral development" and its "precise wiring is coded in the DNA" (p. 10). Scarr and McCartney (1983) claimed that: "Maturational sequence is controlled primarily by the genetic program for development. In development, new adaptations or structures cannot arise out of experience per se" (p. 424). Consistent with the theory of biological intelligence, they maintained that only genes and never experience can specify biological form. Experience may affect performance on psychological tests, but it supposedly does not alter the architecture of the brain itself. The notion of biological intelligence is thus equivalent to a computer model in which there is a stark and inviolable boundary between genetically determined hardware and memories or software stored therein by experience.

AN ALTERNATIVE VIEW OF HEREDITY AND INTELLIGENCE

Several prominent geneticists adopted views clearly contrary to those of Bateson concerning heredity and development. Johannsen (1911) proposed that characters are not themselves inherited; instead, the *genotype* consisting of genes is inherited, whereas the observed character or *phenotype* develops during the life of the individual and may differ greatly among individuals having the same genotype. He held that "the particular organism is a whole, and its multiple varying reactions are determined by its 'genotype' interfering with the totality of all incident factors, may it be external or internal" (p. 133). Woltereck (1909) also argued against the doctrine of preformed characters and proposed that hereditary substance governs how the individual responds to the specific environment encountered during development (the *norm of reaction*; see Platt & Sanislow, 1988; Wahlsten & Gottlieb, 1997). Morgan (1914), having done extensive experimentation with fruit flies, concluded: "a factor, as I conceive it, is some minute particle of a chromosome whose presence in the cell influences the physiological processes that go on in the cell. Such a factor is supposed to be one element only in producing characters of the body. All the rest of the cell or much of it (including the inherited cytoplasm) may take part in producing the characters" (p. 15).

By 1920 an essentially modern conception of heredity had been formulated, one that has endured until the present and been confirmed by numerous discoveries. According to this conception, genes are large molecules that are inherited according to Mendelian principles, and they act at the molecular level as part of a metabolic system in living cells. The developmental consequences of inheriting a certain genotype can vary over a wide range and in many cases are dependent on the organism's environment. Genetic experiments are best done by making the environment as uniform as possible, as Mendel did, in order to reveal the properties of the genes more clearly, but this does not imply that environment is irrelevant.

The crucial distinction between the two conceptions of heredity and development is apparent in the relation between genes at the molecular level and phenomena at the higher and more complex organizational levels of cells, nervous tissues, brain, behavior, and thinking. The reductionist perspective (Bateson, Lorenz) maintains that genes specify the characteristics of things at higher levels, whereas the developmental systems view (Gottlieb, Johannsen, Woltereck) argues that genes act only at the molecular level and participate in a complex system that develops. These theoretical perspectives lead to rather different views of intelligence.

According to the systems view, intelligence is a property that exists at the psychological level, the level of the thinking individual who possesses a complex brain tutored in a human society. Bandura (2000) expressed this well: "Psychological principles cannot violate the neurophysiological capabilities of the systems that subserve them. But the psychological principles need to be pursued in their own right" (p. 2). Because thinking occurs in the brain, a genetic mutation that alters physiological brain development can influence the acquisition and manifestation of intelligence. Nevertheless, the individual's genotype does not code for any particular pathway of development, any specific nervous system structure, or any numerical value of intelligence.

Not all founders of psychological testing were doctrinaire touts of biological intelligence. For example, in applying their famous test of intellectual capacity to a child, Binet and Simon (1905b) stated explicitly: "We have nothing to do either with his past history or with his future; consequently we shall neglect his etiology, and we shall make no attempt to distinguish between acquired and congenital idiocy . . . we leave unanswered the question of whether this retardation is curable, or even improvable. We shall limit ourselves to ascertaining the truth in regard to his present mental state" (p. 191).

After the Second World War, many psychologists rejected the theory of biological intelligence. Stoddard (1945) observed that nature and nurture are "interwoven" from conception and the child is a product of "mutually interacting" heredity and environment. Crow and Crow (1948) presented to their psychology students the view that heredity and environment are interdependent and are not two mutually exclusive classes of causes.

Gates, Jersild, McConnell, and Challman (1948) similarly taught that effects of heredity and environment on intelligence are interwoven and inherited potentialities come to fruition through experience. By the 1950s, it was widely recognized that both hereditary and environmental variations are important for individual differences in intelligence, and leading psychologists, such as Cronbach (1949), taught that the Stanford–Binet and other IQ tests were not measures of innate ability and could be substantially influenced by cultural factors.

Many psychologists thus recognized the great importance of experience for mental development but did not know how strong environmental effects might be on individual differences in the normal, nonclinical range of variation. The concerns of these psychologists were addressed in depth by Fuller and Thompson (1960) in the first text on behavior genetics, where the merits and demerits of research designs that sought to separate influences of heredity and environment or assess their relative strengths were examined. Concerning intelligence, these authors concluded: "In summary, it may be said that the data gathered with human subjects point to heredity as an important determiner of intellectual level though certainly not the only one. From the size of the correlations alone, however, we can infer very little about the extent of its importance, even in very particular cases. Even if all the many relevant variables that may affect the *phenotypic expression of intelligence* were known, the knotty problem of disentangling heredity and environment would still remain" (p. 207; emphasis added).

Recognition of the importance of education and other experiences for IQ test score did not mean the theory of biological intelligence was decisively abandoned, however. The notion of an underlying, true intelligence of biological origin was implicit in many writings during that period. The foregoing statement from Fuller and Thompson (1960) about "the phenotypic expression of intelligence" is a case in point. Goodenough (1954) noted that ". . . divergences in the IQ's of children reared under varying conditions of opportunity and training may likewise result wholly or in part from the fact that the intelligence tests in present use are indirect rather then direct measures. They deal with the results of learning, from which capacity to learn is inferred. When opportunity and incentives have been reasonably similar, the inference is sound, but its validity may be questioned when a comparison is to be made between two or more groups for whom these factors have been markedly different" (p. 486). In the same volume, Jones (1954) observed about verbal test items "that items which in a common environment may be a good index of intelligence may in widely differing environments become predominantly a good index of environment" (p. 653). These authorities evidently continued to think of intelligence as an entity that by definition is *not* altered by experience, a construct whose manifestation can be obscured by differential education. What had changed as a result of many years of research was that experts began to recognize just how very difficult it was to obtain a valid measure of true intelligence because of major environmental impacts on IQ test results.

A clear disavowal of the traditional psychometric doctrine of the true score was made by Tryon (1957), who demonstrated that in evaluating psychological tests, "Postulates of 'underlying factors' are superfluous" (p. 231). Indeed, he proceeded to prove that all the familiar formulae for assessing test reliability could be derived with no reference whatsoever to underlying true scores. He emphatically criticized the prevailing notion of measurement error: "This is a bad term because the experimenter usually has no objective grounds for establishing that the fluctuations of an individual's observed performances are 'errors'—in fact, they are usually *genuine variations* that simply deviate from an average 'true' parameter value" (p. 237; emphasis added). This new conception of test reliability was applied to the problem of selective breeding for geotaxis in fruit flies by Hirsch and Tryon (1956) in the first published of the term "behavior genetics" to signify the emerging discipline in psychology. Cronbach (1970) in his generalizability theory also disputed the concept of "error variance" (see also Shavelson, Webb, & Rowley, 1989). Sadly, Tryon's and Cronbach's views of test reliability were not widely promulgated in behavior genetics, and the present author became one of many hoodwinked by the superfluous and unverified assumptions in the doctrine of a true test score (Wahlsten, 1992).

NERVOUS SYSTEM AND INTELLIGENCE

The theory of biological intelligence asserts that the ability to learn from experience is determined by genetically specified brain structure, whereas true intelligence is only indirectly and imperfectly indicated by standard tests of intelligence. According to this notion, it should therefore be possible to examine the nervous system directly and therein find a better measure of intelligence.

Beginning in the 1960s, neuroscientists discovered that the organization of the nervous system, especially the wiring of synaptic connections in the cerebral cortex, is substantially dependent on and altered by experience (Black & Greenough, 1998; Purves, 1988). For example, many cells in the visual cortex are normally responsive to input from both eyes (binocular cells), but rearing cats with input available from only one eye leads to a rapid change in synapses (Antonini & Stryker, 1993) and a great reduction in the number of binocular cortical cells (a similar condition evidently occurs in the human condition termed *lazy eye*). Early experience with spatially organized sound is crucial for auditory localization in the adult (Knudsen, 1988). Enriched experience leads to a larger and more complex brain with more synaptic connections on more elaborate dendrites of neurons supported by more glial cells and a richer blood supply. A particular kind of experience generally leads to changes in multiple sites in the brain (Klintsova & Greenough, 1999), and there is a multifaceted "brain adaptation" to experience (Greenough, Black, Klintsova, Bates, & Weiler, 1999). There is no critical or sensitive period for experiential effects that are novel or unexpected for the species, and environmental enrichment can increase the number of synaptic connections in the mature or middle-aged animal (Black & Greenough, 1998). Environmental treatments can even increase the number of neurons in the adult brain of experimental animals under certain conditions (Greenough, Cohen, & Juraska, 1999; Kemperman & Gage, 1999; Kemperman, Kuhn, & Gage, 1997), and recent data from taxi drivers in London suggest experience with spatial navigation can enlarge the anterior hippocampus in humans (Freeman, 2000; Maguire et al. 2000). Undernutrition during critical periods can impair brain growth, resulting in fewer and simpler neurons as well as a thinner myelin sheath around the axons of adults (Morgane et al., 1992, 1993).

It has become apparent that the structure of the nervous system is not directly or exclusively specified by genetic information, even though genetic mutations can undoubtedly alter brain structure. The nervous system involves numerous phenotypes that, like all phenotypes, are regulated by both genetic and nongenetic causes. Quantitative analysis of neural phenotypes in different strains or crosses of laboratory animals often reveals that nongenetic variation is substantial (Crusio, Genthner-Grimm, & Schwegler, 1986; Leamy, 1988; Wahlsten, 1989), even when the laboratory environment is carefully controlled to make it as uniform as practically feasible (e.g., Wahlsten, Crabbe, & Dudek, 2001). The earlier opinion that nervous system characteristics are inherently governed by genetic information and impervious to external forces must now be decisively rejected. Consequently, even if researchers were able to identify an array of neural phenotypes that is highly correlated with intelligence, this kind of evidence would not demonstrate a genetic origin of either brain structure or intelligence.

Another challenge to the theory of fixed, biological intelligence has come from well controlled studies of early experience in humans. Large improvements in the early childhood environment, whether caused by adoption into superior homes or random assignment to enriched preschool education, can increase intelligence by as much as one standard deviation or 15 IQ points (Wahlsten, 1997). Smaller but real effects are apparent even when less dramatic differences in experience are considered (Ceci, 1991, 1996). Dropping out of formal schooling or even the summer holidays can lead to a decline in IQ test scores, and starting schooling 1 year earlier can increase IQ test scores. Reports of large environmental effects are consistent with data compiled in quantitative genetic studies of human twins and adopted children that suggest no more than half of phenotypic variance in IQ has genetic associations (Devlin, Daniels, & Roeder, 1997; Plomin & DeFries, 1998; Plomin, DeFries, McClearn, & Rutter, 1997). A large research literature (see Ceci, 1996) has effectively debunked one of the core presumptions of the theory of biological intelligence, that intelligence is fixed by heredity and cannot be enhanced through education. This literature does not prove that heredity is irrelevant, and no expert in this field claims the additive genetic influence is zero. Nevertheless, large treatment effects on mean test scores clearly demonstrate the importance of early experience for mental development. Enriched early experience that confers greater intelligence must in turn lead to superior brain organization.

Efforts to identify intelligence with specific aspects of the nervous system have uncovered a variety of correlations that generally are less than $r = 0.5$ and cannot possibly account for the bulk of variation in intelligence test scores. Speed of nerve conduction and reaction time to visual or tactile stimuli typically show small to moderate correlations with intelligence. These findings are not at all surprising, given that many intelligence tests themselves place a premium on speed of responding. Difficulties of interpretation loom large in many of these studies, however (Mackintosh, 1998). Recent data from Rijsdijk and Boomsma (1997) are particularly interesting. In a large sample of twin pairs, the split-halves reliabilities of different measures of nerve conduction velocity in the forearm were very high ($> .95$), yet the phenotypic correlation with WAIS IQ was only .16. Despite the high within-session consistency of velocity measures, there was very low test–retest correlation between subjects tested at both 16 and 18 years of age ($r = .08$ to $r = .20$), apparently because of continuing developmental change in the peripheral nerves.

Weak correlations are also the rule when comparing IQ with brain size. The literature on brain size measured after death is particularly prone to artifacts, but the advent of in situ methods has provided more credible evidence. A small correlation ($r = .25$) between whole brain volume and IQ was observed by Flashman, Andreason, Flaum, and Swayze (1998) using magnetic resonance imaging (MRI), but no particular brain region showed a markedly higher correlation. In this literature, it is not at all clear whether brain size variation mediates the relation with intelligence or instead both phenotypes are independently influenced by the same causal antecedents, including nutrition and enriched experience. Psychologists know perfectly well that mere correlation does not prove causation, and there is no justification for lowering the methodological standards when one of the variables is a biological measure. Biology should not be automatically granted causal precedence, because we now realize that the psychological environment can sculpt the nervous system and regulate neural activity. As Gottlieb (1992, 1998; Gottlieb, Wahlsten, & Lickliter, 1998) and Rose (1997) have argued, the relation between neural processes and behavior is bidirectional co-action rather than the upward causation from the biological to the psychological level that is proclaimed in reductionist theory.

Eysenck (1988) and others have proposed that the averaged evoked potential (AEP) to sensory stimuli, based on electrical activity recorded from the scalp, gives a purer measure of biological intelligence than IQ tests. Many of the studies reviewed by Eysenck reported correlations with IQ in the range .1 to .5, with one finding a remarkable $r = .8$ between variability in the AEP and IQ. Recently, Jensen (1999) claimed that g is not a psychological variable but rather "a biological one, a property of the brain" (p. 1). His interpretation of evoked potentials was challenged, however, by Verleger (1999), who specializes in the study of human brain electrical activity. Verleger noted that the example of the event related potential (ERP) presented by Jensen (1998) was highly atypical, did not use standard nomenclature for peaks in the record, and was "obviously contaminated by a regular background rhythm" (p. 3). Furthermore, he found that Jensen's index of biological intelligence, the number of zero crossings in the tracing, was mainly an artifact of electrical noise. Verleger did not deny that ERPs might be somehow related to intelligence; rather, he challenged the notion "that ERPs provide a simple biological basis for the measurement of intelligence" (p. 4).

The dynamic functioning of the human brain can now be glimpsed with the technique of functional magnetic resonance imaging (fMRI). The goal of the method is to measure changes in the metabolic activity of small regions of the brain during different kinds of mental activity. Those who hope that this method will provide a foolproof, direct measure of intelligence will be sorely disappointed, however. As illustrated by the study of Rypma and D'Esposito (1999), the measurement is highly indirect, and sophisticated correction for several kinds of artifacts must be used to obtain meaningful data. Because of the extraordinary expense of the apparatus and technician time, most studies involve only a handful of subjects, six in the case of Rypma and D'Esposito (1999), and a very limited array of test conditions. Rather than use correlational methods with large samples, researchers such as Baron-Cohen et al. (1999) find it more effective to equate a few subjects on many potentially important variables in order to isolate the effects of one or two things of central interest in the research.

It is clear that no measure of the nervous system examined to date provides a simple and direct measure of anything remotely resembling general intelligence. Instead, a number of weak neural correlates of IQ have been identified, in many instances so weak that they might inspire speculation about mind-body dualism. Many pitfalls and artifacts in obtaining these neural measures have also been identified, and psychologists without extensive training in neuroscience would be well advised to proceed with caution and seek expert collaborators who really know the brain. Whenever a significant correlation between brain and IQ is detected, the question of causation needs to be addressed in a serious manner, because modern neuroscience has firmly established that experience alters the structure and function of the brain.

Most intelligence tests tap diverse mental functions involving abstract reasoning and a fairly wide variety of language-based skills as well as sensorimotor processes. It thus seems unlikely that neuroscientists will be able to identify any small array of neural phenotypes that fully and fairly represents the same entity as psychometrists measure with mental tests. In a recent interview by Holden (1998), Nathan Brody remarked that: "There are not even any real theories about what are the biological influences" on intelligence. Connectionist models are being addressed to this problem, however (see Elman et al., 1996).

GENES AND INTELLIGENCE

Genetic studies have firmly established that there is no necessary connection between the magnitude of the phenotypic effect of a mutation and the modifiability of the same phenotype by environmental change (Lewontin, 1991; Wahlsten, 1997). Although some devastating mutations do indeed render the organism incapable of benefitting from enhanced environments, there are many others that disrupt homeostatic mechanisms and thereby make the organism more sensitive to external conditions. One important lesson from decades of genetic research is that the metabolic activities of a gene and its relation with phenotypic development are highly specific to the gene in question (Wahlsten, 2001). Thus, our discussion of genetics, neuroscience, and intelligence is best informed by genes whose mode of action is known. On the basis of genes that clearly alter intelligence in humans or learning ability in animals, it is apparent that these genes do not specifically code for intelligence, either biological or psychological.

Consider the well-known example of phenylketonuria (PKU) in humans, where a recessive mutation in the gene coding for the enzyme phenylalanine hydroxylase can impair mental development when the infant inherits two defective copies of the gene. The gene is named PAH to represent the enzyme for which it codes. Even though this is a textbook example of a Mendelian gene causing medical disease, the phenotypic effects are far from simple (Scriver & Waters, 1999). The harmful phenotypic effects can be largely avoided by giving the infant an artificial diet low in the amino acid phenylalanine. In this instance, children with two defective PAH genes are far more sensitive to the level of phenylalanine in the diet than are children with the normal form of the gene. Biochemical methods reveal that the PAH gene is expressed as the enzyme phenylalanine hydroxylase primarily in the liver, not in the brain. When the liver cannot metabolize phenylalanine, it accumulates to high levels in the bloodstream, and this has widespread effects on the physiology of the body and brain. Untreated PKU in an infant has a severe impact on intelligence, but the gene does not in any way code for intelligence and is not specific to neural functioning. Physiologically, the effect of PKU on the brain is quite similar to the effect of severe protein malnutrition, in that it leads to low levels of amino acids being transported into the brain from the bloodstream, and this impairs numerous features of brain development because amino acids are essential for the synthesis of new proteins and many smaller molecules such as neurotransmitters. This example of a genetic defect thus does not deepen our understanding of the relation between brain function and intelligence; instead, it merely confirms what we already know, that normal intelligence depends on having a healthy brain. Knowledge of the gene and its function is invaluable, however, when devising a means to treat the disorder.

The most profound implication of PKU for theories of development arises from the condition known as maternal PKU (Koch et al., 1999; Waisbren, 1999), in which the high levels of phenylalanine in the bloodstream of a pregnant women with PKU, who had been treated effectively in infancy, seriously impairs brain development of her genetically normal fetus. Is this a genetic effect on brain development mediated by the maternal environment external to the affected child or an environmental effect provoked by a genetic defect in the mother? The example demonstrates the extreme difficulty of attempting to partition all differences in brain structure and intelligence into mutually exclusive categories ascribed to either heredity or environment. Once we know how the system of causes works, assigning percentages to the different parts becomes an empty exercise.

Gene action can now be studied in great detail with molecular techniques. The gene is a segment of a DNA molecule, and the first step in its expression occurs when the code in the DNA is transcribed into a large molecule of messenger RNA (mRNA). The presence of mRNA in any tissue in the brain or elsewhere in the body can be detected with the method of *in situ* hybridization. The next step is the translation of the code in the mRNA into the sequence of amino acids in a new protein molecule that is unique to the gene in question. The specific protein can be detected with antibody molecules using the method of immunohistochemistry. It has now become a relatively easy matter to determine the different kinds of tissues wherein a specific gene is expressed and the period during development when it is normally expressed. This knowledge is now readily available for several thousand human and mouse genes. As part of the Human Genome Project, the Genome Database includes this information at the website http://www.gdb.org. In many instances, a homologous gene is also present in mice and can be reviewed at the website http://www.informatics.jax.org. When a gene is claimed to have some effect on intelligence, it is possible to ascertain whether it is a gene expressed exclusively in the brain or widely throughout the body.

An example arises from the report by Chorney et al. (1998) that high IQ score is statistically associated with a specific DNA marker in the IGF2R gene on chromosome 6. The claim was published in *Psychological Science*, a journal directed primarily to psychologists who most likely know little of the intricacies of genetics, and it was cited widely in the mass media as "the first specific gene for human intelligence" (Intelligence genes, 1997). That report also gushed that "The research not only offers new insights into how the brain functions, it could settle the debate about whether genetics or education and lifestyle determine human intelligence." One author of the study (Plomin) was quoted as saying that this discovery should end years of argument over whether genes can affect intelligence because "It is harder to argue with a piece of DNA" (Highfield, 1997). A recent review (Lubbock, 2000) cited this study as showing it is "well established that people with this variant of the normal gene are far more intelligent than average." To the neurogeneticist, however, three aspects of the report rain heavily on the celebration. First, even if the effect is replicated, something that rarely happens in this field, it accounts for only about 2% of variance in IQ in the population. Second, the fine print of the article reveals that the DNA probe associated with IQ was merely a neutral marker and was not actually part of the IGF2R gene that is translated into protein. Consequently, there was no evidence reported to implicate the IGF2R gene itself. Any effect on IQ, if real and replicable by other groups, could very well arise from some other gene located a considerable distance away on the same chromosome. Third, the IGF2R gene codes for the structure of the "insulin-like growth factor II receptor," a kind of protein that allows a cell to detect the presence of hormones similar to insulin that typically circulate widely throughout the body via the bloodstream (see http://www3.ncbi.nlm.nih.gov/htbin-post/Omim for details). A search of recent editions of Current Contents reveals that mutations in the gene are implicated in human cancers of the breast, liver, and prostate. The Gene Expression Data option for the homologous *Igf2r* gene in mice reveals that the gene is widely expressed in the tissues listed in Table 10.2 and is certainly not specific to the brain. No effect of the IGF2R gene on intelligence let alone an effect specific to intelligence has yet been demonstrated by adequate scientific criteria.

Many mutations that alter behavior in the fruit fly *Drosophila* have been discovered, and the molecular mechanisms through which they act have been explored in depth (Pflugfelder, 1998). Some genes, for example *dunce* that codes for the enzyme cyclic AMP-specific phosphodiesterase, are ubiquitously expressed in many kinds of tissue throughout the fly, and most mutant genes known to affect fly behavior show pleiotropic effects on several different phenotypes. The *period* gene alters the length of the endogenous circadian rhythm and is expressed in many kinds of cell that were not previously known to be involved in rhythmic acitivity. Generally speaking, the modes of gene action pertinent to fly behavior are richly varied, and a specific gene generally does not have effects limited to a particular kind of behavior or a single component of a complex behavior (Miklos & Rubin, 1996; Pflugfelder, 1998).

In laboratory mice a large amount of information has been accumulated using the method of targeted mutation in genes known to be relevant to nervous system function (Bolivar, Cook, & Flaherty, 2000; Crusio & Gerlai, 1999; Mak, 1998; see the websites http://tbase.jax.org, http://www.biomednet.com/db/mkmd, and http://165/112/78/61/genetics/ko/ko-index.html). Many of these mutations have surprisingly little effect on behavior and often yield viable animals, despite the total absence of the protein product in "null" mutants known as gene "knockouts." It is now common practice to evaluate the phenotypic effects of a new mutation in mice by screening the animals with an extensive battery of tests of a wide range of physiological and behavioral functions (e.g. Crawley & Paylor, 1997). This literature is somewhat fragmented at present because no two labora-

TABLE 10.2
Tissues of the Mouse in Which the *Igf2r* Gene,
a Homologue of the Human IGF2R Gene, Are Expressed

Adipose tissue	Adrenal gland	Bladder	Cervix	Colon
Duodenum	Epididymis	Eye	Femur	Gall bladder
Heart	Ileum	Incisor	Kidney	Liver
Lung	Mammary gland	Oesophagus	Ovary	Pancreas
Placenta	Skeletal muscle	Skin	Spleen	Testis
Thymus	Tongue			

Brain: cerebellum, cerebral cortex, corpus striatum, hippocampus, midbrain, olfactory bulb, pituitary gland, spinal cord

Source: http://www.informatics.jax.org using the Gene Expression Data option.

tories seem to use the same test battery and details of tests are often idiosyncratic to each lab (see Crabbe, Wahlsten, & Dudek, 1999). Nevertheless, it is apparent that cases where a mutation influences only one kind of
behavior are the exception. The calcium-dependent calmodulin kinase
type II enzyme provides a good example. Knocking out the *Camk2* gene
alters hippocampus-related spatial memory (Mayford et al., 1996) but also
changes the level of fighting behavior (Chen, Rainnie, Greene, & Tonegawa, 1994) and morphine-related behavioral changes (Maldonado et al.,
1996). These kind of widespread phenotypic effects have motivated researchers to invent elaborate experimental methods that can limit the expression of a mutation to a particular kind of cell in the brain or a restricted period of time in order to avoid the difficulty of interpreting data
when diverse developmental effects are involved (Wahlsten, 1999).

One message from genetic investigation of brain and behavior is that
gene action does not occur in a simple one gene-one effect manner expected by reductionist theory (Miklos & Rubin, 1996; Rose, 1997; Strohman, 1997; Wahlsten, 1999). Instead, genes are organized in complex biochemical systems and usually have relevance to a diversity of phenotypes.
Furthermore, the effects of different genes are often interactive, such that
a mutation at one genetic locus has effects that depend on the genotype at
other loci (de Belle & Heisenberg, 1996; Magara et al., 1999). At this stage
of the enterprise, it appears that the complexity of gene action at the molecular level is not likely to tell us a great deal about the nature of intelligence at the psychological level. If an individual encounters difficulty
learning because of a deleterious mutation, then knowing how that specific gene works may provide clues about how to treat the symptoms. In
the vast majority of instances when there is no mutation of major consequence, however, there are probably hundreds or even thousands of genes
involved in the biochemical and physiological processes that result in
learning.

GENERAL VERSUS MULTIPLE FACTOR THEORY

Whether most of the variation in intelligence can be attributed to Spearman's general ability (*g*) factor or some variant of Thurstone's multiple,
primary mental abilities has been a central issue in psychology for decades, and interest in this topic remains at a high level (Das, 1992; Gardner, 1999; Gottfredson, 1997). It has been claimed that there is a "consensus" in the field of psychometrics concerning the reality and importance of
g (Carroll, 1997, p. 33). Gottfredson (1997) presented a statement in support of general intelligence that was signed by 52 people she considered
experts in intelligence, less than half of the 131 people invited to sign. To

me, a consensus means everyone with a certain level of expertise on the topic agrees with a position, and in the field of intelligence there most certainly is no consensus. A poll of specialists seems quite beside the point when several advocates of multiple intelligences are well known and highly respected authorities in the field. In the history of science, virtually all successful theories begin life as minority views and are thwarted by powerful proponents of prevailing beliefs. The more important question is the trend of evidence. Spearman's g has been debated for almost 100 years and still has not won over the field of psychology. There seem to be increasing rumblings of discontent and dissatisfaction with full-scale IQ representations of g.

QUANTITATIVE GENETIC ANALYSIS

The vast majority of the literature on quantitative genetic analysis of human intelligence accepts the validity and importance of g and uses IQ tests that presume to measure mainly a general factor. The statement by Plomin and Petrill (1997) is typical of the field: "What we mean by intelligence is general cognitive functioning (g)" (p. 56). The work of Vandenberg (1968, 1977) with tests of Primary Mental Abilities is a noteworthy exception. I have chosen not to review this entire literature in detail because of serious reservations about the methods typically employed.

Additive genetic models involving genetic correlation (Falconer & McKay, 1996) might be applied to the question of independence of specific abilities, but there are serious doubts about the validity of the assumptions required by the models. Consider the simplest situation where there is only one phenotype being studied, perhaps full scale IQ. Quantitative models seek to separate phenotypic variance into components attributable to additive and dominance genetic variance as well as shared and nonshared environmental effects (Plomin et al., 1997), and they use correlations involving twins and adopted children to achieve this separation. This methodology contains several fatal flaws. There are considerably more relations in the full model than observed correlations in the data set, and the models thus are seriously underspecified (Goldberger, 1978). From a statistical perspective, the human situation does not allow a clean separation of sources of variance (Kempthorne, 1978), and inappropriate formulations are often employed (Schönemann, 1997). The typical practice in human behavior genetics is to assume that certain kinds of correlations are absent or negligible. The usual roster of assumptions includes the following.

1. There is no correlation between scores of the parents (no assortative mating).

2. There is no correlation between genetic similarity of twins and the similarities of their environments (the equal environments assumption).

3. There is no correlation between genotypes of adopted children and their adoptive family environments (no selective placement).

4. There are no effects of the prenatal maternal environment on development.

5. There is no genotype–environment covariance within any class of relative.

6. There is no genotype–environment interaction. Effects are entirely additive.

7. Genes at different loci act independently so that effects are additive (no epistasis).

As reviewed in detail elsewhere, there are good reasons to believe that these assumptions are usually not valid and that violations of the assumptions can have major consequences for the magnitudes of effects in a model (Guo, 1999; Roubertoux & Capron, 1990; Vreeke, 2000; Wahlsten, 1990, 1994; Wahlsten & Gottlieb, 1997). Consequently, quantitative genetic analysis of the factorial structure of tests of multiple intelligences cannot be conclusive. Conclusions from models that are known to incorporate false assumptions are moot. Kempthorne (1990), a leading figure in quantitative genetics, recommended "that most of the literature on heritability in species that cannot be experimentally manipulated, for example, in mating, should be ignored" (p. 139).

ANIMAL LEARNING: GENERAL AND TASK-SPECIFIC

Although learning ability in experimental animals may not be equivalent to human intelligence, there is no doubt that the genetic and cellular mechanisms of acquiring and retaining memories of simple stimulus associations are quite similar in humans and nonhumans (Tully, 1997). Virtually all of the proteins known to be important for synaptic transmission and electrochemical activity of neurons in the central nervous system are present in the brains of humans, mice and rats alike, and most are also found in fruit flies. Methods used with flies and mice make it possible to create a mutation in virtually any gene known to be important in nervous system function, and analysis of the effects of many such mutations will enable us to understand the organization or circuitry of the learning process at the chemical and cellular levels (Crusio & Gerlai, 1999; Gerlai, 1996b;

Tully, 1997; Wahlsten, 1999). Knowing that a particular gene is crucial for learning in mice or flies, we can then ask whether there are different forms (alleles) of that gene in a human population (genetic polymorphism) and whether those alleles are associated with variation in one or many kinds of human intelligences. Most genes in humans are not polymorphic; instead, mutations having harmful effects on brain development tend to be quite rare. Whether intelligence exists in one or many forms is a question about *differences* in intelligence in the human population, and the genetic part of the formula is relevant only to the extent that genetic variants are fairly common.

There is little doubt that different kinds of learning occur in species such as rats and mice, as shown by analyses of brain function with lesions and local application of drugs (Everitt & Robbins, 1997). A large literature on genetic studies of animal learning has examined the question of general learning ability and concluded that most situations are dominated by task-specific abilities (Wahlsten, 1972, 1978, 1999). Selective breeding for high and low rates of acquisition of a task is often successful in obtaining lines of animals that differ greatly in rate of learning, but the line differences are considerably reduced or even reversed when animals are then tested in situations unlike the original task (e.g., the Tryon maze bright and dull lines studied by Searle, 1949). Brush (1991) noted that several selection experiments using the shuttle box with rats yielded lines differentiated primarily by emotionality rather than associative learning ability. This is one reason why few experts in animal behavior genetics today use the term intelligence when describing their findings. It is conceivable that selective breeding for an average score on several kinds of tasks might yield something more general, but available data suggest this would be a very slow and expensive undertaking. That is, it might be possible to uncover evidence of general learning ability in rats or mice, but the variance in this construct would likely be far smaller than task-specific variance.

Inbred strains provide numerous examples of strain-specific reactions to particular kinds of tasks. The A/J strain tends to run when receiving an electric shock, whereas the DBA strain usually jumps, and these unconditioned reflexes can influence the acquisition of an avoidance task (Wahlsten, 1972, 1978). Peeler (1995) found that results with recombinant inbred strains depended on the configuration of the opening between two compartments in the avoidance box. Many mouse strains (e.g., CBA and C3H) suffer from hereditary retinal degeneration and consequently do not perform well on tasks requiring good pattern vision. In the Morris water maze, which is widely applied to assess spatial memory, the A/J strain consistently hugs the walls and therefore fails to learn (Crabbe et al., 1999), whereas the 129 and BALB/c strains often float passively (Francis, Zaharia, Shanks, & Anisman, 1995). Wolfer, Stagljar-Bozicevic, Errington, and Lipp (1998) tested 1,400 mice of different genotypes on the Morris task and then subjected several measures to factor analysis; the first factor accounted for 49% of the variance and reflected thigmotaxis or wall-hugging, the second (19%) represented passive floating, and the third (13%) appeared to be spatial memory, the phenotype of primary interest to researchers who often employ this task to assess gene knockouts. The peculiar reactions to the test situation by the 129 strain is especially problematic because this is the most frequently used strain for producing knockouts (Bolivar et al., 2000; Gerlai, 1996a; Wolfer, Müller, Staglier, & Lipp, 1997).

DOCTRINE OF THE "TRUE" SCORE RECONSIDERED

Given all that is known today about environmental effects on both brain organization and intelligence as well as the nature of gene action, it is apparent that biological intelligence, defined as a stable, genetically specified feature of the individual's brain that determines ability to learn or capacity for achievement, does not exist. Intelligence conceived as an immutable true score is a figment of reductionist dogma. In my opinion, it was a serious mistake in 1904, when so little was known about brain development, to *define* intelligence, a preeminently psychological construct, in terms of its alleged causes at a lower, physiological level of analysis or its stability across age. Building the answer to questions about genetic influence and environmental malleability into a circular definition of intelligence set the stage for decades of möbius discourse. After almost 100 years of intense activity in this field, psychologists are still debating the definition of intelligence (Neisser et al., 1996), and serious doubts are expressed about the commonplace uses of IQ tests (Ceci, 1996; Gardner, 1996; Sternberg, 1996, 1999). The words of Binet and Simon (1905a) still ring true: "The simple fact, that specialists do not agree in the use of the technical terms of their science, throws suspicion upon their diagnoses" (p. 11).

Intelligence is a psychological construct *par excellence*. Its properties need to be defined and measured by psychologists using methods appropriate to the domain of mental activity. Perhaps in the early years of the 20th century, when psychology was an immature discipline lacking self-confidence, there might have been cause to base its doctrines on a more highly respected biology. After a century of growth, however, there is no longer any justification for what Bandura (2000) decried as the "progressive divestiture of different aspects of psychology to biology" (p. 2).

Psychologists would be wise to jettison the true score doctrine and focus on a psychological definition of intelligence. That banal cultural icon, the

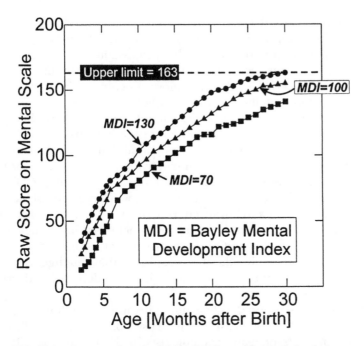

FIG. 10.2.   Raw scores on the Bayley (1969) test of mental development. The test has 163 items with a maximum raw score of 163. Raw scores equivalent to standardized scores of 70 (3rd percentile), 100 (50th percentile), and 130 (98th percentile) are indicated. Because of the rapid growth of mental abilities during this period, children scoring at MDI = 70 are nevertheless well above those at MDI = 130 only a few weeks earlier, and development of those that remain at MDI = 70 over a period of several months is nonetheless quite rapid. Standardization can obscure the pattern of absolute growth. Relations with concomitant brain development should be judged on the basis of growth profiles as well as correlations of standardized scores.

IQ score, is most emphatically not a measure of mental ability. It is a unitless index of relative performance on a test heavily weighted with academic knowledge and scaled in a manner that obscures the current level and rate of growth of intelligence. The Bayley scale of mental development (Fig. 10.2) provides a clear illustration of how dramatic changes in performance can be hidden by a standard score. More illuminating studies on the relation between the nervous system and intelligence would be facilitated if a widely accepted measure of intelligence rather than IQ were available. Looking behind the usual IQ scale, it is apparent that mean level of mental functioning in the population continues to increase rapidly throughout childhood and into the teen years. Many measures of brain structure, on the other hand, show rapidly diminishing changes with age during this same period, whereas the genotype shows no change at all (see Fig. 10.1). To comprehend the neural bases for mental development, we need to examine first and foremost the mean values at different ages. It would be especially instructive to explore changes in the brain wrought by enriched early experiences that are known to enhance intelligence. If a treatment increases intelligence of a group of children by about one standard deviation, a large effect size according to Cohen (1988), there must be some fairly large changes somewhere in the nervous system.

It seems to me that we first need to have a valid measure of a construct; only then might it be useful for comparative purposes to transform the scale into standard deviation units. Unlike the early years of the 20th century when the first IQ tests were constructed, now a large body of literature on intelligence testing and advanced technology for test construction exist. It should be possible to devise an instrument that has a meaningful zero point and an upper limit of performance that is well above the current maximum for highly educated people, so that intelligence can be scored across the complete range of ages, just as is done for body weight and core temperature.

This task will be especially challenging because of the long neglect of fundamental problems of measurement in psychology (Michell, 1997) and the vested interests of many psychologists in the ubiquitous IQ score. Psychometrists have been reluctant to reconsider the matter, as witnessed by this comment of Michell (1997): "When the attitude of turning a deaf ear to criticism becomes entrenched, it can alter patterns of thinking and the way words are used, with the result that criticism may be treated as irrelevant" (p. 356). Perhaps by seeking the source of intelligence in the brain, psychologists will recruit into the debate neuroscientists who are less committed to the standard IQ approach and more interested in the issue of measurement.

REFERENCES

Antonini, A., & Stryker, M. P. (1993). Rapid remodeling of axonal arbors in the visual cortex. *Science, 260,* 1819–1821.

Bandura, A. (2000). Swimming against the mainstream. Accenting the positive in human nature. *HMS Beagle,* Issue 70, January 21. [www.biomednet.com/hmsbeagle/70/viewpts/op_ed]

Baron-Cohen, S., Ring, H. A., Wheelwright, S., Bullmore, E. T., Brammer, M. J., Simmons, A., & Williams, S. C. R. (1999). Social intelligence in the normal and autistic brain: An fMRI study. *European Journal of Neuroscience, 11,* 1891–1998.

Bateson, W. (1913). *Mendel's principles of heredity.* Cambridge, England: Cambridge University Press.

Bayer, S. A., Altman, J., Russo, R. J., & Zhang, X. (1995). Embryology. In S. Duckett (Ed.), *Pediatric neurology* (pp. 54–107). Baltimore: Williams & Wilkins.

Bayley, N. (1969). *Manual for the Bayley Scales of Infant Development*. Berkeley, CA: Institute of Human Development, University of California.

Bayley, N. (1993). *Bayley Scales of Infant Development (2nd ed.) Manual*. San Antonio, TX: Psychological Corporation.

Binet, A., & Simon, T. (1905a). Upon the necessity of establishing a scientific diagnosis of inferior states of intelligence. *L'Année psychologie*, pp. 163–191. [translated by E. S. Kite and reprinted in 1983 in *The development of intelligence in children*, Salem, NH: Ayer Company.]

Binet, A., & Simon, T. (1905b). New methods for the diagnosis of the intellectual level of subnormals. *L'Année psychologie, 12*, 191–244. [translated by E. S. Kite and reprinted in 1983 in *The development of intelligence in children*, Salem, NH: Ayer Company.]

Black, J. E., & Greenough, W. T. (1998). Developmental approaches to the memory process. In J. L. Martinez Jr. & R. P. Kesner (Eds.), *Neurobiology of learning and memory* (pp. 55–88). San Diego: Academic Press.

Bolivar, V., Cook, M., & Flaherty, L. (2000). List of transgenic and knockout mice: Behavioral profiles. *Mammalian Genome, 11*, 260–274.

Bouchard, T. J., Lykken, D. T., McGue, M., Segal, N. L., & Tellegen, A. (1990). Sources of human psychological differences: the Minnesota study of twins reared apart. *Science, 250*, 223–228.

Brody, N. (1992). *Intelligence* (2nd ed.). New York: Academic Press.

Brush, F. R. (1991). Genetic determinants of individual differences in avoidance learning: Behavioral and endocrine characteristics. *Experientia, 47*, 1039–1050.

Burt, C. (1909). Experimental tests of general intelligence. *British Journal of Psychology, 3*, 94–177.

Burt, C. (1934). How the mind works in the adult. In C. Burt (Ed.), *How the mind works*. Freeport, NY: Books for Libraries Press.

Burt, C. (1972). General ability and special aptitudes. In R. M. Dreger (Ed.), *Multivariate personality research: Contributions to the understanding of personality in honor of Raymond B. Cattell* (pp. 411–450). Baton Rouge, LA: Claitor's Publishing.

Burt, C., & Howard, M. (1957). Heredity and intelligence: A reply to criticisms. *British Journal of Statistical Psychology, 10*, 33–63.

Calvin, W. H. (1999). The emergence of intelligence. *Scientific American Presents, 9*, 44–50.

Carroll, J. B. (1997). Psychometrics, intelligence, and public perception. *Intelligence, 24*, 25–52.

Ceci, S. J. (1991). How much does schooling influence general intelligence and its cognitive components? A reassessment of the evidence. *Developmental Psychology, 27*, 702–722.

Ceci, S. J. (1996). *On intelligence. A bioecological treatise on intellectual development* (Expanded ed.). Cambridge, MA: Harvard University Press.

Chen, C., Rainnie, D. G., Greene, R. W., & Tonegawa, S. (1994). Abnormal fear response and aggressive behavior in mutant mice deficient for alpha-calcium-calmodulin kinase II. *Science, 266*, 291–294.

Chorney, M. J., Chorney, K., Seese, N., Owen, M. J., Daniels, J., McGuffin, P., Thompson, L. A., Detterman, D. K., Benbow, C., Lubinski, D., Eley, T., & Plomin, R. (1998). A quantitative trait locus associated with cognitive ability in children. *Psychological Science, 9*, 159–166.

Cohen, J. (1988). *Statistical power analysis for the behavioral sciences*. Hillsdale, NJ: Lawrence Erlbaum Associates.

Cohen, R. J., & Swerdlik, M. E. (1999). *Psychological testing and assessment*. Mountain View, CA: Mayfield.

Crabbe, J. C., Wahlsten, D., & Dudek, B. C. (1999). Genetics of mouse behavior: interactions with laboratory environment. *Science, 284*, 1670–1672.

Crawley, J. N., & Paylor, R. (1997). A proposed test battery and constellations of specific behavioral paradigms to investigate the behavioral phenotypes of transgenic and knockout mice. *Hormones and Behavior, 27,* 201–210.

Cronbach, L. J. (1949). *Essentials of psychological testing.* New York: Harper & Brothers.

Cronbach, L. J. (1970). *Essentials of psychological testing* (3rd ed.). New York: Harper & Row.

Crow, L. D., & Crow, A. (1948). *Educational psychology.* New York: American Book Co.

Crusio, W. E., Genthner-Grimm, G., & Schwegler, H. (1986). A quantitative-genetic analysis of hippocampal variation in the mouse. *Journal of Neurogenetics, 3,* 203–214.

Crusio, W. E., & Gerlai, R. T. (Eds.). (1999). *Handbook of molecular-genetic techniques for brain and behavior research.* Amsterdam: Elsevier Science.

Das, J. P. (1992). Beyond a unidimensional scale of merit. *Intelligence, 16,* 137–149.

de Belle, J. S., & Heisenberg, M. (1996). Expression of *Drosophila* mushroom body mutations in alternative genetic backgrounds: A case study of the mushroom body miniature gene (*mbm*). *Proceedings of the National Academy of Sciences USA, 93,* 9875–9880.

Devlin, B., Daniels, M., & Roeder, K. (1997). The heritability of IQ. *Nature, 388,* 468–470.

Dorfman, D. D. (1978). The Cyril Burt question: New findings. *Science, 201,* 1177–1186.

Elman, J. L., Bates, E. A., Johnson, M. H., Karmiloff-Smith, A., Parisi, D., & Plunkett, K. (1996). *Rethinking innateness. A connectionist perspective on development.* Cambridge, MA: MIT Press.

Encha-Razavi, F. (1995). Fetal neuropathology. In S. Duckett (Ed.), *Pediatric neurology* (pp. 108–122). Baltimore: Williams & Wilkins.

Everitt, B. J., & Robbins, T. W. (1997). Central cholinergic systems and cognition. *Annual Review of Psychology, 48,* 649–684.

Eysenck, H. J. (1988). The biological basis of intelligence. In S. H. Irvine & J. W. Berry (Eds.), *Human abilities in cultural context* (pp. 87–104). Cambridge, England: Cambridge University Press.

Fagan, J. F., III. (1985). A new look at infant intelligence. In D. K. Detterman (Ed.), *Current topics in human intelligence. Volume 1. Research methodology* (pp. 223–246). Norwood, NJ: Ablex.

Falconer, D. S., & MacKay, T. F. C. (1996). *Introduction to quantitative genetics* (4th ed.). Harlow, England: Longman.

Fancher, R. E. (1985). *The intelligence men. Makers of the IQ controversy.* New York: Norton.

Flashman, L. A., Andreasen, N. C., Flaum, M., & Swayze, V. W., II. (1998). Intelligence and regional brain volumes in normal controls. *Intelligence, 25,* 149–160.

Francis, D. D., Zaharia, M. D., Shanks, N., & Anisman, H. (1995). Stress-induced disturbances in Morris water-maze performance: interstrain variability. *Physiology and Behavior, 58,* 57–65.

Freeman, A. (2000). Knowledgeable cabbies get big heads navigating London's 17,000 routes. *Globe and Mail,* March 15, pp. A1, A14.

Fuller, J. L., & Thompson, W. R. (1960). *Behavior genetics.* New York: Wiley.

Galton, F. (1892). *Hereditary genius.* New York: Macmillan.

Gardner, H. (1999). Who owns intelligence? *Atlantic Monthly, 283,* 67–76.

Gates, A. I., Jersild, A. T., McConnell, T. R., & Challman, R. C. (1948). *Educational psychology.* New York: Macmillan.

Gerlai, R. (1996a). Gene-targeting studies of mammalian behavior: is it the mutation or the background genotype? *Trends in Neuroscience, 19,* 177–181.

Gerlai, R. (1996b). Molecular genetic analysis of mammalian behavior and brain processes: Caveats and perspectives. *Seminars in the Neurosciences, 8,* 153–161.

Gesell, A., & Amatruda, C. S. (1947). *Developmental diagnosis. Normal and abnormal child development.* New York: Harper & Row, Hoeber Medical Division.

Goldberger, A. S. (1978). The nonresolution of IQ inheritance by path analysis. *American Journal of Human Genetics, 30,* 442–445.

Goodenough, F. L. (1954). The measurement of mental growth in childhood. In L. Carmichael (Ed.), *Manual of child psychology* (pp. 459–491). New York: Wiley.

Gottfredson, L. S. (1997). Editorial: Mainstream science on intelligence: an editorial with 52 signatories, history, and bibliography. *Intelligence, 24*, 13–24.

Gottlieb, G. (1992). *Individual development and evolution. The genesis of novel behavior.* New York: Oxford University Press.

Gottlieb, G. (1998). Normally occurring environmental and behavioral influences on gene activity: From central dogma to probabilistic epigenesis. *Psychological Review, 105*, 792–802.

Gottlieb, G, Wahlsten, D., & Lickliter, R. (1998). The significance of biology for human development: a developmental psychobiological systems view. In R. M. Lerner (Ed.), *Handbook of child psychology, Vol. 1, Theoretical models of human development* (5th ed., pp. 233–273). New York: Wiley,

Gould, J. L., & Gould, C. G. (1999). Reasoning in animals. *Scientific American Presents, 9*, 52–59.

Greenough, W. T., Black, J. E., Klintsova, A., Bates, K. E., & Weiler, I. J. (1999a). Experience and plasticity in brain structure: possible implications of basic research findings for developmental disorders. In S. H. Broman & J. M. Fletcher (Eds), *The changing nervous system* (pp. 51–70). New York: Oxford University Press.

Greenough, W. T., Cohen, N. J., & Juraska, J. M. (1999b). New neurons in old brains: learning to survive? *Nature Neuroscience, 2*, 203–205.

Guo, S.-W. (1999). The behaviors of some heritability estimators in the complete absence of genetic factors. *Human Heredity, 49*, 215–228.

Harris, D. B. (1963). *Goodenough-Harris Drawing Test manual.* New York: Harcourt, Brace & World.

Hart, V. (1992). Review of the Infant Mullen Scales of Early Development. In J. J. Kramer & J. C. Conoley (Eds), *The eleventh mental measurements yearbook.* Lincoln, Nebraska: Buros Institute of Mental Measurements, University of Nebraska.

Hearnshaw, L. S. (1981). *Cyril Burt. Psychologist.* New York: Vintage Books.

Highfield, R. (1997). First intelligence gene found in 6-year search. *Edmonton Journal*, Nov. 21, p. A2. [reprinted from *Daily Telegraph*, London]

Hirsch, J., & Tryon, R. C. (1956). Mass screening and reliable individual measurement in the experimental behavior genetics of lower organisms. *Psychological Bulletin, 53*, 402–409.

Holden, C. (1998). The first gene marker for IQ? *Science, 280*, 681.

Huttenlocher, P. R., de Courten, C., Garey, L. J., & Van der Loos, H. (1982). Synaptogenesis in the human visual cortex—Evidence for synapse elimination during normal development. *Neuroscience Letters, 33*, 247–252.

Intelligence genes for people. (1997). *Globe and Mail*, Nov. 15, p. D5.

Jacob, F. (1976). *The logic of life. A history of heredity.* New York: Vintage Books.

Jensen, A. (1998). *The g factor: The science of mental ability.* New York: Praeger.

Jensen, A. R. (1999). Precis of: *The g factor: The science of mental ability. Psycoloquy, 10*, Issue 23, Article 1. Available at www.cogsci.soton.ac.uk/cgi/psyc/newpsy?10.023.

Johannsen, W. (1911). The genotype conception of heredity. *American Naturalist, 45*, 129–159.

Jones, D. G. (1989). Brain birth and personal identity. *Journal of Medical Ethics, 15*, 173–178.

Jones, H. E. (1954). The environment and mental development. In L. Carmichael (Ed.), *Manual of child psychology* (pp. 631–696). New York: Wiley.

Kamin, L. J. (1974). *The science and politics of IQ.* New York: Penguin.

Kemperman, G., & Gage, F. H. (1999). New nerve cells for the adult brain. *Scientific American, 280*, 48–53.

Kemperman, G., Kuhn, H. G., & Gage, F. H. (1997). More hippocampal neurons in adult mice living in an enriched environment. *Nature, 386*, 493–495.

Kempthorne, O. (1978). Logical, epistemological and statistical aspects of nature-nurture data interpretation. *Biometrics, 34,* 1–23.

Kempthorne, O. (1990). How does one apply statistical analysis to our understanding of the development of human relationships? *Behavioral and Brain Sciences, 13,* 138–139.

Klintsova, A. Y., & Greenough, W. T. (1999). Synaptic plasticity in cortical systems. *Current Opinion in Neurobiology, 9,* 203–208.

Knudsen, E. I. (1988). Sensitive and critical periods in the development of sound localization. In S. S. Easter, Jr., K. F. Barald, & B. M. Carlson (eds.), *From message to mind. Directions in developmental neurobiology,* (pp. 303–319). Sunderland, MA: Sinauer.

Koch, R., Friedman, E., Azen, C., Hanley, W., Levy, H., Matalon, R., Rouse, B., Trefz, F., Waisbren, S., Michals-Matalon, K., Acosta, P. Buttler, F., Ullrich, K., Platt, L. & de la Cruz, F. (1999). The international collaborative study of maternal phenylketonuria status report 1998. *Mental Retardation and Developmental Disabilities Research Reviews, 5,* 117–121

Kuljis, R. O. (1994). Development of the human brain: the emergence of the neural substrate for pain perception and conscious experience. In F. K. Beller & R. F. Weir (Eds.), *The beginning of human life* (pp. 49–56). Dordrecht, The Netherlands: Kluwer.

Laget, P. (1979). Evoked responses and differential cortical maturation in neonates and children. In E. Meisami & M. A. B. Brazier (Eds.), *Neural growth and differentiation* (pp. 479–492). New York: Raven Press.

Leamy, L. (1988). Genetic and maternal influences on brain and body size in randombred house mice. *Evolution, 42,* 42–53.

Lewontin, R. C. (1991). *Biology as ideology. The doctrine of DNA.* Toronto: Anansi.

Lorenz, K. (1965). *Evolution and modification of behavior.* Chicago: University of Chicago Press.

Lubbock, R. (2000). A helpful tour of the gnomic genome. *Globe and Mail,* March 11, p. D16.

Mackintosh, N. J. (1998). *IQ and human intelligence.* New York: Oxford University Press.

MacWhinney, B. (1998). Models of the emergence of language. *Annual Review of Psychology, 49,* 199–227.

Magara, F., Müller, U., Lipp, H.-P., Weissmann, C., Staliar, M., & Wolfer, D. P. (1999). Genetic background changes the pattern of forebrain commissure defects in transgenic mice underexpressing the β-amyloid-precursor protein. *Proceedings of the National Academy of Sciences USA, 96,* 4656–4661.

Maguire, E. A., Gadian, D. G., Johnsrude, I. S., Good C. D., Ashburner, J., Frackowiak, R. S. J., & Frith, C. D. (2000). Navigation-related structural change in the hippocampi of taxi drivers. *Proceedings of the National Academy of Science U.S.A., 97,* 4398–4403.

Mak, T. W. (1998). *The gene knockout facts book. A-H, I-Z.* New York: Academic Press.

Maldonado, R., Blendy, J. A., Tzavara, E., Gass, P., Roques, B. P., Hanoune, J., & Schütz, G. (1996). Reduction of morphine abstinence in mice with a mutation in the gene encoding CREB. *Science, 273,* 657–659.

Mayford, M., Bach, M. E., Huang, Y., Wang, L., Hawkins, R. D., & Kandel, E. R. (1996). Control of memory formation through regulated expression of a CaMKII transgene. *Science, 274,* 1678–1683.

McCall, R. B., & Carriger, M. S. (1993). A meta-analysis of infant habituation and recognition memory performance as predictors of later IQ. *Child Development, 64,* 57–79.

Mendel, G. (1970). *Versuche über Pflanzenhybriden.* [Studies concerning plant hybrids.] Braunschweig: Friedrich Viewig & Sohn. [reprints of severals papers in German, including the original 1865 classic]

Michell, J. (1997). Quantitative science and the definition of *measurement* in psychology. *British Journal of Psychology, 88,* 355–383.

Miklos, G. L., & Rubin, G. M. (1996). The role of the genome project in determining gene function: Insights from model organisms. *Cell, 86,* 521–529.

Morgan, T. H. (1914). The mechanism of heredity as indicated by the inheritance of linked characters. *Popular Science Monthly,* January, pp. 1–16.

Morgane, P. J., Austin-LaFrance, R. J., Bronzino, J. D., Tonkiss, J., & Galler, J. R. (1992). Malnutrition and the developing central nervous system. In R. L. Isaacson & K. F. Jensen (Eds.), *The vulnerable brain and environmental risks. Vol. 1: Malnutrition and hazard assessment* (pp. 3–44). New York: Plenum Press.

Morgane, P. J., Austin-LaFrance, R., Bronzino, J., Tonkiss, J. Diaz-Cintra, S., Cintra, L., Kemper, T. & Galler, J. R. (1993). Prenatal malnutrition and development of the brain. *Neuroscience and Biobehavioral Reviews, 17,* 91–128.

Neisser, U. (1997). Rising scores on intelligence tests. *Scientific American, 85,* 440–447.

Neisser, U., Boodoo, G., Bouchard, T. J., Jr., Boykin, A. W., Brody, N., Ceci, S. J., Halpern, D. F., Loehlin, J. C., Perloff, R., Sternberg, R. J., & Urbina, S. (1996). Intelligence: knowns and unknowns. *American Psychologist, 51,* 77–101.

O'Rahilly, R., & Müller, F. (1987). *Developmental stages in human embryos.* Washington, DC: Carnegie Institution.

Peeler, D. F. (1995). Shuttlebox performance in BALB/cByJ, C57BL/6ByJ, and CXB recombinant inbred mice: Environmental and genetic determinants and constraints. *Psychobiology, 23,* 161–170

Pflugfelder, G. O. (1998). Genetic lesions in *Drosophila* behavioural mutants. *Behavioural Brain Research, 95,* 3–15.

Platt, S. A., & Sanislow, C. A. (1988). Norm-of-reaction: Definition and misinterpretation of animal research. *Journal of Comparative Psychology, 102,* 254–261.

Plomin, R., & DeFries, J. C. (1998) The genetics of cognitive abilities and disabilities. *Scientific American, 278,* 62–69.

Plomin, R., DeFries, J. C., McClearn, G. E., & Rutter, M. (1997). *Behavioral genetics* (3rd ed.). New York: Freeman.

Plomin, R., & Petrill, S. A. (1997). Genetics and intelligence: what's new. *Intelligence, 24,* 53–78.

Purves, D. (1988). *Body and brain. A trophic theory of neural connections.* Cambridge, MA: Harvard University Press.

Purves, D., & Lichtman, J. W. (1985). *Principles of neural development.* Sunderland, MA: Sinauer.

Rijsdijk, F. V., & Boomsma, D. I. (1997). Genetic mediation of the correlation between peripheral nerve conduction velocity and IQ. *Behavior Genetics, 27,* 87–98.

Rose, S. (1997). *Lifelines. Biology beyond determinism.* Oxford, England: Oxford University Press.

Roubertoux, P. L., & Capron, C. (1990). Are intelligence differences hereditarily transmitted? *Cahiers de Psychologie Cognitive, 10,* 555–594.

Rypma, B., & D'Esposito, M. (1999). The roles of prefrontal brain regions in components of working memory: Effects of memory load and individual differences. *Proceedings of the National Academy of Sciences USA, 96,* 6558–6563.

Samelson, F. (1992). Rescuing the reputation of Sir Cyril Burt. *Journal of the History of Behavioral Sciences, 28,* 221–233.

Sass, H.-M. (1994). The moral significance of brain-life criteria. In F. K. Beller & R. F. Weir (Eds.), *The beginning of human life* (pp. 57–70). Dordrecht, The Netherlands: Kluwer.

Scarr, S., & McCartney, K. (1983). How people make their own environments: a theory of genotype environment effects. *Child Development, 54,* 424–435.

Schönemann, P. H. (1997). On models and muddles of heritability. *Genetica, 99,* 97–108.

Scriver, C. R., & Waters, P. J. (1999). Monogenic traits are not simple—lessons from phenylketonuria. *Trends in Genetics, 15,* 267–272.

Searle, L. V. (1949). The organization of hereditary maze-brightness and maze-dullness. *Genetic Psychology Monographs, 39,* 279–325.

Shavelson, R. J., Webb, N. M., & Rowley, G. L. (1989). Generalizability theory. *American Psychologist, 44,* 922–932.

Spearman, C. (1904). "General intelligence," objectively determined and measured. *American Journal of Psychology, 15,* 201–293.

Spearman, C. (1923). *The nature of 'intelligence' and the principles of cognition.* London, England: Macmillan.

Sternberg, R. J. (1996). *Successful intelligence. How practical and creative intelligence determine success in life.* New York: Simon & Schuster.

Sternberg, R. J. (1999). How intelligent is intelligence testing? *Scientific American Presents, 9,* 12–17.

Stoddard, G. D. (1945). *The meaning of intelligence.* New York: Macmillan.

Strohman, R. C. (1997). The coming Kuhnian revolution in biology. *Nature Biotechnology, 15,* 194–200.

Sturtevant, A. H. (1965). *A history of genetics.* New York: Harper & Row.

Thorndike, E. L. (1924). Measurement of intelligence. I. The present status. *Psychological Review, 31,* 219–252.

Thorndike, E. L., Bregman, E. O., Cobb, M. V., & Woodyard, E. (1926). *The measurement of intelligence.* New York: Teachers College, Columbia University.

Tryon, R. C. (1957). Reliability and behavior domain validity: Reformulation and historical critique. *Psychological Bulletin, 54,* 229–249.

Tully, T. (1997). Regulation of gene expression and its role in long-term memory and synaptic plasticity. *Proceedings of the National Academy of Sciences USA, 94,* 4239–4241.

Vandenberg, S. G. (1968). The nature and nurture of intelligence. In D. C. Glass (Ed.), *Genetics. biology and behavior* (pp. 3–58). New York: Rockefeller University Press.

Vandenberg, S. G. (1977). Hereditary abilities in man. In A. Oliverio (Ed.), *Genetics, environment and intelligence* (pp. 285–304). Amsterdam: Elsevier.

Verleger, R. (1999). The g factor and event-related EEG potentials. *Psycoloquy, 10,* Issue 39, Article 2. Available at www.cogsci.soton.ac.uk/psyc-bin/newpsy?article=10.039.

Vreeke, G. J. (2000). Nature, nurture and the future of the analysis of variance. *Human Development, 43,* 32–45.

Wahlsten, D. (1972). Genetic experiments with animal learning: A critical review. *Behavioral Biology, 7,* 43–182.

Wahlsten, D. (1978). Behavioral genetics and animal learning. In H. Anisman & G. Bignami (Eds.), *Psychopharmacology of aversively motivated behaviors* (pp. 63–118). New York: Plenum.

Wahlsten, D. (1989). Genetic and developmental defects of the mouse corpus callosum. *Experientia, 45,* 828–838.

Wahlsten, D. (1990). Insensitivity of the analysis of variance to heredity-environment interaction. *Behavioral and Brain Sciences, 13,* 109–161.

Wahlsten, D. (1992). The problem of test reliability in genetic studies of brain-behavior correlation. In D. Goldowitz, D. Wahlsten & R. E. Wimer (Eds.), *Techniques for the genetic analysis of brain and behavior: Focus on the mouse* (pp. 407–422). Amsterdam: Elsevier.

Wahlsten D. (1994). The intelligence of heritability. *Canadian Psychology, 35,* 244–58.

Wahlsten, D. (1997). The malleability of intelligence is not constrained by heritability. In B. Devlin, S. E. Fienberg, D. P. Resnick, & K. Roeder (Eds.), *Intelligence, genes, and success. Scientists respond to the bell curve* (pp. 71–87). New York: Copernicus.

Wahlsten, D. (1999). Single-gene influences on brain and behavior. *Annual Review of Psychology, 50,* 599–624.

Wahlsten, D. (2001). Genetics and the development of brain and behavior. In J. Valsiner & K. Connolly (Eds.), *Handbook of developmental psychology,* in press.

Wahlsten, D., & Gottlieb, G. (1997). The invalid separation of effects of nature and nurture: Lessons from animal experimentation. In R. J. Sternberg & E. L. Grigorenko (Eds.), *Intelligence, heredity, and environment* (pp. 163–192). New York: Cambridge University Press.

Wahlsten, D., Crabbe, J., & Dudek, B. (2001). Behavioral testing of standard inbred strains and $5HT_{1B}$ knockout mice: Implications of absent corpus callosum. *Behavioural Brain Research*, in press.

Waisbren, S. E. (1999). Developmental and neuropsychological outcome in children born to mothers with phenylketonuria. *Mental Retardation and Developmental Disabilities Research Reviews*, 5, 125–131.

Wilson, R. S. (1983). Human behavioral development and genetics. *Acta Geneticae Medicae et Gemellologiae*, 32, 1–16.

Wolfer, D. P., Müller, U., Staglier, M., & Lipp, H. (1997). Assessing the effects of the 129/Sv genetic background on swimming navigation learning in transgenic mutants: A study using mice with a modified β-amyloid precursor protein gene. *Brain Research*, 771, 1–13.

Wolfer, D. P. Stagljar-Bozicevic, M., Errington, M., & Lipp, H.-P. (1998). Spatial memory and learning in transgenic mice: fact or artifact? *News in Physiological Science*, 13, 118–122.

Woltereck, R. (1909). Weitere experimentelle Untersuchungen über das Wesen quantitativer Artunterschieder bei Daphniden. *Verhandlungen der Deutschen Zoologischen Gesellschaft 19*, 110–173.

Yakovlev, P. I, & Lecours, A.-R. (1967). The myelogenetic cycles of regional maturation of the brain. In A. Minkowski (Ed.), *Regional development of the brain in early life* (pp. 3–64). Oxford, England: Blackwell.

Yerkes, R. M. (1907). *The dancing mouse. A study in animal behavior*. New York: Macmillan.

Part V

BEHAVIOR–GENETIC
APPROACH

The Case for General Intelligence: A Behavioral Genetic Perspective

Stephen A. Petrill
Wesleyan University

For nearly 100 years, intelligence theorists have debated whether cognitive ability is best conceived as a molar or modular construct. A molar system is one in which a unitary, general process functions across a wide variety of cognitive tasks. A modular system involves numerous distinct cognitive processing units each responsible for certain nonoverlapping cognitive tasks. Modularity is currently the dominant theory in developmental cognitive psychology and neuroscience (e.g., Karmiloff-Smith, 1992). In this chapter, I argue that theories of modularity are based primarily on normative designs or studies of clinical populations, and thus may not apply to variance in the cognitive functioning of unselected populations. More importantly, I argue that theories of modularity have not taken important behavioral genetic results into account. Specifically, behavioral genetic results point strongly to a general factor that becomes more important and more genetic across the lifespan.

LIMITATIONS OF MODULARITY

Evidence for modularity is found when function in one domain is unaffected by damage in another domain. For example, William's Syndrome, an extremely rare genetic disorder (1 in 25,000 births) results in decreased spatial functioning relative to verbal skills. Environmental damage resulting from prenatal trauma and head injury has also been shown

to selectively damage certain cognitive processes, but not others. These results, along with others using alternative neuropsychological and functional methods, have led to the important finding that under certain conditions cognitive skills may be dissociated from one another. Although
these findings have important implications for clinical and educational
applications, these results are based primarily on normative studies (finding average functioning in groups divided by some experimental or quasi-
experimental condition) or clinical populations. As a result, these studies
are potentially limited in their explanation of normal variability in cognitive processing in unselected populations. The fact that cognitive skills
may be dissociated from one another under certain conditions in certain
populations does not necessarily mean that normal variability in cognitive
ability is best characterized by modularity.

More importantly, a recent study published in *Science* contradicts another important assumption made by modularity theory (Paterson,
Brown, Gsodl, Johnson, & Karmiloff-Smith, 1999). As stated by Paterson
et al. (1999), many studies of modularity assume that uneven cognitive
performance found in childhood and adulthood is evidence for genetically influenced modularity beginning in infancy. Examining William's
Syndrome patients, Paterson et al., found a within-syndrome double dissociation: Some William's Syndrome children start out with poor numer-
ocity judgments in infancy but improve in adulthood whereas other William's Syndrome individuals start out with poor verbal skills but improve
by adulthood. This conflicts with the assumption that the DNA marker on
Chromosome 7 associated with Williams's Syndrome is specific to verbal
ability or spatial ability. Additionally these results call into question the assumption that what is found in young children is "more genetic" than
what is found in adulthood.

BEHAVIORAL GENETIC EVIDENCE FOR MOLARITY

Since Galton's (1869) seminal work *Hereditary Genius*, the interface between genes, environment, and cognitive ability has remained a central
tenet of intelligence theory. Although debate initially centered on discussions of nature versus nurture, the data suggest that both genetic and environmental influences are important. When collapsing across all available
twin and adoption studies, heritability estimates for intelligence scores average around 50%, suggesting that genetic influences are responsible for
50% of individual differences in intelligence (Bouchard & McGue, 1981;
Chipuer, Rovine, & Plomin, 1990). These findings are highly stable across
twin versus adoption methods, across diverse populations, and across different measures of intelligence. Indeed, the finding that intelligence is in-

fluenced by both nature *and* nurture is one of the most consistent and highly replicated findings in the psychological literature (Plomin, Owen, & McGuffin, 1994). As a result, few contemporary scientists seriously engage in nature *versus* nurture debates or dispute the overwhelming finding that intelligence shows both genetic and environmental influences.

More importantly, longitudinal and multivariate behavioral genetic studies have begun to examine the genetic and environmental underpinnings of molarity and modularity in cognitive ability. Multivariate studies compare the covariance between family members on *different* variables. For example, genetic influences are implicated if the covariance between verbal and spatial ability is higher for monozygotic (MZ) twins than dizygotic (DZ) twins. Because the correlation between verbal and spatial ability is higher in MZ twins than DZ twins, it is assumed that shared genes are partly responsible for the correlation between verbal and spatial ability. If the correlation between verbal and spatial ability is equal for MZ and DZ twins, then shared environmental influences are implicated. If a correlation between verbal and spatial ability is found within twins but not across twins, then nonshared environmental influences are implicated.

This multivariate behavioral genetic method provides a powerful tool to examine the extent to which cognitive processing is molar or modular. If the same set of genes and environments are operating across different dimensions of cognitive functioning, then a genetic *g* or environmental *g* will emerge, suggesting that a molar explanation best fits the data. If different dimensions of cognitive processing are each associated with independent sets of genes and environments, then a modular explanation best fits the data. Evidence for genetic and environmental modularity would lend support to stringent theories of modularity (Fodor, 1983), which state that modular systems are the result of independent sets of genes responding to different environmental contingencies. Alternatively, evidence for genetic molarity but environmental modularity would support less stringent theories of cognitive development (Karmiloff-Smith, 1992), which suggest that cognitive systems share the same genetic substrate but grow apart as a function of environmental experiences. Genetic and environmental modularity can be assessed by multivariate genetic methods that ask the extent to which a set of variables is driven by the same genetic and environmental factors. Multivariate behavioral genetics examines whether the genes and environments relating to verbal ability at age 10, for example, are the same genes and environments that drive verbal ability at age 18 (Plomin, DeFries, McClearn, & Rutter, 1997).

Multivariate behavioral genetic results provide overwhelming evidence for the importance of general intelligence. Genes point to the importance of general intelligence for the following reasons:

1. The heritability of cognitive abilities increases across the life span.
2. The genetic influences upon cognitive ability become more stable across the life span.
3. The majority of variance in specific cognitive abilities is related to genetic variance underlying g.
4. The proportion of variance in specific cognitive abilities accounted for by genetic g increases across the life span.

The Heritability of Cognitive Ability Increases

As stated earlier, the heritability of cognitive ability is around .50 when collapsing across all studies. However, heritability appears to vary with age, with $h^2 = 40\%$ in early childhood, rising to 60% in early adulthood, finally rising to $h^2 = 80\%$ in later life (Boomsma, 1993; McCartney, Harris, & Bernieri, 1990; McGue, Bouchard, Iacono, & Lykken, 1993; Plomin, 1986; Plomin, Fulker, Corley, & DeFries, 1997). Recently, studies of old–old populations suggest that the heritability of intelligence may begin to decline to around $h^2 = .60$ (Finkel, Pedersen, Plomin, & McClearn, 1998; McClearn et al., 1997). Shared family environmental influences, or c^2 (environmental influences which make family members similar) are significant in early and middle childhood but decrease to zero by adolescence and early adulthood. Nonshared environmental influences, or e^2 (those influences that make family members different) are significant throughout the life span. These results are found not only for general intelligence (e.g., a Full Scale IQ Score), but also for specific cognitive abilities, especially Verbal Ability, Spatial Ability, and Perceptual Speed (Plomin, 1988). Genetic influences become more important throughout the life span, at the expense of the shared environment.

Genetic influences have been examined not only throughout the entire range of ability, but also at the high and low extremes of cognitive ability. Results are similar to those found in the unselected population when examining the extremes of cognitive functioning in early childhood, middle childhood, adolescence, and adulthood (Petrill et al., 1997a; Petrill et al., 1998a; Plomin & Thompson, 1993; Saudino, Plomin, Pedersen, & McClearn, 1994). However, recent data may account for the decline in heritabilty in the very old. Petrill et al. (in press) suggested that this decline may be found only at the low end of cognitive ability. The genetic influences at the low end of cognitive ability approach zero whereas genetic influences at the high end of cognitive ability are around $h^2_g = .80$, which is similar to results found in adult samples.

Cognitive Ability Becomes More Stable Across the Life Span Because of Genetic Influences

Although heritability increases across the life span, more meaningful evidence for the importance of general intelligence may be found by examining longitudinal behavioral genetic studies of cognitive ability. In these studies, the genetic and environmental influences upon stability and change in cognitive ability across time are examined. Fulker, Cherny, and Cardon (1993) examined continuity and change in cognitive ability in infancy and middle childhood using longitudinal sibling data from the Colorado Adoption Project. This study concluded that genes contribute to continuity across child development primarily through general intelligence with two exceptions. The first is the transition from infancy to early childhood as language develops. The second is in middle childhood around 7 years of age. Shared environmental influences contribute primarily to continuity.

These results have also been obtained in other studies. Using twin data drawn from the MacArthur Longitudinal Twin study (Emde et al., 1992), Cherny et al. (1994) examined stability and change in intelligence at 14, 20, and 24 months. Cherny et al. (1994) suggested that genetic influences at 14 months contributed to molarity at 20 months and 24 months, and molarity at 24 months. The shared environment accounted primarily for molarity between 14, 20, and 24 months, while the nonshared environment accounted for modularity. What is important about these findings is that even with the tremendous amount of developmental change that is occurring between 14 and 24 months, there is still stability in cognitive ability across time, and that genetic and shared environmental influences are central to this continuity.

Similarly, Eaves, Long, and Heath (1986) suggested that IQ measures show accumulating effects of "general" genes in a reanalysis of the Louisville Twin Study data (Wilson, 1983). In other words, age specific genes and shared environmental influences decline as a common set of genes emerge. Similar results were obtained in a population-based study of 5- and 7-year-old Dutch twins (Boomsma & van Baal, 1998)

Studies of adult populations provide even more compelling evidence for the importance of continuity based on general intelligence. Plomin, Pedersen, Lichtenstein, and McClearn (1994) examined stability and change in cognitive ability in the Swedish Adoption/Twin Study of Aging (Pedersen et al., 1991). Their study suggests that genes contribute primarily to continuity across time while nonshared environmental influences contribute to change. By adulthood, shared environmental influences have almost no impact.

Taken together, the univariate and longitudinal genetic results suggest that genes become more, not less, important across the life span and that continuity in cognitive ability across time becomes more genetic and more stable. Although these results by themselves do not provide direct evidence for general intelligence, these findings suggest that what is common to cognitive abilities across time becomes more influential, and more genetically influenced.

Genetic *g* Becomes More Important Across the Life Span

As stated earlier, one of the key tenets of modularity is that cognitive ability differentiates across the life span, due to genetic and environmental influences. The behavioral genetic data suggests precisely the opposite. Genes not only account for a greater proportion of variance in cognitive ability across the life span, the stability of cognitive ability across time also becomes more prominent, and more genetic. The behavioral genetic data suggest that this increase in genes is due primarily to genetic variance relating to general intelligence. Shared family environmental influences are also largely molar, but decline to zero by adolescence leaving genetics as the sole influence upon molarity. Modularity is influenced primarily by the nonshared environment with some independent genetic effects (see Fig. 11.1).

Studies of Infancy. There are relatively few multivariate behavioral genetic studies of cognitive ability in infancy. The few studies that have been conducted suggest that a molar general factor is necessary and that shared environment and genetics contribute to this factor. Using the Colorado Adoption Project data, Thompson, Plomin, and DeFries (1985) suggested that 12- and 24-month Bayley scores in adoptive children are correlated with their biological parent's general cognitive ability, but not their parent's specific cognitive abilities, suggesting that genetic influences are mediated by *g*. Reznick, Corley, and Robinson (1997) examined the relationship between verbal and nonverbal intelligence in 14, 20, and 24 month olds drawn from the MacArthur Longitudinal Twin Study. Reznick et al. found that the intercorrelations among verbal and nonverbal tests were driven by both genetic and shared environmental factors. Similarly, Price, Eley, Stevenson, and Plomin (2000) examined more than 6,800 twins participating in the Twins Early Development Study (TEDS; Dale et al., 1998). Price et al. (2000) found substantial shared environmental and genetic overlap between language and non-language-based cognitive ability. In a recent study based on the same TEDS sample, Petrill, Saudino, Wilkerson, and Plomin (2001) conducted a multivariate genetic analysis upon the individual cognitive tests that compose nonverbal intel-

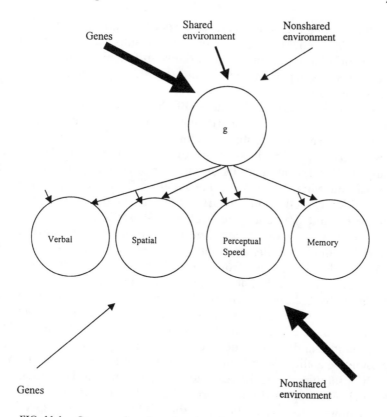

FIG. 11.1. Genes are largely molar, shared environments are largely molar (until adolescence), nonshared environments are modular.

ligence in the TEDS study. The results of this study suggest that, similar to Price et al., genes and shared environment contribute to molarity, whereas the nonshared environment contributes to modularity.

Studies in Early and Middle Childhood. There are many more studies of molarity–modularity in early and middle childhood. Rice, Carey, Fulker, and DeFries (1989) conducted a multivariate genetic analysis of verbal, spatial, perceptual speed, and memory abilities using the 4-year-old data from the Colorado Adoption Project. The data suggest a strong general genetic intelligence factor and a weaker shared environmental factor.

In middle childhood, genetic *g* becomes even more important as heritability increases. Cardon, Fulker, DeFries, and Plomin, (1992) examined the relationship between verbal, spatial, perceptual speed, and memory ability in the Colorado Adoption Project at age 7. Similarly, at age 12, Alarcón, Plomin, Fulker, Corley, and DeFries, (1998) suggested that the covariance among the same measures of specific cognitive abilities may be influenced by a general genetic factor. These results suggest that genetic g accounts for a large portion of the variance in specific cognitive abilities. However, some independent genetic influences for specific cognitive abilities may be found.

Twin studies in early and middle childhood have also suggested that genes and a small amount of shared environment contribute primarily to molarity, whereas the nonshared environment and a small amount of genes contribute to modularity in cognitive ability. Luo, Petrill, and Thompson (1994) examined the importance of genetic g in a sample of 6 to 13 year old twins. Results show that genetic influences on specific cognitive abilities are a reflection primarily of molar genetic g effects with some evidence for independent genetic effects. Shared environmental influences contribute to molarity and nonshared environment contributes to modularity. Similar results were obtained when examining a sample of 7 to 15 year old twins drawn from the Colorado Reading Project (Casto, DeFries, & Fulker, 1995; Labuda, DeFries, & Fulker, 1987).

Additionally, behavioral genetic data in middle childhood suggest that genetic continuity extends beyond measures of intelligence to standardized measures of scholastic performance. Brooks, Fulker, and DeFries (1990) found that the correlation between reading performance and general cognitive ability was influenced solely by shared genetic factors. Similarly, In a sample of 6 to 12 year old twins, Thompson, Detterman, and Plomin (1991) suggested that the correlation between the cognitive tests (broken down into verbal ability, spatial ability, perceptual speed, and memory) and achievement tests (e.g., reading, spelling, and math) was driven largely by shared genetic factors. These results have since been replicated in an adoption study examining roughly 500 adoptive and nonadoptive 7-year-old children (Wadsworth, 1994). Similar effects are obtained when examining the comorbidity between reading and mathematical disability—more than 50% of the observed comorbidy between reading and mathematical disabilities was due to shared genetic influences (Knopik, Alarcón, & DeFries, 1997; Light & DeFries, 1995).

Adulthood.   The influence of genetic g appears to become even more pervasive in adulthood, as shared environmental influences decline. Tambs, Sundet, and Magnus (1986) examined WAIS subtests in a sample of 30 to 57 year-old Norwegian twins. Results suggest that genes account almost entirely for the similarity among WAIS subtests.

Old Age.   Genetic effects are even more intriguing in old age samples. Pedersen, Plomin, and McClearn (1994) found that the majority, but not all of the genetic variance in specific cognitive abilities can still be attributed to *g*. Shared environmental effects were zero while the discrepancy among cognitive abilities was influenced primarily by the nonshared environment.

Even in old–old samples genetic *g* remains important. Petrill et al. (1998b), using the same data employed in the Petrill et al. (2001) study, found even more pronounced general genetic effects when examining nondemented 80+ year-old twins recruited as part of the Octotwin Study (McClearn et al., 1997). The variance in specific cognitive abilities was almost entirely accounted for by genetic *g*, with the differences among specific cognitive abilities influenced primarily by the nonshared environment. Similarly, Finkel, Pedersen, McGue, and McClearn (1995) obtained comparable findings using data from the Swedish Adoption/Twin Study of Aging data to the Minnesota Twin Study of Adult Development (McGue et al., 1993).

Similar to the findings for academic achievement in middle childhood, genetic effects account almost entirely for the correlation between education and intelligence in late adulthood. Lichtenstein and Pedersen (1997) demonstrated that 75% of the correlation between intelligence and educational attainment in a sample of older adult twins is due to genetic overlap between these constructs.

Integration of Multivariate Results Across the Life Span. Putting these multivariate studies together, the data indicate that not only does heritability increase across the life span, but that the genetic influences relating to *g* increase. Molarity becomes even more important with age. In order to display these results more clearly, a set of 9 studies that provide verbal, spatial, perceptual speed, and memory scales are presented in Table 11.1. These studies were selected because they presented heritability,

TABLE 11.1
Multivariate Behavioral Genetic Studies
of Specific Cognitive Abilities

Study	Method	Age of Sample (years)
Rice et al. (1989)	Adoption	4
Cardon et al. (1992)	Adoption	7
Luo et al. (1994)	Twin	6–13
Casto et al. (1994)	Twin	7–16
Tambs et al. (1986)	Twin	40–42
Finkel et al. (1995)	Adoption/Twin	27–88 (MTSADA)
	Adoption/Twin	27–85 (SATSA)
Petrill et al. (1998)	Twin	80+

Note. the Finkel et al., study is divided into Minnesota Twin Study of Adult Development (MTSADA) young, MTSADA older, and Swedish/Adoption Twin Study of Aging (SATSA) subsamples.

genetic correlations, and phenotypic correlations in their results. With these three variables it is possible to calculate the proportion of total variance in each dimension of cognitive ability due to shared genetic factors. As this proportion increases, genetic g, and hence molarity, becomes more important. These data are presented for verbal, spatial, perceptual speed, and memory scales in Figs. 11.2 to 11.5 respectively. With few exceptions, a substantively significant portion of total variance in specific cognitive abilities is due to shared genetic factors. These effects are particularly pronounced for adult populations in verbal, spatial, and perceptual speed scales, accounting from 20% to 60% of the *total* variance, including error. Memory, although influenced by shared genes, is attenuated in its effects. Shared genetic effects are less important in early childhood than in middle childhood and adulthood. Taken together, these data suggest that not only do genetic effects become more important in adulthood, but these effects are increasingly tied to shared genetic factors. In other words, the heritability of a cognitive test appears to be correlated with its g loading, as suggested originally by Jensen (1987). As g loadings increase, the heritability of cognitive ability tests increase.

Collapsing across univariate, longitudinal, and multivariate behavioral genetic studies across the life span, there is overwhelming evidence for the importance of general intelligence. General intelligence not only becomes more (but never entirely) genetically influenced across the life span, but this increase in genetic influence appears to bind cognitive abilities closer together. These findings are in stark contrast to contemporary theories of

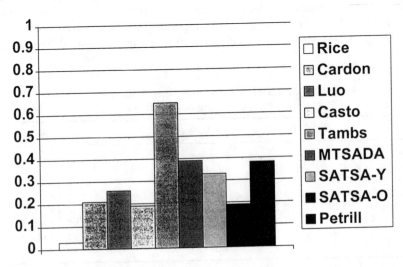

FIG. 11.2.   Percentage of total variance in verbal ability accounted for by general genetic variance.

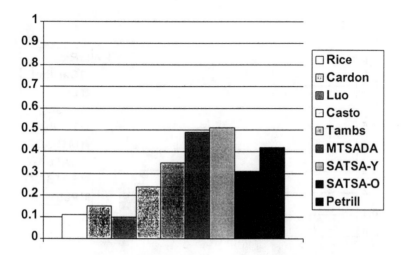

FIG. 11.3. Percentage of total variance in spatial ability accounted for by general genetic variance.

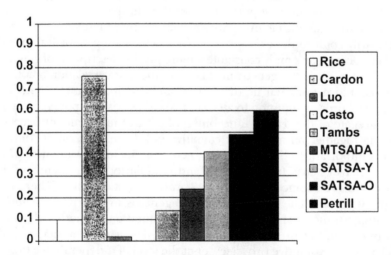

FIG. 11.4. Percentage of total variance in perceptual speed accounted for by general genetic variance.

modularity, which posit that cognitive abilities start out molar, then become modular as genetic and environmental influences drive wedges between cognitive abilities. Genes are increasingly important to cognitive functioning across the life span, and these genes are increasingly correlated across different measures of cognitive abilities.

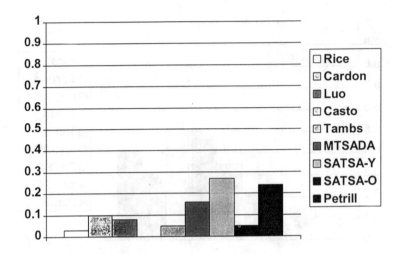

FIG. 11.5.   Percentage of total variance in memory accounted for by general genetic variance.

Although these findings show that intercorrelation among cognitive abilities becomes more important across the life span and is increasingly due to shared genetic factors, critics may argue that these methods do not necessarily confirm the existence of *g*. The behavioral genetic findings described earlier may simply constitute a more precise description of *g* as a statistical entity. Does the genetic mediation of the intercorrelation among diverse cognitive tasks tell us that *g* is a singular, increasingly genetically influenced process common to all cognitive tasks? It is also possible that *g* is an aggregate of the overall functioning of a set of independent processes working together on a complex cognitive task (e.g., Detterman, 1987).

It is important to distinguish between molarity and modularity in the factor analytic sense from molarity and modularity in the neuropsychological sense. At some level, cognitive processing is modular. There is no single "IQ gene." The very fact that intelligence is an additive, polygenetic trait suggests modularity at some level. The question is whether this modularity is found at the level of individual genes or environments, at the level of simple cognitive processes, or at the level of independence in complex cognitive tasks.

BEYOND PAPER AND PENCIL TESTS

Behavioral genetic studies have begun to examine the relationship between elementary cognitive tasks and general intelligence. One approach has been to examine "basic" processes such as reaction time, stimulus discrimination, and decision time and their influence upon general cognitive ability. The results of these behavioral genetic studies mirror what is found when examining paper and pencil psychometric tests. Petrill, Luo, Thompson, and Detterman (1996) suggest that both genes and shared environment are important to the correlation between elementary cognitive ability (ECT), specific cognitive abilities, and general intelligence in a sample of 6 to 13 year-old twins. In contrast, genes become more important to understanding the relationship between ECT's and psychometric intelligence as the population ages (Baker, Vernon, & Ho, 1991; Boomsma & Somsen, 1991; Ho, Baker, & Decker, 1988; McGue, Bouchard, Lykken, & Feuer, 1984; Rijsdijk, Vernon, & Boomsma, 1998; Vernon, 1989). Again, the heritability of elementary cognitive tasks is directly proportional to their *g* loadings.

Other studies have begun to use behavioral genetics to examine brain activity (see Boomsma, Anokhin, & de Geus, 1997; van Baal, de Geus, & Boomsma, 1998; van Beijsterveldt, Molenaar, de Geus, & Boomsma, 1998a; van Beijsterveldt, Molenaar, de Geus, & Boomsma, 1998b). In general, these studies have shown substantial genetic influences on brain electrical activity. One interesting study by Rijsdijk and Boomsma (1997) examined the relationship between peripheral nerve conduction velocity and IQ in a sample of 159 18-year-old Dutch twin pairs. The results of this analysis suggested the small correlation ($r = .15$) between peripheral nerve conduction velocity and general intelligence is entirely due to genetic factors. Although the effect size is small, this study is consistent with earlier intelligence research that hypothesizes genetically influenced neural speed and efficiency is an important factor to general intelligence (Barrett & Eysenck, 1992; Haier, Siegel, Tang, Abel, & Buchsbaum, 1992; Matarazzo, 1992; McGarry-Roberts, Stelmack, & Campbell, 1992; Reed & Jensen, 1992; Vernon & Mori, 1992).

CONCLUSIONS

Almost 100 years of research suggest that diverse cognitive abilities demonstrate a surprising amount of overlap (Carroll, 1993). However, 100 years of research has also demonstrated that cognitive ability may be split into modular units. Factor analytic studies point to the importance of "group" factors such as verbal ability and spatial ability. Neuropsychological studies have demonstrated double dissociations between cognitive skills in clinical populations. Behavioral genetic studies suggest that the nonshared environment is primarily responsible for modularity, especially after adolescence. What are these environments that drive wedges between different aspects of cognitive performance? Can *g* itself be dissected into modular units? So far, the behavioral genetic data suggests that the relationship between elementary cognitive tasks and g is driven primarily by genetic factors, again, especially after adolescence. What are the links between DNA markers, genetic variance, elementary cognitive skills, and psychometric intelligence? Research is only beginning to examine these important issues.

Despite these unresolved issues, it is clear from factor analytic and behavioral genetic studies that general intelligence is also important and that g is likely increasing influenced by shared genetic effects. There is evidence for modularity but this does not take away from the fact that there is a great deal of overlap among diverse cognitive skills. From a molecular genetic perspective, genes are likely to be shared across complex cognitive abilities, and thus it is likely that DNA markers found for one ability will be associated with other abilities (Petrill et al., 1997b). It is also clear that shared genetic influences are important to understanding the intercorrelation among psychometric cognitive abilities, especially in adult and older populations. Given that the vast majority of cognitive assessments administered in schools and in industry involve standardized psychometric tests similar to those found in behavioral genetic studies, it seems prudent to take on board the well-established fact that different skills will correlate, mainly due to shared genes. Building theories of modularity that do not take into account the strong genetic correlation among cognitive skills not only runs counter to the data, but is counterproductive for developing useful theories of intelligence.

REFERENCES

Alarcón, M., Plomin, R., Fulker, D. W., Corley, R., & DeFries, J. C. (1998). Multivariate path analysis of specific cognitive abilities data at 12 years of age in the Colorado Adoption Project. *Behavior Genetics, 28*(4), 255–263.

Baker, L. A., Vernon, P. A., & Ho, H. Z. (1991). The genetic correlation between intelligence and speed of information processing. *Behavior Genetics, 21*(4), 351–368.

Barrett, P. T., & Eysenck, H. J. (1992). Brain evoked potentials and intelligence; the Hendrickson paradigm. *Intelligence, 16*(3–4), 361–382.

Boomsma, D. I. (1993). Current status and future prospects in twin studies of the development of cognitive abilities: Infancy to old age. In T. J., Bouchard Jr. & P. Propping (Eds.), *Twins as a tool of behavioral genetics* (pp. 67–82). Chichester, England: Wiley.

Boomsma, D. I., Anokhin, A., & de Geus, E. (1997). Genetics of electrophysiology: Linking genes, brain, and behavior. Current Directions in *Psychological Science, 6*(4), 106–110.

Boomsma, D. I., & Somsen, R. J. M. (1991). Reaction times measured in a choice reaction time and a double task condition: A small twin study. *Personality and Individual Differences, 12*(6), 519–522.

Boomsma, D. I., & van Baal, C. M. (1998). Genetic influences on childhood IQ in 50- and 7-year old Dutch twins. *Developmental Neuropsychology, 14*(1), 115–126.

Bouchard, J. T., Jr., & McGue, M. (1981). Familial studies of intelligence: A review. *Science, 212,* 1055–1059.

Brooks, A., Fulker, D. W., & DeFries, J. C. (1990). Reading performance and general cognitive ability: A multivariate genetic analysis of twin data. *Personality and Individual Differences, 11*(2), 141–146.

Cardon, L. R., Fulker, D. W., DeFries, J. C., & Plomin, R. (1992). Multivariate genetic analysis of specific cognitive abilities in the Colorado Adoption Project at age 7. *Intelligence, 16,* 383–400.

Carroll, J. B. (1993). *Human cognitive abilities.* New York: Cambridge University Press.

Casto, S. D., DeFries, J. C., & Fulker, D. W. (1995). Multivariate genetic analysis of Wechsler Intelligence Scale for Children—Revised (WISC-R) factors. *Behavior Genetics, 25*(1), 25–32.

Cherny, S. S., Fulker, D. W., Emde, R. N., Robinson, J., Corley, R. P., Reznick, J. S., Plomin, R., & DeFries, J C (1994). A developmental genetic analysis of continuity and change in the Bayley Mental Development Index from 14 to 24 months: The MacArthur Longitudinal Twin Study. *Psychological Science, 5*(6), 354–360.

Chipuer, H. M., Rovine, M. J., & Plomin, R. (1990). LISREL modeling: Genetic and environmental influences on IQ revisited. *Intelligence, 14,* 11–29.

Dale, P. S., Simonoff, E., Bishop, D. V. M., Eley, T. C., Oliver, B. Price, T. S., Purcell, S., Stevenson, J., & Plomin, R. (1998). Genetic influences upon language delay in 2-year-olds. *Nature Neuroscience, 1,* 324–328.

Detterman, D. K. (1987). Theoretical notions of intelligence and mental retardation. *American Journal of Mental Deficiency, 92,* 2–11.

Eaves, L. J., Long, J., & Heath, A. C. (1986). A theory of developmental change in quantitative phenotypes applied to cognitive development. *Child Development, 60,* 993–1004.

Emde, R. N., Plomin, R., Robinson, J., Reznick, J. S., Campos, J. Corley, R., DeFries, J. C., Fulker, D. W., Kagan, J., & Zahn-Waxler, C. (1992). Temperament, emotion, and cognition, at 14 months: The MacArthur Longitudinal Twin Study. *Child Development, 63,* 1437–1455.

Finkel, D., Pedersen, N. L., McGue, M., & McClearn, G. E. (1995). Heritability of cognitive abilities in adult twins: Comparison of Minnesota and Swedish data. *Behavior Genetics, 25*(5), 421–431.

Finkel, D., Pedersen, N L., Plomin, R., & McClearn, G. E. (1998). Longitudinal and cross-sectional twin data on cognitive abilities in adulthood: The Swedish Adoption/Twin Study of Aging. *Developmental Psychology, 34,* 1400–1413.

Fodor, J. A. (1983). *The modularity of mind.* Cambridge, MA: MIT Press.

Fulker, D. W., Cherny, S. S., & Cardon, L. R. (1993). Continuity and change in cognitive development. In R. Plomin & G. E. McClearn (Eds.), *Nature, nurture, and psychology* (pp. 77–97). Washington, DC: American Psychological Association.

Galton, F. (1869). *Hereditary genius: An inquiry into its laws and consequences.* London: MacMillan.

Haier, R. J., Siegel, B., Tang, C., Abel, L., & Buchsbaum, M. S. (1992). Intelligence and changes in regional cerebral glucose metabolic rate following learning. *Intelligence, 16*(3–4), 415–426.

Ho, H. Z., Baker, L. A., & Decker, S. M. (1988). Covariation between intelligence and speed of cognitive processing: Genetic and environmental influences. *Behavior Genetics, 18*(2), 247–261.

Jensen, A. R. (1987). The g beyond factor analysis. In R. R. Ronning, J. A. Glover, J. C. Conoley, & J. C. Witt (Eds.), *The influence of cognitive psychology on testing* (pp. 87–142). Hillsdale, NJ: Lawrence Erlbaum Associates.

Karmiloff-Smith, A. (1992). *Beyond modularity: A developmental perspective on cognitive science.* Cambridge, MA: MIT Press.

Knopik, V. S., Alarcón, M., & DeFries, J. C. (1997). Comorbidity of mathematics and reading deficits: Evidence for a genetic etiology. *Behavior Genetics, 27*(5), 447–453.

LaBuda, M. C., DeFries, J. C., & Fulker, D. W. (1987). Genetic and environmental covariance structures among WISC-R subtests: A twin study. *Intelligence, 11*, 233–244.

Lichtenstein, P., & Pedersen, N. L. (1997). Does genetic variance for cognitive abilities account for genetic variance in educational achievement and occupational status? A study of twins reared apart and twins reared together. *Social Biology, 44*, 77–90.

Light, J. G., & DeFries, J. C. (1995). Comorbidity of reading and mathematics disabilities: Genetic and environmental etiologies. *Journal of Learning Disabilities, 28*(2), 96–106.

Luo, D., Petrill, S. A., & Thompson, L. A. (1994). An exploration of genetic g: Hierarchical factor analysis of cognitive data from the Western Reserve Twin Project. *Intelligence, 18*, 335–347.

Matarazzo, J. D. (1992). Biological and physiological correlates of intelligence. *Intelligence, 16*(3–4), 257–258.

McCartney, K., Harris, M. J., & Bernieri, F. (1990). Growing up and growing apart: A developmental meta-analysis of twin studies. *Psychological Bulletin, 107*, 226–237.

McClearn, G. E., Johansson, B., Berg, S., Pedersen, N. L., Ahern, F., Petrill, S. A., & Plomin, R. (1997). Substantial genetic influence on cognitive abilities in twins 80 or more years old. *Science, 276*, 1560–1563.

McGarry-Roberts, P. A., Stelmack, R. M., & Campbell, K. B. (1992). Intelligence, reaction time, and event related potentials. *Intelligence, 16*(3–4), 289–314.

McGue, M., Bouchard, T. J., Jr., Iacono, W. G., & Lykken, D. T. (1993). Behavioral genetics of cognitive ability: A lifespan perspective. In R. Plomin & G. E. McClearn (Eds.), *Nature, nurture, and psychology* (pp. 59–76). Washington, DC: American Psychological Association.

McGue, M., Bouchard, T. J. Jr., Lykken, D. T., & Feuer, D. (1984). Information processing abilities in twins reared apart. *Intelligence, 16*(3–4), 289–314.

Paterson, S. J., Brown, J. H., Gsodl, M. K., Johnson, M. H., & Karmiloff-Smith, A. (1999). Cognitive modularity and genetic disorders. *Science, 286*, 2355–2358.

Pedersen, N. L., McClearn, G. E., Plomin, R., Nesselroade, J. R., Berg, S., & DeFaire, U. (1991). The Swedish Adoption/Twin Study of Aging: An update. *Acta Geneticae Medicae et Gemellologiae, 40*, 7–20.

Pedersen, N. L., Plomin, R., & McClearn, G. E. (1994). Is there G beyond g? (Is there genetic influence on specific cognitive abilities independent of genetic influences on general cognitive ability?) *Intelligence, 18*, 133–143.

Petrill, S. A., Johansson, B., Pedersen, N. L., Berg, S., Plomin, R., Ahern, F., & McClearn, G. E. (2001). Low cognitive functioning in non-demented 80+ year-old twins is not heritable. *Intelligence, 29*(1), 75–84.

Petrill. S. A., Luo. D., Thompson, L. A., & Detterman, D. K. (1996). The independent prediction of general intelligence by elementary cognitive tasks: Genetic and environmental influences. *Behavior Genetics, 26*(2), 135–148.

Petrill, S. A., Plomin, R., Berg, S., Johansson, B., Pedersen, N. L., Ahern, F., & McClearn, G. E. (1998b). The genetic and environmental relationship between general and specific cognitive abilities in twins age 80 and older. *Psychological Science, 9*(3), 183–189.

Petrill, S. A., Plomin, R., McClearn, G. E., Smith, D. L., Vignetti, S., Chorney, K., Chorney, M. J., Thompson, L. A., Detterman, D. K., Benbow, C., Lubinski, D., Daniels, J., Owen, M., & McGuffin, P. (1997b). DNA markers associated with general and specific cognitive abilities. *Intelligence, 23*(3), 391–204.

Petrill, S. A., Saudino, K. J., Cherny, S. S., Emde, R. N., Hewitt, J. K., Fulker, D. W., & Plomin, R. (1997a). Exploring the genetic etiology of low general cognitive ability from 14 to 36 months. *Developmental Psychology, 33*(3), 544–548.

Petrill, S. A., Saudino, K. J., Cherny, S. S., Emde, R. N., Hewitt, J. K., Fulker, D. W., & Plomin, R. (1998a). Exploring the genetic etiology of high cognitive ability in 14 to 36 month-old twins. *Child Development, 69*(1), 68–74.

Petrill, S. A., Saudino, K. S., Wilkerson, B., & Plomin, R. (2001). Genetic and environmental molarity and modularity of cognitive functioning in two-year-old twins. *Intelligence, 29*(1), 31–44.

Plomin, R. (1986). *Development, genetics, and personality.* Hillsdale, NJ: Lawrence Erlbaum Associates.

Plomin, R. (1988). The nature and nurture of cognitive abilities. In R. J. Sternberg (Ed.), *Advances in the psychology of human intelligence* (pp. 1–33). Hillsdale, NJ: Lawrence Erlbaum Associates.

Plomin, R., DeFries, J. C., McClearn, G. E., & Rutter, M. (1997). *Behavioral genetics* (3rd ed.). New York: Freeman.

Plomin, R., Fulker, D. W., Corley, R., & DeFries, J. C. (1997). Nature, nurture, and cognitive development from 1 to 16 years: A parent-offspring adoption study. *Psychological Science, 8*(6), 442–447.

Plomin, R., Owen, M. J., & McGuffin, P. (1994). Genetics and complex human behaviors. *Science, 264,* 1733–1739.

Plomin, R., Pedersen, N. L., Lichtenstein, P., & McClearn, G. E. (1994). Variability and stability in cognitive abilities are largely genetic later in life. *Behavior Genetics, 24*(3), 207–215.

Plomin, R., & Thompson, L. A. (1993). Genetics and high cognitive ability. *In the origins and development of high ability* (pp. 67–84). New York: Wiley.

Price, T. S., Eley, T. C., Stevenson, J., & Plomin, R. (2000). Genetic and environmental covariation between verbal and non-verbal cognitive development in infancy. *Child Development, 71*(4), 948–959.

Reed, T. E., & Jensen, A. R. (1992). Conduction velocity in a brain nerve pathway of normal adults correlates with intelligence level. *Intelligence, 16*(3–4), 259–272.

Reznick, J. S., Corley, R., & Robinson, J. (1997). A longitudinal twin study of intelligence in the second year. *Monographs of the Society for Research in Child Development, 62*(1).

Rice, T., Carey, G., Fulker, D. W., & DeFries, J. C. (1989). Multivariate path analysis of specific cognitive abilities in the Colorado Adoption Project: Conditional path model of assortative mating. *Behavior Genetics, 19*(2), 195–207.

Rijsdijk, F. V., & Boomsma, D. I. (1997). Genetic mediation of the correlation between peripheral nerve conduction velocity and IQ. *Behavior Genetics, 27*(2), 87–98.

Rijsdijk, F. V., Vernon, P. A., & Boomsma, D. I. (1998). The genetic basis of the relation between speed-of-information processing and IQ. *Behavioural Brain Research, 95*(1), 77–84.

Saudino, K. J., Plomin, R., Pedersen, N. L., & McClearn, G. E. (1994). The etiology of high versus low IQ in the second half of the life span. *Intelligence, 19,* 359–371.

Tambs, K., Sundet, J. M., & Magnus, P. (1986). Genetic and environmental contributions to the covariation between the Wechsler Adult Intelligence Scale (WAIS) subtests: A study of twins. *Intelligence, 16*(4), 475–487.

Thompson, L. A., Detterman, D. K., & Plomin, R. (1991). Associations between cognitive abilities and scholastic achievement: Genetic overlap but environmental difference. *Psychological Science, 2,* 158–165.

Thompson, L. A., Plomin, R., & DeFries, J. C. (1985). Parent-infant resemblance for general and specific cognitive abilities in the Colorado Adoption Project. *Intelligence, 9*(1), 1–13.

van Baal, G. C. M, de Geus, E. J. C., & Boomsma, D. I. (1998). Longitudinal study of genetic influences on ERP-P3 during childhood. *Developmental Neuropsychology, 14*(1), 19–45.

van Beijsterveldt, C. E. M., Molenaar, P. C. M., de Geus, E. J. C., & Boomsma, D. I. (1998a). Genetic and environmental influence on EEG coherence. *Behavior Genetics, 28*(6), 443–453.

van Beijsterveldt, C. E. M., Molenaar, P. C. M., de Geus, E. J. C., & Boomsma, D. I. (1998b). Individual Difference in P300 amplitude: A genetic study in adolescent twins. *Biological Psychology, 47*(2), 97–120.

Vernon, P. A. (1989). The heritability of measures of speed of information processing. *Personality and Individual Differences, 10*(5), 573–576.

Vernon, P. A., & Mori, M. (1992). Intelligence, reaction time, and peripheral nerve conduction velocity. *Intelligence, 16*(3–4), 273–288.

Wadsworth, S. J. (1994). School achievement. In J. C. DeFries, R. Plomin, & D. W. Fulker (Eds.), *Nature and nurture during middle childhood* (pp. 86–101). Cambridge, MA: Blackwell.

Wilson, R. S. (1983). The Louisville twin study: Developmental synchronies in behavior. *Child Development, 54*, 298–316.

Chapter 12

Other Than *g*:
The Value of Persistence

Elena L. Grigorenko
Yale University and Moscow State University

A vast amount of information has been accumulated within the last three decades with respect to scientists' attempt to understand the etiology of variance contributing to the so-called general cognitive ability factor (or general intelligence, *g*). Whether this information is going to be valuable in the long run, and whether it will contribute to our understanding of the origin and the development of cognition, is yet to be determined. At this point, we still do not know what the etiology of the general cognitive ability is, but we have impressive amounts of descriptive information about the general ability's correlates, its links to other cognitive abilities, and its developmental fluctuations.

There is substantially less descriptive information with regard to specific cognitive abilities and their predictive properties, developmental trajectories, and interrelations. However, paradoxically, we know much more about specific origins of a number of cognitive abilities than we do about the etiology of general intelligence. We know, for example, about specific genetic and environmental factors that are causal (at least partially) of the rise of individual variability in specific abilities (e.g., memory) and disabilities (e.g., autism). In contrast, we cannot point out a single specific genetic factor causally involved in the manifestation of variability in *g*.

Even though the overall productivity of the field of general intelligence (at least with respect to understanding the etiology of it) has been somewhat questionable, this field is a very popular domain for scientific inquiry. The dominant model in the field is that of a hierarchy of abilities

(Carroll, 1993; Gustafsson, 1984; Gustafsson & Undheim, 1996), with a general factor (Spearman's g) or with a general factor plus subfactors (Cattell's crystallized and fluid abilities) spanning the higher order g factor. Both positions are extensively represented in the literature (e.g., Brand, 1996; Jensen, 1998 vs. Horn, 1994, 1998), but, for the discussion in this chapter, the distinction is not crucial. I agree with Bouchard in referring to the Cattell model as a truncated g-factor model (Bouchard, 1998) and will refer to both types of hierarchical model here as the g-factor model.

One of the oft-cited findings in the field of intelligence is the 75-year-old convincing evidence that genetic influence on individual differences in the g-factor is significant and substantial (e.g., Plomin & Petrill, 1997). In this chapter, I would like to explore the implications of this finding for the validity of the g-factor model and match these implications with the available empirical evidence.

The following is a set of implications originating within the hierarchical model of intelligence based on the widely accepted assumption of a significant (i.e., different from zero) and substantial (approximately 50%, according to convergent estimates) genetic contribution to the individual variability in g-factor.

If the g-factor forms the basis (in the bottom-to-top paradigm) or the top (in the top-to-bottom paradigm) of other cognitive abilities, then:

1. All genetic influence on specific cognitive abilities should be accounted for by genetic influences on g (i.e., there should not be any significant genetic influence on tests of specific cognitive abilities independent of genetic influence on general cognitive ability). This is, of course, an extreme interpretation of the hierarchy. One might argue, offering a looser interpretation of the hierarchy, that only a specific portion of the genetic variation is preserved in passing through various levels of cognitive hierarchy, and specific genetic variance is added at each level of the hierarchy (see Petrill, chap. 11, this volume). The counterargument to this argument is in the definition of g itself. Given that g originates as a result of decomposing the variance into its general and specific components and throwing specific variance out the window, we, in our attempt to understand the etiology of this general component of the variance, are bound to understanding the etiology of at least those "aspects" of specific abilities which contribute to the general factor. In other words, in the frame of the hierarchical model, genetic variance of interest is only that variance which penetrates all levels of the hierarchy. The assumption that g is the basis of cognitive functioning assumes that we start with a finite quantity of genetic variance, and thus can lose some (through leaks in the hierarchy) but cannot gain any.

2. The *g*-factor should serve the role of the redistributor of genetic variance. If this assumption is correct, then (*a*) specific-abilities' heritability estimates, given that there is a finite quantity of genetic variance contributing to and redistributed by *g*-factor, should not be higher (i.e., should be either equal to or lower than) than that of *g*-factor, and (*b*) a specific ability's heritability estimate should be strongly associated with the ability's correlation with general cognitive ability (i.e., the higher the heritability of a test, the more the test should correlate with general ability).

3. Developmental trajectories of heritability estimates of specific cognitive abilities should resemble the trajectory of *g*-factor heritability estimates. In other words, given that g-related genetic influences in cognition, according to the hierarchy model, are the causal factors for all specific cognitive abilities, developmentally, the heritabilities of specific cognitive abilities should fluctuate in the same way the heritability of *g*-factor does.

In this chapter, these implications of the acceptance of the hierarchical model as an explanatory model for the data accumulated in the field of behavior genetics are evaluated. The evaluation is carried out with regard to specific evidence in the field with regard to (a) answers to the questions underlying these implications and (b) data accumulated from studying specific cognitive abilities.[1] Two conclusions are presented as outcomes of this evaluation. First, heritability estimates of specific cognitive abilities do not support the implications above that are based on the assumption of the validity of hierarchical models of intelligence. There is much more evidence suggesting that individual differences in specific cognitive abilities are controlled by genes to a degree that, at least in some cases, is stronger than that for the *g*-factor. Moreover, specific genetic factors contributing to variability in various specific abilities have been identified, while none have been identified for the *g*-factor. Second, given that the history of the field of individual differences in cognition and the dominant measurement tradition is intimately linked to the hierarchical model of intelli-

---

[1]Even though discussion of the methodological instruments enabling researchers to address these issues is outside the scope of this chapter, I would like to mention the major models the development and usage of which were crucial for testing these implications. These models are: (a) the independent pathway model (Neale & Cardon, 1992)—a single-common-factor model designed to test whether there is genetic variance for the various abilities independent of a common genetic source; (b) the bivariate model—a two-variable model designed to test whether the various tests are influenced by genetic effects independent of genetic effects for *g* (this is an expansion of the independent pathway model, to allow for multiple genetic and environmental factors); and (c) hierarchical models designed to address both the issue of genetic variance independent of genetic variance for *g* as well as the issues of the similarity/dissimilarity of phenotypic, genotypic, and environmental factor structures for different specific abilities across different developmental stages.

gence, the unbalanced situation in the field of behavior genetics, which is replete with studies of g-factors and deficient in studies of specific factors, faces a challenge introduced by the need to validly and reliably quantify these specific factors. Theoretical alternatives to the hierarchical models exist (e.g., taxonomic models of intelligence: Gardner, 1983, 1999; Sternberg, 1997), but the assessment instruments, although available, have not penetrated the field of behavior genetic.

IMPLICATION 1: BRIEF REVIEW OF SPECIFIC ABILITIES

The implications of the two assumptions (a—the best model of intelligence is a hierarchical model where the lower levels of the model are determined by the higher levels of the model; and b—the individual differences at the highest level[s] of intelligence [the g-level] are significantly and substantially accounted for by genetic differences) presented earlier can be reformulated in the form of questions. In this section of the chapter I attempt to answer these questions.

Is there genetic variance for specific cognitive abilities independent of genetic variance for g?

The empirical evidence from eleven twin and adoption studies indicates that the answer is a definite *yes* (Cardon, Fulker, DeFries, & Plomin, 1992; Casto et al., 1995; LaBuda, DeFries, & Fulker, 1987; Loehlin, Horn, & Willerman, 1994; Luo, Petrill, & Thompson, 1994; Lytton, Watts, & Dunn, 1988; Martin & Eaves, 1977; Martin, Jardine, & Eaves, 1084; Pedersen, Plomin, & McClearn, 1994; Rice et al., 1986; Rice, Carey, Fulker, & DeFries, 1989; Tambs, Sundet, & Magnus, 1986). These studies have addressed different abilities (e.g., different subtests of WISC-R, WAIS, scholastic abilities, batteries of specific cognitive abilities) and have investigated samples representative of various developmental stages (e.g., the Colorado Adoption Project, The National Merit Scholarship Qualifying Test sample of Twins, Norwegian twins, and Swedish Adoption/Twin Study of Aging).

In other words, there is considerable evidence suggesting that individual differences in specific cognitive abilities are accounted for, partially but significantly, by genetic influences independent of those contributing to the variance in g. For the sake of the argument in this chapter, however, this evidence will be put in the context of comparing the forming impacts of the g-dependent and g-independent genetic variance on cognitive abilities. In other words, the empirical data should be reanalyzed in such a way that the heritability estimates for specific cognitive abilities are obtained in the presence of the *g*-factor and genetic variance associated with the factor. To my knowledge, very few direct comparisons have been made (Grigorenko & Sternberg, 2000), and when they are made, heritability estimates of specific cognitive abilities decrease negligibly, suggesting the substantiality of those genetic impacts that influence the component of the variance in specific abilities *independent* of *g*.

In addition, there is some indirect support for the claim of the predominance of *g*-independent genetic influences for the formation of individual differences in specific cognitive abilities. This evidence points to specific genes or genetic loci whose function is relevant to specific abilities but not to the *g*-factor (e.g., Grigorenko et al., 2000; Nilsson, Sikström, Adolfsson, Erngrund, Nylander, & Beckman, 1996).

Are some cognitive abilities more heritable than others (i.e., do cognitive abilities have differential heritabilities)? Do these heritability estimates differ from the golden 50% estimated for g?

This question addresses both the issue of the contribution of the genes to specific aspects of cognitive development and the issue of environmental influences on cognitive development.

Results obtained from early twin studies suggest that specific cognitive abilities are differentially heritable (DeFries, Vandenberg, & McClearn, 1976). In addition to twin data, family data have been used in determining heritability estimates for specific cognitive abilities. The largest family study of specific cognitive abilities was the Hawaii Family Study of Cognition (DeFries et al., 1979). This study included data collected from 1,816 families of Americans of European or Japanese descent. A number of familiality coefficients (i.e., regression of offspring on midparent, single-parent/single-child correlations, and sibling correlations) were obtained in this study; all these coefficients provided evidence for the familiality of specific cognitive abilities. For example, midchild–midparent regressions indicated heritability coefficients for families of European descent of .54, .60, .41, and .31, and for families of Japanese descent of .48, .42, .34, and .18, for verbal, spatial, perceptual speed, and memory abilities, respectively. One of the most interesting findings from this study was that within clusters of tests addressing different abilities, various assessments showed dramatic differences in familial resemblance. For instance, a spatial test, the *Paper Form Board*, showed a high index of familial resemblance, whereas another spatial test, *Elithorn Mazes*, showed the lowest level of familiality.

Reviewing this early twin and family studies literature, Plomin summarized that heritability estimates for verbal and spatial abilities tend to be somewhat higher than those for perceptual speed and memory (Plomin, 1988). For example, McGue and Bouchard (1989) reported heritabilities of .57, .71, .53, and .43 for verbal, spatial, perceptual speed, and memory abilities, respectively. However, some later studies contradicted this statement. For example, Thompson, Detterman, and Plomin (1991) found higher heritability estimates for spatial and perceptual speed abilities than for verbal and memory measures in a sample of 6- to 12-year-old twins from the Western Reserve Twin Project. Similarly, the estimates obtained by Pedersen, Plomin, Nesselroade, and McClearn (1992) were .58 (verbal abilities), .46 (spatial abilities), .58 (perceptual speed), and .38 (memory abilities). Likewise, the pattern initially noticed by Plomin was not confirmed in a sample of Swedish twins that were at least 80 years of age (McCelarn et al., 1997). The pattern was .55, .32, .62, and .52, for verbal, spatial, perceptual speed, and memory abilities, respectively.

Similarly, the verbal–spatial versus perceptual–memory differentiation in heritability estimates did not hold for coefficients obtained from the family data. For example, Rice et al. (1989) examined the etiology of individual differences in specific cognitive abilities using the parent–offspring data from the Colorado Adoption Project (offspring at this stage of data collection were 4 years of age). The estimates for verbal, spatial, perceptual speed, and memory abilities obtained under the assumption of isomorphism of the etiology for these cognitive indicators for both adults and children, were .12, .31, .21, and .06, respectively. A set of similar analyses was performed on the data collected when the children were 12 years of age (Alarcón, Plomin, Fulker, Corley, & DeFries, 1998). The heritability estimates were .26, .35, .38, and .53, respectively.

Likewise, there is contradictory evidence with regard to the role of the shared environment. Nichols' review (1978) of twin studies stated that estimates of the shared-environmental proportion of variance ranged from .18 for spatial visualization to .40 for verbal comprehension. However, the contribution of the shared environment was negligible in a number of subsequent studies (Alarcón et al., 1998; Rice et al., 1989; Thompson et al., 1991).

In sum, various specific cognitive abilities demonstrate differential heritability estimates that appear to be age-specific and study/design-specific. Moreover, heritability estimates for specific abilities cover a wide spectrum of possible values (from almost zero to about .70), both not reaching and exceeding the heritability estimates for g-factor.

Interpreting differential heritability estimates within the frame of the hierarchical theories of cognition, two hypotheses originate. First, it is plausible to assume that some basic portion of the g-related genetic variance is distributed within the hierarchy and gets "assigned" to each specific ability (an analogy would be the U.S. Welfare system, where everyone receives the bare minimum), and then this basic "portion" gets extended if other genes contribute to the genetic variance of given specific abilities.

The problem with this hypothesis is that, if such a basic value exists, then it has not been found yet, because the heritability estimates registered could be as low as zero (see memory heritability estimates). So at least some specific abilities do not get a genetic donation from the g-factor. If so, then by definition, these specific abilities must have a different etiology, and therefore will not (cannot!) be a part of the hierarchy.

Second, it is plausible to assume that the heritability estimates of different specific abilities can change along with the degree to which they correlate with g-factor phenotypically: the higher the correlation with g, the higher the heritability estimate (Jensen, 1998). Once again, if such a rule exists, so far it has not been confirmed by empirical data. Even the eye-balling of the indicators presented in this section will show that heritability estimates change within age, and across age and these changes do not demonstrate any apparent links to the level of correlation between specific abilities and the g-factor.

How can the etiology of covariations between various cognitive abilities be explained? Are these covariations g-based?

With respect to these questions, the following findings are relevant. First, it has been shown that the explanation of the etiology of the covariations necessitates the inclusion of both genetic and environmental factors in the model. In other words, both genetic and environmental factors are responsible for the observed correlations between various specific cognitive abilities (e.g., LaBuda et al., 1987; Martin et al., 1984). However, it appears that if genetic factors contribute to similarities between cognitive abilities, than environmental factors differentiate them. In other words, environmental factors commonly impacting various dimensions of specific cognitive abilities appear to be of less importance than are commonly impacting genetic factors. Yet, both specific genetic and specific environmental factors differentiating cognitive abilities from each other have been detected (Cardon et al., 1992; Cardon & Fulker, 1994; Luo et al., 1994).

Using the data from a sample of Norwegian adult twins, Tambs et al. (1986) undertook a multivariate genetic analysis of WAIS scores and reported that the covariation among the subtests was due primarily to a common set of genes. Luo et al.'s (1994) estimates obtained on the data from elementary school twins indicated that specific cognitive abilities are influenced by both common genetic effects and genetic effects specific to each ability. Recently, Casto, DeFries, and Fulker (1995) analyzed WISC-R data from twins with and without reading deficits. According to these data, subtests' phenotypic covariations are explainable by both genetic and shared environmental influences, as well as by specific genetic factors for each subtest.

As described earlier, Rice et al. (1989; Rice, Fulker, & DeFries, 1989) and Alarcón et al. (1998) compared heritabilities of verbal, spatial, perceptual speed, and visual memory indicators in a single sample of biological and adopted families at two points of the children's development—ages 4 and 12. The estimates obtained at age 12 were higher than those at age 4, suggesting that (a) the heritabilities of specific cognitive abilities increase with age (Plomin, 1986) and (b) there is a possible increase in the genetic stability of specific cognitive abilities' indicators as a function of age (DeFries, Fulker, & LaBuda, 1987).

This issue of the etiology of the covariation between specific cognitive abilities is very important in the present context. Specifically, the issue here is whether the presence of the common genetic factors influencing specific cognitive abilities is supportive of the essence of g, or explanatory of the artifact of g? My inclination is to believe (and I stress the subjective nature of this statement—there is not enough data to resolve this issue one way or the other) that the presence of these common genetic factors (as well as the presence of commonly shared environmental influences) is what can explain the artifact of g. There is a growing amount of evidence suggesting that a number of unspecific genetically controlled events happening both prenatally and during the early stages of development (e.g., neuronal movement, neuronal pruning, the formation of the serotonergic system) influence a wide range of psychological outcomes (including personality, cognitive, and behavioral–emotional outcomes). It is possible that the genes controlling these events or a number of other genes of generic importance (e.g., genes involved in the functioning of the autoimmune system) are the genes whose influence is registered under the label of "common genetic influences." These unspecific influences reflect the general condition of the system but fail to differentiate different characteristics of the system.

To illustrate, consider the Human Immunodeficiency Virus (HIV). HIV is a retrovirus that causes the Acquired Immune Deficiency Syndrome (AIDS)—a severe life-threatening illness that suppresses the body's ability to fight infection and can impede neurological functioning. HIV replicates primarily in human macrophages and T4 lymphocytes. Invasion of these two vital components of the immune system gradually depletes the number of cells necessary for normal immune function. As a result, an infected individual's susceptibility to opportunistic infections is increased. It has been shown that individual variability in immune-system responses (which is genetically controlled) is linked to individual responses to the infection and, ultimately, to the severity of the disease. One of the characteristics of the severity of the disease is indicated by the level of the cognitive functioning of the affected person. Thus, the characteristics of the immune system are directly linked with cognitive outcomes, but only through the response to the HIV infection. In other words, there is no direct link between the T4 system and cognitive functioning (neither global, nor specific), but this link becomes active when the organism is challenged by the infection. Thus, genetic differences in the immune system (a candidate for one of the common genetic factors referred to earlier), irrelevant to cognitive functioning in absolute terms, might create the basis for g. If so, g is not the cause of individual differences, it is an artifact of slicing the variance in cognition so that the most general component of this variance (even though it has nothing to do with cognition) is found.

Is the genetic and environmental architecture of specific and general cognitive abilities constant throughout the life span?

This question is related to the third implication of the g-based theories of intelligence: If individual variance in specific cognitive abilities is substantially accounted for by individual variance in g and is linked by the same etiology, then both specific and general abilities should demonstrate identical (or, at least, very similar) developmental profiles of their etiological components.

In an early twin study, Fischbein (1979) administered verbal and inductive tests to male twins at ages 12 and 18 and tests of mathematical reasoning to female and male twins at ages 10 and 13. The correlations showed the following patterns: for verbal ability, the MZ/DZ correlation difference increased slightly (from .10 to .28); for inductive reasoning, the MZ/DZ correlation difference remained approximately the same (.13 versus .22); and for the mathematical reasoning test, differences between MZ and DZ correlations increased (from .08 to .21 for boys and from −.04 to .14 for girls).

The Colorado Adoption Project (CAP) is a longitudinal, prospective study of cognitive development (DeFries, Plomin, & Fulker, 1994; Plomin & DeFries, 1985; Plomin et al., 1988). CAP adults have been extensively tested once, at the onset of the study, whereas CAP children were tested at 1, 2, 3, 4, 7, 9, 10, 11, and 12 years of age (by means of phone, home, or laboratory visits).

To assess the etiology of continuity and change in the development of specific cognitive abilities, Cardon and Fulker (1993, 1994) fitted a longitudinal hierarchical model to CAP data from adopted and nonadopted sibling pairs at ages 3, 4, 7, and 9 and to data from pairs of identical and fraternal twins at ages 3 and 4. Interpreting their results, the authors stated that new genetic variation is manifested at age 7, which results in an increase in heritability estimated with age for verbal, spatial, and perceptual speed, and memory.

According to Cardon and Fulker (1994), different genetic and environmental influences are responsible for the structure of general and cognitive abilities at different times in childhood. It is interesting that when there is evidence for genetic continuity (i.e., the involvement of the same genes at different developmental periods), this continuity is characteristic of specific cognitive abilities rather than *g*.

Another group of researchers (Finkel, Pedersen, Berg, & Johansson, 2000) investigated the heritability of various components of aging. Twelve various markers of aging were factor analyzed and produced 4 factors, 2 of which were cognitive: the fluid abilities factor (with loadings from tests of figure logic, digit symbol [a speed of processing test], and subjective illness summary) and the general knowledge factor (with loadings from indicators of education, occupation, and the test of information). Heritability estimates of fluid abilities factor varied from .67 (in the mid-aged cohort) to .45 (in the old-old cohort) and were significantly lower in the older cohorts. Similarly, estimates of genetic influences on the general knowledge factor varied significantly across all three age groups: from highest in the middle-aged cohort (.76) to lowest in the old-old cohort (.24). Longitudinal analyses across a 3-year interval carried out on a subset of the Swedish Twin/Adoption Study of Aging indicated that the stability of the general cognitive factor is very high (.93) and that genetic factors account for nearly 90% of this stability. Specific cognitive abilities were found to be less stable (about .70) and genetic factors contribute less (about 70%) to their stability (Plomin, Pedersen, Lichtenstein, & McClearn, 1992). Thus, there is a growing amount of evidence in support of decreasing heritability estimates for specific cognitive abilities in very late adulthood (Finkel, Pedersen, McGue, & McClearn, 1995; Finkel, Pedersen, McClearn, Plomin, & Berg, 1996; Finkel, Pedersen, Plomin, & McClearn, 1998; McClearn et al., 1997; Pedersen & Lichtenstein, 1997). Even though the nature of this phenomenon has not yet been understood (e.g., Berg, 1996; Finkel, Pedersen, Berg, & Johansson, in press), there is evidence for the increased heritability of *g*-factors (see Petrill, chap. 11, this volume).

There is a well-articulated position according to which cognitive abilities become less differentiated with age as a result of their more extensive determination by so-called *general cognitive efficiency* (Baltes & Lindenberger, 1997; Baltes, Cornelius, Spiro, Nesselrode, & Willis, 1980; Cunningham, 1980; Lindenberger & Baltes, 1997; Schaie, Willis, Jay, & Chipuer, 1989). According to this position, cognitive aging is a unitary process, resulting, in part, in higher integration and less differentiation of the structure of intelligence in older when compared to younger adults.

A partial confirmation of this statement is also present in the interpretation of some behavior-genetic results. Finkel and McGue (1998), using samples of younger and older twins, compared performance on memory tasks, and correlations between memory tasks and a number of other cognitive variables. In support of the reintegration hypothesis, age differences in the correlations between memory and the cognitive variables were significant in only a few correlations (3 out of 12), but with few exceptions (2 out of 12) the correlations were consistently greater in the older twins than in younger twins. In objection to the reintegration hypothesis, there were no noticeable age differences in the factor structures of the cognitive variables in the younger and the older twins.

In sum, it appears that there is at least some suggestive evidence for differential trajectories of heritability estimates for specific and general abilities across the life span. Specifically, it appears that heritability estimates for both specific and general abilities increase during the transition from early to middle childhood, from childhood to adolescence/youth, and then stabilize during adulthood, but it is plausible that the mechanisms of this increase differ for specific and general abilities. However, during old age the trajectories differ with specific cognitive abilities' heritability estimates decreasing and the g estimates increasing.

To close this section, I would like to summarize the answers to the four preceding questions.

> *Question:* Is there genetic variance for specific cognitive abilities independent of genetic variance for g?
>
> *Answer:* Yes.
>
> *Questions:* Are some cognitive abilities more heritable than others (i.e., do cognitive abilities have differential heritabilities)? Do these heritability estimates differ from the golden 50% estimate obtained for g?
>
> *Answers:* Yes. Yes.
>
> *Questions:* How can the etiology of covariations between various cognitive abilities be explained? Are these covariations g-based?
>
> *Answer:* There is some genetic-based covariation between specific cognitive abilities, but the genes whose effects are responsible for this covariation might have nothing to do with cognition. It is possible that the effects of these genes result in the artifact of the g-factor.
>
> *Question:* Is the genetic and environmental architecture of specific and general cognitive abilities constant throughout the life span?
>
> *Answer:* No.
>
> *Summary:* The data accumulated in behavioral-genetic research does not fit the hierarchy-based models of cognition.

IMPLICATION 2: BRIEF REVIEW WITHIN SPECIFIC ABILITIES

In this portion of the chapter, I would like to review the data originating from studies of heritability estimates obtained for specific cognitive abilities. The intention of this review corresponds to that of the previous section of the chapter: I would like to establish the fit between the empirical data and the hierarchy-based model of cognition. Therefore, this review does not claim to be comprehensive and covers only selected cognitive abilities (reading skills, memory, language skills, and creativity).

READING SKILLS

It is fair to say that the etiology of no other specific cognitive skills has been investigated so extensively as the etiology of reading skills, both in the normal and deficient (i.e., dyslexic or disabled) ranges.

Modern twin studies have been based on the assumption that reading disability is not a categorical disorder, but simply an "extreme" on the continuum of reading ability, normally distributed in populations with broad public schooling. This assumption has required the development of new statistical methods that are appropriate for assessing the etiology of group membership in the tails of the distributions for different skills (the DeFries–Fulker regression method, DeFries & Fulker, 1985). Using this method, researchers applied the classic twins-reared-together design to estimate the relative impact of genetic and environmental effects on the etiology of normal reading achievements (Olson et al., 1999).

DeFries, Fulker, and LaBuda (1987) presented the results of the first twin analyses of specific reading disability, in which the DeFries and Fulker (1985) regression method was utilized. Using small samples of 64 identical and 55 fraternal twin pairs between 8 and 18 years of age, all with English as a first language, they estimated group heritability to be a modest but statistically significant .29. DeFries et al.'s definition of reading disability was based on a cut-off at the 10th percentile on a composite measure based on the word recognition, reading comprehension, and spelling subscales from the Peabody Individual Achievement Test (PIAT; Dunn & Markwardt, 1970). Everyone below the 10th percentile was classified as having specific reading disability. Twenty-three years later the same analyses utilizing the same phenotype were conducted on a much larger sample of twins (223 identical and 169 fraternal twin pairs aged 8 to 18) and yielded a higher estimate of group heritability (58%), with $p < 10^{-12}$ (Wadsworth, Olson, Pennington, & DeFries, 2000).

DeFries and Alarcón (1996), using PIAT subtests for reading comprehension, word recognition, and spelling in order to determine the composite reading performance score, reported the estimated proportion of genetic influence on the group deficit in this score to be 56% (standard error = 9%). Alarcón and DeFries (1997) investigated the heritability of reading performance in both reading disabled and normal samples of Colorado twins. The performance was found to be highly heritable in both the proband (.82) and control (.66) groups. In contrast, corresponding estimates of shared environmental influences were quite low (.01 and .18, respectively). These results are interpreted as strong evidence for a substantial genetic influence on the group deficit in reading.

A vast number of studies have reported MZ and DZ twin correlations for various measures of reading performance (for review, see Grigorenko, 1996). MZ correlations are uniformly greater than DZ correlations, suggesting the presence of genetic influence. However, heritability estimates have varied. Some of this variability can be attributed to the fact that in the majority of studies the sample size was relatively small, so the standard errors of the h^2 estimates[2] are relatively large.

In addition, some twin studies suggest that only certain reading-related skills are inherited. For example, for word recognition, heritability has been estimated at 45% (Brooks, Fulker & DeFries, 1990). Heritability estimates for spelling have ranged from approximately 21% to 62% (Brooks et al., 1990; Petrill & Thompson, 1994). Altogether, for various reading factors and scales, heritability estimates range down from 79% (Martin & Martin, 1975) to 10% (Canter, 1973b).

Olson, Wise, Conners, Rack, and Fulker (1989) explored the genetic etiology for group deficits in phonemic awareness, isolated word recognition, two component reading skills in word recognition (phonological decoding—accuracy and speed in reading nonwords and orthographic coding—accuracy and speed in discriminating a word from a phonologically identical foil), and a related language measure of phonemic awareness. The results revealed heritable group deficits in phonemic awareness, phonological decoding, and word recognition, but not in orthographic coding.

When multivariate analyses were applied, the researchers showed that heritability coefficients estimated jointly for word recognition and phonological decoding were substantially higher than those for word recognition and orthographic coding (DeFries et al., 1991). The low heritability and genetic covariance estimates for orthographic coding suggest that this skill is most likely influenced by environmental forces. Thus, researchers concluded that what is inherited appears to involve the phonological aspects of reading disability. However, this conclusion was challenged in a recent study by Hohnen and Stevenson (1995), who found strong genetic influence on both the phonological and orthographic components of reading processing.

A slightly different pattern of results than that reported in Olson et al.'s 1989 publication was obtained in a more recent behavioral–genetic analy-

---

[2]Broad-sense heritability coefficient, which points to the estimated proportion of the genetic component in the phenotype variation but does not provide any more information beyond this assertion.

sis by Gayán and Olson (1999). This analysis was performed with much larger samples of MZ and DZ twin pairs and revealed evidence for the substantial genetic etiology of all the componential processes studied. Moreover, shared-environmental influences were also significant for all measures. However, the proportions of genetic and shared-environmental influences varied for different processes. Specifically, genetic influence (h^2_g) was lower and shared-environmental influence (c^2_g) was higher for the group deficit in word recognition [.45(.08[3]) versus .49(.10), respectively] when compared to that in phonemic awareness [.56(.14) for genetic influences versus .24(.13) for shared-environmental influences], phonological decoding [.61(.12) for (h^2_g) versus .24(.12) for (c^2_g)], and orthographic coding [(.58(.12) for (h^2_g) versus .20(.12) for (c^2_g)].

Similar results, in terms of the rank order of the magnitude of genetic influences for reading-related processes, were obtained by Grigorenko (1996) in analyses of large extended families. Specifically, the heritability estimates were .55(.15) for phonemic awareness, .44(.14) for rapid naming, .40(.13) for phonological decoding, and .32(.14) for word recognition. In addition, Raskind et al. (2000) have shown in their study of nuclear families that, within a spectrum of reading-related phenotypes, two different phonemic awareness phenotypes showed correlational patterns indicative of genetic influence.

It is important to note that evidence of statistically significant genetic influence on group deficits in different reading-related processes does not imply, necessarily, that the same genes contribute to the variability in different reading skills. Moreover, even when two heritable reading-related processes correlate at the behavioral level, it is as likely that their correlation is due to common environments as it is that they are due to common genes. For example, Olson, Datta, Gayán, and DeFries (1999) have shown that individual differences in phonological decoding and orthographic coding are due to shared as well as to independent genetic influences.

When genetic and environmental correlations between various reading-related processes were estimated, the following patterns were obtained (Grigorenko, 1996). First, the results suggested the presence of common genetic influences for phonemic awareness and decoding [.77(.15)], phonemic awareness, and rapid naming [.77(.13)], and [.92(.06)]. There were no significant genetic correlations between word recognition and any other reading-related processes. Second, the results suggested the presence of common environmental evidence for phonological decoding and rapid naming [.57(.09)]. In addition, at the level of p < .1, there was suggestive evidence for shared environmental influences for word recognition and (1) phonemic awareness [.35(.15)], (2) phonological decoding [.25(.13)], and (3) rapid naming [.32(.13)].

---

[3]Standard errors (SE) are shown in parentheses.

In addition, direct evidence for shared genetic influence was obtained by selecting twins for impaired word recognition and then comparing MZ and DZ cotwin regression to the mean on phonemic awareness, phonological decoding, and orthographic coding (Olson, Forsberg, & Wise, 1994). The results demonstrated significantly greater regression to the population mean for DZ compared to MZ cotwins; thus, there were significant environmental forces orchestrating the overlap between word recognition and the other three deficits. Shared genetic influences were identified for phonemic awareness and phonological coding and phonological decoding and orthographic coding.

As in studies of the etiology of phenotypic correlations between general cognitive ability and reading achievement, the hypothesis was formulated that the phenotypic association between reading achievement and memory may be due, at least partially, to heritable influences (see Thompson, Detterman, & Plomin, 1991 for heritability estimates of memory). This hypothesis has been verified in a number of studies, revealing fairly large genetic correlations between reading performance and memory measures (Thompson et al., 1991; Wadsworth, DeFries, Fulker, Olson, & Pennington, 1995). Analyses of the direction of causation have suggested that differences in reading performance may influence performance on short-memory tasks, but not vice versa (Wadsworth et al., 1995).

Yet another finding suggesting the specificity of relationships between intellectual abilities and memory and reading achievement comes from a study by Gills-Light, DeFries, and Olson (1998). These researchers attempted to understand the etiology of phenotypic correlation between PIAT reading and math composite scores by fitting two models, including (in addition to reading and math scores) (a) indicators of verbal ability (VA) and phonological decoding (PD); and (b) an indicator of short-term memory (STM). The model-fitting was carried out in two samples of normal and disabled readers, but results were similar for both samples. For the VA–PD-reading-math model, after controlling for indicators of verbal intelligence and phonological decoding, the observed correlation between reading and math achievement dropped approximately three times; moreover, about four fifths of the genetic correlations between indicators of reading and math achievement was accounted for by genetic factors common to these skills, verbal abilities, and phonological decoding. In contrast, for the STM-reading-math model, only about one fifth of the genetic correlations between indicators of reading and math achievement was accounted for by genetic factors common to these skills and memory.

The picture of interactions of different reading-related processes appears to be even more complex when age is taken into account. DeFries, Alarcón, and Olson (1997) showed that genetic influence on PIAT word-recognition deficits tends to decline across the 8-year to 20-year age range of the cross-sectional Colorado twin study, whereas genetic influence on PIAT spelling deficits tends to increase with age. The explanation offered for these findings is that word-recognition deficits (as measured by harder PIAT items) are more susceptible to the amount of print exposure, whereas orthographic representation deficits (as measured by higher lever spelling items in the PIAT) are more constrained by genetic factors.

Wadsworth, Gillis, and DeFries (1990) employed multiple regression techniques to test a hypothesis, suggested by Stevenson (Stevenson, Graham, Fredman, & McLoughlin, 1987), that the genetic etiology of reading disability may differ as a function of age. The obtained heritability estimates varied for younger and older twins. This finding was consistent with the hypothesis that genetic factors may be less important as a cause of reading disability in older children (DeFries et al., 1991). However, the power of the sample was not high enough to obtain statistically significant differences between the estimates. This research group also studied the genetic and environmental causes of the phenotypic association between reading performance and verbal short-term memory (Wadsworth et al., 1995). Results of bivariate behavioral genetic analyses indicate that both reading ability and verbal short-term memory are highly heritable, and that a substantial proportion of their phenotypic correlation is due to common genetic influences.

It is a well-established fact that indicators of reading achievement highly correlate with IQ (Lyon, 1989). Naturally, given that heritable factors have been implicated in both reading achievement and general cognitive ability (IQ), the etiology of the observed phenotypic associations between reading achievements and intellectual abilities has been scrutinized. Two main methodological approaches were utilized. First, researchers investigated to what degree the observed IQ-reading achievement phenotypic correlation is attributable to the influence of genetic and/or environmental factors. Using the PIAT reading subtests' scores (Recognition, Comprehension, and Spelling) and the WISC–R full-scale score, Colorado researchers (Brooks et al., 1990) investigated the etiology of associations between IQ and reading performance. The results suggested that observed associations between reading and intelligence factors were largely genetic in origin. Similarly, Cardon et al. (1990) found that about four fifths of the phenotypic correlation between PIAT Reading Recognition and WISC–R full-scale IQ could be accounted for by hereditary influence.

Wadsworth et al. (2000) investigated group estimates of heritability for reading disability in groups of twins ascertained on the basis of the level of IQ of the twin-proband. The researchers discovered that the level of heritability for the group deficit in reading was linked to the probands' Wechsler (1974) full-scale IQ scores. Specifically, in the group of twins with proband IQs below 100, the heritability estimate was .43, whereas in the group of twins with proband IQs above 100, (h^2_g) was .72. Correspondingly, the conclusion was drawn that environmental influences were more important for children with IQs lower than 100. Olson et al. (1999) have replicated this pattern of results for IQ and the genetic etiology for the group deficit in isolated word recognition.

The role of IQ both in the definition of reading disability and in the establishment justification of eligibility for remedial and special education services has been a point of public and academic debate. Public law has required a discrepancy between reading and IQ scores as a condition for obtaining special remedial services. However, there is virtually no evidence that the core phonological reading problems in children with reading disability differ in children with low and high IQ (Siegel & Ryan, 1989; Stanovich & Siegel, 1994). Moreover, there is little or no evidence of differential response to reading remediation in groups of children with low and high IQ (Vellutino, Scanlon, & Lyon, 2000). The findings of the Colorado group described earlier might be of high remedial importance: a policy that denies special-educational services to children with low IQ scores could result in substantial environmental constraints on these individuals' reading development. In fact, offering remedial services to children with lower IQs might help the development of their reading skills substantially.

In summary, all reviewed studies suggest that some components of reading performance (most likely phonemic awareness, phonological decoding, and rapid naming) show high heritability estimates, suggesting the involvement of genetic factors. There is a significant amount of evidence suggesting the presence of reading-specific genetic factors contributing to the variability of reading skills. Moreover, componential reading processes demonstrate differential heritabilities, suggesting a plausibility of at least partially independent genetic and environmental mechanisms operating on different components. Unfortunately, the overwhelming majority of the reading studies have been carried out on younger individuals—there are no estimates of heritabilities obtained on adults and older adults.

MEMORY

Even though there is significant variation from study to study, the results suggest that approximately 45% of the variance in memory performance is attributable to genetic factors, little or none of the variance results from shared (rearing) environmental factors, and the remaining 55% of the variance arises from nonshared (unique) environmental factors (Bouchard, Segal, & Lykken, 1990; Finkel & McGue, 1993; Jarvik, Kallmann, Lorge, & Falek, 1962; Partanen, Bruun, & Markkanen, 1966; Pedersen et al., 1992; Thaper, Petrill, & Thompson, 1994). In addition, researchers have indicated no age differences in the heritability of memory (Finkel & McGue, 1998; Finkel, Pedersen, & McGue, 1995) and the largely genetic origin of the stability in memory performance (Plomin, Pedersen, Lichtenstein, & McClearn, 1994).

Yet, even though the foregoing account is accurate, the story is much more complex. The early behavior–genetic studies of memory (whose total number can be counted on one's fingers) viewed memory as a single construct. The most traditional technique was to administer a set of memory tests or tasks and then to obtain the first principal component as the most "reliable" indicator of memory (for review, see Plomin, DeFries, McClearn, & Rutter, 1997). However, among the very few studies of heritabilities of memory, there are a few that, using a "most-favorite-set-of-memory tasks," provided the reader with differentiated heritability estimates. Let me briefly mention these most popular tasks and summarize the obtained results.

The memory tasks used in behavior genetic studies map on attempts that have been made in the field of general psychology to distinguish separable forms of memory. The most popular distinctions are: (a) the distinction between declarative and nondeclarative memory (e.g., Squire & Zola-Morgan, 1991, also known as the separation of propositional and procedural memory) and (b) the distinction between episodic memory (i.e., remembering events and personal experiences), semantic memory (i.e., remembering factual information), primary memory (i.e., storing incoming information in a highly accessible form; also known as short-term memory or working memory), perceptual representation system (i.e., the system enabling a person to identify objects in the surrounding world), and procedural memory (i.e., remembering actions) [Tulving, 1972, 1993; Tulving & Schacter, 1990].

One of the all-time most popular tasks is that of the Digit Span subtest of the Wechsler intelligence battery. The Digit Span task is used as an indicator of short-term memory (working memory); those researchers who differentiate short-term and working memory view the Backward Digit Span as an indicator of working memory. This task has been used by a number of researchers and has produced contradictory results: some investigators claim there was a significant impact of genetic factors on interindividual variation in this task (Finkel & McGue, 1993; Tambs et al., 1984; Vandenberg, 1962), whereas others failed to find any indication of the heritable nature of this task (e.g., Block, 1968; Bouchard et al., 1990; Mittler, 1969; Thaper et al., 1994).

A cluster of popular memory tasks serve as indicators of episodic memory (Tulving, 1993). These are the Picture Memory Task, Memory for Names and Memory for Faces tasks. In the Picture Memory task, a participant is asked to recognize at the immediate/delayed recall session whether he or she has seen a given picture in his or her "memorizing session." Similarly to the Digit Span task, a few researchers show significant heritability estimates (Bouchard et al., 1990; Pedersen et al., 1992), whereas others could not find any trace of genetic influences (Foch & Plomin, 1980; Garfinkle, 1982; Garfinkle & Vandenberg, 1981; Pedersen et al., 1985; Thapar, Petrill, & Thompson, 1994). Similarly, the heritability estimates obtained for the Memory for Names and Memory for Faces tasks are contradictory: Some researchers reported significant heritability for both immediate and delayed recall (Partanen et al., 1966; Thapar et al., 1994); others, nonsignificant heritability estimates for both immediate and delayed recall (Vandenberg, 1962); and yet others, nonsignificant heritability for immediate recall but significant for delayed (Pedersen et al., 1992) for these tasks.

Researchers (Finkel & McGue, 1998) have investigated which other cognitive variables (e.g., vocabulary, arithmetic, information, comprehension) have largely genetic relationships with memory and which have largely environmental relationships with memory. The reasoning behind that comparison was that if the genetic influences on intelligence and memory were correlated, one could conclude that intelligence and memory arise from the same or similar (genetically influenced) physiological mechanisms, and that if the environmental influences on intelligence and memory were correlated, one could conclude that something in the environment (either shared or nonshared effects) had produced the relationship. The results indicated that the relationship between memory performance and the cognitive variables was entirely genetically mediated in both young and older adults; the magnitude of the correlation between memory and cognitive factors varied across age groups, but the nature of the relationship did not.

Let us revisit the questions posed in the introduction and attempt to answer them using the data accumulated within behavior–genetic studies of memory. In sum, there appears to be genetic variance for memory independent of genetic variance for g. There are certainly different heritability estimates for different types of memory, but there are not enough data that could be instrumental in determining any specific profiles mappable on the current theories of memory. When investigated separately, heritability estimates for various types of memory differ dramatically; when the first principal component obtained on a battery of memory tasks is treated as the general indicator of memory, heritability estimates average around 45%. It appears that the basis of the phenotypic covariation between various memory tasks is genetic, but more data are needed to confirm this observation. Finally, the developmental profiles of heritability for memory tasks differ from those obtained for g.

OTHER SPECIFIC COGNITIVE ABILITIES

Language Skills

A number of studies have estimated heritability coefficients of a variety of language skills. Early twin studies reported a range of heritability estimates, including those of approximately 1.0 (for speech and language comprehension; Lenneberg, 1967), .56 (for indicator of the Illinois Test of Pscyholinguistic Abilities; Mittler, 1969), and .79 (for language comprehension and syntactic abilities; Munsinger & Douglass, 1976). In addition, studies have reported significant heritability coefficients for vocabulary and sentence length (Fischer, 1973) and semantic knowledge (Mittler, 1970, 1971). All these studies, although specific heritability coefficients varied, provided evidence for the presence of a substantial genetic influence for a number of language skills. However, there have also been inconsistent findings regarding the hereditary influence on morphological abilities (Fischer, 1973, Mittler, 1969, 1970, 1971) and articulation skills (Matheny & Bruggeman, 1972)—some studies suggested heritability of these skills, whereas others did not.

Mather and Black (1984) estimated heritability coefficients in a sample of 3- to 6-year-old twins using indicators of vocabulary comprehension, semantic knowledge, morphology, syntax, and articulation. In this study, the only significant heritability coefficient (.68) was that for the PPVT IQ (Peabody Picture Vocabulary Test). However, no other differences occurred between MZ and DZ twin correlations on any other measures.

Bishop and colleagues investigated heritable phenotypes in pairs of twins in which one or both twins met criteria for language impairment and in a set of twins from general population. Behavioral indicators of interest were nonword repetition (Bishop, North, & Donlan, 1996), auditory processing, and phonological short-term memory (Bishop et al., 1999). Results revealed no evidence of a heritable influence on auditory processing in either the general population sample or in extreme groups. In contrast, phonological short-term memory and nonword repetition indicators gave high estimates of group heritability.

Tomblin and Buckwalter (1998) estimated the heritability coefficient for a composite language achievement score (based on receptive and expressive language indicators) in a set of twins and triplets in which at least one member presented poor oral language status. The group heritability was .45. The heritability index changed insignificantly (was estimated at .47) when the estimation was carried out in a subsample containing only children with IQs above 85.

Creativity

There is some evidence of a genetic contribution to creativity (Barron, 1969; Eysenck, 1995; Reznikoff, Domino, Bridges, & Honeyman, 1973). Specifically, a review of 10 twin studies of creativity yielded average twin correlations of .61 for identical twins and .50 for fraternal twins (Nichols, 1978). Grigorenko, LaBuda, and Carter (1992) reported a correlation of .86 for MZ twins and a correlation of .64 for DZ twins for the Torrance Verbal Index of Creativity. Thus, the results indicated only modest genetic influence and substantial influence of shared environment.

Researchers have hypothesized that this modest genetic influence is entirely due to the overlap between tests of creativity and general cognitive ability (Canter, 1973a). To verify, in particular, this hypothesis, Grigorenko and Sternberg (2000) estimated heritability of creativity when only creativity indicators were present and when both crystallized and fluid abilities were controlled for. The heritability estimate for the first case was .25 ($p < .0001$), whereas the heritability estimate for the second case dropped only to .20, remaining significant ($p < .001$). Thus, this result indicated the presence of modest genetic influence even when the overlap is general abilities is controlled for.

Waller, Bouchard, Lykken, Tellegen, and Blacker (1993) argued that creativity is heritable, but in a way that is emergenic rather than strictly linear. This means that the trait emerges from the synergistic interaction among a cluster of more fundamental characteristics, rather than being a single trait in itself. At the same time, Waller and colleagues (Waller et al., 1993) argued that creativity is *not* transmitted through families (see also Bramwell, 1948; Bullough, Bullough, & Mauro, 1981). Such a situation would arise if emergenic traits reflected predictable expressions of certain gene configurations but family members and relatives did not possess enough of the individual traits in common to show them phenotypically. Other investigators, however, have disagreed with the claim of Waller et al. (1993), finding evidence that creativity does run in families (e.g., Dacey, 1989; Scheinfeld, 1973; Vernon, 1989).

In sum, the evidence presented in this section of the chapter only stresses the points made earlier. First, there is weak (or, for some specific cognitive abilities, no) evidence supporting the assumption that the genetic roots of individual variability in specific cognitive abilities originates in a branch of the genetic roots of *g*. Second, there is a noticeable complexity in the structure of heritability estimates for specific cognitive abilities, and this complexity does not resemble the pattern of correlations between specific abilities and g. Third, there is evidence to suggest that the basis of covariation between specific cognitive abilities is genetic, but the mechanism of this covariation is poorly understood. It is possible that the presence of these common genetic effects, characteristic of the whole human organism, result in the illusion of g. The phenomenon of cognitive g resembles the phenomenon of personality g, originating as the first principal component when items on personality inventories are subjected to factorial analyses. It has been suggested that this personality g might have its basis in the way dopaminergic and serotonergic systems get formed (Damberg et al., 2000), and, being global characteristics of a human organism, these systems are "predictive," to a certain degree, of various personality traits. However, no psychologist would argue with the importance of investigating differential personality traits and trying to understand their etiology, simply because specific behaviors are predicted with much higher precision by specific traits than by the personality g. Finally, different specific cognitive abilities demonstrate differential heritability estimates at different stages of development, and the trajectory of these estimates appear not to fit that of the g.

THIS IS TO SAY THAT WE ARE NOT DONE YET

The point of this chapter was to show that much of the evidence accumulated in the field of behavior genetics since the 1980s does not fit the major assumptions of the traditional g (or two g's)-bound hierarchical models of cognition. Unfortunately, there are no behavioral genetic data that would have been applicable for evaluation in the context of taxonomy models of cognition. One of the reasons for the lack of such data is the belief that when working with traditional indicators of cognition, researchers obtain reliable and valid data, while when working with novel models of cognition, they obtain less reliable and valid data (e.g., Bouchard, 1998).

As one of the proponents of the taxonomic approach to cognition, I, of course, strongly disagree with this belief but recognize its origin—indeed, much measurement work needs to be done within taxonomy models of intelligence to overcome this belief. And the proof of the power of the measures will trigger behavior–genetic work that attempts to evaluate the taxonomic models of intelligence by decomposing the etiological variance accountable for individual differences in different intelligences. But all it would take is persistence, because the theoretical foundation of this work and first measurement validation background is in place already (e.g., Sternberg, 1997; Sternberg et al., 2000; Sternberg & Lubart, 1995).

This argument about the reliability and validity requirements for measures prior to their utilization in behavior–genetic research, and an implicit assumption that novel measures will never meet these requirements, reminds me of the story of John Harrison, the man who built a revolutionary time keeper that solved the problem of measuring longitude. During the great age of sea exploration—the 17th and 18th centuries—the longitude problem was one of the greatest measurement challenges. Unequipped with an instrument that could reliably determine their longitude, sailors were lost at sea as soon as land disappeared from their visual field. Ships ended up on rocky shores; the sea killed thousands, punishing them for their inability to determine where they were and to avoid the rocks shown on their maps. The best minds of the period and the scientific establishment (from Galileo to Sir Isaac Newton) were sure that the answer was celestial. The claim was that as soon as the heavens could be mapped longitude would be able to be determined. However, despite the persuasive pressure of the field, John Harrison, an unknown watchmaker, conceived a mechanical solution to the problem. It took Harrison 33 years to built his masterpiece. But when it was built, the problem of measuring longitude was solved.

This is not to say that finding novel ways of measuring cognition will automatically solve the problem of its etiology, but that persistence in pursuing novel ways of thinking pays off.

REFERENCES

Alarcón, M., & DeFries, J. C. (1997). Reading performance and general cognitive ability in twins with reading difficulties and control pairs. *Personality and Individual Differences, 22,* 793–803.

Alarcón, M., Plomin, R., Fulker, D. W., Corley, R., & DeFries, J. C. (1998). Multivariate path analysis of specific cognitive abilities data at 12 years of age in the Colorado Adoption Project. *Behavior Genetics, 28,* 255–264.

Baltes, P. B., & Lindenberger, U. (1997). Emergence of a powerful connection between sensory and cognitive functions across the adult life span. A new window to the study of cognitive aging? *Psychology and Aging, 12,* 12–21.

Baltes, P. B., Cornelius, S. W., Spiro, A. III, Nesselroade, J. R., & Willis, S. L. (1980). Integration versus differentiation of fluid-crystallized intelligence in old age. *Developmental Psychology, 16,* 625–635.

Barron, F. (1969). *Creative person and creative process.* New York: Holt, Rinehart & Winston.

Berg, S. (1996). Aging, behavior, and terminal decline, In J. E. Birren & K. W. Schaie (Eds.), *Handbook of the psychology of aging, 4th edition* (pp. 323–337). New York: Academic Press.

Bishop, D. V. M., Bishop, S. J., Bright, P., James, C., Delaney, T., & Tallal, P. (1999). Different origin of auditory and phonological processing problems in children with language impairment: Evidence from a twin study. *Journal of Speech, Language, and Hearing Research, 42,* 155–168.

Bishop, D. V. M., North, T., & Donlan, C. (1996). Nonword repetition as a behavioural marker for inherited language impairment: Evidence from a twin study. *Journal of Child Psychology and Psychiatry, 4,* 391–403.

Block, J. B. (1968). Hereditary components in the performance of twins on the WAIS. In S. G. Vandenberg (Ed.), *Progress in human behavior genetics* (pp. 221–228). Baltimore, MD: Johns Hopkins University Press.

Bouchard, T. J., Jr. (1998). Genetic and environmental influences on adult intelligence and special mental abilities. *Human Biology, 70*, 257–279.

Bouchard, T. J., Jr., Segal, N. L., & Lykken, D. T. (1990). Genetic and environmental influences on special mental abilities in a sample of twins reared apart. *Acta Geneticae Medicae et Gemellogicae, 39*, 193–206.

Bramwell, B. S. (1948). Galton's *Heredity Genius* and the three following generations since 1869. *Eugenics Review, 39*, 146–153.

Brand, C. (1996). Doing something about *g. Intelligence, 22*, 311–326.

Brooks, A., Fulker, D. W., & DeFries, J. C. (1990). Reading performance and general cognitive ability: A multivariate genetic analysis of twin data. *Personality and Individual Differences, 11*, 141–146.

Bullough, V., Bullough, B., & Mauro, M. (1981). History and creativity: Research problems and some possible solutions. *Journal of Creative Behavior, 15*, 102–116.

Canter, S. (1973a). Personality traits in twins. In G. Claridge, S. Canter, & W. I. Hume (Eds.), *Personality differences and biological variations: A study of twins* (pp. 21–51). New York: Pergamon Press.

Canter, S. (1973b). Some aspects of cognitive function in twins. In G. Claridge, S. Canter, & W. I. Hume (Eds.), *Personality differences and biological variations: A study of twins*. Oxford, England: Pergamon Press.

Cardon, L. R., DiLalla, L. F., Plomin, R., DeFries, J. C., et al. (1990). Genetic correlations between reading performance and IQ in the Colorado Adoption Project. *Intelligence, 14*, 245–257.

Cardon, L. R., & Fulker, D. W. (1993). Genetics of specific cognitive abilities. In R. Plomin & G. E. McClearn (Eds.), *Nature, nurture, and psychology* (pp. 99–120). Washington, DC: American Psychological Association.

Cardon, L. R., & Fulker, D. W. (1994). A model of developmental change in hierarchical phenotypes with application to specific cognitive abilities. *Behavioral Genetics, 24*, 1–16.

Cardon, L. R., Fulker, D. W., DeFries, J. C., & Plomin, R. (1992). Multivariate genetic analysis of specific cognitive abilities in the Colorado Adoption Project at age 7. *Intelligence, 16*, 383–400.

Carroll, J. B. (1993). *Human cognitive abilities: A survey of factor-analytic studies*. New York: Cambridge University Press.

Casto, S. D., DeFries, J. C., & Fulker, D. W. (1995). Multivariate genetic analysis of Wechsler Intelligence Scale for Children-Revised (WISC-R) factors. *Behavior Genetics, 25*, 25–32.

Cunningham, W. (1980). Age comparative factor analysis of ability variables in adulthood and old age. *Intelligence, 4*, 82–86.

Dacey, J. S. (1989). *Fundamentals of creative thinking*. Lexington, MA: Lexington Books.

Damberg, M., Garpenstrand, H., Berggård, C., Åsberg, M., Hallman, J., & Oreland, L. (2000). The genotype of human transcription factor AP –2β is associated with platelet monoamine oxidase B activity. *Neuroscience Letters*.

DeFries, J. C., & Alarcón, M. (1996). Genetics of specific reading disability. *Mental Retardation and Developmental Disabilities Research Reviews, 2*, 39–47.

DeFries, J. C., Alarcón, M., & Olson, R. K. (1997). Genetic aetiologies of reading and spelling deficits: Developmental differences. In C. Hulme & M. Snowling (Eds.), *Dyslexia: Biology, cognition, and intervention* (pp. 156–187). London: Whurr Publishers.

DeFries, J. C., & Fulker, D. W. (1985). Multiple regression analysis of twin data. *Behavior Genetics, 15*, 467–478.

DeFries, J. C., Fulker, D. W., & LaBuda, M. C. (1987). Evidence for a genetic aetiology in reading disability in twins. *Nature, 329*, 537–539.

DeFries, J. C., Johnson, R. C., Juse, A. R., McClearn, G. E., Polovina, J., Vandenberg, S. G., & Wilson, J. R. (1979). Familial resemblance for specific cognitive abilities, *Behavior Genetics, 1,* 23–43.

DeFries, J. C., Olson, R. K., Pennington, B. F., & Smith, S. D. (1991). Colorado Reading Project: An update. In D. D. Duane & D. B. Gray (Eds.), *The reading brain: The biological basis of dyslexia* (pp. 53–88). Parkton, MD: York Press.

DeFries, J. C., Plomin, R., & Fulker, D. W. (1994). *Nature and nurture during middle childhood.* Oxford, England: Blackwell.

DeFries, J. C., Vandenberg, S. G., & McClearn, G. E. (1976). Genetics of specific cognitive abilities. *Annual Review of Genetics, 10,* 179–207.

Dunn, L. M., & Markwardt, F. C. (1970). *Examiner's manual: Peabody Individual Achievement Test,* Circle Pines, MN: American Guidance Service.

Eysenck, H. J. (1995). *Genius: The natural history of creativity.* Cambridge, England: Cambridge University Press.

Finkel, D., & McGue, M. (1993). The origins of individual differences in memory among the elderly: A behavior genetic analysis. *Psychology and Aging, 8,* 527–537.

Finkel, D., & McGue, M. (1998). Age differences in the nature and origin of individual differences in memory: a behavior genetic analysis. *International Journal of Aging and Human Development, 47,* 217–239.

Finkel, D., Pedersen, N. L., Berg, S., & Johansson, B. (2000). Quantitative genetic analysis of biobehavioral markers of aging in Swedish studies of adult twins. *Journal of Aging and Health.*

Finkel, D., Pedersen, N., & McGue, M. (1995). Genetic influences on memory performance in adulthood: Comparison of Minnesota and Swedish twin studies. *Psychology and Aging, 10,* 437–446.

Finkel, D., Pedersen, N., McGue, M., & McClearn, G. E. (1995). Heritability of cognitive abilities in adult twins: Comparison of Minnesota and Swedish data. *Behavior Genetics, 25,* 421–431.

Finkel, D., Pedersen, N., McClearn, G. E., Plomin, R., & Berg, S. (1996). Cross-sequential analysis of genetic influences on cognitive ability in the Swedish Adoption/Twin Study of Aging. *Aging and Cognition, 3,* 84–99.

Finkel, D., Pedersen, N., Plomin, R., & McClearn, G. E. (1998). Longitudianl and corsssectional twin data on cognitive abilities in adulthood: The Swedish Adoption Twin Study of Aging. *Developmental Psychology, 34,* 1400–1413.

Fischbein, S. (1979). Intra-pair similarity in IQ of monozygotic and dizygotic male twins at 12 and 18 years of age. *Annals of Human Biology, 6,* 495–504.

Fischer, K. (1973, March). *Genetic contribution to individual differences in language acquisition.* Paper presented at the biennial meeting of the Society for Research in Child Development,

Foch, T. T., & Plomin, R. (1980). Specific cognitive abilities in 5- to 12-year-old twins. *Behavior Genetics, 10,* 153–162.

Hohnen, B., & Stevenson, J. (1995). Genetic effects in orthographic ability: A second look. *Behavior Genetics, 25,* 271.

Gardner, H. (1983). *Frames of mind: The theory of multiple intelligences.* New York: Basic Books.

Gardner, H. (1999). *Intelligence reframed: Multiple intelligences for the 21st century.* New York: Basic Books.

Garfinkle, A. S. (1982). Genetic and environmental influences on the development of Piagetian logico-mathematical concepts and other specific cognitive abilities. *Acta Geneticae Medicae et Gemellologiae, 31,* 10–61.

Garfinkle, A. S., & Vandenberg, S. G. (1981). Development of Piagetian logicmathematical concepts and other specific cognitive abilities. In L. Gedda, P. Parisi, & W. E. Nance

(Eds.), *Twin Research 3: Intelligence, Personality and Development* (pp. 51–60). New York: Liss.

Gayán, J., & Olson, R. K. (1999). Reading disability: Evidence for a genetic etiology. *European Child & Adolescent Psychiatry*, Suppl. 3, *8*, 52–55.

Gillis-Light, J., DeFries, J. C., Olson, R. K. (1998). Multivariate behavioral genetic analysis of achievement and cognitive measures in reading-disabled and control twin pairs. *Human Biology, 70*, 215–237.

Grigorenko, E. L. (1996). A family study of dyslexia. Unpublished dissertation.

Grigorenko, E. L., LaBuda, M. C., & Carter, A. S. (1992). Similarity in general cognitive ability, creativity, and cognitive style in a sample of adolescent Russian twins. *Acta Geneticae Medicae et Gemellologiae, 41*, 65–72.

Grigorenko, E. L., & Sternberg, R. J. (2000). *Parental influences on children's analytical, creative, and practical intelligence.* Unpublished manuscript, Yale University.

Grigorenko, E. L., Wood, F. B., Meyer, M. S., & Pauls, D. L. (2000). The chromosome 6p influences on different dyslexia-related cognitive processes: further confirmation. *American Journal of Human Genetics, 66*, 715–23.

Gustafsson, J.-E. (1984). A unifying model for the structure of intellectual abilities. *Intelligence, 8*, 179–203.

Gustafsson, J., & Undheim, J. O. (1996). Individual differences in cognitive functions. In D. C. Berliner & R. C. Calfee (Eds.), *Handbook of educational psychology* (pp. 186–242). New York: Simon & Schuster/Macmillan.

Horn, J. L. (1994). Theory of fluid and crystallized intelligence. In R. J. Sternberg (Ed.), *Encyclopedia of human intelligence* (pp. 443–451). New York: Macmillan.

Horn, J. L. (1998). A basis for research on age differences in cognitive abilities. In J. J. McArdle & R. W. Woodcock (Eds.), *Cognitive abilities in theory and practice*. Mahwah, NJ: Lawrence Erlbaum Associates.

Jarvik, L. F., Kallmann, F. J., Lorge, I., & Kalek, A. (1962). Longitudinal study of intellectual changes in senescent twins. In C. Tibbets & W. Donahue (Eds.), *Aging around the world: Social and psychological aspects of aging* (pp. 839–859). New York: Columbia University Press.

Jensen, A. R. (1998). *The g factor. The science of mental ability.* Westport, CT: Praeger.

LaBuda, M. C., DeFries, J. C., & Fulker, D. W. (1987). Genetic and Environmental covariance structures among WISC-R subtests: A twin study. *Intelligence, 11*, 233–244.

Lenneberg, E. (1967). *Biological foundations of language.* New York: Wiley.

Lindenberger, U., & Baltes, P. B. (1997). Intellectual functioning in old and very old age. Cross-sectional results from the Berlin Aging Study. *Psychology and Aging, 12*, 410–432.

Loehlin, J. C., Horn, J. M., & Willerman, K. (1994). Differential inheritance of mental abilities in the Texas Adoption Project. *Intelligence, 19*, 325–336.

Luo, D. Petrill, S. A., & Thompson, L. A. (1994). An exploration of genetic g hierarchical factor analysis of cognitive data from the Western Reserve twin project. *Intelligence, 18*, 335–347.

Lyon, G. R. (1989). IQ is relevant to the definition of learning disabilities: A position in search of logic and data. *Journal of Learning Disabilities, 22*, 504–506, 512.

Lytton, H., Watts, D., & Dunn, B. E. (1988). Stability of genetic determination from age 2 to age 9: A longitudinal twin study. *Social Biology, 35*, 62–73.

Martin, N. G., & Eaves, L. J. (1977). The genetic analysis of covariance structure. *Heredity, 38*, 79–95.

Martin, N. G., Jardine, R., & Eaves, L. J. (1984). Is there one se of genes for different abilities? A re-analysis of the National Merit Scholarship Quantifying Test (NMSQT) data. *Behavior Genetics, 14*, 355–370.

Martin, N. G., & Martin, P. G. (1975). The inheritance of scholastic abilities in a sample of twins. *Annals of Human Genetics, 39*, 219–228.

Matheny, A., & Bruggeman, C. (1972). Articulation proficiency in twins and singletons from families of twins. *Journal of Speech and Hearing Research, 15*, 845–851.

Mather, P. L., & Black, K. N. (1984). Hereditary and environmental influences on preschool twins' language skills. *Developmental Psychology, 20*, 303–308.

McClearn, G. E., Johansson, B., Berg, S., Pedersen, N. L., Ahern, F., Petrill, S. A., & Plomin, R. (1997). Substantial genetic influence on cognitive abilities in twins 80 or more years old. *Science, 276*, 1560–1563.

McGue, M., & Bouchard, T. J. (1989). Genetic and environmental determinants of information processing and special mental abilities: A twin analysis. In R. J. Sternberg (Ed.), *Advances in the psychology of human intelligence* (pp. 7–45). Hillsdale, NJ: Lawrence Erlbaum Associates.

Mittler, P. (1969). Genetic aspects of psycholinguistic abilities. *Journal of Child Psychology and Psychiatry, 10*, 165–176.

Mittler, P. (1970). Biological and social aspects of language development in twins. *Developmental Medicine and Child Neurology, 12*, 741–757.

Mittler, P. (1971). *The study of twins.* Baltimore, MD: Penguin Books.

Munsinger, H., & Douglass, A. (1976). The syntactic abilities of identical twins, fraternal twins, and their siblings. *Child Development, 47*, 40–50.

Neale, M., & Cardon, L. R. (1992). *Methodology for genetic studies of twins and families, NATO ASI Series.* Dordrecht, The Netherlands: Kluwer Academic Press.

Nichols, R. C., (1978). Twin studies of ability, personality, and interests. *Homo, 29*, 158–173.

Nilsson, L. -G., Sikström, C., Adolfsson, R., Erngrund, K., Nylander, P. -O., & Beckman, L. (1996). Genetic markers associated with high versus low performance on episodic memory tasks. *Behavior Genetics, 26*, 555–562.

Olson, R. K., Datta, H., Gayán, J., & DeFries, J. C. (1999). A behavioral-genetic analysis of reading disabilities and component processes. In R. M. Klein & P. A. McMullen (Eds.), *Converging methods for understanding reading and dyslexia* (pp. 133–153). Cambridge, MA: MIT Press.

Olson, R. K., Forsberg, H., & Wise, B. (1994). Genes, environment, and the development of orthographic skills. In V. W. Berninger (Ed.), *The varieties of orthographic knowledge I: Theoretical and developmental issues* (pp. 27–71). Dordrecht, The Netherlands: Kluwer.

Olson, R. K., & Gayán, J. (in press). Brains, genes, and environment in reading development. In S. Newman & D. Dickinson (Eds.), *Handbook for research in early literacy.* New York: Guilford Press.

Olson, R., Wise, B., Conners, F., Rack, J., & Fulker, D. (1989). Specific deficits in component reading and language skills: Genetic and environmental influences. *Journal of Learning Disabilities, 22*, 339–348.

Partanen, J., Bruun, K., & Markkanen, T. (1966). *Inheritance of drinking behavior.* Stockholm: Amqvist & Wiksell.

Pedersen, N. L., & Lichtenstein, P. (1997). Biometric analyses of human abilities. In C. Cooper & V. Varma (Eds.), *Processes of individual differences* (pp. 126–148). London, England: Routledge.

Pedersen, N. L., McClearn, G. E., Plomin, R., & Friberg, L. (1985). Separated fraternal twins: Resemblance for cognitive abilities. *Behavior Genetics, 15*, 407–419.

Pedersen, N. L., Plomin, R., & McClearn, G. E. (1994). Is there G beyond g? (Is there genetic influence on specific cognitive abilities independent of genetic influence on general cognitive ability?). *Intelligence, 18*, 133–143.

Pedersen, N. L., Plomin, R., Nesselroade, J. R., & McClearn, G. E. (1992). Quantitative genetic analysis of cognitive abilities during the second half of the lifespan. *Psychological Science, 3*, 346–353.

Petrill, S. A., & Thompson, L. A. (1994). The effect of gender upon heritability and common environmental estimates in measures of scholastic achievement. *Personality and Individual Differences, 16*, 631–640.

Plomin, R. (1986). *Genes, development, and psychology*. Hillsdale, NJ: Lawrence Erlbaum Associates.

Plomin, R. (1988). The nature and nurture of cognitive abilities. In R. J. Sternberg (Ed.), *Advances in psychology of human intelligence* (Vol. 4, pp. 1–33). Hillsdale, NJ: Lawrence Erlbaum Associates.

Plomin, R., & DeFries, J. C. (1979). Multivariate behavioral genetic analysis of twin data on scholastic abilities. *Behavior Genetics, 9*, 505–517.

Plomin, R., & DeFries, J. C. (1985). *Origins of individual differences in infancy: The Colorado Adoption Project*. Orlando, FL: Academic Press.

Plomin, R., DeFries, J. C., & Fulker, D. W. (1988). *Nature and nurture during infancy and early childhood*. Cambridge, England: Cambridge University Press.

Plomin, R., DeFries, J., McClearn, G., & Rutter, M. (1997). *Behavioral genetics (2nd ed.)*. New York: Freeman.

Plomin, R., Pedersen, N. L., Lichtenstein, P., & McClearn, G. E. (1994). Variability and stability in cognitive abilities are largely genetic later in life. *Behavior Genetics, 24*, 207–215.

Plomin, R., & Petrill, S. A. (1997). Genetics and intelligence: What is new? *Intelligence, 24*, 53–78.

Raskind, W. H., Hsu, Li, Berninger, V. W., Thomson, J. B., & Wijsman, E. M. (2000). Familial aggregation of phenotypes in dyslexia and dysgraphia. *Behavior Genetics, 30*, 385–396.

Reznikoff, M., Domino, G. Bridges, C. Honeyman, M. (1973). Creative abilities in identical and fraternal twins. *Behavior Genetics, 3*, 365–377.

Rice, T., Carey, G., Fulker, D. W., & DeFries, J. C. (1989). Multivariate path analysis of specific cognitive abilities in the Colorado Adoption Project: Conditional path model of assortative mating. *Behavior Genetics, 19*, 195–207.

Rice, T., Fulker, D. W., & DeFries, J. C. (1986). Multivariate path analysis of specific cognitive abilities in the Colorado Adoption Project. *Behavior Genetics, 16*, 107–125.

Schaie, K. W., Willis, S. L., Jay, G., & Chipuer, H. (1989). Structural invariance of cognitive abilities across the adult life span. A cross-sectional study. *Developmental Psychology, 25*, 652–662.

Scheinfeld, A. (1973). *Twins and supertwins*. Baltimore, MD: Penguin.

Siegel, L. S., & Ryan, E. B. (1989). Subtypes of developmental dyslexia: The influence of definitial variables. *Reading and Writing: An Interdisciplinary Journal, 1*, 257–287.

Squire, L. R., & Zola-Morgan, M. (1991). The medial temporal lobe memory system. *Science, 253*, 1380–1386.

Stanovich, K. E., & Siegel, L. S. (1994). Phenotypic performance profile of children with reading disabilities: A regression-based test of the phonological-core variable-difference model. *Journal of Educational Psychology, 86*, 24–53.

Sternberg, R. J. (1997). *Successful intelligence*. New York: Plume.

Sternberg, R. J., Forsythe, G. B., Hedlund, J., Horvath, J., Snook, S., Williams, W. M., Wagner, R. K., & Grigorenko, E. L. (2000). *Practical intelligence in everyday life*. New York: Cambridge University Press.

Sternberg, R. J., & Lubart, T. I. (1995). *Defying the crowd: Cultivating creativity in a culture of conformity*. New York: Free Press.

Stevenson, J., Graham, P., Fredman, G., & McLoughlin, V. (1987). A twin study of genetic influences on reading and spelling ability and disability. *Journal of Child Psychology and Psychiatry, 28*, 229–247.

Tambs, K., Sundet, J. M., & Magnus, P. (1984). Heritability analysis of the WAIS subtests: A study of twins. *Intelligence, 8*, 283–293.

Tambs, K., Sundet, J. M., & Magnus, P. (1986). Genetic and environmental contribution to the covariation between the Wechsler Adult Intelligence Scale (WAIS) subtests: A study of twins. *Behavior Genetics, 16*, 475–491.

Thapar, A., Petrill, S. A., & Thompson, L. A. (1994). The heritability of memory in the Western Reserve Twin Project. *Behavior Genetics, 24,* 155–160.

Thompson, L. A., Detterman, D. K., & Plomin, R. (1991). Associations between cognitive abilities and scholastic achievement: Genetic overlap but environmental differences. *Psychological Science, 2,* 158–165.

Tomblin, J. B., & Buckwalter, P. R. (1998). Heritability of poor language achievement among twins. *Journal of Speech, language, and Hearing Research, 41,* 188–199.

Tulving, E. (1972). Elements and semantic memory. In E. Tulving & W. Donaldson (Eds.), *Organization of memory.* New York: Academic Press.

Tulving, E. (1993). Human memory. In P. Andersen, P. Hvaleby, O. Paulsen, & B. Hökfelt (Eds.), *Memory concepts 1993: Basic and clinical aspects* (pp. 27–45). Amsterdam: Excerpta Medica.

Tulving, E., & Schacter, D. (1990). Priming and human memory system. *Science, 247,* 301–306.

Vandenberg, S. G. (1962). The hereditary abilities study: Hereditary components in a psychological test battery. *American Journal of Human Genetics, 14,* 220–237.

Vellutino, F. R., Scanlon, D. M., & Lyon, R. (2000). IQ scores do not differentiate between difficult to remediate and readily remediated poor readers: More evidence against the IQ achievement discrepancy definition of reading disability. *Journal of Learning Disabilities, 33,* 223–238.

Vernon, P. E. (1989). The nature-nurture problem in creativity. In J. A. Glover & R. R. Ronning (Eds.), *Handbook of creativity. Perspectives on individual differences* (pp. 93–110). New York: Plenum Press.

Wadsworth, S. J., Gillis, J. J., & DeFries, J. C. (1990). Genetic etiology of reading disability as a function of age. *Behavior Genetics, 20.*

Wadsworth, S. J., Olson, R. K., Pennington, B. F., & DeFries, J. C. (2000). Differential genetic etiology of reading disability as a function of IQ. *Journal of Learning Disabilities, 33,* 192–199.

Wadsworth, S. J., DeFries, J. C., Fulker, D. W., Olson, R. K., & Pennington, B. F. (1995). Reading performance and verbal short-term memory: A twin study of reciprocal causation. *Intelligence, 20,* 145–167.

Waller, N. G., Bouchard, T. J., Lykken, D. T., Tellegen, A., & Blacker, D. M. (1993). Creativity, heretability, familiality: Which word does not belong? *Psychological Inquiry, 4,* 235–237.

Wechsler, D. (1974). *Manual for the Wechsler intelligence scale for children (Revised).* New York: The Psychological Corporation.

Part VI

SOCIOCULTURAL APPROACH

g: Highly General and Highly Practical

Linda S. Gottfredson
University of Delaware

The general mental ability factor, *g*, is real. Its existence is no longer a serious question among experts on intelligence (Carroll, 1993). Whatever its underlying nature, psychometric *g* is a reliably measured, replicable phenomenon across all age, race, gender, and cultural groups studied so far (Jensen, 1998). Consequently, among intelligence researchers, it has become the most common working definition of "intelligence." A more important question today is: How *generally useful* are higher levels of *g outside* the realm of paper-and-pencil tests and tasks? The term *intelligence* connotes a very general and broadly useful capacity. Is that the label warranted for *g*? Even if it is, might not the label be warranted for other abilities too, leaving *g* as only one among various intelligences?

This chapter addresses these questions. It first outlines criteria for assessing how broadly useful *g* or any other trait is to individuals in "real life." This is *g's sociological* generality as distinct from its *psychometric* generality, the latter referring to its value in explaining the correlations among mental tests themselves. The former is the *range of life tasks* across which higher levels of *g* meaningfully affect performance. Second, the chapter reviews *g's* utility in one highly studied sphere of life—job performance. The considerable data on *g* in the workplace provide guideposts for understanding the pattern of *g's* generality in other nonacademic realms. The chapter next uses these guideposts to examine *g's* generality in two such realms: the specific tasks in daily life, such as driving and health self-management, and cumulative life outcomes such as socioeconomic success and social pathology.

Theories of intelligence differ considerably in their assertions regarding *g*'s generality. Two theories are compared throughout the chapter: *g* theory, which predicts that *g*'s utility generalizes widely and without regard to a task's manifest content or context, and practical intelligence theory, which postulates that *g* is useful in "academic" tasks but has relatively little value in practical affairs (where a proposed "practical intelligence" is, instead, said to be essential). As will be shown, *g* theory is more consonant with the facts. Whether or not a task seems academic offers scant guidance as to whether its performance is enhanced by higher levels of *g*. In no realm of life is *g* all that matters, but neither does it seem irrelevant in any. In the vast toolkit of human abilities, none has been found as broadly useful—as general—as *g*.

CRITERIA FOR GAUGING THE PRACTICAL IMPORTANCE OF AN ABILITY

Mapping the sociological generality of *g* requires understanding where and why higher levels of *g* are most and least useful to individuals throughout their lives. It is thus a matter of knowing the *pattern* or topography of *g*'s utility, that is, its depth and breadth of impact across diverse arenas of life. Depth of impact is gauged by a trait's *effect sizes* in individual realms of activity; breadth is gauged by the number of realms in which the trait has meaningful effect, which is its *generality*.

Gauging Effect Sizes

Effect size refers specifically to how big a change in the outcome in question is produced by a given change in the predictor (e.g., Cohen, 1988, p. 22; Jensen, 1980, pp. 305–310). In experimental research, where the predictor can be manipulated, effect size is often calculated in terms of standard deviation units of change in the outcome (reading achievement or cigarettes smoked per day) due to some treatment (reading instruction or smoking cessation program). In nonexperimental psychological research, the possible causal importance of a predictor is typically quantified in terms of correlations between predictors and criteria, including regression coefficients (b and beta) and the multiple correlation (R). Odds ratios are often used in other fields, such as epidemiology (Gerstman, 1998).

Although *R* squared (proportion of variance explained) is sometimes mistakenly used to measure effect size, *R* (or its analogs) is the proper measure of a predictor's effect in the real world because it "is directly proportional to the practical value of the [predictor]—whether measured in dollar value of increased output or percentage increase in output"

(Schmidt & Hunter, 1998, p. 272). A correlation of .4 (or .2) means that a one standard deviation change in the predictor (say, *g*) is associated with a .4 (or .2) standard deviation change in the outcome (say, quality of job performance or understanding of a physician's instructions). If the correlation is viewed as the predictor's potential rate of return or leverage for change, a predictor that correlates .4 with the outcome has twice as much leverage as one correlating .2. In the worlds of investing and gambling, these rates would be extraordinary. In the world of psychological intervention, point biserial correlations of this size are respectively considered "large" and "medium" (Lubinski & Humphreys, 1997, Table 2).

Gauging Generality

Generality is the range of human activity across which an ability has meaningful effect sizes. It is greater to the extent that higher levels of *g* provide an advantage to individuals over a greater variety of task domains, ranges of the *g* continuum, ages, generations, and cultures. I focus on the first, partly because the skeptics of *g*'s utility have often focused on task characteristics to press their case.

More importantly, the very definition of an ability is rooted in tasks performed. To abbreviate Carroll's (1993, pp. 3–9) meticulously crafted definition, an *ability* is an attribute of individuals revealed by differences in the levels of task difficulty, on a *defined class of tasks*, that individuals perform successfully when conditions for maximal performance are favorable. The broader the class of tasks, the more general the ability is. Another reason for focusing on tasks is that the other four conditions set forth earlier all influence the configuration of tasks people actually undertake. For instance, the young encounter, seek out, and are expected to master different tasks than their elders. Task expectations and preferences likewise differ for the bright versus the dull, for people entering jobs in the information age rather than the industrial age, and for citizens of widely different economies or cultures. Understanding *g*'s generality across different tasks can therefore help explain any variations in its utility across time, place, age, and range of ability.

Predictions of *g* Theory Versus Practical Intelligence Theory

Theorists of *g* conceptualize it as a general capacity for processing information of any kind. As such, *g* undergirds critical thinking skills such as reasoning, thinking abstractly, spotting and solving problems, and quickly and efficiently learning moderately complex material (see chap. 3 by Jensen, this volume). *g* theory therefore predicts that higher *g* will enhance performance in all tasks that require information processing. It also predicts, however, that task performance will depend more heavily on differences in g (be more "g loaded") when the task requires more complex information processing. Accordingly, a task's g loading would have little to do with its manifest content, including whether it seems school-like or not. Indeed, it is well known that g loadings are low for some manifestly academic tasks (such as spelling and arithmetic computation among adults) but high for others with the same kind of content (reading comprehension, mathematical reasoning).

In contrast, practical intelligence theorists tend to conceptualize g as only an "academic" intelligence ("book smarts"), as distinct from "practical" intelligence ("street smarts" or common sense), which they posit is relatively independent of g (Sternberg, Wagner, Williams, & Horvath, 1995). Thus narrowing g to mere book smarts or "inert" rather than active intelligence, they assert that highly g-loaded tests tap only "a tiny and not very important part" of the intellectual spectrum (Sternberg, 1997, p. 11).

The proponents of practical intelligence have clarified the g-is-only-book-smarts thesis by defining what they mean by academic versus practical tasks (Sternberg & Wagner, 1993; Sternberg et al., 1995). As shown in Table 13.1, academic tasks are said to call for thought and not action, are imposed rather than chosen, are esoteric, and their answers and means of solution are highly circumscribed. In contrast, both the nature of the problem and the solution of practical tasks are said to be more ambiguous, and their solution (of which there may be several) requires everyday experience and personal interest. The difference between academic and practical is thus a distinction between, on the one hand, the narrow, pedantic, disconnected theoretical and, on the other, the messy, meaningful reality

TABLE 13.1
Sternberg and Wagner's (1993) Definition
of Academic Versus Practical Tasks

"Academic" problems tend to:	*"Practical"* problems tend to:
1. Be formulated by other people	1. Require problem recognition and formulation
2. Be well-defined	2. Be ill-defined
3. Be complete	3. Require information seeking
4. Possess only a single correct answer	4. Possess multiple acceptable solutions
5. Possess only a single method of obtaining the correct answer	5. Allow multiple paths to solution
6. Be disembedded from ordinary experience	6. Be embedded in and require prior everyday experience
7. Be of little or no intrinsic interest	7. Require motivation and personal involvement

in which people actually live. Whereas *g* may be crucial in the former, it is not in the latter, posit the proponents of practical intelligence theory. Their prediction would seem to be that *g*'s criterion validities (its correlations with outcomes) will be higher when tasks are more academic (e.g., are well-defined, disembodied from ordinary experience, and of little intrinsic interest) and smaller when they more practical (e.g., require problem recognition and formulation, information seeking, and personal involvement).

In short, both *g* theory and practical intelligence theory agree that *g*'s impact is moderated by task attributes, but they disagree on which ones. The latter suggests that the effect sizes for *g* rise for more academic tasks, whereas the former suggests that they rise for more complex ones, whether academic or not. Practical intelligence theory suggests that *g* is therefore not very general because academic tasks are confined mostly to school settings. *g* theory suggests, in contrast, that higher *g* has pervasive value because people face complex tasks in many aspects of life; it is not only an academic ability, but also a highly practical one.

g and Job Performance

Outside of education, the most intensely studied sphere of intelligent performance has been job performance. For many decades, teams of military, public, and private sector researchers have spent incalculable person-years documenting the determinants of performance in training and on the job. The century-old field of personnel selection psychology has been devoted to just this effort.

THE NATURE OF RESEARCH ON JOB PERFORMANCE

Initial Reluctance to Entertain *g* Theory

Many personnel psychologists have turned to *g* theory in recent years, but for many decades the field was ruled by the *theory of situational specificity*. This was the belief that there are many independent abilities and that the particular mix of abilities that is relevant to a job—and even to the individual positions within a job classification—depends on the detailed specifics of the position's duties and setting. Intelligence was viewed as only one among many aptitudes affecting performance, and its importance was thought spotty and unpredictable—as was that of all other predictors. By this theory, no trait had general utility. Schmidt and Hunter (1998), among others, showed via meta-analysis that the specificity doctrine was sustained by statistical artifacts owing to most research samples being small and somewhat homogeneous in mental ability. Once those artifacts are taken into account, g's importance is seen to be pervasive and lawfully patterned. The specificity doctrine did not die for lack of enthusiasm, but from the crush of accumulating evidence (e.g., see Humphreys' personal account, 1986).

Personnel psychologists as a group never expected intelligence to be important and many wish that it were not. As g has shown ever greater promise for explaining job performance, it has become more subject to concerted efforts to *disconfirm* its functional importance and to find alternatives to mental tests for selecting and promoting workers. The major reason for such efforts, often bordering on the desperate, has been that g-loaded employee selection typically screens out proportionately many more Blacks and Hispanics (has "disparate impact"), which makes an employer vulnerable to legal and political attack (Sharf, 1988). Although useful for prompting more interest in how non-g traits affect job performance, this effort to negate the apparent functional impact of g has, ironically, only further confirmed it (e.g., Schmitt, Rogers, Chan, Sheppard, & Jennings, 1997). All but a few personnel psychologists now accept that g has special importance for work performance (e.g., see the special issue of *Human Performance* by Viswesvaran & Ones, in press), but that acceptance has been for the most part a grudging concession to empirical evidence. The move to g theory therefore cannot be attributed to any so-called "g-ocentric" enthusiasm (Sternberg & Wagner, 1993) on the part of personnel psychologists.

The Body of Evidence

Evidence has gone far beyond showing that g has a big overall impact on job performance to showing where it has its largest impact, and why. The major discoveries about g's gradients of effect are listed in Table 13.2 and are discussed later. In presenting the evidence for the generalizations in Table 13.2, I have relied on meta-analyses of thousands of small studies and on two very large military projects. All the correlations with g in this chapter's Job Performance section have been corrected, except where noted otherwise, for two statistical artifacts that depress correlations below their true level: unreliability and restriction in range of mental ability. Most personnel selection research has measured job performance with supervisor ratings, so, unless specified otherwise, all correlations with performance reported here refer to performance measured subjectively rather than objectively. As we shall see, subjective measures of performance lead to underestimating g's impact on job competence.

The Measurement of **g**.   Only a small proportion of job performance studies have actually correlated job performance with *g* scores, because estimating *g* scores requires administering a broad battery of tests from which the *g* factor can be extracted. However, many kinds of studies have shown, over and again, that *g* is by far the biggest component of all mental tests (Carroll, 1993). So great is their *g* component that mental tests are usually just "flavored" by the special abilities they are meant to measure. Moreover, it is the *g* component of mental tests that usually accounts almost entirely for their predictive value (e.g., Jencks et al., 1979, chap. 4; Jensen, 1998; Ree & Carretta, 1997; Thorndike, 1986). Tests differ in the degree to which they are *g* loaded (that is, in their ability to measure *g*), but the highly *g*-loaded ones can be treated as interchangeable, albeit imperfect, measures of *g*, no matter how they are labeled (verbal, quantitative, spatial, and the like). I shall therefore refer to all mental tests as de facto measures of *g*. One test that will figure prominently in discussions to follow is the Armed Forces Qualifying Test (AFQT), which is derived from the Armed Services Vocational Aptitude Battery (ASVAB). The AFQT is as highly correlated with IQ as IQ tests are with one another (Herrnstein & Murray, 1994, appen. 3), and it has been shown to measure the *g* factor well (Jensen, 1988; Ree, Carretta, & Doub, 1998/1999). Because any single test such as the AFQT can only approximate *g*, such tests *underestimate* *g*'s effects to some extent. Virtually all the estimates to follow therefore understate the impact of *g* for this reason as well.

Two Especially Important Research Projects.   The Army's Project A (Campbell, 1990) and the Joint-Service Job Performance Measurement/ Enlistment Standards (JPM) Project (Wigdor & Green, 1991) bear a detailed look because both used the expensive and hence rarely used gold standard in measuring job performance, namely, hands-on job-sample tests, and not just the inexpensive and hence much-used job knowledge tests and supervisor ratings. So, for example, the 4- to 8-hour hands-on tests might include having a naval machinist's mate respond to an alarm signaling loss of pressure in the main engine lube oil pump. These projects also systematically investigated the dimensionality of both performance criteria and their predictors, which had never before been done so systematically. Different criteria are predicted best by different personal traits, so understanding the relative value of *g* hinges on understanding the dimensionality of both performance and its determinants. The two projects are also especially pertinent because they were motivated by a practical intelligence perspective, in particular, by a concern that the military's seemingly *academic* selection tests might not actually predict workers' *practical* performance.

Both of these huge, interrelated projects had their origins in Congressional concern that the military services needed to improve and better validate their procedures for selecting and classifying recruits. At the time, the ASVAB had been validated only against performance in military training, not on the job. The new collective research effort required developing and evaluating multiple ways of assessing performance (including job samples, job simulations, job "walk-through" interviews, job knowledge tests, and ratings by self, peers, and supervisors) for a wide variety of occupational specialties (military police, jet engine mechanic, administrative specialist, rifleman, etc.) in each of the four services; developing a wider array of cognitive and non-cognitive predictors; and then validating all predictors (or subsets thereof) against all the performance criteria available for each service. The validation research was based on relatively large samples of recruits with longitudinal data.

A Crucial Distinction Among Outcome Criteria: Core Technical Versus Noncore "Citizenship" Dimensions of Performance.

The JPM project found that its different performance criteria were far from perfectly correlated, even when corrected for unreliability. The median (uncorrected) correlation of hands-on (objectively measured) performance was .57 with job walk-through interviews (where workers describe how they would perform certain tasks), .47 with paper-and-pencil job knowledge tests, .37 with training (school knowledge) scores, and .26 with supervisor ratings (Wigdor & Green, 1991, tables on pp. 151–155; note that the four correlations tend to be for different sets of jobs). The four criteria therefore measure somewhat different aspects of performance, but job knowledge and training grades—the most academic criteria—share more in common with the practical gold standard than do supervisor ratings.

Army Project A systematically investigated the dimensionality of these criteria in 19 entry-level Army jobs via LISREL modeling of 32 criterion scores for 9,430 job incumbents (Campbell, McHenry, & Wise, 1990). The latent structure modeling yielded five factors: (1) core technical task proficiency (job-specific proficiency, such as an armor crewman starting and stopping a tank's engines), (2) general soldiering (proficiency in common duties, such as determining grid coordinates on military maps; Campbell et al., 1990, p. 322), (3) peer support and leadership, effort, and self development, (4) maintaining personal discipline, and (5) physical fitness and military bearing. Correlations among the five dimensions suggest that job performance tends to be divided into technical versus nontechnical dimensions (the first two vs. the last two factors, with the third being intermediate). The latter, noncore kinds of performance were measured mostly by ratings and are often characterized as the "citizenship" or "contextual" aspect of job performance (Organ, 1994).

Precisely because citizenship behaviors tend to be "extra-role, discretionary" behaviors that are *not* part of a job description (essentially, working above and beyond the call of duty), some researchers question whether they ought to be used as criteria in developing selection batteries (Borman & Motowidlo, 1993, pp. 93–94; Schmidt, 1993, p. 505). The noncore dimensions of performance are nonetheless relevant for our purposes here, because they affect people's lives by affecting both their supervisors' ratings and their job satisfaction (Borman & Motowidlo, 1993; Organ & Konovsky, 1989).

A Crucial Distinction Among Predictors: Cognitive Versus "Noncognitive" Predictors of Performance. The military services, like civilian employers, have been criticized in the past for perhaps relying too heavily on cognitive ability measures, especially paper-and-pencil tests, when selecting workers. The concern was that batteries of paper-and-pencil tests, such as the ASVAB, might measure academic abilities not actually relevant to the job while omitting useful noncognitive predictors. This would lead to weak selection batteries as well as to undue emphasis on academic talent. Army Project A addressed these concerns by developing an experimental test battery that measured not only a wide array of personal attributes that the ASVAB does not, but also specific mental skills that are manifestly perceptual–psychomotor rather than academic in content (e.g., choice reaction time and accuracy, target tracking). The trial predictor battery included 65 scales for a wide variety of personality, interest, and other nonacademic traits that an extensive review of the literature had identified as potentially useful predictors. Scores on these scales were combined, together with 4 ASVAB composites, to create a total of 24 predictor composites for 400–600 incumbents in each of nine high-volume Army jobs (McHenry, Hough, Toquam, Hanson, & Ashworth, 1990, Table 2). The predictor composites fell into six categories: general cognitive ability (4 ASVAB composites), spatial ability (1 composite), perceptual–psychomotor abilities (6), temperament–personality (4), vocational interests (6), and job reward preferences (3). The first three categories are highly *g* loaded but the last three are not. There is much other research on the importance of noncognitive traits, some of which is discussed later, but Project A is still the largest and most thorough single study of the relative utility of cognitive and noncognitive traits.

A Crucial Question: Is g Causal? The answer is "yes." Ample research, particularly from the military services, shows that performance in training and on the job is correlated with mental ability assessed *before* entering training or the job. Mental ability also predicts job performance controlling for all other factors ever studied, the most important of which are examined shortly. There have also been large-scale quasi-experiments in which the emphasis on *g* in selecting workers was either increased or decreased (Schmidt & Hunter, 2000; see also the results of Project 100,000, Laurence & Ramsberger, 1991). Aggregate performance plummets when *g* is ignored, and it improves substantially in mid- to high-level jobs when *g* is weighted more heavily. The question among personnel researchers now is not whether *g* has a causal role, but instead how much, where, and why.

THE *g*-BASED THEORY OF JOB PERFORMANCE

The breadth and stability of the evidence in personnel selection psychology has led to the causal modeling of job performance (e.g., Hunter, 1983a, 1986; Hunter & Schmidt, 1996; Ree & Carretta, 1997; Ree, Earles, & Teachout, 1995). Figure 13.1 extracts the essence of this modeling. This model helps to explain *g*'s pattern of impact in both work and nonwork realms of life because it is, at heart, a *learning* theory and the need to learn is incessant in modern life (Hunter & Schmidt, 1996). *g* is important because it reflects the ability to learn (cf. Carroll, 1997). By this theory, job *performance* depends chiefly on job-specific *knowledge* that workers have learned either in training or through experience on the job. Differences in both knowledge and performance depend, in turn, on three kinds of differences among workers, summarized here as the "can do" (ability), "will do" (interest), and "have done" (training and experience) components of developed competence. All three precursors are important because they all affect the accumulation of job knowledge: the first affects workers' *rate* of learning from experience; the second, their *effort* to learn when given the opportunity; and the third, their *opportunity* to have learned. The one task attribute that shifts the relative importance of these person-precursors is task complexity. More complex jobs require more learning.

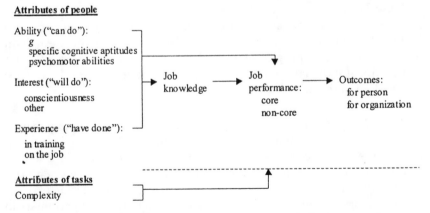

FIG. 13.1.   Job performance model based on personnel selection research.

g is the predominant *can do* factor, and it affects job performance primarily via its strong effect on job knowledge. This is g's indirect effect, and it is analogous to *crystallized* intelligence. However, learning is not enough. Past learning never fully prepares people for the challenges they will face on the job (or in life). Many jobs (and life situations) require considerable adaptation and improvisation. Workers must spot and solve new problems that require going beyond merely applying old knowledge. More complex jobs impose more such demands because they are less "automatable." This is g's *direct* effect on performance, and it is analogous to *fluid g*. The indirect effect of g on hands-on performance is at least twice as big as its direct effect in the typical job (e.g., Hunter, 1986).

This imbalance of indirect to direct effects is found for both *rated* performance and *actual* hands-on performance. The big difference in g's prediction of the two criteria is that g has considerably stronger effects, both direct and indirect, on objectively measured performance than on supervisory ratings. Supervisors' perceptions of performance generally are only moderately responsive to either worker knowledge or worker performance, perhaps because few supervisors have much opportunity to actually observe their subordinates (Borman, White, Pulakos, & Oppler, 1991, p. 870). On the other hand, ratings are much more sensitive to worker personality traits that substantially affect employees' apparent "citizenship" but not their performance of core duties.

KEY DISCOVERIES ABOUT g'S GENERALITY

With this model as an organizing guide, the 18 major discoveries in Table 13.2 can be used to chart g's degree of generality across different dimensions of work.

Discoveries 1–3a: g Has Full Generality Across All Jobs, Performance Criteria, Ability Levels, and Lengths of Experience

The first meta-analyses of job performance showed that g's ability to predict job performance does not vary across time or place for different positions within the same or substantially similar job category (e.g., Hunter & Hunter, 1984, p. 80; Schmidt & Hunter, 1984; Schmidt, Hunter, & Pearlman, 1981; Schmidt, Hunter, Pearlman, & Shane, 1979). That is, criterion validities are not subject to the vagaries of situational specificity, as had long been thought. Since then, repeated meta-analyses have demonstrated even wider generality for g, in particular, that g is useful in predicting job performance across (1) the full range of jobs in the United States

TABLE 13.2
Major Findings on *g*'s Impact on Job Performance[a]

Utility of g

1. Higher levels of *g* lead to higher levels of performance in all jobs and along all dimensions of performance. The average correlation of mental tests with overall rated job performance is around .5 (corrected for statistical artifacts).
2. There is no ability threshold above which more *g* does not enhance performance. The effects of *g* are linear: successive increments in *g* lead to successive increments in job performance.
3. (a) The value of higher levels of *g* does not fade with longer experience on the job. Criterion validities remain high even among highly experienced workers. (b) That they sometimes even appear to rise with experience may be due to the confounding effect of the least experienced groups tending to be more variable in relative level of experience, which obscures the advantages of higher *g*.
4. *g* predicts job performance better in more complex jobs. Its (corrected) criterion validities range from about .2 in the simplest jobs to .8 in the most complex.
5. *g* predicts the core technical dimensions of performance better than it does the non-core "citizenship" dimensions of performance.
6. Perhaps as a consequence, *g* predicts objectively-measured performance (either job knowledge or job sample performance) better than it does subjectively-measured performance (such as supervisor ratings).

Utility of g *relative to other "can do" components of performance*

7. Specific mental abilities (such as spatial, mechanical, or verbal ability) add very little, beyond *g*, to the prediction of job performance. *g* generally accounts for at least 85–95% of a full mental test battery's (cross-validated) ability to predict performance in training or on the job.
8. Specific mental abilities (such as clerical ability) sometimes add usefully to prediction, net of *g*, but only in certain classes of jobs. They do not have general utility.
9. General psychomotor ability is often useful, but primarily in less complex work. Its predictive validities fall with job complexity while those for *g* rise.

Utility of g *relative to the "will do" component of job performance*

10. *g* predicts core performance much better than do "non-cognitive" (less *g*-loaded) traits, such as vocational interests and different personality traits. The latter add virtually nothing to the prediction of core performance, net of *g*.
11. *g* predicts most dimensions of non-core performance (such as personal discipline and soldier bearing) much less well than do "non-cognitive" traits of personality and temperament. When a performance dimension reflects both core and non-core performance (such as leadership), *g* predicts to about the same modest degree as do non-cognitive (less *g*-loaded) traits.
12. Different non-cognitive traits appear to usefully supplement *g* in different jobs, just as specific abilities sometimes add to the prediction of performance in certain classes of jobs. Only one such non-cognitive trait appears to be as generalizable as *g*: the personality dimension defined by conscientiousness and integrity. Its effect sizes for core performance are substantially smaller than *g*'s, however.

(Continued)

TABLE 13.2
(Continued)

Utility of g *relative to job knowledge*

---

13. *g* affects job performance primarily *indirectly* through its effect on job-specific knowledge.
14. *g*'s *direct* effects on job performance increase when jobs are less routinized, training is less complete, and workers retain more discretion.
15. Job-specific knowledge generally predicts job performance as well as does *g* among experienced workers. However, job knowledge is not generalizable (net of its *g* component), even among experienced workers. The value of job knowledge is highly job specific; *g*'s value is unrestricted.

Utility of g *relative to the "have done" (experience) component of job performance*

---

16. Like job knowledge, the effect sizes of job-specific experience are sometimes high but they are not generalizable.
17. In fact, experience predicts performance less well as all workers become more experienced. In contrast, higher levels of *g* remain an asset regardless of length of experience.
18. Experience predicts job performance less well as job complexity rises, which is opposite the trend for *g*. Like general psychomotor ability, experience matters least where *g* matters most to individuals and their organizations.

---

[a]See text for citations.

(e.g., Hunter & Hunter, 1984); (2) all levels of experience on the job (e.g., Schmidt, Hunter, Outerbridge, & Goff, 1988); and (3) all broad performance criteria, whether they emphasize *content* (core technical vs. noncore; McHenry et al., 1990) or *method* of assessment (paper-and-pencil tests, hands-on job samples, or ratings; Wigdor & Green, 1991).

The impact of *g* is also linear, that is, brighter job incumbents always perform better on the average, controlling for other factors (e.g., Coward & Sackett, 1990). There is evidence that additional increments in *g* are useful even at highest reaches of *g* and cultural achievement. Simonton (1994, chap. 8) reviews historiographic research indicating that the greatest Western composers, political leaders, and U.S. Presidents were brighter than eminent compatriots of lesser renown. He points out that greatness requires zeal and persistence too, but that additional intelligence enhances performance even at the highest levels of cultural achievement.

No meta-analysis has documented any limits to *g*'s generality in predicting job performance. Effect sizes vary from small to very large, depending on the kind of job and performance criterion considered (as is discussed next), but they are never zero. In fact, average effect sizes are substantial: the average correlation between mental test scores and ratings of overall job performance hovers around .5 in broad collections of jobs (Hunter & Hunter, 1984; Schmidt & Hunter, 1998).

Discoveries 3b–6: g's Effect Sizes Vary
by Job Complexity, Length of Experience,
and Performance Criterion

Although higher levels of g are at least somewhat useful in all job circumstances, they are much more useful in some than others. This variability behaves lawfully, creating predictable gradients of effect size across the topography of work.

Job Complexity. The best known variation in predictive validities for g is that higher levels of g are a bigger advantage in more complex jobs. When Hunter (1983b; Hunter & Hunter, 1984) classified civilian jobs into five broad levels of complexity, average criterion validities for mental tests ranged from .23 in the simplest work (feeding/offbearing work) to .58 in the most complex (synthesizing/coordinating work). Almost 63% of the workforce held middle-complexity jobs. These jobs had an average criterion validity of .51 and included skilled blue collar occupations as well as midlevel white collar occupations. When narrower job families and more objective performance criteria are considered, validities range more widely—from about .2 in the simplest jobs to almost .8 in the most complex.

This complexity-related gradient of effect sizes is especially important because research in both sociology and psychology has shown that the major distinction among occupations in the U.S. economy is the complexity of their duties (e.g., Miller, Treiman, Cain, & Roos, 1980). The complexity dimension among jobs is highly correlated with their prestige or general social desirability. It is also moderately highly correlated to a job's criticality to the employer (Gottfredson, 1997, Table 7) and the dollar value of differences in worker performance in a job (Hunter, Schmidt, & Judiesch, 1990). In short, g tends to give the "biggest bang for the buck" in the jobs most highly valued by workers and their employers.

Job analyses indicate that g is more important in more complex jobs for reasons that g theory would predict: The key to a job's complexity is how much information processing the work demands. As seen in Table 13.3, these information-processing skills are prototypical of g. Compiling and combining information, advising, reasoning, planning, analyzing, and decision making all correlated at least .8 with job complexity level in a wide array of civilian jobs (Gottfredson, 1997, Table 7). This result mirrors Arvey's (1986, p. 418) earlier finding, also shown in Table 13.3, that the strongest correlates of complexity across jobs in the petrochemical industry (his "Reasoning and Judgment" factor) were requirements for dealing with unexpected situations (.75), learning and recalling job-related information (.71), reasoning and making judgments (.69), identifying problem situations quickly (.69), and reacting swiftly when unexpected problems occur

TABLE 13.3
Selected Correlates of Job Complexity

Task requirements	Correlation (uncorrected)
With Job "Complexity" factor: PAQ Job Analysis Data for 276 Broad Census occupations[a]	
Compiling information (importance of)	.90
Combining information (importance)	.88
Advising (importance)	.86
Writing (importance)	.86
Reasoning (level of)	.83
Planning/scheduling (amount)	.83
Analyzing (importance)	.83
Decision making (level)	.82
Negotiating (importance)	.79
Persuading (importance)	.79
Oral information (extent of use)	.68
Coding/decoding (importance)	.68
Instructing (importance)	.67
With "Judgment and Reasoning" factor: Analysis of 140 Jobs in Petrochemical Industry[b]	
Deal with unexpected situations	.75
Able to learn and recall job-related information	.71
Able to reason and make judgements	.69
Able to identify problem situations quickly	.69
React swiftly when unexpected problems occur	.67
Able to apply common sense to solve problems	.66
Able to learn new procedures quickly	.66
Alert and quick to understand things	.55
Able to compare information from two or more sources to reach a conclusion	.49

[a]From Gottfredson (1997, pp. 100–101), with permission of Elsevier Science. PAQ = Position Analysis Questionnaire.
[b]From Arvey (1986, p. 418), with permission of Academic Press.

(.67). These specific task requirements seem to defy classification as consistently academic, which practical intelligence theory would seem to require.

Another finding also seems to reflect the fact that greater complexity yields greater effect sizes for *g*. Namely, both experience and ability level predicted performance better in civilian than in military jobs of roughly comparable (moderate) complexity (Hunter, 1983a; Schmidt, Hunter, & Outerbridge, 1986). For example, the average correlations of mental ability with work sample performance and supervisor ratings were, respectively, .75 and .47 in 10 civilian jobs but .53 and .24 in 4 Army jobs (Hunter, 1983a). This civilian–military difference in effect sizes is thought to result from the military's more intense training and its greater insistence on following standard operating procedures. Both would reduce the *g* loadedness of military work, the first by reducing how much recruits must learn on their own after they start the job and the second by reducing their discretion in performing the job, that is, their opportunity to use their own judgment in deciding which problems to tackle and how (Schmidt et al., 1986, p. 433).

Experience. The skeptics of *g* might logically predict that its value would fade, especially in nonacademic jobs, as workers confront problems in the messy real world for which they were not specifically trained (e.g., Table 13.3's "dealing with unexpected situations" and "decision making"). Decaying criterion validities on the job, if confirmed, would be a matter of great concern in personnel selection. Hunter, Schmidt, and their colleagues (Hunter & Schmidt, 1996; Schmidt, Hunter, Outerbridge, & Goff, 1988) examined whether lengthier experience would, in fact, wash out the advantages of higher *g* for later job performance. In a meta-analysis of civilian work, they found that criterion validities for *g* actually *increased* with length of experience. The criterion validities for *g* ranged from .35 among incumbents with 0 to 3 years of job-specific experience to .59 for workers with an average of over 12 years of experience (Hunter & Schmidt, 1996). Hunter and Schmidt suggest that this increase is probably artifactual, however, at least for midlevel jobs, because the trend across experience categories disappears when differences in experience within the categories are controlled. A study of four Army jobs found that, when such differences in experience were controlled, *g*'s correlations with hands-on performance held steady at about .4 throughout the 5 years of experience for which the study had data (Schmidt et al., 1988, Table 6).

Effect sizes for experience, and their consequent ability to disguise the role of *g*, seem to increase when incumbents vary more widely in *relative* experience. When experience is not controlled, effect sizes for *g* increase as relative experience becomes more similar, as happens, for instance, when all incumbents have 10 to 12 rather than 0 to 2 years of experience. An additional year of experience makes a much bigger difference when the average tenure on a job is 1 year rather than 11.

What this means in pragmatic terms is that even lengthy experience does not compensate for below-average IQ. Differences in experience can hide but never nullify the value of higher *g*. Moreover, the advantages of higher *g* remain substantial in all but perhaps the simplest jobs. In 23 military jobs of moderate complexity, low-ability recruits (CAT IV, which is AFQT percentiles 10–30) with over 36 months of experience still performed notably worse than bright men (CAT I–II, which is AFQT percentiles 65–99) with only 0 to 12 months of experience (Wigdor & Green, 1991, pp. 163–164). When jobs are simpler than these, low-*g* workers may eventually catch up with sufficient practice, but when jobs are more complex, such workers are apt to be left hopelessly behind as their more able peers continue to advance in mastery.

Core Versus Noncore Dimensions of Performance (Army Project A Data).

Most of the criterion validities discussed so far come from civilian studies, and they are based almost entirely on supervisor ratings of job performance. However, both Army Project A and the JPM research program developed a wide range of performance criteria, as described earlier. They found that *g*'s effect sizes were two to four times as large for some criteria as for others in these moderately complex military jobs. (Keep in mind that the effect sizes for military jobs may underestimate those for civilian jobs.)

Table 13.4 summarizes Army Project A's pertinent findings for nine jobs, whose average validities were all essentially the same (McHenry et al., 1990). Column 1 shows that general cognitive ability, as measured by the ASVAB, is a strong predictor of *core* task performance, whether the tasks be job-specific (core technical proficiency) or common across the variety of Army jobs (general soldiering proficiency). The predictive validities of general cognitive ability were .63 and .65, respectively, for these two proficiency criteria. Moreover, the *predictive* component of *g*, so measured, was also captured well by mental test composites that are *not* paper-and-pencil or even verbal in format, in this case, the set of computerized perceptual–psychomotor tests, which had concurrent validities, respectively, of .59 and .65 for the same two criteria (see column 3). Although these two sets of cognitive composites, the ASVAB and the experimental, are quite different in content and format, their predictive component must be essentially identical—and probably consists almost entirely of *g*—because the experimental cognitive battery adds only .01 to .04, net of the ASVAB, to the prediction of performance, no matter which of the five performance criteria are considered (compare columns 1 and 6). That small incremental validity is due almost entirely to the spatial composite in the experimental cognitive battery (compare columns 5 and 6).

The results for the noncore dimensions of performance are very different. The *g* factor, as represented in the ASVAB composites, is not nearly as strong a predictor of the *noncore, nontechnical* aspects of performance as it is the core technical aspects, whether job specific or general: the predictive validities are, respectively, .31, .16, and .20 for effort–leadership, personal discipline, and fitness–bearing (column 1). As the study authors suggest (McHenry et al., 1990, p. 352), *g*'s higher validity for effort–leadership than for the other two criteria may be due to the effort–leadership measure including ratings of core task performance. To summarize, Project A's results suggest that *g* has a small effect (about .2) on job-related self-control (the last two criteria), a moderate effect on being an effective team

TABLE 13.4

The Abilities of Different Cognitive and Noncognitive Ability Composites to Predict
5 Dimensions of Job Performance: Army Project A Data for 9 Mid-Level Jobs

	Predictor Sets[a]							
	ASVAB	Project A's New Composites			ASVAB Plus New Composites			All
Dimension of Job Performance	General Cognitive Ability Composites (K = 4) (1)	New Spatial Composite (K = 1) (2)	7 New Cognitive Composites (Includes spatial) (K = 7) (3)	13 New Temperament/Interest-Reward Preferences (TIR) Composites (K = 13) (4)	New Spatial Composite plus 4 ASVAB Composites (K = 5) (5)	7 New Cognitive Composites Plus 4 ASVAB Composites (K = 11) (6)	13 New Temperament-Interest-Reward (TIR) Composites Plus 4 ASVAB Composites (K = 17) (7)	(K = 24) (8)
Core technical proficiency	.63	.56	.59	.44	.65	.65	.65	.67
General soldiering	.65	.63	.65	.44	.68	.69	.67	.70
Effort and leadership	.31	.25	.27	.38	.32	.32	.43	.44
Personal discipline	.16	.12	.13	.35	.17	.17	.37	.37
Physical fitness and military bearing	.20	.10	.14	.38	.22	.23	.41	.42

Source: From McHenry et al. (1990, Tables 4–7). Reprinted with permission of Personnel Psychology, copyright (1990).
[a]Multiple R's were corrected for range restriction and adjusted for shrinkage. K = number of composites.

leader or team member (.3), and a very strong effect on the core technical performances for which workers bear individual responsibility (.6).

Objective Versus Subjective Measures of Performance (JPM Project Data). Predictive validities from the JPM project flesh out the picture of the relation of *g* to different performance criteria. The Project A core proficiency criteria (job-specific and general) were based on a combination of job knowledge and hands-on proficiency tests. In contrast, the JPM project kept these two types of criteria separate when examining the predictive validity of *g*. It thus provides a more direct test of the skeptics' hypothesis that *academic* ability tests (such as the ASVAB) do not predict *practical* (hands-on) performance well, only other paper-and-pencil performances (such as job knowledge tests). The JPM reports that the median (uncorrected) correlation of hands-on (job-sample) performance with the AFQT was .38 for the 23 jobs studied across the four services (Wigdor & Green, 1991, p. 161). Predictive validity was as high in the Army and Marine jobs, few of which could be construed as academic, as it was in the Air Force and Navy jobs.

AFQT (uncorrected) predictions of hands-on performance in the four Marine jobs reinforce the point that the supposedly academic AFQT actually predicts performance on practical as well as academic tasks: rifleman (.55), machinegunner (.66), mortarman (.38), and assaultman (.46; Wigdor & Green, 1991, p. 161). These jobs are hardly the picture of esoteric academic work. To illustrate that the criterion tasks actually chosen for measurement were not mostly school-like, the two tasks that were most highly correlated with overall hands-on performance among rifleman were "land navigation" and "live rifle fire" (Wigdor & Green, 1991, p. 148).

Hunter (1986, p. 352) summarized data showing, further, that the predictive validity of *g* is higher for objectively measured than subjectively measured job performance, regardless of whether the objective measures are paper-and-pencil (academic) or hands-on (practical). *g* correlated .80 and .75, respectively, with job knowledge and work sample performance but only .47 with supervisory ratings in 10 civilian jobs, and it correlated .63 and .53 with the two objective measures but only .24 with ratings in four military jobs. As noted earlier, skeptics of *g* had long predicted the opposite pattern, based on the mistaken assumption that supervisors are unduly impressed by intelligence.

Discoveries 7–9: Generality of *g* is High Relative to Other Ability ("Can Do") Factors

Assessing *g*'s practical value requires knowing how large its effects typically are *relative* to other personal traits that might also create differences in task performance. Meta-analyses have been consistent in showing, not only that g has very general value for job performance, but also that narrower mental abilities (such as verbal, spatial, and mechanical aptitude) do *not* have general value after removing their large g component. Examples would include the clerical, mechanical, and electrical composites of the ASVAB. Tests of specific aptitudes seldom predict performance as well as does g, and they generally predict only to the extent that they measure g (Hunter, 1983c, 1983d; Schmidt, Ones, & Hunter, 1992). They seldom add more than .01 to .03 to the prediction of job performance beyond g, no matter how performance is measured, as is illustrated by spatial ability in Table 13.4 (compare columns 1 and 5) for Army Project A data. Such weak incremental validity is a consistent finding from research for the other military services (Ree, Earles, & Teachout, 1994) and civilian jobs (Schmidt et al., 1992, pp. 646–647). The finding should not be surprising in view of the moderately high correlations among all mental abilities (their "positive manifold"), which means that once a mental test's g component is removed, it retains little with which to predict anything. The only meta-analytically-derived exception to the .03 ceiling so far has been for speeded clerical tests in clerical work. They are among the least g-loaded mental tests, which gives them greater opportunity to add to criterion validity beyond what g contributes, but even here the addition is small (e.g., from .64 to .68 in Hunter, 1985, p. 15). The typical finding is that an aptitude composite that is tailored for one family of jobs (say, mechanical) predicts performance about equally well in all others (say, clerical or general technical; e.g., Hunter, 1985, 1986, p. 357).

In fact, the g factor always carries the freight of prediction in any full battery of mental tests. Thorndike's (1986) systematic analysis of the issue is particularly illuminating. Criterion validities for entire aptitude batteries, such as the U.S. Employment Service's General Aptitude Test Battery (GATB), are often higher than those for the g factor alone, although g always accounts for the lion's share of a battery's validity. Thorndike's special contribution was to calculate how superior (or inferior) a battery is to g alone after cross-validating the battery's prediction equations in new samples (in order to eliminate the capitalization on chance that occurs in deriving a prediction equation, which capitalization increases with the number of tests in a battery). The apparent superiority of batteries whose prediction equations are tailored to specific school subjects, sexes, or jobs is much reduced or disappears with cross-validation. In two large samples, g yielded 85% to 95% of the criterion validity of the cross-validated aptitude batteries for predicting grades in high school and military training. In small samples of incumbents from various jobs, a single g factor predicted job performance *better* than did the cross-validated GATB prediction equations developed for each job.

The point is not that *g* is the only mental ability that matters. It is not. Rather, the point is that no other well-studied mental ability has average effect sizes that are more than a tiny fraction of *g*'s (net of their large *g* component), and none has such general effects across the world of work. Narrower aptitudes, such as verbal, spatial, and quantitative ability, may make special contributions to core job performance in some jobs, net of *g*, but—as with clerical speed—they would contribute only in limited domains of activity. As argued earlier, generality is gauged by the variety of tasks in which an aptitude enhances performance. Special aptitudes have quite circumscribed generality, net of their *g* component.

A largely *non*-mental ability—general psychomotor ability (which includes eye–hand coordination and manual dexterity)—is the only ability that meta-analyses have shown to be general and also have effect sizes that sometimes exceed those of *g* (Hunter & Hunter, 1984). As with *g*, its effect sizes vary systematically with job complexity—but in the *opposite* direction: Criterion validities of psychomotor ability *fall* from .48 to .21 as those for *g* rise from .23 to .58 across Hunter's five levels of increasing job complexity (Hunter & Hunter, 1984, p. 83). In other words, the general psychomotor factor tends to provide the biggest competitive advantages in the lowest level, least attractive jobs.

Discoveries 10–12: Generality of *g* is High Relative to Interest ("Will Do") Factors

Personnel researchers have devoted keen attention lately to personality traits and vocational interests because they are correlated little or not at all with either *g* or race and therefore hold out the greatest hope of improving the prediction of performance while simultaneously reducing disparate impact. Meta-analyses for vocational interests reveal very low validities for predicting supervisor ratings—.10 (Schmidt & Hunter, 1998, Table 1). Army Project A's vocational interest composite predicted core performance much better (.35), but the authors note that their interest composite behaved more like a test of cognitive ability than like one of temperament and personality (McHenry et al., 1990, Table 4 & pp. 351–352).

Of the "big five" personality factors (extraversion, agreeableness, conscientiousness, neuroticism, and openness to experience), only conscientiousness and its variants seem to have general validity across the world of work. However, that validity is substantial: .31 for tests of conscientiousness and .41 for tests of integrity. Meta-analyses show that these tests add, respectively, .09 and .14 to the prediction of supervisor ratings, beyond *g*, to yield multiple Rs of .60 and .65 (Schmidt & Hunter, 1998, Table 1). Conscientiousness and integrity capture both the willingness to expend the effort to learn and work harder (which enhances core knowledge and performance) and the citizenship behaviors that impress supervisors, regardless of a worker's core performance.

Other personality traits have been found useful in predicting performance in particular jobs or job families, but they appear not to have general utility (Hogan, 1991, p. 898). Their value is more local, that is, more specific to the job family in question, such as sales or management. In short, conscientiousness–integrity has broad importance, but no noncognitive trait rivals *g* in *both* generality and effect size.

Although restricted primarily to midlevel jobs, the military research provides a more systematic confrontation between cognitive and noncognitive predictors of performance. (Putatively *non*-cognitive factors such as Army Project A's are actually only *less* cognitive—less *g* loaded—than are mental tests. The *g* loadings of so-called noncognitive tests are seldom ascertained, however.) The research is more systematic because it includes a wide array of both criteria and predictors, something which civilian research seldom if ever does. As described earlier, Army Project A developed three sets of noncognitive predictor composites: temperament/personality (T), vocational interests (I), and job reward preferences (R). All are measured by paper-and-pencil, multiple-choice inventories. The TIR composites represent dispositions or motivations to perform different tasks. They thus reflect primarily the willingness ("will do") rather than the ability ("can do") to perform a job or task well. As shown in Table 13.4, the TIR composites were much weaker than *g* in predicting core performance, whether job specific or general (compare column 4 to 1). They added virtually nothing, whether singly or in combination, to the explanation of core performance beyond that afforded by general cognitive ability (column 7 vs. 1). On the other hand, together they greatly outperformed *g* in predicting discipline (.35 vs. .16, column 4 vs. 1) and fitness/bearing (.38 vs. .20), indicating that performing well along these lines may be primarily a matter of motivation rather than ability. General mental ability added very little (.02–.03) to their prediction (column 7 vs. 4). In contrast, performance on the effort/leadership criterion was about equally responsive to both will do and can do factors, although slightly more to the former (.38) than to the latter (.31, column 4 vs. 1). This is the only criterion out of the five on which *both* the *can do* and *will do* traits were necessary for distinguishing better from worse performers.

Note that the criterion validities for the TIR composites, which range from .35 to .44 for the five performance criteria (column 4 of Table 13.4), are comparable to those mentioned earlier for conscientiousness (.31) and integrity (.41). In fact, much of the predictive value of the TIR composites lay in their measurement of dependability (McHenry et al., 1990, pp. 344 and 349). The Army and civilian results thus seem quite consistent regarding the relative utility of *g* versus noncognitive traits.

In summary, the noncognitive traits add little to the prediction of core technical performance but may be superior predictors of noncore discretionary behaviors. It would seem, then, that *g*'s effects tend to be high at the core of job performance but fade toward the periphery, whereas the opposite is true for noncognitive traits.

Discoveries 13–15: Generality of *g* is High Relative to Job Knowledge

As discussed earlier, *g* is a good predictor of job knowledge; correlations are generally around .5 to .8 (Hunter, 1986, p. 352; Schmidt & Hunter, 1998, p. 265). Job knowledge, in turn, is the chief precursor of hands-on performance, with correlations somewhat higher. As noted, *g* influences performance primarily indirectly via job knowledge, although its (smaller) direct effects seem to increase when jobs are more complex and less routinized, training is less complete, and incumbents retain more discretion.

Job knowledge is sometimes viewed as a performance criterion, one which is intermediate between *g* and hands-on performance or supervisor ratings. However, it can also be viewed as a competitor to *g* in predicting these criteria. It should come as no surprise that it can outpredict *g* among experienced workers, because job-specific knowledge—*expertise*—is a function of both ability and experience (e.g., Hunter, 1986, p. 352). The correlations of job knowledge and *g* with hands-on performance are, respectively, .80 versus .75 (10 civilian jobs) and .70 versus .53 (4 Army jobs); and with supervisor ratings they are .56 versus .47 (civilian) and .37 versus .24 (Army).

However, job knowledge is not general, because it is always specific to a job or occupation. Although we can use one test of *g* to predict performance in all jobs, there must be as many job knowledge tests as there are jobs or job families, because all jobs are by definition comprised of different core duties with different content to be learned. A knowledge test that does not cover required core knowledge is not "content valid." Knowledge tests are thus a general *strategy* for assessing job competence, but their *content* must always be specific to a job or job family. Moreover, they are suitable only for persons who are already trained or experienced. By necessity, they are highly local—unlike *g*, which crosses all boundaries of content. To the extent that job knowledge is general at all, it is because it measures *g*, the facility with which people have learned that knowledge.

The *g*-based theory of job performance would predict a moderately strong correlation between job knowledge and hands-on performance in mid- to high-level jobs, because complexity of information processing is the most distinctive feature of those jobs and because *g* is the ability to process information. *g* is useful not only in learning jobs, but also in solving the new problems they continually present, especially when the jobs are highly complex. Recall, however, that the massive military studies were prompted by the opposite expectation—that simply *knowing*, especially when assessed by paper-and-pencil methods (*academic* knowledge), might not be much related to actually *doing* (*practical* action). The research has now shown a strong connection between the knowing and doing: *g* and *g*-based knowledge are highly practical. *g* theory was correct.

Discoveries 16–18: Generality of *g* is High Relative to Experience ("Have Done") Factors

Experience functions somewhat like *g* in enhancing job performance: It leads to more learning and thus more job knowledge, which in turn increases both hands-on performance and supervisor ratings. However, it is a weak competitor to *g*, even when its effect sizes are comparable. Like job knowledge, it is content valid only when it is job specific. It is not general. There are two other major differences between experience and *g*.

First, higher *g* always leads to better average performance, as was noted earlier, but lengthier experience does not. Specifically, further analyses of the four midlevel Army jobs found that average absolute levels of performance stop rising by the time incumbents have been on a job about 5 years, meaning that differences in experience lose much of their predictive validity after 5 years, at least for midlevel military jobs. In contrast, *g*'s validity remains strong (Schmidt et al., 1986, p. 436; see also McDaniel, Schmidt, & Hunter, 1988). In a meta-analysis of civilian jobs, *g*'s correlation with supervisory ratings rose, as noted earlier, from .35 for workers with 0 to 3 years of experience to .59 for workers with more than 12 years of experience, but the validities for experience *dropped* from .49 to .15 (Hunter & Schmidt, 1996, Table 5). Only in the least experienced group (0–3 years) did experience outpredict *g*; this is the average level of experience at which *relative* disparities in experience are typically at their maximum.

The second difference between experience and *g* is that the criterion validities for experience are higher in *less* complex jobs (as is the case for psychomotor ability too), which is opposite the pattern for *g*: they average .39 in low complexity jobs and .28 in high complexity jobs (McDaniel et al., 1988, Table 2). The reason for this inversion is probably that workers in low-level jobs receive little formal training and therefore must learn their jobs mostly through experience once on the job (McDaniel et al., 1988, p. 330).

Job-specific experience may be essential to good performance in most jobs, but differences in experience are generally useful in distinguishing better from worse workers only in the first few months or years on the job. In contrast, differences in *g always* matter. Their impact can, however, be concealed by differences in experience, especially in groups including people with almost no job-specific experience.

SUMMARY FOR JOB PERFORMANCE

Ample evidence has shown that *g* predicts core job performance widely and well, overall. The personality dimension of conscientiousness–integrity may possibly rival *g* in generality, but not in average effect size. Psychomotor ability may have both generality and occasionally big effect sizes, but it matters least where *g* matters most—in complex jobs. These are precisely the prestigious jobs for which individuals compete most avidly and whose good performance is most critical to the organization. Job knowledge and experience are important, but they are highly specific. They are general only to the extent that they tap *g* or the opportunity to use it in order to learn a job's essentials.

Effect sizes for *g* vary systematically according to the complexity of tasks, but not whether they seem academic (e.g., well defined, have only one right answer) or practical (e.g., require diagnosing and solving ill-defined problems). Indeed, the so-called academic attributes in Table 13.1 do not apply even to many school subjects, from history to science, which often involve ill-defined problems with more than one solution or means to it. What at least five of the seven supposedly academic attributes represent are actually strategies for creating *test items* that will be reliable (e.g., items have a single correct answer) and unbiased (e.g., tasks are disembedded from personal experience and require no outside knowledge), and thus more valid. Practical intelligence theorists have confused *how* tests measure traits well with *what* traits they measure.

There is no body of evidence even remotely comparable to that for *g* that there exists any other highly general "intelligence," if by intelligence we mean a primarily mental ability. Gardner, for instance, has not yet even measured his eight "multiple intelligences" (Gardner, 1997), let alone shown them independent of *g* or able to predict anything. Research on *practical intelligence*, as described by Sternberg and his colleagues (Sternberg et al., 2000), has been limited to looking at the concurrent validity of "tacit knowledge" in school and work settings. Their five studies (8 samples) relating tacit knowledge to job performance in the civilian sector (they also have one study on three samples of Army officers) have focused on only four narrow and mostly high-*g* occupations (academic psychologists, business managers, bank managers, and life insurance salespeople) and relied on small samples (average $N = 55$) and mostly careerist rather than core technical performance criteria (e.g., reputation, salary; see Gottfredson, in press-a, for a detailed critique). In any case, that research program has provided far too few correlations for a meta-analysis of job performance and therefore cannot support its claim that practical intelligence "is at least as good a predictor of future success as is the academic form of intelligence [g]" (Sternberg et al., 2000, pp. xi–xii; also Sternberg, 2000).

Moreover, that program has provided no data at all for performance in everyday activities outside school and work. In contrast, as we see next, large bodies of evidence show that high g provides tremendous advantages throughout the breadth and length of life, and that low g constitutes a very practical, very pervasive disadvantage.

g and Life Performance

No other personal trait has been shown to correlate with so many valued outcomes as has g. The outcomes include altruism, breadth of interests, educational attainment, emotional sensitivity, leadership, moral reasoning, motor skills, musical abilities, occupational success, social skills, and much more (Brand, 1987). g also correlates, negatively, with a wide range of problem behaviors, including accident-proneness, delinquency, dogmatism, racial prejudice, smoking, and truancy. The correlations range from strong to weak, but seem pervasive. (Recall that correlations in this section will be *uncorrected* unless otherwise noted.) Although g's generality would thus seem to be quite broad, there is yet little systematic mapping of g's gradients of effect across social life. The job performance model provides a start, because the individual duties in a job are analogous to individual tasks in life. In addition, jobs themselves (limited but somewhat fluid subsets of duties) are analogous to people's lives (the reasonably circumscribed ebb and flow of activities and challenges over a person's lifetime).

RISKS IN MANAGING INDIVIDUAL LIFE TASKS

Many work activities are life tasks as well: managing people and money, selecting products and paying bills, preventing and responding to accidents, driving, teaching, and the like. Many of these activities require the complex information processing skills in Table 13.3, including advising, reasoning, planning, analyzing information, negotiating, persuading, coordinating, and instructing—not to mention "dealing with unexpected situations" and "applying common sense to solve problems." Because higher levels of *g* enhance performance of jobs in which these are key duties, they can be expected to enhance performance of analogous tasks in daily life. There is indeed evidence, for instance, that higher *g* is advantageous in driving. A longitudinal study of Australian servicemen, none of them in the retarded range, found that IQ correlated with rate of death by automobile accident, even after controlling for other characteristics (O'Toole, 1990). The auto fatality rate for men of IQ 85 to 100 (92.2 per 100,000) was double that for men of IQ 110 to 115 (51.5 per 100,000). The rate for men of IQ 80 to 85 was three times as high (146.7 per 100,000).

The discoveries about *g*'s impact on job performance (Table 13.2) provide a roadmap for collecting, classifying, and interpreting data on *g*'s gradients of effect in everyday affairs. They suggest, most importantly, that *g* will be useful wherever information processing is required, and that its impact will be highest when tasks are complex or novel and lower when they are simple, routine, repetitive, much practiced, and supervised. For instance, they predict that higher levels of *g* will be a bigger advantage (controlling for experience) when driving an unfamiliar route during rush hour or bad weather than when driving a familiar route when traffic is light and the weather good. The research thereby also suggests that knowing more about the distribution of task demands and opportunities across daily life can speed our understanding of *g*'s generality in practical affairs.

A Matrix of Life Tasks

The two important dimensions of tasks discussed earlier, and shown here in Fig. 13.2, are their complexity and whether they entail mostly technical matters rather than citizenship. The latter distinction seems to correspond roughly to the difference between *instrumental* and *socioemotional* tasks. The job performance validity data suggested that *g*'s impact is highest for complex technical tasks and that it drops gradually as tasks become simpler or more socioemotional, in which case they depend increasingly on "will do" (personality) factors such as conscientiousness. It is not clear, however, that the advantages of greater mental competence ever fall to zero either on the job or in the myriad details of managing one's way in life.

Research on individuals' adaptation and adjustment illustrate how this matrix can illuminate *g*'s effects in daily life as well as paid employment. As described next, *adaptation* probably falls more toward the instrumental side of the matrix than does *adjustment*, and its correlation with *g* is correspondingly higher. The latter, personal adjustment, is measured in many ways, but refers to "a complex of behaviors involving such features as emotional stability, freedom from neurotic symptoms, responsibility, getting along with people, social participation, realistic self-confidence, absence

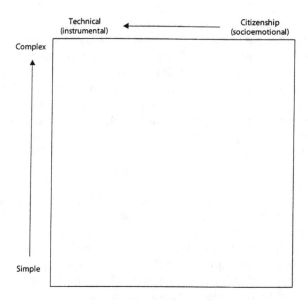

FIG. 13.2.   The matrix of life tasks.

of socially disruptive and self-defeating behavior, . . . [and much more, including] displaying a capacity for self-discipline and planful and sustained goal-directed effort" (Jensen, 1980, pp. 357–358). This seems similar to the "citizenship" dimension of job performance, which is very much dependent on "will do" (personality) traits. However, adjustment still correlates .4 to .6 with IQ, even when IQ is measured in childhood and adjustment in adulthood (Jensen, 1980, p. 357).

Adaptive behavior is similar to adjustment, but emphasizes instrumental competence more heavily relative to emotional adjustment than does the concept of adjustment. Typical measures focus, for instance, on "everyday skills such as handling money, personal care and hygiene, telling time, domestic skills, ability to go shopping alone, and the like" (Jensen, 1980, p. 358). Most adaptive behavior measures have been developed in the context of diagnosing mental retardation, but they correlate .6 to .7 with IQ in normal children. In short, socioemotional outcomes may depend less on g than do more strictly instrumental ones, but both seem to be enhanced by higher g. There is also a sizeable literature on competence in late adulthood (Diehl, 1998), when mental powers fade, which also seems to reflect this instrumental–socioemotional gradient in effect sizes for g. Studies show that "everyday problem-solving" late in life correlates from .3 (Cornelius & Caspi, 1987) to .8 with fluid g (Willis & Schaie, 1986), with the latter studies using measures that seem to more closely represent the instrumental side of the life-task matrix.

Other socioemotional tasks and behaviors may be simpler (not require much information processing) than those captured in research on adjustment, and therefore depend little on *g* but a lot on personality traits such as sociability and dependability. These would be located to the lower right of the matrix. So, although the interpersonal task of persuading people may be moderately to highly *g* loaded (see Table 13.3), being a pleasant and dependable coworker or companion may not. And just as the latter can increase one's ratings as a worker, being a "good citizen" can gain one regard and resources elsewhere in life regardless of one's mental competence. Indeed, they may be especially important for retarded individuals, whose successful adjustment often depends on good will and regular help from others (Edgerton, 1981; Koegel & Edgerton, 1984).

Performance of life tasks throughout this matrix would often depend, of course, on more than "can do" and "will do" factors." For instance, "have done" factors (previous training and experience) can also affect performance, the prior evidence suggesting that their relative advantages are greatest when tasks are simple and one's peers have little or no such experience. Help from family, friends, and organizations matter, too, as do other aspects of people's circumstances (Gottfredson, in press-b), but they are beyond the scope of this chapter.

Functional Literacy

The literature on functional literacy is especially illuminating because it has examined the relation of everyday competence to various task characteristics, finding the academic–practical distinction irrelevant but complexity crucial. The study of literacy in recent decades has been driven by a growing concern that a high proportion of Americans is unable to meet many of the daily demands of modern life that most of us take for granted. *Functional literacy* refers, most broadly, to using the written word effectively (literacy) for everyday (functional) purposes. Literacy research focuses on practical tasks, and ignores merely *academic* reading, which does not affect understanding of or effective adaptation to one's options and circumstances in life. By focusing on reading, which is a solitary technical activity, functional literacy research targets tasks primarily to the left (technical) side of the matrix in Fig. 13.2.

There are three independent research literatures on functional literacy, referred to as work literacy (Sticht, 1975), adult literacy (Kirsch, Jungeblut, Jenkins, & Kolstad, 1993), and health literacy (National Work Group on Literacy and Health, 1998). They involve reading and understanding prose, documents, forms, and other written materials, respectively, at work, in everyday activities, and in the health system. All three fields of research began with the same belief in situational specificity, in particular, that there are as many types of literacy as there are major types of written material. All three have therefore taken pains to develop scales whose items simulate tasks in the relevant settings: for example, their tests have workers read the tables of contents of their technical manuals, citizens read bus schedules and menus, and patients read the labels on vials of prescription medicine. Like personnel psychologists, then, literacy researchers started out skeptical of, even hostile to, anything like *g* theory. Also like personnel researchers, their findings have nonetheless turned out to support *g* theory. They do so by revealing that literacy is the ability to process information (*g*) and that it has enormous practical importance.

Although largely independent in personnel, aims, and methods, all three literatures tell the same story. All initially sought to measure multiple dimensions of literacy, but their evidence reveals that literacy is unidimensional. For instance, the three scales (Prose, Document, and Quantitative) comprising the U.S. Department of Education's National Adult Literacy Survey (NALS) correlate over .9 *before* correction for unreliability despite the developers' effort to create three independent scales. As a result, "major [NALS] survey results are nearly identical for each of the three scales . . . with findings appearing to be reported essentially in triplicate, as it were" (Reder, 1998, pp. 39, 44).

Work literacy and health literacy researchers have both investigated whether delivering information orally rather than in written form might enhance comprehension, but they have found that "poor readers" comprehend information no better when they listen to it instead. Army research on the matter was quite extensive (Sticht, 1975, chap. 7). The NALS adult literacy researchers also did a detailed task analysis showing that the difficulty of NALS items does not depend on their readability per se (Kirsch, Jungeblut, & Mosenthal, 1994). As has been shown many times (e.g., Jensen, 1980, pp. 325–326), "reading ability" for native speakers is far more than decoding skill. Rather, it is comprehension. Speech and written symbols are just different vehicles for transmitting information.

All three literatures also eventually identified complexity as the crucial distinction among literacy tasks. The NALS researchers did an excellent analysis in which they detailed the task characteristics that account for the relative difficulty of NALS items. Described as "process complexity," the attributes include the abstractness of information, its embeddedness in lengthy or irrelevant information, and the difficulty of the inferences it requires (Kirsch & Mosenthal, 1990). These results are summarized in Table 13.5, which illustrates both the items and their information-processing demands at each of the five NALS literacy levels.

Work and health literacy researchers have not performed any formal task analyses of their scales, but they have focused on making everyday materials more readable for poor readers by reducing their complexity

TABLE 13.5
Sample Items and Information-Processing
Demands at Five Levels of NALS Literacy

Proficiency Level	Sample Items[a]	Information-Processing Demands[b]
0 > >	69 Sign your name (D)	
	191 Total a bank deposit entry (Q)	Level 1 (NALS ≤225) tasks require identifying or matching single pieces of information or performing a single, simple, specified arithmetic operation (like addition) in contexts where there is little or no distracting information. (Includes about 14% of white and 38% of black adults aged 16 and over.[c])
	224 Underline sentence explaining action stated in short article (P)	
225	232 Locate intersection on a street map (D)	
	250 Locate two features of information in sports article (P)	Level 2 (NALS 226–275) tasks introduce distractors, more varied information, and the need for low-level inferences or to integrate two or more pieces of information. Information tends to be easily identifiable, despite the presence of distractors, and numeric operations are easily determined from the format of the material provided (say, an order form). (Includes about 25% of white and 37% of black adults.)
	270 Calculate total costs of purchase from an order form (Q)	
275	280 Write a brief letter explaining error made on a credit card bill (P)	
	308 Using calculator, determine the discount from an oil bill if paid within 10 days (Q)	Level 3 (NALS 276–325) tasks require integrating multiple pieces of information from one or more documents, which themselves may be complex and contain much irrelevant information. However, the matches to be made between information and text tend to be literal or synonymous, and correct information is not located near incorrect information. (Includes about 36% of white and 21% of black adults.)

(Continued)

TABLE 13.5
(Continued)

Proficiency Level	Sample items[a]	Information-Processing Demands[b]
325	323 Enter information given into an automobile mainte-nance record form (D) 328 State in writing an argument made in lengthy newspa-per article (P) 348 Use bus schedule to deter-mine appropriate bus for given set of conditions (D) 368 Using eligibility pamphlet, calculate the yearly amount a couple would receive for basic supplemental security income (Q)	*Level 4* (NALS 326–375) tasks require more inferences, multiple-features matches, in-tegration and synthesis of information from complex passages or documents, and use of multiple sequential operations. (Includes about 21% of white and 4% of black adults.)
375	387 Using table comparing credit cards, identify the two cat-egories used and write two differences between them (D) 410 Summarize from text two ways lawyers may challenge prospective jurors (P) 421 Using calculator, determine the actual cost of carpet to cover a room (Q)	*Level 5* (NALS 376–500) tasks require the application of specialized background knowledge, disembedding the features of a problem from text, and drawing high-level inferences from highly complex text with multiple distractors. (Includes about 4% of white and less than 0.5% of black adults.)
> > 500		

[a]*Source:* Brown, Prisuta, Jacobs, & Campbell (1996, p. 10). P = prose scale, D = documents scale, Q = quantitative scale.

[b]*Source:* Brown et al. (1996, p. 11).

[c]*Source:* Kirsch, Jungleblut, Jenkins, & Kolstad (1993, Table 1.1A). Percentages are for Prose Scale.

(Doak, Doak, & Root, 1996; Sticht, 1975, chap. 7). Their methods, separated by decades and specific purpose, are strikingly similar and include limiting information to the bare essentials and then providing it in a concise, standardized manner that breaks down all complex material into small, carefully sequenced, concretely illustrated chunks that tell people exactly what to do. Health literacy specialists suggest that materials be written at the fifth-grade level, although they concede that this is beyond the capabilities of a substantial proportion of urban and elderly patients, even when they average 10 years of schooling.

Discovering that neither task content nor modality affect literacy demands but that complexity is key, analysts turned to the language of learning, problem solving, and critical thinking (although without actually mentioning *intelligence* or *g*) to describe the meaning of literacy. NALS analysts describe adult literacy in terms such as "problem solving," "complex information processing," and "verbal comprehension and reasoning, or the ability to understand, analyze, interpret, and evaluate written information and apply fundamental principles and concepts" (Baldwin, Kirsch, Rock, & Yamamoto, 1995, p. xv; Venezky, Kaestle, & Sum, 1987, pp. 25, 28). Health literacy researchers now suggest that health literacy is the "ability to acquire new information and complete complex cognitive tasks," and that low literacy reflects "limited problem-solving abilities" (Baker, Parker, Williams, & Clark, 1998, pp. 795–797).

The three fields have shown that their seemingly different literacies all mimic *g*. Two of the fields have specifically correlated literacy with tests known to be highly *g*-loaded. Work literacy, as intensively studied several decades ago by the Army, is measured well by the AFQT, its (uncorrected) correlations with job-specific work literacy being .6 to .8 (Sticht, 1975, pp. 46–48, 75). Although the data are less extensive for measures of health literacy, the various health literacy scales also correlate .7 to .9 with each other and with tests of known high *g* loading (Davis, Michielutte, Askov, Williams, & Weiss, 1998), such as the Wide Range Achievement Test (WRAT). "Literacy" appears to be a surrogate measure of *g*.

Impact of Adult Literacy. The adult literacy scales reveal the stark meaning of low *g* in many daily activities, because the scales are criterion-referenced. Table 13.5 samples the tasks that people at each of the five NALS literacy levels are able to perform on a routine basis (with 80% proficiency). The longer list from which they are drawn (Brown, Prisuta, Jacobs, & Campbell, 1996, p. 10) shows that they represent skills needed to carry out routine transactions with banks, social welfare agencies, restaurants, the post office, and credit card agencies; to understand contrasting views on public issues (such as parental involvement in schools); and to comprehend the public events of the day (such as stories about sports and fuel efficiency) and one's personal options (welfare benefits, discount for early payment of bills, and so on). As shown in the table, almost 40% of White adults and 75% of Black adults are able to function routinely at no higher than Level 2, which limits them to making only low-level inferences and integrating only a few pieces of clearly identifiable information—a clear disadvantage in the Information Age. In fact, NALS researchers note that individuals at Levels 1 or 2 "are not likely to be able to perform the range of complex literacy tasks that the National Education Goals Panel considers important for competing successfully in a global economy and exercising fully the rights and responsibilities of citizenship" (Baldwin et al., 1995, p. 16).

The socioeconomic correlates of NALS literacy level suggest that low literacy does, in fact, greatly affect individuals' overall life chances. Table 13.6 shows that the likelihood of White adults working only part-time, not even looking for work, using food stamps, and living in poverty rises steadily as literacy falls. For instance, less than 4% of adults with Level 5 literacy live in poverty, but more than 10 times that proportion with Level 1 literacy do. The odds ratios in the table show that the *relative risks* posed by low literacy are greater for some outcomes (living in poverty as an adult) than others (working part-time), but they are substantial for all (see Gottfredson, in press-b, for further explanation and analysis of these odds ratios). Epidemiologists consider any factor that doubles risk relative to a comparison group to be a "moderately strong" risk factor and one that quadruples risk to be a "strong" risk factor (Gerstman, 1998, pp. 127–

TABLE 13.6
Economic Outcomes at Different Levels of NALS Literacy:
Whites Aged 16 and Over (% and Odds Ratios)

Outcome		Prose Literacy Level				
		1 (≤ 225)	*2* (226–275)	*3* (276–325)	*4* (326–375)	*5* (376–500)
Employed only	%	70	57	46	36	28
part-time	OR	2.7	1.6	1.0	0.7	0.5
Out of labor force	%	52	35	25	17	11
	OR	3.2	1.6	1.0	0.6	0.4
Uses food stamps	%	17	13	6	3	1
	OR	3.2	2.3	1.0	0.5	0.2
Lives in poverty	%	43	23	12	8	4
	OR	5.5	2.2	1.0	0.6	0.3
Employed *not* as pro-	%	95	88	77	54	30
fessional or manager	OR	5.6	2.2	1.0	0.4	0.1

Source of percentages: Kirsch, Jungleblut, Jenkins, & Kolstad (1993, Figures 2.5, 2.6, 2.7, 2.9, & 2.10).

128). The comparison group here is Level 3, which probably averages around IQ 105.

Everyday Effects of Health Literacy. A recent overview of health literacy in *Patient Care* (Davis, Meldrum, Tippy, Weiss, & Williams, 1996, p. 94) concluded that "[m]edication errors and adverse drug reactions may be due in no small measure to the patient's inability to read and follow written and oral instructions. Poor compliance with medical recommendations, long the bane of well-intentioned physicians, may not be so much a matter of willful disobedience as one of failure to understand the clinician's instructions and expectations." Such risks owing to low *g* are illustrated in Table 13.7, which samples items on the major test of health literacy, the Test of Functional Health Literacy in Adults (TOFHLA; Williams et al., 1995). In this case, the "adequate" literacy group is of roughly average IQ, so it is the comparison group for gauging the relative risks of low

TABLE 13.7

Percentage and Relative Risk (Odds Ratios) of Patients Incorrectly Answering Test Items on the TOFHLA, by Level of Health Literacy

Test Item		Literacy Level		
		Inadequate	Marginal	Adequate
Numeracy items				
How to take medication on an empty stomach	%	65.3	52.1	23.9
	OR	6.0	3.2	1.0
How to take medication four times a day	%	23.6	9.4	4.5
	OR	6.6	2.2	1.0
How many times a prescription can be refilled	%	42.0	24.7	9.6
	OR	6.8	3.1	1.0
How to determine financial eligibility	%	74.3	49.0	31.5
	OR	9.0	3.0	1.0
When next appointment is scheduled	%	39.6	12.7	4.7
	OR	13.5	3.0	1.0
How many pills of a prescription should be taken	%	69.9	33.7	13.0
	OR	15.6	3.4	1.0
Prose Cloze passages				
Instructions for preparing for upper gastrointestinal tract radiographic procedure	%	57.2	11.9	3.6
	OR	36.2	3.7	1.0
Rights and Responsibilities section of Medicaid application	%	81.1	31.0	7.3
	OR	54.3	5.7	1.0
Standard informed consent document	%	95.1	72.1	21.8
	OR	70.5	9.4	1.0

From Williams, Parker, Baker, Parikh, Pitkin, Coates, & Nurss (1995, Table 3), *Journal of the American Medical Association, 274*, pp. 1677–1682. Copyrighted 1995, American Medical Association.

g. The data are for the walk-in and emergency care center patients of two large urban hospitals. Of the 2,659 patients, 26% did not understand information about when a next appointment is scheduled, 42% did not understand directions for taking medicine on an empty stomach, and 60% could not understand a standard informed consent document (data not shown in table). Table 13.7 shows how patients with "inadequate" health literacy were from 2 to 15 times more likely to fail the items than were individuals with "adequate" literacy. Even the flattest risk gradients in Table 13.7 reveal that low health literacy is more than a "very strong" risk factor (odds ratios of 6.0–6.8) for being unable to follow even the simplest medical instructions.

Table 13.8 provides even more disturbing data on the risks posed by low *g*, because it illustrates that low-ability patients being treated for seri-

TABLE 13.8
Percentage and Relative Risk (Odds Ratios) of Patients
Incorrectly Answering Selected Questions about their
Chronic Disease, by Level of Health Literacy

		Literacy Level		
Patient does not know that		*Inadequate*	*Marginal*	*Adequate*
Diabetes				
If you feel thirsty, tired, and weak, it usually	%	40.0	30.8	25.5
means your blood glucose level is high	OR	2.0	1.3	1.0
When you exercise, your blood glucose level	%	60.0	53.8	35.3
goes down	OR	2.7	2.1	1.0
If you suddenly get sweaty, nervous, and	%	62.0	46.1	27.4
shaky, you should eat some form of sugar	OR	4.3	2.3	1.0
Normal blood glucose level is between	%	42.0	23.1	11.8
3.8–7.7 mmol/L (70–140 mg/dL)	OR	5.4	2.2	1.0
If you feel shaky, sweaty, and hungry, it usu-	%	50.0	15.4	5.9
ally means your blood glucose level is low	OR	15.9	2.9	1.0
Hypertension				
Canned vegetables are high in salt	%	36.7	24.0	19.2
	OR	2.4	1.1	1.0
Exercise lowers blood pressure	%	59.7	56.0	32.0
	OR	3.1	2.7	1.0
Blood pressure of 130/80 mm Hg is normal	%	58.2	32.0	28.8
	OR	3.4	1.2	1.0
Losing weight lowers blood pressure	%	33.2	16.0	8.3
	OR	5.5	2.1	1.0
Blood pressure of 160/100 mm Hg is high	%	44.9	30.0	8.3
	OR	9.0	4.7	1.0

From Williams, Baker, Parker, & Nurss (1998, Tables 2 and 3), *Archives of Internal Medicine, 158,* pp. 166–172. Copyrighted 1995, American Medical Association.

ous chronic illnesses, such as diabetes and hypertension, often do not understand the most basic facts about their disease and how to manage it. Being in long-term treatment, these patients presumably have been instructed in how to care for themselves and are motivated to do so. That the odds ratios for many of these questions are more favorable than those for the easier TOFHLA items (fall below 6.0 for patients with "inadequate" literacy) probably results from "have done" factors, including training and practice, and possibly higher than normal motivation ("will do" factors). They are nonetheless still high. It is shocking, for instance, that about half of the diabetic patients with inadequate literacy do not know how to recognize the daily symptoms of their disease that require quick management (shakiness, thirst, and the like).

Research relating literacy to broad health outcomes suggests that the sorts of risks identified earlier do indeed cumulate in some manner to damage health. For example, low-level readers (reading grade level 0–3) who were enrolled in basic education classes had sickness profiles similar to people with serious chronic illnesses (Weiss, Hart, McGee, & D'Estelle, 1992). In a study of Medicaid patients, the worst readers (Grades 0–2) had annual health care costs of $12,974 compared to the average of $2,969 for the whole sample (Weiss, Blanchard, McGee et al., 1994). A third study that prospectively followed 958 urban hospital patients for 2 years found that patients with *inadequate* TOFHLA literacy were twice as likely (31.5%) to be admitted to the hospital during the next 2 years as were patients with *adequate* literacy (14.9%; Baker et al., 1998). Controlling for all demographic factors yielded a risk ratio for hospitalization of 1.7, which is a moderately strong effect.

Health literacy researchers worry that the disadvantages of low literacy are rising because the explosive growth in new treatments and technologies has created "tremendous learning demands." "For example, a patient who was lucky enough to survive an acute myocardial infarction in the 1960s was typically discharged with only a pat on the back and wishes for good luck. In the 1990s, such a patient is likely to be discharged on a regimen of aspirin, a beta-blocker, an angiotensin-converting enzyme inhibitor, and possibly a low-salt and low-cholesterol diet and medications to control hypertension, diabetes, and hypercholesterolemia. A patient's ability to learn this regimen and follow it correctly will determine a trajectory toward recovery or a downward path to recurrent myocardial infarction, disability, and death" (Baker et al., 1998, p. 791).

CUMULATIVE RISKS OVER THE LIFE COURSE

The literacy research suggests how differences in performance on discrete everyday tasks in self-management can cumulate to produce serious long-term disadvantages for living a long and good life. Just as the typical IQ item is not by itself a good measure of *g* (the typical item correlates only weakly with IQ), no one daily episode of competence may reflect mostly *g* at work. However, as long as items *consistently* tap *g* but not any other one thing, as apparently do the NALS items, their bits of *g* loading pile up while their "specificities" cancel each other out. With sufficient items, the result is a test that measures virtually nothing but *g*.

The issue here, then, is the consistency with which *g* runs through life's many daily activities, whether simple or complex and whether technical or socioemotional, and thereby consistently tilts the odds of success in favor of the more able. As is apparent from the example of IQ test items, *g* does-n't need to tilt the odds very much in any particular instant to have a dramatic impact as those instants accumulate. Even small effect sizes, when their effects add up, can produce big gains over the long run—as do the small odds favoring the house in gambling (Gordon, Lewis, & Quigley, 1988). A big cumulative impact for *g* does not rule out the possibility, of course, that other consistent attributes of people (conscientiousness) and their surrounds (family assistance) also cumulate in the same manner—as would be the case, for example, when both ability and effort influence the many individual grades that cumulate to produce a high school grade point average (GPA). As with job performance, one must always assume that other things matter too.

The following pages look at evidence on how *g* tilts the odds of success in different domains of life as well as how those odds can themselves multiply across domains. I focus on social outcomes that emerge from long, cumulative histories of behavior and specifically on the nexus of good outcomes (higher education, occupation, and income) and the nexus of bad outcomes (unemployment, crime, welfare use, and illegitimacy) that so concern policy researchers. Only the barest summary can be provided because each major outcome represents a huge literature in itself.

The Nexus of Good Outcomes

Correlations of IQ with socioeconomic outcomes vary in size depending on the outcome in question, but they are consistent and substantial: years of education (generally .5–.6), occupational status (.4–.5), and earnings, where the correlations *rise* with age (.2–.4; see especially the reanalysis of 10 large samples by Jencks et al., 1979, chap. 4). The predictions are the same whether IQ is measured in Grades 3 to 6, high school, or adulthood (Jencks et al., 1979, pp. 96–99). Moreover, they are underestimates, because they come from single tests of uncertain *g* loading (Jencks et al., 1979, p. 91). Various specific aptitude and achievement tests (both academic and nonacademic) also predict education, occupation, and earnings, but essentially only to the extent that they also measure *g* (Jencks et al., 1979, pp. 87–96; Gottfredson & Crouse, 1986). In short, *g* is what drives a test's predictions of socioeconomic success, and the predictions are substantial when *g* is reasonably well measured, even in childhood.

A large body of work in sociology and economics (e.g., Behrman, Hrubec, Taubman, & Wales, 1980; Jencks et al., 1972; Jencks et al., 1979; Sewell & Hauser, 1975; Taubman, 1977) has painted what might be called an augmented-chain-reaction portrait of *g*'s effects. IQ has a very large effect on years of education obtained; education in turn has a strong effect on occupational level attained; which in turn has a modest effect on income. That is the chain reaction. IQ's effects are carried through at each stage of the process, indirectly. This *indirect* effect of IQ, via education or occupation, diminishes down the line as other non-*g* forces come into play to determine level of occupation and earnings. The other forces include structural ones, such as employers relying on cheap but fallible signals of talent (educational credentials) to hire workers (Gottfredson, 1985) and using set salary schedules to pay them, regardless of their actual job performance.

However, IQ also has *direct* effects at each stage; that is, it helps to predict occupational status *net* of education and earnings *net* of occupation. Via these direct effects, *g* has a "modest influence" through age 25 in boosting young adults up the occupational ladder (Jencks et al., 1979, p. 220) and a "substantively important" one through at least middle age for upping their relative earnings (p. 119). Thus, *g* tilts the odds of success far down the chain of outcomes by tilting the odds of success at each stage along the way, but it also gives an independent boost at each stage of the process. For example, *g*'s independent boost toward higher earnings may be partly via the better job performance that higher *g* produces. *g* is like a persistent tailwind—or headwind, as the case may be.

Criterion-referenced data yield a portrait of life chances that differ dramatically for people of different IQ levels. They are summarized in the upper part of Fig. 13.3 for five segments of the IQ continuum: IQ 75 and below ("high risk" zone), IQ 76 to 90 ("up-hill battle"), IQ 91 to 110 ("keeping up"), IQ 111 to 125 ("out ahead"), and IQ above 125 ("yours to lose"). Occupational opportunities are virtually unlimited, when only *g* is considered, for people with IQs above 125 (95th percentile), but opportunities become quite restricted and unfavorable for persons of IQ 76 to 90 (5th to 25th percentile). No jobs routinely recruit individuals below IQ 80 (10th percentile), the military is forbidden to do so, and it currently accepts no one below about IQ 85.

A major reason for these differences in employment opportunities is that, as shown in the figure, trainability falls quickly at lower levels of *g*. As was reaffirmed by the literacy research, instruction must be drastically simplified for low-*g* people and stripped of anything abstract or "theoretical."

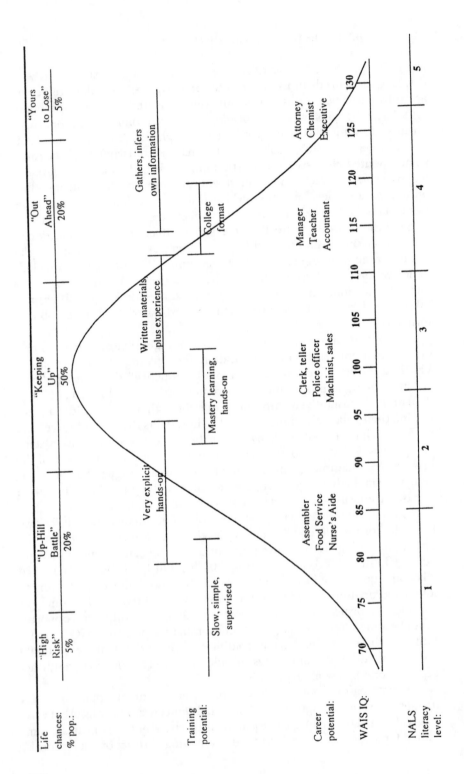

Ever incarcerated (%, white men)	7	7	3	1	0
Chronic welfare recipient (%, white mothers)	31	17	8	2	0
Had illegitimate child (%, white women)	32	17	8	4	2
High school dropout (%, whites)	55	35	6	0.4	0

FIG. 13.3. Life chances in different ranges of the IQ bell curve. *Note.* Adapted from Gottfredson (1997, Figure 3) by permission of Elsevier Publishing.

Whereas the learning of low-g individuals must be carefully guided and highly supervised, high-g individuals can essentially train themselves when given access to the requisite information.

The Nexus of Bad Outcomes

Just as high g is associated with a nexus of good socioeconomic outcomes, so too is low g associated with a nexus of social pathologies. Juvenile delinquency, for instance, correlates about −.25 with IQ (Gordon, 1986) and −.3 with poor school deportment (frequency of disciplinary actions; Roberts & Baird, 1972; see also Herrnstein & Murray, 1994, chap. 11; Moffitt, Gabrielli, Mednick, Schulsinger, 1981; Moffitt & Silva, 1988). Although those correlations might seem low, they are equal to or higher than that between social class background and delinquency (Gordon, 1997), which social commentators generally consider important. In any case, small correlations can represent big shifts in odds of success and failure across the IQ continuum.

This is shown in the lower part of Fig. 13.3, which gives the g-related risks of incarceration and several other social pathologies that are typically treated as dichotomous (either–or) outcomes. The rows show the percentage of young White adults in each broad IQ range who exhibit each of the bad outcomes. The data, which are from the National Longitudinal Survey of Youth (NLSY; Herrnstein & Murray, 1994), reveal that the prevalence of these serious problems typically doubles at *each* successively lower range of IQ. This serial doubling was also seen for poverty and use of food stamps in the NALS research (Table 13.6), which included a large sample of white adults from a much wider age range (Kirsch et al., 1993).

Table 13.9 provides data for yet other outcomes from the NLSY research, particularly for welfare use and attachment to the labor force. The figure and two tables tell the same story: lower levels of cognitive skill are associated with substantially higher rates of social pathology. Looking down the columns in all three arrays of data suggests how risks *compound* across outcomes. Compared to the average person, low-IQ people have many times the risk of not just one bad outcome, but many, and they are at correspondingly little risk of good outcomes, such as employment in managerial or professional work. Exactly the reverse is true for high-g persons. The lower one's g level is, the higher one's risk of tripping at least one of the landmines littering the fields of life.

Table 13.9 lists the outcomes in roughly ascending order according to how strongly g affects the *relative* risks of these outcomes for people of very low IQ. The odds ratios (ORs) range from less than 2.0 for men being out of the labor force (not looking for work) or unemployed, to around 5.0 to 6.0 for illegitimacy, poverty, and welfare use, to 19.0 for dropping out of

TABLE 13.9

Relative Risk of Bad Outcomes Associated With Lower IQ:
Prevalence (%) and Odds Ratios (OR) for Young White Adults

Outcome		IQ Level				
		≤ 75	76–90	91–110	111–125	> 125
Bell Curve data: General population[a]						
Out of labor force 1+	%	22	19	15	14	10
mo/yr (men)	OR	1.6	1.3	1.0	0.9	0.6
Unemployed 1+ mo/yr	%	12	10	7	7	2
(men)	OR	1.8	1.5	1.0	1.0	0.3
Ever incarcerated	%	[7][b]	7	3	1	0
(men)	OR	[2.4]	2.4	1.0	0.3	0.1[c]
Chronic welfare recipi-	%	31	17	8	2	0
ent (women)	OR	5.2	2.4	1.0	0.2	0.05[d]
Had illegitimate chil-	%	32	17	8	4	2
dren (women)	OR	5.4	2.4	1.0	0.5	0.2
Lives in poverty as an	%	30	16	6	3	2
adult	OR	6.7	3.0	1.0	0.5	0.3
Went on welfare after	%	55	21	12	4	1
1st child (women)	OR	9.0	2.0	1.0	0.3	0.1
High school dropout	%	55	35	6	0.4	0
	OR	19.0	8.4	1.0	0.1	0
Bell Curve data: Sibling pairs[e]						
Not working in profes-	%	100	99	98	92	77
sional job	OR	hi[f]	2.0	1.0	0.2	0.1
Not a college graduate	%	100	97	81	50	18
	OR	hi[f]	7.6	1.0	0.2	0.1

[a]Source of percentages: Herrnstein & Murray (1994, respectively, pp. 158, 163, 247, 194, 180, 132, 194, & 146).

[b]See text for explanation.

[c]Assuming that % rounded to zero from 0.4, which yields odds of .004 and an odds ratio of .13.

[d]Assuming that % rounded to zero from 0.4, which yields odds of .004 and an odds ratio of .046.

[e]Source of percentages: Murray (1997b).

[f]OR can not be calculated because the odds of 100:0 (its numerator) cannot be calculated.

high school. ORs for people of *above* average IQ are approximately the mirror image of those for people of below-average IQ. Just as a below-average IQ creates a disadvantage relative to the average person, an above-average IQ confers a relative advantage.

g is clearly at the center of the nexus of both good and bad outcomes, but social scientists generally resist attributing it causal power. Sibling studies provide strong evidence, however, that *g* has a big causal influence and social class a comparatively weak one in determining socioeconomic outcomes. Biological siblings differ two thirds as much in IQ, on the average, as do random strangers (12 vs. 17 IQ points). Despite siblings growing up in the very same households, their differences in IQ portend differences in life outcomes that are almost as large as those observed in the general population (Jencks et al., 1979, chap. 4; Murray, 1997a, 1997b; Olneck, 1977, pp. 137–138). Even in intact, nonpoor families, siblings of above average intelligence are much more likely to have a college degree, work in a professional job, and have high earnings than are their average-IQ siblings, who in turn do much better than their low-IQ siblings (Murray, 1997b). Table 13.9 provides the sibling data for holding a college degree and a high-level job. The story is the same for bad outcomes: lower-IQ siblings have much higher rates of bearing illegitimate children, living in poverty, and the like (Murray, 1997a).

TASK, PERSON, AND STRUCTURAL FACTORS THAT TILT *g*'S GRADIENTS OF RELATIVE RISK

The *g* factor relates, often strongly, to a wide range of important outcomes in life. However, *g*'s effect sizes vary across different dimensions of personal life just as they do across tasks in the workplace. The correlational data suggest, for instance, that some good outcomes, such as level of education and occupation, depend more on *g* level than others, such as income. The odds ratios likewise indicate that some bad outcomes, such as chronic welfare dependence, are more sensitive to differences in *g* than are others, such as unemployment. The relative risk of misunderstanding standard hospital documents is greater than the relative risk of misunderstanding medicine labels and the daily signals of whether one is maintaining good control of a chronic illness.

Understanding the practical impact of *g* requires understanding the pattern of these different gradients of risk across the landscape of people's lives. The job performance model discussed earlier (Fig. 13.1) provides some guides. Relative risks can be pushed up or down by both the nature of the *tasks* and the range of variation in the *people* studied. Among task attributes, complexity may be the most crucial. More cognitively demanding tasks (consent forms vs. prescription labels) always tilt the odds of competent behavior in favor of bright people, all else equal. A task's complexity can be pushed downward over time for the individuals performing it, however, when people get much experience with (that is, learn) the task at hand, whether it be a job or a chronic illness. Complexity can also be pushed upward by, among other things, diverting people's cognitive resources away from the task (multitasking) or by granting them more free-dom—freedom to use their "judgment"—in performing the task as they wish. As shown earlier, the validity of *g* for predicting job performance was higher in civilian jobs than in comparably complex military jobs, where people have to "work by the book." Social norms and mores can also be seen as pressure to work by the book. They vary over time and place (the acceptability of bearing illegitimate children), so we might expect to see corresponding shifts in relative risk for low *g* people when supervision and social pressure wax and wane.

Gradients of relative risk can also steepen or flatten for reasons having nothing to do with task complexity, as the job performance model indi-cates. Risk gradients can tilt when the people being studied differ in other traits that affect performance on a particular task: special abilities (other "can do" factors), personality and interests ("will do" factors), and task-specific experience ("have done" factors). When they are task-relevant, these other person factors will cause *g*-related shifts in relative risks, how-ever, only when they are correlated with *g* itself. Relative odds will become steeper when those other factors are *positively* correlated with *g* (bright people are more motivated or experienced at a task than are dull people). Conversely, relative risks will be leveled somewhat if these factors are *nega-tively* correlated with *g* (dull people are more motivated or have more ex-perience at the task). In certain extreme conditions, such as when bright people have no experience but dull people a lot, the relative risks can be reversed.

We have to go beyond the job performance model for the institutional and contextual factors that moderate *g*'s influence on outcomes such as in-come or welfare use. Personnel researchers try to eliminate such factors in their studies in order to better understand task performance itself, but such contextual factors can be expected to moderate the impact of *g* in many arenas of life. Perhaps most important among them is the degree to which different life outcomes are even sensitive to a person's *performance* rather than to institutional dictates. To take an example, a salesman's in-come may be quite sensitive to his sales performance, but a teacher's may depend exclusively on years of tenure and education, regardless of per-formance in the classroom. The more responsive institutions are to differ-ences in performance, whether that be raising salary for a job well done or increasing welfare for more children borne, the more likely it is that dif-ferences in *g* will steepen the gradients of relative risk (for income, welfare dependence). As discussed earlier, the more freedom society gives individ-uals to make unconstrained choices (to get more education, to bear chil-dren out of wedlock), the bigger the impact any differences in *g* will have. Personal freedom increases *g*'s already vast generality.

REFERENCES

Arvey, R. D. (1986). General ability in employment: A discussion. *Journal of Vocational Behavior, 29*(3), 415–420.

Baker, D. W., Parker, R. M., Williams, M. V., & Clark, W. S. (1998). Health literacy and the risk of hospital admission. *Journal of General Internal Medicine, 13*, 791–798.

Baldwin, J., Kirsch, I. S., Rock, D., & Yamamoto, K. (1995). *The literacy proficiencies of GED examinees: Results from the GED-NALS comparison study.* Washington, DC: American Council on Education and Educational Testing.

Behrman, J. R., Hrubec, Z., Taubman, P., & Wales, T. (1980). *Socioeconomic success: A study of the effects of genetic endowments, family environment, and schooling.* New York: North-Holland.

Borman, W. C., & Motowidlo, S. J. (1993). Expanding the criterion domain to include elements of contextual performance. In N. Schmitt & W. C. Borman (Eds.), *Personnel selection in organizations* (pp. 71–98). San Francisco: Jossey-Bass.

Borman, W. C., White, L. A., Pulakos, E. D., & Oppler, S. H. (1991). Models of supervisory job performance ratings. *Journal of Applied Psychology, 76*(6), 863–872.

Brand, C. (1987). The importance of general intelligence. In S. Modgil & C. Modgil (Eds.), *Arthur Jensen: Consensus and controversy* (pp. 251–265). New York: Falmer Press.

Brown, H., Prisuta, R., Jacobs, B., & Campbell, A. (1996). *Literacy of older adults in America: Results from the National Adult Literacy Survey.* Washington, DC: U.S. Department of Education, National Center for Education Statistics.

Campbell, J. P. (Ed.). (1990). Project A: The U. S. Army Selection and Classification Project. *Personnel Psychology, 43*(2) [special issue].

Campbell, J. P., McHenry, J. J., & Wise, L. L. (1990). Modeling job performance in a population of jobs. *Personnel Psychology, 43*(2), 313–333.

Carroll, J. B. (1993). *Human cognitive abilities: A survey of factor-analytic studies.* New York: Cambridge University Press.

Carroll, J. B. (1997). Psychometrics, intelligence, and public perception. *Intelligence, 24*(1), 25–52.

Cohen, J. (1988). *Statistical power analysis for the behavioral sciences.* Hillsdale, NJ: Lawrence Erlbaum Associates.

Cornelius, S. W., & Caspi, A. (1987). Everyday problem solving in adulthood and old age. *Psychology and Aging, 2*(2), 144–153.

Coward, W. M., & Sackett, P. R. (1990). Linearity of ability-performance relationships: A reconfirmation. *Journal of Applied Psychology, 75*, 295–300.

Davis, T. C., Meldrum, H., Tippy, P. K. P, Weiss, B. D., & Williams, M. V. (1996). How poor literacy leads to poor health care. *Patient Care, 30*(16), 94–127.

Davis, T. C., Michielutte, R., Askov, E. N., Williams, M. V., & Weiss, B. D. (1998). Practical assessment of adult literacy in health care. *Health Education & Behavior, 25*(5), 613–624.

Diehl, M. (1998). Everyday competence in later life: Current status and future directions. *The Gerontologist, 38*(4), 422–433.

Doak, C. C., Doak, L. G., & Root, J. H. (1996). *Teaching patients with low literacy skills* (2nd ed.). Philadelphia: J. B. Lippincott.

Edgerton, R. B. (1981). Another look at culture and mental retardation. In M. J. Begab, H. D. Haywood, & H. L. Garber (Eds.), *Psychosocial influences in retarded performance. Vol. I: Issues and theories in development* (pp. 309–323). Baltimore: University Park Press.

Gardner, H. (1997). A multiplicity of intelligences. *Scientific American Presents, 9*(4), 18–23.

Gerstman, B. B. (1998). *Epidemiology kept simple: An introduction to classic and modern epidemiology.* New York: Wiley.

Gordon, R. A. (1986). Scientific justification and the race-IQ-delinquency model. In T. F. Hartnagel & R. A. Silverman (Eds.), *Critique and explanation: Essays in honor of Gwynne Nettler* (pp. 91–131). New Brunswick, NJ: Transaction Books.

Gordon, R. A. (1997). Everyday life as an intelligence test: Effects of intelligence and intelligence context. *Intelligence, 24*(1), 203–320.

Gordon, R. A., Lewis, M. A., & Quigley, A. M. (1988). Can we count on muddling through the *g* crisis in employment? *Journal of Vocational Behavior, 33*, 424–451.

Gottfredson, L. S. (1985). Education as a valid but fallible signal of worker quality: Reorienting an old debate about the functional basis of the occupational hierarchy. In A. C. Kerckhoff (Ed.), *Research in sociology of education and socialization: Vol. 5* (pp. 119–165). Greenwich, CT: JAI Press.

Gottfredson, L. S. (1997). Why *g* matters: The complexity of everyday life. *Intelligence, 24*(1), 79–132.

Gottfredson, L. S. (in press-a). Dissecting practical intelligence theory: Its claims and evidence. *Intelligence.*

Gottfredson, L. S. (in press-b). *g*, jobs, and life. In H. Nyborg (Ed.), *The scientific study of general intelligence: Tribute to Arthur R. Jensen.* Elmsford, NY: Pergamon Press.

Gottfredson, L. S., & Crouse, J. (1986). The validity versus utility of mental tests: Example of the SAT. *Journal of Vocational Behavior, 29*(3), 363–378.

Herrnstein, R. J., & Murray, C. (1994). *The bell curve: Intelligence and class structure in American life.* New York: Free Press.

Hogan, R. T. (1991). Personality and personality measurement. In M. D. Dunnette & L. M. Hough (Eds.), *Handbook of industrial and organizational psychology: Volume 2* (2nd ed., pp. 873–919). Palo Alto, CA: Consulting Psychologists Press.

Humphreys, L. G. (1986). Commentary. *Journal of Vocational Behavior, 29*(3), 421–437.

Hunter, J. E. (1983a). A causal analysis of cognitive ability, job knowledge, job performance, and supervisor ratings. In F. Landy, S. Zedeck, & J. Cleveland (Eds.), *Performance measurement and theory* (pp. 257–266). Hillsdale, NJ: Lawrence Erlbaum Associates.

Hunter, J. E. (1983b). *Overview of validity generalization for the U.S. Employment Service.* (USES Test Research Report No. 43). Washington, DC: U. S. Department of Labor, Employment and Training Administration, Division of Counseling and Test Development.

Hunter, J. E. (1983c). *The dimensionality of the General Aptitude Test Battery (GATB) and the dominance of the general factors over specific factors in the prediction of job performance for USES* (Test Research Report No. 44). Washington, DC: U.S. Department of Labor, U.S. Employment Service.

Hunter, J. E. (1983d). *The prediction of job performance in the military using ability composites: The dominance of general cognitive ability over specific aptitudes* (DOD Contract No. F41689-83-C-0025). Rockville, MD: Research Applications, Inc.

Hunter, J. E. (1985). *Differential validity across jobs in the military.* Unpublished report, Department of Psychology, Michigan State University.

Hunter, J. E. (1986). Cognitive ability, cognitive aptitudes, job knowledge, and job performance. *Journal of Vocational Behavior, 29*(3), 340–362.

Hunter, J. E., & Hunter, R. F. (1984). Validity and utility of alternative predictors of job performance. *Psychological Bulletin, 96*(1), 72–98.

Hunter, J. E., & Schmidt, F. L. (1996). Intelligence and job performance: Economic and social implications. *Psychology, Public Policy, and Law, 2*(3/4), 447–472.

Hunter, J. E., Schmidt, F. L., & Judiesch, M. K. (1990). Individual differences in output variability as a function of job complexity. *Journal of Applied Psychology, 75*, 28–42.

Jencks, C., Bartlett, S., Corcoran, M., Crouse, J., Eaglesfield, D., Jackson, G., McClelland, K., Mueser, P., Olneck, M., Schwartz, J., Ward, S., & Williams, J. (1979). *Who gets ahead? The determinants of economic success in America.* New York: Basic Books.

Jencks, C., Smith, M., Acland, H., Bane, M. J., Cohen, D., Gintis, H., Heyns, B., & Michelson, S. (1972). *Inequality: A reassessment of the effect of family and schooling in America*. New York: Basic Books.

Jensen, A. R. (1980). *Bias in mental testing*. New York: Free Press.

Jensen, A. R. (1988). Review of the Armed Services Vocational Aptitude Battery. In J. T. Kapes & M. M. Mastie (Eds.), *A counselor's guide to career assessment instruments* (pp. 59–62). Alexandria, VA: The National Career Development Association.

Jensen, A. R. (1998). *The g factor: The science of mental ability*. Westport, CT: Praeger.

Kirsch, I. S., Jungeblut, A., Jenkins, L., & Kolstad, A. (1993). *Adult literacy in America: A first look at the results of the National Adult Literacy Survey*. Princeton, NJ: Educational Testing Service.

Kirsch, I. S., Jungeblut, A., & Mosenthal, P. B. (1994, March). *Moving towards the measurement of adult literacy*. Paper presented at the National Center for Education Statistics, U.S. Department of Education, Washington, DC.

Kirsch, I. S., & Mosenthal,. T. B. (1990). Exploring document literacy: Variables underlying the performance of young adults. *Reading Research Quarterly, 25*, 5–30.

Koegel, P., & Edgerton, R. B. (1984). Black "six hour retarded children" as young adults. In R. B. Edgerton (Ed.), *Lives in progress: Mildly retarded adults in a large city* (pp. 145–171). Washington, DC: American Association on Mental Deficiency.

Laurence, J. H., & Ramsberger, P. F. (1991). *Low-aptitude men in the military: Who profits, who pays?* New York: Praeger.

Lubinski, D., & Humphreys, L. G. (1997). Incorporating general intelligence into epidemiology and the social sciences. *Intelligence, 24*(1), 159–201.

McDaniel, M. A., Schmidt, F. L., & Hunter, J. E. (1988). Job experience correlates of job performance. *Journal of Applied Psychology, 73*(2), 327–330.

McHenry, J. J., Hough, L. M., Toquam, J. L., Hanson, M. A., & Ashworth, S. (1990). The relationship between predictor and criterion domains. *Personnel Psychology, 43*(2), 335–366.

Miller, A. R., Treiman, D. J., Cain, P. S., & Roos, P. A. (Eds.). (1980). *Work, jobs, and occupations: A critical review of the Dictionary of Occupational Titles*. Washington, DC: National Academy Press.

Moffitt, T. E., Gabrielli, W. F., Mednick, S. A., & Schulsinger, F. (1981). Socioeconomic status, IQ, and delinquency. *Journal of Abnormal Psychology, 90*(2), 151–156.

Moffitt, T. E., & Silva, P. A. (1988). IQ and delinquency: A direct test of the differential detection hypothesis. *Journal of Abnormal Psychology, 97*(3), 330–333.

Murray, C. (1997a). IQ will put you in your place. *Sunday London Times*. May 25. Available online.

Murray, C. (1997b). IQ and economic success. *The Public Interest*, No. 128, 21–35.

National Work Group on Literacy and Health (1998). Communicating with patients who have limited literacy skills: Report of the National Work Group on Literacy and Health. *The Journal of Family Practice, 46*(2), 168–176.

Olneck, M. R. (1977). On the use of sibling data to estimate the effects of family background, cognitive skills, and schooling. In P. Taubman (Ed.), *Kinometrics: Determinants of socioeconomic success within and between families* (pp. 125–162). New York: North-Holland.

Organ, D. W. (1994). Organizational citizenship behavior and the good soldier. In M. G. Rumsey, C. B. Walker, & J. H. Harris (Eds.), *Personnel selection and classification* (pp. 53–67). Hillsdale, NJ: Lawrence Erlbaum Associates.

Organ, D. W., & Konovsky, M. (1989). Cognitive versus affective determinants of organizational citizenship behavior. *Journal of Applied Psychology, 74*(1), 157–164.

O'Toole, B. J. (1990). Intelligence and behavior and motor vehicle accident mortality. *Accident Analysis and Prevention, 22*, 211–221.

Reder, S. (1998). Dimensionality and construct validity of the NALS assessment. In M. C. Smith (Ed.), *Literacy for the twenty-first century* (pp. 37–57). Westport, CT: Praeger.

Ree, M. J., & Carretta, T. R. (1997). What makes an aptitude test valid? In R. F. Dillon (Ed.), *Handbook on testing* (pp. 65–81). Westport, CT: Greenwood.

Ree, M. J., Carretta, T. R., & Doub, T. (1998/1999). A test of three models of the role of *g* and prior job knowledge in the acquisition of subsequent job knowledge. *Training Research Journal, 4*, 1–16.

Ree, M. J., Carretta, T. R., & Teachout, M. S. (1995). Role of ability and prior job knowledge in complex training performance. *Journal of Applied Psychology, 80*(6), 721–730.

Ree, M. J., Earles, J. A., & Teachout, M. S. (1995). Predicting job performance: Not much more than *g*. *Journal of Applied Psychology, 79*, 518–524.

Roberts, J., & Baird, J. T., Jr. (1972). *Behavior patterns in children in school.* DHEW publication no. 72-1042. Washington, DC: U.S. Government Printing Office.

Schmidt, F. L. (1993). Personnel psychology at the cutting edge. In N. Schmitt & W. C. Borman (Eds.), *Personnel selection in organizations* (pp. 497–515). San Francisco: Jossey-Bass.

Schmidt, F. L., & Hunter, J. E. (1984). A within setting empirical test of the situational specificity hypothesis in personnel selection. *Personnel Psychology, 37*, 317–326.

Schmidt, F. L., & Hunter, J. E. (1998). The validity and utility of selection methods in personnel psychology: Practical and theoretical implications of 85 years of research findings. *Psychological Bulletin, 124*(2), 262–274.

Schmidt, F. L., & Hunter, J. E. (2000). Select on intelligence. In E. A. Locke (Ed.), *The Blackwell handbook of principles of organizational behavior* (pp. 3–14). Malden, MA: Blackwell.

Schmidt, F. L., Hunter, J. E., & Outerbridge, A. N. (1986). Impact of job experience and ability on job knowledge, work sample performance, and supervisory ratings of job performance. *Journal of Applied Psychology, 71*(3), 432–439.

Schmidt, F. L., Hunter, J. E., Outerbridge, A. N., & Goff, S. (1988). Joint relation of experience and ability with job performance: Test of three hypotheses. *Journal of Applied Psychology, 73*(1), 46–57.

Schmidt, F. L., Hunter, J. E., & Pearlman, K. (1981). Task differences and validity of aptitude tests in selection: A red herring. *Journal of Applied Psychology, 66*, 166–185.

Schmidt, F. L., Hunter, J. E., Pearlman, K., & Shane, G. S. (1979). Further tests of the Schmidt-Hunter Bayesian validity generalization model. *Personnel Psychology, 32*, 257–281.

Schmidt, F. L., Ones, D. S., & Hunter, J. E. (1992). Personnel selection. *Annual Review of Psychology, 43*, 627–670.

Schmitt, N., Rogers, W., Chan, D., Sheppard, L., & Jennings, D. (1997). Adverse impact and predictive efficiency of various predictor combinations. *Journal of Applied Psychology, 82*(5), 719–730.

Sewell, W. H., & Hauser, R. M. (1975). *Education, occupation, and earnings: Achievement in the early career.* New York: Academic Press.

Sharf, J. C. (1988). Litigating personnel measurement policy. *Journal of Vocational Behavior, 33*(3), 235–271.

Simonton, D. K. (1994). *Greatness: Who makes history and why.* New York: Guilford Press.

Sternberg, R. J. (1997). *Successful intelligence: How practical and creative intelligence determine success in life.* New York: Penguin Putnam.

Sternberg, R. J. (2000). Human intelligence: A case study of how more and more research can lead us to know less and less about a psychological phenomenon, until finally we know much less than we did before we started doing research. In E. Tulving (Ed.), *Memory, consciousness, and the brain: The Tallinn Conference* (pp. 363–373). Philadelphia, PA: Taylor & Francis, Psychology Group.

Sternberg, R. J., Forsythe, G. B., Hedlund, J., Horvath, J. A., Wagner, R. K., Williams, W. M., Snook, S. A., & Grigorenko, E. L. (2000). *Practical intelligence in everyday life.* New York: Cambridge University Press.

Sternberg, R. J., & Wagner, R. K. (1993). The *g*-ocentric view of intelligence and job performance is wrong. *Current Directions in Psychological Science, 2*(1), 1–5.

Sternberg, R. J., Wagner, R. K., Williams, W. M., & Horvath, J. A. (1995). Testing common sense. *American Psychologist, 50,* 912–926.

Sticht, T. (Ed.). (1975). *Reading for working: A functional literacy anthology.* Alexandria, VA: Human Resources Research Organization.

Taubman, P. (Ed.). (1977). *Kinometrics: Determinants of socioeconomic success within and between families.* New York: North-Holland.

Thorndike, R. L. (1986). The role of general ability in prediction. *Journal of Vocational Behavior, 29*(3), 332–339.

Venezky, R. L., Kaestle, C. F., & Sum, A. M. (1987). *The subtle danger: Reflections on the literacy abilities of America's young adults.* Princeton, NJ: Educational Testing Service.

Viswesvaran, C., & Ones, D. S. (Eds.). (in press). Role of general mental ability in industrial, work, and organizational (IWO) psychology [Special issue]. *Human Performance.*

Weiss, B. D., Blanchard, J. S., McGee, D. L., Hart, G., Warren, B., Burgoon, M., & Smith, K. J. (1994). Illiteracy among Medicaid recipients and its relationship to health care costs. *Journal of Health Care for the Poor and Underserved, 5,* 99–111.

Weiss, B. D., Hart, G., & McGee, D., & D'Estelle, S. (1992). Health status of illiterate adults: Relation between literacy and health status among persons with low literacy skills. *Journal of the Board of Family Practice, 5,* 257–264.

Weiss, B. D., Reed, R. L., & Kligman, E. W. (1995). Literacy skills and communication methods of low-income older persons. *Patient Education and Counseling, 25,* 109–119.

Wigdor, A. K., & Green, B. F., Jr. (Eds.). (1991). *Performance for the workplace. Volume 1.* Washington, DC: National Academy Press.

Williams, M. V., Baker, D. W., Parker, R. M., & Nurss, J. R. (1998). Relationship of functional health literacy to patients' knowledge of their chronic disease. *Archives of Internal Medicine, 158,* 166–172.

Williams, M. V., Parker, R. M., Baker, D. W., Parikh, N. S., Pitkin, K., Coates, W. C., & Nurss, J. R. (1995). Inadequate functional health literacy among patients at two public hospitals. *Journal of the American Medical Association, 274*(21), 1677–1682.

Willis, S. L., & Schaie, K. W. (1986). Practical intelligence in later adulthood. In R. J. Sternberg & R. K. Wagner (Eds.), *Practical intelligence: Nature and origins of competence in the everyday world* (pp. 236–268). New York: Cambridge University Press.

Chapter 14

Contextual Variability in the Expression and Meaning of Intelligence

Cynthia A. Berg
University of Utah

Paul A. Klaczynski
Western Carolina University

Julie struggles and incorrectly completes an arithmetic word problem, but easily completes the same problem (2 × 30 + 157), when it is abstracted from the word problem. Tom quickly identifies the logical fallacy in an evolutionary argument that contradicts his religious beliefs, but accepts the validity of another, equally flawed, argument that supports his beliefs of creationism. In an everyday problem situation where Kevin is trying to perform competently on a task that is performed (with others with whom he is having difficulty getting along), Kevin focuses in on the task to be performed when the problem occurs at school, but focuses on the interpersonal difficulty when solving the same problem at home. After watching the first half hour of a movie for which he paid $10, Todd is utterly bored but refuses to leave the theater because (so his argument goes) he'd be "throwing money away." Later, after Sophie argued that he should view the situation more logically, Todd realized that the costs he already sunk should not influence his current decision, so, together with Sophie, he walked out of the theater.

These examples serve to illustrate the intraindividual variability that exists in the expression of intelligent performance. Individuals across the developmental age span and across cultures clearly demonstrate highly intelligent performance under some contextual conditions and evince less intelligent performance in other contexts. Variability in intellectual performance across contexts and tasks has been reported in numerous literatures including everyday problem solving (Blanchard-Fields, Chen, &

Norris, 1997; Ceci & Roazzi, 1994), cognitive development (Biddell & Fischer, 1992; Gelman & Baillargeon, 1983; Siegler, 1996), educational psychology (Brown, Bransford, Ferrara, & Campione, 1983; Stanovich & West, 1997), and cross-cultural psychology (Irvine & Berry, 1988; Rogoff, 1982). As we illustrate here, cognitive variability is not merely an individual difference attribute associated with low psychometric intelligence; rather, across levels of measured ability, variability is the norm in everyday cognition.

The variability in the expression and meaning of intelligence across developmental and cultural contexts is used to address the question, "How General is Intelligence?" We interpret this question in the following way. Evidence for the generality of intelligence would be demonstrated if those with high intelligence (measured via traditional intelligence assessments) displayed consistently high performance across tasks that were thought to tap components of intelligence. Furthermore, consistency in the meaning of intelligence as a construct across developmental ages and cultural contexts would lend further evidence for the notion of intelligence as a general construct that transcends different contexts. That is, evidence that most people—regardless of cultural background and age—have similar beliefs or "naive theories" concerning intelligence and its components, can be taken as evidence that laypersons, consistent with numerous g theorists, intuitively believe that there exists a domain-general aspect of cognition that enables adaptation across multiple contexts.

The body of literature that we present, however, presents a picture of immense variability in both the expression and meaning of intelligence in response to context. Thus, this work does not support the view that intelligence is a general factor that transcends contexts. We argue instead that variability—moment-to-moment fluctuations in cognitive performance as a function of context and task content—is the norm in everyday intelligence. Cognitive inconsistency is as typical of individuals of high psychometric intelligence as it is of individuals who score poorly on standardized intelligence tests. Further, cognitive flexibility is a critical ingredient for attaining one's goals in the face of rapid changes in contextual demands and social resources.

In the present chapter, we briefly review some of the findings that lead us to the conclusion that *intelligence is specific, situated, contextualized, and variable rather than general.* We begin by reviewing sociocultural research that demonstrates that intelligence differs often dramatically across cultural contexts both in its expression and its meaning. The sociocultural perspective will be useful in understanding the variability in intelligence across cultures, across ethnic groups within a single culture, and across developmental age groups within the American culture. We then explore in our own research how the same individuals vary in their intellectual performance in response to subtle contextual differences (e.g., as a function of problem domain, consistency with personal belief systems, instructions to "think logically"). This body of research clearly demonstrates that intelligence is not a general phenomenon that exists across contexts that differ in their intellectual or motivational demands. The research, however, does challenge researchers to begin to address the variability in the expression of intelligence that has been apparent in the field for a very long time (see Siegler, 1996, for a review). We conclude the chapter with two frameworks that address the variability in intelligence across context that may guide research as to when to expect intelligence to look general versus to look more variable.

Sociocultural Findings Demonstrating Variability in Intelligence Across Cultures or Contexts

A central idea to the sociocultural position on intelligence is that "intelligence will be different across cultures (and across contexts within cultures) insofar as there are differences in the kinds of problems that different cultural milieus pose their inhabitants" (Laboratory of Comparative Human Cognition, 1982, p. 710). Cross-cultural psychologists for decades searched for a "culture-free" test that could measure the intelligence of individuals that span various cultures with different physical ecologies and thus different opportunities and demands. Berry (1966) concluded, however, that "the search for a 'culture-free' test is futile insofar as it is hoped to find a universally valid test" (p. 229). Thus, the notion that intelligence is a single entity that is demonstrated similarly across cultures or contexts is antithetical to the sociocultural perspective.

By tying intelligence to the particular contexts in which it is expressed, the sociocultural perspective advanced a view of intelligence that was more situated in the everyday activities of its inhabitants (Rogoff & Lave, 1984) than previous positions to intelligence. Intelligence was measured in new and ecologically relevant ways such as filling milk delivery orders (Scribner, 1986), making mathematical calculations while grocery shopping (Lave, 1988), performing mental arithmetic skills while selling wares on the street (Nunes, Schliemann, & Carraher, 1993), reasoning while betting on horses (Ceci & Liker, 1986), and using tacit knowledge concerning how to succeed in one's occupation (Wagner & Sternberg, 1986). Measures of intelligence as it is demonstrated in the daily lives of individuals are often known as measures of "everyday intelligence" (Berg & Klaczynski, 1996; Rogoff & Lave, 1985; Sternberg & Wagner, 1986). Thus, measures of everyday intelligence have been of central focus for those adopting loosely a sociocultural or contextual view of intelligence and its development.

Variability in the Expression of Intelligence
Across Contexts

The field of cross-cultural psychology is replete with examples of variability in intellectual performance. This variability is most evident when performance on standard intelligence test items is contrasted with performance on problems that should assess the same cognitive processes in the ecological context of people's daily lives. We briefly (but by no means exhaustively) describe several of these examples to illustrate that intelligence is not demonstrated similarly across contexts. We include some of the most compelling examples, although several others exist (see Ceci, 1990; Irvine & Berry, 1988; and Laboratory of Comparative Human Cognition, 1982, for reviews).

In cross-cultural psychology, most studies illustrate greater competence when intellectual skills are measured in the daily lives of inhabitants than when cognitive skills are taken out of their normal ecology. For instance, Gladwin (1970) found that Micronesian navigators performed at a high level on complex memory, inference, and calculation skills required to travel from island to island and yet performed poorly on standard intelligence tests. Reuning (1988) similarly reported complex problem-solving abilities of !Hung San hunters (searching clues regarding an animal, planning complex courses of action) who performed at levels similar to Western children on Piagetian tasks, information-processing tasks and intelligence items. Thus, the overwhelming message of this cross-cultural research is that *intelligence* is not something that is demonstrated similarly across contexts.

Compelling evidence for the context-specificity of intelligence exists in research where individuals within Western industrialized cultures are compared on tasks that involve similar cognitive operations but that are differentially situated within the daily lives of individuals. For instance, Lave and her colleagues (Lave, 1988; Lave, Murtaugh, & de la Rocha, 1984; Murtaugh, 1985) studied the everyday mathematical operations of individuals as they "comparison shopped" at the grocery store at a time prior to the availability of unit pricing. Evidence for accurate judgments regarding "best buys" was overwhelming, despite the quite complex mental division that was demanded by the task. Not only was the accuracy of shoppers' judgments unrelated to scores on a standardized test of arithmetic performance, but "expert" shoppers (i.e., homemakers) outperformed college students from an elite university who had received considerably more formal training in mathematics and logic.

Similar results are reported by Scribner (1984, 1986) among dairy deliverers who had to mentally compute prices of dairy orders. Few dairy drivers computed the price of orders based on the exact algorithm of multiplying quantities of items by ordered category by unit prices and then summing products across categories. Instead, drivers used heuristic solutions where strategies were fit adaptively to the precise nature of orders and how the orders deviated from full case prices. Their ability to perform arithmetic operations for dairy orders was not predictive of their arithmetic skills as assessed through traditional paper and pencil tests (Scribner, 1986). Ceci and Liker (1986) examined the complex cognitive processes of expert horse racing handicappers. In predicting the "post-time" odds of hypothetical horses—calculations involving as many as 30 variables per horse—expert handicappers were able to take into consideration as many as seven variables (in a nonadditive manner comparable to computations performed in multiple regression analyses) to generate odds directly comparable to computer-generated odds. Although their IQs ranged from 80 to 130, IQ was unrelated to the ability to predict race track odds, suggesting that the cognitive processes are not a manifestation of an underlying g, but rather evolved within that domain.

Such results extend across the developmental life span. For example, similar to the mathematical abilities mentioned earlier for adults, Carraher, Carraher, and Schlieman (1985) studied the everyday mathematics of Brazilian children (ages 9–15) who worked as street vendors. The everyday arithmetic required of these children (mental addition, subtraction, and multiplication) is remarkable given these children's limited education (typically less than 5 years of education). Carraher et al. compared the mathematic skills of the children in story problems that mimicked the problems required in their daily work to that of isomorphs that were context free. Children performed 98% of the word problems correctly, but only 37% of the decontextualized math problems. Perret-Clermont (1980) reported the complementary results for middle-class Western children who had no difficulty performing decontextualized problems (e.g., 5 + . . . = 8), but had extensive difficulty solving the same addition problems when couched in real-life examples.

Thus, research findings from cross-cultural or sociocultural psychology illustrate the variability in the expression of intelligence that exists across different contexts, even when tasks are made to be similar in terms of the underlying cognitive demands. Individuals perform best when the intellectual operations required by the task are part of their daily context and perform less well when such operations are unfamiliar or removed from their typical context. From this perspective there is little evidence for a view of intelligence that is general and is expressed similarly across contexts.

Contextual Variations in the Meaning of Intelligence Across Ethnic and Age Groups

The view that intelligence depends on the particular contexts in which it is displayed, is consonant with research on how laypeople who vary in cultural context and age perceive intelligence. What intelligence means as a construct varies by cultural and developmental context and intelligence is not viewed as a monolithic construct that contains some limited small number of key essential components. The work on laypeople's views of intelligence came, in part, from Neisser's (1979) view that intelligence as a concept exists largely as a resemblance to a prototype of an intelligent person. A person's intelligence, then, is the degree to which the individual corresponds to his or her culture's prototype of an exceptionally intelligent person. Irvine (1970) also argued that psychologists could benefit from an examination of the layperson's use of the word intelligence as a "key to the way in which society designates acts as intelligent" (p. 24). From the contextual perspective (Berg & Calderone, 1994; Berry, 1984; Sternberg, 1984), people's conceptions of intelligence are particularly useful as they provide somewhat of an insider's perspective to the mental activity it takes to adapt to life contexts. Layperson's views about the nature of intelligence are also important as they serve as the basis for informal assessments of the intelligence of others and self (Sternberg, Conway, Ketron, & Bernstein, 1981).

Research has now demonstrated that laypeople (across cultures and age groups) do not believe that intelligence is a single construct that is displayed similarly across contexts. Berry (1984) reviewed research that examines people's views of intelligence in different cultural contexts (groups in Africa, Australia, China, Latin America, Malaysia). He concluded that cultures differ in what they perceive as constituting intelligent thought and that most cultures deviate from the view that intelligence is a single construct reflecting abstract judgment and thought. Further, all cultures view intelligence as multifaceted, often containing characteristics rarely identified with Western notions of intelligence. In many African cultures, intelligence during childhood is associated with characteristics such as obedience, responsibility, and respect (Berry, 1984). Mundy-Castle (1983, as cited in Berry, 1984) distinguished between social (tact, social ease, behavior that is in accordance with accepted social values) and technical intelligence to refer to two different facets of intelligence found in African folk conceptions of intelligence. Research on Chinese conceptions of intelligence (see Keats, as cited in Berry, 1984) indicated that Chinese teachers and students stress perseverance, effort, and determination, together with attitudes of social responsibility in their conceptions of intelligence more so than Australian teachers and students (for more detail on Chinese conceptions see Stevenson & Lee, 1990).

Within a single culture, intelligence is viewed as multifaceted containing many characteristics not traditionally associated with "general" intelligence. In one of the first empirical studies to examine layperson's conceptions Sternberg et al. (1981) found that lay adults believed that intelligence comprised characteristics such as practical problem solving (e.g., reasons logically and well, identifies connections among ideas), verbal ability (e.g., speaks clearly and articulately), and social competence (e.g., accepts others for what they are, admits mistakes). Developmental work has found that both adults and children stress different characteristics in their perceptions of intelligence in childhood, young adulthood, and late adulthood (Berg & Sternberg, 1992; Siegler & Richards, 1982; Yussen & Kane, 1983). Siegler and Richards (1982) and Yussen and Kane (1983) found that adults and children agree that the characteristics that constitute intelligence during child development shift from sensorimotor and language skills in infancy, academic and social skills in grade school, and social motivational and cognitive factors in young adulthood. Berg and Sternberg (1992) found that more traditional intellectual characteristics (such as ability to deal with novelty) were perceived as more important during young adulthood, whereas more practical or everyday intellectual characteristics (e.g., ability to cope with disastrous life situations, using common sense) were more likely in middle-aged and older adulthood. Furthermore, Berg and Sternberg found that adults perceived that intelligence is modifiable in that individuals can become more or less intelligent with time depending on contextual conditions (e.g., reading, education, lack of stimulating environment, and contact with other stimulating people). Such developmental differences are important as some have argued that different developmental epochs represent different contextual conditions (Berg & Calderone, 1994).

Further evidence for both the diversity of characteristics that laypeople believe constitute intelligence and cultural specificity comes from research by Okagaki and Sternberg (1993) where immigrant parents from Cambodia, Mexico, the Philippines, and Vietnam, and native-born Anglo-American and Mexican American parents were asked what characterized an intelligent child. Parents coming from different cultures placed a different relative weight on the characteristics defining intelligence. All parents (except the Anglo-American parents) emphasized noncognitive characteristics (i.e., motivation, social skills, and practical school skills) as equally important or as more important than cognitive characteristics (e.g., problem-solving skills, verbal ability, creativity) to their conceptions of an intelligent first-grade child. Further, for Filipino and Vietnamese parents, motivation (working hard to achieve goals) was the most important component of their conception of an intelligent child.

Thus, work from laypeople's conceptions of intelligence suggests that people's conceptions vary by context. People of different cultural groups vary in the types of characteristics that they believe constitute intelligence and in the relative weighting of these characteristics. Individuals of different ages (often described as comprising different contexts, see Berg & Calderone, 1994) also differ in the types of characteristics that are thought to comprise intelligence. We should note that not only do laypeople differ in what they believe characterizes intelligence, but experts do as well (Sternberg & Berg, 1986).

INTER- AND INTRADOMAIN VARIABILITY
AND INTELLIGENCE

The previous sections illustrate, first, that many scholars in both developmental and cross-cultural psychology are disenchanted with the concept of general intelligence and, second, that the views of these psychologists coincide with those of laypersons from an assortment of cultural and subcultural contexts and age groups. Like academic psychologists, laypersons recognize that everyday demands, societal resources, and opportunities for learning collude to create forms of intelligence appropriate to and functional within particular contexts. Also like academic psychologists, it should be clear that despite areas of substantial overlap, people are of the opinion that no single definition of intelligence suffices to capture the richness and variability of "real-world" intelligence.

In the present section we begin to explore in our own research, the inter- and intradomain variability in the expression of everyday intelligence. Our findings of task variability are compelling as they span tasks that comprise ill-structured everyday problem-solving tasks as well as more well-structured reasoning tasks. Our research with ill-structured tasks has involved tasks where diversity can exist both in the goals for accomplishing the tasks and in the means for accomplishing those goals. Such problems are ones that individuals encounter in their daily lives and which are embedded in interpersonal contexts (Berg, Strough, Calderone, Sansone, & Weir, 1998). Our research with more well-structured problems has involved reasoning and decision-making tasks where performance is examined in terms of normative versus heuristic responses. In both cases, diversity exists across problem isomorphs in how individuals perform such tasks. Specifically, cognitive variability on these tasks is related to (a) the contexts in which the problems are embedded and individuals' goals within those contexts, (b) the theoretical beliefs that individuals hold about particular content domains (e.g., religion, social classes), and (c) individuals' motivation to reason "logically and accurately." Such variability in everyday intellectual performance exists across the intellectual spectrum (i.e., variability in responding is not limited to those of low intellectual ability).

The theme of the present section is this: The quality of intellectual performances, both in relatively novel domains and in domains with which individuals have considerable familiarity, varies on a problem-to-problem basis. Consistently higher order reasoning is the hallmark of remarkably few individuals of any age group; instead, even those who purportedly possess superior "raw" intellectual resources are no more consistent in the application of their abilities than individuals whose measured intelligence is lower. Findings from different theoretical and methodological traditions are used to illustrate and refine this point.

The Role of Problem Interpretations in Understanding Contextual Variations in Everyday Problem-Solving Strategies

Research on everyday problem solving has focused on the strategies that individuals use to solve problems that are complex and multidimensional and are frequently encountered in daily life (see Berg & Klaczynski, 1996, for a review). Strategy selection is a measure of everyday problem-solving performance that deals with knowledge of strategy effectiveness and utilization among a broad range of strategies for dealing with everyday problems. Many different distinctions have been drawn for how people approach everyday problems, some of which draw extensively from research on stress and coping and control literatures (Heckhausen & Schulz, 1995; Lazarus & Folkman, 1984).

Several studies have found that the context in which an everyday problem occurs (e.g., family, work, school) impacts strategy selection (Berg, 1989; Blanchard-Fields, Chen, & Norris, 1997; Blanchard-Fields, Chen, Schocke, & Hertzog, 1998; Cornelius & Caspi, 1987; Folkman, Lazarus, Pimley, & Novacek, 1987) as well as the specific problem within each context (Berg, 1989; Cornelius & Caspi, 1987). The importance of context in understanding strategy selection extends across hypothetical everyday problems (Berg, 1989; Berg & Calderone, 1994) as well as problems that individuals have actually experienced (Aldwin, Sutton, Chiara, & Spiro, 1996; Berg et al., 1998). In addition, how individuals solve hypothetical problems often does not generalize to how individuals solve actual problems that they experience (Berg, Meegan, & Strough, 1997; Saltzstein, 1994). Thus, individuals do not use the same type of strategy across all problem contexts. Much of our research examining everyday problem solving for ill-structured problems has examined the role of problem interpretations in understanding context effects on task performance (Berg & Calderone, 1994; Berg et al., 1998). Everyday problems that are actually encountered in daily life are often interpreted in diverse ways, ways that have consequences for how such problems are solved.

One approach to examining the role of context in strategy selection has been to compare individuals who occupy different subcontexts as everyday problem-solving strategies are construed as intellectual efforts to achieve specific goals within the greater confines of culturally or subculturally specific developmental tasks. In Klaczynski (1994), first and fourth year medical school students drew qualitatively different interpretations of and made qualitatively distinct decisions regarding both moral dilemmas and problems encountered by both types of students on a daily basis, despite similarly high levels of "general" ability. Similarly, educational "track" (e.g., college preparatory vs. vocational training) impacted adolescents' values, control beliefs, and goals. These social–cognitive differences lead, in turn, to both between-track and within-subject variations in interpretations of and solutions to everyday problems (Klaczynski, Laipple, & Jurden, 1992; Klaczynski & Reese, 1991).

Another approach to examining the effect of context on strategy selection is to compare individuals as they describe problems that exist in different contexts. Our research finds that context differences may occur as different contexts hold different opportunities and goals for problem solution. Berg et al. (1998) asked preadolescent, young, middle-aged, and older adults to describe an everyday problem they had recently experienced in one of six domains (school, family, friends, work, leisure, and health), to describe their goals for the problem, and how they solved the problem. To assess problem definitions, participants' problem descriptions and goals were examined in terms of whether they reflected competence (purpose of accomplishing, achieving, or getting better at something) or interpersonal concerns (purpose to bring about some outcome involving others). Participants' strategies for dealing with the environment were coded as cognitive self-regulation (thoughts of the problem solver directed at regulating how he or she thought about the problem), behavioral self-regulation (self-initiated action by the problem solver aimed at changing his or her behavior to fit with the demands of the problem), or regulation or inclusion of others (behavior by the problem solver to influence or include other people's behavior, beliefs, or feelings). Strategies varied depending on the domain in which problems were described. However, these domain effects arose because problem domains were associated with different goals, which, in turn, were associated with particular strategies. Problems mentioned in the friend domain were almost exclusively associated with interpersonal problem definitions, whereas other domains such as school were predominately associated with competence problem definitions (either alone or in combination with interpersonal definitions see Fig. 14.1). The interpersonal nature of individuals' problem definitions was important also for understanding whether individuals used strategies that involved regulating or including other individuals (e.g., interpersonal goals were associated with greater use of regulating or including others). Thus, domain variability was related to the ways that individuals interpreted or represented everyday problems.

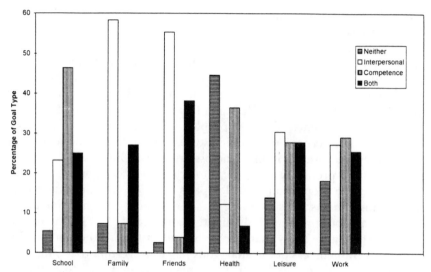

FIG. 14.1. Percentage of reported goals within domain. From Berg, Strough, Calderone, Sansone & Weir (1998). Reprinted with permission of the American Psychological Association.

In another study, we examined how the same individuals interpreted problems and viewed strategy effectiveness across two domains (Berg & Calderone, 1994), where problems were written to be analogs of each other (see Table 14.1 for problem analogs in the family and school domain). Thus, we were able to examine consistency in problem definitions across problems that were isomorphs. Fifth-, eighth-, and eleventh-grade students were presented with hypothetical everyday problems that pre-

TABLE 14.1
Problem Analogs Across Family and School Domains
Used in Berg and Calderone (1994)

School

You and your friend are swimming in P. E. class. Your friend is a much better swimmer than you and is very competitive. Your friend has challenged you to a race. You would really like to win, but you are not sure you are good enough to even make a race worthwhile. Every time you see your friend at school, your friend teases you about how you are going to lose the race.

Family

You and your brother/sister are going skiing with your family. Your brother/sister is a much better skier than you and always cares about winning. He/she has dared you to a race. You would really like to win, but you are not sure you are good enough to even make the race worthwhile. Every evening your brother/sister teases you about how you are going to lose the race.

---

sented a conflict involving an interpersonal component (e.g., a conflict with a project partner) and a task component (e.g., needing to complete a group project to be competitive for a class prize). Individuals were asked to define what was the "real" problem in the project and their responses were coded as to whether they focused on some aspect of the task (e.g., need to get the reading done), on an interpersonal component (e.g., my friend is mad at me), on the self (e.g., I forgot), or a combination of one of the three components. Although problems were all written to contain a task versus an interpersonal conflict, students were largely not consistent in how they interpreted problems across problems. Only 3 of 163 students defined all 16 problems using the same definition category.

The average proportion of analog pairs to which participants gave the same definition was .61, suggesting that participants gave the same definition to analogous problems only slightly more than half of the time. Fifth graders were more likely than eleventh graders to give the same definitions to both members of the analogous pairs, suggesting that older adolescents were more variable than younger children (see also Rogoff, Gauvain, & Gardner, 1987). Thus, those likely to possess a more advanced cognitive level were found to be more variable. Problem interpretations were important for understanding the strategies that students perceived would be effective for solving the problem. Individuals who interpreted problems in interpersonal or task terms rated higher those strategies that were congruent with their problem interpretations (i.e., interpersonal interpretation resulted in higher effectiveness ratings for interpersonally oriented strategies than task-oriented strategies and vice versa). The only relation between problem interpretations and standardized test scores (Stanford Achievement Test), indicated that those who focused on the interpersonal components of the problem in their definitions scored higher on the standardized tests ($r = .25$).

Problem interpretations are not only important when examining qualitative aspects of problem solution such as the content of the person's strategies, but extend to more quantitative aspects of everyday performance. A frequently used criterion for everyday problem-solving performance has been the number of strategies that a person can generate in response to a hypothetical problem (Denney & Pearce, 1989; Spivack & Shure, 1982). The idea is that the ability to generate large numbers of strategies reflects effective problem solving as it allows for flexibility in action and optimal adjustment to obstacles (Spivack & Shure, 1982). Berg, Meegan, and Klaczynski (1999), however, examined whether such an exhaustive reasoning style related to a particular way of representing the problem, namely staying within the formal requirements of the problem. However, the tendency to generate fewer problem solutions (as is characteristic of older adults) might relate to interpreting problems within one's everyday experiences that might increase the frequency of heuristic reasoning and cognitive short-cuts (Scribner, 1986).

Berg et al. (1999) presented hypothetical problems to young and older adults. Individuals' interpretations of the problems were examined in terms of whether they stayed within the formal or stated elements of the problem or brought in additional information from their own experience. To uncover strategy generation, individuals were extensively probed to generate strategies they would use to deal with the problem. Two different approaches to these problems were uncovered. One approach was described as an exhaustive processing style, where the problem was interpreted largely by drawing inferences from the stated problem and was associated with high numbers of strategies generated and large numbers of requests for additional information about the problem. A second approach is a more selective or experiential processing style where individuals interpreted the problem within the confines of their experience, often making extensive outside references to persons, contexts, and constraints, which indicated that experience permeated how the person thought about the problem. When individuals used an experiential processing approach they generated fewer numbers of strategies and requested less information to solve the problem. These two approaches to the problem, however, could not be considered differences between individuals, but differences that individuals exhibited across problems, in that few individuals could be characterized as adopting the experiential approach across all problems. The only correlation between a measure of verbal intelligence and interpretations indicated that those who interpreted more problems within the confines of the problem (as opposed to drawing inferences or interpreting the problem within their own experience) scored lower in verbal intelligence than those who made fewer such interpretations.

Problem interpretations are also important in understanding performance variability on more well-structured, formal reasoning problems. Laipple (1991) found that old adults were less likely to interpret logical problems (isolation of variables problems) within the confines of the problem, but instead imputed elements of their own experience in the problems. In Laipple (1991), differences in the experiential nature of individuals' problem interpretations accounted for all of the age differences in problem-solving performance between young and older adults (see also Sinnott, 1989). In Klaczynski and Narasimham (1998a), older adolescents were more likely than younger adolescents to interpret correctly certain conditional reasoning rules as conditionals and to solve them correctly. For instance, more middle adolescents than early adolescents correctly interpreted such conditional statements as, "If a student drives a car, then that student must be at least 16 years old" and correctly solved problems associated with the conditional (e.g., drew uncertainty inferences to the problem,

"John does not drive a car. Is John at least 16 years old?"). The same adolescents were also more likely than younger adolescents to misinterpret other conditional rules as biconditionals (e.g., "If a person exercises frequently, then that person will be in good shape" was interpreted as also entailing, "If a person is in good shape, then that person exercises frequently."). As a consequence of these interpretations, older adolescents proposed more solutions that were correct—only if the rules had actually been biconditionals (thus, reasoning was "correct" given subjects' interpretations).

Thus, problem interpretations are one factor that help to understand the variability in task performance across different contexts. Individuals differ in their problem interpretations in ways that relate to their solutions of specific problems. However, it appears that variability in problem interpretations is not a property of the individual, but that the variability exists at the transaction of the individual with the specific problem at hand (see the following discussion of frameworks to guide variability).

Intelligence and "Task Variability": Moment-to-Moment Shifts in Reasoning

Variability in problem solving is not limited to domain-related variation, but also exists as variability is examined on a problem to problem basis. The phenomenon of task variability has been well documented in numerous areas of cognitive and developmental psychology (Reyna & Brainerd, 1995). In essence, task variability is seen when reasoners use sophisticated, normatively appropriate strategies on some problems (e.g., as a function of familiarity) and less sophisticated or fallacious reasoning on logically isomorphic problems. For example, studies of Wason's (1966) infamous selection task have repeatedly shown that people reason consistently with the dictates of formal logic under some conditions (e.g., when problems concern prescriptive rules regarding what should or ought to be done in a situation), but not under other conditions (e.g., when problems involve arbitrary conditional rules; Evans [1989] and Evans & Over [1996] reviewed this literature).

In what follows, we refer to studies of motivated reasoning and ask the question, Is this type of variability less common among individuals of higher than of lower psychometric ability? In motivated reasoning research, problems contain conclusions that are either consistent, inconsistent, or neutral with respect to participants' beliefs. In contrast to traditional social psychological research in this area, problem type (e.g., belief-consistent) varies within-, rather than between-, subjects. Reasoning biases are apparent when sophisticated reasoning is used to reject belief-inconsistent evidence (e.g., Klaczynski & Narasimham, 1998b) or everyday arguments (e.g., Klaczynski, in press-a), but heuristic strategies are used to facilitate the acceptance of belief-consistent evidence and arguments. Central to the present discussion, then, biases are manifested in the form of task variability—shifts from sophisticated reasoning to heuristics, personal experiences, and other relatively simple arguments (e.g., assertions that belief-consistent evidence is true) on a problem-to-problem basis (see also Kuhn, 1993; Kuhn, Amsel, & O'Loughlin, 1988; Kuhn, Garcia-Mila, Zohar, & Andersen, 1995).

Example problems of evidence used in investigations of adolescents' and adults' beliefs concerning the effects of belonging to their particular religious groups are presented in Table 14.2. These examples were specifically created for individuals who had indicated that they were Catholic and who held strong convictions that belonging to that religion positively impacted numerous social behaviors and personality attributes. The first example describes evidence that supports this belief system; in the second example, however, the belief system is clearly contravened.

Responses to the first example typically have a heuristic, experiential flavor (e.g., "That's pretty true because I don't know any good Catholics who

TABLE 14.2
Example Problems Used in Investigations of Beliefs Reasoning

Belief-Consistent Evidence

Dr. Bill R. is a psychologist interested in determining whether sexual harassment is more likely to occur in some religions than in others. To conduct his research, he included in his study Baptists, Hindus, Methodists, Catholics, and Lutherans. In each religion group, he asked 80 people to be in the study. To measure sexual harassment, Dr. R. observed people in each group at church picnics and counted the number of times each person told jokes with sexual content. At the end of his study, Dr. R. found that the Catholics told an average of only 2.0 sexual jokes per month. On the other hand, members of the other religions, told an average 6.5 sexual jokes per month. Therefore, people from other religions told more than three times as many sexual jokes than the Catholics. Based on this, Dr. R. concluded that Catholics are involved in less sexual harassment than people who belong to other religions.

Belief-Inconsistent Evidence

Dr. T. is a psychologist interested in determining whether some religious groups have more faith in God than others. To conduct his research, he included in his study Baptists, Catholics, Methodists, Hindus, Muslims, and Lutherans. In each religious group, he asked 80 people to be in the study. To measure faith in God, Dr. T. went to the home of each person in each religious group 7 times and observed the number of prayers each person told per week. At the end of his study, Dr. T. found that the average Catholic told only 3.5 prayers per week. Members of the other religions, on the other hand, told an average of 8.0 prayers per week. Therefore, people in other religions told more than twice as many prayers as Catholics. Based on this, Dr. T. concluded that Catholics have less faith in God than people who are members of other religions.

---

joke around about sex," and "From what I know that's the way those other religions are. Catholics are much more devout; that's pretty well-known."). The typical response of participants to the second problem is to denounce it because, among other flaws, the measure of sexual harassment lacks construct validity (e.g., This research is worthless because just because a person tells jokes about sex doesn't mean anything about sexual harassment.). These different approaches to judging the evidence occur on a within-subjects basis as individuals shift from relatively superficial arguments to relatively more complex arguments as a function of evidence type.

In this research, general intellectual ability has been determined by assessing formal operational capacities (Klaczynski, 1997; Klaczynski & Fauth, 1997) and dimensions of fluid and crystallized intelligence (Klaczynski, 1997; Klaczynski & Gordon, 1996a, 1996b; Klaczynski & Robinson, 2000). Belief-consistent and inconsistent problems have been structured in such ways that their conclusions could be refuted by various forms of scientific reasoning—by invoking statistical principles (e.g., intuitive versions of the law of large numbers) and by explaining validity threats (as in the examples)—and by detecting flaws in critical thinking (e.g., the domino fallacy). A number of different belief systems have been assessed, involving social classes, religions, occupational aspirations, and tastes in music.

Across multiple studies, no significant relationships between reasoning biases and intellectual ability have been found. This null result has been replicated with several ability assessment instruments, across numerous types of reasoning that objective reasoners should use on belief-relevant problems, and with each of the belief systems listed earlier. Furthermore, the small role of intellectual ability does not appear to vary by age, as it fails to predict biases from early adolescence (Klaczynski, 1997, 2000) through old age (Klaczynski & Robinson, 2000). Such biases may relate, however, to individual difference characteristics such as the difference between "belief-driven" and "truth-driven" individuals (Klaczynski, 2000). Truth-driven individuals are more likely than belief-driven individuals to subordinate domain-specific belief systems to general epistemological goals such as remaining open-minded, reasoning consistently, understanding that knowledge is indeterminate and monitoring reasoning for quality (note similarity of this cognitive style to those discussed by Baron [1988], Stanovich & West [1997] and Perkins, Jay, & Tishman [1993]).

The Roles of Motivation and Perspective-Switching in Understanding Variability in Everyday Reasoning Biases and Decision Making

The foregoing discussion highlights a number of recent insights into the nature of variability in problem solving and reasoning. Regardless of whether confronted with "everyday" problems, designed to have relatively imprecise processing demands, or formal problems, intended to provide relatively straightforward assessments of reasoning competencies, individuals' goals, beliefs, and experiences impinge on task interpretations that vary by context and problem type. In turn, these interpretations have fairly dramatic effects on the cognitive operations performed to solve tasks "successfully." The problem by problem variability suggests that interpretations may vary on a problem to problem basis. Shifts may occur within subjects on a problem to problem basis from interpretations consistent with experimenter's definitions to interpretations that are "contextualized" to participants' goals and beliefs. Questions that arise from these findings are: To what extent are these shifts in interpretations under subjective control? and Are individual differences in the extent of subjective control related to psychometric intelligence? Note that both questions imply that metacognitive monitoring of one's cognitive operations is paramount to managing interpretations and re-interpretations successfully.

Research with college students provides some support for the conjecture that individuals can consciously adapt their interpretations of certain decision making problems to coincide with experimentally intended interpretations. For instance, Epstein, Lipson, Holstein, and Huh (1992) found that, when asked to view problems from their "usual perspective," most participants committed the contrary-to-fact fallacy when assessing the causes of previously occurring events. However, in the vast majority of cases, the reasoning of the same participants was normatively correct when they were instructed to adopt the perspective of a "perfectly logical person" (see also Denes-Raj & Epstein, 1994).

In a recent extension, Klaczynski (2001) presented early adolescents, middle adolescents, and college students a series of contrary-to-fact, sunk cost, and probability decision-making tasks. Participants responded to problems of each type from either their "usual" perspective or from the "logical person perspective." Consider the following "sunk cost" problem (adapted from Frisch, 1993):

Problem 1: You are staying in a hotel room on vacation. You paid $10.95 to see a movie on pay TV. After 5 minutes, you are bored and the movie seems pretty bad. How much longer would you continue to watch the movie?

Problem 2: You are staying in a hotel room on vacation. You turn on the TV and there is a movie on. After 5 minutes, you are bored and the movie seems pretty bad. How much longer would you continue to watch the movie?

In the example, the sunk cost fallacy is indicated by the decision to continue watching the movie in the first scenario, but not in the second scenario (Stanovich & West, 1999). Because sunk costs (i.e., money paid for the movie) are irrelevant (i.e., they are irretrievable and should be ignored), decisions in the two situations should be the same.

As in Epstein et al. (1992), across ages normative responding was poor in the usual perspective frame, but increased substantially in logical perspective frame. Despite these increases, only on the contrary-to-fact problems did the majority of the oldest—and presumably most intelligent—participants respond normatively. The low rates of normative responding to the probability judgment and sunk cost problems were unlikely the result of poorly developed analytic competencies; basic probabilistic reasoning abilities are generally acquired by early adolescence (Kreitler & Kreitler, 1986) and children as young as eight years grasp the rationale for avoiding the sunk cost fallacy (Arkes & Ayton, 1999; Baron, Granato, Spranca, & Teubal, 1993).

In addition to assessing the influence of perspective shifting on normative responding, Klaczynski (2001) also assessed variability in the responses. The amount of variability in the responding of the middle adolescents and young adults was no less than in the responding of the early adolescents. The sources of variability, however, were age-related as most of the responses of the two older groups were either normative or fallacies typically shown by adults; the early adolescents' responses were either typical fallacies or more idiosyncratic errors (see Fig. 14.2).

A second set of investigations (Klaczynski & Gordon, 1996b; Klaczynski & Narasimham, 1998a) relevant to the metacognitive control of reasoning resources and decision quality focused on the relationships between motivation and belief-based reasoning biases. In this work, adolescents were presented a series of hypothetical "experiments" relevant to subjectively important belief systems (e.g., concerning religion). Reasoning quality was assessed by the extent to which flaws built into the scenarios were detected; reasoning biases were measured as differences in the detection of flaws in scenarios that depicted belief systems positively or negatively. First, when asked to evaluate the quality of the "research" and to justify their evaluations, adolescents in control conditions evidenced the typical "motivated reasoning" effect: Reasoning was more sophisticated on belief-inconsistent than on belief-consistent problems, a bias that enabled the preservation of the existing belief system. In "accuracy motivation" conditions, participants were told that they would be punished if they displayed biases in their reasoning (e.g., by having to re-take the various assessment instruments and having to justify their reasoning before a panel of adult judges in a formal interview).

Not surprisingly, reasoning quality on both belief-consistent and belief-inconsistent problems improved. The accuracy manipulation thus "worked" in one sense: Participants put more cognitive effort into evaluating the experiments regardless of the direction of the conclusions. Critically, however, disparities (i.e., biases) in reasoning were no smaller in these condi-

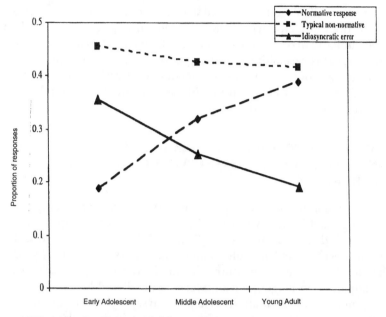

FIG. 14.2. Developmental differences in sources of variability across three types of decision making tasks (i.e., sunk cost, probability judgment, contrary-to-fact), collapsed across the "usual" and "logic" framing conditions. From Klaczynski (2001). Reprinted with permission from Elsevier.

tions than in control conditions. A second, equally important, finding was that extrinsic accuracy pressure improved overall reasoning quality more for higher than for lower general ability adolescents. Like lower ability adolescents, however, the motivated reasoning biases of high-ability adolescents were as prevalent in the accuracy as in the control condition (Klaczynski & Gordon, 1996b). These data point to limitations on the extent to which individuals, regardless of psychometric ability, can exert metacognitive control over the representations upon which their reasoning operates: Despite knowing that they needed to reason objectively, neither high- nor low-ability individuals successfully inhibited the interfering effects of beliefs.

Summary

The foregoing research demonstrates quite convincingly that intelligence is variable in its expression across problems that vary in terms of their context, whether problems are consistent or inconsistent with one's beliefs, and whether one is encouraged to be accurate in one's logical reasoning. Thus, to the extent that a general view of intelligence would predict that intelligence is displayed in general across a broad range of contexts, this research does not support a view of intelligence as general and demonstrated similarly across contexts. The challenge for researchers is how to characterize this variability and to begin to understand why intelligence is variable across contexts. In the next section we describe two different theoretical frameworks that begin to address why intelligence might be variable across contexts and problems.

FRAMEWORKS TO ADDRESS VARIABILITY IN INTELLIGENCE ACROSS CONTEXTS AND PROBLEMS

Although variability in the expression and meaning of intelligence has been recognized for many years within many different perspectives to intelligence (Biddell & Fisher, 1992; Siegler, 1996), recently theorists have begun to develop new metaphors and frameworks to specifically address variability. For instance, in contrast to the ladder metaphor advanced by Piagetian and neo-Piagetian frameworks, Biddell and Fisher (1992) liken development to a web of alternative pathways. Siegler uses the metaphor of overlapping waves to capture the idea that individuals use multiple strategies at the same time, although some strategies will become differentially frequent across development.

In this final section, we describe two frameworks that help understand the variability that we have uncovered in our research. These frameworks were developed separately to help explain variability in ill-structured problems (Model of Everyday Problem Solving Adaptation) and more formal reasoning problems (Two-process Theories of Cognition). Although developed for different types of problems, both frameworks focus attention on how individuals define, represent, and encode problems in understanding variability in strategy selection and normative versus heuristic reasoning. We illustrate how variability in problem solving and logical reasoning is fully expected in such frameworks, rather than being the annoyance that variability is in other frameworks to intelligence (e.g., Piagetian framework).

Model of Everyday Problem-Solving Adaptation

The model of everyday problem solving (graphically presented in Fig. 14.3) seeks to understand variability in how individuals select strategies for solving everyday problems through individuals' definitions of everyday problems and tasks (Berg, Strough, Calderone, Meegan, & Sansone, 1997; Sansone & Berg, 1993). As already described, our research has examined several different facets of problem definitions including whether the content of the problem is focused on interpersonal versus competence com-

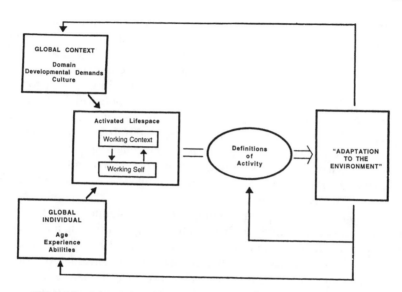

FIG. 14.3. Schematic representation of the model of Everyday Problem Solving Adaptation. From "Adapting to the Environment Across the Life Span," by C. Sansone & C. Berg, 1993, *International Journal of Behavioral Development, 16*(2), p. 219. Copyright 1993. Reprinted with permission of The International Society for the Study of Behavioural Development.

ponents (Berg et al., 1998; Berg & Calderone, 1994) and whether experience is imputed into the problem definition (Berg et al., 1999). Individuals define everyday problems through a transactional process whereby features of the context (e.g., domain of problem) and of the individual (e.g., age, experience, abilities) combine. Although a particular problem definition may derive from all of the possible contextual and individual factors present at the time, it may not include all such features. Thus, we suggest a distinction between "global" contextual and individual factors (i.e., the set of all possible contextual and individual factors) and the subset of those factors that are activated at any single point in time ("working context" and "working self"). The distinction between global and working self reflects researchers' suggestions that only a portion of the self may be represented in awareness at any given point in time (Markus & Wurf, 1987; Rhodewalt, 1986). The notion of working context adds to this work on the self that only part of the context is perceived and processed at any point in time.

Our research has shown that problem-solving outcomes, such as strategies for solving everyday problems, will vary depending on one's problem definition and will not be optimal or nonoptimal across problem-solving contexts or individuals with different abilities, personalities, and experiences. Mischel (1984), in fact, argued that such flexibility in responses across situations "is adaptive and functional, more indiscriminate responding may indicate ineffective coping and inadequate competence for dealing more appropriately with the specific situation" (p. 360).

This model of everyday problem solving is able to accommodate the fact that individuals show such intraindividual variability across problems in their problem definitions and strategies. As problem definitions and strategies occur due to a transaction between individual and contextual characteristics, in fact, variability is the predicted norm not the exception. Two different problem contexts may focus awareness on a subset of self-knowledge particularly relevant to that context (Bargh, Lombardi, & Higgins, 1988; Markus & Wurf, 1987). This awareness can be conscious or unconscious. That is, contextual cues may activate aspects of the self-concept (e.g., affiliative vs. competence components, epistemic beliefs) without awareness on the part of the individual that they are thinking about a certain aspect of the self. For instance, in Berg et al. (1998) the contexts of school versus friends may have differentially focused individuals on competence versus affiliative aspects of their self-concept (see Roberts & Donahue, 1994), leading to different problem definitions and strategies. Reciprocally, the specific cognitive and affective schemas and attitudes that are activated at a single point in time for the individual may focus attention to specific features of the context, rather than others. Individual differences in the differentiation and complexity of the self-concept (Campbell et al., 1996; Labouvie-Vief, Chiodo, Goguen, Diehl, & Orwoll, 1995) may help to understand differences in the extent of intraindividual variability in problem definitions and strategies across problem contexts. For instance, individuals with a more complex and differentiated self-concept may be more variable in their problem definitions and strategies, as different aspects of the self can be accessed at any particular point in time.

Take the example of the hypothetical problems from the Berg and Calderone (1994) study, in which problem analogs were constructed across two domains. How could it be that individuals would not define these problems similarly, given their similar structure and content? Perhaps these two problems activate different aspects of the individual's self-concept, thereby focusing individuals on different components of the problem. For instance, the friend problem at school, may activate feelings of competence in competition, thereby focusing the individual on the specific task of winning the race. However, the sibling problem may activate relational schemas for sibling, thereby focusing the individual on the interpersonal aspects of the problem, rather than winning the race. These different problem definitions are associated with different strategies for the solution of the problem that focused differentially on dealing with the interpersonal issue or completing the task.

Two-Process Theories of Cognition

Another approach that not only anticipates cognitive variability, but that also views such variability as sometimes (but not always) adaptive relies on a function distinction between conscious and unconscious processing. In cognitive and social psychology, the past decade has witnessed increased development and usage of two-process theories to explain variability in phenomena ranging from persuasion (Chen & Chaiken, 1999), decision making (Stanovich, 1999), reasoning (Evans & Over, 1996; Stanovich & West, 1999), implicit and explicit memory (Reyna & Brainerd, 1995), and numerous aspects of cognitive development (Klaczynski, 2001; Reyna, Lloyd, & Brainerd, in press). In two-process theories, cognition is seen as developing along two dissociated trajectories—one directed toward increases in computational processing and in the capacity to decontextualize reasoning from problem content; the second directed toward heuristic, highly contextualized processing (Stanovich, 1999).

In two-process approaches, decision making is jointly determined by interactions between two cognitive systems (Epstein, 1994) and preconsciously extracted representations often form the basis for consciously made decisions (Evans, 1996). Task characteristics (e.g., familiarity), context (e.g., social demands for accuracy), and individual difference variables (e.g., epistemic beliefs, intelligence) interact to determine which processing system is predominant on a given task (Stanovich, 1999).

The properties and characteristics of the two systems differ at several levels. Heuristic system processing is relatively rapid, enables automatic recognition of environmental features (e.g., facial cues), and facilitates information mapping onto and assimilation into existing knowledge categories. Relative to analytic processing, heuristic processing occurs at the periphery of awareness, requires little cognitive effort, and thus frees attentional resources for computationally complex reasoning.

When heuristic processing is predominant on a task, responses have no basis in reasoning in the "usual" sense; that is, computational analyses and attempts to break problems down into discrete components are absent, little or no attention is paid to formal rules of inference or decision making. Although some heuristics may derive from well-learned, automated rules, such rules are applied "thoughtlessly" (i.e., without concern for their limitations; see Arkes & Ayton, 1999). Heuristic processing also may predominate when tasks activate stereotypes, personal "theories" (e.g., of personalities), and vivid or salient memories (Kahneman & Tversky, 1972; Klaczynski, in press-a). Phenomenologically, judgments arrived at heuristically feel intuitively correct, but the basis for this feeling is often difficult to articulate (Epstein, 1994).

Analytic processing is consciously controlled, effortful, and deliberate. Successful analytic reasoning depends on the acquisition of abilities that are frequently prescribed as normative for reasoning and decision making (Epstein, 1994). Analytic competencies include the higher order abilities that enable reasoning consistent with the rules of formal logic, decisions based on comparisons between a priori probabilities, and accurate calibration of one's abilities. Unlike heuristic processing, analytic processing is directed toward precise inferences.

The two systems are assumed to operate on different task representations. Heuristic processing generally operates on "contextualized" representations that are heavily dependent on problem content (e.g., familiarity) and semantic memory structures (e.g., stereotypes). Analytic processing operates on "decontextualized" representations in which the underlying structure of a task is decoupled from superficial content and which thereby facilitate logico-computational operations (Stanovich & West, 1997). The two systems may also be related to different forms of encoding information (Brainerd & Gordon, 1994, with analytic processing more related to verbatim traces (which entail correspondence to problem details), whereas heuristic processing is more related to gist traces (i.e., holistic abstractions of patterns).

The representation–processing system relationship is considerably more complex than portrayed here. For example, decontextualized representations increase the probability of analytic processing, but do not guarantee such processing. Even if analytic processing is engaged, normative solutions are not ensured because representations may be misleading, inappropriate reasoning principles may be applied, appropriate principles may be misapplied, or heuristic processing may interfere with reasoning despite conscious attempts to reason analytically (Evans & Over, 1996; Reyna et al., in press). For instance, in the motivated reasoning research of Klaczynski and Gordon (1996a), although participants in the accuracy motivation engaged in more complex, analytic processing than their control counterparts, they were unable to inhibit the interfering effects of their prior beliefs, which presumably occurred without participants' conscious awareness.

To further illustrate the applicability of the two-process model to motivated reasoning research and to explaining variability of everyday cognition, consider the model of motivated reasoning presented in Fig. 14.4. Confronted with evidence consistent with prior beliefs, heuristic processing—the "default" processing system—remains predominant. The evidence is processed at a relatively cursory level and is accompanied by little or no motivation to scrutinize the quality of the evidence. At presentation, the evidence activates a set of beliefs (e.g., concerning religion); as the evidence is processed, these beliefs remain activated and enable/justify the

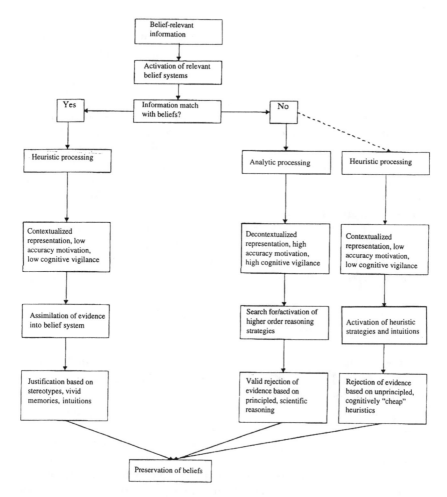

FIG. 14.4. A two-process model of motivated reasoning biases. From Klaczynski (2000). Adapted with permission of Elsevier Science.

acceptance of the evidence; that is, through heuristic processing, prior beliefs sometimes serve as "proof" for evidence that supports them (Klaczynski, 2000).

By contrast, incongruent evidence usually leads to predominantly analytic processing (as indicated by the dotted line from the belief/evidence match box to heuristic processing, there are exceptions to this general rule). The data are inspected closely as individuals search for flaws in evidence quality. Part of this search entails the abstraction of a decontextualized task representation in which the logical structure of the evidence is considered independently from evidence content. Use of such representations enables the construction of principled reasons or the activation of sophisticated reasoning strategies; application of these strategies allows reasoners to reject the evidence on an apparently rational basis (Klaczynski, in press-a).

Isomorphic evidence that differs only in its consistency with prior beliefs thus elicits predictable variability in the quality of reasoning on a problem-to-problem basis. In the case of belief-based reasoning, variability is a product of both motivational and representation differences fostered by belief-consistent and inconsistent evidence. More generally, the two-process perspective argues that variability in responding thus arises, in part, as a function of changes in the processing system predominant at a particular moment and, in part, from various types of "breakdowns" in analytic system processing (e.g., retrieval of incorrect reasoning principles; see Reyna et al., in press). Critically, although indices of general ability may predict various types of analytic processing failures, it is unrelated to responding under conditions that elicit predominately heuristic processing (Klaczynski, 2000).

SUMMARY AND CONCLUSIONS

To return to the question posed earlier, "How General is Intelligence?", we have reviewed research from very different literatures that demonstrates convincingly that intelligence is not a general capacity that is exhibited similarly across widely varying contexts. In fact, intelligence is not a general capacity that is similar across contexts with rather subtle differences (e.g., problem analogs in the family and school domain, logical reasoning problems in the same domain that simply are consistent with or inconsistent with one's beliefs). Everyday problem solving and reasoning is replete with variability that occurs from moment to moment as a function of context and tasks. Variability is not restricted to specific cultures, individuals of specific ages, nor to those of low intellectual ability.

The ubiquity of variability is important and leads us to a different question than the one with which this chapter began. The new question is, "When does intelligence look general and when does it look specific to particular contexts?" Two frameworks developed for different types of intellectual problems (everyday ill-structured problems versus more formal reasoning problems) assist in addressing this new question. Both frameworks predict that intellectual performance will look similar across contexts and problems to the extent that the problems are interpreted and represented in a similar fashion. Problems that are encoded in different ways and that activate different aspects of people's beliefs and self-concepts, are not likely to display similar intellectual performances. However, problems where goals, beliefs, and self-concepts are more similar should produce more similar intellectual performance.

The research and theory reviewed in this chapter recognizes and embraces the variability that is inherent in individuals' adaptation efforts across cultures and development. Although the issue of variability may at times seem chaotic in that individuals vary in their intellectual efforts as much (if not more) as they are consistent, such variability may reflect the adjustments that occur as individuals navigate the changing environment of their daily lives. Such an approach may shift the focus from identifying the most "optimal" intellectual performances and documenting their developmental growth, to identifying the processes whereby individuals adapt to the changing circumstances of their lives.

ACKNOWLEDGMENTS

Research reported in this paper was supported by grant HD 25728 from the National Institute of Child and Human Development and the National Institute of Aging, awarded to Carol Sansone and Cynthia A. Berg, by a University of Research Committee Grant awarded to Berg and by a Spencer Fellowship awarded from the National Academy of Education to Berg. We would like to thank Robert Sternberg and Elena Grigorenko for their comments on an earlier draft of this chapter.

REFERENCES

Aldwin, C. M., Sutton, K. J., Chiara, G., & Spiro, A. (1996). Age differences in stress, coping, and appraisal: Findings from the normative aging study. *Journal of Gerontology: Psychological Sciences, 51B*, 179–188.

Arkes, H., & Ayton, P. (1999). The sunk cost and Concorde effects: Are humans less rational than lower animals? *Psychological Bulletin, 125*, 591–600.

Bargh, J. A., Lombardi, W. J., & Higgins, E. T. (1988). Automaticity of chronically accessible constructs in person X situation effects on person perception: It's just a matter of time. *Journal of Personality and Social Psychology, 55*, 599–605.

Baron, J. (1988). *Thinking and deciding*. New York: Cambridge University Press.

Baron, J., Granato, L., Spranca, M., & Teubal, E. (1993). Decision-making biases in children and early adolescence: Exploratory studies. *Merrill-Palmer Quarterly, 39*, 22–46.

Berg, C. A. (1989). Knowledge of strategies for dealing with everyday problems from childhood through adolescence. *Developmental Psychology, 25*, 607–618.

Berg, C. A., & Calderone, K. S. (1994). The role of problem interpretations in understanding the development of everyday problem solving. In R. J. Sternberg & R. K. Wagner (Eds.), *Mind in context: Interactionist perspectives on human intelligence* (pp. 105–132). New York: Cambridge University Press.

Berg, C. A., & Klaczynski, P. (1996). Practical intelligence and problem solving: Searching for perspectives. In F. Blanchard-Fields & T. M. Hess (Eds.), *Perspectives on cognition in adulthood and aging* (pp. 323–357). New York: McGraw-Hill.

Berg, C. A., Meegan, S. P., & Klaczynski, P. (1999). Age and experiential differences in strategy generation and information requests for solving everyday problems. *International Journal of Behavioral Development, 23*, 615–639.

Berg, C. A., Meegan, S. P., & Strough, J. (1997, April). Practical problem solving in the school context: Do perceptions accurately reflect behavior? In C. Berg (Chair), *The role of intelligence, representations, and motivation in everyday problem solving across the life span*. Presented at the meeting of Society for Research in Child Development, Washington, DC.

Berg, C. A., & Sternberg, R. J. (1992). Adults' conceptions of intelligence across the life span. *Psychology and Aging, 7*, 221–231.

Berg, C. A., Strough, J., Calderone, K. S., Meegan, S. P., & Sansone, C. (1997). The social context of planning and preventing everyday problems from occurring. In S. L. Friedman & E. K. Scholnick (Eds.), *Why, how, and when do we plan? The developmental psychology of planning* (pp. 209–236). Mahwah, NJ: Lawrence Erlbaum Associates.

Berg, C. A., Strough, J., Calderone, K. S., Sansone, C., & Weir, C. (1998). The role of problem definitions in understanding age and context effects on strategies for solving everyday problems. *Psychology and Aging, 5*, 334–370.

Berry, J. W. (1966). Temne and Eskimo perceptual skills. *International Journal of Psychology, 1*, 207–229.

Berry, J. W. (1984). Towards a universal psychology of cognitive competence. *International Journal of Psychology, 19*, 335–361.

Biddell, T. R., & Fischer, K. W. (1992). Beyond the stage debate: Action, structure, and variability in Piagetian theory and research. In R. J. Sternberg & C. A. Berg (Eds.), *Intellectual Development* (pp. 100–140). Cambridge, England: Cambridge University Press.

Blanchard-Fields, F., Chen, Y., & Norris, L. (1997). Everyday problem solving across the life span: Influence of domain specificity and cognitive appraisal. *Psychology and Aging, 12*, 684–693.

Blanchard-Fields, F., Chen, Y., Schocke, M., & Hertzog, C. (1998). Evidence for content-specificity of causal attributions across the adult life span. *Aging, Neuropsychology and Cognition, 5*, 241–263.

Brainerd, C. J., & Gordon, L. L. (1994). Development of verbatim and gist memory for numbers. *Developmental Psychology, 30*, 163–177.

Brown, A., Bransford, J., Ferrara, R. A., & Campione, J. C. (1983). Learning, remembering, and understanding. In J. H. Flavell & E. M. Markman (Eds.), *Handbook of child psychology: Vol. 3. Cognitive Development* (pp. 77–166). New York: Wiley.

Campbell, J. D., Trapnell, P. D., Heine, S. J., Katz, I. M., Lavallee, L. F., & Lehman, D. R. (1996). Self-concept clarity: Measurement, personality correlates, and cultural boundaries. *Journal of Personality and Social Psychology, 70*, 141–156.

Carraher, T. N., Carraher, D., & Schliemann, A. D. (1985). Mathematics in the streets and in the schools. *British Journal of Developmental Psychology, 3*, 21–29.

Ceci, S. J. (1990). *On intelligence more or less*. Englewood Cliffs, NJ: Prentice-Hall.

Ceci, S. J., & Liker, J. (1986). Academic and nonacademic intelligence: An experimental separation. In R. J. Sternberg & R. K. Wagner (Eds.), *Practical intelligence: Nature and origins of competence in the everyday world* (pp. 119–142). New York: Cambridge University Press.

Ceci, S. J., & Roazzi, A. (1994). The effects of context on cognition: Postcards from Brazil. In R. J. Sternberg & R. K. Wagner (Eds.), *Mind in context: Interactionist perspectives on human intelligence* (pp. 74–101). New York: Cambridge University Press.

Chen, S., & Chaiken, S. (1999). The heuristic-systematic model in its broader context. In S. Chaiken & Y. Trope (Eds.), *Dual process theories in social psychology* (pp. 73–96). New York: Guilford Press.

Cornelius, S. W., & Caspi, A. (1987). Everyday problem solving in adulthood and old age. *Psychology and Aging, 2,* 144–153.

Denes-Raj, V., & Epstein, S. (1994). Conflict between intuitive and rational processing: When people behave against their better judgment. *Journal of Personality and Social Psychology, 66,* 819–829.

Denney, N. W., & Pearce, K. A. (1989). A developmental study of practical problem solving in adults. *Psychology and Aging, 4,* 438–442.

Epstein, S. (1994). Integration of the cognitive and psychodynamic unconscious. *American Psychologist, 49,* 709–724.

Epstein, S., Lipson, A., Holstein, C., & Huh, E. (1992). Irrational reactions to negative outcomes: Evidence for two conceptual systems. *Journal of Personality and Social Psychology, 62,* 328–339.

Evans, J. B. St. T. (1989). *Bias in human reasoning: Causes and consequences.* London: Routledge.

Evans, J. B. St. T. (1996). Deciding before you think: Relevance and reasoning in the selection task. *British Journal of Psychology, 87,* 223–240.

Evans, J. B. St. T., & Over, D. E. (1996). *Reasoning and rationality.* Hove, England: Psychology Press.

Folkman, S., Lazarus, R. S., Pimley, S., & Novacek, J. (1987). Age differences in stress and coping processes. *Psychology and Aging, 2,* 171–184.

Frisch, D. (1993). Reasons for framing effects. *Organization Behavior and Human Decision Processes, 54,* 399–429.

Gelman, R., & Baillargeon, R. (1983). A review of some Piagetian concepts. In P. H. Mussen (Series Ed.) & J. Flavell & E. M. Markman (Vol. Eds.), *Handbook of child psychology: Vol. 3. Cognitive development* (pp. 167–230). New York: Wiley.

Gladwin, T. (1970). *East is a big bird.* Cambridge, MA: Belknap Press.

Heckhausen, J., & Schulz, R. (1995). A life-span theory of control. *Psychological Review, 102,* 284–304.

Irvine, S. H. (1970). Affect and construct-across-cultural check on theories of intelligence. *Journal of Social Psychology, 80,* 23–30.

Irvine, S. H., & Berry, J. W. (1988). The abilities of mankind: A reevaluation. In S. H. Irvine & J. W. Berry (Eds.), *Human abilities in cultural context* (pp. 3–59). New York: Cambridge University Press.

Kahneman, D., & Tversky, B. (1972). Subjective probability: A judgement of representativeness. *Cognitive Psychology, 3,* 430–454.

Klaczynski, P. A. (1994). Cognitive development in context: An investigation of practical problem solving and developmental tasks. *Journal of Youth and Adolescence, 23,* 141–168.

Klaczynski, P. A. (1997). Bias in adolescents' everyday reasoning and its relationships with intellectual ability, personal theories, and self-serving motivation. *Developmental Psychology, 33,* 273–283.

Klaczynski, P. A. (2000). Motivated scientific reasoning biases, epistemological beliefs, and theory polarization: A two-process approach to adolescent cognition. *Child Development, 71,* 1347–1366.

Klaczynski, P. A. (2001). Framing effects on adolescent task representations, analytic and heuristic processing, and decision making: Implications for the normative-descriptive gap. *Journal of Applied Developmental Psychology, 22,* 289–309.

Klaczynski, P. A., & Fauth, J. (1997). Developmental differences in memory-based intrusions and self-serving statistical reasoning biases. *Merrill-Palmer Quarterly, 43,* 539–566.

Klaczynski, P. A., & Gordon, D. H. (1996a). Goal-directed everyday problem solving: Motivational and general ability influences on adolescent statistical reasoning. *Child Development, 67,* 2873–2891.

Klaczynski, P. A., & Gordon, D. H. (1996b). Self-serving influences on adolescents' evaluations of belief-relevant evidence. *Journal of Experimental Child Psychology, 62,* 317–339.

Klaczynski, P. A., Laipple, J. S., & Jurden, F. H. (1992). Educational context differences in practical problem solving during adolescence. *Merrill-Palmer Quarterly, 38,* 417–438.

Klaczynski, P. A., & Narasimham, G. (1998a). Problem representations as mediators of adolescent deductive reasoning. *Developmental Psychology, 34,* 865–881.

Klaczynski, P. A., & Narasimham, G. (1998b). The development of self-serving reasoning biases: Ego-protective versus cognitive explanations. *Developmental Psychology, 34,* 175–187.

Klaczynski, P. A., & Reese, H. W. (1991). Educational trajectory and "action orientation": Grade and track differences. *Journal of Youth and Adolescence, 20,* 441–462.

Klaczynski, P. A., & Robinson, B. (2000). Personal theories, intellectual ability, and epistemological beliefs: Adult age differences in everyday reasoning biases. *Psychology and Aging, 15,* 400–416.

Kreitler, S., & Kreitler, H. (1986). Development of probability thinking in children 5 to 12 years old. *Cognitive Development, 1,* 365–390.

Kuhn, D. (1993). Connecting scientific and informal reasoning. *Merrill-Palmer Quarterly, 39,* 74–103.

Kuhn, D., Amsel, E., & O'Loughlin, M. (1988). *The development of scientific thinking skills.* Orlando, FL: Academic Press.

Kuhn, D., Garcia-Mila, M., Zohar, A., & Andersen, C. (1995). Strategies of knowledge acquisition. *Monographs for the Society for Research in Child Development, 60* (serial no. 245).

Laboratory of Comparative Human Cognition (1982). Culture and intelligence. In R. J. Sternberg (Ed.), *Handbook of human intelligence* (pp. 642–719). Cambridge, England: Cambridge University Press.

Labouvie-Vief, G., Chiodo, L. M., Goguen, L. A., Diehl, M., & Orwoll, L. (1995). Representations of self across the life span. *Psychology and Aging, 10,* 404–415.

Laipple, J. S. (1991). *Problem solving in young and old adulthood: The role of task interpretation.* Unpublished doctoral dissertation, West Virginia University.

Lave, J. (1988). *Cognition in practice: Mind, mathematics, and culture in everyday life.* Cambridge, England: Cambridge University Press.

Lave, J., Murtaugh, M., & de la Rocha, O. (1984). The dialectic of arithmetic in grocery shopping. In B. Rogoff & J. Lave (Eds.), *Everyday cognition: Its development in social context* (pp. 67–94). Cambridge, NA: Harvard University Press.

Lazarus, R. S., & Folkman, S. (1984). *Stress, appraisal, and coping.* New York: Springer.

Markus, H. R., & Wurf, E. (1987). The dynamic self-concept: A social psychological perspective. *Annual Review of Psychology, 38,* 299–337.

Mischel, W. (1984). Convergences and challenges in the search for consistency. *American Psychologist, 39,* 351–364.

Murtaugh, M. (1985). The practice of arithmetic by American grocery shoppers. *Anthropology and Education Quarterly,* Fall.

Neisser, U. (1979). The concept of intelligence. In R. J. Sternberg & D. K. Detterman (Eds.), *Human intelligence* (pp. 179–189). Norwood, NJ: Ablex.

Nunes, T., Schliemann, A. D., & Carraher, D. W. (1993). *Street mathematics and school mathematics.* Cambridge, England: Cambridge University Press.

Okagaki, L., & Sternberg, R. J. (1993). Parental beliefs and children's school performance. *Child Development, 64,* 36–56.

Perkins, D. N., Jay, E., & Tishman, S. (1993). Beyond abilities: A dispositional theory of thinking. *Merrill-Palmer Quarterly, 39,* 1–21.

Perret-Clermont, A. N. (1980). *Social interaction and cognitive development in children.* London: Academic Press.

Reuning, H. (1988). Testing bushmen in the central Kalahari. In S. H. Irvine & J. W. Berry (Eds.), *Human abilities in the cultural context* (pp. 453–486). New York: Cambridge University Press.

Reyna, V. F., & Brainerd, C. J. (1995). Fuzzy-trace theory: Some foundational issues. *Learning and Individual Differences, 7*, 145–162.

Reyna, V. F., Lloyd, F. J., & Brainerd, C. J. (in press). Memory, development, and rationality: An integrative theory of judgment and decision making. In S. Schneider & J. Shanteau (Eds.), *Emerging perspectives on decision research* (pp.). Cambridge University Press.

Reyna, V. F., & Brainerd, C. J. (1995). Fuzzy-trace theory: An interim synthesis. *Learning and Individual Differences, 7*, 1–75.

Rhodewalt, F. T. (1986). Self-presentation and the phenomenal self: On the stability and malleability of self-conceptions. In R. F. Baumeister (Ed.), *Public self and private self* (pp. 117–142). New York: Springer.

Roberts, B. W., & Donahue, E. M. (1994). One personality, multiple selves: Integrating personality and social roles. *Journal of Personality, 62*, 199–218.

Rogoff, B. (1982). Integrating context and cognitive development. In M. E. Lamb & A. L. Brown (Eds.), *Advances in developmental psychology* (Vol. 2, pp. 125–170). Hillsdale, NJ: Lawrence Erlbaum Associates.

Rogoff, B., Gauvain, M., & Gardner, W. (1987). Children's adjustment of plans to circumstances. In S. L. Friedman, E. K. Scholnick, & R. R. Cocking (Eds.), *Blueprints for thinking* (pp. 303–320). Cambridge, England: Cambridge University Press.

Rogoff, B., & Lave, J. (Eds.). (1984). *Everyday cognition: Its development in social context.* Cambridge, MA: Harvard University Press.

Sansone, C., & Berg, C. A. (1993). Adapting to the environment across the life span: Different process or different inputs? *International Journal of Behavioral Development, 16*, 215–241.

Saltzstein, H. D. (1994). The relation between moral judgment and behavior: A social-cognitive and decision-making analysis. *Human Development, 37*, 299–312.

Scribner, S. (1984). Studying working intelligence. In B. Rogoff (Ed.), *Everyday cognition: Its development in social context.* Cambridge, MA: Harvard University Press.

Scribner, S. (1986). Thinking in action: Some characteristics of paractical thought. In R. J. Sternberg & R. Wagner (Eds.), *Practical intelligence: Origins of competence in the everyday world* (pp. 143–162). New York: Cambridge University Press.

Siegler, R. S. (1996). *Emerging minds: The process of change in children's thinking.* New York: Oxford University Press.

Siegler, R. S., & Richards, D. D. (1982). The development of intelligence. In R. J. Sternberg (Ed.), *Handbook of human intelligence* (pp. 897–971). New York: Cambridge University Press.

Sinnott, J. D. (1989). A model for solution of ill-structured problems: implications for everyday and abstract problem solving. In J. D. Sinnott (Ed.), *Everyday problem solving: Theory and applications* (pp. 72–79). New York: Praeger.

Spivack, G., & Shure, M. B. (1982). The cognition of social adjustment: Interpersonal cognitive problem solving thinking. In B. Lahey & A. E. Kazdin (Eds.), *Advances in clinical child psychology* (Vol. 5, pp.). New York: Plenum Press.

Stanovich, K. E. (1999). *Who is rational? Studies of individual differences in reasoning.* Mahwah, NJ: Lawrence Erlbaum Associates.

Stanovich, K. E., & West, R. F. (1997). Reasoning independently of prior belief and individual differences in actively open-minded thinking. *Journal of Educational Psychology, 89*, 342–357.

Stanovich, K. E., & West, R. F. (1999). Discrepancies between normative and descriptive models of decision making and the understanding/acceptance principle. *Cognitive Psychology, 38*, 349–385.

Sternberg, R. J. (1984). A contextual view of the nature of intelligence. In P. S. Fry (Ed.), *Changing conceptions of intelligence and intellectual functioning: Current theory and research* (pp. 7–34). Amsterdam: North-Holland.

Sternberg, R. J., & Berg, C. A. (1986). Definitions of intelligence: A quantitative comparison of the 1921 and 1986 symposia. In R. J. Sternberg & D. K. Detterman (Eds.), *What is intelligence? Contemporary viewpoints on its nature and definition* (pp. 155–162). Norwood, NJ: Ablex.

Sternberg, R. J., Conway, B. E., Ketron, J. L., & Bernstein, M. (1981). People's conceptions of intelligence. *Journal of Personality and Social Psychology, 41,* 37–55.

Sternberg, R. J., & Wagner, R. K. (Eds.). (1986). *Practical intelligence.* New York: Cambridge University Press.

Stevenson, H. W., & Lee, S. (1990). Contexts of achievement. *Monographs of the Society for Research in Child Development, 55,* (1-2, Serial No. 221), 1–123.

Wagner, R. K., & Sternberg, R. J. (1986). Tacit knowledge and intelligence in the everyday world. In R. J. Sternberg & R. K. Wagner (Eds.), *Practical intelligence.* New York: Cambridge University Press.

Wason, P. C. (1966). Reasoning. In B. Foss (Ed.), *New horizons in Psychology.* Harmondworth: Penguin Books.

Yussen, S. R., & Kane, P. T. (1983). Children's ideas about intellectual ability. In *The child's construction of social inequality.* New York: Academic Press.

Part VII

SYSTEMS APPROACH

g: Knowledge, Speed, Strategies, or Working-Memory Capacity? A Systems Perspective

Patrick C. Kyllonen
Educational Testing Service

PRELIMINARIES: DOES *g* EXIST?

At one level, it is difficult to understand what all the fuss is about. *g* can be thought of as simply a label for the empirical phenomenon of "positive manifold."[1] This is the ubiquitous finding of positive correlations among scores on tests of cognitive ability, first noted by Spearman (1904). Take any set of cognitive tests, and the correlations among them will all be positive, unless there is something very odd about the sample of test takers (e.g., sample too small, test takers prescreened to be identical in ability level) or the tests (e.g., unreliable, much too hard or too easy for the group of test takers).

Is this an interesting finding? Yes! First, it is not some kind or artifact of correlations, something about correlations that just has to be. As evidence, consider that cognitive test scores do not correlate positively with every human performance or expression. They do not correlate with personality scales, for example (with the one exception of the "openness" or "intellect" factor). Nor do they typically correlate with perception measures,

---

[1]More precisely, though without altering the basic argument, *g* is the name of a hypothetical factor in a particular model of these correlations. Consider that *n* tests require *n* [*n* − 1] / 2 correlations to describe all their interrelationships. By positing a hypothetical factor, let's call it *g*, those *n* [*n* − 1] / 2 correlations can be accounted for by only *n* correlations ("factor loadings"), and thus the model positing a *g* factor is a more parsimonious description of the correlation matrix. "Centrality" is another description of an analogous phenomenon from the multidimensional scaling and clustering literature (Tversky & Hutchinson, 1986).

such as sensory acuity, flicker fusion, or sensitivity, as has been known since Galton's time. But, even though cognitive measures do not correlate with everything, they do correlate with a lot of things, namely each other. This makes positive manifold a very general finding, with broad reaching implications. A considerable amount of important human activity is cognitive in nature. Thus, scores on cognitive tests predict important human activities such as performance in education, training, and on the job (e.g., Ree & Earles, 1994), as well as a lot of other places (Brand, 1987).

Another important point is that positive manifold, and therefore the existence of g, is not dependent on any particular statistical technique, other than some measure of association between scores, such as the correlation coefficient. One does not need factor analysis to show positive manifold. It certainly can be that besides positive manifold there is additional organization or structure in a correlation matrix of test scores. Methods such as factor analysis, multidimensional scaling, and clustering can be useful in identifying such additional structure. And these methods may be helpful in more precisely quantifying g, and in identifying variability in the degree to which tests reflect or measure g. But, these are simply refinements. The existence of g per se is not affected by these refinements.

If g exists, in some sense, an important question is, what is it? The fact that cognitive tests correlate positively does not tell us much, if anything at all, about why they correlate positively. Nor does it provide much insight into the true generality of g, which is the topic of this book. We can conduct studies showing how much of the person-to-person variability in a wide variety of performance contexts can be accounted for by g, as many have (e.g., Ree & Earles, 1994; Schmidt & Hunter, 1998). But without knowing what g is, we cannot have much confidence in the underlying generality of these kinds of findings. We cannot know, for example, whether cultural changes, such as transforming from a paper-based to a web-based economy, increasing nutrition levels, or providing education to uniform curriculum standards will modify these findings, because we will not know the source of these findings in the first place.

THE SYSTEMS PERSPECTIVE

> In the most general sense system means a configuration of parts or components joined together in a web of relationships.
> —Instructional System Designers, Inc.

This chapter reviews one particular approach to addressing the question of what g is: the systems approach. The basic idea is this. Cognitive psychology has settled on a view, or framework, characterizing humans as information-processing systems. What this means is that any cognitive activity, such as reading a text passage, or learning a programming technique by studying examples, can be analyzed by considering the flow and transformation of information as it passes through the human mental apparatus. Much of cognitive psychology can be seen as an attempt to define the various processing stages and storage operations, and the various forms information takes as it is processed during the course of human learning, problem solving, and performance.

Over the years, cognitive psychologists have proposed general models of this process to account for the wide range of empirical phenomena characterizing the difficulties people have in solving various kinds of problems, learning various kinds of materials, or performing various kinds of tasks. As would be expected, the scope of many of the earlier models was modest, focusing on a relatively small class of tasks, such as memory (e.g., Atkinson & Schiffrin, 1968). Over time the scope expanded to include learning and problem solving (e.g., Anderson, 1983, Newell, 1990) and, more recently, dual-task and perceptual-motor performance (e.g., Byrne & Anderson, 1998; Kieras & Meyer, 1997). The scope of such models, which have become so complex they are now referred to as "architectures" (i.e., schemes from which models for particular tasks can be built), is now such that they encompass just about the entire domain of cognitive and even psychomotor tasks.

How does all this relate to the study of g? As far back as Cronbach (1957), observers have noted that scientific psychology has distributed itself into two independent disciplines, the correlational and the experimental. Whereas the existence of g is an assertion emanating from the correlational tradition, human information-processing models and architectures have developed out of the experimental tradition. That is, the data such models have been formulated to account for have been exclusively experimental data, typically contrasting average performance levels of participants on various experimentally manipulated tasks, without regard to individual differences in performance levels.

One way to *explain* something, or to say what something is, is to recast it in terms of another system, for example, one developed on the basis of other data, using other methodologies. Consider g. It can be understood, as suggested earlier, as simply the observation of positive manifold in a correlation matrix of cognitive test scores. But there is a certain tautological quality to this statement that makes it less than satisfying. One is reminded of Boring's (1923) oft-cited proclamation that "intelligence is what the tests test" (p. 5). However, if we can define g in terms of the components or parameters of another system, the system that gave rise to cognitive information-processing models and architectures, we will have gained insight into what g is. This is the purpose of the chapter—to explain g, by examining it from an alternative perspective, a systems perspective.

There is not a single systems perspective or approach with respect to the study of human intelligence. Rather, there have been various perspectives. In this chapter we sort those into three. A "cognitive components" approach, pioneered by Sternberg (1977), is based on what is essentially a detailed step-by-step task analysis of performance on cognitive test items. The idea is to identify the various processing steps examinees engage in, and to treat these as new "ability variables." One can then correlate these new ability variables with g, for example, as a way of gaining insight into what g is. A second approach, "components of cognitive architectures," is one my colleagues and I (Kyllonen, 1995), and a group from Mannheim University (Wittman & Süß, 1999) have used. It is based on developing measures of the major components of information-processing models. These measures then are indicators of proficiency with respect to the various architecture components, and one can correlate these components with g to determine which component or combination aligns most closely with g. A third, more recent entry, is a "parameters of cognitive architectures" approach used by Daily, Lovett, and Reder (1998) based on Anderson's (1993) ACT–R model. The approach involves examining parameters from the ACT–R model, and correlating those parameters to external criteria. This approach differs from the componential approach in that the models from which the parameters are derived are very general models, designed to accommodate essentially all cognitive tasks, rather than a small, specific set of tasks, such as analogies tasks. The third approach differs from the second one in that the model parameters, rather than proficiency scores measured on major model components, are the new ability variables.

These three approaches are best characterized not as warring but as complimentary camps. In current work there is considerable blending of methods and concepts and acknowledgment of findings from all three approaches. Still, the approaches are distinct enough that it is useful to review them, and particularly for the purposes of this chapter, their conclusions regarding g, separately.

The approaches are perhaps best illustrated in reference to the analysis of an interesting cognitive task, one that could be considered similar to what might be found on general aptitude batteries, such as the Armed Services Vocational Aptitude Battery, but at the same time, is more challenging. A more difficult task may make it easier for the reader to appreciate the issues of strategy selection, the role of knowledge, and the importance of working-memory capacity in task performance.

A Quantitative Word Problem

Consider the following problem taken from the Quantitative section of the Graduate Record Examination (GRE; Educational Testing Service, 1995, p. 1072):

If t tablets cost c cents, then at this rate how many cents will 5 tablets cost? (A) $5ct$, (B) $5c/t$, (C) $c/5t$, (D) $5t/c$, (E) $t/5c$

There are many different strategies for tackling this problem, but we can roughly sort them into three categories: "remembering," "figuring it out," and "doing a little bit of both." A step-by-step description of how the problem could be solved using each of the three strategies is presented in Table 15.1.

It is clear that the remembering strategy is the shortest and most reliable, and therefore would be an attractive strategy choice. The difficulty is that it requires knowledge of a particular problem form (the "if x things cost y amount, how much do z things cost? zy/x" problem form). The problem is difficult because many examinees do not possess such knowledge, or, if they do, do not recognize the problem as requiring it, due to the mismatch between the form of the problem in their memory, and the form of the problem on the test. In either event they cannot use this strategy, and must resort to the longer, and more unreliable *mixed* or *figure it out* strategies. Also note that while applying this strategy minimizes the memory burden, compared to using the other strategies, there still is a working-memory demand. In particular, "doing the substitutions" (Step 3) is unlikely to be a completely automatic process, but instead is one requiring the examinee to maintain one (or more) substitutions in memory (e.g., $x = t$), while performing the other substitutions.

The mixed strategy requires partial knowledge. As can be seen, the examinee recognizes the problem's requirement for the cost formula (total cost = number of items × cost per item) and after a false start, the cost-per-item formula (cost-per-item = total cost / number of items). (The fact that these formulas are simply rearrangments of the same terms does not preclude their being stored separately in memory.) Problem solution also involves combining these two formulas, which is a tricky step in itself, in that it increases the working-memory burden. Thus, this strategy is bound to lead to more errors, as it could become easy to forget the results of one of the substitutions, while doing the others.

The figure-it-out strategy is a kind of last resort when one does not possess knowledge of the formulas being asked for. One basically must figure out the formulas on one's own. As is typical in novel problem-solving situations, the first step is to recognize that one does not know "the answer," and then to call upon one's storehouse of very general problem-solving heuristics as a way of getting started. In this case, the examinee thinks to substitute in constants for variables, which is an instance of a kind of "simplify the problem" heuristic. The choice of small numbers that divide into each other evenly is another example of this kind of heuristic. Breaking the problem down into parts (the *if* and *then* parts) is still another exam-

TABLE 15.1
Three Strategies for Solving Quantitative Word Problems

Problem

"If t tablets cost c cents, then at this rate how many cents will 5 tablets cost?
(A) $5ct$, (B) $5c/t$, (C) $c/5t$, (D) $5t/c$, (E) $t/5c$"

"Remembering" Strategy

---

1. You read the problem statement, and recognize a certain form from the words, "If . . . then," "cost" etc.
2. You recognize it as an instance of the, "If x things cost y amount, then how much will z things cost?" problem, to which you know the answer is "zy/x."
3. You do the substitutions ($x = t$; $y = c$; $z = 5$), and out pops the answer, "$5c/t$."

"Mixed Strategy"

---

1. You spot some key words in the problem statement, such as "If . . . then," "cost," and the variables, "c" and "t."
2. You therefore recognize this as a particular type of problem, the "cost" problem.
3. You know, from experience in mathematics, or from studying test preparation materials, that the solution to cost problems is "cost = number of items × cost per item."
4. You plug in the variables and numbers and get "cost = $5c$."
5. You look through the choices and there is no "$5c$."
6. So you reread the problem, and you notice that the cost per item is not really "c", but instead, something involving both "t" and "c."
7. You might right away recognize the "cost-per-item" rule, which is that the cost-per-item = total cost / the number of items.
8. You plug the problem specifics into this memorized formula to get cost-per-item = c/t.
9. Now you can go back to the "cost" formula, and plug this answer back in, to get, $5c/t$.

"Figuring-It-Out" Strategy

---

1. Reading the statement, you realize you do not know how to categorize the problem, let alone the formula needed to solve it.
2. Therefore, you decide to restate the problem to yourself with real numbers rather than variables, because you do know that substituting real numbers for variables is a generally useful problem-solving heuristic.
3. You plug in some "plausible numbers" (small numbers, numbers you might actually use in such a problem in the real world), by restating the problem to yourself, "If 3 tablets cost 7 cents, then at this rate, how many cents will 5 tablets cost."
4. While looking at the problem statement, you divide 3 into 7, and realize that the answer is not an integer. You also try to divide 7 into 3, and you realize that that answer is not an integer, either.
5. You decide that it will be easier to work with integers, and that you will therefore have to find numbers that divide into each other as integers.
6. You try 4 and 12, knowing that they divide into each other, and you say to yourself, "If 4 tablets cost 12 cents, then at this rate, how many cents will 5 tablets cost?"
7. You focus attention on the "If" clause and say to yourself, "If 4 tablets cost 12 cents, that would mean that each tablet costs 12/4 = 3 cents."
8. While remembering that each tablet costs 3 cents, you turn your attention to the "then" part of the statement, and say to yourself, "how many cents will 5 tablets cost?"

(Continued)

420

TABLE 15.1
(Continued)

"Figuring-It-Out" Strategy (Continued)

---

9. You say to yourself, if each tablet costs 3 cents, then 5 tablets would cost 3 × 5 = 15 cents.

10. You review the alternative responses, and realize that knowing the answer, per se, is not helpful for solving the problem, because the problem is asking you to provide the formula, not the answer (besides, your numbers are "made up" not from the problem statement).

11. You try to recall what steps you just went through, and remember that you first focused on the "If" part of the statement, and you said to yourself, "If 4 tablets cost 12 cents, then . . . each tablet must cost 3 cents, so it was 12 / 4."

12. You map variables from the problem statement onto 12 and 4 (12 = c; 4 = t), and that gives you c/t.

13. While keeping "c/t" in mind, mentally rehearsing, or writing it down, you recall that you next attended to the "Then" part of the statement, which was "how many cents will 5 tablets cost?"

14. While still rehearsing "c/t", and realizing that 5 must be part of the answer, as must be "c/t," you search through the alternatives, and realize that the only one you can eliminate is "(A) 5ct", (and perhaps "(C)" and "(E)", which have "5" in the denominator). That is not enough uncertainty reduction, and so you decide to go ahead and try to continue solving the problem.

15. You remember that you're remembering "c/t", and you remember that you're focusing on the "Then" part of the problem, which is "how many cents will 5 tablets cost?"

16. You remember that what "c/t" stood for was the cost for one item, so you realize that because the problem is asking for the cost of 5 items, 5 must therefore be multiplied with c/t, giving "5c/t."

---

ple. Note also that the strategy outlined here is quite long, compared to the others. There are many opportunities for missteps, forgotten results from previous steps, and losing one's place in the problem solving sequence (i.e., losing track of the goals one is working on).

Let's review what this informal analysis of performance of a somewhat complex cognitive task tells us. First, the task itself is almost certainly a good measure of *g*. For one thing, mathematical reasoning tests are often included in general aptitude batteries, such as the ASVAB or GATB. For another, rate problems, and cost problems, such as this one are typically included as items in such tests. Second, we can see that there are several potential sources of problem difficulty, and any of these therefore could be candidates for telling us what *g* is. There may be others, but what appear to stand out are knowledge, strategies, and working memory capacity.

g could be equated with knowledge. That is, individuals vary in the knowledge they bring to a task—some bring more, some less—and this variance could be what produces positive manifold. It seems clear that the best solution strategy is the first one, in that it is shortest, and therefore likely to be both the quickest executed, and the one least prone to errors. It also is the strategy that happens to depend on having the most specialized knowledge. Extrapolating from this example, one could imagine that a person with lots of specialized knowledge of this type (e.g., rate problems, specific algebraic manipulations) would do very well on mathematical reasoning problems. And it could be that performance of problems in other realms, such as matrices, or series problems, could also be seen as being facilitated by having some kind of specialized knowledge that the problem is calling upon. This is not to say that such problems demand such knowledge. As can be seen from the Table 15.1 example, one can still solve the problem without specialized knowledge. It is just that having such knowledge will tend to increase performance levels.

   g could be equated with strategies. Some examinees come into the testing situation with better strategies at their disposal, and this could be what produces positive manifold. Assuming that the remembering strategy is the best, and the figure-it-out strategy is the worst, one could argue that strategic choice drives performance on this task and, more generally, on many kinds of intelligence test items. We might distinguish three kinds of strategic choices. One is driven by knowledge, or ability, another is more capricious, and a third is the "trick"—driven by knowledge, but knowledge that is easily instilled (e.g., teaching mnemonic strategies for a free-recall task). The choice of the remembering versus figure-it-out strategies is driven by knowledge. One can imagine other strategic choices driven by abilities, such as working-memory capacity. For these situations we would conclude that strategy choice is determined by ability—strategy would not be an explanation of *g*, but a side effect. There are also some examples of capricious strategy choices in Table 15.1. One is looking at the alternatives before completing the solution to the problem (mixture strategy, Step 5; and figure-it-out strategy, Step 15). There are no examples of tricks available for the item in Table 15.1, and for good reason. The minimization of the possibility of tricks is built into the design of large-scale high-stakes tests, such as the GRE.

   g could be equated with working-memory capacity. All three strategies include steps requiring information to be maintained in working memory, while other processing is occurring. A good example is the substitions (Step 3 in the remembering strategy, Steps 4 and 8 in the mixed strategy, and Steps 7, 9, and 12 in the figure-it-out strategy). Another example is, "remember the solution to one part of the problem while trying to work out the solution to another part of the problem" (Step 8 in the mixed strategy; Step 8 in the figure it out strategy). And in all three strategies, particularly the latter two, the examinee is constantly having to keep track of what subgoal is being worked on, and what subgoal is to be accomplished next once the current subgoal is completed.

There are still other possibilities, "dark-horse candidates." Speed is one—imagine an examinee so mentally quick that he or she was able to execute the seemingly laborious 16-step figure-it-out strategy in less time than someone else might execute the 3-step remembering strategy. Learning ability is another one. Imagine being able to learn while doing the figure-it-out strategy so that the next time a similar problem is encountered one would be able to employ the remembering strategy.

This informal analysis of what might be involved in solving cognitive test items is a good preview of the candidates for the meaning of g. Some seem more likely than others. For example, working memory seems the most important, but speed seems less so. Knowledge is obviously important, but it's not clear that it would replace g, because it seems that the character of knowledge being called upon is domain specific. Strategies seem to be incidental to the process—driven by the possession of knowledge, rather than driving the problem solving. But this is an informal analysis. We now turn our attention toward what the various systems approaches tell us about the nature of g.

COGNITIVE COMPONENTS AND THE ANALYSIS
OF TEST ITEMS

> Rather than looking to learning or physiological theory for some correlate of intelligence, I should like to focus attention on intellectual activity itself. . . . The simplest and most direct approach, it seems, is to begin with the specific behaviors involved in responding to items on intelligence tests.
> —Estes (1974, pp. 742–743)

> I foresee our compiling a relatively small catalogue of information-processing components that in various combinations account for performance on tasks requiring intelligence
> —Sternberg (1978, p. 56)

> The effort to dislodge g has been less than successful.
> —Brody (1992, p. 125)

During the late 1970s there was a flurry of information-processing analyses of cognitive tasks, at least partly stimulated by Sternberg's (1977) seminal book on componential analysis. These included examinations of reading (Fredericksen, 1982), mental rotation (Cooper, 1976), analogies (Mullholland, Pellegrino, & Glaser, 1980), deductive reasoning (Egan & Grimes-Farrow, 1982), and numerous other tasks that were essentially intelligence tests. The reason for the high level of activity was the belief, widely shared at the time, that information-processing analyses would serve as a key to unlock the mysteries of intelligence. Individual differences psychologist saw "an almost totally new methodology" appearing "to offer a greater possibility of isolating processes than traditional factor-analytic methodology" (Carroll, 1978). Experimental psychologists (e.g., Underwood, 1975) saw an opportunity to validate theoretical constructs using individual differences as a litmus test. The testing community, particularly, the military testing community, saw an opportunity to revamp extant notions of intelligence testing, and replace dated conceptions of aptitude with a new, more theoretically grounded concept of information-processing proficiencies. For example, Marshall Farr, the director of the individual-differences program at the Office of Naval Research, funded much of this research with the expectation that it might lead to changes in the military personnel selection and classification system.

Method

There are many varieties of componential analysis, but it is useful to consider them all as being defined by several essential features. First, one begins with the task of interest, say an intelligence test, or a quantitative word problem task, as shown in Table 15.1. Next, one creates a simpler variant of that task. For example, Sternberg created analogies problems that allowed examinees to study parts of the analogy before the full analogy was presented. An example of a simpler variant of the quantitative word problem might be one that replaced constants with variables, for example, "If 10 tablets cost 5 cents, then at this rate how many cents would 20 tablets cost?"

One then computes the difference between performance scores for the two variants, and the result is a component score. These component scores reflect a process, or processing stage, isolated as a result of creating the two task variants. For example, in the analogies case, the process so isolated might be the one of *applying* a relationship (the relationship between A and B, encoded as the result of prior study) to the C and D terms. In the quantitative word problem, the process might be some process associated with using variables, rather than constants. These component (difference) scores (e.g., application, using variables) then can be correlated with other variables, such as *g*. Clearly, the interestingness of such a correlation is related to the meaning and interpretability of the component scores. For example, one may have theoretical reasons for believing that applying relationships (in analogies), or using variables (in quantitative word problems) is an interesting or meaningful component process.

In much of the earlier work, scores were response times. For example, the time taken to solve a full analogy (A:B::C:D) could have subtracted from it the time to solve a partial analogy (one in which one is allowed to study, say, the A:B terms before being presented the full A:B::C:D problem). It is a bit less straightforward but nevertheless possible to compute error scores (e.g., Embretson, 1995), a point we return to later.

There are several ways to compute difference scores in these kinds of studies. One is simple subtraction. However, there are cases when regressing one task's scores on the other's, and taking the residual as the component score is advantageous for conceptual or score reliability reasons (e.g., Donaldson, 1983; Kyllonen, Tirre, & Christal, 1991; Woltz, 1988, 1999).

Findings

Pellegrino and Lyon (1979) and Brody (1992) provided good reviews of some of the early work on componential analysis of ability tests. In general, to make a long story short, the considerable research done did not provide an adequate account of the general factor in terms of elementary components. One somewhat surprising, yet reliable finding was that the component scores did not correlate as highly with the total score or with the general factor as did the "residual" scores (Lohman, 1994). Let us review exactly what this means. In componential analysis, a score (response time, or error rate) is divided into two parts: the isolated component(s), and the rest of the score, the residual. In many contexts (such as Sternberg's [1977] original work on analogies), there can be more than one component, created by more than one partial task, but there is always the component part(s) and the remaining part. It is this remaining part, the residual, that tends to correlate highest with both total task score, and with g.

This finding is instructive. Consider that in the componential approach there are always two tasks, the full task, and the partial task. The component is the difference between the two tasks. That is,

Full task score = partial task score + component score.[2]

And, the typical finding coming out of these analyses is that the correlation between the partial task score (i.e., the residual, or the remaining part) and the full task score is greater than the correlation between the component score and the full task score. There are two reasons this is not surprising, in retrospect. First, the partial task is still a cognitive measure, just as the full task is. The partial task will be easier, but it is still a cognitive task. Because of positive manifold (i.e., g) two cognitive tasks will tend to correlate positively. The component score, on the other hand, is not a cognitive task. In fact, using the regression approach to estimating a compo-

---

[2]I am glossing over a technicality here, which is that slope scores are often used rather than simple differences; but this really has no implications for the argument because slopes are simply averages of a set of difference scores.

nent score, the component is defined as being independent of at least one cognitive task, namely the partial task. Therefore it should not be surprising that the correlation between two cognitive tasks is greater than the correlation between a cognitive task and something defined as independent of a cognitive task.

Second, partial tasks are typically fairly similar to the full tasks, and scores from the two tasks therefore tend to be highly correlated. The reliability of a difference score is dependent on the correlation between scores from the two tasks that produce the difference score. As the correlation between two tasks increases, the reliability of the difference score between them decreases. Therefore, not only should component scores tend to correlate less with total task score, they also should tend to have low reliability, another consistent finding in this literature.

A second problem plaguing these studies was that componential analysts worked on the wrong problems! The intention, remember, was to analyze intelligence tests. However, there was a problem with working on intelligence tests. They tend to be defined by whether people can do them or not (i.e., errors), but componential analysis is tailor made for response times. It is possible to do a componential analysis with errors, but the math is more difficult. Consider (RT is response time, and PC is probability correct):

$$RT \text{ (full task)} = RT \text{ (partial task)} + RT \text{ (component 1)}$$
$$+ RT \text{ (component 2)} + \ldots, \text{ vs.}$$

$$PC \text{ (full task)} = PC \text{ (partial task)} \times PC \text{ (component 1)}$$
$$\times PC \text{ (component 2)} \times \ldots.$$

Multiplication is more difficult to work with than addition. Not only that, but RT scores are continuous, whereas PC scores are binary. That means that standard linear multiple regression, the tool of choice for componential analysis, is not the proper analytic tool for componential analyses of error scores. To deal with this problem, what early componential analysts did was to create tasks that looked like intelligence tests, but were much easier than intelligence tests. The idea was to make them so easy that hardly any errors were committed, and the variability between people would as a result shift from the error score to a response time measure. A problem with this approach of course, is that by doing this, the whole nature of the enterprise changed, as componential analysts were no longer analyzing intelligence tests. Speed and level aspects of performance have long known to be separate—those who can quickly solve easy problems are not necessarily those who can solve the most difficult problems (Lohman, 1988).

Embretson (1995) avoided this problem by developing a multiplicative (to deal with error scores) logistic (to deal with their binary character) componential modeling technique, tailor made to handle error scores. This enabled componential analysis to be applied to the true tasks of interest, intelligence tests. And interestingly, she chose as her target of analysis a task modeled after Raven's Progressive Matrices (via Carpenter, Just, & Schell, 1990), one of the best measures of *g* there is. Further, the substantive topic of her research, a bullseye with respect to the topic of this chapter, was to evaluate the relative importance of working memory and what she called "control processes" in determining matrices task performance. To make matters even better, she avoided still another problem plaguing this line of research, the small sample problem. Unfortunately, the conclusion she reached, that control processes were more important than working-memory capacity in determining performance, is more tenuous than we might wish it to be. The way Embretson set up her design and analysis, working memory was the component process, and control processes was the "residual." As I attempted to demonstrate earlier, this design more or less preordained the conclusion.

In summary, componential analysis has not shed much light on the nature of *g*, per se. This is not to say that it has not proved useful as a technique. To the contrary, the approach has turned out to be one of the lynchpins of item difficulty modeling and item-generation theory; a critical breakthrough for applied testing (Irvine & Kyllonen, 2002). The considerable effort that has gone into componential analysis has provided a wealth of information on the sources of difficulty in cognitive tests. Exploiting this knowledge is already proving invaluable in test item development, both in decreasing costs and in increasing our understanding of what items measure. However, the fundamental problem of componential analysis as a way of understanding g is that an analysis of the difference between two measures of *g* is not the best way to find out about what *g* is.

CORRELATES OF COMPONENTS OF COGNITIVE ARCHITECTURES

> From the scientific point of view we will be on much firmer footing when we try to relate individual differences to a general model of cognition.
> —Hunt, Frost, & Lunneborg (1973, p. 120)

> A consensus information-processing model would be an ideal source from which to hypothesize components.
> —Kyllonen (1995)

In the 1970s, Hunt and colleagues (e.g., Hunt, 1978; Hunt, Frost, & Lunneborg, 1973) proposed a new approach to studying intelligence. They took models from experimental cognitive psychology, computed individuals' scores on tasks giving rise to those models, then correlated those scores with intelligence test scores, an approach subsequently referred to as cognitive correlates (Pellegrino & Glaser, 1979). The cognitive models available at the time tended to be rather narrow in scope, in some cases applying to only a single task. So what resulted was a set of intriguing correlations between information-processing tasks and task parameters and intelligence tests, but without an overarching framework in which to help determine patterns and consistencies.

Some time later cognitive psychologists began expressing disenchantment with the potential for cumulative progress with models designed to accommodate narrow issues, such as memory retrieval or scanning, in isolation (Newell, 1973). This lead to an evolution in cognitive psychology toward increasingly comprehensive modeling systems or frameworks, as exemplified in production system models like SOAR (Newell, 1990), CAPS (Just & Carpenter, 1992), and ACT (Anderson, 1983). This proved fortuitous for intelligence research. These more complex and comprehensive information-processing systems served as a much more fruitful basis from which to posit sources of individual differences, and hence to potentially get closer to an understanding of the nature of g.

Method

There is disagreement in cognitive psychology over the details and implementation, but there is some consensus about broad architectural features of the human information-processing system. One is the distinction made between short-term, or *working memory*, representing the current focus of attention, and *long-term* memory representing the storehouse of knowledge that can be called upon in problem solving and performance. Another is the distinction between two types of long-term memory, *declarative*, which stores facts, and *procedural*, which stores procedures, skills, and automatic processes. A third feature is the time-dependent character of problem solving. To these cognitive features, we can add perceptual (governing the input) and motor (governing the output) processing capabilities.

Figure 15.1 presents an architecture for this "consensus information processing model." People, for example, test examinees, take in information from the environment through the perceptual processing system, which is then temporarily stored in working memory. This triggers the activation of relevant facts and procedures from the two long-term memories, which join the perceptual representation in working memory, and through additional associations new facts and procedures, and perhaps perceptual inputs, shuffle through working memory. At some point a motor response, such as selecting an answer to a test item, is executed. During this information-processing activity declarative and procedural learn-

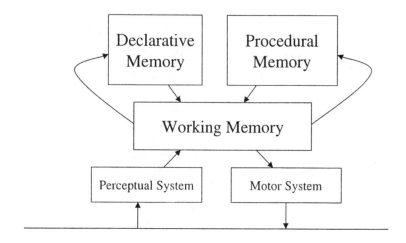

FIG. 15.1. Consensus human information-processing model illustrating the flow of information through the perceptual, memory, and motor systems.

ing occurs, more or less automatically, as a result of items entering working memory. This is represented by the arrows going from working memory to declarative and procedural memory.

Figure 15.2 suggests potential sources of individual differences in this processing system, that is, candidates for g. First, it is clear that all information processing goes through working memory. In keeping with this central role, Anderson (1993) pointed out that in ACT, a major cause for errors is working-memory failures. At one time there was a debate over whether errors were caused by "slips" (working memory failures) or "bugs" (misconceptions), but the tide has turned against the misconception account, based on analyses of errors during intelligent tutoring instruction (Anderson, 1993). I reached the same conclusion in an analysis of errors on mental paper folding items (Kyllonen, 1984). The cause for working memory being a source of error is its limited capacity. Increasing capacity reduces error, and we can imagine that people varying in working-memory capacity therefore vary in their likelihood of committing errors. This makes working-memory capacity a good candidate for g.

A second potential source of individual differences is in the declarative knowledge people bring to the testing situation. There are many dimensions of a knowledge base, such as its breadth, depth, accessibility, and organization. All are worthy of being investigated as sources of individual differences. However, breadth seems on first consideration to be the most likely candidate for g, as captured in the sentiment, "x is smart, x knows

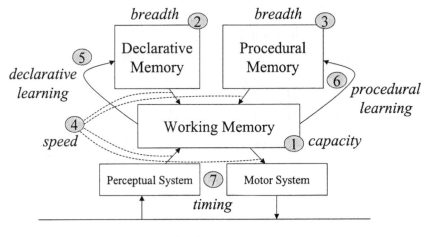

FIG. 15.2.   Human information-processing system with hypothesized performance-affecting parameters governing the efficacy of the system numbered 1 ("capacity") to 7 ("timing").

lots of stuff." Depth of knowledge would reveal itself as expertise in a particular area, and would not therefore seem to be a good candidate for general ability. Similar could be said about organization. A case can be made for the role of knowledge organization in achieving expertise (Britton & Tidwell, 1995; Glaser, 1987). However, it is difficult to think about what it would mean to have a generally well organized knowledge base across the board. Accessibility and breadth are confounded—accessibility depends on availability. But for available knowledge, such as common vocabulary or simple facts, accessibility would reveal itself as retrieval speed, and is therefore treated under the processing speed heading.

A third potential source of individual differences is in the procedural knowledge one brings to the testing situation. One could posit the same dimensions as for declarative knowledge, but declarative and procedural knowledge are different. Declarative knowledge can be tested by asking people if they know something (e.g., what is the meaning of defenestrate?). Procedural knowledge, by definition (in the cognitive world) is tacit, not explicit—the test of the possession of procedural knowledge is not whether one can talk about it but whether one can use it. The most general kind of procedural knowledge, and therefore the most likely candidate for being g, is general problem-solving heuristics. We can imagine that people vary in the degree to which they possess these. However, we cannot test for this by asking people whether they know such and such a heuristic. That would be a declarative knowledge test. Rather, we have to test for procedural knowledge by putting examinees in a novel problem-solving situation where specific problem-solving procedures are not available, and they therefore must resort to the use of these general heuristics. Table 15.1 shows an example of this (the figure-it-out-strategy, in general, but particularly Steps 2 ["replace variables with constants"], 5 ["simplify'] and 7 ["divide & conquer']). Inductive reasoning items are also cases of novel problems that call upon the use of these procedures for their solution.

A fourth potential source of individual differences variance is in the speed with which information is processed. All the arrows in Fig. 15.2 represent the flow of information, and therefore all of them indicate a possible role for the rate of information processing. In principle, there could be several different processing speeds: speed of retrieval from declarative or procedural memory, speed of moving percepts into working memory, and speed of executing a motor response. And in fact, such a partitioning of processing speed has been demonstrated (Kyllonen, 1985; Kyllonen et al., 1991). However, there is a strong general processing-speed factor (Roberts, 1995), which could serve as a candidate for g.

The fifth and sixth potential sources of individual differences are found in the declarative and procedural learning mechanisms, which govern both the likelihood that a particular fact, or procedure will be learned in the first place, and the incremental benefit of additional exposures of that fact or procedure. Initial learning and incremental benefit then are potentially separate sources of individual differences. In practice, however, it seems difficult to tease these apart, without resorting to componential type approaches (e.g., subtracting initial learning from outcome to estimate incremental benefit), and so we might simply think of declarative and procedural learning ability per se as candidates for g.

The seventh potential source of individual differences variance listed in the architectural diagram is not really a good candidate for g, but it is included here for completeness. It is inspired by recent work in the EPIC (Kieras & Meyer, 1997) and ACT–R/PM (Byrne & Anderson &, 1998) architectures to accommodate perceptual-motor and dual-task performance. Though almost certainly not g, this factor may nevertheless be important in certain important tasks, such as psychomotor tasks, that require careful coordination and temporal synchronicity between the perceptual and motor systems. For lack of a better label, we can call this source *timing*.

Finally, there is the issue of content. On the one hand, there is a very reliable individual-differences phenomenon regarding content effects: (a) tasks cluster into verbal, spatial, and quantitative categories; and (b) the importance of these category distinctions decreases as task complexity (g-loading) increases (Kyllonen, 1993; Marshalek, Lohman, & Snow, 1983; Snow, Kyllonen, & Marshalek, 1984). On the other hand, the existing architectures do not explicitly accommodate this. At one time, Anderson (1983) sorted knowledge into propositions, spatial images, and temporal strings, which is close to reflecting the individual-differences result, but he has apparently since abandoned that categorization. Baddeley (1986) proposed two separate storage systems for working memory, spatial and verbal, but he did not distinguish quantitative as a third. In any event, probably the most important aspect of the content finding regarding the search for g, is that whatever g is must be separable from, or independent of content. It would therefore seem to be hard to argue that (breadth of) declarative knowledge is the same as g, even though vocabulary tests are typically excellent measures of g.

The discussion to this point has focused on the sources of individual differences. There is the additional issue of how these sources can be measured with actual tests. This is an extremely interesting topic in its own right, but it is not possible to go into great detail here due to space limits (see Kyllonen, 1991, 1994, 1995 for discussion). In general it is possible to identify measures of these various factors from the literature. It is also possible to create variants of such measures in the different content areas. For example, Daneman and Carpenter (1980) developed a widely used working-memory test, later adapted by Turner and Engle (1989). I and my colleagues on the Learning Abilities Measurement Project (LAMP) developed verbal, quantitative, and spatial variants of such a task that could be group-administered on computer. In fact we have produced a comprehensive test battery (the CAM battery) consisting of 9 to 12 measures of each of the factors listed in Fig. 15.2, with each of the three contents. Making variants across contents, and developing several measures for each factor allows one to remove content and method (task) effects from the ability factors, which allows more straightforward interpretations of the correlations between the ability factors and each other or external criteria. (It also allows one to re-confirm the individual-differences content phenomenon referred to earlier.)

Findings

The approach is fairly straightforward. It involves finding or creating measures based on definitions of these factors from the literature, with multiple measures for each category, then correlating factor or composite scores from these measures with g and other criteria. Major problems encountered in the individual-differences literature are too few measures, and too few subjects. For the most part we avoided both of these problems by creating hundreds of different measures of the various factors over the past 15 years, and administering them to tens of thousands of subjects at the (unfortunately now defunct) Test Development Center at Lackland Air Force Base in San Antonio, Texas. A detailed summary of the results of those studies is provided elsewhere (Kyllonen, 1995). Here I briefly summarize those findings, and provide an update. I also review results from the Mannheim group (Wittman & Süß, 1999).

The major finding was that g correlated highly with working-memory capacity. We (Kyllonen & Christal, 1989), in a paper entitled "g is (little more than) working-memory capacity?!," reported this based on a series of large-N studies using a variety of working-memory measures (6) and a variety of reasoning measures (15). We estimated correlations of $r = .82$, .88, .80, and .82, on four samples of Air Force enlistees ($N = 723$, 412, 415, and 594, respectively). However, these were underestimates due to restriction of range (enlistees were prescreened on ability, using the ASVAB). Also, the criterion measure was not true g, measured by a broad sample of tests, but reasoning, measured by tests purported to measure that factor—reasoning is highly correlated with g, but it is not the same factor (e.g., Carroll, 1993). In a followup (Kyllonen, 1993), using 310 civilians drawn from the community to get an unrestricted sample, we estimated working memory with 9 measures, and g with the 10-test ASVAB, and found a correlation between them of .99. This suggests that the parenthetical qualifier in the title of the Kyllonen-Christal paper may have been an error.

No other cognitive factor—knowledge, speed, or learning ability—correlated with g after the working-memory factor was partialed out. Thus, we have our answer to the question of what g is. It is working-memory capacity.

The trust we can put in this conclusion obviously depends on the operationalization of working-memory capacity by the tasks used. Although, as noted, we have employed numerous and varied indicators of working-memory capacity, some have argued that the measures themselves are "complex" and that is what accounts for the high correlation with g (e.g., Süß, Oberauer, Wittman, Wilhelm, & Schultze, 1996). It is true that the design of the working-memory measures was rather casual (the principles simply were that [a] they require only common knowledge, [b] they show minimal learning effects, and [c] they involve "simultaneous processing and storage" following Baddeley, 1986). However, Süß et al. replicated the basic finding with what they considered simpler measures of working-memory capacity. Süß et al. (1996) constructed working memory tasks "based on very simple elements and cognitive operations with limited degrees of freedom for the test [taker]" (p. 7). Süß et al. also used a different general aptitude battery, the BIS (Jäger, Süß, & Beaducel, 1997), on German University students. The correlation they estimated between working memory and g was .92 to .96 ($N = 128$). An important point is that it probably doesn't matter how one measures working memory (beyond the principles just listed). If the construct were so fragile that minor methodological decisions affected the outcome we hardly would be in a position to say that the construct was g!

Another issue, and one that gets to the theme of this book is how general is working-memory capacity? In the information-processing architectures, working-memory is quite general. It is involved in every cognitive activity in that it represents the current focus of thought or attention. From an individual-differences standpoint, we can say that working memory is involved in virtually every cognitive test. Like g, the involvement will vary. And the question of the generality of g, or the generality of working memory is how much variance is that?

A second potential criticism of the working-memory-g studies discussed thus far is that they all occur within a closed, self-contained world, of short-term (typically less than 15 minutes) somewhat artificial cognitive tests administered in a laboratory setting. All we have shown is that one set of tests correlates highly with another set. What would happen if we examined more realistic learning, such as what might occur in a college classroom or in military technical training? How important would the 15-minute measures of working memory capacity prove to be in predicting significant learning that occurred over days rather than over several minutes?

We conducted a series of studies examining this issue of the importance of working memory in learning. We began with fairly simple learning tasks, such as learning a set of if–then classification rules (Woltz, 1988), and logic gates (Christal, 1991; Kyllonen & Stephens, 1990). But we progressed to more complex learning such as computer programming that occurred during 20 to 40 hours of instruction (Kyllonen, 1995; Shute, 1991). To summarize, we found that working-memory capacity was the most important determinant of how much was learned. For example, in the computer programming study we found that a working-memory factor predicted more than 80% of the variance in overall learning ($N = 350$) (Kyllonen, 1995). There also was a significant secondary role played by domain-specific knowledge: Those who entered the study knowing more math and programming concepts (e.g., another programming language) learned faster. No other factor, such as general declarative or procedural knowledge, or processing speed, added to the prediction of learning.

Wittman and Süß (1999) reported on a study in a similar vein involving 136 University students in which they examined learning on three complex simulation tasks occuring over two 5- to 6-hour days. The simulations were (a) operating a power plant (to keep supply and demand in balance), (b) managing a tailor shop, and (c) managing a competitive high-technology company. The simulations represented anywhere between a year and 15 years worth of decision making interacting with fluctuating economic cycles.

On a third day they administered an extensive test battery that consisted of measures of working memory (9 tasks, verbal, spatial, and quantitative), domain-specific knowledge (economics), and assorted other intelligence tests. Although their analysis is a bit complicated, basically they also found, as we did, that working-memory capacity and domain-specific knowledge together accounted for a substantial amount of overall learning ($R^2 = .70$), and that no other ability factor added to that prediction.

The tasks discussed to this point have been cognitive. Psychomotor tasks, or dynamic operator tasks are another important class of performance tasks. They include driving, piloting, air traffic control, and other tasks requiring continuous responding to a changing perceptual display. Psychomotor tasks are treated as a separate category of tasks in the psychometrics literature (Carroll, 1993), and in fact, have their own separate taxonomies (e.g,. Fleishman & Quintannce, 1984). Few studies have looked at the role of working memory (or g) on such tasks (though see Ree & Carretta, 1994). Partly that was due to the fact that during the period of active interest in this area (Fleishman, 1954), the g concept had been moribund, replaced by a Thurstonian multiple-factors view. We (Chaiken, Kyllonen, & Tirre, 2000), thought it would be useful to re-evaluate this area. We developed a set of 16 psychomotor tests taken from Fleishman's (1954) battery, and administered these and a comprehensive cognitive abilities battery to 161 recent high-school graduates. Contrary to the earlier work, we found that a single psychomotor factor provided a good account of the correlations among the psychomotor tests. Path analyses suggested that the general psychomotor factor could be largely accounted for by two cognitive factors, general working-memory capacity ($r = .67$), and an orthogonal time estimation factor ($r = .32$). We concluded that psychomotor performance is constrained by working-memory limits and the ability to keep track of time.

To summarize the findings presented in this section, we found that g can be identified as working-memory capacity. We also found that the importance of working-memory capacity is not limited to other cognitive tests, but is a key determinant of a broad range of complex learning and performance activities including learning computer programming, and performing on simulations of the management of power plants, tailor shops, and high-technology companies. We found that working memory plays a key role in governing success on psychomotor tasks as well as more purely cognitive ones. In all these studies we found an additional role for other factors: In the cognitive tasks the other factor was domain-specific knowledge; in the psychomotor task the other factor was a timing factor.

What about the other factors—procedural knowledge and the two learning factors (declarative and procedural)? They simply did not correlate with g, once the effects of the common working-memory factor was eliminated. The problem is that working memory accounts for almost all the individual-differences variability in these factors—the average correlation among them ranges in the .90s (Chaiken et al., 2000; Kyllonen, 1993). We operationalized strategy knowledge as the possession of general problem-solving heuristics, observed through performance on tasks requiring novel problem-solving skills. These did not provide any independent prediction of g or of learning. We can conclude that the possession of good general strategies is not related to g independently of working-memory capacity.

PARAMETERS FROM COGNITIVE ARCHITECTURES

> The domain-general [parameter] W would be like Spearman's (1904) g in theories of intelligence.
> —Anderson & Lebiere (1998, p. 447)

Our apparent finding that g is working-memory capacity, and that as such, working-memory capacity plays an important role in governing learning and performance begs the question, what is working-memory capacity?

ACT–R does not have separate working memories per se. In ACT–R (Anderson & Lebiere, 1998) working memory is represented as a temporary high level of activation of items in long-term declarative memory. Working memory is in effect the small set of items that are currently available by virtue of their temporarily high activation levels. Three factors determine the temporary activation level of an item:

- The baseline strength of the item in long-term memory (a parameter called B). This is the parameter corresponding to what was referred to earlier as "knowledge," or perhaps more precisely the "accessibility" facet of that knowledge. B varies with frequency (learning exposures) and recency (strength decays over time).
- The strength of the item's associations to other items that are currently active (i.e., "in working memory") (a parameter called S). This is the spreading activation parameter, which governs the flow of thought—items become active to the degree to which they are associated with items currently in focus.
- Source activation, or the amount of attention the person has available to give to the item (a parameter called W)

That is, the first two parameters concern the strength of an item and its associations with other items that currently are the focus of thought. The third parameter represents the activation available to put on the item. The total activation (W) is split up among the items currently in focus, and so if there are numerous items being considered simultaneously, each gets only a small fraction of W. This leads to the phenomenon of working-memory overload. For example, consider the dual-task situation, in which each item in focus has only a small amount of activation available to sustain it, resulting in a high probability of loss of that information.

In ACT–R, W is a constant, divided among all the items being attended to. Lovett, Reder, and Lebiere (1999) proposed that W could vary from individual to individual, and hence could be the parameter reflecting individual differences in working-memory capacity. That is, this is the parameter instantiating Spearman's (1927) concept of "mental energy." This differs from other possible explanations to account for individual differences on cognitive tasks, such as variability in knowledge. But the explanation is consistent with the data presented in this chapter.

To test this concept, Lovett et al. (1999) developed a letter span task, similar in form to Daneman and Carpenter's (1980) reading span task, but simpler. Instead of reading sentences, examinees read single letters, and instead of remembering the last word in the sentences, examinees remembered a final single digit. For example, examinees might be shown the strings, "a f 3" then "d e 5" then "c k 6." Their task was to articulate the characters as they were rapidly presented, 2 per second. Then, after all the characters were presented, they were to recall the last character in each set, which was a digit. For example, they would have to recall "3," "5," and "6." As with the Daneman–Carpenter task, set size (i.e., the number of digits) varied from 3 to 6 (the example shown was a set size of 3). As is typically the case with this kind of task, there were two key empirical results. First, the probability of recalling the digits decreased as set size increased. Second, there were large differences between examinees in the degree to which they could do this. Lovett et al. developed a model of the task using the ACT–R architecture. The model fit the average data well, when W was set to a constant amount. However, they also let W vary across individuals and found that the model fit the individual data as well. Daily et al. (1998) replicated this finding, and in addition, accounted for individual differences in serial position effects. Further, they found that W correlated ($r = .55$) with at least one external cognitive measure, a spatial matrix test, a measure of g.

This study was small, and only suggestive, but still, there are many potential advantages to this approach to understanding working memory. First, it explains why working memory could be g. Insofar as W plays a central role in all cognitive tasks, so should the working-memory capacity factor predict performance, to at least some degree, of all cognitive tasks.

A second advantage is in the prediction of a task's working-memory requirements and hence construct validity. As noted earlier, the working-memory tasks referred to earlier in this chapter were constructed in a fairly casual manner: designed to conform to Baddeley's (1986) definition requiring simultaneous storage and processing, to be resistant to learning, and to only require overlearned (well known) material, but not much else. It has been a purely empirical enterprise to determine whether tasks and items within those tasks actually are good working-memory measures, as indicated, for example, by their correlations with a working-memory factor. The use of an ACT–R type modeling approach, specifying various items' B and S parameters could help determine a task or even item's working-memory requirement, and its validity as a working-memory task or item, in advance of collecting data to assemble a large correlation matrix. For example, items with low individual-differences variance in B and S, but high in W would be good working-memory measures. It is not there yet, but the framework seems promising.

A third advantage is that the approach provides a coherent system in which to evaluate the relative importance of experimental, environmental, and individual-differences effects. For example, one can imagine evaluating the effects of stressors and unusual environments (e.g., space, the deep sea) on the different parameters (B, S, and W), and comparing those effects with the individual-differences effects (cf. Kyllonen, 2002). It would be interesting to evaluate, for example, whether the onset of some stressor (e.g., fatigue) translated directly to a loss of g, by the W metric.

Fourth, the approach provides interesting predictions that could be validated from correlational studies. For example, W in ACT–R affects both the speed and accuracy of memory retrieval, suggesting a strong correlation between working-memory capacity and processing speed. For example, Lovett et al. (1999) proposed that "If the amount of attentional energy, W, decreases . . . , then all retrieval latencies will be slower (not to mention more error prone)" (p. 157). In fact, there is a relationship between processing speed and g, and its cause has been the subject of considerable speculation in the intelligence literature (e.g., Jensen, 1993). However, the relationship is not perfect, and it may be that at least part of the reason for the attenuation in the relationship between working memory (or g) and processing speed is the importance of the speed–accuracy tradeoff decision (Dennis & Evans, 1996).

TRAINABILITY OF g: EFFECTIVE VERSUS UNDERLYING WORKING-MEMORY CAPACITY

One of the promises of the information-processing approach to the study of intelligence has been that it might serve to inform us of ways to improve intelligence. Past attempts to improve intelligence have not been extremely successful (e.g., Herrnstein, Nickerson, deSanchez, & Swets, 1986; Nickerson, Perkins, & Smith, 1985). In contrast, there have been remarkable successes in improving working-memory capacity, as noted in the expertise literature (e.g., Ericsson, 1996). If working memory capacity is g, why should there be this kind of discrepency?

To address this issue it is useful to distinguish effective versus general, or underlying, working-memory capacity. Underlying working-memory capacity is g. Effective working-memory capacity is what improves with practice and experience, and therefore represents a combination of g plus knowledge, or in ACT–R terms, $W + B$ (and perhaps S). One improves one's effective working-memory capacity by practicing the skill, or rehearsing the facts, over and over. Although underlying working memory is important, task performance obviously depends on one's effective working-memory capacity, not on one's underlying working-memory capacity. Consider the example presented in Table 15.1. By having the requisite knowledge for the problem ("if x things cost y amount, the answer to how much z things cost is zy/x") and by having practiced using that knowledge on actual problems, one increases one's effective working memory capacity for problems of that type. It may be, and undoubtedly is the case that having high underlying capacity enables one to achieve expertise on problems like this faster, with fewer learning opportunities compared with someone with less underlying capacity. But, underlying capacity is no substitute for effective capacity, and one with lower underlying capacity, with more experience, could certainly surpass one with more capacity and less experience.

CONCLUSIONS

g exists. That is to say, performance scores on all cognitive tasks correlate positively—those who do better than average on any one cognitive task will most likely do better than average on any other cognitive task. A critical question is why? The answer proposed here is that g is working-memory capacity, and the bottleneck to all cognition is the limited capacity of working memory. In this chapter I have presented considerable evidence for the assertion that g is working-memory capacity and that it is important in many different learning and performance contexts. Numerous studies have shown that measures of working-memory capacity correlate quite highly with measures of g (e.g., Kyllonen, 1993; Kyllonen & Christal, 1990). Predictive validity studies examining complex criterion performances, lasting from 10 to 20 hours, such as learning computer programming (Kyllonen, 1995; Shute, 1991) and managing businesses in simulation games (Süß et al., 1996; Wittman & Süß, 1999) have demonstrated the generality of working memory, or *g*. Working memory's scope of influence is not limited to traditional "static" cognitive tasks, but can be extended to account for dynamic, psychomotor, and dual tasks as well (Chaiken et al., 2000; Tirre & Gugerty, 1998; Tirre & Ikomi, 1999).

There are probably many possible challenges to this hypothesis, but four stand out (roughly corresponding to the hypotheses stated in this chapter's title):

1. *Working-memory capacity is vaguely (or even circularly) defined.* Working-memory capacity here was defined as performance on tasks that (a) require simultaneous processing and storage, (b) do not involve learning, and (c) require knowledge that everyone is presumed to have. This is admittedly an informal definition. One could argue that this is, nevertheless, a considerably more precise definition than one that could be made about tests of *g*. Further, there is the promise of still increased precision based on the work pinpointing working-memory capacity as the source activation parameter within the ACT–R production-system model of cognition (Anderson & Lebiere, 1998; Daily et al. (1998); Lovett et al. (1999).

2. *A vocabulary test does not require simultaneous processing and storage—Why is it such a good measure of* g? This is basically the fluid–crystallized distinction. The standard response is that crystallized measures, such as knowledge measures (e.g., vocabulary tests), represent the results of past processing. That is, working-memory capacity affects initial vocabulary acquisition (Marshalek, 1981; Sternberg & Powell, 1983).

3. *Aren't strategies important?* There is considerable work attesting to the importance of strategies in expert performance. But expertise and intelligence are not synonymous. Expertise is characterized by the availability of considerable domain knowledge and efficient strategies in the specific domain of expertise. Intelligence—or *g*, or working-memory capacity—crosses multiple domains. We found that the availability of very general strategic knowledge, or procedures—what might be called general problem-solving heuristics—correlated very highly with working-memory capacity, and did not predict performance independently of working-memory capacity.

4. *How does this explain the reaction time and inspection time results?* As Brody (1992) pointed out in discussing Carpenter et al.'s (1990) analysis of the Raven's Progressive Matrices test, the consistently high correlations found between the very simple visual and auditory perceptual tasks (reaction time and inspection time) and *g* (Deary, 1999; Vernon, 1987) stands as a challenge to any explanations of *g* that invoke only complex, higher order functions. We have not found any circumstances where processing speed predicts complex criterion tasks (learning or performance) once the effects of *g*, or working memory are removed. Still, the high correlation

between processing speed and working memory, or *g*, warrants an explanation. Conceptualizing working-memory capacity as source activation may indicate a promising direction for explaining this correlation—the same "attentional energy" parameter, source activation (W) in the ACT–R model (Anderson & Lebiere, 1998; Lovett et al., 1999), underlies both task accuracy and speed, even on the simplest tasks. One can still ask, as Jensen (2000) did of *g*, whether "mental speed" is a cause of working memory capacity, or an epiphenomenon. It is interesting in that regard to note the parallels between the search for neuroscience explanations of mental speed (e.g., Jensen, 1993) and working memory (e.g., all the chapters in Miyake & Shah, 1999).

In conclusion, two lines of research are likely to flow from the working memory and *g* connection. First, in addition to further analyses of information-processing correlates of working memory (Conway et al., in press; Engle et al., 1999) there will be a continued pursuit and examination of the generality and implications of parameters representing individual differences in working-memory capacity in complex information-processing frameworks such as ACT–R and 3CAPS (Just & Carpenter, 1992). It would be interesting if the reaction time and inspection time results could be accounted for by this approach (Point 4 above). Second, the equating of working memory with *g* should spur continued work in the more applied discipline of item difficulty modeling. Under this scheme, much of item difficulty on complex aptitude and achievement tests could be accounted for by items' working memory and knowledge requirements. Some promising results along these lines are already in (Irvine & Kyllonen, 2002), and further work promises to provide a better understanding of what items measure, along with a technology for automatic item generation.

REFERENCES

Anderson, J. R. (1983). *The architecture of cognition*. Cambridge, MA: Harvard University Press.

Anderson, J. R. (1993). *Rules of the mind*. Hillsdale, NJ: Lawrence Erlbaum Associates.

Anderson, J. R., & Lebiere, C. (1998). *The atomic components of thought*. Mahwah, NJ: Lawrence Erlbaum Associates.

Atkinson, R. C., & Schiffrin, R. M. (1968). Human memory: A proposed system and its control processes. In K. W. Spence & J. T. Spence (Eds.), *The psychology of learning and motivation: Advances in research and theory, Vol. 2* (pp. 89–195). New York: Academic Press.

Baddeley, A. D. (1986). *Working memory*. Oxford, England: Clarendon Press.

Boring, E. G. (1923, June). Intelligence as the tests test it. *The New Republic*, 35–37.

Brand, C. (1987). The importance of general intelligence. In S. Modgil & C. Modgil (Eds.), *Arthur Jensen: Consensus and controversy*. New York: Falmer.

Britton, B. K., & Tidwell, P. (1995). Cognitive structure testing: A computer system for diagnosis of expert-novice differences. In P. D. Nichols & S. F. Chipman (Eds.), *Cognitively diagnostic assessment* (pp. 251–278). Hillsdale, NJ: Lawrence Erlbaum Associates.

Brody, N. (1992). *Intelligence* (2nd ed.). San Diego, CA: Academic Press.

Byrne, M. D., & Anderson, J. R. (1998). Perception and action. In J. R. Anderson & M. D. Byrne (Eds.), *The atomic components of thought* (pp. 167–200). Mahwah, NJ: Lawrence Erlbaum Associates.

Carpenter, P. A., Just, M. A., & Schell, P. (1990). What one intelligence test measures: A theoretical account of the processing in the Raven Progressive Matrices test. *Psychological Review, 97*, 404–431.

Carroll, J. B. (1978). How shall we study individual differences in cognitive abilities? Methodological and theoretical perspectives. *Intelligence, 2*, 87–115.

Carroll, J. B. (1993). *Human cognitive abilities*. Cambridge, England: Cambridge University Press.

Chaiken, S. R., Kyllonen, P. C., & Tirre, W. C. (2000). Organization and components of psychomotor ability. *Cognitive Psychology, 40*, 198–226.

Christal, R. E. (1991). *Comparative validities of ASVAB and LAMP tests for logic gates learning* (Tech. rep. No. AL-TP-1991-0031). Brooks AFB, TX: Armstrong Laboratory, Human Resources Directorate.

Conway, A. R. A., Cowan, N., Bunting, M. F., Therriault, D., & Minkoff, S. (in press). A latent variable analysis of working memory capacity, short-term memory capacity, processing speed, and general fluid intelligence. *Intelligence*.

Cooper, L. A. (1976). Individual differences in visual comparison processes. *Perception and Psychophysics, 19*, 433–444.

Cronbach, L. J. (1957). The two disciplines of scientific psychology. *American Psychologist, 12*, 671–684.

Daily, L. Z., Lovett, M. C., & Reder, L. M. (1998). *Modeling individual differences in working memory capacity*. Paper presented at the Fifth Annual ACT–R Workshop, Pittsburgh, PA: Carnegie Mellon University. (http://www.andrew.cmu.edu/user/ldaily/workmem.html)

Daneman, M., & Carpenter, P. A. (1980). Individual differences in working memory and reading. *Journal of Verbal Learning and Verbal Behavior, 19*, 450–466.

Deary, I. (1999). Intelligence and visual and auditory information processing. In P. L. Ackerman, P. C. Kyllonen, & R. D. Roberts (Eds.), *Learning and individual differences* (pp. 111–134). Washington, DC: American Psychological Association.

Dennis, I., & Evans, J. St. B. T. (1996). The speed-error trade-off problem in psychometric testing. *British Journal of Psychology, 87*, 105–129.

Donaldson, G. (1983). Confirmatory factor analysis models of information processing stages: An alternative to difference scores. *Psychological Bulletin, 94*, 143–151.

Educational Testing Service (1995). *GRE: Practicing to take the general test, big book*. Princeton, NJ: Educational Testing Service.

Egan, D. E., & Grimes-Farrow, D. D. (1982). Differences in mental representations spontaneously adopted for reasoning. *Memory and Cognition, 10*, 297–307.

Embretson, S. E. (1995). Working memory capacity versus general central processes in intelligence. *Intelligence, 20*, 169–189.

Engle, R. W., Tuholski, S. W., Laughlin, J. E., & Conway, A. R. A. (1999). Working memory, short-term memory and general fluid intelligence: A latent variable approach. *Journal of Experimental Psychology: General, 128*, 309–331.

Ericsson, K. A. (Ed.). (1996). *The road to excellence: The acquisition of expert performance in the art and sciences, sports and games*. Mahwah, NJ: Lawrence Erlbaum Associates.

Estes, W. K. (1974). Learning theory and intelligence. *American Psychologist, 29*, 740–749.

Fleishman, E. A. (1954). Dimensional analysis of psychomotor abilities. *Journal of Experimental Psychology, 48*, 437–454.

Fleishman, E. A., & Quaintance, M. K. (1984). *Taxonomies of human performance: The description of human tasks*. Orlando, FL: Academic Press.

Fredericksen, J. R. (1982). A componential theory of reading skills and their interactions. In R. S. Sternberg (Ed.), *Advances in the psychology of human intelligence, Vol. 1* (pp. 125–180). Hillsdale, NJ: Lawrence Erlbaum Associates.

Glaser, R. (1987). Learning theory and theories of knowledge. In E. DeCorte, J. G. L. C. Lodewijks, R. Parmentier, & P. Span (Eds.), *Learning and instruction* (pp. 397–414). Oxford/Leuven: Pergamon Press/Leuven University Press.

Herrnstein, R. J., Nickerson, R. S., deSanchez, M., & Swets, J. A. (1986). Teaching thinking skills. *American Psychologist, 41*, 1279–1289.

Hunt, E. (1978). Mechanics of verbal ability. *Psychological Review, 85*, 109–130.

Hunt, E. B., Frost, N., & Lunneborg, C. (1973). Individual differences in cognition: A new approach to intelligence. In G. Bower (Ed.), *The psychology of learning and motivation: Advances in research and theory* (Vol. 7, pp. 87–123). New York: Academic Press.

Irvine, S., & Kyllonen, P. C. (2002). *Generating items for cognitive tests: Theory and practice*. Mahwah, NJ: Lawrence Erlbaum Associates.

Jäger, A. O., Süß, H. -M., & Beauducel, A. (1997). *Berliner Intelligenzstruktur-Test: BIS-Test, Form 4 [Test for the Berlin model of intelligence structure]*. Göttingen, Germany: Hogrefe.

Jensen, A. (1993). Why is reaction time correlated with psychometric g? *Current Directions in Psychological Science, 2*, 53–56.

Jensen, A. (2000). Jensen on "Jensenism." *Intelligence, 26*, 181–208.

Just, M. A., & Carpenter, P. A. (1992). A capacity theory of comprehension: Individual differences in working memory. *Psychological Review, 99*, 122–149.

Kieras, D., & Meyer, D. E. (1997). An overview of the EPIC architecture for cognition and performance with application to human-computer interaction. *Human-Computer Interaction, 12*, 391–438.

Kyllonen, P. C. (1984). Information processing analysis of spatial ability. *Dissertation Abstracts International, 45* (3-A): 819 (Issue 0420-073X).

Kyllonen, P. C. (1985). *Dimensions of information processing speed* (Tech. Paper No. 85-57). Brooks AFB, TX: Air Force Human Resources Laboratory.

Kyllonen, P. C. (1991). Principles for creating a computerized test battery. *Intelligence, 15*, 1–15.

Kyllonen, P. C. (1993). Aptitude testing based on information processing: A test of the four-sources model. *Journal of General Psychology, 120*, 375–405.

Kyllonen, P. C. (1994). Cognitive abilities testing: An agenda for the 1990s. In M. G. Rumsey, C. B. Walker, & J. H. Harris (Eds.), *Personnel selection and classification* (pp. 103–125). Hillsdale, NJ: Lawrence Erlbaum Associates.

Kyllonen, P. C. (1995). CAM: A theoretical framework for cognitive abilities measurement. In D. Detterman (Ed.), *Current topics in human intelligence: Vol. IV, Theories of intelligence* (pp. 307–359). Norwood, NJ: Ablex.

Kyllonen, P. C. (1996). Is working-memory capacity Spearman's g? In I. Dennis & P. Tapsfield (Eds.), *Human abilities: Their nature and measurement* (pp. 49–76). Mahwah, NJ: Lawrence Erlbaum Associates.

Kyllonen, P. C. (2002). Item generation for repeated-measures performance testing. In S. Irvine & P. C. Kyllonen (Eds.), *Generating items for cognitive tests: Theory and practice* (pp. 251–276). Mahwah, NJ: Lawrence Erlbaum Associates.

Kyllonen, P. C., & Christal, R. E. (1990). Reasoning ability is (little more than) working memory capacity?! *Intelligence, 14*, 389–433.

Kyllonen, P. C., & Stephens, D. L. (1990). Cognitive abilities as determinants of success in acquiring logic skill. *Learning and Individual Differences, 2*, 129–160.

Kyllonen, P. C., Tirre, W. C., & Christal, R. E. (1991). Knowledge and processing speed as determinants of associative learning. *Journal of Experimental Psychology: General, 120,* 57–79.

Lohman, D. F. (1988). Spatial abilities as traits, processes, and knowledge. In R. J. Sternberg (Ed.), *Advances in the psychology of human intelligence, Vol. 4* (pp. 181–248). Hillsdale, NJ: Lawrence Erlbaum Associates.

Lohman, D. F. (1994). Component scores as residual variation (or why the intercept correlates best). *Intelligence, 19,* 1–12.

Lovett, M. C., Reder, L. M., & Lebiere, C. (1999). Modeling working memory in a unified architecture: An ACT–R perspective. In A. Miyake & P. Shah (Eds.), *Models of working memory: Mechanisms of active maintenance and executive control* (pp.). New York: Cambridge University Press.

Marshalek, B. (1981). Trait and process aspects of vocabulary knowledge and verbal ability. *Dissertation Abstracts International, 42* (5-A): 2094 (Issue: 0420-073X).

Marshalek, B., Lohman, D. F., & Snow, R. E. (1983). The complexity continuum in the radex and hierarchical models of intelligence. *Intelligence, 7,* 102–127.

Miyake, A., & Shah, P. (Eds.). (1999). *Models of working memory: Mechanisms of active maintenance and executive control.* New York: Cambridge University Press.

Mullholland, T. M., Pellegrino, J. W., & Glaser, R. (1980). Components of geometric analogy solution. *Cognitive Psychology, 12,* 252–284.

Newell, A. (1973). You can't play 20 question with nature and win: Projective comments on the paper of this symposium. In W. G. Chase (Ed.), *Visual information processing* (pp. 463–526). New York: Academic Press.

Newell, A. (1990). *Unified theories of cognition.* Cambridge, England: Cambridge University Press.

Nickerson, R. S., Perkins, D. N., & Smith, E. E. (1985). *The teaching of thinking.* Hillsdale, NJ: Lawrence Erlbaum Associates.

Pellegrino, J. W., & Glaser, R. (1979). Cognitive correlates and components in the analysis of individual differences. In R. J. Sternberg & D. K. Detterman (Eds.), *Human intelligence: Perspectives on its theory and measurement* (pp. 61–88). Norwood, NJ: Ablex.

Pellegrino, J. W., & Lyon, D. R. (1979). The components of a componential analysis. *Intelligence, 3,* 169–186.

Ree, M. J., & Carretta, T. R. (1994). The correlation of general cognitive ability and psychomotor tracking tests. *International Journal of Selection and Assessment, 2,* 209–216.

Ree, M. J., & Earles, J. A. (1994). The ubiquitous predictiveness of *g.* In M. G. Rumsey, C. B. Walker, & J. H. Harris (Eds.), *Personnel selection and classification.* Hillsdale, NJ: Lawrence Erlbaum Associates.

Roberts, R. D. (1995). *Speed of processing within the structure of human cognitive abilities.* Unpublished doctoral dissertation. Sydney, Australia: University of Sydney.

Schmidt, F. L., & Hunter, J. E. (1998). The validity and utility of selection methods in personnel psychology: Practical and theoretical implications of 85 years of research findings. *Psychological Bulletin, 124,* 262–274.

Shute, V. (1991). Who is likely to acquire programming skills? *Journal of Educational Computing Research, 7,* 1–24.

Snow, R. E., Kyllonen, P. C., & Marshalek, B. (1984). The topography of learning and ability correlations. In R. J. Sternberg (Ed.), *Advances in the psychology of human intelligence, Vol. 2* (pp. 47–103). Hillsdale, NJ: Lawrence Erlbaum Associates.

Spearman, C. (1904). "General intelligence," objectively determined and measured. *American Journal of Psychology, 15,* 201–293.

Spearman, C. (1927). *The abilities of man.* New York: Macmillan.

Sternberg, R. J. (1977). *Intelligence, information processing, and analogical reasoning: The componential analysis of human abilities.* Hillsdale, NJ: Lawrence Erlbaum Associates.

Sternberg, R. J. (1978). Intelligence research at the interface between differential and cognitive psychology: Prospects and proposals. *Intelligence, 2,* 195–222.

Sternberg, R. J., & Powell, J. (1983). Comprehending verbal comprehension. *American Psychologist, 38,* 878–893.

Süß, H. -M., Oberauer, K., Wittman, W. W., Wilhelm, O., & Schultze, R. (1996). *Working memory capacity and intelligence: An integrative report based on Brunswik symmetry* (Research rep. No. 8). Mannheim, Germany: University of Mannheim.

Tirre, W. C., & Gugerty, L. J. (1998). *A cognitive correlates analysis of situation awareness* (AFRL-HE-AZ-TR-1998-0086). Brooks Air Force Base, TX: Air Force Research Laboratory - Human Resources Directorate.

Tirre, W. C., & Ikomi, P. A. (1999, May). *The measurement of timesharing ability in a synthetic piloting task.* Paper presented at the 10th International Aviation Psychology Symposium, Columbus, OH.

Turner, M. L., & Engle, R. W. (1989). Is working memory capacity task dependent? *Journal of Memory and Language, 28,* 127–154.

Tversky, A., & Hutchinson, J. W. (1986). Nearest neighbor analysis of psychological spaces. *Psychological Review, 93,* 3–22.

Underwood, B. J. (1975). Individual differences as a crucible in theory construction. *American Psychologist, 30,* 128–134.

Vernon, P. A. (Ed.). (1987). *Speed of information processing and intelligence.* Norwood, NJ: Ablex.

Wittman, W. W., & Süß, H. -M. (1999). Investigating the paths between working memory, intelligence, knowledge, and complex problem-solving performances via Brunswik Symmetry. In P. L. Ackerman, P. C. Kyllonen, & R. D. Roberts (Eds.), *Learning and individual differences: Process, trait, and content determinants* (pp. 77–104). Washington, DC: American Psychological Association.

Woltz, D. J. (1988). An investigation of the role of working memory in procedural skill acquisition. *Journal of Experimental Psychology: General, 117,* 319–331.

Woltz, D. J. (1999). Individual differences in priming: The roles of implicit facilitation from prior processing. In P. L. Ackerman, P. C. Kyllonen, & R. D. Roberts (Eds.), *Learning and individual differences: Process, trait, and content determinants* (pp. 135–156). Washington, DC: American Psychological Association.

Chapter 16

Beyond *g*: The Theory of Successful Intelligence

Robert J. Sternberg
Yale University

Suppose all of human intelligence were reducible to just a single thing. How simple things would be! People could be ranked on intelligence just as they are ranked on height. People could be chosen for jobs as physicists, literary editors, artists, business executives, lathe operators, accountants, lawyers, psychiatrists, and interpreters, among other things, on the basis of just a single test. Of course, there might be a few annoying specific abilities that would distinguish these folks. But presumably, they would be relatively small in importance. After all, there have been two books entitled *The g Factor* (Brand, 1996; Jensen, 1998) during the past few years, not two books entitled *The s Factors* (Nobody, No Year).

Many psychometric researchers studying intelligence believe there is overwhelming evidence for a conventional psychometric view, positing a general ability, or *g*, at the top of a hierarchy and then successively more narrow abilities below that. The thesis of this chapter is that conventional notions of intelligence as headed by an all-encompassing *g* factor are incomplete and hence inadequate. I argue further that a construct of *successful intelligence* better captures the fundamental nature of human abilities.

Although many different definitions of intelligence have been proposed over the years (see, e.g., "Intelligence and its measurement," 1921; Sternberg & Detterman, 1986), the conventional notion of intelligence is built around a loosely consensual definition of intelligence in terms of generalized adaptation to the environment. Theories of intelligence extend this definition by suggesting that there is a general factor of intelligence, often labeled *g*, which underlies all adaptive behavior. As mentioned earlier, in many theories, including the theories most widely accepted today (e.g., Carroll, 1993; Gustafsson, 1994; Horn, 1994), other mental abilities are hierarchically nested under this general factor at successively greater levels of specificity. For example, Carroll suggested that three levels can nicely capture the hierarchy of abilities, whereas Cattell (1971) and Vernon (1971) suggested two levels were especially important. In the case of Cattell, nested under general ability are fluid abilities of the kind needed to solve abstract reasoning problems such as figural matrices or series completions and crystallized abilities of the kind needed to solve problems of vocabulary and general information. In the case of Vernon, the two levels corresponded to verbal: educational and practical: mechanical abilities. These theories, and others like them, are described in more detail elsewhere (Brody, 2000; Carroll, 1993; Embretson & McCollam, 2000; Herrnstein & Murray, 1994; Jensen, 1998; Sternberg, 1994, 2000), but are called into question in this chapter.

I argue here that the notion of intelligence as adaptation to the environment and as operationalized in narrowly based intelligence tests is incomplete. Instead, I argue for a concept of *successful intelligence*, according to which intelligence is the ability to achieve success in life, given one's personal standards, within one's sociocultural context (Sternberg, 1997, 1999a, 1999d). One's ability to achieve success depends on capitalizing on one's strengths and correcting or compensating for one's weaknesses through a balance of analytical, creative, and practical abilities in order to adapt to, shape, and select environments.

This chapter is divided into three main parts. First, I argue that conventional and some other notions of intelligence are, at best, incomplete, and, at worst, wrong. Second, I suggest an alternative notion of successful intelligence that expands upon conventional notions of intelligence. Third, I draw some conclusions about the nature of intelligence.

NOTIONS OF INTELLIGENCE THAT ARE INADEQUATE

In this section I argue that conventional notions of intelligence are incomplete. I suggest that intelligence is not a unitary construct and so theories based on notions of general intelligence, dating back to Spearman (1904) and up to the present (e.g., Brand, 1996; Carroll, 1993; Jensen, 1998), cannot be complete either.

Conventional Notions

There now has accumulated a substantial body of evidence suggesting that, contrary to conventional notions, intelligence is not a unitary construct. This evidence is of a variety of different kinds, most of which suggest that the positive manifold (pattern of positive correlations) among ability tests is likely not to be a function of some inherent structure of intellect. Rather, it reflects interactions among the kinds of individuals tested, the kinds of tests used in the testing, and the situations in which the individuals are tested.

One kind of evidence suggests the power of situational contexts in testing (see also Ceci, 1996; Gardner, 1983; Lave, 1988; Nuñes, Schliemann, & Carraher, 1993). For example, Carraher, Carraher, and Schliemann (1985; see also Ceci & Roazzi, 1994; Nuñes, 1994) studied a group of children that is especially relevant for assessing intelligence as adaptation to the environment. The group was composed of Brazilian street children. Brazilian street children are under great contextual pressure to form a successful street business. If they do not, they risk death at the hands of so-called "death squads," which may murder children who, unable to earn money, resort to robbing stores (or who are suspected of resorting to robbing stores). The researchers found that the same children who are able to do the mathematics needed to run their street business are often little able or unable to do school mathematics. In fact, the more abstract and removed from real-world contexts the problems are in their form of presentation, the worse the children do on the problems. These results suggest that differences in context can have a powerful effect on performance.

Such differences are not limited to Brazilian street children. Lave (1988) showed that Berkeley housewives who successfully could do the mathematics needed for comparison shopping in the supermarket were unable to do the same mathematics when they were placed in a classroom and given isomorphic problems presented in an abstract form. In other words, their problem was not at the level of mental processes but at the level of applying the processes in specific environmental contexts.

Ceci and Liker (1986; see also Ceci, 1996) showed that, given tasks relevant to their lives, men would show the same kinds of effects as were shown by women in the Lave studies. These investigators studied men who successfully handicapped horse races. The complexity of their implicit mathematical formulas was unrelated to their IQs. Moreover, despite the complexity of these formulas, the mean IQ among these men was only at roughly the population average or slightly below. Ceci also subsequently found that the skills were really quite specific: The same men did not successfully apply their skills to computations involving securities in the stock market.

In our own research, we have found results consistent with those just described. These results have emanated from studies both in the United States and in other countries. We describe here our international studies because we believe they especially call into question the straightforward interpretation of results from conventional tests of intelligence that suggest the existence of a general factor.

In a study in Usenge, Kenya, near the town of Kisumu, we were interested in school-age children's ability to adapt to their indigenous environment. We devised a test of practical intelligence for adaptation to the environment (see Sternberg & Grigorenko, 1997; Sternberg et al., 2001). The test measured children's informal tacit knowledge for natural herbal medicines that the villagers believe can be used to fight various types of infections. At least some of these medicines appear to be effective (Dr. Frederick Okatcha, personal communication), and most villagers certainly believe in their efficacy, as shown by the fact that children in the villages use their knowledge of these medicines an average of once a week in medicating themselves and others. Thus, tests of how to use these medicines constitute effective measures of one aspect of practical intelligence as defined by the villagers as well as their life circumstances in their environmental contexts. Middle-class Westerners might find it quite a challenge to thrive or even survive in these contexts, or, for that matter, in the contexts of urban ghettos often not distant from their comfortable homes.

We measured the Kenyan children's ability to identify the medicines, where they come from, what they are used for, and how they are dosed. Based on work we had done elsewhere, we expected that scores on this test would not correlate with scores on conventional tests of intelligence. In order to test this hypothesis, we also administered to the 85 children the Raven Coloured Progressive Matrices Test, which is a measure of fluid or abstract-reasoning-based abilities, as well as the Mill Hill Vocabulary Scale, which is a measure of crystallized or formal-knowledge-based abilities. In addition, we gave the children a comparable test of vocabulary in their own Dholuo language. The Dholuo language is spoken in the home, English in the schools.

We did indeed find no significant correlation between the test of indigenous tacit knowledge and the fluid-ability tests. But to our surprise, we found statistically significant correlations of the tacit-knowledge tests with the tests of crystallized abilities. The correlations, however, were *negative*. In other words, the higher the children scored on the test of tacit knowledge, the lower they scored, on average, on the tests of crystallized abilities. This surprising result can be interpreted in various ways, but based on the ethnographic observations of the anthropologists on our team, Geissler and Prince, we concluded that a plausible scenario takes into account the expectations of families for their children.

Many children drop out of school before graduation, for financial or other reasons, and many families in the village do not particularly value formal Western schooling. There is no reason they should, as many of these children will for the most part spend their lives farming or engaged in other occupations that make little or no use of Western schooling. These families emphasize teaching their children the indigenous informal knowledge that will lead to successful adaptation in the environments in which they will really live. Children who spend their time learning the indigenous practical knowledge of the community generally do not invest themselves heavily in doing well in school, whereas children who do well in school generally do not invest themselves as heavily in learning the indigenous knowledge—hence the negative correlations.

The Kenya study suggests that the identification of a general factor of human intelligence may tell us more about how abilities interact with patterns of schooling and especially Western patterns of schooling than it does about the structure of human abilities. In Western schooling, children typically study a variety of subject matters from an early age and thus develop skills in a variety of skill areas. This kind of schooling prepares the children to take a test of intelligence, which typically measures skills in a variety of areas. Often intelligence tests measure skills that children were expected to acquire a few years before taking the intelligence test. But as Rogoff (1990) and others have noted, this pattern of schooling is not universal and has not even been common for much of the history of humankind. Throughout history and in many places still, schooling, especially for boys, takes the form of apprenticeships in which children learn a craft from an early age. They learn what they will need to know in order to succeed in a trade, but not a lot more. They are not simultaneously engaged in tasks that require the development of the particular blend of skills measured by conventional intelligence tests. Hence it is less likely that one would observe a general factor in their scores, much as we discovered in Kenya. Some years back, Vernon (1971) pointed out that the axes of a factor analysis do not necessarily reveal a latent structure of the mind but rather represent a convenient way of characterizing the organization of mental abilities. Vernon believed that there was no one "right" orientation of axes, and indeed, mathematically, an infinite number of orientations of axes can be fit to any solution in an exploratory factor analysis. Vernon's point seems perhaps to have been forgotten or at least ignored by later theorists.

The test of practical intelligence we developed for use in Kenya, as well as some of the other practically based tests described in this chapter, may seem more like tests of achievement or of developing expertise (see Ericsson, 1996; Howe, Davidson, & Sloboda, 1998) than of intelligence. But I have argued that intelligence is itself a form of developing expertise—that there is no clearcut distinction between the two constructs (Sternberg, 1998a, 1999b). Indeed, all measures of intelligence, one might argue, measure a form of developing expertise. Crystallized-ability tests, such as tests of vocabulary and general information, certainly measure developing and developed knowledge base. And available data suggest that fluid-ability tests, such as tests of abstract reasoning, measure developing and developed expertise even more strongly than do crystallized-ability tests. Probably the best evidence for this claim is that fluid-ability tests have shown much greater increases in scores over the last several generations than have crystallized-ability tests (Flynn, 1984, 1987; Neisser, 1998). The relatively brief period of time during which these increases have occurred (about 9 points of IQ per generation) suggests an environmental rather than a genetic cause of the increases. And the substantially greater increase for fluid than for crystallized tests suggests that fluid tests, like all other tests, actually measure an expertise acquired through interactions with the environment. This is not to say that genes do not influence intelligence: Almost certainly they do (Bouchard, 1997; Plomin, 1997; Scarr, 1997). Rather, the point is that the environment always mediates their influence and tests of intelligence measure gene–environment interaction effects. The measurement of intelligence is by assessment of various forms of developing expertise.

The forms of developing expertise that are viewed as practically or otherwise intelligent may differ from one society to another or from one sector of a given society to another. For example, procedural knowledge about natural herbal medicines, on the one hand, or Western medicines, on the other, may be critical to survival in one society, and irrelevant to survival in another (e.g., where one or the other type of medicine is not available). Whereas what constitutes components of intelligence is universal, the content that constitutes the application of these components to adaptation to, shaping, and selection of environments is culturally and even subculturally variable.

The developing world provides a particularly interesting laboratory for testing theories of intelligence because many of the assumptions that are held as dear in the developed world simply do not apply. A study we have done in Tanzania (see Sternberg & Grigorenko, 1997; Sternberg, Grigorenko, Ngorosho et al., in press) points out the risks of giving tests, scoring them, and interpreting the results as measures of some latent intellectual ability or abilities. We administered to 358 school children between the ages of 11 and 13 years near Bagamoyo, Tanzania, tests including a formboard classification test, a linear syllogisms test, and a Twenty Questions Test, which measure the kinds of skills required on conventional tests of intelligence. Of course, we obtained scores that we could analyze and evaluate, ranking the children in terms of their supposed general or other abilities. However, we administered the tests dynamically rather than statically (Brown & Ferrara, 1985; Budoff, 1968; Day, Engelhardt, Maxwell, & Bolig, 1997; Feuerstein, 1979; Grigorenko & Sternberg, 1998; Guthke, 1993; Haywood & Tzuriel, 1992; Lidz, 1987, 1991; Sternberg & Grigorenko, 2002; Tzuriel, 1995; Vygotsky, 1978). Dynamic testing is like conventional static testing in that individuals are tested and inferences about their abilities made. But dynamic tests differ in that children are given some kind of feedback in order to help them improve their scores. Vygotsky (1978) suggested that the children's ability to profit from the guided instruction the children received during the testing session could serve as a measure of children's zone of proximal development (ZPD), or the difference between their developed abilities and their latent capacities. In other words, testing and instruction are treated as being of one piece rather than as being distinct processes. This integration makes sense in terms of traditional definitions of intelligence as the ability to learn ("Intelligence and its measurement," 1921; Sternberg & Detterman, 1986). What a dynamic test does is directly measure processes of learning in the context of testing rather than measuring these processes indirectly as the product of past learning. Such measurement is especially important when not all children have had equal opportunities to learn in the past.

In our assessments, children were first given the ability tests. Then experimental group children were given instruction by which they were able to learn skills to enable them to improve their scores. Then they were tested again. Because the instruction for each test lasted only about 5 to 10 minutes, one would not expect dramatic gains. Yet, on average, the gains were statistically significant. Uninstructed control children gained significantly less. More importantly, scores on the pretest showed only weak although significant correlations with scores on the posttest. These correlations, at about the .3 level, suggested that when tests are administered statically to children in developing countries, they may be rather unstable and easily subject to influences of training. Such children are not accustomed to taking Western-style tests, and so profit quickly even from small amounts of instruction as to what is expected from them. Of course, the more important question is how the scores correlated with other cognitive measures. In other words, which test was a better predictor of transfer to other cognitive performance, the pretest score or the posttest score? We found the posttest score to be the better predictor.

Dynamic testing can perform successfully in the United States as well as abroad. In one of our studies, we devised a test of foreign-language learning ability that dynamically measured participants' ability to learn an artificial language at the time of test. The language was quite complex and required learning of many different facets, presented both orally and visually (Grigorenko, Sternberg, & Ehrman, 2000). We found that scores on our test correlated more highly with a test of foreign-language learning ability (the Modern Language Aptitude Test—MLAT) than with a test of general ability. Scores also significantly predicted success in foreign-language classrooms.

What, then, is intelligence? This question is addressed in the next section.

THE NATURE OF SUCCESSFUL INTELLIGENCE

The theory of successful intelligence has four key elements (see also Stern-berg, 1997). These elements are summarized in Fig. 16.1.

1. *Intelligence is defined in terms of the ability to achieve success in life in terms of one's personal standards, within one's sociocultural context.* The field of in-telligence has at times tended to put "the cart before the horse," defining the construct conceptually on the basis of how it is operationalized rather than vice versa. This practice has resulted in tests that stress the academic aspect of intelligence, as one might expect, given the origins of modern intelligence testing in the work of Binet and Simon (1916) in designing an

Definition of Successful Intelligence

　　　The ability to achieve success in life

　　　According to one's personal standards

　　　Within one's sociocultural context

Types of Processing Skills Contributing to Successful Intelligence

　　　Analytical

　　　Creative

　　　Practical

Uses of Processing Skills for Successful Intelligence

　　　Adaptation to Environments

　　　Shaping of Environments

　　　Selection of Environments

Mechanisms for Utilization of Processing Skills in Successful Intelligence

　　　Capitalization on Strengths

　　　Correction of Weaknesses

　　　Compensation for Weaknesses

FIG. 16.1.　The theory of successful intelligence.

instrument that would distinguish children who would succeed from those who would fail in school. But the construct of intelligence needs to serve a broader purpose, accounting for the bases of success in all of one's life.

The use of societal criteria of success (e.g., school grades, personal income) can obscure the fact that these operationalizations often do not capture people's personal notions of success. Some people choose to concentrate on extracurricular activities such as athletics or music and pay less attention to grades in school; others may choose occupations that are personally meaningful to them but that never will yield the income they could gain doing work that is less personally meaningful. Although scientific analysis of some kinds requires nomothetic operationalizations, the definition of success for an individual is idiographic. In the theory of successful intelligence, however, the conceptualization of intelligence is always within a sociocultural context. Although the processes of intelligence may be common across such contexts, what constitutes success is not. Being a successful member of the clergy of a particular religion may be highly rewarded in one society and viewed as a worthless pursuit in another culture.

2. *One's ability to achieve success depends on one's capitalizing on one's strengths and correcting or compensating for one's weaknesses.* Theories of intelligence typically specify some relatively fixed set of abilities, whether one general factor and a number of specific factors (Spearman, 1904), seven multiple factors (Thurstone, 1938), or eight multiple intelligences (Gardner, 1999). Such a nomothetic specification is useful in establishing a common set of skills to be tested. But people achieve success, even within a given occupation, in many different ways. For example, successful teachers and researchers achieve success through many different blendings of skills rather than through any single formula that works for all of them.

3. *Success is attained through a balance of analytical, creative, and practical abilities.* Analytical abilities are the abilities primarily measured by traditional tests of abilities. But success in life requires one not only to analyze one's own ideas as well as the ideas of others, but also to generate ideas and to persuade other people of their value. This necessity occurs in the world of work, as when a subordinate tries to convince a superior of the value of his or her plan; in the world of personal relationships, as when a child attempts to convince a parent to do what he or she wants or when a spouse tries to convince the other spouse to do things in his or her preferred way; and in the world of the school, as when a student writes an essay arguing for a point of view.

4. *Balancing of abilities is achieved in order to adapt to, shape, and select environments.* Definitions of intelligence traditionally have emphasized the role of adaptation to the environment (Intelligence and its measurement, 1921; Sternberg & Detterman, 1986). But intelligence involves not only

modifying oneself to suit the environment (adaptation), but also modifying the environment to suit oneself (shaping), and sometimes, finding a
new environment that is a better match to one's skills, values, or desires
(selection).

Not all people have equal opportunities to adapt to, shape, and select
environments. In general, people of higher socioeconomic standing tend
to have more opportunities and people of lower socioeconomic standing
have fewer. The economy or political situation of the society also can be
factors. Other variables that may affect such opportunities are education
and especially literacy, political party, race, religion, and so forth. For example, someone with a college education typically has many more possible
career options than does someone who has dropped out of high school in
order to support a family. Thus, how and how well an individual adapts to,
shapes, and selects environments must always be viewed in terms of the
opportunities the individual has.

More details regarding the theory can be found in Sternberg (1985a,
1997). Because the theory comprises three subtheories—a componential
subtheory dealing with the components of intelligence, an experiential
subtheory dealing with the importance of coping with relative novelty and
of automatization of information processing, and a contextual subtheory
dealing with processes of adaptation, shaping, and selection, I have referred to the theory from time to time as *triarchic*.

PROCESSES OF SUCCESSFUL INTELLIGENCE

According to the proposed theory of human intelligence and its development (Sternberg, 1980b, 1984, 1985a, 1990, 1997), a common set of processes underlies all aspects of intelligence. These processes are hypothesized
to be universal. For example, although the solutions to problems that are
considered intelligent in one culture may be different from the solutions
considered to be intelligent in another culture, the need to define problems
and translate strategies to solve these problems exists in any culture.

Metacomponents, or executive processes, plan what to do, monitor things
as they are being done, and evaluate things after they are done. Examples
of metacomponents are recognizing the existence of a problem, defining
the nature of the problem, deciding on a strategy for solving the problem,
monitoring the solution of the problem, and evaluating the solution after
the problem is solved.

Performance components execute the instructions of the metacomponents.
For example, inference is used to decide how two stimuli are related and
application is used to apply what one has inferred (Sternberg, 1977).

Other examples of performance components are comparison of stimuli, justification of a given response as adequate although not ideal, and actually making the response.

Knowledge-acquisition components are used to learn how to solve problems or simply to acquire declarative knowledge in the first place (Sternberg, 1985a). Selective encoding is used to decide what information is relevant in the context of one's learning. Selective comparison is used to bring old information to bear on new problems. And selective combination is used to put together the selectively encoded and compared information into a single and sometimes insightful solution to a problem.

Although the same processes are used for all three aspects of intelligence universally, these processes are applied to different kinds of tasks and situations depending on whether a given problem requires analytical thinking, creative thinking, practical thinking, or a combination of these kinds of thinking. Individuals' abilities to use these processes can be compromised by various factors, such as poor nutrition and illness (Sternberg et al., 1997). Data supporting the theory cannot be presented fully here but are described elsewhere (Sternberg, 1977; Sternberg, 1985a; Sternberg et al., 2000).

ANALYTICAL, CREATIVE, AND PRACTICAL
ASPECTS OF INTELLIGENCE

In this section, I consider the analytical, creative, and practical aspects of intelligence, first, in combination, and then, individually.

The Three Aspects of Intelligence Viewed in Combination

An important foundation of the theory of successful intelligence is the importance of analytical, creative, and practical abilities to intellectual functioning. A number of the studies described next show both the internal validity and the external validity of these constructs.

Internal Validity. Three separate factor-analytic studies support the internal validity of the theory of successful intelligence.

In one study (Sternberg, Grigorenko, Ferrari, & Clinkenbeard, 1999), we used the so-called Sternberg Triarchic Abilities Test (STAT—Sternberg, 1993) to investigate the internal validity of the theory. Three hundred twenty-six high school students, primarily from diverse parts of the United States, took the test, which comprised 12 subtests in all. There were four subtests each measuring analytical, creative, and practical abilities. For each type of ability, there were three multiple-choice tests and one essay test. The multiple-choice tests, in turn, involved, respectively, verbal, quantitative, and figural content. Consider the content of each test:

1. Analytical–Verbal: Figuring out meanings of neologisms (artificial words) from natural contexts. Students see a novel word embedded in a paragraph, and have to infer its meaning from the context.

2. Analytical–Quantitative: Number series. Students have to say what number should come next in a series of numbers.

3. Analytical–Figural: Matrices. Students see a figural matrix with the lower right entry missing. They have to say which of the options fits into the missing space.

4. Practical–Verbal: Everyday reasoning. Students are presented with a set of everyday problems in the life of an adolescent and have to select the option that best solves each problem.

5. Practical–Quantitative: Everyday math. Students are presented with scenarios requiring the use of math in everyday life (e.g., buying tickets for a ballgame), and have to solve math problems based on the scenarios.

6. Practical–Figural: Route planning. Students are presented with a map of an area (e.g., an entertainment park) and have to answer questions about navigating effectively through the area depicted by the map.

7. Creative–Verbal: Novel analogies. Students are presented with verbal analogies preceded by counterfactual premises (e.g., money falls off trees). They have to solve the analogies as though the counterfactual premises were true.

8. Creative–Quantitative: Novel number operations. Students are presented with rules for novel number operations, for example, "flix," which involves numerical manipulations that differ as a function of whether the first of two operands is greater than, equal to, or less than the second. Participants have to use the novel number operations to solve presented math problems.

9. Creative–Figural: In each item, participants are first presented with a figural series that involves one or more transformations; they then have to apply the rule of the series to a new figure with a different appearance, and complete the new series.

We found that a confirmatory factor analysis on the data was supportive of the triarchic theory of human intelligence, yielding separate and uncorrelated analytical, creative, and practical factors. The lack of correlation was due to the inclusion of essay as well as multiple-choice subtests.

Although multiple-choice tests tended to correlate substantially with multiple-choice tests, their correlations with essay tests were much weaker. We found the multiple-choice analytical subtests to load most highly on the analytical factor, but the essay creative and performance subtests to load most highly on their respective factors. Thus, measurement of creative and practical abilities probably ideally should be accomplished with other kinds of testing instruments that complement multiple-choice instruments.

We have now developed a revised version of this test, which, in a preliminary study of 53 college students, shows outstanding internal and external validation properties (Grigorenko, Gil, Jarvin, & Sternberg, 2000). This test supplements the creative and practical measures described earlier with performance-based measures. For example, creative abilities are additionally measured by having people write and tell short stories, by having them do captions for cartoons, and by having them use computer software to design a variety of products. Practical skills are measured additionally by an everyday situational-judgment inventory and a college-student tacit-knowledge inventory. These tests require individuals to make decisions about everyday problems faced in life and in school. We found that the creative tests are moderately correlated with each other and the practical tests are highly correlated with each other. The two kinds of tests are distinct from one another, however. Interestingly, the performance-based assessments tend to cluster separately from multiple-choice assessments measuring the same skills (similar to our earlier findings of essay measures tending to be distinctive from multiple-choice measures). These results further suggest the need for measuring not only a variety of abilities, but also, for measuring these abilities through various modalities of testing.

In a second and separate study, conducted with 240 freshman-year high school students in the United States, Finland, and Spain, we used the multiple-choice section of that STAT to compare five alternative models of intelligence, again via confirmatory factor analysis. A model featuring a general factor of intelligence fit the data relatively poorly. The triarchic model, allowing for intercorrelation among the analytic, creative, and practical factors, provided the best fit to the data (Sternberg, Castejón, Prieto, Hautakami, & Grigorenko, 2001).

In a third study, we tested 511 Russian school children (ranging in age from 8 to 17 years) as well as 490 mothers and 328 fathers of these children. We used entirely distinct measures of analytical, creative, and practical intelligence. Consider, for example, the tests we used for adults. Similar tests were used for children (Grigorenko & Sternberg, 2001).

Fluid analytical intelligence was measured by two subtests of a test of nonverbal intelligence. The *Test of g: Culture Fair, Level II* (Cattell & Cattell, 1973) is a test of fluid intelligence designed to reduce, as much as possible, the influence of verbal comprehension, culture, and educational level, although no test eliminates such influences. In the first subtest we used, *Series*, individuals were presented with an incomplete, progressive series of figures. The participants' task was to select, from among the choices provided, the answer that best continued the series. In the *Matrices* subtest, the task was to complete the matrix presented at the left of each row.

The test of crystallized intelligence was adapted from existing traditional tests of analogies and synonyms–antonyms used in Russia. We used adaptations of Russian rather than American tests because the vocabulary used in Russia differs from that used in the United States. The first part of the test included 20 verbal analogies (KR20 = 0.83). An example is: *circle— ball = square—? (a) quadrangular, (b) figure, (c) rectangular, (d) solid, (e) cube.* The second part included 30 pairs of words, and the participants' task was to specify whether the words in the pair were synonyms or antonyms (KR20 = 0.74). Examples are: *latent—hidden,* and *systematic—chaotic.*

The measure of creative intelligence also comprised two parts. The first part asked the participants to describe the world through the eyes of insects. The second part asked participants to describe who might live and what might happen on a planet called "Priumliava."[1] No additional information on the nature of the planet was specified. Each part of the test was scored in three different ways to yield three different scores. The first score was for originality (novelty); the second was for the amount of development in the plot (quality); and the third was for creative use of prior knowledge in these relatively novel kinds of tasks (sophistication). The mean interstory reliabilities were .69, .75, and .75 for the three respective scores, all of which were statistically significant at the $p < .001$ level.

The measure of practical intelligence was self-report and also comprised two parts. The first part was designed as a 20-item, self-report instrument, assessing practical skills in the social domain (e.g., effective and successful communication with other people), in the family domain (e.g., how to fix household items, how to run the family budget), and in the domain of effective resolution of sudden problems (e.g., organizing something that has become chaotic). For the subscales, internal-consistency estimates varied from 0.50 to 0.77. In this study, only the total practical intelligence self-report scale was used (Cronbach's alpha = .71). The second part had four vignettes, based on themes that appeared in popular Russian magazines in the context of discussion of adaptive skills in the current society. The four themes were, respectively, how to maintain the

---

[1]In Russian, the word *Priumliava* is a nonsense word. It does, however, contain the root *um* which is similar to the English root *mind*. This feature of the word *Priumliava* was detected and played out by a few participants in the study. This accomplishment, however, was not incorporated in the rating scheme—those who capitalized in their writing on the presence of the root *um* in *Priumliava* were rated on the same bases as everybody else.

value of one's savings, what to do when one makes a purchase and discovers that the item one has purchased is broken, how to locate medical assistance in a time of need, and how to manage a salary bonus one has received for outstanding work. Each vignette was accompanied by five choices and participants had to select the best one. Obviously, there is no one "right" answer in this type of situation. Hence we used the most frequently chosen response as the keyed answer. To the extent that this response was suboptimal, this suboptimality would work against us in subsequent analyses relating scores on this test to other predictor and criterion measures.

In this study, exploratory principal-component analysis for both children and adults yielded very similar factor structures. Both varimax and oblimin rotations yielded clearcut analytical, creative, and practical factors for the tests. Thus, a sample of a different nationality (Russian), a different set of tests, and a different method of analysis (exploratory rather than confirmatory analysis) again supported the theory of successful intelligence. Now consider in more detail each of three major aspects of successful intelligence: analytical, creative, and practical.

External Validity.   We have done three studies that look simultaneously at the external validity of analytical, creative, and practical abilities.

In the first set of studies, we explored the question of whether conventional education in school systematically discriminates against children with creative and practical strengths (Sternberg & Clinkenbeard, 1995; Sternberg, Ferrari, Clinkenbeard, & Grigorenko, 1996; Sternberg, Grigorenko, Ferrari, & Clinkenbeard, 1999). Motivating this work was the belief that the systems in schools strongly tend to favor children with strengths in memory and analytical abilities.

We used the Sternberg Triarchic Abilities Test, as already described. The test was administered to 326 children around the United States and in some other countries who were identified by their schools as gifted by any standard whatsoever. Children were selected for a summer program in (college-level) psychology if they fell into one of five ability groupings: high analytical, high creative, high practical, high balanced (high in all three abilities), or low balanced (low in all three abilities). Students who came to Yale were then divided into four instructional groups. Students in all four instructional groups used the same introductory psychology textbook (a preliminary version of Sternberg [1995]) and listened to the same psychology lectures. What differed among them was the type of afternoon discussion section to which they were assigned. They were assigned to an instructional condition that emphasized either memory, analytical, creative, or practical instruction. For example, in the memory condition, they might be asked to describe the main tenets of a major theory of depression. In the analytical condition, they might be asked to compare and contrast two theories of depression. In the creative condition, they might be asked to formulate their own theory of depression. In the practical condition, they might be asked how they could use what they had learned about depression to help a friend who was depressed.

Students in all four instructional conditions were evaluated in terms of their performance on homework, a midterm exam, a final exam, and an independent project. Each type of work was evaluated for memory, analytical, creative, and practical quality. Thus, all students were evaluated in exactly the same way.

Our results suggested the utility of the theory of successful intelligence. First, we observed when the students arrived at Yale that the students in the high creative and high practical groups were much more diverse in terms of racial, ethnic, socioeconomic, and educational backgrounds than were the students in the high-analytical group, suggesting that correlations of measured intelligence with status variables such as these may be reduced by using a broader conception of intelligence. Thus, the kinds of students identified as strong differed in terms of populations from which they were drawn in comparison with students identified as strong solely by analytical measures. More importantly, just by expanding the range of abilities we measured, we discovered intellectual strengths that might not have been apparent through a conventional test.

We found that all three ability tests—analytical, creative, and practical—significantly predicted course performance. When multiple-regression analysis was used, at least two of these ability measures contributed significantly to the prediction of each of the measures of achievement. Perhaps as a reflection of the difficulty of deemphasizing the analytical way of teaching, one of the significant predictors was always the analytical score. (However, in a replication of our study with low-income African-American students from New York, Deborah Coates of the City University of New York found a different pattern of results. Her data indicated that the practical tests were better predictors of course performance than were the analytical measures, suggesting that what ability test predicts what criterion depends on population as well as mode of teaching.) Most importantly, there was an aptitude–treatment interaction whereby students who were placed in instructional conditions that better matched their pattern of abilities outperformed students who were mismatched. In other words, when students are taught in a way that fits how they think, they do better in school. Children with creative and practical abilities, who are almost never taught or assessed in a way that matches their pattern of abilities, may be at a disadvantage in course after course, year after year.

In a follow-up study (Sternberg, Torff, & Grigorenko, 1998a, 1998b), we looked at learning of social studies and science by third graders and eighth graders. The 225 third graders were students in a very low-income neighborhood in Raleigh, North Carolina. The 142 eighth graders were students who were largely middle to upper-middle class studying in Baltimore, Maryland, and Fresno, California. In this study, students were assigned to one of three instructional conditions. In the first condition, they were taught the course that basically they would have learned had we not intervened. The emphasis in the course was on memory. In a second condition, they were taught in a way that emphasized critical (analytical) thinking. In the third condition, they were taught in a way that emphasized analytical, creative, and practical thinking. All students' performance was assessed for memory learning (through multiple-choice assessments) as well as for analytical, creative, and practical learning (through performance assessments).

As expected, we found that students in the successful-intelligence (analytical, creative, practical) condition outperformed the other students in terms of the performance assessments. One could argue that this result merely reflected the way they were taught. Nevertheless, the result suggested that teaching for these kinds of thinking succeeded. More important, however, was the result that children in the successful-intelligence condition outperformed the other children even on the multiple-choice memory tests. In other words, to the extent that one's goal is just to maximize children's memory for information, teaching for successful intelligence is still superior. It enables children to capitalize on their strengths and to correct or to compensate for their weaknesses, and it allows children to encode material in a variety of interesting ways.

We have now extended these results to reading curricula at the middle-school and the high-school level. In a study of 871 middle-school students and 432 high-school students, we taught reading either triarchically or through the regular curriculum. At the middle-school level, reading was taught explicitly. At the high-school level, reading was infused into instruction in mathematics, physical sciences, social sciences, English, history, foreign languages, and the arts. In all settings, students who were taught triarchically substantially outperformed students who were taught in standard ways (Grigorenko, Jarvin, & Sternberg, 2000).

In the third study—the Grigorenko–Sternberg (2001) study in Russia described before—the analytical, creative, and practical tests we employed were used to predict mental and physical health among the Russian adults. Mental health was measured by widely used paper-and-pencil tests of depression and anxiety and physical health was measured by self-report. The best predictor of mental and physical health was the practical-intelligence measure. Analytical intelligence came second and creative intelligence came third. All three contributed to prediction, however. Thus, we again concluded that a theory of intelligence encompassing all three elements provides better prediction of success in life than does a theory comprising just the analytical element.

Thus the results of three sets of studies suggest that the theory of successful intelligence is valid as a whole. Moreover, the results suggest that the theory can make a difference not only in laboratory tests, but in school classrooms and even the everyday life of adults as well. Consider further the elements of the theory independently.

Analytical Intelligence

Analytical intelligence is involved when the components of intelligence (which are specified by the componential subtheory of the triarchic theory) are applied to analyze, evaluate, judge, or compare and contrast. It typically is involved when components are applied to relatively familiar kinds of problems where the judgments to be made are of a fairly abstract nature.

In some of my early work, I showed how analytical kinds of problems, such as analogies or syllogisms, can be analyzed componentially (Guyote & Sternberg, 1981; Sternberg, 1977, 1980b, 1983; Sternberg & Gardner, 1983), with response times or error rates decomposed to yield their underlying information-processing components. The goal of this research was to understand the information-processing origins of individual differences in (the analytical aspect of) human intelligence. With componential analysis, one could specify sources of individual differences underlying a factor score such as that for "inductive reasoning." For example, response times on analogies (Sternberg, 1977) and linear syllogisms (Sternberg, 1980a) were decomposed into their elementary performance components so that it was possible to specify, in the solving of analogies or other kinds of problems, several sources of important individual or developmental differences:

1. What performance components are used?
2. How long does it takes to execute each component?
3. How susceptible is each component to error?
4. How are the components combined into strategies?
5. What are the mental representations upon which the components act?

Studies of reasoning need not use artificial formats. In a more recent study, we looked at predictions for everyday kinds of situations, such as when milk will spoil (Sternberg & Kalmar, 1997). In this study, we looked at both predictions and postdictions (hypotheses about the past where information about the past is unknown) and found that postdictions took longer to make than did predictions.

Research on the components of human intelligence yielded some interesting results. For example, in a study of the development of figural analogical reasoning, we found that although children generally became quicker in information processing with age, not all components were executed more rapidly with age (Sternberg & Rifkin, 1979). The encoding component first showed a decrease in component time with age and then an increase. Apparently, older children realized that their best strategy was to spend more time in encoding the terms of a problem so that they later would be able to spend less time in operating on these encodings. A related finding was that better reasoners tend to spend relatively more time than do poorer reasoners in global, up-front metacomponential planning, when they solve difficult reasoning problems. Poorer reasoners, on the other hand, tend to spend relatively more time in local planning (Sternberg, 1981). Presumably, the better reasoners recognize that it is better to invest more time up front so as to be able to process a problem more efficiently later on. We also found in a study of the development of verbal analogical reasoning that, as children grew older, their strategies shifted so that they relied on word association less and abstract relations more (Sternberg & Nigro, 1980).

Some of our studies concentrated on knowledge-acquisition components rather than performance components or metacomponents. For example, in one set of studies, we were interested in sources of individual differences in vocabulary (Sternberg & Powell, 1982; Sternberg, Powell, & Kaye, 1982; see also Sternberg, 1987b). We were not content just to view these as individual differences in declarative knowledge because we wanted to understand why it was that some people acquired this declarative knowledge and others did not. What we found is that there were multiple sources of individual and developmental differences. The three main sources were in knowledge-acquisition components, use of context clues, and use of mediating variables. For example, in the sentence, "The blen rises in the east and sets in the west," the knowledge-acquisition component of selective comparison is used to relate prior knowledge about a known concept, the sun, to the unknown word (neologism) in the sentence, "blen." Several context cues appear in the sentence, such as the fact that a blen rises, the fact that it sets, and the information about where it rises and sets. A mediating variable is that the information can occur after the presentation of the unknown word.

We did research such as that described here because we believed that conventional psychometric research sometimes incorrectly attributed individual and developmental differences. For example, a verbal analogies test that might appear on its surface to measure verbal reasoning might in fact measure primarily vocabulary and general information (Sternberg, 1977). In fact, in some populations, reasoning might hardly be a source of individual or developmental differences at all. And if we then look at the sources of the individual differences in vocabulary, we would need to understand that the differences in knowledge did not come from nowhere: Some children had much more frequent and better opportunities to learn word meanings than did others.

The kinds of analytical skills we studied in this research can be taught. For example, in one study, we tested whether it is possible to teach people better to decontextualize meanings of unknown words presented in context (Sternberg, 1987a). In one study, we gave 81 participants in five conditions a pretest on their ability to decontextualize word meanings. Then the participants were divided into five conditions, two of which were control conditions that lacked formal instruction. In one condition, participants were not given any instructional treatment. They were merely asked later to take a posttest. In a second condition, they were given practice as an instructional condition, but there was no formal instruction, per se. In a third condition, they were taught knowledge-acquisition component processes that could be used to decontextualize word meanings. In a fourth condition, they were taught to use context cues. In a fifth condition, they were taught to use mediating variables. Participants in all three of the theory-based formal-instructional conditions outperformed participants in the two control conditions, whose performance did not differ. In other words, theory-based instruction was better than no instruction at all or just practice without formal instruction.

Research on the componential bases of intelligence was useful in understanding individual differences in performance on conventional tests of intelligence. But it became increasingly clear to me that this research basically served to partition the variation on conventional tests in a different way, rather than serving to uncover previously untapped sources of variation. Children develop intellectually in ways beyond just what conventional psychometric intelligence tests or even Piagetian tests based on the theory of Piaget (1972) measure. So what might be some of these other sources of variation in intelligence? Creative intelligence seems to be one such source of variation, a source that is almost wholly untapped by conventional tests.

Creative Intelligence

Intelligence tests contain a range of problems, some of them more novel than others. In some of our work we have shown that when one goes beyond the range of unconventionality of the tests, one starts to tap sources of individual differences measured little or not at all by the tests. According to the theory of successful intelligence, (creative) intelligence is particularly well measured by problems assessing how well an individual can cope with relative novelty. Thus it is important to include in a battery of tests problems that are relatively novel in nature. These problems can be either convergent or divergent in nature.

In work with convergent problems, we presented 80 individuals with novel kinds of reasoning problems that had a single best answer. For example, they might be told that some objects are green and others blue; but still other objects might be *grue*, meaning green until the year 2000 and blue thereafter, or *bleen*, meaning blue until the year 2000 and green thereafter. Or they might be told of four kinds of people on the planet Kyron, *blens*, who are born young and die young; *kwefs*, who are born old and die old; *balts*, who are born young and die old; and *prosses*, who are born old and die young (Sternberg, 1982; Tetewsky & Sternberg, 1986). Their task was to predict future states from past states, given incomplete information. In another set of studies, 60 people were given more conventional kinds of inductive reasoning problems, such as analogies, series completions, and classifications, and were told to solve them. But the problems had premises preceding them that were either conventional (dancers wear shoes) or novel (dancers eat shoes). The participants had to solve the problems as though the counterfactuals were true (Sternberg & Gastel, 1989a, 1989b).

In these studies, we found that correlations with conventional kinds of tests depended on how novel or nonentrenched the conventional tests were. The more novel the items, the higher the correlations of our tests with scores on successively more novel conventional tests. Thus, the components isolated for relatively novel items would tend to correlate more highly with more unusual tests of fluid abilities (e.g., that of Cattell & Cattell, 1973) than with tests of crystallized abilities. We also found that when response times on the relatively novel problems were componentially analyzed, some components better measured the creative aspect of intelligence than did others. For example, in the *grue–bleen* task mentioned earlier, the information-processing component requiring people to switch from conventional green–blue thinking to *grue–bleen* thinking and then back to green–blue thinking again was a particularly good measure of the ability to cope with novelty.

In work with divergent reasoning problems having no one best answer, we asked 63 people to create various kinds of products (Lubart & Sternberg, 1995; Sternberg & Lubart, 1991, 1995, 1996) where an infinite variety of responses were possible. Individuals were asked to create products in the realms of writing, art, advertising, and science. In writing, they would be asked to write very short stories for which we would give them a choice of titles, such as "Beyond the Edge" or "The Octopus's Sneakers."

In art, they were asked to produce art compositions with titles such as "The Beginning of Time" or "Earth from an Insect's Point of View." In advertising, they were asked to produce advertisements for products such as a brand of bow tie or a brand of doorknob. In science, they were asked to solve problems such as one asking them how people might detect extraterrestrial aliens among us who are seeking to escape detection. Participants created two products in each domain.

We found that creativity is relatively although not wholly domain-specific. Correlations of ratings of the creative quality of the products across domains were lower than correlations of ratings and generally were at about the .4 level. Thus, there was some degree of relation across domains, at the same time that there was plenty of room for someone to be strong in one or more domains but not in others. More importantly, perhaps, we found, as we had for the convergent problems, a range of correlations with conventional tests of abilities. As was the case for the correlations obtained with convergent problems, correlations were higher to the extent that problems on the conventional tests were nonentrenched. For example, correlations were higher with fluid than with crystallized ability tests, and correlations were higher, the more novel the fluid test was. These results suggest that tests of creative intelligence have some overlap with conventional tests (e.g., in requiring verbal skills or the ability to analyze one's own ideas—Sternberg & Lubart, 1995) but also tap skills beyond those measured even by relatively novel kinds of items on the conventional tests of intelligence.

The work we did on creativity revealed a number of sources of individual and developmental differences.

1. To what extent was the thinking of the individual novel or nonentrenched?
2. What was the quality of the individual's thinking?
3. To what extent did the thinking of the individual meet the demands of the task?

We also found, though, that creativity, broadly defined, extends beyond the intellectual domain. Sources of individual and developmental differences in creative performance include not only process aspects, but aspects of knowledge, thinking styles, personality, motivation, and the environmental context in which the individual operates (see Sternberg & Lubart, 1995, for details).

Creative-thinking skills can be taught and we have devised a program for teaching them (Sternberg & Williams, 1996). In some of our work, we divided 86 gifted and nongifted fourth-grade children into experimental and control groups. All children took pretests on insightful thinking.

Then some of the children received their regular school instruction whereas others received instruction on insight skills. After the instruction of whichever kind, all children took a posttest on insight skills. We found that children taught how to solve the insight problems using knowledge-acquisition components gained more from pretest to posttest than did students who were not so taught (Davidson & Sternberg, 1984).

Tests of creative intelligence go beyond tests of analytical intelligence in measuring performance on tasks that require individuals to deal with relatively novel situations. At the same time, they probably measure creativity that is, for the most part, within existing paradigms (see Sternberg, 1999c). But how about situations that are relatively familiar, but in a practical rather than an academic domain? Can one measure intelligence in the practical domain, and if so, what is its relation to intelligence in more academic kinds of domains?

Practical Intelligence

Practical intelligence involves individuals applying their abilities to the kinds of problems that confront them in daily life, such as on the job or in the home. Practical intelligence involves applying the components of intelligence to experience so as to (a) adapt to, (b) shape, and (c) select environments. Adaptation is involved when one changes oneself to suit the environment. Shaping is involved when one changes the environment to suit oneself. And selection is involved when one decides to seek out another environment that is a better match to one's needs, abilities, and desires. People differ in their balance of adaptation, shaping, and selection, and in the competence with which they balance among the three possible courses of action.

Much of our work on practical intelligence has centered on the concept of tacit knowledge. We define this construct, for our purposes, as what one needs to know, in order to work effectively in an environment, that one is not explicitly taught and that often is not even verbalized (Sternberg et al., 2000; Sternberg & Wagner, 1993; Sternberg, Wagner, & Okagaki, 1993; Sternberg, Wagner, Williams, & Horvath, 1995; Wagner, 1987; Wagner & Sternberg, 1986). We represent tacit knowledge in the form of production systems, or sequences of "if-then" statements that describe procedures one follows in various kinds of everyday situations.

We typically have measured tacit knowledge using work-related problems that present problems one might encounter on the job. We have measured tacit knowledge for both children and adults, and among adults, for people in more than two dozen occupations, such as management, sales, academia, secretarial work, and the military. In a typical tacit-knowledge problem, people are asked to read a story about a problem someone faces and to rate, for each statement in a set of statements, how adequate a solution the statement represents. For example, in a paper-and-pencil measure of tacit knowledge for sales, one of the problems deals with sales of photocopy machines. A relatively inexpensive machine is not moving out of the show room and has become overstocked. The examinee is asked to rate the quality of various solutions for moving the particular model out of the show room. In a performance-based measure for sales people, the test-taker makes a phone call to a supposed customer, who is actually the examiner. The test-taker tries to sell advertising space over the phone. The examiner raises various objections to buying the advertising space. The test-taker is evaluated for the quality, rapidity, and fluency of the responses on the telephone.

In our studies we found that practical intelligence as embodied in tacit knowledge increases with experience, but it is profiting from experience, rather than experience per se, that results in increases in scores. Some people can have been in a job for years and still have acquired relatively little tacit knowledge. We also have found that subscores on tests of tacit knowledge—such as for managing oneself, managing others, and managing tasks—correlate significantly with each other. Moreover, scores on various tests of tacit knowledge, such as for academics and managers, are also correlated fairly substantially (at about the .5 level) with each other. Thus, tests of tacit knowledge may yield a general factor across these tests. However, scores on tacit-knowledge tests do not correlate with scores on conventional tests of intelligence, whether the measures used are single-score measures or multiple-ability batteries. Thus, any general factor from the tacit-knowledge tests is not the same as any general factor from tests of academic abilities (suggesting that neither kind of g factor is truly general, but rather, general only across a limited range of measuring instruments). Despite the lack of correlation of practical–intellectual with conventional measures, the scores on tacit-knowledge tests predict performance on the job as well as or better than do conventional psychometric intelligence tests. In one study done at the Center for Creative Leadership, we further found that scores on our tests of tacit knowledge for management were the best single predictor of performance on a managerial simulation. In a hierarchical regression, scores on conventional tests of intelligence, personality, styles, and interpersonal orientation were entered first and scores on the test of tacit knowledge were entered last. Scores on the test of tacit knowledge were the single best predictor of managerial simulation score. Moreover, they also contributed significantly to the prediction even after everything else was entered first into the equation. In recent work on military leadership (Hedlund et al., 1998), we found that scores of 562 participants on tests of tacit knowledge for military leadership predicted ratings of leadership effectiveness, whereas scores on a conventional test of intelligence and on our tacit-knowledge test for managers did not significantly predict the ratings of effectiveness.

One might expect performance on such tests to be hopelessly culture-specific. In other words, it might be expected that what is adaptive in the workplace of one culture may have little to do with what is adaptive in the workplace of another culture. This appears not to be the case, however. In one study, we gave a tacit-knowledge test for entry-level employees to workers in a wide variety of jobs in the United States and in Spain. We then correlated preferred responses in the two countries. The correlation was .91, comparable to the reliability of the test (Grigorenko, Gil, Jarvin, & Sternberg, 2000)!

We also have done studies of social intelligence, which is viewed in the theory of successful intelligence as a part of practical intelligence. In these studies, 40 individuals were presented with photos and were asked to make judgments about the photos. In one kind of photo, they were asked to evaluate whether a male–female couple was a genuine couple (i.e., really involved in a romantic relationship) or a phony couple posed by the experimenters. In another kind of photo, they were asked to indicate which of two individuals was the other's supervisor (Barnes & Sternberg, 1989; Sternberg & Smith, 1985). We found females to be superior to males on these tasks. Scores on the two tasks did not correlate with scores on conventional ability tests, nor did they correlate with each other, suggesting a substantial degree of domain specificity in the task.

Practical-intelligence skills can be taught. We have developed a program for teaching practical intellectual skills, aimed at middle-school students, that explicitly teaches students "practical intelligence for school" in the contexts of doing homework, taking tests, reading, and writing (Williams, Blyth, White, Li, Sternberg, & Gardner, 1996). We have evaluated the program in a variety of settings (Gardner, Krechevsky, Sternberg, & Okagaki, 1994; Sternberg, Okagaki, & Jackson, 1990) and found that students taught via the program outperform students in control groups that did not receive the instruction.

I would add that individuals' use of practical intelligence can be to their own gain in addition to or instead of the gain of others. People can be practically intelligent for themselves at the expense of others. It is for this reason that wisdom needs to be studied in its own right in addition to practical or even successful intelligence (Baltes & Staudinger, 2000; Sternberg, 1998b).

In sum, practical intelligence, like analytical intelligence, is an important antecedent of life success. Because measures of practical intelligence predict everyday behavior at about the same level as do measures of analytical intelligence (and sometimes even better), we believe that the sophisticated use of such tests roughly could double the explained variance in various kinds of criteria of success. Using measures of creative intelligence as well might increase prediction still more. Thus, tests based on the construct of successful intelligence might take us to new and higher levels of prediction. At the same time, expansions of conventional tests that stay within the conventional framework of analytical tests based on standard psychometric models do not seem likely to expand our predictive capabilities (Schmidt & Hunter, 1998). But how did we get to where we are, both with respect to levels of prediction and with respect to the kinds of standard psychometric tests used to attain these levels of prediction?

CONCLUSION

The time has come to move beyond conventional theories of intelligence. In this chapter I have provided data suggesting that conventional theories and tests of intelligence are incomplete. The general factor is an artifact of limitations in populations of individuals tested, types of materials with which they are tested, and types of methods used in testing. Indeed, our studies show that even when one wants to predict school performance, the conventional tests are somewhat limited in their predictive validity (Sternberg & Williams, 1997). I have proposed a theory of successful intelligence and its development that fares well in construct validations, whether one tests in the laboratory, in schools, or in the workplace. The greatest obstacle to our moving on is in vested interests, both in academia and in the world of tests, where testing companies are doing well financially with existing tests. We now have ways to move beyond conventional notions of intelligence; we need only the will.

What is especially interesting is that lay conceptions of intelligence are quite a bit broader than ones of psychologists who believe in g (Berry 1974; Sternberg & Kaufman, 1998). For example, in a study of people's conceptions of intelligence (Sternberg, Conway, Ketron, & Bernstein, 1981; see also Sternberg, 1985b), we found that lay persons had a three-factor view of intelligence as comprising practical problem solving, verbal, and social-competence abilities. Only the first of these abilities is measured by conventional tests. In a study of Taiwanese Chinese conceptions of intelligence (Yang & Sternberg, 1997a, 1997b), we found that although Taiwanese conceptions of intelligence included a cognitive factor, they also included factors of interpersonal competence, intrapersonal competence, intellectual self-assertion, and intellectual self-effacement. In a study of Kenyan conceptions of intelligence (Grigorenko et al., 2001), we found that four distinct terms constitute rural Kenyan conceptions of intelligence—*rieko* (knowledge and skills), *luoro* (respect), *winjo* (comprehension of how to handle real-life problems), *paro* (initiative)—with only the first directly referring to knowledge-based skills (including but not limited to the academic). Even more importantly, perhaps, we discovered in a study among different ethnic groups in San Jose, California, that although the 359 parents in different ethnic groups have different conceptions of intelligence, the more closely their conception matches that of their children's teachers, the better the children do in school (Okagaki & Sternberg, 1993). In other words, teachers value students who do well on the kinds of attributes that the teachers associate with intelligence. The attributes they associate with intelligence are too limited.

In considering the results of implicit-theories research, it is important to remember that implicit theories provide a starting point, not an ending point, for explicit theories (Sternberg, 1985b; Sternberg, Conway, Ketron, & Bernstein, 1981). In other words, they can suggest directions in which to expand (or, in theory, contract) our notions about intelligence, but they do not directly test those notions, per se. The reason, quite simply, is that people's implicit theories may be wrong. There are many historical illustrations of this fact. Implicit theories regarding the reality of phlogiston as the basis of fire provided the incentive for scientifically testing for the existence of phlogiston: These beliefs did not confirm or disconfirm the existence of this substance. Scientific testing of explicit theories was needed to provide such tests.

The time perhaps has come to expand our notion and everyone's notion of what it means to be intelligent. Exactly what kind of expansion should take place? I have suggested here an expansion of the conventional conception of intelligence to include not just memory and analytical abilities, but creative and practical abilities as well. My original conceptualization of this expansion derived from personal experience working with students, but the confirmation of its feasibility came from psychometric and experimental studies of its internal and external validity. Other expansions are also possible. For example, research is ongoing with regard to emotional intelligence (Davies, Stankov, & Roberts, 1998; Mayer, Caruso, & Salovey, 1999), with promising although as yet mixed results. Hopefully, predictive empirical research also will be forthcoming regarding the theory of multiple intelligences (Gardner, 1983). Ultimately, the answer to the question of how to expand our conception of intelligence will depend in part on the imagination of theorists, but more importantly, on the data showing incremental internal and external validity over the conventional notions that have dominated theory and research on intelligence to date. The memory and analytical abilities measured by these tests have been and likely will continue to matter for many forms of success in life. They never have been, and are unlikely ever to be, the only intellectual abilities that matter for success. It is for this reason that we have needed and will continue to need theories such as the theory of successful intelligence, not only theories of a "general" ability that is not truly general.

ACKNOWLEDGMENTS

Preparation of this essay was supported by Grant REC-9979843 from the National Science Foundation and by a grant under the Javits Act Program (Grant No. R206R000001) as administered by the Office of Educational Research and Improvement, U.S. Department of Education. Grantees undertaking such projects are encouraged to express freely their professional judgment. This article, therefore, does not necessarily represent the position or policies of the Office of Educational Research and Improvement or the U.S. Department of Education, and no official endorsement should be inferred. Preparation of the article was further supported by funds from Contract MDA 903-92-K-0125 from the U.S. Army Research Institute and a grant from the Partnership for Child Development.

REFERENCES

Baltes, P. B., & Staudinger, U. M (2000). Wisdom: A metaheuristic (pragmatic) to orchestrate mind and virtue toward excellence. *American Psychologist, 55*, 122–135.

Barnes, M. L., & Sternberg, R. J. (1989). Social intelligence and decoding of nonverbal cues. *Intelligence, 13*, 263–287.

Berry, J. W. (1974). Radical cultural relativism and the concept of intelligence. In J. W. Berry & P. R. Dasen (Eds.), *Culture and cognition: Readings in cross-cultural psychology* (pp. 225–229). London: Methuen.

Binet, A., & Simon, T. (1916). *The development of intelligence in children*. Baltimore: Williams & Wilkins. (Originally published 1905)

Bouchard, T. J. (1997). IQ similarity in twins reared apart: Findings and responses to critics. In R. J. Sternberg & E. L. Grigorenko (Eds.), *Intelligence, heredity, and environment* (pp. 126–160). New York: Cambridge University Press.

Brand, C. (1996). *The g factor: General intelligence and its implications*. Chichester, England: Wiley.

Brody N. (2000). History of theories and measurements of intelligence. In R. J. Sternberg (Ed.), *Handbook of intelligence* (pp. 16–33). New York: Cambridge University Press.

Brown, A. L., & Ferrara, R. A. (1985). Diagnosing zones of proximal development. In J. V. Wertsch (Ed.), *Culture, communication, and cognition: Vygotskian perspectives* (pp. 273–305). New York: Cambridge University Press.

Budoff, M. (1968). Learning potential as a supplementary assessment procedure. In J. Hellmuth (Ed.), *Learning disorders* (Vol. 3, pp. 295–343). Seattle, WA: Special Child.

Carraher, T. N., Carraher, D., & Schliemann, A. D. (1985). Mathematics in the streets and in schools. *British Journal of Developmental Psychology, 3*, 21–29.

Carroll, J. B. (1993). *Human cognitive abilities: A survey of factor-analytic studies*. New York: Cambridge University Press.

Cattell, R. B. (1971). *Abilities: Their structure, growth and action*. Boston: Houghton Mifflin.

Cattell, R. B., & Cattell, A. K. (1973). *Test of g: Culture fair, Level 2*. Champaign, IL: Institute for Personality and Ability Testing.

Ceci, S. J. (1996). *On intelligence: A bioecological treatise on intellectual development* (expanded ed.). Cambridge, MA: Harvard University Press.

Ceci, S. J., & Liker, J. (1986). Academic and nonacademic intelligence: an experimental separation. In R. J. Sternberg & R. K. Wagner (Eds.), *Practical intelligence: Nature and origins of competence in the everyday world* (pp. 119–142). New York: Cambridge University Press.

Ceci, S. J., & Roazzi, A. (1994). The effects of context on cognition: Postcards from Brazil. In R. J. Sternberg & R. K. Wagner (Eds.), *Mind in context: Interactionist perspectives on human intelligence* (pp. 74–101). New York: Cambridge University Press.

Davidson, J. E., & Sternberg, R. J. (1984). The role of insight in intellectual giftedness. *Gifted Child Quarterly, 28*, 58–64.

Davies, M., Stankov, L., & Roberts, R. D. (1998). Emotional intelligence: In search of an elusive construct. *Journal of Personality and Social Psychology, 75*, 985–1015.

Day, J. D., Engelhard, J. L., Maxwell, S. E., & Bolig, E. E. (1997). Comparison of static and dynamic assessment procedures and their relation to independent performance. *Journal of Educational Psychology, 89*, 358–368.

Embretson, S., & McCollam, K. (2000). Psychometric approaches to the understanding and measurement of intelligence. In R. J. Sternberg (Ed.), *Handbook of intelligence* (pp. 16–33). New York: Cambridge University Press.

Ericsson, K. A. (Ed.). (1996). *The road to excellence*. Mahwah, NJ: Lawrence Erlbaum Associates.

Feuerstein, R. (1979). *The dynamic assessment of retarded performers: The learning potential assessment device, theory, instrument, and techniques*. Baltimore, MD: *University* Park.

Flynn, J. R. (1984). The mean IQ of Americans: Massive gains 1932 to 1978. *Psychological Bulletin, 95*, 29–51.

Flynn, J. R. (1987). Massive IQ gains in 14 nations: What IQ tests really measure. *Psychological Bulletin, 101*, 171–191.

Gardner, H. (1983). *Frames of mind: The theory of multiple intelligences*. New York: Basic Books.

Gardner, H. (1999). Are there additional intelligences? The case for naturalist, spiritual, and existential intelligences. In J. Kane (Ed.), *Education, information, and transformation* (pp. 111–131). Englewood Cliffs, NJ: Prentice-Hall.

Gardner, H., Krechevsky, M., Sternberg, R. J., & Okagaki, L. (1994). Intelligence in context: Enhancing students' practical intelligence for school. In K. McGilly (Ed.), *Classroom lessons: Integrating cognitive theory and classroom practice* (pp. 105–127). Cambridge, MA: Bradford Books.

Grigorenko, E. L., Jarvin, L., & Sternberg, R. J. (in press). School-based tests of the triarchic theory of intelligence: Three settings, three samples, three syllabi. *Contemporary Educational Psychology*.

Grigorenko, E. L., Gil, G., Jarvin, L., & Sternberg, R. J. (2000). *Toward a validation of aspects of the theory of successful intelligence*. Manuscript submitted for publication.

Grigorenko, E. L., Geissler, W., Prince, R., Okatcha, F., Nokes, C., Kenny, D., Bundy, D., & Sternberg, R. J. (2001). The organization of Luo conceptions of intelligence: A study of implicit theories in a Kenyan village. *International Journal of Behavioral Development, 25*, 367–378.

Grigorenko, E. L., & Sternberg, R. J. (1998). Dynamic testing. *Psychological Bulletin, 124*, 75–111.

Grigorenko, E. L., & Sternberg, R. J. (2001). Analytical, creative, and practical intelligence as predictors of self-reported adaptive functioning: A case study in Russia. *Intelligence, 29*, 57–73.

Grigorenko, E. L., Sternberg, R. J., & Ehrman, M. (2000). A theory-based approach to the measurement of second-language learning ability: The CANAL-S theory and test. *The Modern Language Journal, 84*, 390–405.

Gustafsson, J. E. (1994). Hierarchical models of intelligence and educational achievement. In A. Demetriou & A. Efklides (Eds.), *Intelligence, mind and reasoning: Structure and development* (pp. 45–73). Amsterdam: North-Holland/Elsevier Science Publishers.

Guthke, J. (1993). Current trends in theories and assessment of intelligence. In J. H. M. Hamers, K. Sijtsma, & A. J. J. M. Ruijssenaars (Eds.), *Learning potential assessment* (pp. 13–20). Amsterdam: Swets & Zeitlinger.

Guyote, M., & Sternberg, R. J. (1981). A transitive-chain theory of syllogistic reasoning, *Cognitive Psychology, 13*, 461–525.

Haywood, H. C., & Tzuriel, D. (Eds.). (1992). *Interactive assessment*. New York: Springer-Verlag.

Herrnstein, R. J., & Murray, C. (1994). *The bell curve*. New York: Free Press.

Horn, J. L. (1994). Theory of fluid and crystallized intelligence. In R. J. Sternberg (Ed.), *The encyclopedia of human intelligence* (Vol. 1, pp. 443–451). New York: Macmillan.

Howe, M. J. A., Davidson, J. W., & Sloboda, J. A. (1998). Innate talents: Reality or myth? *Behavioral & Brain Sciences, 21*, 399–442.

Intelligence and its measurement: A symposium. (1921). *Journal of Educational Psychology, 12*, 123–147, 195–216, 271–275.

Jensen, A. R. (1998). *The g factor: The science of mental ability*. Westport, CT: Praeger/Greenwood.

Lave, J. (1988). *Cognition in practice: Mind, mathematics, and culture in everyday life*. New York: Cambridge University Press.

Lidz, C. S. (Ed.). (1987). *Dynamic assessment: An interactional approach to evaluating learning potential*. New York: Guilford Press.

Lidz, C. S. (1991). *Practitioner's guide to dynamic assessment*. New York: Guilford Press.

Lubart, T. I., & Sternberg, R. J. (1995). An investment approach to creativity: Theory and data. In S. M. Smith, T. B. Ward, & R. A. Finke (Eds.), *The creative cognition approach* (pp. 269–302). Cambridge, MA: MIT Press.

Mayer, J. D., Caruso, D. R., & Salovey, P. (1999). Emotional intelligence meets traditional standards for an intelligence. *Intelligence, 27*, 267–298.

Neisser, U. (Ed.). (1998). *The rising curve*. Washington, DC: American Psychological Association.

Nuñes, T. (1994). Street intelligence. In R. J. Sternberg (Ed.), *Encyclopedia of human intelligence* (Vol. 2, pp. 1045–1049). New York: Macmillan.

Nuñes, T., Schliemann, A. D., & Carraher, D. W. (1993). *Street mathematics and school mathematics*. New York: Cambridge University Press.

Okagaki, L., & Sternberg, R. J. (1993). Parental beliefs and children's school performance. *Child Development, 64*, 36–56.

Piaget, J. (1972). *The psychology of intelligence*. Totowa, NJ: Littlefield Adams.

Plomin, R. (1997). Identifying genes for cognitive abilities and disabilities. In R. J. Sternberg & E. L. Grigorenko (Eds.), *Intelligence, heredity, and environment* (pp. 89–104). New York: Cambridge University Press.

Rogoff, B. (1990). *Apprenticeship in thinking: Cognitive development in social context*. New York: Oxford University Press.

Scarr, S. (1997). Behavior-genetic and socialization theories of intelligence: Truce and reconciliation. In R. J. Sternberg & E. L. Grigorenko (Eds.), *Intelligence, heredity, and environment* (pp. 3–41). New York: Cambridge University Press.

Schmidt, F., & Hunter, J. (1998). The validity and utility of selection methods in personnel psychology: Practical and theoretical implications of 85 years of research findings. *Psychological Bulletin, 124*, 262–274.

Spearman, C. E. (1904). "General intelligence" objectively determined and measured. *American Journal of Psychology, 15*, 201–293.

Sternberg, R. J. (1977). *Intelligence, information processing, and analogical reasoning: The componential analysis of human abilities*. Hillsdale, NJ: Lawrence Erlbaum Associates.

Sternberg, R. J. (1980a). Representation and process in linear syllogistic reasoning. *Journal of Experimental Psychology: General, 109*, 119–159.

Sternberg, R. J. (1980b). Sketch of a componential subtheory of human intelligence. *Behavioral and Brain Sciences, 3,* 573–584.

Sternberg, R. J. (1981). Intelligence and nonentrenchment. *Journal of Educational Psychology, 73,* 1–16.

Sternberg, R. J. (1982). Natural, unnatural, and supernatural concepts. *Cognitive Psychology, 14,* 451–488.

Sternberg, R. J. (1983). Components of human intelligence. *Cognition, 15,* 1–48.

Sternberg, R. J. (1984). Toward a triarchic theory of human intelligence. *Behavioral and Brain Sciences, 7,* 269–287.

Sternberg, R. J. (1985a). *Beyond IQ: A triarchic theory of human intelligence.* New York: Cambridge University Press.

Sternberg, R. J. (1985b). Implicit theories of intelligence, creativity, and wisdom. *Journal of Personality and Social Psychology, 49,* 607–627.

Sternberg, R. J. (1987a). Most vocabulary is learned from context. In M. G. McKeown & M. E. Curtis (Eds.), *The nature of vocabulary acquisition* (pp. 89–105). Hillsdale, NJ: Lawrence Erlbaum Associates.

Sternberg, R. J. (1987b). The psychology of verbal comprehension. In R. Glaser (Ed.), *Advances in instructional psychology* (Vol. 3, pp. 97–151). Hillsdale, NJ: Lawrence Erlbaum Associates.

Sternberg, R. J. (1990). *Metaphors of mind: Conceptions of the nature of intelligence.* New York: Cambridge University Press.

Sternberg, R. J. (1993). *Sternberg Triarchic Abilities Test* (STAT). Unpublished test.

Sternberg, R. J. (Ed.). (1994). *Encyclopedia of human intelligence.* New York: Macmillan.

Sternberg, R. J. (1995). *In search of the human mind.* Orlando, FL: Harcourt Brace.

Sternberg, R. J. (1997). *Successful intelligence.* New York: Plume.

Sternberg, R. J. (1998a). Abilities are forms of developing expertise. *Educational Researcher, 27,* 11–20.

Sternberg, R. J. (1998b). A balance theory of wisdom. *Review of General Psychology, 2,* 347–365.

Sternberg, R. J. (1999a). Human intelligence: A case study of how more and more research can lead us to know less and less about a psychological phenomenon, until finally we know much less than we did before we started doing research. In E. Tulving (Ed.), *Memory, consciousness, and the brain: The Tallinn Conference* (pp. 363–373). Philadelphia, PA: Psychology Press.

Sternberg, R. J. (1999b). Intelligence as developing expertise. *Contemporary Educational Psychology, 24,* 259–375.

Sternberg, R. J. (1999c). A propulsion model of creative contributions. *Review of General Psychology, 3,* 83–100.

Sternberg, R. J. (1999d). The theory of successful intelligence. *Review of General Psychology, 3,* 292–316.

Sternberg, R. J. (Ed.). (2000). *Handbook of intelligence.* New York: Cambridge University Press.

Sternberg, R. J., Castejón, J., & Prieto, M. D., Hautakami, J., & Grigorenko, E. L. (2001). Confirmatory factor analysis of the Sternberg Triarchic Abilities Test (multiple-choice items) in three international samples: An empirical test of the triarchic theory of intelligence. *European Journal of Psychological Assessment, 17,* 1–16.

Sternberg, R. J., Clinkenbeard, P. R. (1995). A triarchic model of identifying, teaching, and assessing gifted children. *Roeper Review, 17,* 255–260.

Sternberg, R. J., Conway, B. E., Ketron, J. L., & Bernstein, M. (1981). People's conceptions of intelligence. *Journal of Personality and Social Psychology, 41,* 37–55.

Sternberg, R. J., & Detterman D. K. (Eds.). (1986). *What is intelligence? Contemporary viewpoints on its nature and definition.* Norwood, NJ: Ablex.

Sternberg, R. J., Ferrari, M., Clinkenbeard, P. R., & Grigorenko, E. L. (1996). Identification, instruction, and assessment of gifted children: A construct validation of a triarchic model. *Gifted Child Quarterly, 40,* 129–137.

Sternberg, R. J., Forsythe, G. B., Horvath, J., Hedlund, J., Snook, S., Williams, W. M., Wagner, R. K., & Grigorenko, E. L. (2000). *Practical intelligence in everyday life.* New York: Cambridge University Press.

Sternberg, R. J., & Gardner, M. K. (1983). Unities in inductive reasoning. *Journal of Experimental Psychology: General, 112,* 80–116.

Sternberg, R. J., & Gastel, J. (1989a). Coping with novelty in human intelligence: An empirical investigation. *Intelligence, 13,* 187–197.

Sternberg, R. J., & Gastel, J. (1989b). If dancers ate their shoes: Inductive reasoning with factual and counterfactual premises. *Memory and Cognition, 17,* 1–10.

Sternberg, R. J., & Grigorenko, E. L. (1997, Fall). The cognitive costs of physical and mental ill health: Applying the psychology of the developed world to the problems of the developing world. *Eye on Psi Chi, 2,* 20–27.

Sternberg, R. J., & Grigorenko, E. L. (2002). *Dynamic testing.* New York: Cambridge University Press.

Sternberg, R. J., Grigorenko, E. L., Ferrari, M., & Clinkenbeard, P. (1999). A triarchic analysis of an aptitude-treatment interaction. *European Journal of Psychological Assessment, 15,* 1–11.

Sternberg, R. J., Grigorenko, E. L., Ngorosho, D., Tuntufue, E., Mbise, A., Nokes, C., & Bundy, D. A. (in press). Hidden intellectual potential in rural Tanzanian school children. *Intelligence.*

Sternberg, R. J., & Kalmar D. A. (1997). When will the milk spoil? Everyday induction in human intelligence. *Intelligence, 25,* 185–203.

Sternberg, R. J., & Kaufman, J. C. (1998). Human abilities. *Annual Review of Psychology, 49,* 479–502.

Sternberg, R. J., & Lubart, T. I. (1991). An investment theory of creativity and its development. *Human Development, 34,* 1–31.

Sternberg, R. J., & Lubart, T. I. (1995). *Defying the crowd: Cultivating creativity in a culture of conformity.* New York: Free Press.

Sternberg, R. J., & Lubart, T. I. (1996). Investing in creativity. *American Psychologist, 51,* 677–688.

Sternberg, R. J., & Nigro, G. (1980). Developmental patterns in the solution of verbal analogies. *Child Development, 51,* 27–38.

Sternberg, R. J., Nokes, K., Geissler, P. W., Prince, R., Okatcha, F., Bundy, D. A., & Grigorenko, E. L. (2001). The relationship between academic and practical intelligence: A case study in Kenya. *Intelligence, 29,* 401–418.

Sternberg, R. J., Okagaki, L., & Jackson, A. (1990). Practical intelligence for success in school. *Educational Leadership, 48,* 35–39.

Sternberg, R. J., & Powell, J. S. (1982). Theories of intelligence. In R. J. Sternberg (Ed.), *Handbook of human intelligence* (pp. 975–1005). New York: Cambridge University Press.

Sternberg, R. J., Powell, J. S., & Kaye, D. B. (1982). The nature of verbal comprehension. *Poetics, 11,* 155–187.

Sternberg, R. J., Powell, C., McGrane, P. A., & McGregor, S. (1997). Effects of a parasitic infection on cognitive functioning. *Journal of Experimental Psychology: Applied, 3,* 67–76.

Sternberg, R. J., & Rifkin, B. (1979). The development of analogical reasoning processes. *Journal of Experimental Child Psychology, 27,* 195–232.

Sternberg, R. J., & Smith, C. (1985). Social intelligence and decoding skills in nonverbal communication. *Social Cognition, 2,* 168–192.

Sternberg, R. J., Torff, B., & Grigorenko, E. L. (1998a). Teaching for successful intelligence raises school achievement. *Phi Delta Kappan, 79,* 667–669.

Sternberg, R. J., Torff, B., & Grigorenko, E. L. (1998b). Teaching triarchically improves school achievement. *Journal of Educational Psychology, 90,* 374–384.

Sternberg, R. J., & Wagner, R. K. (1993). The *g*-ocentric view of intelligence and job performance is wrong. *Current Directions in Psychological Science, 2,* 1–4.

Sternberg, R. J., Wagner, R. K., & Okagaki, L. (1993). Practical intelligence: The nature and role of tacit knowledge in work and at school. In H. Reese & J. Puckett (Eds.), *Advances in lifespan development* (pp. 205–227). Hillsdale, NJ: Lawrence Erlbaum Associates.

Sternberg, R. J., Wagner, R. K., Williams, W. M., & Horvath, J. A. (1995). Testing common sense. *American Psychologist, 50,* 912–927.

Sternberg, R. J., & Williams, W. M. (1996). *How to develop student creativity.* Alexandria, VA: Association for Supervision and Curriculum Development.

Sternberg, R. J., & Williams, W. M. (1997). Does the Graduate Record Examination predict meaningful success in the graduate training of psychologists? A case study. *American Psychologist, 52,* 630–641.

Tetewsky, S. J., & Sternberg, R. J. (1986). Conceptual and lexical determinants of nonentrenched thinking. *Journal of Memory and Language, 25,* 202–225.

Thurstone, L. L. (1938). *Primary mental abilities.* Chicago: University of Chicago Press.

Tzuriel, D. (1995). *Dynamic-interactive assessment: The legacy of L. S. Vygotsky and current developments.* Unpublished manuscript, Bar-Ilan University.

Vernon, P. E. (1971). *The structure of human abilities.* London: Methuen.

Vygotsky, L. (1978). *Mind in society: The development of higher order processes.* Cambridge, MA: Harvard University Press.

Wagner, R. K. (1987). Tacit knowledge in everyday intelligent behavior. *Journal of Personality and Social Psychology, 52,* 1236–1247.

Wagner, R. K., & Sternberg, R. J. (1986). Tacit knowledge and intelligence in the everyday world. In R. J. Sternberg & R. K. Wagner (Eds.), *Practical intelligence: Nature and origins of competence in the everyday world* (pp. 51–83). New York: Cambridge University Press.

Williams, W. M., Blythe, T., White, N., Li, J., Sternberg, R. J., & Gardner, H. I. (1996). *Practical intelligence for school: A handbook for teachers of grades 5–8.* New York: HarperCollins.

Yang, S., Sternberg, R. J. (1997a). Conceptions of intelligence in ancient Chinese philosophy. *Journal of Theoretical and Philosophical Psychology, 17,* 101–119.

Yang, S., & Sternberg, R. J. (1997b). Taiwanese Chinese people's conceptions of intelligence. *Intelligence, 25,* 21–36.

Author Index

A

Abel, L., 240, 242, 293, 295
Abelson, R. P., 210, 219
Ackerman, P. L., 34, 36, 189, 198, 215
Acland, H., 369, 378
Acosta, P., 262, 274
Adolfsson, R., 303, 325
Ahern, F., 284, 289, 296, 304, 308, 325
Alarcón, M., 287, 288, 294, 296, 304, 306, 310, 313, 321, 322
Alderton, D. L., 156, 177
Aldwin, C. M., 389, 407
Allan, K. M., 27, 36, 168, 169, 178
Allport, A., 192, 206, 207, 209, 213
Altman, J., 246, 271
Amatruda, C. S., 247, 273
Amsel, E., 395, 410
Anastasi, A., 80, 81
Andersen, C., 395, 410
Anderson, J. R., 209, 210, 212, 213, 417, 418, 429, 431, 432, 436, 440, 441, 442
Anderson, M., 203, 213
Anderson, S. W., 199, 207, 208, 213, 220
Andreasen, N. C., 258, 273
Andrist, C. G., 237, 241
Angleitner, A., 165, 166, 180
Anisman, H., 268, 273
Anjoul, F., 32, 37
Anokhin, A., 293, 294
Anstey, K. J., 174, 177
Antonini, A., 256, 271
Antonis, B., 192, 207, 213
Apfelblat, D., 206, 207, 212, 213, 217
Arkes, H., 398, 403, 407
Arvey, R. D., 344, 345, 376

Ashman, A., 68, 74, 79, 81, 83
Ashworth, S., 339, 343, 347, 348, 351, 353, 378
Askov, E. N., 363, 376
Atkinson, R. C., 190, 206, 213, 417, 441
Austin, E. J., 202, 215
Austin-LaFrance, R. J., 257, 275
Ayton, P., 398, 403, 407
Azen, C., 262, 274

B

Bach, M. E., 264, 275
Baddeley, A. D., 137, 145, 162, 177, 200, 206, 208, 212, 213, 214, 432, 433, 438, 441
Baillargeon, R., 138, 147, 382, 409
Baird, J. T., Jr., 372, 379
Baker, D. W., 363, 365, 366, 367, 376, 380
Baker, L. A., 293, 294, 295
Baldwin, J., 363, 364, 376
Baltes, P. B., 172, 174, 175, 177, 179, 189, 201, 202, 214, 217, 308, 321, 324, 471, 474
Bandura, A., 254, 269, 271
Bane, M. J., 369, 378
Bardon, G., 141, 145
Bargh, J. A., 402, 407
Barkley, R. A., 65, 81
Barnes, M. L., 471, 474
Baron, J., 396, 398, 407
Baron-Cohen, S., 259, 271
Barrett, P. T., 293, 294
Barron, F., 319, 321
Bartlett, S., 337, 368, 369, 374, 377, 378

Bates, E. A., 260, 272
Bates, T. C., 194, 214, 231, 241
Bateson, W., 252, 271
Bayer, S. A., 246, 271
Bayeux, C., 131, 138, 140, 148
Bayley, N., 246, 270, 271
Beauducel, A., 433, 443
Beckan, L., 303, 325
Becker, K. A., 80, 84
Behrman, J. R., 369, 376
Benbow, C., 262, 272, 294, 296
Benson, D. F., 208, 219
Benton, A., 199, 207, 208, 220
Benzecri, J. P., 130, 145
Berg, C. A., 383, 386, 387, 388, 389,
    390, 391, 392, 393, 400, 401, 402,
    407, 408, 411, 412
Berg, S., 284, 285, 289, 296, 304, 308,
    321, 323, 325
Bernieri, F., 284, 296
Bernstein, M., 386, 412, 472, 473, 477
Berry, J. W., 382, 383, 386, 408, 409,
    472, 474
Bickley, P. G., 202, 214
Biddell, T. R., 382, 400, 408
Binet, A., 246, 254, 269, 271, 454, 474
Bishop, D. V. M., 286, 295, 318, 321
Bishop, S. J., 318, 321
Bjorklund, D. F., 202, 214
Black, J. E., 256, 271
Black, K. N., 318, 325
Blacker, D. M., 319, 327
Blanchard, J. S., 367, 380
Blanchard-Fields, F., 381, 382, 389,
    408
Blendy, J. A., 264, 275
Block, J. B., 316, 322
Blythe, T., 472, 479
Bobbitt, B. L., 196, 216
Boden, C., 73, 81
Bodmer, W. F., 268, 272
Bolig, E. E., 452, 475
Bolivar, V., 264, 268, 271
Boodoo, G., 152, 179, 246, 269, 275
Boomsma, D. I., 166, 180, 258, 275,
    284, 285, 293, 294, 297

Boring, E. G., 417, 441
Borkenau, P., 165, 166, 180
Borman, W. C., 339, 341, 376
Bors, D. A., 27, 36
Bouchard, J. T., Jr., 152, 179, 246,
    251, 269, 271, 275, 282, 284, 293,
    295, 296, 301, 303, 319, 320, 322,
    325, 327, 452, 474
Boykin, A. W., 152, 179, 246, 269, 275
Braden, W., 237, 242
Bradmetz, J., 134, 145
Bradshaw, J., 171, 178
Bradway, P., 29, 37
Brainerd, C. J., 394, 404, 406, 408, 411
Brammer, M. J., 259, 271
Bramwell, B. S., 319, 322
Brand, C. R., 21, 36, 97, 113, 154,
    177, 194, 202, 214, 215, 300, 322,
    356, 376, 416, 441, 447, 474
Bransford, J. D., 197, 214, 382, 408
Bregman, E. O., 250, 276
Bridges, C., 319, 326
Bright, P., 318, 321
Britton, B. K., 430, 442
Brody, N., 28, 36, 58, 66, 81, 152,
    179, 246, 269, 271, 275, 423, 425,
    440, 442, 448, 474
Bronzino, J. D., 257, 275
Brooks, A., 288, 295, 311, 314, 322
Brown, A., 382, 408
Brown, A. L., 197, 198, 214, 452, 474
Brown, H., 362, 363, 376
Brown, I., 199, 215
Brown, J. H., 282, 296
Browning, H. L., 240, 242
Bruggeman, C., 318, 325
Brush, F. R., 268, 272
Bruun, K., 316, 317, 325
Buchsbaum, M. S., 240, 242, 293, 295
Bucik, V., 194, 218
Buckner, R. L., 209, 214
Buckwalter, P. R., 318, 327
Budoff, M., 452, 474
Bullmore, E. T., 259, 271
Bullough, B., 319, 322
Bullough, V., 319, 322

Bundy, D. A., 450, 452, 472, 475, 478
Bunting, M. F., 441, 442
Burgess, P., 199, 206, 207, 208, 209, 219
Burgoon M., 367, 380
Burns, N. R., 27, 29, 37, 170, 177
Burt, C., 25, 36, 41, 52, 202, 214, 249, 250, 272
Butler, F., 262, 274
Byrd, M., 201, 214
Byrne, M. D., 417, 431, 442

C

Cain, P. S., 344, 378
Calderone, K. S., 386, 387, 388, 389, 391, 400, 402, 407, 408
Calvin, W. H., 246, 247, 272
Campbell, A., 362, 363, 376
Campbell, J. D., 402, 408
Campbell, J. P., 94, 113, 337, 376
Campbell, K. B., 167, 179, 293, 296
Campione, J. C., 197, 198, 214, 382, 408
Campos, J., 285, 295
Canter, S., 311, 319, 322
Cantor, J., 137, 140, 145, 146
Capron, C., 267, 276
Cardon, L. R., 287, 289, 295, 301, 302, 305, 307, 314, 322, 325
Carey, G., 287, 289, 297, 302, 304, 326
Carlson, J. S., 68, 69, 71, 74, 81, 82
Caroff, X., 136, 147
Carpenter, P. A., 138, 146, 157, 178, 427, 428, 432, 437, 440, 441, 442, 443
Carraher, D. W., 383, 385, 408, 410, 449, 474, 476
Carraher, T. N., 385, 408, 449, 474
Carretta, T. R., 162, 180, 337, 340, 379, 444
Carroll, J. B., 10, 17, 21, 24, 25, 26, 27, 28, 29, 36, 42, 43, 52, 53, 89, 90, 114, 121, 122, 123, 124, 144, 145, 152, 165, 166, 178, 194, 202, 214, 225, 234, 241, 265, 272, 293, 295, 300, 322, 331, 333, 337, 340, 376, 433, 435, 442, 448, 474

Carullo, J. J., 140, 146
Caruso, D. R., 232, 242, 473, 476
Caryl, P. G., 167, 168, 171, 178
Case, R., 11, 12, 14, 17, 136, 137, 138, 139, 144, 145, 146
Caspi, A., 358, 376, 389, 409
Castejón, J., 459, 477
Casto, S. D., 288, 289, 295, 302, 305, 322
Cattell, A. K., 459, 467, 474
Cattell, R. B., 34, 36, 46, 53, 199, 214, 459, 467, 474
Cavalli-Sforza, L. L., 268, 272
Ceci, S. J., 28, 36, 152, 179, 186, 214, 230, 241, 246, 257, 269, 272, 275, 382, 383, 384, 385, 408, 449, 474, 475
Cerella, J., 201, 202, 214
Chaiken, S. R., 403, 408, 435, 436, 440, 442
Challman, R. C., 254, 273
Chan, D., 336, 379
Chen, C., 264, 272
Chen, S., 403, 408
Chen, Y., 381, 382, 389, 408
Cherny, S. S., 284, 285, 286, 289, 295, 296
Chiara, G., 389, 407
Chiodo, L. M., 402, 410
Chipuer, H. M., 282, 295, 308, 326
Chorney, K., 262, 272, 294, 296
Chorney, M. J., 262, 272, 294, 296
Christal, R. E., 140, 146, 158, 160, 161, 179, 425, 431, 432, 434, 439, 442, 443, 444
Cibois, P., 134, 147
Cintra, L., 257, 275
Clark, W. S., 363, 367, 376
Cleary, T. A., 93, 114
Clinkenbeard, P. R., 461, 452, 457, 461, 477, 478
Coates, W. C., 365, 380
Cobb, M. V., 250, 276
Cohen, D., 369, 378
Cohen, J., 105, 114, 332, 376
Cohen, N. J., 256, 273

Cohen, R. L., 212, 214
Conelly, S., 201, 216
Conners, F., 232, 242, 311, 325
Conway, A. R. A., 162, 178, 199, 215, 441, 442
Conway, B. E., 386, 412, 472, 473, 477
Conway, R. N. F., 74, 81
Cook, M., 264, 268, 271
Cooper, C. J., 170, 177
Cooper, L. A., 423, 442
Corcoran, M., 337, 368, 369, 374, 377, 378
Corley, R. P., 284, 285, 286, 287, 294, 295, 297, 304, 306, 321
Cormier, P., 68, 69, 71, 81
Cornelius, S. W., 308, 321, 358, 376, 409
Court, J. H., 188, 218
Cowan, N., 137, 144, 146, 441, 442
Coward, W. M., 343, 376
Crabbe, J. C., 257, 264, 268, 272, 277
Craik, F. I. M., 201, 214
Crawford, J. R., 27, 36, 168, 169, 170, 178
Crawley, J. N., 262, 272
Crinella, F. M., 239, 243
Cronbach, L. J., 67, 81, 212, 215, 254, 272, 414, 442
Crouse, J., 337, 368, 369, 374, 377, 378
Crow A., 254, 272
Crow, L. D., 254, 272
Crusio, W. E., 257, 264, 267, 272
Cunningham, W., 308, 322

D

D'Esposito, M., 259, 276
D'Estelle, S., 367, 380
Dacey, J. S., 319, 322
Daily, L. Z., 418, 440, 442
Dale, P. S., 286, 295
Damasio, H., 208, 213
Daneman, M., 138, 146, 432, 437, 442
Daniel, M. H., 21, 36, 202, 215, 235, 242

Daniels, J., 262, 272, 294, 296
Daniels, M., 257, 272
Danthiir, V., 29, 36
Das, J. P., 59, 61, 62, 63, 64, 66, 68, 69, 70, 71, 72, 73, 74, 77, 80, 81, 82, 83, 265, 272
Dash, U. N., 68, 69, 71, 82
Datta, H., 310, 312, 315, 325
Davenport, E. C., 94, 114
Davey, T. C., 96, 98, 114, 121, 146
Davidson J. W., 451, 476
Davidson, J. E., 193, 219, 469, 475
Davies, M., 473, 475
Davis, T. C., 363, 365, 376
Day, J. D., 452, 475
de Belle, J. S., 265, 272
de Courten, C., 237, 242, 246, 274
de Geus, E. J. C., 293, 294, 297
de la Cruz, F., 262, 274
de la Rocha, O., 384, 410
De Ribaupierre, A., 131, 137, 138, 140, 147, 148
De Vries, R., 121, 122, 123, 124, 145, 146
Dean, P. R., 151, 180
Dearborn, W. F., 98, 114
Deary, I. J., 21, 27, 36, 52, 53, 163, 167, 168, 169, 170, 171, 178, 188, 190, 194, 195, 202, 203, 204, 214, 215, 219, 440, 442
Decker, S. M., 293, 295
DeFaire, U., 285, 296
DeFries, J. C., 257, 266, 275, 284, 285, 286, 287, 288, 289, 294, 295, 296, 297, 302, 303, 304, 305, 306, 307, 308, 310, 311, 312, 313, 314, 315, 316, 321, 322, 323, 324, 325, 326, 327
Delaney, T., 318, 321
Demetriou, A., 11, 17, 144, 146
Dempster, F. N., 144, 146, 198, 200, 201, 208, 213, 215
Denes-Raj, V., 397, 409
Denney, N. W., 392, 409
Dennis, I., 438, 442
deSanchez, M., 439, 443

Detterman, D. K., 21, 36, 202, 215, 230, 232, 233, 235, 237, 241, 242, 243, 262, 272, 292, 293, 294, 295, 296, 304, 313, 327, 447, 453, 455, 477
Devlin, B., 257, 272
DeVries, R., 120, 121, 146
Diamond, S., 183, 215
Diaz-Cintra, S., 257, 275
Diehl, M., 358, 376, 402, 410
DiLalla, L. F., 314, 322
Dillon, R. F., 80, 81
Doak, C. C., 363, 376
Doak, L. G., 363, 376
Dolan, R. J., 56, 81
Dolph, B., 25, 29, 31, 37
Domino, G., 319, 326
Donahue, E. M., 402, 411
Donaldson, G., 425, 442
Donlan, C., 318, 321
Dorfman, D. D., 251, 272
Doub, T., 340, 379
Douglass, A., 318, 325
Doyle, J., 210, 217
DuBois, P., 107, 114
Dudek, B. C., 257, 264, 268, 272, 277
Duncan, J., 157, 178, 198, 199, 200, 206, 208, 215
Dunn, B. E., 302, 324
Dunn, L. M., 310, 323

E

Eaglesfield, D., 337, 368, 369, 374, 377, 378
Earles, J. A., 340, 350, 379, 416, 444
Eaves, L. J., 285, 295, 302, 305, 324
Edgarton, R. B., 359, 376, 378
Efklides, A., 3, 4, 11, 12, 13, 17
Egan, V., 21, 36, 195, 202, 215
Egan. D. E., 423, 442
Ehrman, M., 453, 475
Eley, T. C., 262, 272, 286, 295, 297
Elliott, C. D., 66, 81
Elman, J. L., 260, 272
Embretson, S. E., 158, 159, 178, 231, 242, 426, 442, 448, 475

Emde, R. N., 284, 285, 286, 289, 295, 296
Emslie, H., 157, 178, 198, 199, 200, 215
Encha-Razavi, F., 246, 272
Engelhard, J. L., 452, 475
Engle, R. W., 137, 140, 145, 146, 162, 178, 199, 215, 432, 441, 442, 445
Epstein, S., 397, 398, 403, 404, 409
Ericsson, K. A., 439, 442, 451, 475
Erngrund, K., 303, 325
Estes, W. K., 423, 442
Evans, G., 195, 215
Evans, J. B., St. T., 394, 403, 404, 409, 438, 442
Evans, S. W., 237, 241
Everitt, B. J., 267, 273
Eysenck, H. J., 154, 178, 189, 193, 194, 212, 214, 215, 258, 273, 293, 294, 319, 323

F

Faber, C., 202, 217
Fagan, J. F., III, 230, 242, 246, 273
Fancher, R. E., 249, 273
Fantuzzo, J. W., 64, 82
Farrar, M. J., 136, 146
Fauth, J., 396, 409
Ferrara, R. A., 382, 408, 452, 474
Ferrari, M., 452, 457, 461, 477, 478
Ferraro, F. R., 202, 215
Ferrera, R. A., 197, 198, 214
Feuer, D., 284, 293, 296
Feuerstein, R., 68, 81, 452, 475
Finkel, D., 284, 289, 295, 308, 316, 317, 323
Fischbein, S., 307, 323
Fischer, K., 318, 323
Fischer, K. W., 136, 144, 146, 382, 400, 408
Fisher, D. L., 202, 215
Fisk, A. D., 202, 215
Flaherty, L., 264, 268, 271
Flanagan, D. P., 64, 82
Flashman, L. A., 258, 273

Flaum, M., 258, 273
Flavell, E. R., 12, 17
Flavell, J. H., 12, 17
Fleishman, A. I., 100, 114
Fleishman, E. A., 435, 442, 443
Flynn, J. R., 110, 114, 452, 475
Foch, T. T., 317, 323
Fodor, J. A., 202, 209, 283, 295
Fogarty, G. J., 21, 36, 190, 215
Folkman, S., 389, 409, 410
Forness, S. R., 64, 82
Forrin, B., 27, 36
Forsberg, H., 313, 325
Forsythe, G. B., 320, 326, 355, 356, 379, 457, 469, 478
Fountas, I., 78, 83
Frackowiak, R. S. J., 56, 81, 208, 216
Francis, D. D., 268, 273
Fredericksen, J. R., 423, 443
Fredman, G., 314, 326
Freer, P., 198, 199, 200, 215
Frensch, P. A., 188, 201, 215, 219
Friberg, L., 317, 325
Friedman, E., 262, 274
Frisch, D., 397, 409
Friston, K. J., 56, 61, 208, 216
Frith, C. D., 208, 209, 216
Frost, N., 427, 443
Fulker, D. W., 283, 284, 285, 286, 287, 288, 289, 294, 295, 296, 297, 302, 304, 305, 306, 307, 308, 310, 311, 313, 314, 321, 322, 324, 325, 326, 327
Fuller, J. L., 250, 255, 273
Furneaux, W. D., 154, 178

G

Gabrielli, W. F., 372, 378
Gage, F. H., 256, 274
Galanter, E., 59, 82, 188, 217
Galconer, D. S., 266, 273
Galilei, Galileo, 19, 36
Galler, J. R., 257, 275
Galton, F., 153, 178, 249, 273, 282, 295

Garcia-Mila, M., 395, 410
Gardner, H., 5, 17, 25, 36, 153, 178, 189, 216, 265, 269, 273, 302, 323, 355, 376, 449, 455, 472, 473, 475, 479
Gardner, M. K., 154, 156, 180, 196, 197, 219, 464, 478
Gardner, W., 392, 411
Garey, L. J., 237, 242, 246, 274
Gass, P., 264, 275
Gastel, J., 467, 478
Gates, A. I., 254, 273
Gathercole, S., 162, 177
Gauvain, M., G392, 411
Gayán, J., 310, 312, 315, 324, 325
Gazzaniga, M. S., 200, 209, 216
Geary, D. C., 71, 81
Geissler, P. W., 450, 472, 475, 478
Gelman, R., 382, 409
Genthner-Grimm, G., 257, 264, 272
Gerlai, R. T., 267, 268, 272, 273
Gerstman, B. B., 332, 364, 376
Gesell, A., 247, 273
Gibson, G. J., 21, 36, 167, 168, 178, 202, 215
Gil, G., 471, 475
Gillis, J. J., 314, 327
Gillis-Light, J., 313, 324
Gintis, H., 369, 378
Gladwin, T., 384, 409
Glaser, R., 196, 218, 423, 428, 430, 443, 444
Glass, G. V., 119, 120, 121, 124, 146, 148
Glass, J., 206, 207, 212, 213, 217
Globerson, T., 139, 146
Glutting, J. J., 64, 68, 81, 82
Gmeindl, L., 206, 207, 212, 213, 217
Goff, G. N., 32, 37
Goff, S., 343, 345, 346, 379
Goguen, L. A., 402, 410
Goldberger, A. S., 266, 273
Goldman, S. R., 156, 177
Goldstein, S., 79, 81
Goodenough, F. L., 25, 273

Gordon, D. H., 396, 398, 399, 404, 409, 410
Gordon, L. L., 404, 408
Gordon, R. A., 368, 372, 377
Goschke, T., 205, 216
Gottfredson, L. S., 152, 178, 265, 273, 344, 345, 359, 369, 371, 377
Gottlieb, G., 252, 253, 258, 267, 273, 277
Gottling, S. H., 68, 69, 70, 71, 80, 83
Gould, C. G., 247, 273
Gould, J. L., 247, 273
Gould, S. J., 101, 114, 226, 242
Grafinkle, A. S., 317, 323
Graham, P., 314, 326
Granato, L., 398, 407
Grasby, P. M., 209, 216
Green, B. F., Jr., 337, 338, 343, 346, 349, 380
Green, F. L., 12, 17
Greenacre, M. J., 130, 146
Greene, R. L., 210, 216
Greene, R. W., 264, 272
Greenough, W. T., 256, 271, 273
Grigorenko, E. L., 303, 311, 312, 319, 320, 324, 326, 355, 356, 379, 448, 450, 452, 453, 457, 459, 461, 462, 463, 469, 471, 472, 475, 477, 478, 479
Grimes-Farrow, D. D., 423, 442
Grotzer, T. A., 198, 218
Gsodl, M. K., 282, 296
Gugerty, L. J., 440, 445
Guilford, J. P., 21, 22, 23, 24, 28, 36, 89, 114
Guo, S. -W., 267, 273
Gustafsson, J. -E., 10, 17, 27, 36, 47, 53, 144, 146, 165, 168, 169, 178, 300, 324, 448, 475
Gutentag, S., 80, 82
Guthke, J., 452, 476
Guttman, L., 20, 23, 36
Guyote, M. J., 196, 216, 464, 476

H

Hagen, E. P., 58, 83

Haier, R. J., 237, 240, 242, 293, 295
Haiken-Vasen, J., 230, 242
Hald, M. E., 68, 70, 71, 80, 82
Hale, S., 202, 217, 218
Halford, G., 11, 17
Halpern, D. F., 152, 179, 246, 269, 275
Hamagami, F., 29, 37
Hanley, W., 262, 274
Hanoune, J., 264, 275
Hanson, M. A., 339, 343, 347, 348, 351, 353, 378
Harnishfeger, K. K., 200, 214
Harris, D. B., 247, 273
Harris, M. J., 284, 296
Hart, G., 367, 380
Hartigan, J. A., 111, 114
Hartley, A. A., 201, 202, 216
Hasher, L., 200, 201, 216, 220
Hauser, R. M., 369, 379
Hautakämi, J., 459, 477
Hawkins, R. D., 264, 275
Haygood, R. C., 197, 216
Haywood, H. C., 452, 476
Hazlett, E., 240, 242
Hearnshaw, L. S., 251, 273
Heath, A. C., 285, 295
Heckhausen, J., 389, 409
Hedlund, J., 320, 326, 355, 356, 379, 469, 478
Heine, S. J., 402, 408
Heisenberg, M., 265, 272
Hemmingway, T., 171, 181
Hendrickson, A. E., 237, 242
Hendrickson, D. E., 237, 242
Herrnstein, R. J., 97, 114, 372, 373, 377, 439, 443, 448, 476
Hertzog, C., 389, 408
Hewitt, J. K., 284, 286, 289, 296
Heyns, B., 369, 378
Hick, W. E., 163, 178
Higgins, E. T., 402, 407
Highfield, R., 263, 274
Hirsch, J., 256, 274
Ho, H. Z., 293, 294, 295
Hodder, S. L., 27, 36
Hofer, S. M., 48, 53

Hoffman, M. B., 68, 81
Hogan, R. T., 352, 377
Hohnen, B., 311, 323
Holden, C., 259, 274
Holstein, C., 397, 398, 409
Holzman, P. S., 153, 178
Honeyman, M., 319, 326
Horn, J. L., 20, 21, 22, 23, 29, 34, 36, 37, 48, 53, 64, 82, 199, 216, 301, 324, 448, 476
Horn, J. M., 302, 324
Horvath, J. A., 145, 148, 320, 326, 334, 355, 356, 379, 380, 457, 469, 478, 479
Hough, L. M., 339, 343, 347, 348, 351, 353, 378
Howard, M., 250, 272
Howe, M. J. A., 195, 216, 451, 476
Hsieh, S., 207, 209, 213
Huang, Y., 264, 275
Huh, E., 397, 398, 409
Humphreys, L. G., 23, 37, 87, 89, 90, 93, 94, 95, 96, 97, 98, 100, 103, 104, 108, 114, 115, 120, 121, 122, 123, 124, 143, 146, 333, 336, 337, 378
Hunt, E. B., 26, 37, 105, 115, 151, 164, 178, 179, 190, 192, 203, 211, 216, 427, 443
Hunter, J. E., 94, 115, 333, 335, 340, 341, 343, 344, 345, 346, 349, 350, 351, 352, 353, 354, 377, 378, 379, 416, 444, 472, 476
Hunter, R. F., 343, 344, 351, 377
Husen, T., 98, 114
Hutchinson, J. W., 415, 445
Huttenlocher, P. R., 237, 242, 246, 274

I

Ikomi, P. A., 440, 445
Inhelder, B., 118, 146
Inman, W. C., 124, 135, 143, 146
Irvine, S. H., 383, 383, 386, 409, 427, 441, 443

J

Jackson, A., 471, 478
Jackson, G., 337, 368, 369, 374, 377, 378
Jacob, F., 252, 274
Jacobs, B., 362, 363, 376
Jäger, A. O., 433, 443
James, C., 318, 321
Jardine, R., 302, 305, 324
Jarvik, L. F., 316, 324, 463, 471, 475
Jay, E., 396, 410
Jay, G., 308, 326
Jencks, C., 337, 368, 369, 374, 377, 378
Jenkins, L., 359, 362, 364, 372, 378
Jennings, D., 336, 379
Jensen, A. R., 5, 17, 25, 37, 46, 48, 49, 47, 50, 51, 52, 53, 66, 82, 87, 95, 100, 114, 115, 154, 164, 165, 167, 168, 170, 171, 177, 179, 193, 194, 201, 213, 216, 217, 223, 225, 234, 242, 243, 258, 259, 274, 290, 293, 295, 297, 301, 305, 324, 331, 332, 337, 358, 378, 438, 441, 443, 447, 448, 476
Jersild, A. T., 254, 273
Johannsen, W., 253, 274
Johansson, B., 284, 289, 296, 304, 308, 323, 325
Johnson, D., 68, 69, 70, 71, 80, 83
Johnson, D. F., 197, 216
Johnson, M. B., 64, 66, 84
Johnson, M. H., 260, 272, 282, 296
Johnson, R., 198, 199, 200, 215
Johnson, R. C., 303, 323
Jones, D. G., 245, 246, 274
Jones, L. V., 94, 114
Jones, L. W., 183, 219
Jones, R. D., 208, 213
Jonides, J., 206, 209, 216
Judiesch, M. K., 34, 377
Jungeblut, A., 359, 360, 362, 364, 372, 378
Juraska, J. M., 256, 273
Jurden, F. H., 390, 410
Juse, A. R., 303, 323

Just, M. A., 157, 178, 427, 428, 440, 441, 442, 443

K

Kaestle, C. F., 363, 380
Kagan, J., 285, 295
Kahana, M. J., 237, 241
Kahneman, D., 190, 216, 403, 409
Kail, R., 145, 146, 172, 179, 231, 242
Kalek, A., 316, 324
Kallmann, F. J., 316, 324
Kalmar, D. A., 464, 478
Kamin, L. J., 250, 274
Kandel, E. R., 264, 275
Kane, M., 201, 216
Kane, P. T., 387, 412
Kantor, L., 165, 181, 194, 220
Kar, B. C., 68, 69, 71, 82
Karmiloff-Smith, A., 260, 272, 282, 283, 295, 296
Kashima, E., 96, 114
Katz, I. M., 402, 408
Kaufman, A. S., 59, 66, 74, 75, 82, 118, 121, 134, 146
Kaufman, J. C., 472, 478
Kaufman, N. L., 59, 66, 74, 75, 82
Kavale, K. A., 64, 82
Kaye, D. B., 465, 478
Kazi, S., 4, 11, 12, 15, 17, 144, 146
Keating, D. P., 196, 216
Keith, T. Z., 64, 82, 202, 214
Kellaghan, T., 21, 36, 202, 215
Kemper, T., 257, 275
Kemperman, G., 256, 274
Kempthorne, O., 266, 267, 274
Kendrick, S. A., 93, 114
Kenny, D., 472, 475
Ketron, J. L., 472, 473, 477
Kieras, D. E., 206, 207, 212, 213, 217, 417, 431, 443
Kirby, J. R., 63, 68, 72, 73, 75, 76, 77, 78, 81, 82
Kirsch, I. S., 359, 360, 362, 363, 364, 372, 376, 378

Klaczynski, P. A., 383, 389, 390, 392, 393, 394, 396, 397, 398, 399, 401, 403, 404, 405, 406, 408, 409, 410
Kliegl, R., 201, 202, 203, 216, 217
Kline, P., 156, 179
Kluwe, R. H., 205, 217
Knapp, J. R., 21, 37
Knevel, C. R., 237, 241
Knopik, V. S., 288, 296
Knorr, E., 165, 180
Knudsen, E. I., 256, 274
Koch, R., 262, 274
Koegel, P., 359, 378
Kohlberg, L., 121, 122, 123, 124, 145, 146
Kolstad, A., 359, 362, 364, 372, 378
Konovsky, M., 339, 378
Krampe, R. T., 202, 216
Kranzler, J. H., 47, 53, 168, 171, 179, 193, 194, 217, 234, 243
Kray, J., 201, 202, 215, 216, 217
Krechevsky, M., 471, 475
Kreitler, H., 398, 410
Kreitler, S., 398, 410
Kruber, Z., 369, 376
Kuhn, D., 395, 410
Kuljis, R. O., 245, 246, 274
Kyllonen, P. C., 32, 37, 140, 146, 158, 160, 161, 179, 231, 242, 418, 425, 427, 429, 431, 432, 433, 434, 436, 439, 441, 443, 444, 435, 436, 440, 442

L

Labouvie-Vief, G., 402, 410
LaBuda, M. C., 288, 296, 302, 305, 306, 307, 310, 319, 322, 324
Laget, P., 246 274
Laipple, J. S., 390, 393, 410
Laird, J. E., 153, 179, 210, 212, 217
Laird, P. S., 205, 218
Lane, D. M., 203, 217
Lansman, M., 190, 216
Larivée, S., 125, 135, 147
Larson, G. E., 193, 201
Lashley, K. S., 56, 82

Lauber, E., 206, 207, 212, 213, 217
Laughlin, J. E., 162, 178, 199, 215, 441, 442
Laurendeau, M., 118, 147
Lautrey, J., 129, 130, 131, 134, 136, 147, 146
Laux, L. F., 203, 217
Lavallee, L. F., 402, 408
Lave, J., 383, 384, 411, 420, 449, 476
Law, D. J., 105, 115
Lay, W., 151, 180
Lazarus, R. S., 389, 409, 410
Leamy, L., 257, 269, 274
Lebiere, C., 436, 437, 438, 440, 441, 444
LeBuffe, P. A., 75, 83
Legree, P. J., 232, 242
Lehman, D. R., 402, 408
Leiman, J. M., 44, 53, 88, 90, 115
Lenneberg, E., 318, 324
Levy, H., 262, 274
Levy, P., 171, 179
Lewis, J., 164, 179
Lewis, M. A., 368, 377
Lewontin, R. C., 260, 274
Lhermitte, F., 207, 208, 217
Li, J., 472, 479
Lichtenstein, P., 285, 289, 296, 297, 308, 316, 325, 326
Lichtman, J. W., 245, 275
Lickliter, R., 258, 273
Liddle, P. F., 208, 216
Lidz, C. S., 68, 82, 452, 476
Lienert, G. A., 202, 217
Liker, J., 230, 241, 383, 384, 385, 408, 449, 475
Lima, S. D., 202, 217
Lin, P., 100, 114
Lindenberger, U., 172, 174, 175, 177, 179, 189, 201, 202, 203, 204, 214, 215, 216, 217, 308, 321, 324
Linn, M. C., 105, 115
Lipp, H. -P., 265, 268, 274, 277
Lipson, A., 397, 398, 409
Lloyd, F. J., 403, 404, 406, 411

Loehlin, J. C., 112, 115, 152, 179, 246, 269, 275, 302, 324
Lohman, D. F., 156, 167, 179, 189, 190, 192, 199, 200, 217, 425, 426, 431, 444
Lombardi, W. J., 402, 407
Long, J., 285, 295
Longeot, F., 118, 126, 127, 128, 130, 147
Lorenz, K., 252, 274
Lorge, I.., 316, 324
Lovett, M. C., 418, 437, 438, 440, 441, 442, 444
Lubart, T, I., 320, 326, 467, 468, 476, 478
Lubinski, D., 94, 95, 97, 103, 104, 108, 114, 115, 262, 272, 294, 296, 333, 378
Lunneborg, C., 164, 179, 427, 443
Luo, D., 29, 37, 166, 167, 171, 179, 230, 237, 241, 243, 288, 289, 293, 296, 302, 305, 324
Luria, A. R., 56, 59, 60, 61, 82
Lykken, D. T., 251, 271, 284, 293, 296, 315, 316, 317, 319, 322, 327
Lynn, R., 202, 217
Lyon, D. R., 425, 444
Lyon, G. R., 314, 324
Lyon, R., 315, 327
Lytton, H., 302, 324

M

MacKay, T. F. C., 266, 273
Mackintosh, N. J., 27, 37, 258, 274
MacLeod, C. M., 163, 164, 179
MacWhinney, B., 247, 274
Magara, F., 265, 274
Magnus, P., 288, 289, 297, 302, 305, 316, 326
Mak, T. W., 264, 275
Maldonado R., 264, 275
Markkanen, T., 316, 317, 325
Markus, H. R., 401, 402, 410
Markwardt, F. C., 310, 323
Marr, D. B., 200, 201, 202, 217

Marshalek, B., 156, 179, 189, 190, 192, 199, 200, 217, 431, 440, 444
Martin, N. G., 302, 305, 311, 324
Martin, P. G., 311, 324
Massaro, D. W., 153, 179
Massiotta, J. C., 56, 81
Masters, M. S., 105, 115
Mastropieri, M. A., 68, 82
Matalon, R., 262, 274
Matarazzo, J. D., 293, 296
Matheny, A., 318, 325
Mather, N., 79, 81
Mather, P. L., 318, 325
Mauro, M., 319, 322
Maxwell, S. E., 452, 475
Mayer, J. D., 232, 242, 473, 476
Mayford, M., 264, 275
Mayr, U., 201, 202, 203, 216, 217
Mbise, A., 452, 478
McArdle, J. J., 29, 37
McCartney, K., 253, 276, 284, 296
McClearn, G. E., 257, 266, 275, 284, 285, 288, 289, 294, 295, 296, 297, 302, 303, 304, 308, 316, 317, 323, 325, 326
McClelland, K., 337, 368, 369, 374, 377, 378
McCollam, K., 448, 475
McConnell, T. R., 254, 273
McCrimmon, R. J., 171, 178
McDaniel, M. A., 354, 378
McDermott, D., 210, 217
McDermott, P. A., 64, 68, 81, 82
McGarry-Roberts, P. A., 167, 179, 293, 296
McGee, D. L., 367, 380
McGrane, P. A., 457, 478
McGregor, S., 457, 478
McGrew, K. S., 64, 66, 82
McGue, M., 251, 271, 282, 284, 289, 293, 295, 296, 303, 308, 316, 317, 323, 325
McGuffin, P., 262, 272, 283, 294, 296, 297
McHenry, J. J., 337, 339, 343, 347, 348, 351, 353, 376, 378

McLaughlin, J. A., 119, 120, 121, 124, 148
McLoughlin, V., 314, 326
Mednick, S. A., 372, 378
Meegan, S. P., 388, 389, 392, 393, 400, 401, 408
Meldrum, H., 365, 376
Meredith, W., 29, 37
Meyer, D. E., 206, 207, 212, 213, 217, 417, 431, 443
Meyer, M. S., 303, 324
Michals-Matalon, K., 262, 274
Michelson S., 369, 378
Michielutte, R., 363, 376
Miklos, G. L., 264, 275
Miller, A. R., 344, 378
Miller, C. K., 119, 120, 121, 124, 148
Miller, G., 59, 82, 188, 217
Milner, B., 208, 217
Minkoff, S., 441, 442
Mischel, W., 401, 410
Mishra, R. K., 68, 72, 73, 74, 81
Mitchell, R. F., 163, 180
Mittler, P., 316, 318, 325
Miyake, A., 141, 142, 148, 441, 444
Moffitt, T. E., 372, 378
Molenaar, P. C. M., 202, 217, 293, 297
Montanelli, R. G., Jr., 90, 115
Moody, J., 202, 215
Morgan, T. H., 253, 275
Mori, M., 293, 298
Morra, S., 139, 140, 147
Mosenthal, P. B., 360, 378
Motowidlo, S. J., 339, 376
Mueser, P., 337, 368, 369, 374, 377, 378
Mulaik, S. A., 42, 53
Mulholland, T. M., 423, 444
Müller, F., 246, 275
Müller, U., 265, 268, 274, 277
Munsinger, H., 318, 325
Murray, C., 97, 113, 114, 115, 372, 373, 374, 377, 378, 448, 476
Murtaugh, M., 384, 410
Myerson, J., 202, 217, 218
Myors, B., 31, 37

N

Naglieri, J. A., 53, 59, 60, 62, 63, 64, 66, 68, 71, 72, 73, 75, 79, 80, 82, 83, 84
Narasimham, G., 393, 394, 398, 410
Nassefat, M., 118, 147
Navon, D., 192, 218
Neale, M., 301, 325
Necka, E., 198, 218
Neisser, U., 152, 179, 203, 204, 212, 218, 246, 251, 269, 275, 386, 410, 452, 476
Nesselroade, J. R., 285, 296, 308, 321
Nettelback, T., 27, 29, 37, 168, 170, 177, 179, 181, 194, 195, 215, 218
Neubauer, A. C., 164, 165, 166, 171, 180, 193, 194, 218
Neumann, O., 207, 218
Newell, A., 153, 179, 205, 209, 210, 212, 217, 218, 417, 428, 444
Newsome, W. T., 176, 180
Ngorosho, D., 452, 478
Nichols, M. J., 176, 180
Nichols, R. C., 304, 319, 325
Nickerson, R. S., 439, 443, 444
Nigro, G., 465, 378
Nilsson, L. -G., 303, 325
Nimmo-Smith, I., 199, 215
Nokes, C., 452, 472, 475, 478
Nokes, K., 450, 478
Noll, J., 64, 82
Norman, D. A., 183, 184, 206, 207, 210, 212, 218
Normandeau, S., 125, 135, 147
Norris, L., 381, 382, 389, 408
North, T., 318, 321
Novacek, J., 389, 409
Nuechterlein K. H., 240, 242
Nuñes, T., 383, 410, 449, 476
Nurss, J. R., 365, 366, 380
Nylander, P. -O., 303, 325

O

O'Loughlin, M., 395, 410

O'Rahilly, R., 246, 275
O'Toole, b. J., 357, 378
Oakhill, J., 142, 147
Oberauer, K., 433, 439, 445
Okagaki, L., 387, 410, 469, 471, 473, 475, 476, 478, 479
Okamoto, Y., 3, 4, 11, 12, 14, 15, 17
Okatcha, F., 450, 472, 475, 478
Oliphant, G. W., 31, 37
Oliver, B., 286, 295
Olneck, M., 337, 368, 369, 374, 377, 378
Olson, R. K., 310, 311, 312, 313, 314, 315, 322, 323, 324, 325, 327
Ones, D. S., 350, 379
Oppler, S. H., 341, 376
Organ, D. W., 338, 339, 378
Orwoll, L., 402, 410
Outerbridge, A. N., 343, 345, 346, 379
Over, D. E., 394, 403, 404, 409
Owen, M. J., 262, 272, 283, 294, 296, 297

P

Paek, J., 240, 242
Pallier, G., 25, 26, 27, 29, 32, 36, 37
Paolitto, A. W., 65, 76, 80, 83
Papadopoulos, T. C., 74, 83
Parent, S., 125, 135, 147
Parikh, N. S., 365, 380
Parisi, D., 260, 272
Park, R. K., 98, 114
Parker, R. M., 363, 365, 366, 367, 376, 380
Parkin, A., 142, 147
Parrila, R. K., 74, 83
Parsons, C. K., 120, 121, 122, 123, 124, 143, 146
Partanen, J., 316, 317, 325
Pascual-Leone, J., 11, 17, 136, 137, 138, 140, 147
Paterson, S. J., 282, 296
Pauls, D. L., 303, 324
Pavlov, I. P., 56, 83

Paylor, R., 264, 272
Pearce, K. A., 392, 409
Pearlman, K., 341, 379
Pedersen, N. L., 284, 285, 288, 289, 295, 296, 297, 302, 304, 308, 316, 317, 323, 325
Peeler, D. F., 268, 275
Pellegrino, J. W., 105, 115, 156, 177, 190, 196, 216, 218, 423, 425, 444
Pennington, B. F., 310, 311, 314, 323, 327
Perfect, T. J., 202, 218
Perkins, D. N., 198, 218, 396, 410, 439, 444
Perloff, R., 152, 179, 246, 269, 275
Perret-Clermont, A. N., 385, 410
Persanyi, M. W., 237, 241
Petersen, A. C., 105, 115
Peterson, P. L., 68, 83
Petrill, S. A., 29, 37, 166, 167, 171, 179, 230, 243, 265, 275, 284, 286, 288, 289, 293, 294, 296, 297
Petrill, S. A., 300, 302, 304, 305, 308, 311, 316, 317, 324, 325, 326, 327
Pfeiffer, S. I., 75, 83
Pflugfelder, G. O., 264, 275
Piaget, J., 466, 476
Pietsch, A., 171, 181
Pimley, S., 389, 409
Pinard, A., 118, 147
Pinnell, G., 78, 83
Pintner, R., 58, 59, 83
Pitkin, K., 365, 380
Platsidou, M., 3, 11, 12, 13, 17, 144, 146
Platt, L., 262, 274
Platt, S. A., S253, 275
Plomin, R., 230, 243, 257, 262, 265, 266, 272, 275, 282, 283, 284, 285, 286, 287, 288, 289, 294, 295, 296, 297, 300, 302, 303, 304, 305, 306, 307, 308, 313, 314, 316, 317, 321, 322, 323, 325, 326, 327, 452, 476
Plunkett, K., 260, 272
Polovina, J., 303, 323
Pool, J. E., 68, 72, 73, 74, 81

Posner, M. I., 163, 180
Pötter, U., 202, 204, 217
Powell, C., 457, 465, 478
Powell, J. S., 196, 219
Pressley, M. P., 68, 77, 79, 83
Pribram, H., 188, 217
Pribram, K., 59, 82
Price, T. S., 286, 295
Prieto, M. D., 459, 477
Prince, R., 450, 472, 475, 478
Prisuta, R., 362, 363, 376
Pulakos, E. D., 341, 376
Pulos, S., 140, 143, 148
Purcell, S., 286, 295
Purves, D., 245, 256, 275

Q

Quaintance, M. K., 435, 443
Quartetti, D. A., 42, 53
Quigley, A. M., 368, 377

R

Rack, J., 311, 325
Raftopoulos, A., 12, 14, 17
Rainnie, D. G., 264, 272
Rand, Y., 68, 81
Raven, J. C., 156, 180, 188, 218
Reber, A. S., 187, 218
Reder, L. M., 418, 437, 438, 440, 441, 442, 444
Reder, S., 360, 378
Ree, M. J., 162, 180, 337, 340, 350, 379, 416, 435, 444
Reed, T. E., 293, 297
Reese, H. W., 390, 410
Reitan, R., 199, 207, 208, 218
Reuning, H., 384, 411
Reyna, V. F., 394, 404, 406, 411
Reynolds, 192, 207, 213
Reznick, J. S., 285, 286, 295, 297
Reznikoff, M., 319, 326
Rhodewalt, F. T., 401, 411
Rice, T., 287, 289, 297, 302, 304, 326

Rich, S. A., 141, 146
Richards, D. D., 387, 411
Rieben, L., 131, 147, 148
Riemann, R., 165, 166, 180
Rifkin, B., 465, 478
Rijsdijk, F. V., 166, 180, 258, 275, 293, 297
Ring, H. A., 259, 271
Roazzi, A., 382, 408, 449, 475
Robbins, T. W., 267, 273
Roberts, B. W., 402, 411
Roberts, J., 372, 379
Roberts, R. D., 6, 18, 22, 25, 26, 27, 28, 29, 31, 32, 33, 36, 37, 153, 165, 166, 180, 431, 444, 473, 475
Robinson, B., 396, 410
Robinson, D. L., 237, 242
Robinson, J., 285, 286, 295, 297
Rock, D., 363, 364, 376
Roeder, K., 257, 272
Rogers, W., 336, 379
Rogoff, B., 382, 383, 392, 411
Rojahn, J., 80, 83
Roos, P. A., 344, 378
Root, J. H., 363, 376
Roques, B. P., 264, 275
Rose, S. P., 144, 146, 258, 264, 275
Rosenbloom, P. S., 153, 179, 205, 210, 212, 217, 218
Rothney, J. W. M., 98, 114
Roubertoux, P. L., 267, 276
Rouse, B., 262, 274
Rovine, M. J., 282, 295
Rubin, G. M., 264, 275
Russo, R. J., 246, 271
Rutter, M., 257, 266, 275, 316, 326
Ryan, E. B., 315, 326
Rypma, B., 200, 201, 216, 259, 276

S

Saccuzzo, D. P., 193, 201
Sackett, P. R., 343, 376
Salovey, P., 473, 476
Salthouse, T. A., 145, 146, 172, 173, 179, 180, 201, 202, 218

Saltzstein, H. D., 389, 411
Samelson, F., 251, 276
Sanders, B., 105, 115
Sanilow, C. A., 253, 275
Sansone, C., 388, 400, 401, 408, 411
Sass, H. -M., 245, 276
Sattler, J. M., 58, 83
Saudino, K. J., 284, 286, 289, 296, 297
Sauffer, J. M., 162, 180
Scanlon, D. M., 315, 327
Scarr, S., 253, 276, 452, 476
Schacter, D., 316, 327
Schafer, E. W. P., 50, 53
Schaie, K. W., 201, 219, 308, 326, 358, 380
Schank, R. C., 210, 219
Scheid, K., 68, 83
Scheinfeld, A., 319, 326
Schell, P., 427, 440, 442
Schiffrin, R. M., 417, 441
Schliemann, A. D., 383, 385, 408, 410, 449, 474, 476
Schmid, J., 44, 53, 88, 90, 94, 115
Schmidt, F. L., 333, 335, 339, 340, 341, 343, 345, 346, 350, 351, 352, 353, 354, 377, 378, 379, 416, 444, 472, 476
Schmitt, N., 336, 379
Schneider, W., 206, 219
Schocke, M., 389, 408
Schönemann, P. H., 266, 276
Schulsinger, F., 372, 378
Schultze, R., 433, 439, 445
Schulz, R., 389, 409
Schumacher, E. H., 206, 207, 212, 213, 217
Schütz, G., 264, 275
Schwartz, J., 337, 368, 369, 374, 377, 378
Schwegler, H., 257, 264, 272
Schweizer, K., 31, 37
Scopesi, A., 140, 147
Scribner, S., 383, 384, 385, 393, 411
Scriver, C. R., 260, 276
Scruggs, T. E., 68, 82
Searle, L. V., 268, 276

Sechenov, I., 60, 83
Secrest, T., 124, 135, 143, 146
Seese, N., 262, 272
Segal, N. L., 251, 271, 315, 316, 317, 322
Seizova-Cajic, T., 25, 29, 37
Sewell, W. H., 369, 379
Shah, P., 141, 142, 148, 441, 444
Shallice, T., 199, 206, 207, 208, 209, 212, 218, 219
Shane, G. S., 341, 379
Shanks, N., 268, 273
Sharf, J. C., 336, 379
Shell, P., 157, 178
Sheppard, L., 336, 379
Shiffrin, R. M., 190, 206, 213, 219
Shure, M. B., 392, 411
Shute, V., 434, 439, 444
Shuttleworth, F. K., 98, 114
Siegel, B. V., 240, 242, 293, 295
Siegel, L. S., 57, 64, 83, 315, 326
Siegler, R. S., 382, 383, 387, 400, 411
Sikström, C., 303, 325
Silva, P. A., 372, 378
Simmons, A., 259, 271
Simon, H. A., 209, 210, 218
Simon, T., 246, 254, 269, 271, 454, 474
Simonoff, E., 286, 295
Simonton, D. K., 343, 379
Simpson, C. R., 195, 209
Sinha, S. N., 49, 53, 53
Sinnott, J. D., 393, 411
Sloboda, J. A., 451, 476
Smith, C., 471, 478
Smith, D. L., 294, 296
Smith, E. E., 439, 444
Smith, E. F., 206, 209, 216
Smith, G. A., 174, 177
Smith, K. J., 367, 380
Smith, M., 369, 378
Smith, P. L., 153, 167, 181, 195, 220
Smith, S. D., 311, 314, 323
Snook, S. A., 320, 326, 355, 356, 379, 457, 469, 478

Snow, R. E., 67, 68, 69, 71, 81, 83, 156, 179, 189, 190, 192, 199, 200, 217, 431, 444
Somsen, R. J. M., 293, 294
Sowell, T., 108, 115
Spearman, C. E., 48, 52, 53, 151, 153, 155, 156, 167, 180, 183, 196, 202, 203, 219, 249, 276, 415, 437, 444, 448, 455, 476
Spinath, F. M., 165, 166, 180
Spiro, A., 308, 321, 389, 407
Spivack, G., 392, 411
Spranca, M., 398, 407
Spry, K. M., 237, 241
Squire, L. R., 210, 219, 316, 326
Staglier, M., 268, 277
Staliar, M., 265, 274
Stankov, L., 6, 18, 21, 22, 25, 28, 29, 31, 32, 33, 36, 37, 153, 165, 166, 180, 190, 192, 215, 219, 473, 475
Stanovich, K. E., 315, 326, 382, 396, 403, 404, 411
Staudinger, U. M., 201, 214, 471, 474
Stelmack, R. M., 167, 179, 293, 296
Stephens, B., 119, 120, 121, 124, 146, 148
Stephens, D. L., 434, 443
Sternberg, R. J., 26, 37, 59, 66, 83, 145, 148, 152, 154, 155, 156, 158, 163, 179, 180, 188, 189, 190, 193, 194, 195, 196, 197, 198, 200, 216, 217, 219, 246, 269, 275, 276, 302, 303, 320, 324, 326, 334, 336, 355, 356, 379, 380, 383, 386, 387, 388, 408, 410, 412, 418, 423, 425, 440, 444, 445, 447, 448, 450, 451, 452, 453, 454, 455, 456, 457, 459, 461, 462, 463, 464, 465, 466, 467, 468, 469, 471, 472, 473, 474, 475, 476, 477, 478, 479
Stevenson, J., 286, 295, 297, 311, 314, 323, 326
Sticht, T., 359, 360, 363, 380
Stoddard, G. D., 254, 276
Stokes, T. L., 27, 36
Stolzfus, E., 200, 201, 216

Stough, C., 168, 178, 188, 190, 194, 195, 203, 204, 215, 231, 247
Strohman, R. C., 264, 276
Stroop, J. R., 200, 219
Strough, J., 388, 389, 390, 391, 400, 402, 408
Stryker, M. P., 256, 271
Sturtevant, A. H., 251, 276
Stuss, D. T., 208, 219
Styles, E. A., 207, 209, 213
SüB, H. -M., 418, 433, 434, 439, 443, 445
Sum, A. M., 363, 380
Sundet, J. M., 288, 289, 297, 302, 305, 316, 326
Suton, K. J., 389, 407
Swales, M., 198, 215
Swayze, V. W., II, 258, 273
Sweets, J. A., 439, 443

T

Tallal, P., 318, 321
Tambs, K., 288, 289, 297, 302, 305, 316, 326
Tang, C., 240, 242, 293, 295
Tanner, J. M., 98, 115
Taubman, P., 369, 376, 380
Taylor, R., 232, 242
Teachout, M. S., 340, 350, 379
Tellegen, A., 251, 271, 319, 327
Terman, L. M., 96, 115
Tetewsky, S. J., 467, 479
Teubal, E., 398, 407
Thapar, A., 316, 317, 327
Thatcher, R. W., 144, 148
Therriault, D., 441, 442
Thompson, L. A., 230, 243, 262, 272, 284, 286, 288, 289, 293, 294, 296, 297, 302, 304, 305, 311, 313, 316, 317, 324, 325, 327
Thompson, R., 239, 243
Thompson, W. R., 250, 255, 273
Thomson, G. A., 26, 37
Thomson, G. H., 101, 115
Thorndike, E. L., 151, 180, 250, 276

Thorndike, R. I., 58, 83
Thorndike, R. L., 46, 53, 106, 115, 337, 350, 380
Thurstone, L. L., 41, 53, 455, 479
Tidwell, P., 430, 442
Tippy, P. K. P., 365, 376
Tirre, W. C., 431, 435, 436, 440, 442, 444, 445
Tishman, S., 396, 410
Tomblin, J. B., 318, 327
Tonegawa, S., 264, 272
Tonkiss, J., 257, 275
Toquam, J. L., 339, 343, 347, 348, 351, 353, 378
Torff, B., 462, 478, 479
Tranel, D., 199, 207, 208, 213, 220
Trapnell, P. D., 402, 408
Trefz, F., 262, 274
Treiman, D. J., 344, 378
Tryon, R. C., 255, 256, 274, 276
Tuddenham, R. D., 118, 148
Tuholski, S. W., 162, 178, 199, 215, 441, 442
Tully, T., 267, 276
Tulving, E., 209, 210, 214, 220, 316, 317, 327
Tuntufue, E., 452, 478
Turner, M. L., 432, 445
Tversky, A., 415, 445
Tversky, B., 403, 409
Tzavara, E., 264, 275
Tzuriel, D., 452, 476, 479

U

Ullrich, K., 262, 274
Underwood, B. J., 424, 445
Undheim, J. O., 10, 17, 300, 324
Urbina, S., 80, 81, 152, 179, 246, 269, 275

V

Van Baal, G. C. M., 285, 293, 294, 297
Van Beijstereveldt, C. E. M., 293, 297
Van der Loos, H., 237, 242, 246, 274

van der Molen, M. W., 202, 217
Van Luit, J. E. H., 71, 84
Vandenberg, S. G., 246, 266, 276, 303, 316, 317, 323, 327
Vanderwood, M., 64, 82
Vellutino, F. R., 315, 327
Venezky, R. L., 363, 380
Verleger, R., 258, 276
Vernon, P. A., 47, 53, 165, 166, 180, 181, 193, 194, 201, 220, 231, 243, 293, 294, 297, 298, 440, 445
Vernon, P. E., 95, 115, 319, 327, 448, 451, 479
Vickers, D., 153, 171, 177, 167, 168, 171, 181, 195, 220
Vignetti, S., 294, 296
Vinh Bang, 118, 148
Vreeke, G. J., 267, 276
Vygotsky, L., 452, 453, 479

W

Wadsworth, S. J., 288, 298, 310, 313, 314, 327
Wagner, R. K., 145, 148, 320, 326, 334, 336, 355, 356, 379, 380, 383, 412, 457, 469, 478, 479
Wagstaff, D., 202, 218
Wahlsten, D., 253, 256, 257, 258, 260, 262, 264, 267, 268, 269, 272, 273, 276, 277
Waisbren, S. E., 262, 274, 277
Wales, T., 369, 376
Waller, N. G., 319, 327
Wang, L., 264, 275
Ward, S., 337, 368, 369, 374, 377, 378
Warren, B., 367, 380
Wason, P. C., 394, 412
Wasserman, J. D., 80, 84
Waters, P. J., 260, 276
Watts, D., 302, 324
Wechsler, D., 58, 64, 66, 84, 314, 327
Wechsler, W., 187, 220
Weir, C., 389, 390, 391, 400, 402, 408
Weiskrantz, L., 209, 220
Weiss, B. D., 363, 365, 367, 376, 380

Weissmann, C., 265, 274
Wellman, H. M., 12, 18
Weng, L. -J., 41, 42, 44, 45, 53, 193, 216, 225, 242
Werder, J. K., 66, 82
Wesman, A., 93, 114
West, R. F., 382, 396, 403, 404, 411
Wheelwright, S., 259, 271
White, L. A., 341, 376
White, M., 171, 181
White, N., 472, 479
Wickens, C. D., 192, 220
Wigdor, A. K., 111, 114, 337, 338, 343, 346, 349, 380
Wilhelm, O., 433, 439, 445
Wilkerson, B., 284, 297
Willerman, K., 302, 324
Williams, D., 237, 242
Williams, J., 337, 368, 369, 374, 377, 378
Williams, M. V., 363, 365, 366, 367, 376, 380
Williams, N. H., 68, 75, 76, 77, 78, 82
Williams, P., 157, 178, 198, 199, 200, 215
Williams, S. C. R., 259, 271
Williams, W. M., 145, 148, 198, 219, 320, 326, 334, 355, 356, 379, 380, 457, 468, 469, 472, 478, 479
Willis, S. L., 308, 321, 326, 358, 380
Willson, R. G., 168, 181
Wilson, J. R., 303, 323
Wilson, R. S., 252, 277, 285, 298
Wise, B., 311, 313, 325
Wise, L. L., 337, 376
Wittman, W. W., 418, 433, 434, 439, 445
Wolfer, D. P., 265, 267, 274, 275, 277
Wolfle, L. M., 202, 214
Wolfson, D., 199, 207, 208, 218
Woloshyn, V., 68, 77, 79, 83
Woltereck, R., 253, 277
Woltz, D., 425, 434, 445
Wood, F. B., 303, 324
Woodcock, R. W., 64, 66, 82, 84
Woodyard, E., 250, 276

Wu, J. C., 240, 242
Wurf, E., 401, 402, 410

Y

Yamamoto, K., 363, 364, 376
Yang, S., 472, 479
Yao, G., 95, 114
Yeates, K. O., 80, 82
Yee, P. L., 190, 216
Yerkes, R. M., 58, 84, 252, 277
Yoakum, C. S., 58, 84
Young, R., 195, 218
Yu, J., 239, 243
Yuill, N., 142, 147
Yussen, S. R., 387, 412

Z

Zacks, R., 200, 201, 216, 220
Zaharia, M. D., 268, 273
Zahn-Waxler, C., 285, 295
Zhang, X., 246, 271
Zohar, A., 395, 410
Zola-Morgan, M., 210, 219, 316, 326
Zurbriggen, E., 206, 207, 212, 213, 217
Zutell, J., 77, 78, 84

Subject Index

A

ADHD children, 64, 65, 76
Ambiguity of single-process
    account, 32-34
American and French approach to
    test measurement, 125-129
Analogical reasoning, 7
Animal learning
    general and task specific, 267-269
Architecture of mind
    interdependencies of, 13, 14
Architecture
    levels of, 10
    microarchitecture, 9, 10
    operations of, 12, 13
    three level, 12-14
    time neutral, 10
    time-dependent, 10
Architectures of intellect, 8-10
    complementarity of, 8
    organization on flow of events,
        8
    processing speed (PS), 8, 12
    psychometrics, 8
    structural 8
Attention, 6-8, 10
Attitude-treatment interaction
    (ATI), 67, 68

B

Behavioral definitions, 100, 101
Behavioral genetic perspective,
    281-294
    evidence for molarity, 282-284
    limitations of modularity, 281,
        282

Biased selection of tasks, 24
Biological basis for intelligence, 35,
    245-271
Biological intelligence, 248-251
    heredity and, 248-251
    psychometric tests and statistical
        adjustment, 248
    structure of nervous system, 248-
        251
Biological variables of g, 240, 241
Black-White differences in testing,
    97, 99, 100, 108, 109
Brain
    functional organization of, 56, 57
Brain function and g, 236-240
    as single brain process, 237
    as derivative of brain processes,
        239, 240
    as multiple brain processes, 238
    fMRI and PET, 238, 239

C

Causal modeling errors, 112, 113
    primary basis for, 113
Child measurement, 246-248
Children with learning disorders
    (LD), 64, 65
Cognition
    components of, 12
    monitoring and regulatory
        components, 12
Cognitive ability (and genetic
    influences)
    decision time, 293
    reaction time, 292
    stability across the life span, 285,
        286

stimulus discrimination, 293
twin studies, 285, 286, 289, 293
Cognitive architecture, 8-10
Cognitive development
working memory capacity, 11
Cognitive elements of information
processing, 151-177
discrimination and cognitive
aging, 172-174
experimental level of cognitive
constructs, 163-167
inspection times and cognitive
ability test scores, 167-171
psychometric-level cognitive
constructs, 154-162
psychophysical-level cognitive
constructs, 167-174
Cognitive explanations of *g*, 229-236
as multiple cognitive process,
232-235
as single cognitive process, 230-
232
cognitive processes and, 229, 230
in terms derivative of cognitive
processes, 232-235
summary, 236
Cognitive factors
psychological nature of, 30
Cognitive inconsistency, 383
see Intelligence, variability of
Cognitive manifestations of *g*
attentional resources (structural
properties), 190-192
cognitive components, 196, 197
developmental considerations,
201-204
metacognition, 197, 198
processing properties located in
subsystems of brain, 198-201
speed of processing, 193, 194
visual processing, 196-198
Cognitive tests, 20-24
sampling of participants, 20-24
sampling of cognitive tasks, 20-
24
Core capacities, 12

Correlated vectors method, 49-52
Correlates of proficient cognitive
performance, 93
educational correlates, 94
miscellaneous correlates, 95-98
neural events, 95, 96
proficiency in civilian occupations, 94
proficiency in military assignments, 94, 95
Correlates
achievement motivation to
values, 97
Cross-cultural, 386-388, 451-453
contextual variability, 381, 383-388
Kenyan conceptions, 450, 471, 472
Crystallized intelligence, 34, 46-48
fluid and, 46-48
Russia, 460-464

D

Development of *g* factor, 11-14
domain-specific factors, 12
see g factor
Domain-specific (DS) abilities, 8, 12
numerical, 8
reasoning, 8
spatial, 8
verbal, 8
Domain-specific systems, 15

E

Errors from restriction of range of
talent, 105, 108
handling restriction, 108
kinds of restriction, 106, 107
restriction in longitudinal
perspective, 107, 108
Evolutionary perspective, 247
External validity of g, 48, 49

F

Factor loadings, 30-32

Factor methods, 88, 90
Factor models, 40-45
  general and specific factors, 40
  hierarchical and nonhierarchical
    models, 40
  orthogonalized hierarchical
    model, 42, 43
  primary or first-order factors, 41,
    42
  second-order factors, 42
  simple structure, 41
Factor-analytic basis, 20
Fair tests, 99
Familiarity and experience, 10
Fluid and crystallized intelligence,
  12, 46-48
Fluid intelligence, 12
Functional literacy, 359-365
  National Adult Literacy Survey
    (NALS), 360-365

G

g factor
  and brain function, 236-240
  as a distillate of scores, 40
  as a scientific construct, 224-229
  as statistical artifact, 226, 227
  based on factor analysis, 225, 226
  biological variables, 240, 241
  current status of, 223, 224
  defined, 6-8, 184-187, 224, 225
  dependent on test battery, 227
  does it exist? 4-8
  focusing ability, 6
  no such thing as, 227, 228
  sociological generality of, 331-375
  speed of processing, 6, 7
  variance beyond *g*, 228, 229
  working memory, 6, 7
g in cognitive terms (criteria for),
  187-212
  cognitive explanations of, 229-236
  control of third variable, 189
  need for empirical demonstra-
    tion, 188, 190

need for multiple measures of *g*,
  189
need for plausibility, 190
theoretical rather than empirical,
  188, 189
g in comparison to PASS, 55-81
  evidence relevant to *g*, 63-81
  Luria's work as blueprint, 59-61
Gender
  high-school measurement, 96, 97
General vs. multiple factor theory,
  265
General/narrow abilities, 88
Genes and intelligence, 260-265
  DNA and, 262, 267
  doctrine of "true" score recon-
    sidered, 269-271
  Gene Expression Data, 263, 264
  Human Genome Project, 262
  interactive effects of genes, 264, 265
  mutations in genes, 263, 264
  phenylketonuria (PKU) and PAH
    gene, 260-262
Genetic research, 14
Genetics
  and physical structure, 251-253
  see Life span and genetics
Group factors
  individual differences in devel-
    opmental pathways, 129-136

H

Health literacy
  test of functional health literacy
    (TOFHLA), 365-367
Height and intelligence, 98
Heredity and intelligence
  alternative view, 253-256
  biological intelligence, 245-271
  environment, 254, 255, 257
  genotype/phenotype, 253, 255
  Hawaii, Family Study of Cog-
    nition, 303
  test reliability, 255, 256

Heritability estimates for specific
    cognitive abilities
    creativity, 319, 320
    language skills, 318, 319
    memory, 315-318
    reading, 309-315
Heritability of cognitive ability,
    101, 284, 304, 307
Hierarchical model
    assumptions based on, 300-320
    constancy of genetic and environ-
        mental architecture, 309-320
    explaining etiology of covari-
        ations between cognitive
        abilities, 307-309
    genetic variance for specific
        cognitive abilities, 302
    heritability estimates, 309-320
    item selection, 93
    statistical criticism, 91, 93
Historical views, 24, 25
HIV/AIDS, genetically controlled
    outcomes, 306
Human Genome Project, 262
Hypercognitive processes (HP), 8,
    9, 12
    and cognitive abilities, 8

                    I

Information processing skills,
    life tasks, 356-375
    reaction time, 99
    see Job performance
Intellectual success, 15, 16
Intelligence as an emergent property,
    245-248
    EEG and, 246
    from birth to age 2, 246-248
    genetic perspective, 247
    tests for, 247
    see Genetics
Intelligence
    analytical aspects of, 457-466
    conventional notions, 448-453
    creative aspects of, 457-469

inadequate notions, 448
    nature of successful, 454-456
    practical aspects of, 457-464, 469-
        472
    processes of successful, 456, 457
    Sternberg Triarchic Abilities Test
        (STAT). 457-459
    see Nervous system, Genes
Intelligence, variability of, 381-407
    across cultures and contexts, 381,
        383-388
    across ethnic and age groups,
        385-388
    biases and decision making, 396,
        399
    frameworks that address varia-
        bility, 400
    in problem solving, 389-394, 400,
        403
    inter and intradomain variability,
        388, 389
    motivation and perspective
        switching, 396-399
    representation-processing
        system, 404-406
    shifts in reasoning, 394-396
    strategy selection, 390-394
    two-process approaches to
        decision making, 403-406
Interventions
    see PASS, PREP
Invariance of g
    across methods, 45
    across tests, 46
    across populations, 46
IQ tests, 58, 59, 66, 67
    alternative tests, 59
    test outcome, 368-374
    see also PASS

                    J

Job performance, 335-375
    g scores, 336, 337
    g-based theory of, 340-355
    pilot training, 107, 108

see also Military, Personnel selection, Functional literacy

K

Knowledge and reasoning processes, 7
Knowledge handling, 12

L

Language development, 246, 247
Life course tasks
adaptation-adjustment, 357-359
bad/good outcomes, 372-375
management of, 356-359
risks over the life span, 367-375
Life phases
integrating, 11
Life span and genetics
adulthood, 288
early and middle childhood, 287, 288
infancy, 286, 287
integration of multivariate results, 289-292
old age, 288, 289
Long-term memory, 10
Lower order processes, 25-30
arbitrariness of classification, 26, 27
as more tractable than higher order processes, 27
Elementary Cognitive Tasks (ECT), 25, 26, 29
microlevel reductionism 28
reductionism, 27, 28

M

Measurement ability of g, 16, 17
Measurement data
different use of r, 102-105
errors in interpreting correlations, 101, 102
individual differences in, 101
what r and r^2 provide, 102
Memory, 315-318
long-term, 10
see working memory
Metarepresentation, 12
Military experience, 346, 347
Military
Armed Forces Qualifying Test (AFQT), 337, 349
can do, will do, have done, factors, 349-354
cognitive vs. noncognitive performance measures, 339-348
job complexity, 344-346
Joint-Service Job Performance Measurement/Enlistment Standards (JPM), 337, 338
Project A, 337, 338, 347
see Job performance
Modern theories of cognition, 205-213
computer simulation models, 208, 209
models of attentional control, 206-208
neuropsychological research, 208, 209

N

Nervous system and intelligence, 256-260
averaged evoked potential (AEP) and IQ, 258-260
genetic information, 257
heredity/environment, 257
myelin sheath, 256, 257
twin studies, 257
visual cortex, 256
Neural correlates
brain/head size, 98, 99
Noncognitive influences, 35
Novel tasks, 10
slower processing, 10
Novel tasks

planning, organization, and
  regulation, 10

O

One-factor vs. multifactor systems,
  19, 20
Operational definitions, 88
  factor methods, 89, 90
  hierarchical transformation, 90, 91
  observations required, 89
  standard psychometric methods,
    89

P-Q

PASS theory, 55-81
  assessment and intervention, 67,
    68
  attention, 62
  case illustration, 74-81
  cognitive assessment system
    (CAS), 69-80
  evidence relevant to g, 63-81
  PASS Reading Enhancement
    Program (PREP), 72-80
  planning facilitation and inter-
    vention, 68-73
  planning, 61, 62
  relationships to test achievement,
    66, 67
  sensitivity to children's cognitive
    variation, 64-66
  simultaneous processing, 62
  successive processing, 62
Perception, 10
Personnel selection
  g-based theory of, 340, 341
  theory of situational specificity,
    335, 336
Physique
  correlates with intelligence, 98
Piagetian stages of development, 11
Piagetian test measures
  American approach, 119-125

French approach, 125
  hypothesis of Reuchlin, 125-129
Piagetian tests, 117-145
Planning and control, 7, 12
Positive manifold, 20, 28, 183, 186
Premature choices, 88
PREP (PASS Reading Enhancement
    Program), 72-80
  case illustration, 74-81
  cognitive assessment system
    (CAS), 69-80
  efficacy of, 73, 74
  reading failure, 72-76
  strategy planning and focus
    development, 72, 73
  word sorting and story mapping,
    77, 78
Primary abilities as empirical basis,
  88
Processing capacity, 136, 137
  plurality of processing capacities,
    140-142
  studies pointing to unity of, 139,
    140
  task measurement, 137-139
Project Talent background Question-
    naire, 96, 97
Properties of the general factor, 91-
    93
  measurement of the general
    factor, 91, 92
  residuals in hierarchical theory,
    92
Psychometric g, 39-52
  distinctions between intelligence
    and g, 39, 40
Psychometrics
  as nondevelopmental, 11
Quantitative genetic analysis, 265-
    267

R

Race differences in testing, 97-100,
  108, 109

Raven's Progressive Matrices, 99, 427
  and reification errors, 99, 110, 111
Regulatory processes, 10
Reification errors, 109
  academic performance and, 111
  and intelligence tests, 109, 110
  example of reification, 109, 110
  job performance and, 111, 112
  Raven's Progressive matrices
    and, 110, 111

S

Self-concept, 15
Self-monitoring skills, 10
Self-regulation skills, 10
Short and long-term goals, 16
Single-score measures of intelligence, 55
Social phenomena
  effects of, 97, 98
  see Sociological generality of g
Socioeconomic status and test
  scores, 97, 98
Sociological generality of g, 331, 332
  functional literacy, 365-367
  gauging effect sizes, 332, 333
  gauging generality, 333
  gradients of risk, 374, 375
  health literacy, 365-367
  IQ and bad outcome, 372-374
  IQ and good outcome, 368-372
  job performance, 335-356
  practical intelligence theory,
    333-335
  risks in managing life tasks, 356-
    375
Structure of mind, 8-10
System-handling metacomponents,
  12
Systems perspective to g, 416-418
  analysis of test items, 423-427

cognitive components approach,
  418, 423-427
components of cognitive architectures, 418, 427-436
effective vs. underlying working
  memory capacity, 438, 439
figure-it-out strategy, 419
mixed strategy, 419
parameters of cognitive architectures, 418, 436-438
remembering strategy, 419
solving quantitative word
  problems, 418-423

T

Testing
  race differences in, 97, 99, 100
  fair tests, 99
Theoretical understanding of
  intelligence, 55, 56
Theory of mind, 12
Twin studies, 302, 303
  cognitive ability and genetic
    influences, 285, 286, 288, 293
  Colorado Adoption project, 285-
    287, 304, 307, 310, 314, 314, 318
  genetic influences, 285, 286, 289,
    293
  MacArthur Longitudinal Twin
    Study, 285, 286
  Octotwin Study, 289
  Twins Early Development Study
    (TEDS). 286, 287
  see Cognitive ability and genetic
    influences

V-Z

Variability of g, 7, 8
Working memory 6-8,10, 415-451
  capacity, 11
Zone of proximal development
  (ZPD), 453